LOOKING FOR
ARTHUR

LOOKING FOR

ARTHUR

A ONCE AND FUTURE
TRAVELOGUE

RICHARD LEVITON

STATION HILL OPENINGS

BARRYTOWN, LTD.

Published under the Station Hill Openings imprint of Barrytown, Ltd., Barrytown, New York 12507, as a project of The Institute for Publishing Arts, Inc., a not-for-profit, federally tax exempt, educational organization.

Web: www.stationhill.org
E-mail: Publishers@stationhill.org

Grateful acknowledgement is due to the National Endowment for the Arts, a Federal Agency in Washington, DC, and by the New York State Council on the Arts for partial financial support of the publishing program of The Institute for Publishing Arts, Inc.

Distributed by Consortium Book Sales & Distribution, Inc. 1045 Westgate Drive, Saint Paul, MN 55114-1065.

Cover design by Susan Quasha with Vicki Hickman.
Typesetting by Alison Wilkes.

Library of Congress Cataloging-in-Publication Data

Leviton, Richard.
    Looking for Arthur : a once and future travelogue / Richard Leviton.
        p. cm.
    ISBN 1-886449-13-9
    1. Glastonbury Region (England)—Antiquities, Celtic. 2. Arthur, King—Homes and haunts—England—Glastonbury Region. 3. Leviton, Richard—Journeys—England—Glastonbury Region. 4. Britons—Kings and rulers—Legends. 5. Arthurian romances—Sources. I. Title.
DA690.G45L38 1997
914.23'83—dc21   96-48775
                                                                  CIP

Printed in the United States of America.

Contents

OTHER BOOKS BY THE AUTHOR

The Imagination of Pentecost:
Rudolf Steiner & Contemporary Spirituality

Weddings By Design:
A Guide to Nontraditional Ceremonies

Environment:
Where Personal & Planetary Health Meet (forthcoming)

Brain Builders!
A Lifelong Guide to Sharper Thinking, Better Memory,
And an Age-Proof Mind

To the Blaise babies when they come
—may you remember it all

1

GLASTONBURY IS IN MY HEART

ne day, Glastonbury, long after all this happened, I looked inside my heart and there you were. I hadn't thought about you for so long and it had been many years since I last set foot on your magic soil. My chest seemed to expand until it encompassed the whole of you and I am here again in Glastonbury, breathing the charmed air of this uniquely troubling town. I know you, your cranky weather, green-tufted hills, your anomalous Tor and its hollow tower, red-roofed homes, your forlorn Abbey and its "grave" of Arthur, the earnest pilgrims and fervent mystics crowding your High Street, the arcane temples, disguised caves, and forgotten tunnels just beneath your skin, and the Grail—that antique holiness occulted within the lovely folds of Chalice Hill. We did so much on its behalf.

But most of all I remember bloodred Chalice Well, your exquisite garden floriate with angels, their wingtips bedewed with healing drops of Eden trickling through my courtyard. How many times did Blaise span the disparate realms of Avalon and Logres for us in that little grotto, their wings arcing between the worlds, granting us passage? So here, in the eye of my heart, I see you, expectant as always, but this time for good reason, because the millennium draws near and Joseph's seed is sprouting and we are returning and you shall at last come into your own.

How can all this fit inside my unextraordinary chest? Even so, I contain this colossus of myth and history, pagan exploit and High Church drama, Arthurian spectacle and millennialist expectation, this infectious breeding ground of Celtic prophets and new age vi-

2 ✤ Richard Leviton

sions, this dizzying span of centuries and repetition that stretches back to the beginning. Is it all going to happen again, you ask me? Yes, I think so, but with some changes. It is as unstoppable as spring leaves. It is as if someone planted a fabulous seed in my heart, which is your heart, dear Glastonbury, knowing that when the time is right in my life and in the world, it will sprout and grow rapidly into the mythic tableau of contemporary Glastonbury and Arthurian Avalon. So that here I am again on Wearyall Hill by the Holy Thorn planted by Joseph of Arimathea, that seed-sowing emissary of the Christ mystery from two thousand years ago, surveying, as he did, the geomythic landscape of Avalon, looking for Arthur.

2

A Town, A Myth & A Life:
Looking for Arthur

The bus pulls out of Bristol coach station with only three of us aboard. When I clamber into the bus with my luggage, fresh from the train out of London and, from there, just off the plane from San Francisco, two dear mums in their seventies are already installed in a rear seat chatting animatedly about "Harry and his trips down Winchester, you see." Their friendly gossiping pulls me welcomingly into England, its voices and landscape. The bus pulls out of its grimy hangar and begins its winding potter through the cozy, ancient hills and stone-walled villages of Avon and Somerset as we make for its enigmatic jewel called Glastonbury.

This region is rife with attributions, declaimed in many tongues. It all rings with intrigue, mysticism, and a secret destiny. Glastonbury, and to an extent, all of Celtic Somerset, is the Region of the Summer Stars, the Sanctuary of Our Lord, the Summer Country, The White Land, Avalon. More enigmatically, Glastonbury will be the site of the prophecied New Jerusalem when it dawns in the Golden Age, said by some to be just around the corner. Maelwas is the King of the Summer Country (*Aestiva Regio*) and Lord of the Island of Glass (*Ynys Wydrin*), but so is Avallach and so is Gwyn ap Nudd, King of the Fairies—they're probably all the same. Glastonbury is "this holiest Erthe in England," the Mother of Saints, *Domus Dei*—the Home of God, *Secretum Domini*—the Secret of Our Lord, and of course Avalon, the Isle of Apples, island of the Blessed and portal to the

Otherworld. The epithets are numerous and expansive and probably without end. England herself is sometimes called Our Lady's
Dowry and the Lord's Vineyard—at least that's what you're likely to
hear in Somerset, which seems intoxicated with this lush Celtic heritage.

Not only names but legends abound here, too. There is the legend
that Joseph of Arimathea, the reputed uncle and benefactor to Jesus
of Nazareth and a Jewish political leader of consequence, once travelled to Glastonbury bearing the Holy Grail sanctified by Jesus the
Christ—and some claim he brought Jesus with him—then cultivated
the Lord's Vineyard in Glastonbury, founded Britain's first Christian
ecclesia in Glastonbury in the first century A.D., and converted the
Celtic natives to the new teachings of Christ. A great deal of
Glastonbury's history and expectancy turns on this great deed of
Joseph, assuming any of it's true, of course. The atmosphere of Avalon
at Glastonbury—I would quickly appreciate how intimately the two
interpenetrate each other—is pendulant with portent, like an apple
tree at harvest time, and among the sweet fruits of this mythic orchard on the Glass Island is Arthur, the once and future. Glastonbury
still conceals many mysteries, says English Earth Mysteries researcher
John Michell, but "when times are ripe, something wonderful will
be unearthed at Glastonbury."

When I decided to come here, I knew I'd be entering a region lushly
foliated with myths about Arthur, asleep in the womb of Avalon
until his destined moment of awakening. The mythic tableau is complex and so much of it has been played out in this landscape and
born into the present as folk memory. As I sit here in the lurching
bus, figures from the Arthurian canon parade through my jet-lagged
memory. Arthur the white-clad king on horseback slaying the dragon.
Arthur withdrawing Excalibur the Kingsword from the adamant
stone in the London churchyard. The Lady of the Lake emerging
mistily from the waters, a bold sword held aloft in her samite-gloved
hand. Arthur's contrived, secret birth at Tintagel in Cornwall and
his midnight abduction by Merlin who lived by the prophecy of the
once and future king—*rex quondam, rex futurus*. Arthur's Pendragon

banner, his twelve battles to secure his kingship at a young age. His sister Morgan, "the great clerk of necromancy," as Sir Thomas Malory described her, battling him throughout his life, then bearing him as he died on her spectral barge into Avalon. Arthur returning, too, beyond anyone's expectations, from *Annwyn*, the Celtic Otherworld, sailing on *Prydwen*, his crystal ship, with sword and cauldron. The Grail manifesting numinous and beckoning at Camelot on Pentecost, the day the Grail Knights gathered every year for fresh inspiration. The angels winging haloes about Galahad, the consummate *Parfait* Grail Knight on his ascension into Heaven, the Quest completed. Arthur's fatal encounter with his rejected, bastard son, Mordred. Bedivere, Arthur's bosom companion since childhood, returning Excalibur the King Sword to the deeps of Avalon, flinging it into the astral waters for a future time, a future Arthur. Arthur asleep with his knights in the hollow hills of the Summer Country, awaiting the alarm call, the summons to rise and return.

These mythic events float nebulously, prodigally, like irritating pollen in the Avalon airs, never achieving the kind of substantiability that might persuade the stodgy Arthurian scholars of their truth. All this that's claimed fabulously in legend may have happened here in Glastonbury, Somerset's intoxicated heart—in some fashion. That's the key, to figure out how to understand these myths, to sense in what nonordinary way they might be true, even useful. How to approach the Arthurian myth has vexed scholars and inflamed mystics for centuries; fortunately, a few of Glastonbury's hoard of outrageous attributions may be defensible in ordinary terms. So as I lean my head against the window, I tick off the more *relatively* certifiable Arthurian attractions of Glastonbury, not that this means that they are any more historically concrete. They simply might be.

Arthur had a vision of the Virgin Mary and the Grail at Beckery Chapel on Bee-Keeper's Island at the back end of town, out past the area now dominated by sheepskin factories. Camelot reportedly once occupied a bare, grassy hilltop twelve miles from here at South Cadbury. Bedivere may have tossed Excalibur from Pomparles Bridge, near Beckery, into the River Brue, which still trickles anemically through the cow pastures in the Levels today. Joseph of Arimathea brought the Grail, which perhaps was a cup or serving vessel blessed by Jesus at his Last Supper, and buried it in a secret cave within Chalice Hill. His staff turned into a flowering thorn tree when he implanted it in the magical soil of Wearyall Hill. Arthur and his wife Guinivere, according to the Abbey monks some 800 years ago, were buried on the church grounds in a place of honor. Arthur's legendary Round Table may have been a 20 mile wide configuration of zodiacal effigies sculpted in the Somerset landscape around Glastonbury according to standard star patterns. Glastonbury Tor was the entrance to Morgan's Avalon, the healing isle of apples and necromantic priestesses.

This is the extent of my textbook knowledge of Arthurian Glastonbury. Whether any of it is true is anybody's guess. The idea of a zodiac imprinted in the landscape is a proposition best suited to an esoteric specialist to contemplate. The Abbey, Beckery, Chalice Well, Camelot, the Tor—these have been meticulously excavated in recent decades by archeologists seeking to authenticate or discredit the Arthurian nimbus for once and the future. But all this assiduous cataloguing of shards and cross-checking of dates in ancient manuscripts and drafting of probable occupation scenarios may have substantiated Arthur's probable, speculative Celtic milieu, but frankly it hasn't brought *him* any closer to real life. His reality, his autobiography, remains shrouded in a mist of uncertainty and rank speculation, yet the vague imminence of his return continues to burn within many hearts, and not exclusively British either. The expectancy of Arthur inspires an unending deluge of books, theories, tours, movies, dreams, retellings, definitive explanations, authoritative debunkings—not to overlook the U.S. Presidency and its quest for another Kennedyian Camelot—and these in turn generate an incessant pilgrimage of Arthurian fans from around the world to the otherwise insignificant Somerset market town called Glastonbury.

But what would a town be like, I'm wondering, as we roll and bump over the perdurable Somerset hills, today, after the collapse of the Empire, after the Falkland's bravado, after the Thatcher years, the erratic dotage of the sterling, the terrorist bombings in London, when England's biggest export seems to be culture in the form of BBC TV movies—what would life be like in an English town weighted down with centuries of expectations and claims and the interweaving drama of Celtic paganism, Druidic magic, and foundational British Christianity leavened with new age boosterism? Like John Cowper Powys, the prodigious chronicler of myth-laden Glastonbury of the 1930s, I want to hear the reverberations of Arthur in the bakeshop, I want to sense the Grail in the laundromat. Powys devoted eleven hundred earnest pages to pondering "the effect of a particular legend, a special myth, a unique tradition, from the remotest past in human history upon a particular spot on the surface of this planet, together with its crowd of inhabitants of every age and every type of character."

In his *A Glastonbury Romance,* Powys characterized the town as "a material center of force." Its psychic chemistry was mutable by human interaction, yet it was still somehow an independent, if not ineffable, entity "by reason of the creative energies pouring into it from the various cults, which consciously or unconsciously, sucked their life-blood from its wind-blown gossamer-light vortex." The essence of Glastonbury, the pearl gleaming secretly in its bowered heart, said Powys, is the Grail, the source of all seeking, the end of all questing. Perennially, the Grail is just beyond comprehension, a celestial carrot dangled ravishingly by a starry hand before our awestruck gaze. "It refers us to things beyond itself and to things beyond words. The Grail is older than Christianity as it is older than Glastonbury Tor. The Grail represents a lapping up of one perfect drop of noonday happiness," Powys added, glossing a fine phrase by Nietzsche. The Grail is "a recognized alien resident" in secular Glastonbury. Yet despite Glaston-bury's obstreperous Grail Killers, the denyers, the realists, the debunkers, the scholars, the Grail has "not only stained, dyed, impregnated the atmosphere of this particular spot but has associated itself with every detail of its local history."

I would have said at first that Arthur drew me to Glastonbury, yet as I've looked closer over the months I find Arthur holding the Grail, offering it to me. Powys is right: the Grail is the magnet; even Arthur is held in its grip. I've journeyed through the membranes of career, preconception, culture, time, and passed beyond these, untangling myself to set out after this recognized alien resident and noonday elixir in a town just as revelatory, gorgeously lunatic, and mystically aswirl in this time as it was for Powys and his *dramatis personae* in the 1930s.

The fact is I *had* to come to Glastonbury. I was flooded out of my life, swept involuntarily across the Atlantic, rolled up wet and breathless and curious on the psychic sands of Avalon. My work, my projects, my friends, my opinions, my presumed future—nothing held me fixed on that old life track, that worn out trajectory. I think often of Sam Gamgee's rapture in *The Lord of the Rings* when he first saw Elves. It was for this unassuming Hobbitt as good as peering into Heaven, because when he saw the Elves, he felt his past life, so cozy but parochial in his roundhouse in Hobbiton, widen into an astonishing vista of a vast world. Sam's delight exceeded his ability at description—isn't it always so with mystics?—so the closest he came to articulating the splendor revealed to him was his gnomic remark, "Well, sir, if I could grow apples like that, I would call myself a gardener. But it was the singing that went to my heart, if you know what I mean."

Yes, I know what you mean, Sam, and I, too, want to see Elves. I want to watch wide-eyed as the landscape of my life widens out into a fabric of myth, history, and destiny, when figures from legend suddenly spring up from the tall grass and beckon me to follow them into the unknown. On my first trip to England in my early twenties, I walked voluntarily enchanted through the countryside of Wales and Cornwall—and I mean *walked*, at least a hundred miles with backpack and Whitman's *Leaves of Grass*, along the public cliff paths, pitching my tent at night. I was scouting for echoes, looking for doorways, on the trail of Tolkien's inspiration; why couldn't Tolkien's world happen in real life? I thought I might find his secret in the landscape itself, in the vapors of the place. Privately I sang with the indefatigably happy Hobbitts, "Home is behind, the world ahead. And there are so many paths to tread!"

It was my maiden voyage into the outskirts of the Celtic otherworld. I wanted that intoxicating sense of living in a story that was growing, still alive, of breathing inside an event already ballooning rapidly beyond my comprehension into something of portent. I wanted to jump into a myth. "What a tale we have been in, Mr. Frodo, haven't we?" says Sam. "I wish I could hear it told! Do you think they'll say, 'Now comes the story of Nine-Fingered Frodo and the Ring of Doom?' And then everyone will hush, like we did, when in Rivendell they told us the tale of Beren One-Hand and the Great Jewel. I wish I could hear it! And I wonder how it will go after our part?"

Frodo set off on his journey because somebody handed him a very hot potato—a stolen ring capable of destroying the world. Bilbo, his foster-uncle, gave him the ring, and Gandalf the wizard told him how dangerous it was, then pushed him out of the door of secure Hobbiton into a tremendous initiation experience in the wide world that changed his life. It was, as Tolkien was fond of saying, a eucatastrophe, personally apocalyptic but in a positive way. Frodo had a destiny, an obligation in the world; the context for his great deed was so large that only a myth could contain it. I can't claim such a precipitous inception into the Arthurian world, but I know the seed of intention showed early signs of sprouting on that Friday night in March when I sat alone yet another night in my New England farmhouse in the western hills of Massachusetts. Winter was finally breaking up and so, I saw later, were the structure and habits of my life. The woodstove kept the room toasty, my fourth bottle of Guinness stood half-empty on the table, my rocking chair creaked with each new shove of my toe against the floor, and Jasper, my golden retriever, lay curled up beside the stove, his head golden baked and presently retrieving dog dreams. I see now that was the moment when I saw *how* I could find the time and money to make a window in my life to spend a summer in England on an exploratory, possibly flirtatious, reconaissance of Glastonbury, poking around in Arthur country. Tolkien invented his world using mythic figures from various Nordic cultures, but the Arthurian mythos inhabits a real landscape and draws on possibly real figures.

Nor have I forgotten that moment, that second of poetic insight on an earlier October afternoon deep in the autumn woods behind my house. I was perched on an old, loping, spinish stone wall that was draped in orange and red leaves as still more leaves fluttered down from birch and maple trees overhead. I felt a connection like a rivet between epochs, a sudden chilled breath from unknown past generations of New Englanders who had stood at this same spot in the woods and laid these heavy stones to form a wall which I would encounter as an organic document of their history centuries later. It was the first time the idea of the past assumed a palpable reality for me; I sensed a link, a continuity, a thread of connection. The stone wall was like a dark, running ridge, an exposed bone of earth, a boundary marker, flowing back into their time establishing a continuum of habitation, expectation, even leaf falls.

Perspiring, shivering, I felt empathy with these faceless forebears standing ghostly with me in the drifting autumnal hills. In their day, of course, there were no woods but open pastures; they built the stone walls in lieu of fencing for livestock. Now the second-growth forest has grown up around their stone fences, but this wall was a golden bough granting me imaginative passage into their earlier days, into a time before my life and dreams, and in such a way I could feel the pulse of their lives right now in my own. They touched me and I quaked—and laughed because, as one doubting friend said as I announced my evidently quixotic intention to look for Arthur in the vale of Avalon: "What are you going to do, interview King Arthur himself?" I didn't know what I meant, really, but I knew I had to do it. I wanted to find some stone wall in Glastonbury that would conduct me sinuously back through the same place into the different time of Avalon.

I don't have any methodology. Maybe I'll drink some Avalonian hard cider, the pride of Somerset, and summon up a fanciful vision of Arthur. Maybe I'll be an Arthurian lepidopterist and dash around the fields of Avalon with my swift net swooping up every nuance that flutters, hoping it's Arthur's. I'll look behind old thorn trees, under bridges, inside Abbey arches, within apocryphal gravesites, into ancient springs, atop barren hillforts, in the noisy cafes, in the beer-sloshed, darts-punctuated pubs, in the green and muddy landscape—in my self. My days will be a record of a crazy man chasing an ancient story through the hollow hills, circling, dipping, disappearing, sighing, shouting, pausing, circling, over and over in a merry, unjustifiable exhalation of myth-living. I'm going to jump into the rabbitt-hole of Arthur and pull the door in with me until no trace remains. Why not? It won't cost much anyway: only my life.

All that remained after that inspiration by the woodstove were the phone calls, the planning, the doubts, the mounting excitement, the turning of the weeks on the calendar as the day finally approached when I would enter that jumbo jet in San Francisco—I had moved here some months earlier—bound for Avalon and sit on the wafting plane for a dozen hours, cross-legged, my attention on the breath, and stay awake thanks to strategically consumed cups of black coffee and contemplate my three hundred and twenty-two fellow myth-livers on board. I warmed to the knitwork of their secret plans, their anxieties, the slips of paper reminding them not to forget the traveller's checks, the bits of toast left uneaten on the breakfast plate, the final laundry tumbled and dried late last night, the rush to the airport at dinnertime for the night flight, the seat assignment, the boarding of this giant aerial ocean liner, this massive *Prydwen*, and the beginning of our shared destiny, this momentary cache of lives high above the Atlantic of leaping dolphins and the promise of new life. With the dawn it would be Easter.

3

SETTLING INTO A NEW HOME
ON EASTER SUNDAY

I washed into Glastonbury on an Easter tide. Curmudgeonly Buddhist, I was raised antiseptically Protestant and appalled by the prospect of any intimacy with organized Christianity; I protested even Protestantism. What spartan Protestantism didn't provide, ascetic Buddhism took away, leaving me twice lapsed, a non-participant, and mortally hungry. With my nose pressed against the window of the rippling bus, I sense the Tor is about to emerge into sight if only for an astonished eyeblink. The Great Pyramid of England, the Atlantean Lion, the Hill of Evil—so have people dubbed this strange sculpted hill, this 521 foot high Celtic prominence slalomed into fading terraces and spiked with a hollow stone tower. The Tor would be for me in the early months of my myth-jumping and Avalonian wanderings a physical symbol of both the apparently knowable and the exasperatingly unknowable about Avalon and its Arthur. The Tor is Glastonbury's own enigmatic snow leopard; it isn't that you almost never see it, but you never see the same Tor twice. It would be a daily checkpoint for me, visible from my breakfast porch at the Level's View Bed and Breakfast, a geomythic barometer of grass and stones and sheep and hikers registering the psychic swirls and innuendoes wafting through the Glastonbury ethers. Over toast, tea, and boiled eggs, I would contemplate this anomaly like a Samurai in training—safely, from a distance, sizing it up.

The bus lurches, dips, and rolls up again across this oscillating landscape and I see the Tor, suddenly: vague, white, a spiked peak, an insinuation on a pedestal amidst the low-slung clouds. Until a hedgerow swipes my view. We pass on sedately through somber, stony villages with orange lichen ensconced on ancient grey rock and along fresh-scented narrow lanes girted with furrowed spring fields. Now comes Wells, the city built upon sacred water, an ecclesiastical town whose triumph in the millennial battle for hegemony over rival Glastonbury is enshrined in its lagoon-girt cathedral, hale and much visited unlike Glastonbury's Abbey ruins. Today Wells is crammed with Easter visitors roaming every byway. A snarly cluster of skinhead teenagers, sullen in leather, denim, and purple patches, occupies the fountain bench, billboarding faces of defiance and bewilderment.

We lumber out of Wells and amongst yellow eyefuls of forsythias and daffodils, young oak leaf sprouts, and the ubiquitous hedgerow in spring regeneration; I catch a second glimpse of the Tor. It holds itself steady for a longer contemplation, this green knob steepled in grey—until it's swept away by a looming chimney and then washed back yet again into sight, unnatural, chilling, only to shrink with each mile, its stone tower dedicated to the Archangel Michael, first thimbling, now vacating, the horizon as the Tor sinks into the expanding hills like a foreign sun. Tor gazers of Glastonbury constantly report bizarre alterations in perspective like this. Looking for Arthur would be like this, too, a similar interrupted contemplation of something that at heart is elusive, tantalizing, probably ungraspable, as one minute the legendary Arthur careens into sight, approaching palpability, only to vanish into the Celtic Otherword the next.

The bus pulls up before Glastonbury Town Hall, and I drag my luggage and body, now thirty hours since its last unpacking into sleep, down the street two blocks to the tourist office on Northload. I don't want to walk very far with all this luggage, I explain to the clerk, hoping to find accommodations pretty much around the corner. Papers, books, typewriter, files, clothes, boots—it all weighs a lot and I'm tired, I tell her. Obliging, impeccably pleasant, she books me in at the Level's View, "a lovely, quiet little place" half a mile away up Fisher's Hill. Theoretically some luggage-lugging would do me good, if I only had the energy and interest. I set off, over-loaded and groaning, wondering if the hill has been named in honor of the Maimed Fisher King, chief resident and probable owner of the Grail Castle and despondent ruler of the Wasteland of Logres for whose redemption and healing all of Arthur's knights and the great king himself annually departed Camelot in fervent quest—and on whose behalf this quirky journalist has, perhaps belatedly, arrived from America to cover the story as it breaks.

I rest in the shade of Abbey Park, about halfway to the Level's View. From my bench under a large beech, I watch five children busy on swings, slides, and astride a beachball, passively supervised by two adults. Chalice Hill frames this two acre park like a crescent belly graced with downy trees. Behind, the Tor scowls like a prickly jutting chin with one thick bristle unscathed by the razor: St. Michael's tower, all that remains from the Abbey outpost that crumbled in Glastonbury's only recorded earthquake. Both hills— how clearly they state the lineaments of their temperament—abide, silent, direct, and vivid. A one-year-old toddler staggers up to me, confident and stubby in his lurching mobility; he stares at me with strong intent as if trying to remember something or as if wanting to tell me something. Then the fat little Buddha waddles away, stops, returns for another penetrating glance at this American traveller; I encourage him with a smile. The old, little man of Glastonbury, wizened with infancy, claiming a memory from a distant time. Glastonbury would be like this, the enigmatic meeting frought with unclaimed portent. His two sitters whisk him off in a flutter of giggles and embarassment.

Lorries downshift in regular pulsation, climbing Magdalene Street behind me. A farm tractor lows past with a hay wagon stacked seven-tiered with fresh bales. I continue my trudge up Hillhead, another name for Fisher's Hill, which is the residential end of Wearyall Hill, the greater topographical prominence on which Fisher's Hill, sits like a shoulder. Wearyall is one of Glastonbury's four antique promi-nences, inscribed with mythic portent as if from the first moment of creation. Wearyall's companions in ancient significance are the Tor,

Chalice Hill, and Edmund's Hill; together they constitute the four islands of the Summer Country. The reference to summer was once partly geological. In the old days of Avalon, around the time Joseph of Arimathea made his legendary visit here, the winter rains and swollen rivers—Brue, Parrett, Axe—flooded the lowlands, leaving only the four hills unsoaked and habitable, virtual islands in a shallow inland sea. It was only in the summer months, really, that Glastonbury was accessible to people by means other than boat. Even now the Levels, as they call the flatlands where they farm peat, are soggy in January, but I doubt you'll see a boat drawing into Glastonbury unless it's some cider-induced vision from Avalon.

Hillhead is lined with strange cars, and I suppose I don't know England that well because all the car names—Vauxhall, Woseley, Triumph, Hillman, Morris Minor—are unfamiliar and a little exotic. Rose Cottage, on my right half-way up Hillhead, is a textbook specimen of preserved English quaintness. It's squat, stoney, flowered, hundreds of years old, and the front door is wide open; inside, a woman's legs stretch luxuriantly out from a stuffed chair towards a television from which the news is announced in crisply enunciated British. Next door, someone plunks away at a stiff-keyed manual typewriter; elsewhere in the house, somebody clinks dishes in a recessed kitchen. Finally, I stand in the portico of a mottled, Grecian-white, architecturally rambling house, roofed with red tiles and fronted with rose trellises. I set my bags down, wipe the sweat from my brow, and, fairly worn out, ring the bell of the Level's View.

A tall, handsome maternal woman in her fifties opens the door, welcoming me with a gracious smile. I'm prepared to like her at once. Nickie Smithson, she's the kind of bed and breakfast hostess you feel life-long, inseparable friends with after the first five minutes of tea, biscuits, and conversation. We sit in her public room with a view overlooking the Levels, fairly dry and dotted with grazing cows. During my stay in Glastonbury, Nickie would be my guide, interpreter, confidant, aunt-in-residence in whose "lovely" two-storied cottage I would ruminate and from whose nest I would make my exploratory incursions into the feverish heart of Avalon.

In this room where we take our tea, two framed posters hang on the wall. One is a map of England decorated with figures and paragraphs about the Arthur legend, events and people anchored, if only by local tradition, to specific localities. If this map is true, then Arthur was chopped into a hundred pieces and claimed equally by a hundred places on the island as having lived, loved, fought, and died in their neighborhood. The concept, Nickie tells me, is that the Arthur story continues to live in the landscape like incorrigible dandelions, blossoming perennially as attributions at hillforts, stone circles, medieval villages by the hundredfold. The other poster depicts an ovoid, circus-like procession of animal shapes, tumbling in a perpetual zodiacal circuit superimposed on the Somerset landscape on a swath about 20 miles wide. This is a map of Glastonbury's Temple of the Stars, says Nickie, a decidedly controversial thesis put forth in the 1920s by a Canadian researcher named Katherine Maltwood.

Maltwood's researches into Somerset esoterica and mythic topography led her to propose that a replica of the stellar zodiac, with its twelve Houses or signs such as Taurus, Scorpio, and Capricorn, was somehow written hugely, elliptically in the immediate landscape. An imprint of the stars is overlaid on the Glastonbury Levels, Maltwood declared, who published maps, sketches, aerial photographs, and several books to make her case. Hills, paths, waterways, ditches, lanes had been inexplicably sculpted, when seen from above or in Ordnance Survey maps, into the traditional animal shapes of the zodiac. And this landscape circuit of effigies, Maltwood claimed, was none other than King Arthur's Round Table, and the Grail Quest was a clutch of field accounts of Knights making their way through its fantastic domain, what Church historians once called Glaston's Twelve Hides. Between the implications of these two posters (and the intruiging discipline of what Anthony Roberts calls "geomythics"—the myth living in the landscape) and the comfort of Nickie's tea and talk, I would take my bearings in Arthurian Glastonbury for the next few months.

"But you know at least a few people knew about this long before Maltwood picked up the idea again," says Nickie. "Back in the fifteenth century, the Elizabethan magus Dr. John Dee was aware of the Glastonbury zodiac. He seems to have visited it, made some discoveries, even prepared a starmap. He called the zodiac Merlin's Secret." Around 1580, Dee, who was court astrologer to Queen Elizabeth and allegedly a regular communicant with angels, wrote in his diary: "The starres which agree with their reproductions on the ground do lye onlie on the celestial path of the Sonne, moon and planets, with the notable exception of Orion and Hercules.... All the greater starres of Sagittarius fall in the hinde quarters of the horse, while Altiar, Tarazed, and Alschain from Auilaa do fall in its cheste.... Thus is astrologie and astronomie carefullie and exactely married and measured in a scientific reconstruction of the heavens which shews that the ancients understoode all which today the lerned know to be factes." Among the learned today, John Dee himself is a "facte" not well known while his zodiacal exegesis is ignored—except for iconoclastic enclaves like Glastonbury.

"That's where Joseph of Arimathea landed, they say, in A.D. 32 or 64, with the Grail," says Nickie, standing by the window and gesturing towards the grassy crest of Wearyall Hill. Joseph stuck his staff into the soil of Wearyall, which zodiacal advocates say is part of Pisces the Fish, and it was immediately transformed into a flowering thorn tree, which remains today, or at least a botanical descendant. That's the folk legend. King Arthur himself spent a night in a nunnery formerly situated where the Level's View Bed & Breakfast now stands, Nickie adds. Early one morning, after being visited for three nights running by a persistent angel urging him to get up, Arthur walked over dewy Wearyall at sunrise and down the other side to Beckery Chapel, another Abbey outpost, and received a vision of Mary, Mother of Christ, the Christ child, the Grail, all in an otherworld chapel in the same place as the tangible one he thought he was sitting down in. That's another local story attested to by monastic historians down at the Abbey, says Nickie. And for good measure, she's fairly confident that a few of the foundation stones in this building originally came from the once imperial Abbey, from the terrible moment in 1539 when it was literally dismembered and its sacred stones carried into diaspora as public property for builders and its last abbott, the unfortunate Richard Whiting, regrettably lost his head due to hanging on the Tor.

These orientations completed, Nickie invites me into their private living room, where several other guests and her husband, William, are watching the crucifixion of Jesus on television—a BBC dramatization, that is. How enwrapped they all are in this archetypal drama staged with all the trappings of an American Superbowl. By a strange coincidence, a week ago I watched the first installment of this same program at a friend's house in the Sierra Nevada mountains of California. I watched it fitfully, walking away often, restless, frowning, probing the refrigerator for a beer, standing watch on the porch under the twinkling stars—seeking distraction. It's a powerful drama, I won't argue that, but it makes me squirm the way this televisionized mythos manipulates my emotional reactions. I couldn't document it nor had I ever investigated it properly, but I felt this was a travesty of the real story, which, when understood, would justifiably take one's breath away and bring tears—but not this literalization. That's how I felt about Arthur, too; as readers and fans we react only to a cultural facade, a convenient fable, not the real story; that's hidden yet potentially world transformative.

I have other things to occupy my attention than fretting over the Stations of the Cross. Like settling into my new home. The Level's View perches on a narrow ridge at the end of a kind of isthmus of habitation that juts out from the higher grassy knob of Wearyall Hill. Nickie's place is two-storied, rectangular, white, its front graced with roses and ivy and little black-rimmed, unshuttered windows erratically placed, from which we can peer out upon passers-by from the white-walled bulk. From the Smithson's car park, which accommodates three small cars and a brace of bicycles, I can survey the Levels, those flat, peaty moorlands parcelled into numerous fields for miles until the gentle rise of the Polden Hills in the south or the Mendips in the north, while in the east the mound of Chalice Hill smiles like a green rainbow.

On Wearyall, it feels as if you're walking on a mountain ridge enjoying intimate views of the environs—shops, houses, traffic, churches, weather, other hills. You get the commanding confidence and information of a vista even though the hill itself soars only one hundred feet above the flatlands. From the carpark I see one of my two bedroom windows on the second floor; my study window over- looks the Levels and the River Brue. I've claimed my space, unpack- ing my researcher's tools: the torn Malory, the weighty Powys, the twice read Bradley, the stacks of articles, the commentators' books. The bed is lumpy, jerry-built from four unrelated mattress segments, the lights are low wattage, but there is a small desk for my type- writer, a tiny bookshelf, an extra quilt—it's a fine room for looking for Arthur.

On the second floor balcony among the back garden foliage on my first morning at myth-living headquarters, I keep my eyes trained on Wearyall, Chalice Hill, and the Tor, in case there are signs of Arthur. "We always say, 'Thank goodness for the Tor,'" says Nickie, leaning against the doorjamb, "because it keeps people away from all the real treasures of Glastonbury like our Wearyall Hill." The Tor is performing its public service admirably this morning, I note, look- ing off to my left, as it draws a steady bead of visitors up its pyrami- dal flanks, keeping them all away from our Wearyall. The Tor—its name derives from an old Celtic generic term for any hilltop or earthen prominence—is treeless, grassy, muscular, bumpy, peculiar. The St. Michael tower spikes its crown as the last brooding, hollow vestige from the Abbey's twelfth century intention to establish an ecclessiastical beachhead there. In pre-Christian days, local legend claims, a stone circle fit the peak like a pagan coronet; human-made landscape engineering, possibly from as early as Atlantis some 10,000 years ago, produced the hill's distinctive asymmetry; the zigzagging septenate terracing across its slopes represents an old initiatory maze used in Celtic initiations. So say the legends. A local commentator named Wright noted in 1888: "One thing that clings to me was go- ing up the Tor and penetrating through a low-lying cloud, which shed its heavy rain on the town, while we were above in a bright sun shining on the upper part of the cloud which had the appearance of a sea of silver. Or again of going over the old road by the side of Wearyall Hill one autumn morning, before it was light, and when the water had flooded all the low-lying lands, we saw the Will-O-the-Wisp." Now, a century later, locals talk about UFOs and spectral lights around the Tor.

This morning I count thirty people milling about the base of the St. Michael tower. Children in red jackets and yellow dresses, their voices trailing after them kites lofted in the wind. Suddenly they flutter like a dispersal of pigeons down the slope into a waiting schoolbus. The Tor is like a big, patient dog, abiding these intruders as if they were mewling kittens scrambling over its shanks. Tawny puffballs of Dorset sheep seem flung out on the Tor's shoulders like furry yoyos. A few solitary climbers pick their way up its steep slope, often deviating from the foot-pounded, tourist-compacted trail on their way to the summit, intersecting at times the heptatic weavings of the labyrinth coiled around the Tor like a somnolent dragon. The Tor, says another legend, is hollow, with a large stone chamber inside once used for initiations; finding the precise location entrance to this presumed cave is the desire of all the magicians of Glastonbury. Even the archeologists wouldn't mind unearthing it, should it exist, which they strenuously doubt. The Tor's ambiguity, along with Wright's mysterious Will-O-the-Wisp, attracts visitors by the hundreds, and a lot of them end up at Nickie's.

"I wonder why the Level's View is such a magnet?" Nickie asks, pouring herself a cup of tea. "We get such special, nonordinary people, you know—why do you suppose that is? Are we supposed to learn from them or is it they're getting things from staying with us? I don't know. Maybe we're just tidying up their beds and serving them a hot breakfast and that's all. It often seems that living in Glastonbury is like unravelling such a big ball of yarn, except you find there's nothing at the center. It's all the threads flung out all over. It can be terribly frustrating. We get all the stereotypes: the romantic Hebrew from the Holy Land wanting to see the New Jerusalem, the anorexic runaway from Brixton, the White One (that's what he called himself), two women, at different times, claiming to be

Mary Magdalene reincarnated. I've almost forgotten what a normal guest is like. Every situation in Glastonbury is heightened, exaggerated, overdone, blown out of proportion. Everything is more vivid, more dramatic, more fraught with coincidence."

Nickie gazes out over the Levels, sipping her tea. "Oh dear. I suppose I must get things ready for the other guests. It takes all my effort just to maintain any sense of balance living here. The longer I stay in Glastonbury, the less I seem to know about anything. I can't reject things out of hand but I can't automatically take everything on board, all the strange things people go on about. They take themselves *so* seriously. A high-ranking Druid stayed here last June. He left his white cape in his room, forgot it when he left. It was covered in manure from his rolling about on the Tor at midnight during their solstice ritual. I laundered it with plenty of bleach but good Lord, bleach plus cow make pink. I was so embarassed. I put his pink Druid's robe in the washer again just as he knocked at my front door asking for it. 'Do you have it?' he asked in such a low voice, as if it were a government secret. I wrapped it up wet, praying it wasn't pink anymore, but it probably was. I tried frightfully hard to be cheery. I really must get the eggs boiling for breakfast."

Nickie's breakfast eggs are well-boiled but what buoys my spirits is the joy of being here in Nickie's pink Druid salon. "This is the best bed and breakfast in town for people who are not normal," I declare with American cheek to my breakfast companions. If challenged on the spot just then, perhaps I wouldn't have been able to substantiate my case, but over the weeks my dossier on Nickie's clientele would shore things up. I watch, curious about my fellow questers in Avalon. There's Betty: fiftysomething, Californian, recently divorced, adrift on a midlife wanderlust, unmoored from family, friends, and job, floating around the Celtic high places like Iona, Findhorn, Glastonbury. Gregory, a New Zealander, is mildly fanatical with his Rosicrucian diagrams documenting the uncanny presence of faces— Merlin's, Arthur's, among others—in the mottled surface of stone number 53 of Stonehenge. There's Rosalyn from London, a vegetarian, her eyes thickly made up in blue cosmetics under bouffant red hair, she's a trance medium on assignment for "them." They sent Rosalyn to Glastonbury to "clean up the energy" on the Tor. Mrs. Margaret Pallow, 82, is a British Israelite: a tiny, dignified woman, she rocks contentedly in Nickie's creaky old chair in the darkening public room in the evenings until William helps her up to her room. Joan, retired from fifteen years of marriage and child-raising, reads Qabala at Chalice Well, soaks up its "healing vibrations," remembers her flusher days when she could afford to stay at the posh George & Pilgrim's on High Street. Upstairs, in the single room with the hillocky bed, there's that quirky fellow, possibly eccentric, and certainly American, a little cheeky, the one with errant, thinning curly hair, wrinkled corduroys, wool sweaters, wire-rimmed glasses, the one who arrived on Easter Sunday laden with expectations, requesting miso soup and brown rice for dinner, who said he was looking for Arthur.

Everything is enhanced in Glastonbury, Nickie says. At Level's View if there's one thing that gets seriously enhanced every day it's the dishes and laundry. At the end of a busy weekend, the Smithson's miniscule, medieval kitchen is crammed with tottering stacks of dirty plates and bowls, the wicker baskets are overloaded with sheets and pillow cases queuing for the wash, and the detritus of breakfast for twelve prompts the fainthearted to flee the entropic kitchen forever. Guests roam the house shamelessly as if touring a museum, so in a bid for privacy, William frequently retreats to his sacrosanct Cedar Room, sliding the door shut with an antisocial click. In his domain, he's surrounded by the tools of his joy: three harps, a piano, shelves of astrology books, manuscripts in progress, natal charts. Nickie, too, retreats to their private drawingroom, booklined, cozy with sofas and stuffed chairs and curtained windows. I'm sure they yearn for late morning when the guests file out for their appointments in town, or the bus back to London, and the Level's View exhales into silence, except for the clacking of a typewriter on the second floor.

In the lull between the breakfast rush and late afternoon arrivals, I often catch an uxorial exchange between Nickie and William. They set up two ironing boards in the second floor hallway outside my room, and together they steam and fold and stack their way through a mound of sheets, shirts, handkerchiefs, towels, murmuring "Yes, my darling" and "Oh, isn't that simply lovely?" as the iron hisses. William is sudsing through a shoulder-high stack of dishes, humming a Bach cantata, and says to Nickie, who dries: "She wants us over to lunch tomorrow to meet several others. She says we'll talk about our past lives but I told her we have too much cleaning and maybe we can't come." William calls out from the bathtub, in the spirit of a frolicking whale, "Coffee, Nickie. Coffee, please!"

One night the Level's View has no guests, so we make an outing to Wells Cathedral to hear a forty-part motet by Thomas Tallis by a choir distributed among the transepts. Their voices resound against the stone walls, sculpting the cathedral's ethers with Tallis' medieval reverence. This is music written for angels, William declares. I loved the music so much I left my body, he muses on the drive back to Glastonbury. I left the cathedral with some angels, celestial women with streaming chestnut hair and faces almost terrifying with beauty, he adds. Did you get the phone numbers of these heavenly maidens, I ask, probably spoiling the moment. It's not that I disbelieve him; my thoughts are iridescent with mermaid angels with beatific smiles and Tallis voices and diaphanous wings enfolding Glastonbury. William and Nickie would be ground base and anchor for me as I tossed myself into the Avalonian fray.

In the evening of my first day on the quest, I tramp down Hillhead to the Queen's Head pub, picking it randomly among Glastonbury's dozen public houses. I fortify myself with Rev. Lionel Smithett-Lewis' 1920 speculative book on the activities of Joseph of Arimathea in Glastonbury; many people read the Reverend, who was once vicar here, but few believe him. He amassed his "evidences" for Joseph's projects, secret traditions, and the Grail fraternities in Glastonbury, and on the strength of his ecclesiastical experiences and reputation, he hoped people would accept them. Smithett-Lewis was short on convincing footnotes and proofs so most Arthurian scholars tend to cite him sparingly, with tweezers. As for the Queen's Head's four other patrons tonight and the bristly publican in this miniscule, hops-swollen room, I would guess the Reverend's veracity is not a burning issue. Over a pint of Wadsworth's Best Bitter, I track Joseph's possible peripatetry from Jersusalem to Glastonbury, but the jukebox competes strenuously for my attention. "The crystal chandelier lights up the paintings on your wall," someone from Texas croons, not offering any footnotes for his claim either. "Marble statuettes are hanging daintily in the hall," the syrupy voice continues. I cock my ear for any mention of Arthur, but the country-and-western twang owns the airwaves tonight and the King draws his pint in private at some other pub in Avalon.

4

JOSEPH'S MILLENNIAL VIEW FROM WEARYALL HILL

t's a double birthday—April 23—when I make my first visit
to the mythic end of Wearyall Hill. The day commemorates
the birthday of Wellesley Tudor Pole, a Christian initiate and
Glastonbury benefactor, tea merchant, wartime advisor to
Winston Churchill, founder of Chalice Well; he died, regrettably, in 1969 in his eighties, because I'd love to have met him. The
second birthday is for St. George, exemplar of chivalry, dragon-slayer,
and British patron saint since 1222, who died, if he ever lived, a long
time ago, possibly in the third century A.D. I couldn't know it at the
time, but both figures would be my patron saints as a Grail Knight—
but that's looking ahead. So it's with their birthdays in mind, perhaps in their honor, that I'm making a preliminary reconaissance to
Wearyall, ferreting for clues that might substantiate Joseph of
Arimathea's reputed visit here two thousand years ago, starting with
the Holy Thorn, which used to be his staff.

The thorn's legend is ancient but it's not sensible to suppose, as the
legend persistently maintains, that this particular *Crataegus
monogyna*, or white thorn, is the original one magically transformed
from Joseph's staff in 31 A.D. or 64 A.D. depending on which unreliable source you consult. The earliest printed notice of this tree's
forebear and its peculiar trait of flowering at Christmas dates from
1520 when Richard Pyerson wrote in his *Life of Joseph Arimathea*:
"The Hawthorne also, that groweth in Werall, do burge and bere
grene leaves at Christmas." We're a long way from Christmas in
either direction, and today the thorn's arthritic branches are as if

frozen motionless after being windblown; the trunk is wrapped in a rusted metal cage five feet high with an inner slip of old chicken wire. A large, flat stone, half-buried in the tall grass and supposedly laid by a local farmer in 1800 to commemorate his faith in Joseph's arrival, is adorned with fresh cow flops. Cows and tourists have equal, unscheduled access to Wearyall. A warbler trills in a branch of the Holy Thorn within a cave formed of shiny dark-green leaves; it's of no significance to this warbler that its roost was once a magical staff brought from Jerusalem.

The residential strip of Wearyall, which includes the Level's View, resembles the backbone of a giant animal ferreting just beneath the landscape surface. "Wirral Hill, like the hump of a great sacred dromedary," wrote Powys. He also said of Wirral, using its older, shorter name, that it was "the actual site of that Terre Gastee of the medieval romances, which became withered and blighted after the Dolorous Blow delivered by the unlucky Balin upon King Pelleas, Guardian of the Grail." Powys was talking shop here to the Grail Knights, referring to the tradition that once the Grail Castle flourished in a verdant land, presided over by a wise, hale monarch, the Fisher King; the Dolorous Blow, which was the misuse of a powerful sword, grievously wounded the king, who became known ever after as the Maimed Fisher King; the wounding cast his dominions into ruin, known afterwards as the Wasteland. Powys suggested that Wearyall itself played a crucial role in this antique disaster. Meanwhile, the standard folk etymology for Wearyall derives from the reported—or imagined—exclamations of exhaustion by Joseph of Arimathea and his band as they beached their coracle at the base of the hill, *very weary all* from having journeyed from the Holy Land through Marseilles to the Bristol Channel and then inland to this Summer Country island, bearing the Holy Grail.

Literary scholars and Grail historians find stories like this sufficient occasion to smirk and debunk and the debate about Joseph's doings has raged inconclusively through the centuries. Joseph's official biography portrays him as a wealthy, politically influential elder of the Sanhedrin in Palestine who became mentor and financier to young Jesus in his formative years, taking him on journeys, including a famous one to Britain, poetically remembered in a famous poem by William Blake: "And did those feet in ancient time/Walk upon England's mountains green/And was the Holy Lamb of God/On England's pleasant pastures seen."

The Crucifixion was political disaster for Joseph who had publicly backed Jesus. According to the eleventh century A.D. *Gospel of Nicodemus*, "The Jews set Joseph up in a windowless cell, sealed the door, and set a guard. When they opened the cell, he was not there." Joseph later explained that the angels had "translated" him out of jail and back to Arimathea. "Four angels lifted the cell into the air, whilst he stood in prayer; and the Lord had appeared to him." Joseph gathered a retinue that allegedly included Mary, mother of Jesus, Lazarus, the resurrected, and several others; they left the Holy Land in secret, bearing a precious relic christened by Jesus when he bore the Christ within him. This relic may have been the Grail chalice or two silver and white cruets; either way, Joseph bore a sacred vessel containing blood and sweat of the dying Jesus. In Marseilles, the apostle Philip encouraged Joseph to establish a Christian settlement in Druidic Glastonbury; arriving here and explaining his apostolic mission, Joseph was greeted favorably by King Arviragus, who awarded him the Twelve Hides of Glaston, which was about 1440 acres.

"The place Arviragus assigned them was an island, rude and uncultivated," noted A. Herne in 1772, trying to clarify the Glastonbury legends, "called by the Britons for the color of it, Iniswitryn, that is, the Glassy Island, compassed by the bay full of woods, bushes, and fens." Apparently the Archangel Gabriel had comforting words for Joseph, too, and promised support such that only thirty-one years after the Crucifixion, Joseph of Arimathea founded Britain's first Christian church. It was modest, a circular compound, an oratory of wicker wands twisted together with a straw roof, situated somewhere between the present Abbey and Chalice Well. Joseph dedicated his tiny ecclesia to the Virgin Mary whose body was buried in Glastonbury after she ascended to Heaven. "Nor can we forget," adds Rev. Lionel Smithett-Lewis, "that King Arthur, and indeed every one of the Knights of the Round Table, claimed descent from Joseph of Arimathea."

Smithett-Lewis evidently was familiar with Sir Thomas Malory's florid description of Joseph as the heavenly Bishop of the Grail mysteries in his classic fifteenth century compendium of Arthuriana, *Le Morte d'Arthur*, which runs to one thousand pages. Scholars rank Smithett-Lewis' work as equivalent to Malory's—a faithful compilation of fancy, supposition, and myth. As Malory recounted Joseph's apotheosis: "And therewithal beseemed them that there came a man and four angels from heaven, clothed in the likeness of a bishop, and had a cross in his hand; and these four angels bare him up in a chair, and set him down before the table of silver whereupon the Sangrail was; and it seemed that he had in the midst of his forehead letters which said, 'See ye here, Joseph, the first bishop of Christendom, the same which our Lord succoured in the city of Sarras in the spiritual place.'"

Once in Glastonbury, Joseph assumed his duties as Christendom's first abbott in Britain, burying the Grail (or cruets) in a secret chamber near Chalice Well so that Jesus the Christ's sacred blood could perpetually stain the well waters red, or chalybeate, thereafter known as Blood Spring. When he died, Joseph was buried in a place of prophetic significance, according to Maelgwyn, the sixth century A.D. Glaston-bury monk, astronomer, historian, and mystic. "He lies on a forked line, next the south corner of an oratory fashioned of wattles. For Joseph has in his sarcophagus with him two cruets, white and silver, filled with blood and sweat of the prophet Jesus." The fact is nobody has found Joseph's tomb, although many have looked and speculated. Maelgwyn, perhaps waxing gnomic, predicted the eventual discovery of Joseph's occulted grave as an event of momentous consequence. "When his sarcophagus shall be found complete and intact in future days it shall be seen and open to all the world. Thenceforth neither water nor the dew of heaven shall fail the dwellers in that most noble isle."

I walk up to the last bench on the crest of Wearyall to a point just beyond the avuncular clump of bushes flourishing like side whiskers on the smooth green face of the hill. Before me lies all of Glastonbury, red-shingled and spired, huddled around the base of the four Summer Country islands. The aroma of chimney smoke wafts past, the rattle of an empty hay rick trails across the hill, and my gaze sways along the silent cow paths that meander down the slope and out onto the Levels where a farmer mows his peat field, criss-crossing, never missing a swath. What am I really looking at? It's as if the physical landscape is a veil and something portentous lives beneath this facade—but what? Somerset: *Sumorsaete, Sumortun-saete*, land of the summer dwelling folk, land of the ancient Sumers; for the Welsh, the original "countrymen," it is *Gwylad yr Haf*, the White Land; and for Taliessin, radiant-browed Celtic bard, it is the Region of the Summer Stars. The brightest star in the *Aestiva Regio* might have been Gwyn ap Nudd, King of the Celtic fairies, Master of *Annwn*, the Otherworld deep within the Tor, Lord of the Dead, spectral leader of the Wild Hunt with his infernal red-eared white hounds of Hell. Gwyn's name means "white" or "light," which accords with another old term for Somerset: *Gwynfa*, "place of light."

So Buddhist scholar Stephen Jenkins isn't making that big an associative leap in *The Undiscovered Country* when he calls Somerset "the place of bliss." Jenkins boldly speculates that possibly there is a fundamental affinity between Somerset and the Buddhist sacred city, Shambhala, domain of perfected humans, known in the East as a place of unalloyed bliss, the "source of happiness," and a spiritual paradise. Jenkins astonished his readers in 1977 when he reported that certain high-ranking Mongolian lamas he had personally studied with had given him this assurance: "The millennarian teachings of the realm of Shambhala were preserved (albeit in veiled form) in Britain, which they regarded as the White Island of Central Asian legend. It is weird to think that the great Arthurian *Matter of Britain* just might be the locked treasure house he spoke of." But the Mongolian lamas told him more. The kingdom of Shambhala had once been in Britain in the last centuries before Christ, "when Gwynfa, the Place of Bliss, was located in the Summer Country, about that ancient site of Glastonbury."

Jenkins' seemingly outlandish suggestion that Buddhist Shambhala might be connected, possibly identical with, Avalonian Somerset is buttressed by another name, this one indigenously British: Albion, the White Island, anciently the name for the British Isles. Holding Glastonbury and its four islands in my gaze, I'm struck with how this red-roofed enclave, cradled between the two long hills of Wearyall and Edmunds, resembles a giant, recumbent earthen figure. Wearyall and Edmunds are the legs, the Abbey its groin, Chalice Hill the plump belly, the Tor the prominent chest, while the head rests massively somewhere out in Maltwood's Temple of the Stars. Male or female, I can't say, but human, yes: the landscape as the giant figure of a human, Albion.

"Chained within the hills and valleys of his native realm," writes John Michell in *The View Over Atlantis*, "the great spirit, Albion, lay powerless in fetters of iron-mortality, his form obscured by the encroaching fog of a grey enchantment, his kingdom usurped by a host of petty tyrants." Albion: the once and future white island, the geomythic figure of a human giant whose body is the landscape, the islands, the Summer Country, Glastonbury; the geomythos of Albion, whose legend lives in the topography of the landscape. Joseph, implanting his staff on Wearyall, on the figure's upper thigh, must have perceived this clone of Albion, Gwynfa's divine Man. Maybe that's what brought him to Glastonbury; maybe the staff had to needle the giant's thigh to accomplish a great healing of the land itself. "The shadow of Albion, whether as deva, giant or god," writes Anthony Roberts in *Sowers of Thunder* (the Glastonbury historian who first introduced the term "geomythics" in the 1970s), "covers all these holy centers, not being specifically associated with any one location but rather symbolizing the power of them all through the body of a giant whose lineaments are shaped by the contours of the living earth itself."

5

A HELICOPTER FOR GWYN ON AVALON'S CRYSTAL MOUNTAIN

'm clacking away at my typewriter one morning when Nickie peers through the doorway, which is ajar. A giant Army helicopter has been buzzing around the St. Michael tower for the last hour dropping off mysterious roped bundles; she and William are off to investigate—would I like to come? At last, an opportunity to meet the Tor firsthand. I've deliberately kept myself away from the Tor, Gwyn's ambiguous hill, content to scrutinize it daily from my porch until the right moment presents itself. First impressions after all are formative.

The Tor is inexplicably protean, subject to imaginative viewing. From one vantage point, it's a spiked war helmet; from another, in the early morning shadows, its maze-terraced slopes are the intricate folds of a shawl wrapped around a woman's shoulders. Yet as we step out the front door of the Level's View this morning, the dirt trail up the Tor is a delicate umbilical cord, a lifeline pulling pilgrims up the steep hill, up the spiritual path. My viewmaster clicks again with a new impression: it's a tawny ribbon trailing in a light breeze, each hiker is one color sparkle among a myriad of Avalonian ornaments. And again: the Tor trail is an artery whose diastolic flow pumps human corpuscles to its central heart cavity. Through William's binoculars I see that a half dozen men in green uniforms are at work at the base of the tower easing down pallets from the hovering helicopter.

"The elemental spirits up there must be going mad with all this hopping about," says Nickie. "It looks like the Army is chasing them *off* the Tor today," I quip as we drive down Hillhead. It's not like the Army or anything else could chase away the primordial devic beings Wellesley Tudor Pole observed there, "radiant and magnificent in all the ancient beauty of mind and power." Pole saw the apricot light of the Christ's aura blend with the residual smoke-blue of the Glastonbury vibration to form a "most astonishing pattern, resembling a huge flower with tendrils reaching out in all directions."

We park by the hedgerow on Wellhouse Lane, then stand at the edge of a broad grassy field at the bottom of the Tor's northern slope. Two dozen other people have taken an hour off to watch the event. The Army is transporting pallets of dry cement for the National Trust to fortify the eroding foundations of the tower, a man tells us; it turns out he's the National Trust warden in charge of Somerset properties, including the Tor. The constant heavy feet of thousands of tourists milling about its base has destabilized the foundation. "I've been on this job seven years now and I'll tell you that in every season, every kind of weather, I've never seen the Tor without somebody on it. Four years ago somebody actually drove a Subaru up the Tor for a TV commercial but it got stuck near the top." A twin-propellered cargo plane lumbers past at barely two hundred feet, from our vantage point seemingly lower than the base of the Tor itself. "They like to challenge each other who can fly the lowest," the warden adds.

The field is roped off, and inside the cordon are two Army jeeps, a large Army truck with canvas sides, a sun-yellow Royal Navy Avcat fuel truck, and the Helly, as the crowd calls it, hovering titanically twenty feet above the field, as six yellow-helmeted men attach a dangling hook to the ropes around the pallet. Awesome in its crudity, this fierce insectal tube lifts off sideways, backing its way up the Tor's shoulders, as if about to ritually thread its maze, then disappears behind its crown, leaving us only the constant whirring as proof of its existence. As we stand at the base of our sacred mountain and glass island, intrigue ignites us. Nothing happens in Glastonbury that isn't varnished with extra significance, with unspoken import. "She will draw a magnetic life from her Three Hills strong enough to attract all the world to her side," said Powys of Glastonbury. "Where the guide books make their great mistake is in treating Glastonbury as a fragment of history, instead of something that's *making* history."

All that's visible of the helicopter from here are its blade tips beating the air behind the tower. It hovers beyond sight, infernally, like Gwyn's spectral hounds snapping at the leash, yelping in expectation of the Wild Hunt, about to burst the veil into our reality just as the helicopter is whirring at the threshold of theirs. Is the helicopter still there or has it joined Gwyn's horde? No wonder Dion Fortune, occult novelist and Qabalist who lived in the house at the base of the Tor in the 1930s, called the Tor the hill of dreams. The Tor is "shaped like a couchant lion bearing a tower upon its crest," said Fortune in *Avalon of the Heart*; it is "the most pagan of hills which keeps its spiritual freedom." The Tor is indeed "the Hill of Vision for anyone whose eyes have the least inclination to open upon another world. Many times the tower is reported to have been rimmed in light; a warm glow, as of a furnace, beats up from the ground on wild winter nights, and the sound of chanting is heard from the depths of the hill."

In recent decades, Glastonburians have attributed that glow and chanting to extraterrestrials. People report seeing orange balls of light, egg-shaped objects, they hear droning sounds—it's the standard impedimenta of a presumed UFO presence. But what we call UFOs today, the folk of Somerset once called the Little People, the Shining Folk, or Devas. Around 650 A.D. St. Collen occupied a hermitage on the then wooded slopes of the Tor. One day he was invited to a grand feast and musical entertainment at Gwyn ap Nudd's palace of enchantments within the Tor. The hermitic St. Collen was a bit of a curmudgeon because when he met Gwyn in his golden chair, he behaved poorly. He found Gwyn, as the voice of legend recounts it, "with the best appointed troops, steeds with young men riding them of the handsomest description, maidens also of the most gentle and sprightly aspect, and in addition all else that became the state appertaining to the court of a sumptuous king." Unimpressed, St. Collen sprinkled a bottle of holy water upon the pagan apparition and

Gwyn, vaguely nonplussed, took his party elsewhere and vanished.

Glastonbury Tor as Avalon's crystal mountain, *Ynys Witrin*, the primordial sacred mountain as glass island rising translucently above the misty inland sea of the Summer Country—the tradition persists, despite St. Collen's ban. Another monastic emissary to *Ynys Witrin* was St. Patrick, the evangelizing Irishman and one-time abbott of Glastonbury Abbey—again, if you believe the Abbey myth-makers of one thousand years ago for whose saintly pantheon St. Patrick was a prize catch. One day St. Patrick and his companion Wellias climbed "with great difficulty" up through "the dense wood" of the Tor and found "an ancient oratory well-nigh ruined, yet fitting for Christian devotion." The oratory's interior (this was before the St. Michael tower was built) was suffused with "so sweet an odor that we believed ourselves to be set in the beauty of Paradise." That night Jesus told him in a dream that he had designed the oratory "to the honor of my name, and here men should honorably invoke the aid of my archangel, Michael." There is no record of St. Patrick spritzing Jesus with holy water as a banishment for ecclesiastically incorrect visions.

Suddenly, monstrously, our patience is rewarded as the source of the droning becomes visible again. First, the helicopter's whipping blades appear, then the olive-skinned machine itself emerges rude and dark from behind the Tor as if it had been closeted with Gwyn in the Otherworld. Blades and fusilage parallel the tower as if pinned to the airspace; the visual juxtaposition is unnerving, as if the seam between realities is unravelling. The helicopter wails down the Tor to us, fanning bystanders at an elevation of five feet; its windwake stirs up a confetti of spring dandelions in seed stage. After the helicopter lands, things get ordinary. The helicopter is in our world again but nobody discusses events in Annwn. The flight crew eats lunch, invites us to circumambulate the grounded brute, sets a three-year-old boy to pose cockily at the doorway with flight goggles and helmet. Then it's time to go: the helicopter roars into life like a jet, its blade spinning a furious circlet in the air, blurring vision; fifteen feet off the ground, the pilot leans out his cockpit window and waves.

Arcing past Gwyn's Tor, will it flash us a rainbow like the globular spaceship in *E.T.* as it flashed homeward into another dimension? No, you only get rainbows in Glastonbury when somebody has achieved the Holy Grail, say the legends.

But who can you trust in a place so glamorously seductive, so rampant with spectral chieftains, Otherworld castles, and Army helicopters—the legends, the scholars, the myth-makers? "Into this blue-purple vapor, into the bosom of these fields lower than the sea," says Powys, "floated, drifted upon the wind, all those dangerous enervating myths, here caught by these fatal, low-lying flats they had lingered... these tender-false mandragoras lulled to sleep the minds of generations!"

6

OLD FRIENDS WRITE
IN THE GROUND

erky and frothy after two Guinnesses one evening, I arrive home at Level's View from the pub and find Nickie waving me into the living room. "Come meet Henry DeForest," she says, indicating an empty chair for me. Henry is about seventy, slender, wiry, with sparkling blue eyes, a broad, high forehead, and swept-back wavy white hair; his face is sensitive and inquiring. He wears a baggy rainbow sweater into whose amorphous folds his body seems to vanish, leaving only the intelligent head. Apparently Nickie has briefed him on my Arthurian project, because he launches without preamble into a discussion of Arthurian arcana, like the Parsafalian archetype and Merlin's hierophantic responsibility, before I even get the teacup to my lips. "Glastonbury is living in hell at this moment," he says. "Its healing, loving energy is unbalanced, coupled with its failure to radiate its own glory. The crucifixion of Glastonbury needs to be completed, the devastation and misery of soul must be more heart-rending, and the experience of the rock-bottom of despair more absolute than elsewhere." Silence around the table; then Henry smiles and relaxes. "But I'm hoping for the best. So much depends on Glastonbury's final resurrection. Look, I have to run along but I want to come back tomorrow with a special book. I couldn't find it tonight."

The next evening before Henry arrives, I amble up Wearyall at sunset and perch on a west-facing bench to smoke my pipe. Unsociable insects punctuate my reverie by dive-bombing my neck. I'm so startled by their first attack, I fall off the bench trying to swipe my way to safety. Let's try another bench further up the hill; but it's no improvement, soon a swarm of buzzing black things hovers noisily inches from my eyes. Maybe the smoke will drive them away but the tobacco haze from extra puffing only makes me dizzy. Inexplicably, there's a lull in the nipping and I'm free to contemplate the evening mists engulfing the Tor and its tower. Then something shifts and the dusk feels radically different; I feel impelled to flee Wearyall, to *run*. I barrel down the slope through the queer dusk, the benches disappearing into the thickening dark. What kind of Celtic bogeyman am I running from—Gwyn and his awful red-eared hounds? I scramble over the turnstile, dash down the lane, turn my key in the lock, jump inside, close the door quickly, and catch my breath. But I'm not home safe yet. I sit in the guests' living-room and notice Henry, Nickie, and William talking in the next room; I can't see them, only their reflections in the glass door; they don't know I'm back. Somebody arrives at the front door and they all depart, still not seeing me. The queerness deepens: have I become invisible? As if I'm straddling two worlds with an eye in each, I lay down on my bed in confusion to calm my breathing and find my center again.

Voices downstairs call my name—suddenly the unnerving mists from Wearyall disperse, and, as if nothing has happened, I join Nickie, William, and Henry at the candlelit table. Henry reads aloud with a warm trill of bardic power from a book by Wellesley Tudor Pole called *Writing on the Ground* that describes the discovery in Glastonbury of a peculiar blue sapphire bowl of uncertain age but undoubted numinosity. The bowl, which appeared in Glastonbury in 1906, is now kept in the Upper Room in Little St. Michael's at Chalice Well. "It's an uncannily powerful object," says Henry. "It's only known by word of mouth and only a few can see it. I've been using it in my work over the last year but I haven't actually held it for several months. Tudor Pole mentions it in only a few places in his books; it's absolutely shrouded in mystery. Let's try and see it tomorrow."

The bowl was discovered at St. Bride's Well along the River Brue by friends of Tudor Pole. At least one version of St. Bride's Well is situated behind the former site of Beckery Chapel on Bee-Keeper's Island, which is about one-quarter mile behind Wearyall. This "island" is a nondescript tussocky mound, basically an empty field behind Beckery Burrows, Glastonbury's old sheep-processing neighborbood; horses and sheep are pastured here, alternately; immediately adjacent is the town's wastewater processing unit. Hardly anybody visits Beckery and it's not on the new age roster of Glastonbury sacred sites. The blue bowl, Pole contended, had been physically blessed by Jesus the Christ then brought to Glastonbury through Italy by a cabal of secret dispatches; ultimately, it was buried at the Well for a later, intended rediscovery. One day, in his Bristol office, Pole suddenly knew precisely where the bowl was located and that it was time to unearth it; he had already seen this in a dream.

"I regard the discovery of the glass vessel as a promise or forerunner, symbolically, of Avalon's renewable destiny, as a 'sign upon the wind,'" Pole said in 1963. "For me, this vessel provides a direct link with the time Jesus was on Earth. For some undisclosed reason, the vessel's true origin has been purposely concealed." Pole didn't think the sapphire bowl was the Holy Grail. "The Grail has never materialized in mortal form to be handled by man. Nor ever will. This celestial symbol of Love and Unity has had its prototypes or earthly reflections from very ancient times. It's humbling to realize that a supposedly inanimate object can play the stupendous role of focus for the manifestation of such an event. This vessel is the symbol of the heavenly and eternal Grail. It is the Chalice of Christ, the promise of the future." Evidently Joseph's silver cruets or chalice from the Last Supper were also earthly reflections of this heavenly reality, and probably not the Grail either.

"I'm feeling adventurous," Henry declares, setting the book down. "Let's slip into town for something to eat," he says to me. We drive down Hillhead in Henry's rattling blue van whose gear box, he tells me, is subject to sudden seizures. "It bloody well better not act up tonight because I'm hungry and no mechanic," Henry says. Were you ever married? I ask him. Once, but his wife died seven years ago; but that doesn't stop them from communicating because she visits him often in dreams and he feels her presence frequently. Henry is basically retired and collects a government pension, but he's by no means an inactive septuagenarian. He's embroiled in numerous projects, travels, secret societies, seminars, and obscure causes; he manages a butterfly sanctuary and leads pilgrimages to the French Pyrenees. "I always seem to be working with younger people, practically two generations behind me. It's part of a larger pattern and anyway I feel ageless." He acted when he was younger, studied Rudolf Steiner's Anthroposophy, taught in Steiner's Waldorf schools, was a mental health therapist, is a lifetime philosopher.

"Clairvoyants lack the judgement of historians but they lack the insight of the psychics," Henry explains as we stride into the fish-and-chips shop on Maidlode Street. "Clairvoyance is psychological but the historian who cannot intuit a different level of information is compelled to seek tangible, consistent, and reproducible proofs. Double chips with lots of vinegar."

Henry's flat is at the Golden Gate, formerly the secret, privileged entrance to the Abbey. Now it's a small housing project just beyond the Abbey wall, Henry says, opening the door. I deposit myself in a sagging armchair in his tiny livingroom. "Have some tea and cake and if the cream on the cake is sour, just ignore it." As Henry makes phone calls from another room, I examine a stack of books on the table: they're all by Tudor Pole. "I left them out for you," he calls out. I don't know why, but this delights me; in fact, since I first heard his name, I've felt a glow, a recognition, a familiarity with this man who died when I was a teenager and whom I couldn't possibly have met, except in dreams.

Born in 1884, Pole had been a writer, traveller, archeologist, industrialist, soldier, seer, healer, and occult advisor to Winston Churchill during the war. In 1940, he orchestrated the Big Ben Silent Minute, which mobilized millions of British—whose country was then under aerial siege by Germany and worried about an imminent land invasion—to pray silently for one minute at nine o'clock every night. After the war, the German high command, which also em-

ployed occultism in their war efforts, admitted this had been a formidable weapon. In 1959, Pole purchased the Chalice Well property
from the Belgian Order of the Sacred Heart; fifty-five years earlier he
had decided to acquire it but he knew the time wasn't ripe. He created the Chalice Well Trust to manage the property, thereby fulfill-
ing his 1904 intuition that these two acres sandwiched between
Chalice Hill and the Tor possessed an innate sanctity and destiny.
Throughout his life, Pole was the Well's spiritual guardian, and, to a
large degree, Glastonbury's, too. "In 1904, Glastonbury was dead or
anyway in a coma, spiritually speaking," reflected Pole in 1960. "It
is my hope that Chalice Well may once more fulfill the inspiring
mission of acting as a gateway through which revelation for the
coming times may flow, radiating from there across Britain and the
world."

The next morning we have an appointment to spend some reflective time in the Upper Room at Little St. Michael's, which Pole established as a residency for the managers, a small bed-and-breakfast
service for visitors, and as a conference center. The Upper Room, on
the top floor of Little St. Michaels, was Pole's unique inspiration in
which he designed a small chamber based on a vision he had of the
actual room in which Jesus held his Last Supper. Stillness and high
aspiration permeate Pole's Upper Room; the penetrative sense of the
spiritual worlds, the insinuation of a doorway between worlds are
ambient. In one half of the room stands a long wooden table with
empty wooden bowls and a dozen simple chairs along its perimeter.
This area is roped off; we're to sit in chairs on the other side of the
small room. "There is a Presence already apparent in the Upper
Room, now taking on its destined shape and atmosphere," Pole said.
One Christmas, Pole found the room "thronged by friends and visitors from far and wide in unseen realms." Henry opens a drawer in
a small cabinet, closes it abruptly, frowns, then leaves the room. I
don't know what's upset him, but I ease into the stillness and soon
forget about it.

I rejoin Henry a half hour later outside. He's clearly annoyed; invisible tongues of fire lick at his bushy eyebrows, casting doleful shad-

ows on his elfin face. "They removed the bowl. The custodian has actually taken the bowl away from public view. He says people are drawn to the Room solely to use the bowl, which is idolatrous. To me, that's spiritual censorship, and I told him because I was quite put out to find the bowl removed. The blue sapphire bowl is part of the hierophantic alchemical transformation work underway in Glastonbury." The controversy seems remote to me because I'm beginning to feel into Pole's remarks about the symbolic Grail and the various physical artifacts created as reflections. If Pole's right, the real Grail is beyond the realm of physical objects and should be our true focus. Anyway, I'm eager to experience the gardens upon which Pole set a nimbus of destiny when he wrote in 1966: "Chalice Well is *already* being used as a platform for a renewal of the Christ message and will continue so to be used." I tell Henry I'll rejoin him later.

I love the gardens of the Well at first sight, this sliver of eternal joy wedged between the Glastonbury hills, this vale of paradise in Avalon's lap. The garden is landscaped into four distinct sections through which the chalybeate water flows in sculpted tiers and channels from the actual pentagonal well at the far end, through the mouth of a stone lion, tumbling into the grotto called Arthur's Courtyard, then into a *vesica piscis* spillway near the gatehouse. The water gurgles and cascades through a panoply of flowers, bushes, fruit trees, cobbled paths, benches, the drone of bees, a sussurus of visitors—and my rapt attention. Color, sound, smell, sensation are amplified to an acuteness of being; the air is redolent with blossoms, sanctity, and spiritual expectation. Expectancy: as if the flowers will speak, as if the angels will materialize. As if Arthur....

Over the gateway into Arthur's Courtyard is a metal sculpture of a sword passing between two interlocking circles called a *vesica piscis*, a key symbol in sacred geometry and Gothic architecture. You stand at the gateway as if on the verge of a vast room with an atmosphere of its own. At the other end of the Courtyard is a stairway made of fourteen broad steps laid a little eccentrically. "Since the Arthur Courtyard at Chalice Well has been regenerated," wrote Pole in 1964, "the avenue between it and its astral counterpart has been reopened. Invaluable energies are now flowing in both directions once more."

What's also flowing copiously through the Courtyard are 25,000 gallons a day of Blood Spring waters widely regarded to be sanctified and innately healing, like the waters of Lourdes; visitors are constantly filling flasks at the Lion's Head fountain.

I sit on a bench near the Lion's Head to watch the steady spume of holy water through its stone mouth. Amidst a sashay of apple blossoms, daffodils, gurgling water, and the warm blaze of sunshine, I exhale into an intense relaxation. My eyes shut and I'm an ecstatic frog floating eyes up in the afternoon pond. Something pours into the garden coating me in liquid feeling. I sit in a cone of loveliness. I'm inside, enveloped, tucked lovingly within the cooing wings of a white dove the size of the garden. Blue irises quiver, unspoken words poise on the tips of stamens. Everywhere I look, here it is, this indwelling, lilting seriousness, this feeling beyond laughing, crying, self-reflecting, that wafts me inward, into the angelic soul of things.

Mellow from this infusion, I stroll up the garden to the last section, to the Well itself. Its inner pentagonal chamber, once used for baptisms, is capped by a heavy lid overlaid with another metalwork *vesica piscis*, this one designed in 1919 by Abbey excavator Frederick Bligh Bond. With both hands, I lift the cover and peer into its ancient interior of square-cut stones lapped perennially by bloodred holy water. Nobody knows for sure where this prodigious flow of water originates. Mendip Hills, some suggest; others say it's a secret spring inside Chalice Hill or the Tor; either way, most of it is wasted, spilling out into the gutters because town officials consider it insanitary for general consumption and entrepreneurs haven't bothered to exploit it. "No sacred pool, in Rome, or Jerusalem, or Mecca, or Tibet," said Powys, "has gathered such an historic continuum of psychochemical force about it as this spot contained then and contains still." Powys acknowledged the Well's "thick psychic aura of magical vibrations" and suggested it represented "a crack, that cranny, that slit in Time through which the Timeless had broken the laws of Nature."

7

AN OLD GIANT WHO LIKES APPLE TREES

olden apples—I've had them on my mind all morning here at Chalice Hill. Glastonbury and Avalon may be named with apples in mind. According to one etymology, Glasteing, one of twelve brothers from northern Britain long ago, tracked his eight-legged pregnant sow through all of Somerset along a wandering path since called *Suggaweg*, or Sow's Way. The peripatetic sow eventually nestled under an apple tree to suckle her thirty newborn piglets.

In honor of this bovine perspicacity, Glasteing founded his new settlement around this apple tree: *Glasteingaburg*, now Glastonbury. The scholars dismiss the fable outright as a fairy tale, but it's the oldest surviving Just-So story about the origins of Glastonbury. *Insula Avallonia*, the Island of Apples, was founded upon an abundance of apples, contends William of Malmesbury, the Abbey's own meticulous thirteenth century resident historian. Geoffrey of Monmouth, a twelfth century concocter of pseudo-historical fancies, (most historians say), took William's speculations one step further, proposing that Avalon's foundation may be attributable to a famous personality in the Arthurian stories: Morgan.

"The island of apples, which men call 'The Fortunate Isle,' gets its name from the fact it produces all things of itself, and apple trees grow in its woods from the close-clipped grass," wrote Geoffrey in his *Vita Merlini*. "There nine sisters rule by a pleasing set of laws those who come to them from our country. She who is first of them is more skilled in the healing art and excels her sisters in the beauty of her person, Morgan is her name." In the Arthurian canon, Morgan le Fay is Arthur's sister and arch enemy, a witch who steals his power, undermines his rule, and saves his soul for Avalon; but for Geoffrey, Morgan is the matriarchal dispenser of the apples of wisdom and thus the spiritual benefactor of all Celtic heroes. Morgan's father, says Geoffrey, was Avallach, King of the *Aestiva Regio*, the apple-rich and magical Summer Country. The legends unequivocally equate Avalon with Glastonbury, while Avallach's name permutates and gets adulterated over the centuries, ending up as Melwas. As he lays dying on her barge, Morgan ferries the mortal Arthur back to Avalon and outside of time. Morgan's eight sisters, according to Celtic myth, grant wondrous passage to humans to their Blessed Realms. Irish bards once spoke of *echtrai*, tales of adventure, and *imramma*, tales of voyages, when they recounted the miraculous translation of antique heroes through the nebulous Celtic Otherworld, variously called The Land of the Living, The Land of Women, The Land of Promise. With irresistible blandishments of immortality and unending delight—symbolized by the golden apple—one of Morgan's sisters inducts the hero into undertaking the perilous journey.

In this paradaisal world, there is no death, sin, or transgression, an otherworldly woman told Conle the Redhaired, tossing him an apple as an inducement. Bran, Son of Febal, wakes one afternoon to find a branch of silver apple wood, white with blossoms, plucked from the apple trees of Emain on the Island of Joy, which he subsequently visits. King Cormac is awarded a branch of silver apple wood from which hang three golden apples. This grants him passage into the Land of Promise. In *The Dream of Rhonabwy*, Eiryn Wych, servant to Arthur, spreads a mantle of brocaded silk with an apple of red-gold at each of its corners before Arthur, inviting him to step upon it; should he wrap himself up in this magic mantle, Arthur would become invisible yet able to see everything. The golden bough may have been mistletoe for Aeneas, but here in the Celtic homeland, the golden apple with silver leaves is the ticket into Avalon.

It's only early May, so if Avalon is to produce a bounty of golden apples this season surely the harvest won't come until the fall. Even so, the apple trees on the rim of Chalice Hill are aflutter with white expectation. The stout old trees are strung like necklace beads around the soft throat of the hill. Chalice Hill, Morgan's hill, your lush green mound spotted with dandelion and buttercup, silently gestates the Holy Grail. I sit under a mature beech in spring leaf and look over Glastonbury three hundred feet below. It's so close you can almost peer into the back lanes and laundry rows from this position of intimate loftiness. The Abbey fishpond is a flat, shiny dish sparkling in the swart lawn amidst collapsed transepts. Solitary walkers about the molten pond are moats in the unblinking eye of a huge, green fish. Beyond is Wearyall like a whale's back, sheets of water streaming off its emerald flanks.

There is a roaring, as if a giant flame-thrower were belching furnaces of heat. It's the strangest sound and impossible to identify until I see what's making it: a hot air balloon, orange-skinned and striped in blue and red, floats like an aerial golden apple before me just off the hill. Two adventurers in the bucket survey Glastonbury with binoculars. I envy them their elevation and the opportunity to survey the countryside, to whoof off into the Land of the Living, should they wish, accepting the blandishments of Morgan's priestesses, collecting signs of Arthur on the way. Arthur left traces throughout the Celtic landscape; surely they'll find one.

In the Welsh legend *Culhwch and Olwen*, Arthur, his dog Cafall, and "the hosts of the world, the champions of Britain," set out on a wild hunt through Ireland, Wales, and Cornwall, overland by horse, oversea by *Prydwen*, Arthur's crystal ship. They're after Twrch Trwyth, a wild boar whom they eventually drive into the sea. The Welsh remember Arthur in their *Triads* as one of the Three Generous Men of the Island of Britain, as one of the "nine bravest and most notable warriors of the whole world," and as the most fearsome of the Three Red Ravagers. "For a year neither grass nor plants used to spring up where one of the three would walk; but where Arthur went, not for seven years." *Arth Vawr*, the Heavenly Bear—that's what the Celtic myth-makers called Arthur, borne in the celestial wain of Ursa Major, the great She-bear among the stars who stalks the Pole Star under the baleful eye of Draco, the celestial dragon. But if the wanderers in the golden balloon have seen Arthur, they're not saying and soon drift away over Edmunds Hill in a whoof of indifference.

8

GOG AND MAGOG OPEN THEIR OAKEN GATES

iants—I've always loved stories about them. Here at the bottom of Stonedown Lane at the base of the uplift that ends in the Tor, I'm standing between Gog and Magog, two ancient oaks and onetime sentinels of Avalon. I can't help wondering if the Tor, perhaps Glastonbury itself, was originally built by giants; perhaps Glasteing was an antediluvian giant. It's the names—Gog and Magog—so rich in association, that prompt my thoughts in this direction because originally their names belonged to giants.

Geoffrey of Monmouth described the wrestling confrontation between Corineus and the "repulsive, deadly monster Gogmagog," a Cornish giant. Gogmagog was so strong that "once he had given it a shake, he could tear up an oak tree as though it had been a hazel wand." Britain, in the first days after the Romans Brutus and Corineus arrived here intent on colonization, was "uninhabited except for a few giants," adds Geoffrey. Some of those few giants, including Gogmagog, evidently needed to be removed from the land. King Arthur was summoned to Brittainy to dispatch a great giant who had vanquished fifteen kings, embroidered his jewelled coat with their beards, and liked to gnaw on human limbs for dinner. "This was the fiercest giant that ever I met with, save one in the mount of Araby, which I overcame, but this was greater and fiercer," exclaims Arthur afterwards, according to Malory.

World mythology is replete with giant myths. The Norse recount the giants of Jotunheim such as Eggther the Warder, Thrym the Lord,

Ymir the First; the Greeks had their Hundred Handed Ones, Titans, and one-eyed Cyclops; and in the British Isles practically the origin of the entire megalithic landscape of stone circles, hills, mounds, forts, ditches, henges, and cairns is attributed to the architectural might of a vanished race of industrious, quarrelsome giants. Hebrew tradition does not remember Gog and Magog so fondly. The Bible portrays them as the brutish enemies of Israel: Og, a fifteen foot tall giant and remnant of the vanished race of Rephaim, is the King of Bashan. Og probably lost his "g" and was once Gog. Og, Sihon, and Anak, says William Blake, were among the giants of the White Island. Jehovah placed them as guards at the arches of Albion's tomb, "binding the Stars/In merciful Order, bending the Laws of Cruelty to Peace."

Og, says the Talmud, descended from a fallen angel while Rabbinical myths contend that Og was a giant six miles high who drank water from the clouds and toasted fish by holding them against the sun's rays; and when the Deluge was at its floodtide, its waters reached only to his knees. Noah refused Og entry to the Ark but allowed the giant to sit on the roof as they floated on top of the world ocean, and he fed him every day. In return Og pledged that he and his descendants would be Noah's servants in perpetuity. Somehow the mythic portent of all this got loaded onto these two ancient oaks at the end of Stonedown.

As the last two of presumably dozens of Avalon Oaks, Gog and Magog look like stout Tolkienesque Ents, fat, squished in, thirty-feet tall, wide-girthed sentient trees. Local legend says these two stalwarts once marked the beginning of a Druidic processional, two parallel lines of oaks from here to the bottom swirls of the Tor. That's why, says a legend, the town was formerly spelled *Glastanbyrie*, Hill of Oaks. According to the antiquarian Eyston writing in 1714, Gog and Magog, and not Wearyall, mark the place where Joseph and his band disembarked from their coracle; from Stonedown, they trekked across the Glastonbury islands to Wearyall. Lionel Smithett-Lewis claims once there stood here an additional tree, the Oak of Avalon, installed as a memorial to Joseph's arrival in Glastonbury. Over the centuries the oaks died, were removed and not replaced, so that by 1906 the last of the avenue of oaks, excepting Gog and Magog, were chopped down to prepare the field for agriculture; the felled trees, eleven feet in diameter, exhibited more than two thousand seasonal growth rings; and J. Snow & Sons of Glastonbury transformed the hoary oakwood into chairs, candlesticks, bowls, and picture frames. So vanished the remains of Glastonbury's Druidic "Patriarchal Pillars & Oak Groves," as Blake called them, the teaching sanctuaries of the *dervo-vidos*, Druids with "knowledge of the oak."

Today, both Gog and Magog sport shiny yellow leaves, but of this old couple, half of Gog, on my left facing the Tor, is missing. She's still alive and cussing no doubt, but about half her limbs have been removed and the remaining limbs are hollow and inert. Magog, on my right, is healthier, resembling an inverted Nantes carrot, with green stems waving lustily from its narrowed crown. Magog is a molten tree that solidified tentatively, in lumps, in midpour; Magog is a paradox of senesence and virility.

When Powys stood here, vicariously, through a character, between these "gigantic living creatures whose topmost branches were already thickly sprinkled with small, gamboge-yellow leaf buds," he felt they were "conversing together in that golden sun-haze." Powys presumed the trees were bandying their rich knowledge of Glastonbury history, having witnessed it all. He felt "the immense repository of this huge tree's vast planetary experience." One of Powys' characters, visiting Gog and Magog in an evening windstorm, senses the branches are deliberately making sounds: "a cumulative, rustling sigh, as if a group of sorrowful Titans had lifted up their united voices in one lamentable dirge over the downfall of their race." Were Gog and Magog remembering the days when giants walked Albion, built the temples, heaped high the hills, and left shreds of memories of their colossal deeds in the form of myths? Powys doesn't say.

Standing about ten feet behind Gog and Magog, facing the Tor, a shred of memory suddenly surfaces in my mind. It was a dream from last night. I was standing here in the same place in daylight except the two oaks were much younger, hugely healthy, vibrant, in full-spring leaf. As if made of light, a white pillar, forty feet high, rises in the same place as each tree, sheathing them so that each tree is inside a white pillar. One pillar is Gog, the other Magog. At the top of the right-hand pillar stands a winged horse, atop the left, a lion; both are alive, presumably guardians. A massive double door, white, closed, and latched at the handles, connects the two pillars. Through the double doors, though closed, I see a broad avenue of light, thirty feet across, flowing out from this gateway flanked by a double column of oak trees from Stonedown up to the Tor.

I walk along this oak-lined promenade, two rows of trees on each side, as part of a ritual procession; hundreds of Celts, men on the right, women on the left, stand among the trees watching our progress with an intent reverence. I realize I'm not walking alone. On my left walks a handsome young woman robed in blue, her thick, dark brown hair braided at the nape; she focusses on her slow, meditative walking. To her left walks another young woman, her dark hair tied in a bun at the back of her head, her lips bright red, and her cheeks rouged. On my right is an older man whose floppy white hair falls in boyish bangs over his ears and forehead. "Merlin has a fresh robe today, we see," somebody snickers from among the trees. Merlin? And who am I in this phantom procession? I feel like myself, yet it feels as if I'm inside somebody else's body. I have a thick, red beard, my body is stout, perhaps twenty years older, my clothes are fine but unfamiliar and not of this century; a gold circlet sits on my full head of auburn hair, and I walk with an inexplicable confidence, a regality.

The four of us escort a cheerful young man robed in white with a green waistband. His brown hair is long and he wears a jewelled necklace, a torc perhaps. We are here to acknowledge his graduation from a long course of study at a Celtic academy. I can't quite see them, but I'm sure there are angels about; the ethers feel aflutter with the insinuation of wings and twinkling stars. We reach the base of the Tor, halting before a white archway on which the image of a red dragon rearing on its hind legs is painted; the dragon's arrow-tipped tail curves around the archway like a vine. For a fleeting moment, I sense there is, impossibly, a real dragon, flaming and animate, behind the archway looming as big as the Tor. An apple tree in pink spring dimple grows on each side of the archway. The white-haired man, whom the voice in the crowd called Merlin, inspects the new apple leaves with an expression of rapture. That's true to character, certainly: Merlin was an orchardist. In *Avallenau*, a sixth century poem ascribed to Myrddin (a variant spelling of Merlin), the old magus says he was shown "seven score and seven delicious apple trees" at dawn—"sweet apples, for those who can digest them."

The way the fields and hedges are laid out, it's difficult to retrace the probable course of this ancient oak-girted processional to the Tor. The topography seems designed to defeat the attempt, as if the landscape has lost interest in the initiation its configuration once provided. When I came down here along Basketfield Lane, which curves along the backside of the Tor, it was like seeing the dark side of the moon. The Tor appeared as a coned pyramid with three fat midriff bulges. I ambled along a footpath off Ashwell Lane that was supposed to deposit me near Stonedown, but it vanished unaccountably into hillocks and barbed wire. Scrambling sideways across a tough green knoll to its crest, I found St. Michael's tower at the same height as the fenceposts ten feet before me. I climbed another ten feet up the next rise, and the Tor swelled into full, familiar stature, shouldering itself out of the gentle valley like a greenclad giant mollusced with three dozen Dorset sheep flung out like a handful of marbles over its short-clipped slopes.

That's typical of the anamolous, unsettling perspectives Glastonbury habitually serves up. The Tor is Glastonbury's consummate shape-shifter. The Glastonbury landscape, says Arthurian historian and Glastonbury scholar Geoffrey Ashe, who lives nearby, is weird, a monstrous refraction, full of bizarre practical jokes that throw the mind off balance. "Subconsciously prompted, it interprets the landscape into something truly alien to common experience. The irrational scene loosens the grip of the Ordinary and gives scope to the Fantastic. Just by a matter of an inch, it jars open the magic casements."

The walk home is less disorienting as Ashe's magical casements reveal a jewel of beauty this time. I set off from Gog and Magog, picking my way over Stonedown Hill and along its high fields and across a long, bumpy ridge that overlooks a scattering of cottages and the hills enclosing Wells a dozen miles away. The vista from here is gorgeous: a horseshoe valley with steep shelving pastures bathed in chiaroscuric greens, creamy, softly luminous shanks of lawn ridged in shadow and hedge, a miniscule bowl of delight backlit by the gods. The beauty is palpable, intimate, a glimpse of paradise on the verge of Glastonbury. Alfred Lord Tennyson was similarly appalled by his prospect of Avalon: "The island-valley of Avilion/Where falls not hail or rain or any snow/Nor wind ever blows loudly; but it lies/Deep-meadow'd, happy, fair with orchard lawn/And bowery hollows crown'd with summer sea."

The footpath terminates, too soon, at a cow gate because I feel I could walk within this luminiscent contentment for centuries, inhaling the landscape through all my senses. With each swing of the arm, each stride of my legs, it's as if I step ever fuller into my paradaisal body. Six heifers congregate by the gate and just beyond them I see a small road sign: Paradise Lane. Down the lane through Wick Hollow into Bove Town, I behold uncanny Glastonbury, Powys' market town of Grail-seekers and Grail-killers, Ashe's spiritual Los Angeles of England, and the giant Glasteing's settlement. "Mr. Geard could see the roofs of Glastonbury," wrote Powys, "looking, with all their bright red tiles, as if a great wave of spray from the chalybeate fountain had washed over them."

9

"NOT WISE THE THOUGHT, A GRAVE FOR ARTHUR"

nd like invaluable debris cast up on the shore and claimed by the lowtide sands, the Abbey clasps Arthur's bones and memory possessively to its bosom. Once imperial, her 592 feet of stone ruins now houses Arthur's supposed grave in the midst of transepts and within preaching distance of the vanished high altar. A little metal sign announces it, in understated pride: Arthur's grave.

It's wrong, of course. Arthur wasn't buried here by the altar and he wasn't buried near the Lady Chapel either, near the base of the church, as the medieval historians contend. Heed the old Celts, they knew. "A grave for Mark, a grave for Gwythur," says the *Black Book of Carmarthen*, a compendium of Welsh myths, "a grave for Gwgawn of the ruddy Sword. Not wise the thought, a grave for Arthur." Malory echoed this contention concisely in his formulation, *rex quondam, rexque futurus*—once king, always king, so how could he be buried?

William of Malmesbury—the Abbey hired him, in the wake of their disastrous fire of 1184, as a pubic relations specialist to help refurbish its legendary past to incorporate more of Arthur and Camalate—observed: Arthur's grave is "nowhere to be seen." That was before the monks edited his text to their advantage; afterwards he wrote seemingly more as a publicist than chronicler: "I pass over Arthur, famous king of the Britons, buried with his wife in the monks' cemetery between two pyramids." Then in 1191 the presumed bones of Arthur and his golden-haired wife, Queen Guinivere, were miraculously disinterred from a depth of 18 feet, both lying within a hollow oak coffin; it nonplussed nobody that one skeleton was eight feet long. After this discovery, the Abbey's mythopolitical fortunes dramatically increased as ecclesia wed royalty. "The Abbot and convent, raising up the remains," wrote Adam of Domerham in 1300, "joyfully translated them into the great church, placing them in a double tomb, magnificently carved. The king's body was set by itself at the head of the tomb, that of the queen at the foot or the eastern part, and there they remain to the present day." The clerical monks then further translated the Celtic, pagan Arthur into the heart of the Christian Grail Mystery where he's been embedded ever since.

The Abbey is a forty acre arboretum bounded by an eccentric stone wall eight feet high that meanders along the fringe of the property, bobbing left, weaving right, maintaining itself mostly upright. At certain points in its desultory passage about the Abbey, flowers blossom like whiskers from its crevices as they bloom, like randomly flung bouquets, in the grass-carpeted, broken walls and toppled columns, nosegays upon the paltry remains of what was once the largest and among the wealthiest of cathedrals in medieval Britain. A feeling of sanctuary swells within me as I pace the skeletal remains of the cloister at eight in the morning. The Abbey's sanctity, William of Malmesbury said, derived from the fact it was the repository of so many saints, making it "a heavenly shrine on Earth." Its age and the multitude of interred saints, William added, "have called forth such reverence for the place that at night scarcely anyone presumes to keep watch there."

At the Edgar Chapel, out beyond the transepts and vanished high altar (and the closest the Abbey extended towards Chalice Hill), I survey the supine body of the church, imagining it intact—cloister, chapter house, transepts, nave, presbytery, galilee, frater sub-vault—vibrant with people, holy with choirs, prayers, and spiritual mission. "Glastonbury Abbey is like a man struck down in his prime," observed Dion Fortune. "Its ghost walks.... To stand in the center of the great Nave, looking towards the high altar, is like standing waist deep in a swift mountain stream."

Frederick Bligh Bond stood in that stream and heard voices. Director of Excavations at Glastonbury Abbey from 1908 to 1922, he found corroboration for his architectural intuitions from some of the former Glastonbury monks who had lived here during the Abbey's prime. Bond, a reputable architect and scholar, teamed up with psychic John Alleyne to conduct what he later called a psychological experiment. Alleyne reportedly received scripts through automatic writing from the Company of Avalon, the Watchers, whose most voluble brother was Johannes de Glaston, who died in 1533. "And because he was of nature his soul was pure and he is of the Company that doth watch and wait for the glories to be renewed. Johannes Bryant is striving for the glory of Glaston." And he gave Bond a hot tip that would cost him his career. "There is much under the grass deep down and unrifled."

Johannes and his Brothers showed Bond where to excavate and by these unconventional means they unearthed the Loretto and Edgar Chapel foundations and resolved various other architectural mysteries of the Abbey. His remarkable discoveries were applauded by church and colleagues who didn't know about his use of psychism as a research tool. The Company of Avalon, from its detached perspective, claimed they constantly beheld the Abbey in its original splendor, which meant in its ideal, eternal form. Records indicate that even before the Abbey burned down in 1184 it was incomplete, and still under construction; the final Edgar Chapel that was to crown the Abbey was never finished. "Alle of the Company who loved and love our Abbey as it standeth to us, see all its glory, though ye see but woeful ruins. We who walked and yet do walk in the fleshly tabernacle in which, by thought, we clothe ourselves withal, can still dwell in the cloysters where we were wont to contemplate. We who observe the Laws tell you that the Image of the Building remains always, because it is a genuine symbol of the Divine impulse which gave it birth." When the truth came out, Bond's colleagues were shocked by his heretical means and discounted the revelations from Johannes' "gate of remembrance;" in 1922, Bond's employers fired him, discredited his discoveries, and tried to carry on as if the scandal had never happened and the missing chapels were never discovered.

Outside the Abbey grounds, Glastonbury swells with pilgrims. Fifteen buses crammed with visitors roll down Magdalene Street in both directions queuing at the gates with ecclesiastical synchrony. The sidewalks of Glastonbury groan under the weight of clergymen. Can it be the spiritual prospects of the Pilgrimage alone that draw these men, women, and children to the "Holy House at the Head of the Moors Adventurous," as the Abbey was somewhat colorfully once called—or are they responding to yet a deeper call? Men in ankle-length black robes, red streaks pleating their staid uniforms, stride funereally through the town. How did these somber men get away with stealing the blood and dark earth of the matriarchal Mysteries?

By early afternoon, the High Street is impassably dense with people. When the bells toll at three-thirty, the formal procession rolls out on a wave of organ music. Under plumes of incense, hundreds of robed men and boys carrying banners and scepters parade by; it will take an hour before the entire Pilgrimage wends its solemn way into the waiting chairs on the Abbey lawn. This is probably the closest to a Christian agapé you're likely to encounter in England outside of Canterbury. Anglicans have converged on Glastonbury for this single-day pilgrimage since 1924 when the event's founders, a group of thirty members of the Guild of Servants of the Sanctuary in Bristol, joined, serendipitously, members of the Salisbury branch of the English Church Union, when they both arrived at the Abbey gates for a pilgrimage on the same day. A multitude of banners, each embroidered with the name of a parish, ripple like fronds against a backdrop of intent faces, ancient stone, and broken spires. "Let us proclaim the mystery of faith," intones a male voice over the loudspeaker. The crowd responds in catechism: "Christ has died. Christ is risen. Christ will come again." So the Crusades march into the Abbey led by a man bearing a gold-painted cross upon which an effigy of Jesus is spiked obscenely like an emaciated animal basted for the barbecue.

"And by death to life immortal they were born and glorified," continues the liturgist, but my thoughts drift back, in imagination at least, to that cataclysmic moment on May 25, 1184, when the *velum sanctuarium* caught fire from a candle borne by the Prior at High Mass. A sudden wind whipped it into a conflagration of flames "fiercer than any kindled from a Danish battle brand, which swept the monastery on a night of high winds," Brother Symon of the Company of Avalon recalled. "For miles across the fen blazed the fortress, a monstrous torch in the darkness before it fell in a blackened ruin."

Among the few Abbey treasures preserved from the flames was "the sword of Arthur ye Kynge, and that our Kynge Henrie took." A later King Henry took away the whole Abbey in his infamous Dissolution of the Monasteries proclamation of 1539. In fact, starting in April 1536 and finishing in April 1540, King Henry VIII, then in his twenty-seventh year of reign, closed down 800 religious houses, monasteries, nunneries, and friaries, and sent about 10,000 monks, canons, nuns, and friars packing. He left Arthur's grave at Glastonbury Abbey intact, though. Arthur remains caught in the crossfire between church and state even today where his grave, if only symbolic, lies a few feet behind the red-carpeted dais from which the catechism is directed. "Hail Mary, full of grace, blessed is the fruit of thy womb, Jesus," continues the minister. Hail Ygraine, full of grace, blessed is the fruit of thy womb, Arthur, I respond. The priest's subdued fervor is momentarily eclipsed as four jets streak menacingly low overhead, ripping the sky and his prayers apart in a thrust of Celtic anger. "Almighty God, we have sinned against you, through our own fault..."

I withdraw to the far end of the grounds out of earshot of the Marian liturgy upon Arthur's grave and out of sight of the masses of pilgrims whose presence magically recreates the ghostly outlines of the Abbey's glorious Image. I perch happily on the edge of the ovate fishpond—Almoner's Pond, it was once called—paved with lilies on the verge of opening yellow-eyed under the noonday sun. The monks dug this contemplative pond centuries ago, lined it with stones and stocked it with fish, whose finger-thin descendants still ripple redmouthed through the olive-hued water. A flock of puffy cumulous clouds drift languidly among the lilies so that for a moment the little fish stream and wriggle through sculpted mist into a wide blue sky. I clasp my hands behind me and perambulate the pond, noting the two lifejackets on posts at either end, in case I fall in. Legend says the pond is incalculably deep; it also says there is a secret doorway at its bottom that opens into a tunnel, and that the Abbey's prolific treasures may have been hidden down there when King Henry VIII—"that incredible fool!" exclaims Powys—inspected the Abbey for proofs (and spoils) of the Dissolution. But he didn't find Arthur.

Where is Arthur? Where is Arthur? I intone my query in rhythm with my breathing as I pace the stone-edged pond. "He passes to be King among the dead/And after healing of his grievous wound, He comes again," Tennyson answers me, adding, "From the great deep to the great deep he goes." Did Arthur escape to Avalon through the Abbey's fishpond? In his mysterious passage between the great deeps, Arthur found himself appropriated and duly humbled by the Christian hagiographers; his wild Celtic reputation was diminished by the spiritual light of the Abbey's pre-eminent saints. St. Padarn, for example, rescued the tyrant Arthur from being devoured by the Earth. St. Cadocus tricked Arthur into compliance by transforming a ransom of one hundred cattle into bundles of fern. Those were the friendly accounts; the less charitable clerics waxed slanderous, calling Arthur a church looter, an opportunist, a malicious schemer, a rebel king.

Maybe the truth of Arthur is buried in the Abbey's secret, unexcavated heart, in an arcane chamber untainted by clerical aspersion. It's possible. Didn't the Company of Avalon allude to unsuspected secrets inscribed in tile and geometry within the Abbey, physical or ghostly, mysteries originating with Joseph of Arimathea's original *ecclesia,* "the symbolic circle of the Holy Twelve?" Citing the correct configurations of the St. Mary and Lady Chapels, the Glaston monks teased Frederick Bligh Bond with this clue: "Know that in this designing of the Floor lies the future prophecy of Glastonbury, together with the inward secrets of Christianity."

10

AN ANGEL BIDS ARTHUR TO
VISIT BECKERY CHAPEL

For three nights running, an angel woke Arthur, who was sleeping in a room on Wearyall Hill, and bid him visit Beckery Chapel. This remarkable story comes from John of Glastonbury, an Abbey historian writing in 1400. "There was at that time in Wirral within the island of Avallonia, a monastery of holy virgins, dedicated in the name of the Apostle Peter, wherein Arthur oftentimes rested and abode, attracted by the amenity of the place." According to Rev. John Collinson, writing in 1784, St. Peter's monastery was situated "where the thorn grew without the pale of Weriel Park, belonging to the Abbey." She can't prove it, but Nickie suspects that monastery was close to Level's View, if not in practically the same place. The angel visited Arthur three nights, each time requesting him to visit the hermitage of St. Mary Magdalen of Beckery to "behold and understand what there shall be done."

It took the angel three visits to persuade Arthur, evidently too cozy in St. Peter's amenities, to rouse himself at dawn and set off across Wearyall Hill to Beckery. According to John, Gawain, one of Arthur's knights, at first dissuaded him from crediting the angelic visitation; then John describes Gawain's reconnaissance visit to Beckery Chapel on Arthur's behalf. He returned with a gold candlestick in his hand and a dagger in his groin, crying loudly "even as a madman;" afterwards he "expired" and was buried among the deceased nuns in Wirral. "The king, then, feeling that God was unwilling that anyone should enter the chapel except to the salvation of his soul, immediately went there alone at dawn."

Maybe it's because I like getting up early, but the prospect of a dawn outing to Beckery strikes me as a good ercise in mythopoeic identification with the elusive Arthur. I figure if Arthur could, on the third attempt, rouse himself out of his comfortable quilt before dawn and tramp over Wearyall to keep an appointment made by angel, so can I *sans* angel. It's four-forty five as I slip out the front door of the Level's View, so early the eggman and milkman haven't been around yet. In the predawn half-light, the air is fresh, moist, as if Avalon has been misted with a floral scent. Out on the Levels, a ribbon of mist trails the Brue. Arthur would have to dress warmly on a morning like this and wear a hat, too. I make my way up Wearyall, avoiding the fresh cow splats. At the crest, looking out to the sheepworks and the ten circular tanks of the wastewater treatment plant, I make out a slight ridge of land, a green ripple like a finger outstretched across a still belly of land—Beckery Island, unoccupied, all of forty feet above sea level.

Traditionally, Beckery was one of Glastonbury's smaller, minor islands, yet it was topographically important enough for the Abbey to establish an outpost there, secure it would not be flooded when the Summer Country was awash in winter waters. Godney, Marchey, Nyland, Panborough, Redlake, Clewer, Northlode, Bleadney, Merewistia, Ferramere—these were among the islands of greater Glastonbury according to thirteenth century Somerset charters. Islands or no, Arthur would have needed Wellingtons on this soggy outing as I discover my sneakers are thoroughly soaked from the calf-high dew-drenched grass.

I stride down Wearyall's western slope and into Beckery, a workingman's district "down round the back" of Glastonbury and its empty brick factories. I saunter over Bumbaley Bridge that spans a tiny tributary of the Brue and the remnant of an extensive water diversion project undertaken by the medieval Abbey, then walk past the Northover buildings, a vacant, tilting collection of derelict stone cottages, until I reach the empty parking lot across the street from the three-storied Morlands' sheepworks, most of its windows darkened with bluebrown shades. At the end of the car park, I climb over a flabby barbed wire fence, take a confident step into the tussocky field, and fall straight over into the wet grass. The footing is treacherous in this terrain of unfriendly hillocks; deep, ankle-breaking coombs gape between them. I lurch gracelessly through the pimpled field. Behind me, Wearyall is a green whaleback swimming away with decisive fin strokes from the tarred and jumbled ugliness of the factories.

Three white swans lift off from the Brue, wings whistling like saxophones, as I arrive at the grassy site of Beckery Chapel. Beckery Island is an undistinguished green lump in the peaty Levels girted by fields called Brides in honor of Beckery's patron saint, the Irish St. Bridget (or Bride). Allegedly she consecrated her chapel here in 488 A.D., directing the Christian nuns in their contemplations. After she died, St. Bridget's relics—a bag, necklace, handbell, embroidery tools—were displayed and "adored" in later years in the Beckery oratory until they disappeared, along with the chapel and Abbey, in 1549, although a local benefactor named Alice Buckton reportedly found the handbell in 1920. St. Bridget may have been that same Brighid about whom Cormac in his celebrated ninth century A.D. *Glossary* said, "Among all the Irish a goddess used to be called Brighid." Among the Scots and Irish, Brighid was revered on a par with the Virgin Mary; she was called the Queen of Heaven, one of the Three Blessed Ladies of Britain, one of the Three Mothers; she was often portrayed with golden hair, a blue mantle, with girdle and staff, a wheatsheaf and harp in her hands. Her name and its various cognates—Brigid, Brigit, Bride, Briginda, Brigidu, Brigantia, Brihati—suggest "fiery arrow, the Bright One, the Exalted One," a woman of light.

For reasons obscure, yet intriguing, this site is also known as Bee-Keeper's Island. King Cenwalh of the West Saxons granted *Beokeri* and other lands to Abbot Berthwald of Glastonbury in 670 A.D., while another charter from 971 A.D. refers to Bridget's chapel as Little Ireland, presumably in honor of the plethora of Irish saints resident here. Alternatively, the designation may derive from *Becc-*

eriu or *Eo Beocere*, which means Bee-Keeper's Island, a designation that baffles nearly everyone because of the suspicion that somehow it isn't literally honey bees the name commemorates.

It's not only bees that are associated with Beckery, but fish. According to Dr. John A. Goodchild, a British physician and Celtic mystic, Beckery (this entire district of Glastonbury) marks the spot of the "ancient salmon of St. Bride," as he claimed around 1904. The salmon is a three thousand foot long earthen fish effigy that extends approximately from Bride's Hill (Beckery Island) towards the Abbey girting Wearyall Hill on its right. Bride's Well—"more like a rather muddy pond into which the water from nearby fields used to drain through a sluice," notes Patrick Benham in *The Avalonians*—marks the Salmon's Eye and was formerly known as the Women's Quarter, the presumed templic site of earlier Druidic priestesses.

Fish or bees aside, some of the old accounts suggest that in Arthur's day, approximately the early sixth century A.D., his young knights sat in vigil through the night at St. Mary Magdalene's Church, as Beckery Chapel was renamed, on the eve of their induction into the company of Camalate. Whatever its original name, Beckery Island lapsed into near oblivion until 1887 when Glastonbury archeologist John Morland excavated two chapels here, discovering unsuspected outbuildings, even skeletons, all of which significantly substantiated the medieval claims of the Abbey. Morland wrote: "The chapel was situated at the highest point of the island in a field called Chamberlain's Hill; a beautiful site with a free view across the Levels right to the Bristol Channel."

Once he arrived here, no doubt Arthur was curious as to what kind of vision the angel had cooked up for him at Beckery Chapel. I'm convinced, however, that if his manner of arriving at Bee-Keeper's Island was anything like mine, he would have sat down for his clairvoyance with cold, wet feet. Being a king with a reputation to uphold back among the fellows at Camalate, not to mention the necessity of at least seeming to be a macho *dux bellorum* in the face of the invading Saxons, Arthur probably kept his grumblings about conditions at Beckery to himself, as I will. So he sat here, respectfully, waiting for the angel to part the curtains between the worlds; and so I sit here, too, equally respectful, hoping for a glimpse of my quarry.

Arthur had good reason to feel penitential: when he drew near the chapel, he saw two hands holding swords on either side of the door "that smote against each other and struck out fire," according to John of Glastonbury. As I sit here, following my breathing with attention and warmth, the suggestion of choirs and deep droning chants wells up from the ground, cathedralic voices rumbling the ethers. Maybe it's my imagination, but then, according to the anonymous author of the thirteenth century *High History of the Holy Grail*, which recounts Arthur's visit to the chapel of St. Augustine (possibly Beckery under another name), "King Arthur was in the little house beside the chapel, and had heard the voice of the sweet Mother of God and the angels." Apparently something was remiss in his behavior because they wouldn't let him in. "But sore it irketh him of this that he may not enter therewithin, and he heareth, there where the holy hermit was singing the mass, right fair responses, and they seem to him to be the responses of angels."

In John's account, Arthur fared better. After kneeling before the door and praying for heavenly mercy, he was admitted inside where he beheld a holy place "adorned beyond compare." He was greeted by a venerable old man in black raiment, with long, grey hair and white beard; once Arthur was seated, the old man put on priestly robes and said Mass. Mary Mother of God appeared bearing the infant Jesus in her arms, presenting the child to the priest who set him on the altar. "This is my Body," the priest said, raising the infant in his arms. "Take and eat," and he ate the infant, literally consuming the Host, except that as soon at Communion was completed, the Christ child reappeared on the altar, "unharmed and entire, the spotless paschal Lamb." Mary awarded the astonished Arthur a crystal cross in honor of his witnessing of the divine office, then departed, leaving Arthur with the priest who explained the situation to him.

Arthur felt so "visited by manifold joy" and "mightily rejoiced" on account of this vision that he vowed to change his armorial bearings, which had been silver with three red lions, to green to include a silver cross and an image of the Virgin Mary with child over the cross' right arm. In later years, the crystal cross, kept in the Abbey's treasury, was carried proudly in Lenten processions. Arthur departed Beckery Chapel "confirmed in the faith of the Lord," says John. After that, I think he probably went home, changed into dry socks, and had a hot breakfast.

11

AN ORDINARY GLASTONBURY DAY ON THE QUEST

fter a mythopoeic breakfast at Level's View in honor of our joint expedition to Beckery—Arthur's and mine—I walk into Glastonbury to do my laundry, including the wet socks. Lugging my duffel bag of shirts, trousers, and towels up High Street, I remember what Dion Fortune once said of Glastonbury: "The past lives on at Glastonbury. All about us it stirs and breathes, quiet, but living and watching. God has been thought about so much in this island in the marshes that he is very near, and the veil that hides the sanctuary is very thin. Glastonbury has ever been the home of men and women who have seen visions. The veil is thin here, and the Unseen comes very near to earth." Humming to myself, I wonder if any of the visionaries here have encountered Arthur on either side of the veil. Meanwhile, the domestic affairs of living go on.

I cram myself into one of those stout, red, upright, inimitably British telephone booths that crop up irregularly in Glastonbury. I stack my ten pence coins on the little counter and dial a number in London, calculating it will take one coin for every eleven seconds to keep the connection open. Except that I've overlooked the degree of dexterity and patience required to get the clanky coin to stay inserted in the slot and to not pop out a fourth time stranding my London party on a silent line. If you want to reach out and touch someone in England, your local pay phone is not the ticket. After more attempts, I get the money to stay in the telephone and launch my conversation with the party in London until I'm distracted by something in the street. Six Army tanks—genuine, metal-tracked tanks with turreted guns, around which a half dozen uniformed, helmeted, and goggled soldiers perch like ravens of war—clatter imperiously down High Street. A military helicopter flies deafeningly low overhead, not more than two hundred feet above the shops. Further up the street, a half dozen tractor trailer trucks and two tourist buses are jammed tight in the narrow road. Just outside my phone box there's a clutch of young mothers, with eight-wheeled prams and grinning, indolent children aboard, packed four deep in matronly consternation on the sidewalk. Gridlock on High Street. My line goes dead for want of coins.

As I push open the heavy folding door of the booth, a very tall man with long grey hair, robed in ankle-length somber black cloth with a gold cross bobbing like a beachball against his chest, strides up my corner of High Street, a man of the cloth clearly brimming with fresh revelations. Right behind him come a tangle of Army boys, thick young men with mustaches, rakish grey berets, splotchy yellow-green fatigues, and heavy black boots. The sects are out in full dress today. The Army lads beach at H. J. Janes the Bakers for doughnuts while the priest ascends into Lloyds Bank.

With a little hesitation, I finish getting out of the phone booth and queue at the zebra crossing. Technically, the blinking light at both ends of this black-and-white barred pedestrian safety zone guarantees me safe passage across Glastonbury's clogged and dangerous two-lane superhighway, but as Dion Fortune warns, the veil is thin here and I want to stay on this side of it at least until I find Arthur. Like Arthur, I feel confirmed in my faith in the Lord when I place my besneakered feet upon the zebra zone and nobody runs me over. Avalon's High Street is often infernally loud, smelly, dirty, dark, unkempt, dangerous. The sheer grimy physicality of the trucks and buses and commuters is a jolting counterbalance to mystical abstraction, of which there is much in this town. As I step into safety on the far sidewalk, an ambulance storms across the zebra zone, its two-tiered clanging horn raucous and merry as if produced by trumpeters on its roof. Just outside the laundromat is a troop of Romans.

That's what they call the punkers with their Mohican hedgerows and jewellry made from used automobile parts. I enter the laundromat and offer thanks to Arthur's Beckery angel that I be spared any further visions through the veil.

As my corduroys slosh happily in the machine, I glance through an old local newspaper called the *Glastonbury Communicator*. It's the latest incarnation in a series of new age interpretive publications that periodically appear in town only to disappear after a few issues. An anonymous contributor with a perky sense of humor discusses the Glastonbury Reincarnate Hero. "This is a typical Tor Town Type, dressed up in heroic war gear and armlets, striding up and down the ley lines. The Reincarnate Hero claims to have reincarnated as great leaders or manipulators of events many times before. They see themselves as manifestations of Divine archetypes and great public cosmic instruments. They see the advent of the Millennium here in the New Jerusalem as a glorious opportunity to manifest their powers, to take their rightful place center-stage and be revealed to the world as the Creatures of Destiny they know themselves to be." O lamentable reincarnate heros! What happens when a creature of destiny turns out to be a pawn of fate? Like old King Pellinor who spent seventeen years in quest of the *Beste Glatissant*, the elusive Questing Beast of the medieval Grail stories, the uncatchable quarry whose belly grumbled "like unto the questing of thirty couple hounds." All Pellinor got as the manifestation of his reincarnate Tor Town Type powers was fewmets, the droppings of the beast pursued.

I spend most of the afternoon in the laundromat engrossed in T.H. White's whimsical *The Once and Future King*, waiting for my corduroys to dry on the rack. Somehow the day edges itself up against five o'clock and, as if by master switch, the streets of Glastonbury empty, swept clean at closing time, except for an interesting puddle of men and women with wine glasses trickling out of the bookstore, evidently constituting a cocktail party. It's a reception and book launch for a well-known geomancy scholar and Earth Mysteries expert who in teeshirt and baggy trousers looks more like a housepainter than a prophet of the New Jerusalem. Here, I would guess, is the cream of

Glastonbury's congeries of Grail-seekers, the magicians, witches, geomancers, and savants, fortified with wine, cheese, and the holy regalia of their spiritual engagements.

I feel daring, after my afternoon hermitage at the laundromat, and dive into the sea of conversation and innuendoes, wondering as always, if anybody has seen Arthur. "No one has come to Glastonbury and not been surprised by the depth and range of activity here," says the bookstore owner, a grinning bear of a man and *chef d'cuisine* of this new age salon. "People come here to look beyond the veil of reality. People always say, 'Glastonbury is my spiritual home.' Whatever is going on with you, Glastonbury magnifies it a thousand times. So you need to enhance your judgement if you plan to survive."

A man in Harris tweed, yellow shirt, and bow tie, who has overheard our conversation, nods his head and launches forth. "It's the same conflict between the spiritual quest and the sensible tourist trade as it was in Powys' day. People come to Glastonbury to follow their dream. There are so many little seed groups of six people. The place is packed with strange types, each person desperately into his own quest. People dash about with synchronicity in their eyes; they see significant coincidences in everything. The energy fields are dense, so full of things being battled out. And it's an ego-shattering town. Glastonbury rejects the ones she doesn't want." A middle-aged woman in a green sweater and tan slacks tells me with a flash of disdain, "Glastonbury on all levels is the great seducer. The Tor is a gigantic faucet. Energy is available for any purpose to anyone with a bucket, but watch out, it's an absolutely undisciplined, unfocussed energy."

Another man compares Glastonbury to a tangle of telephone wires that connect one to all the psychic planes. The trouble is, frayed cables lie everywhere, through which flow too many kilowatts of spiritual energy. Fueled by this energy, people zoom off in all directions, he says. Glastonbury is a thousand-armed demon with something up every sleeve. "The only way people keep their sanity around here is by becoming aggressively normal, desperately ordinary. In a magical culture it's a recipe for instant insanity if you don't know how to shield yourself."

A man who could be mistaken for a thirty-something Mick Jagger and who tells me he's writing a book on astrology, characterizes Glast-onbury's demography as "Glastafaria." Glastonbury dances to Celtic reggae: dread-knotted, marijuana-fueled psychic cowboys can buckaroo freelance through psychedelic Avalon and not even cowgirls get the blues in stoned Tor Town. This crazy town, in which materialists meet magic and visionaries meet the ground, offers everybody happiness and bumptious joy courtesy of the Glastonbury Angel, the astrologer explains. "Through this social cohesion, the Angel squirts her vision, which in this locality overpowers all other visions and employs, even unconsciously, every single person here, Glastonian and Glastafarian."

As I drift through the group, I recognize a face I saw on a poster: Robert Coon, an American. He describes himself as a "Qabalist magickian and alchemical poet" striving for physical immortality as he makes his elliptical navigations through the multitudinous ethers of Avalon. The poster had announced a workshop on prophecy and magic that he gave a few weeks ago. Tufts of white flop out at ear level from under a leonine mane of shoulder-length sable-black hair. Coon stands in a crouch, slightly hunched over, in brown corduroy jacket, black teeshirt inscribed with a tricolor pentagram, jeans, and orange sneakers. He's a student of the Glastonbury zodiac, currently researching Earth chakra points. Glastonbury, he tells me, is the planet's heart center through which Teilhard de Chardin's mystical Omega point of global synoptic awareness and noöspheric epiphany will be fulfilled. "The heart flower of Glastonbury opened to its fullness of maturity and crystallized into an eternally stable jewel this Easter. The green Philosopher's Stone is now fully operative on the Tor."

If anybody could appreciate that newly functional Philosopher's Stone surely it's Tony Roberts, whom I met weeks ago through Nickie. Tony is loud and large, bursting with verbal energy and intellectual enthusiasms. He wears a baseball cap and leather jacket, sports a thick Saxon beard, smokes cigars nonstop; he's a rogue Tom Bombadil, spitfire polymath, and, by his own description, "a neo-Blakean elegiac and magical geomancer." You just plug him in, point him at a set of attentive ears, and he'll passionately spume a universe of concerns, anecdotes, preci, and denunciations. "I'm trying to avoid controversy tonight although I've heard a few people might make incantations against me, try a little dark magic."

The Tor is the great pyramid of Albion, a multidimensional gateway through which the achievement of the Grail is still possible, Roberts says. UFOs cluster about its summit like bees around a flower. The Tor is a psychic lightning rod, a channeler of cosmic potentizing energies dispersing them throughout the recumbent body of a dreaming Earth. Glastonbury's zodiac is a spiritual matrix for the planet, an ancient Atlantean alchemical temple newly reinvigorated, "rebirthing the psycho-geomantic strata of the Glastonbury geomythic." As I pick myself up off the floor onto which I have been swept by the fulsomeness of Robert's oratory, he adds, puckishly, "Have a pleasant trek through Glastonbury, but remember you have to pick your way through a spiritual minefield out there." Regrettably, Roberts himself fared poorly in the minefield because he died suddenly one night a few years later while meditating on his mystical Tor.

I disengage myself from the Avalonian street fair as a jag of lightning flashes over the Tor. Streaks of orange band the western horizon as dusk settles and the full moon climbs into prominence. I hoist up my laundry sack and am about to cross High Street when somebody calls my name. It's Theodore, and he invites me to join he and Tim at the Lamb on Northlode Street. I met Theodore one day at Kopp's Courtyard, the Little Covent Garden of Glastonbury as it's fondly called. I was nursing a cup of Earl Grey far beyond what the dregs might deliver and wishing the cafe had more apple scones. Theodore is a kind of bemused, disgruntled aristocrat with a florid, urbane banter, an immaculately enunciated voice, the kind of privileged accent that lands him unexpectedly, now and then, in tight corners and sudden brawls in certain pubs of his acquaintance, he told me with a grin. He's dapper, thirty, unemployed, genteel in tweed, ascot, and running shoes. "I'm a bit of a mystic myself," he replied when I asked him how he negotiates the Glastonbury minefields. "I just don't like people parading about with their enlightenment philosophy on their sleeves."

The Lamb is a pub with a bare basement ambiance under a faded yellow, stained ceiling. If I weren't in the company of Theodore, I'd call it a tough place, the kind of bar I'd normally avoid. In fact, I hardly ever visit bars. It's rough-and-tumble and Theodore's posh accent infiltration here is a stroke of sociological bravura. It's early, and only a handful of Lamb stalwarts are on hand to handle the pints. Three young women in punkish cropped yellow hair joke with a bare-chested man with a black Mohican strip across his shiny scalp. The landlord draws Theodore a pint of Draught Bass in his can, a two hundred year old bronze mug. The can set on a counter leans honestly to one side as if from the weight of centuries of inebriation; its underside is somewhat squashed in, perhaps from being used to bang pub counters or pubmate's heads.

"There's really nobody here I would consider inviting up to the flat for an intellectual chat," Theodore confides, banging his empty can on the counter to rouse the landlord. "But there are types here it's nice to have a drink with. I come here to escape being a hermit. The rowd-iness is refreshing." I have to lean in close to Theodore to hear him as suddenly the Lamb has swollen with at least forty patrons. Elvis Presley commands the jukebox and the Romans are singing with enough force to blow out the windows.

Around nine-thirty, Theodore leaves for the Mitre for a darts game. "I've been carefully controlling my drinking tonight to stay functionally sober," he says with a slurred twinkle. "The Lamb's best have been called upon to defend our mother pub's honor against the heathen dart tossers at the Mitre," he adds, squeezing a black pouch in which he keeps his private dagger-tipped anti-heathen darts. As for myself, I'm working diligently on my second draught Guinness wondering if being detached is a safe position to assume in this mercurial environment. Tim emerges like a jungle explorer through the dense underbrush of drinkers still on their feet. He's a lanky six-foot-three, sports a flared-collar blue shirt, tight jeans, and size twelve peppermint green high top sneakers. Hanging out with Theodore and Tim is like *Upstairs, Downstairs* live. We join some Lambsters in a dice game.

Nigel, one of the guys, is assailed at intervals by the pub dog, an ill-mannered Corgi who clamps his teeth into his trousers, snarling and wringing his head until Nigel blushes from all the attention. He fidgets in mock pain, shrugs his shoulders helplessly, then, cheered on by his friends, tries to beat off the chewing Corgi with his cap. The uproar subsides and Nigel chucks his dice to the boisterous applause of Ned. Ned is twenty-five, recently married, pot-bellied, tattooed, with a round head, stubbly chin, gold earrings, and a rough, infectious amiability. He rolls up his denimed sleeves, leans forward, chucks the dice, raises his fists, scoring a cool five thousand. He throws again—"Five thousand and rolling!" But he loses it and slumps into a grumbled "Zilch!" So we down our pints, chuck the wayward dice, pound the table, fight off the pub dog, make jokes, visit the toilet, smoke, spin tunes, and try not to trip over my laundry bag. Theodore returns from the Mitre and immediately loses thousands of points in one flamboyant chuck. "Silly game," he comments.

"Last drinks, gentlemen!" shouts the landlord. For the next fifteen minutes, he bustles efficiently, topping pints, collecting coins. The evening swells into a slurred crescendo as all the sodden men are raving on about how long a way it is to Tipperary even if it is bloody French. The Mohican is dancing, maybe bear-hugging, possibly strangling, another man with silver earrings. A wispy man with receding hairline surveys the scene from a bar stool with teary eyes. Five minutes before eleven, closing time, the last ten stalwarts stagger obediently out and the Lamb is closed for the night.

The fresh evening air and comparative quiet restores me at once. We call in at a party on Benedict Street where Theodore collects a woman who is monumentally drunk and occasionally coherent. She doesn't want to go home because she's convinced her husband is in bed this minute with another woman. Therefore she will stay the night with Theodore. A gentleman in all circumstances, Theodore smiles over his silken ascot and says dryly, "I'll fluff up another pillow."

Two hours have vanished and it's one in the morning. Tim feels chatty. "It doesn't bloody matter how you get here, as long as you're *here*. Do you know what I think living is all about? It's absurd. It's amazing. It's a privilege. The question is, are you watching the movie or getting on with what you're here for?" With Tim the rhetorical slips seamlessly into the personal and I realize he's talking about me. "Intuition is dangerous, you know, because it changes you. Once you start following it, it happens more. You're breaking all the patterns, aren't you? You don't know where you'll be in six months. Send me a postcard, man. Keep visiting. Watch the changes." Tim's focus is unnerving and I wonder how he can know me so well. "You can't run away from it because it's already here. Glastonbury spits out the people who can't change, who can't deal with the pressures of looking at who they really are. Don't worry. You already know all the answers to your questions. I can see it in your eyes."

It's three a.m. as I leave their flat, my bundle of fresh, folded laundry faithfully in tow, the answers to all my questions ablaze in my eyes if I could but see them. Tim's prescience is unsettling but intoxicating. If I already know the answers, that means I know where Arthur is, but where is that? I feel so dull, so rooted in materiality. The consummate Grail Knight Parsifal has to evolve through three stages of spiritual development before he achieves the Grail. "He must evolve upwards from dullness, through doubt, to the third stage, *Saelde*, to win security of soul once more," says Grail scholar Walter Johannes Stein. Here I am, a man with warm blood lugging a bag of laundry, looking for Arthur—in Glastonbury, in the landscape, in books, histories, poems, fantasies, interviews, pubs, mythopoeic reconstructions, sixteen hundred years after the fact. And I'm looking for Arthur reflexively, in my own style of searching, watching myself looking for Arthur in this paper-strewn *imramma*. Recognition is paramount, maybe imminent.

The real Arthur could be radically different from his legend, from the millennial expectations of the once and future king. Arthur might walk the streets of Glastonbury tonight, in disguise, looking for himself, in a new body, an unfamiliar time, under changed circumstances. He's astir in the hollow hills, struggling to remember, to reconnect, reassemble. Here we are, both dazed, amnesiac, wandering in dullness. Arthur remembering himself and myself looking for Arthur by automythopoeic excavation—are they the same or different? Two men dig a tunnel each from the opposite end, hoping to meet. We break through the last clumps of dense earth and knock our shovels together in a joyful recognition. "Oh, it's you, then," echoes mind to mind.

I trudge up Fisher's Hill with an unaccountable edge of apprehension weighing on me. The streets are too empty, too silent, ambivalent. I feel as if Powys' "Invisible Watchers" or Bond's Company of Avalon loom invisibly large behind me, their heads protruding through the veil. Ironically, in the late 1800s, Hillhead was a dangerous place, "a tough spot of Glastonbury," according to local historian Ray Burrows. "In those days the local police had to go there in twos. Had an ill-advised Bobby gone there alone, the Hillhead folk would crowd around him in order to place a rolled newspaper spiel up under his belt from behind—and then set fire to it!" Tail Piping, they called it, a Hillhead specialty.

Maybe the Hillhead ghosts are tail-piping me, because I feel a brooding, ambiguous presence, ghostly fingers reaching through from another world to touch my shoulders or wrap its giant wings around me, squeezing out perplexity. God is frightening, the mystics report. Anxiety ripples electrically across my back and I break into a jog, my laundry bag banging my knees with each pumping stride. "You can't run away from it because it's already here," Tim had said gnomically. He's right. There's no outrunning this presence, not this time, not this life, not here.

I wake up in the middle of the night, furious with Glastonbury. This town is one giant *makyo* simultaneously occupying everyone's attention, I shout inside my head. I take a big Zen stick, the Buddhist baseball bats they call *kyosaku*, and give Glastonbury a strong thump on its shoulders. Then I walk up and down the streets giving all the people, the buildings, the hills, the air, myself, a *makyo*-busting whack. Wake up! We're dreaming, misconstruing everything.

"*Makyo*" are the phenomena—visions, hallucinations, illusory sensations—which the practitioner of Zen is apt to experience at a particular stage in his sitting," says Yasutani Roshi, a twentieth-century Japanese Zen master. "There are innumerable different kinds of *makyo*—indeed each person may experience *makyo* peculiar to his own nature." Indeed: entire towns may experience illusions of mind, strange shapes like wild beasts, demons, angels, visions of Buddha and his disciples chanting sutras, or of ancient Celtic heroes suddenly waking up in the hollow hills to resume their lives.

12

GLIMPSING ARTHUR'S SWORD FROM THE PERILOUS BRIDGE

omparles Bridge endures the rattling of traffic this morning as it has for centuries, with indifference. A stout, white truck labelled Bray's Sheepskin Products downshifts gratingly, followed by Sovereign Motors, then a long, dark blue tractor trailer, a flaming red Royal Mail stepvan, a tottering grey station wagon, a woman in knee-boots, black dress, and tan sweater on bicycle, then an elderly man in tweed and woolen cap, walking a Corgi—they all make their passage across the dangerous bridge, *Pont Perillieux* as Pomparles (it was called *Pons Periculosis* in 1415) has been known for centuries. What's less well known is that it's the swinging doorway into geomythic Avalon.

It was from this spot upon an antecedent of the bridge, claims Somerset legend, that Bedivere, Arthur's oldest friend and most faithful knight, threw Excalibur into the mere of the River Brue. Bedivere vacillated at first, reluctant to throw away the invaluable king sword, but Arthur commanded it. He thought to hide Excalibur under a tree for posterity but the dying Arthur wouldn't hear of it and ordered Bedivere, again, to throw the sword into the water. "There came an arm and a hand above the water and met it, and caught it, and so shook it thrice and brandished, and then vanished away the hand with the sword in the water," wrote Malory. That was the Lady of the Lake, Arthur's lifelong mentor: she gave him the sword when he claimed his kingship and she reclaimed it when his reign was over.

From Pomparles, there's no sign of Excalibur or the Lady of the Lake brandishing the invincible blade; the Brue, barely fifteen feet across, flows sluggishly, murkily, a couple feet below the surface slime, like a stream in retirement. A clutch of mustard on each bank cheerily encourages the desultory channel to keep the faith and keep flowing. If there is a sword lying in the mud of the Brue, I should think I'd be able to see it—but, of course, there isn't, that's taking things literally.

I set off down a cow lane that meanders along the phlegmatic Brue. Buttercups sway at foot-level; St. Michael's tower is a Gothic kite flying a green sky, trailing a long, silvery-tailed footpath. A cirrus cloud takes the form of a sleek greyhound in full racing stride over the Tor invoking Gwyn's dogs, the *Cwn Annwn*. One of Powys' characters came out to Pomparles on a sunny day. He was a Grail-killer, a disbeliever, a debunker who found the whole Grail business and "that damned sword" the absurd consequences of "the heady opiate fumes of the Glastonbury Legend." He was lucky despite himself. Something touched him at Pomparles, filling him with "an intense, disturbed, bewildered curiosity." Surveying the Brue and the Levels, he saw "literally shearing the sun-lit air with a whiteness like milk" an object resembling a sword fall into the mud of the river then disappear. "John felt that *something* had touched him from beyond the limits of the known."

I look up from the Brue and there's a man sitting on the bank with a fishing rod a few feet away from me. White-haired with sparkling eyes, he looks directly at me with a penetrating gaze and smiles. He looks sixty and very healthy; he wears blue trousers, a white flannel shirt, denim vest, and old brown shoes; his hair flops over his forehead in disorderly bangs. I feel as if I've just woken up from a trance I barely knew I was in.

"The sword isn't in the Brue," he says, gesturing for me to sit down next to him. "It's pointless fishing for it this way." He studies me with a friendly, subdued grin, like an antique expert appraising a new find. "It's in the dragon's mouth. In the crystal finger. In the Avenue of Cedars. In the Stone. In the bull's eye. In the Fisher King's groin. I see you have no idea what I'm talking about. Good. Call me Ben.

He laughs as incomprehension captures my face. He seems to have been expecting me. "Of course I was. You're looking in all the wrong places. What you're looking for isn't even what you think it is, either. Still, you're close. Are you ready to cross the dangerous bridge and go for broke?" Chuckling, he stands up. "It could be big trouble, you know. Then again, it could be the point of your life. You just never know in this business. Anyway, you're not getting anywhere the way you're going about it now, are you? So what's there to lose?"

I stood up. That's too many questions to answer. How does he know all this about me? What's strangest is that I feel I've known Ben for a long time even though it's been only three minutes. That I once knew him, then forgot, and now can't remember what it was about. "Remembering takes time," Ben says. He tracks every dribble of my thinking like a basketball guard on the man with the ball. "Especially if you're not used to it."

"Where do you live?" I ask him, as we walk back to Pomparles.

"Around here. Why don't you come visit, have a proper pot of English tea? I'll even provide transportation. Unless you'd rather cogitate more about some literary version of an imaginary event? It's this old box on wheels." Ben points to a dented blue Morris Minor parked near the bridge. As we drive off, I feel inexplicably happy, relieved, expectant: this man, this Ben, whoever he is, might have some answers; he certainly knows my questions. Maybe he's seen Arthur or knows where to look. How he knows so much about my mental processes, that's a mystery whose solution will have to wait.

Hours later, late afternoon, we've been talking nonstop in Ben's kitchen about everything—the Grail, meditation, the weather, myths, the landscape, the zodiac, Arthur. We've drunk our way through several pots of Earl Grey. It's a tiny cottage, centuries old, with little square windows, set in a village called East Lyng, about twenty miles from Glastonbury. We relax into a lull, silently reflecting on the import of our conversation. Ben blows intricate smoke rings from his pipe, dividing his attention between his smokecraft and me, in case

I do or say anything interesting. "Do you know why I'm in Glastonbury, really why?" I ask him.

Ben closes his eyes, draws on his pipe, blows more rings, then answers. "I see the Tor. You walk around its base, feeling the vibrations, happy. You are at home with these energies. You have an inner knowing of purpose, a deep sense of belonging as you feel the Earth beneath your feet. There's something you want to draw up from the Earth. It's as if with each step you want to uproot something pure from deep inside the Earth and bring it into your body. You look back at your footprints and see they make a picture, tell a story, but there's a piece missing. The sun makes a full circle around you and has a message for you. Maybe it's not the sun as you know it; maybe it's a bright star. It makes another circle around you then rises to a point straight above you. It has a corona of yellow and orange. This star begins to move information through you, fresh inspiration, such that you put everything aside and start looking for that missing piece. The Earth, sensing this change, opens and takes you along a new, gentle, very subtle path."

Ben pauses to clean and refill his pipe, studying me for my reaction. I'm with him inside this strange image of a star guiding me along new paths within the Earth. Why is it I sense angels inside this star?

"Now, on this new path a crystal just ahead shows you the way. This crystal or energy field has a feminine quality and gradually leads you to all the creatures of the Earth, the elementals. They lead you to something they hold as a great secret. The Earth has many beautiful things within it, riches perhaps, diamonds, emeralds, sources of insight. All these form the pyramid. You're asked to look inside, to gaze upon the Mystery. Standing before the pyramid is the Fairy Queen and the Little Folk; she teaches them to guide you. Anubis, the Queen's dog, opens the door to the pyramid and invites you to enter. You walk inside, penetrating ever deeper while the elementals protect you with their pure vibration. You reach a deep point, the center of the pyramid. You stand there and grow into your true self."

Ben's mesmerizing words have projected me in an imaginative sense into Glastonbury and the secret, unsuspected pyramidal recesses of the Tor, at least momentarily, until he finishes speaking. I open my eyes again and look around the kitchen to make sure it's still there. It feels like I've been away for hours. "Right. Well, then, why am I looking for Arthur? That's my big question."

"First, for yourself," says Ben. "You should be clear about this. It would be best for you to clear away everything inside you that doesn't feel this way. Look, say you were a dog and somebody dangled a sausage in front of your nose to get your attention to lure you to a new place. It's like that. They wanted to entice you here from America to undergo a complete transformation as part of a training process. Arthur is the bait. What you gather and write about will become part of yourself as the story starts to be with you. You are all the actors in the drama about Arthur and the Grail. But it's also about the actual experience of the Grail, what Arthur did for the Grail, how this changed the experience of the group around him, how this influenced the history of the Earth and the lives of its people—each time, many times, this coming time. You could see a completely different aspect of the Grail than what is generally known.

"But you'll have to use your inspiration, your psychic attunement, your love, your desire to serve, your meditation practice, to make it happen. If your motivation is weak, things won't unfold for you. When you are in touch with the true value of this work for Glastonbury and the Earth, then you will have all you need. Then you will remember. You see, you're here for a good reason. Take strength. Be patient. I see a crown placed on your head. This will be a means to something whose validity will be revealed in the light of your new experiences. How about another cup of tea?"

It's a relief to get up and stretch. My attention roams indolently through Ben's tiny kitchen. As the kettle heats up, I examine the breadbox. Good, he's sensible about bread, especially if I'm going to stay here for a couple of weeks. Ben suggested it an hour ago. I couldn't come up with any reason not to. I slice two thick wedges of Ben's evidently homemade whole wheat bread, spread a layer of tahini on them, and describe a gleeful ballet around the raindrop of floor space, balancing the food tray of honey pot, milk jug, and lemons on my palm. I nod my head like a metronome to some inaudible Bach partita, as a shiver of excitement regarding what might be in store for me shakes my frame.

Ben's loaned me his couch as my new bedroom, saying it might be convenient for me to stay here while I get acquainted with Anubis. That's the Girt Dog of Langport, as they call it in Somerset, the watchdog of the Avalon zodiac whose landscape body is made of stars and hills. Caball or Cafal, Arthur called the Dog, his dog. Progress at last. It doesn't matter that I don't know what Ben is talking about or why or how he knows all this. Something is finally happening. Before I meet the Dog, I must encounter the dragon, Ben adds, the Aller Dragon. The zodiac figures all have names as if they've been domesticated. I shuffle into the living room to which Ben has relocated and pour the tea. "This ought to fortify us. Got any more Delphic nuggets for me? Here's your lemon."

Ben's face dimples in merriment. "Oh, you Americans are a cheeky lot. Don't you have any reverence for the oracle seated venerably before you, for the hoary seer of Vortigern's tower?" He squeezes two lemon wedges into his tea, leans back in his chair, and after a long chuckle like underground rumbling, he says, "Go on then. What's your question?"

"Did I have a lifetime in connection with Arthur or his Grail group?"

"This is something that should hardly concern you. When you realize who and what you were, and are, from your personal experience of remembering, you'll understand why it is of only minor importance in relation to what you are here for this time. Still, whatever role you have played and will play is central to the plot. But it would be helpful if you could accept the fact that you are beginning a process of transformation. You may not recognize yourself when you're finished. I hope you don't. This is not a change in the nature of your path but in its quality. It now grows more subtle, enlivened, *wet*. In this lifetime your path has been dry with only occasional pools. You are about to take the first step into the water, into the wet quality of your path, off the Pomparles into the Brue.

"Look, see it as a series of three Gothic arches. This is your process of transformation. You look through two of these arches, the one in the distance and the one in the foreground, but you don't see the middle one, the path of beauty. You stand under this middle arch wearing a crown. 'Myth-Making'—that's written across the middle arch, in blue neon against a green background inside a purple heart.

"But there is another level behind this. You dive head first into your Egyptian past. A being comes into focus, a huge bird, a falcon perhaps, maybe Horus, enveloped in a blue ray. At its side stands a woman of a high spiritual order. You sit next to her, cross-legged, and eat from a bowl. You're hungry for information, as if starving, but you eat so fast you can't absorb anything. There is a desperation about your demand for more food, more knowledge, more insight.

"Attendants dress you in Egyptian clothes then lift you onto a throne, gently reminding you of who you are. You take long rests to absorb energy and information in a daydream state. People visit you, give you presents. Each person stirs a memory and you remember them. The attendants tie a white band around your head, knotting it in the back in a particular way. They place four white feathers in the band at the back of your head and draw your purple cloak around you. Inside the cloak there is an embroidered image, in two layers. First, a golden heart inside a white equal-armed cross; then an Egyptian ankh. The two are superimposed. Camalate."

Ben gives this word a strange inflection. He opens his eyes and smiles. "Surely you're not taking any of this seriously! God, I hope not. I mean, you don't even remember me yet, despite the oak trees and the fresh robe." Before I can protest, Ben holds up his palm. "Wait. There's little more. The house isn't burning down. Settle back in your chair. Pay attention to your breathing. You studied meditation. Act like you remember what it's all about. Breathe calmly, with attention. Picture a still lake with a smooth, unruffled surface. The rays of the sun and moon harmoniously strike its surface together."

As I picture the lake, the scene shifts at once. I see a golden human figure, as if a man wore a gold-plated deep-sea diving outfit. I study his face. At first it's grotesque, ugly, damaged, wounded, scary, then it's only unusual, strange, not so intimidating. The mask falls away, revealing the face of a handsome, friendly, familiar man—myself when much younger.

"Drop a pebble in the lake," Ben says. "Tell me what you see."

"A pink rose on a long stalk. Its blossom is about to unfurl. Behind the rose stands a stout, red-bearded man in a white tunic; he holds a flaming torch."

"Go to the bottom of the lake," Ben suggests.

In my imagination, I dive down into the lake. Instead of water, the lake is full of white light, which exerts a strong pressure on me from all sides. Or maybe it's that my body is swelling with light activated from inside; it struggles with the weight of gravity impinging on me from the outside. A treasure chest sits on the lake bottom; it's overgrown with seaweed, encrusted, ancient; I see traces of gold underneath its exterior. The chest sits on an opened white lotus flower.

"Here is the key," says Ben. "Open the chest."

Waves of intense anticipation converge with an inexplicable happiness in me. I feel as if I'm in a pressure cooker, in the middle of a dark, black sphere. I open the chest. A myriad of bubbles sparkle out followed by a congeries of human faces, some known, some unfamiliar, then green, frond-like hands clasped in prayer rise elegantly before me. There is a mirror at the bottom of the chest.

"Look into the mirror," says Ben.

The light in the mirror implodes into a single point—a blazing star.

13

IMPROVING EYESIGHT
EARNS ME A SWORDFIGHT

ince I moved into Ben's house, my eyesight has been improving. I don't mean I'm getting around without my glasses but a different kind of myopia is getting markedly better. Inner vision. "We have to do something about your eyes," Ben said the first morning. "You have to start *seeing*."

We were drinking tea in the kitchen when Ben handed me a palm-sized green crystal and told me to concentrate on its inner facets. Then he grinned. "What do you think?" he said, looking at me inquisitively. "About the lion." I didn't know what he meant. "The lion that just walked into the room." Ben? "The one standing in front of the meditation room door." That was on my left. I was used to Ben announcing apparitions in the house. "Did I say something offensive about lions?" I quipped. So far the fact that I couldn't see any lions to my left hadn't produced a disaster. "Breathe to that crystal; let it become a screen," said Ben. After a few minutes, nothing appeared on the crystal screen, so I looked up. There was a tawny male lion stretched full length up from the doorsill scratching the walls like a housecat. "I think this means it's time we meditated, don't you?" said Ben. He opened the lion-pelted door confidently and the three of us tromped into the room.

We spend a great deal of our time meditating, at all hours of the day and night. It reminds me of the days at the Zen center except here our focus is different. Now we go out looking for *makyo*, for imaginal images. If I carried on like this when I was a bona fide Zen student, they would have broken the *kyosaku* on me before they felt they'd pounded me enough. The irony is I never had *makyo* back then, just hours of dullness on the *zafu*.

Ben sits next to me, motionless; even his breathing is undetectable. Yet the way he carries on adds meaning to the Zen phrase "leaping like a tiger while sitting still." My eyes are closed, my attention poised on the inhale-exhale of the breath at my belly when suddenly Ben appears before me in a child's body with wings, hovering cherubically overhead. He pours milk (or light) over me from a two-handled cauldron; he holds a luminous egg that flashes like a beacon then turns into a brilliant torch with a searing white flame. Ben uses this to cauterize the room. Ben seems to be clothed in white, but as he moves, his body scintillates with color; he hands me a flaming orange torch as he steps down from a ladder. Next, he spins a crystal in his palm into an umbrella and is instantly airborne, riding the sky, waving grandly, making the clown of an arc across my mind.

This would have passed the time better for me during those meditation retreats when I would fret over those insoluble, reason-defeating *koans* the Zen master liked to inflict upon us. In a sense, things aren't that different with Ben. My *koan* is Arthur. The *makyo* are instructive, too. "First you learn to see, then you master discrimination," Ben says.

Serious business is swiftly heading my way. My knees are symphonic with pain; they are Bruckner at his most raging. I'm driving the Cadillac of meditation postures, the full lotus, because it's stable and heightens my concentration, even while it squeezes my knees in a painful grip. My attention rushes out of my belly like a fire truck barrelling down the pike towards the jabbing furnace devouring my patellas. Firemen unload water hoses at the towering flames while I nudge myself into the painless interstices between the flames. That's the point, anyway: dramatically concentrate your attention to a single point. Pain in the knees isn't the only route there, but it's a fast one.

Just as I find precarious relief, Ben stands before me with a long, sharp knife—and rams it all the way into my sternum. Then he turns the blade *in situ*, as if gouging out a cavity, making a scabbard in a region of my body so sensitive and off-limits that I never feel comfortable touching it myself, not in even the most gingerly of ways. Mind you, when I say Ben rammed a sword into my chest, I don't mean my physical body; but whatever body he's penetrated, I'm squirming with discomfort. The room grows hot, perspiration rolls down my face, my glasses steam up. Like a surgeon, Ben opens up the first red layer of skin around the sternum. Finally, he backs off and winks in a friendly way, with the knife still in place.

Meanwhile, neither of us have physically stirred from our meditation seats, except for some twitching and squirming on my part. I open my eyes, relieved that I am not actually impaled through the sternum, except, paradoxically, I am: I can see the glinting knife, its blade plung-ed like the famous sword in the stone into the anvil of my very ordinary chest. There is no pain, yet I am terrifically uncomfortable. Later, Ben says, "I wanted to bring something to your attention. I think you got my point."

We sit without further incident for awhile. This gives Ben time to think up new parlor tricks for my benefit. Now he appears before me, standing, and hangs a circle of white curtains that form a crown around my head; they leap into a blazing corona of hundreds of gold, orange, and topaz flames. Once again my attention wanders away from my diligent work at the belly to this conflagration around my head. Out of the flames arise two intertwined cobras, one golden, the other silver, uncoiling, flicking dreadful tongues at my eye level. I would fall over backwards with fright, except the full lotus keeps me rivetted for the full extent of the visual torture. The cobras dissolve into emptiness—thank God Buddha was right: form *is* emptiness. In their place appears a man: he's red-haired, bearded, stocky, about fifty, in antique medieval clothing, looking straight at me. Until he's fiercely decapitated with a single ax stroke; his unwashed, scruffy head plunks into a pail.

Ben reappears like a diligent hunter checking his traps and inspects his handiwork at my sternum. His knife has swollen, transformed itself into a thick sword that skewers my heart. Unbelievably, Ben takes another sword and rams it through my right ear until the tip comes out the left ear. Not content with a deposit of two swords in me, Ben takes another blade and rams it straight into my chest as if it's a bean bag. Groaning, I wobble on my cushion. I figure I ought to remain in the ring in case more swords are heading my way, but the imminent explosion of my knees commandeers my attention. Providentially. "Gotta go. Sorry, Ben. It's the knees," I tell him mentally. "Don't be silly," he replies in my mind. "Your knees are fine."

This *makyo* is getting out of hand, but before I can whistle for the nearest Zen master to whack Ben with the *kyosaku*, I surprise myself. Suddenly I strike out at Ben with a pathetic wooden sword of my own, guarding myself with a wobbly shield. We leap around the meditation room, swords jabbing. I ding Ben on the eyebrow; he laughs when I apologize and look concerned, then rams his hilt through my well-perforated sternum and leaves it in place. That makes three swords in my chest. Their weight knocks me over. I'm down on the mat for the count as Ben rings the bell. End of meditation.

I stagger out of the room on wooden knees and crash into the door because my glasses are so steamed up I can't see anything. Why can't they make glasses with built-in windshield wipers? I am a human pin cushion. A sword through my head, ear-to-ear, three broadswords sheathed in my chest, my knees aflame with daggers—it's complicated getting through the doorframe without being knocked sideways or getting the sword handles hung up on something. I collapse on the couch exhausted beyond explanation. Feverish, disoriented, sleepy, my head throbs, my breathing is logjammed with anxiety. Momentarily, I see myself as a gawky teenager stumbling out of Ben's meditation room, beaten up, dejected, pouting, grouchy, ornery, wingeing, miserable. Zazen was never this rough. Those tigers may have leapt but they never gored me like this.

Ben stands over me as I twitch and sweat on his couch. He's laughing. He holds his stomach, it hurts to laugh this much. "Have a hot bath. Use pine oil," he says. "You'll feel yourself again, more or less, in an hour." A mischievous twinkle lurks behind his solicitude. He's slashed me to bits, I realize as I slide my damaged body into the hot

suds. "You should have let me finish with my knives and not re-
sisted me," Ben says, standing in the bathroom doorway. "Especially when you don't know the first thing about swords or how to
use one. Or when you don't even have one. You need a sword. Next
time you see something happening you don't like, hold up a mirror.
Visualize one as big as your body. It's a good defense in most cases,
unless you're up against somebody like me. Then forget it. Pray. That
might help. But not much. I've got friends in high places. Lots of
connections."

"You find it very amusing," I grumble, only my mouth visible above
the pine foam. "At the least I'm glad you know what you're doing."

"Whatever makes you say that?" Ben replies, closing the door.

That night I dream I walk along a small ridge overlooking a construction site about twenty feet below. Within the site, a vast snake
begins to writhe, shaking off dirt and stones, revealing its terrible
shape, six feet thick, speckled silver, grey, and black amidst white
scales. I can't believe how big it is. In the morning I remember Ovid's
description of Python in his *Metamorphoses*. "A serpent never known
before, the huge Python, a terror to men's new-made tribes, so far it
sprawled across the mountainside... the bloated Python, whose vast
coils across so many acres spread their blight."

"Well. I think we're ready for the dragon, or snake if you prefer,
don't you?" Ben announces at breakfast. "I presume you know that
Arthur was a dragon-slayer."

"Sure. And I know that in the hagiographies they always talk
about his exploits against dragons," I answer, my mouth full of toast
and marmalade. "He was off in Brittainy hunting dragons and various monsters. Arthur sought a terrible serpent that had laid waste
twelve parts of the land, says one source."

"Good. But did you know Arthur slew a dragon, right here in our
back garden? The Aller Dragon."

Somerset is packed with dragon lore; in fact, so is much of Britain.
Folk memory and the survival of alleged artifacts corroborate the
former existence of eight dragons in Somerset alone, at Crowcombe,
Church, Carhampton, Castle Neroche, Shervage Wood,

Churchstanton, Kilve, Aller. Legend says a dragon once flew between Curry Rivel and Aller, a distance of a few miles, poisoning
trees, blackening crops, terrorizing villagers. Some legends claim it
still lives in the Sedgemoor bogs near Athelney and a queer old hill
called Burrowbridge Mump five miles from here. A doughty fellow
named John Aller (alternatively, he was called Hext) slew the dragon
with a spear, which, the church at Lower Ham claims, is the same
one hanging on their wall. Most dragons are fond of milk, and the
Aller Dragon was no exception. Knowing this, John Aller covered
himself in pitch, put on a mask to protect himself from the dragon's
noxious fumes, then speared the beast in its den one night; afterwards, he sealed the cave with an iron harrow. That's the myth; but
what is the reality of the Aller Dragon, or of any of the dragons?

There are famous dragons like the Serpent Mound in America's
Ohio, a landscape feature sculpted to look like a huge snake when
seen from above; or Dragon Hill in England's Wiltshire, so named
because of a chalk figure of an ancient horse (or dragon) etched in
the grass. "Is this Aller Dragon part of the Glastonbury zodiac in
some way? I ask."

"That's right," says Ben. "It's part of the Somerset star temple,
which happens to be a lot bigger and more starry than most people
think. The Aller Dragon is an Earth figure that corresponds, approximately, with the constellation Hydra, the Water Snake. It's not
a one hundred percent correspondence, as above so below, nor does
it have to be. When the old geomancers developed this zodiac, they
made their own adaptations. There's some flexibility to the system.
The landscape changes over time, too, and we're dealing with a considerable block of time here. Even so, the run of the hills and some of
the place-names still recall the stellar body of Hydra laid over the
landscape. It goes from Hatch Beauchamp to Aller; that's about ten
miles from tail to tongue."

In the Greek myths, Hercules' second labor was to kill the Lernaean
Hydra. This water snake's dog-like body was prodigious, sporting
eight or nine heads, one of which was golden and immortal. So noxious was this dragon that its breath or even the smell of its tracks

could be fatal to humans. Iolaus drove Hercules to Hydra's lair in his chariot while Pallas Athena advised him on technique. Hercules' problem was that every time he cut off one head, Hydra sprouted another two or three in its place. Iolaus helped him cauterize each root with flaming branches so that no more heads could spring forth. Hercules finally severed the Hydra's immortal head, then buried it, still hissing, under a massive rock. He dipped his arrows in the Hydra's gall so that henceforth a wound from one of his arrows would be fatal to his enemies.

The Greek legends imply that Hercules' Hydra is equivalent to the dragon at the Spring of Ares, near Thebes, the one Cadmus slew. "Hidden in the cave, there dwelt a snake, a snake of Mars," writes Ovid. "Its crest shone gleaming gold; its eyes flashed fire; its whole body was big with venom, and between its triple rows of teeth its three-forked tongue flickered." After the serpent killed most of Cadmus' men, he crushed its head with a boulder. Pallas Athena advised Cadmus to plow the soil then plant the serpent's teeth like seed in the furrows, "from which a future people should arise." They did: the Sparti, or Sown Men, were a combative folk who sprang up instantly, clashing their weapons; only five Sown Men survived the eventual carnage, but they unanimously offered their services to Cadmus and helped him build the Theban acropolis called Cadmea.

But that was myth and long ago. What relation it has to the ten mile span of hills between Hatch Beauchamp and Aller I couldn't fathom.

"Let's tidy up the kitchen and then go walk through a myth in the landscape," said Ben.

14

WALKING IN THE DRAGON'S FIRELIT BACK

rimson Hill is a couple miles past the village of Hatch Beauchamp, between Currey Mallet and Wrantage. Ben pulls off the road by an unmarked ridge, and we walk silently along the edge of a pasture and into the woods. The hill slumps into moorland below on the right while straight ahead runs a footpath that leads us to the mossy wreck of an old stone foundation. We sit down amidst narcissi and garlic-scented ransom. "It glared down the whole wide wood, as huge, if all its size were seen, as in the sky, the Snake that separates the two bright Bears," writes Ovid of Cadmus' Hydra. Ben explains that we have arrived at the tail of the Water Snake such that the land between Hatch Beauchamp and Crimson Hill encompasses approximately the last seven stars in its tail. "Let's have a look at this tail, shall we?" suggests Ben.

I close my eyes and settle down into my breathing until my mind clears, then empties. A large, thick golden arrow appears, pointing skywards; joined to it is a similar green arrow, pointing groundwards.

"That's right, the tail is golden," comments Ben. "It was purified long ago in the flames of the dragon's breath. The tail was once in its mouth; Hydra in its infancy was oroboric. The tail was the dragon's golden crown. The worm oroboros, tail in its mouth, a closed loop, a complete circuit. Then she gradually uncoiled herself like a spring fern, piercing each energy node in her serpentine body with the tail. Now the tail points heavenward to receive cosmic and solar energy and it forks earthward to ground this energy. The angels assist with the golden point and the gnomes help with the green point. Everything in geomancy is reciprocal and multilayered like that. Think of this as a cycling of energy from above to below and back up to above again. Where we sit here at the tail is the junction of the green and gold energy circuits, the creative, blending point. The dragon circulates cosmic and solar energies received here up through the higher nodes in its body."

"Ben, how can a series of hills be a dragon? I don't understand that."

"The dragon is a figure of light superimposed on the hill of matter. The original superimposition itself helped shape the contours of this landscape. Except that at the risk of confusing you, this isn't precisely correct. It's more correct to say the physical hill was superimposed on the light body of Hydra. Each node on the landscape body of this Water Snake is a doorway into the light body of the figure, which, remember, is really a constellation in the zodiac. Each node in Hydra, like Crimson Hill, represents a star point in its landscape body. The tail has the power to pierce and activate each star node in its body so that eventually the life fire can flame throughout its body. That enlivens the dragon; it becomes a flame from tail to crown, capable of magnetically charging the landscape. Now, that activation can only happen with human help. Hydra is, ultimately, an aspect of yourself as a human being, a partial reflection of yourself seen in a cosmic mirror. Each star in Hydra is a point in human consciousness. But the snake, as all geomantic figures, must be periodically renewed in the Earth, as if reborn, through the efforts of people."

"Was Arthur aware of the Aller Dragon?"

"Indeed he was. The Aller Dragon was a key aspect in Arthur's system of training for the Grail Knights. Here they not only learned geomancy but practiced it because the star nodes require regular maintenance and calibration as times change. The act of making geomantic adjustments was synchronous with their own initiations into the landscape mysteries. Each node in Hydra, like Crimson Hill, is a star and a stage in the progressive unfoldment of consciousness within the stage called Hydra. Now, the village of Aller was the templic seat for the Somerset dragon fellowship, for the Pendragon rituals. That's why it was once called Arthur's Village. Arthur's reputation as a dragon-slayer—and Cadmus' too—pertains in part to his mastery of the *energies* of Hydra, both in the landscape and in himself. The Hydra outside, the Hydra within: they are not different, only mirror reflections."

"So Arthur didn't actually slay dragons."

"No. You know the popular image of St. Michael, one of Britain's patron saints, renowned for his dragon-slaying? Same business. First, he wasn't a saint at all. He was—and still is—an archangel. Second, he didn't slay the dragon but energized it with the cosmic light of his sword. There's no point in destroying dragons; they have a role in the energetics of the planet. On the other hand, you want to let the dragon know who's the boss because it also represents the lower self. Michael, Arthur, and the other dragon heroes like Cadmus and St. George, imparted light and energy to the landscape figure, thereby animating it for the benefit of the environment and its residents. Arthur and his knights awoke the Hydra, especially in the spring. They roused the dormant fire of consciousness stored in its root. They awoke the dragon that slept in the hills with their swords. Each knight had a sword. Again, don't take this literally. Just as Hydra is a figure in light, so were the swords. Light swords, forged by insight. The knights walked the landscape nodes of Hydra—through these same woods, actually—starting as we are at Crimson Hill. They aligned their consciousness with the quality of consciousness represented by each node in Hydra's geomythic body; by the time they reached the crown, they had fully identified with the figure in consciousness and energetically aligned themselves with its stages in consciousness. Her wings, by the way, are huge, red canvas sails billowing in the etheric winds. Maybe you'll see them."

"Why did they call Hydra the Aller Dragon?"

"People once had a poetic feeling for the possibilities of language. You find it in the old British place names. They called the dragon Aller to mean *All Hers*, in respect of her expansiveness, for the vista in consciousness she gave. She was capable of transporting the knights when they and the dragon had simultaneously reached a point of ripeness. They were *all hers*. That's because Hydra is an aspect of the cosmic dragon, Draco, the one Ovid meant when he said it was the snake that separates the two bears, Ursa Major and Ursa Minor. This is the world serpent. The Egyptians called it *Sata* or *Tuat* on whose back the Sun rode at night through the underworld. For the Greeks, it was Oceanos, the sea serpent of the outermost waters. She was *Mat Chinoi*, the Serpent Mother; *Kadru*, the Indian serpent Goddess who birthed the immortal Nagas; *Per Uatchet*, the Egyptian Great Mother of Creation; Ninhursag, for the Akkadians, 'She Who Gives Life to the Dead;' for the Hebrews, Leviathan, the wriggly one, for whom the Levites, of the tribe of Levi, were the 'Sons of the Great Serpent.' You see how quickly things move into the mythic in this business? The Hebrew Qabalists had another deeper meaning for the Aller Dragon which maybe you'll work out later."

"How did Arthur deploy his knights across Hydra?"

"He sent them out to the various nodes on Hydra while he sat at Aller, the dragon's crown. The knights moved the energy up the dragon to Arthur who grounded it. When the dragon was lit, aflame with cosmic energy, it breathed fire into the landscape. Everything prospered: crops, livestock, inhabitants, the evolution of human consciousness. Now, although the Aller Dragon is rooted to this ridge overlooking the moor, at times she could lift herself off the ground and travel around like a tongue of fire with Grail Knights astride her brilliant form. This is tricky to understand: it's not literally true yet it's much more than imaginatively true. You'll have to experience it yourself to know what I mean. Enough background. Let's get practical. Hydra is here to be of service to you. Bring your attention to the tail of the dragon within yourself. Sink your attention down into your root, the source of the creative."

As I sink deep into my breathing, my body widens out into the landscape. Crimson Hill, with its gold and green arrows, sits in my groin. There are paving stones at the base of a tree. I pry them loose. Underneath is a nest with two snakes, each a foot long and two inches thick with amber-black scales; one is male, one female, making a circle; each is awake. The scene shifts: I'm in a sidewalk drawing competition at an oceanside promenade. I've chalked the figure of a yellow dragon. The dragon stands up, turns into a man in golden armor standing inside the St. Michael tower on Glastonbury Tor; flames envelop him, rising to the crown of the tower high above. A third image comes into focus. I'm about to cross a street. As my right foot steps onto the curb, I notice a pool of fresh blood underneath. I pull off my sock; it's bloodstained—with my blood, flowing from a lateral cut above the ankle and from my big toe.

"Well, that gives us an indication of where you need work," comments Ben who appears to have followed my imagery as if watching it on closed-circuit TV. "The dragon mirrors you. It shows you where you stand in relation to the dragon within, to the energy and its elaboration within your being at this point in time and as the result of cumulative experience from this lifetime and previous ones. The intertwining snakes, that's your potential, the equipoise of wisdom, male and female energies in harmony. The flaming man in the tower is your process of transformation and purification, barely begun. You saw an image of the soul of man within the stone tower of the body. The bleeding ankle: here you observe your present limitation. An old wound that hinders your outward expression and movement as a man—right foot stepping forward into the world. A hobble, a stutter in the execution of your purpose. An instability in your masculine self, a loss of male vitality. Could use a little healing, don't you think? Let's walk up the spine of Hydra and visit the next star."

Perhaps it's my imagination, but with each step I make in these aromatic spring woods, it's as if I am walking in two worlds. In one world, soft, moist earth, dry twigs, crinkled oak leaves, thick green shoots; in another, stars, shiny scales, a serpentine life-form miles long. "And now it coils in giant spirals, now it towers up tall as a tree, now like a stream in spate after a storm it rushes surging on, and breasts aside the woods that bar its way," writes Ovid, describing Cadmus' dragon. Even without Ovid's imagery, the landscape evokes the Aller Dragon: the abrupt uprising of the moors into a spiny, undulant ridge of hills with suggestive names like Crimson and Swell make it easy to construe this topography as that of a recumbent watersnake. After walking about two miles, we reach a grassy knoll and Ben gestures for me to sit down.

There is a distinct inner light about this place, although it lacks the mellow stability of Crimson Hill. After breathing quietly with a relaxed inner focus, I see a thirty-foot high crystalline vertical form with three sides terminating in a single sky-piercing tip. Inside this sculpted cone of light, I see a jet airplane as if from underneath, its massive engines hung like testicles from silvery wings.

"Welcome to Lord Wood, another starpoint close to Hydra's tail," announces Ben, chuckling. "Balls, that's right, but not hanging off a jet. You have had a little glimpse, with filtering, of the energy nature of this point. Hydra's generative center at this time is somewhat dormant."

That was all for Lord Wood, just the recognition. We walk for another hour in silence until we reach a nature preserve at Swell Wood, owned by the Royal Society for the Preservation of Birds. My first step into this wood sends a dozen great blue herons gliding majestically overhead to circle their treetop nests. This copse is lovely, intoxicating, maternal. We sit down inside a natural grass circle amidst a stand of beeches; a half hour passes in happy silence, then Ben asks me for my impressions.

"It's elegant, motherly, nurturing, like the inside of a belly: pink, warm, and soft," I reply. "It feels like a reservoir of mothering. The place has a hushed loveliness as if this mother were swelling with fruit. It feels like the omphalos of Hydra, the center that sees the tail and the crown, the source of her breath. It's *so* feminine." I remember Tolkien on the soft spot of the drake Foalókë: "The armor of these vile worms is of little worth upon their bellies."

It takes us two hours to walk through the woods along Hydra's back to Ben's Morris Minor. Over a sandwich and tea, Ben explains that Swell Wood is another aspect of the dragon's generative center. Then we drive up the dragon for six miles, pulling off the narrow road beside a large estate and wheatfield a little past the miniscule village of Heale, in between Burton Wood and Stoneley Copse and on the verge of what the Ordnance Survey calls Burton Pynsent Monument, a decrepit stone obelisk. We pick our way along the edge of the field, cross a fence, and enter a sloping five acre greensward tussocked by a hundred grazing sheep. The monument is derelict, a collapsing stone tower a hundred feet high barred by a locked iron gate inserted into its cracked, unstable base. Its internal spiralling staircase is closed permanently to the public; in its decline, the monument forlornly surveys the north moors, the River Parett, Burrowbridge Mump, and the indifferent sheep, who barely flinch as we slip through their ranks.

"Where are we now in Hydra?" I ask Ben as I survey the landscape below, sweeping from Burrowbridge Mump to Glastonbury Tor, minutely visible beyond a range of hills.

"This is *Al Sharasif*, the Ribs, as the Arabic astronomers called it," Ben tells me. "We could call it the dragon's solar plexus. As you're noticing, each node is an energy point and a reservoir of light with a different taste or feel. Each has its specific function within the life of the landscape figure. Hydra sucks in solar energy through this point— and so should you. Let the sun enter your solar plexus from the heart. Take this hill into your solar plexus. As the placename says, this place heals. You heal the wounds of the solar plexus by awakening the love in the heart."

We sit silently for an hour. My solar plexus grows tight and thick, as if knotted in dozens of places. Nothing else happens until we return to Ben's car and are about to drive off. Suddenly and involuntarily my legs start thrashing against the inside door and floorboards as if possessed in a spastic fit. The rear-view mirror, inches from my forehead, threatens to slice into my eyes like a dagger. I can't bear being this close to it. Nor can I bear staying in Ben's car another second. I shove open the door and stagger away, clutching my stomach as if I've been stabbed. I collapse on the ground in a clump, breathing hard, perspiring, shaking.

Ben kneels at my side, waiting silently. There are metal shackles around my ankles attached to a long chain. I am in China, being carted off to die, against my will, unfairly. I am a strong man, physically powerful, probably an accomplished warrior, maybe a martial artist. My masculine powers are well-honed. I've been condemned unjustly by my peers; my jailers convey me, bound and straitjacketed, a great distance in this cramped carriage, out into the wasteland. It is maddeningly claustrophobic, so I thrash about trying to upset the carriage but fail. We travel endlessly across a flat, barren plain until we reach a solitary shack. My captors castrate, disembowel, blind, then chain me, leaving a thick spear embedded in my upper belly, leaving me to bleed to death in torment. In the moments before I die, I vow never again to manifest my powers or reveal my true identity because it is too dangerous.

A series of subsequent lifetimes flicker past like fragments from an epic movie. Lives as a monastic contemplative, Buddhist, Christian, Islamic, in England, Tibet, France, Japan, Burma, Iraq—lives in whose celibate aura I begin to heal this profound wound. The somber procession of hermitic lives is occasionally punctuated by the antic gestures of a clown or trickster in which I allowed a little irony and witty bile to percolate through this damaged solar plexus. Self-confidence swells and I take on lives embedded in books, papers, ideas, scholarly investigations, as I attempt to redress the iniquities of the world through the safety of writing. Voices across the lifetimes congeal into Gregorian chanting, echoing in stone cathedrals as a dirge for my pain. Somebody has remained obdurately unborn through this rosary of lives. I'm sad, mournful, seeing how this devastating experience in China sits like triple-headed Cerberus before the gates of my own development. It growls at the gates of my solar plexus preventing me from reclaiming innate powers: my identity. I put the watchdog in place, I keep him fed; only I can remove him.

In light of this recognition, the contours of my present life reconfigure: the physical meekness, the poor eyesight, the reclusive writer's lifestyle, the ambivalent engagement with the world, the sullen resentment, the incorrigible wit. My head lies in the soft grass, tears form, and my chest heaves with sobs. Ben lays crystals along my body then squeezes a large stone in his palm, moving it in circles around my solar plexus and heart. I lie as if under a filmy brown blanket of karmic toxins.

"Breathe the toxins out through the bottom of your feet, as you exhale," Ben advises gently.

The sheath of toxins slowly turns grey, then white, then dissipates as I flush the wounds out of my system, from the memory of my cells. Smoke swirls out of my sternum from the hole left by the Chinese spear. My body is uncomfortable, fidgety, like a cornered animal, flinching in the shadow of an inexorable predator. I keep breathing calm into my belly, to a tiny point of brilliant light, like a pinprick, like a blazing star just above the navel. Somehow I am peaceful and agitated simultaneously. Gnarled hands reach into my body and yank out the intestines, the stomach, liver, heart. Then a beam of strong yellow light projects out of Ben's hands into my body cavity, healing the inflamed tissue; there is always another layer of woundedness within: I am a battered, hemorrhaging onion. Strike me here, it's already soft and used to your spear point; my suppurating flesh swells for another thrust. Scar tissue draws a cartilaginous veil across each previous wounding, helping me to forget why I pain. I examine the bloodied tissue, flaming under the light of day, and the exposed ribs beneath, futile shield.

I grab the spear with both hands and yank it, shouting: "You'll never do that to me again, damn you!" I fling the bloodied spear into the woods as my Chinese body goes stiff and death takes me off. A half hour later I'm recovered sufficiently to sit up and smile feebly at Ben.

"Some spear," Ben says.

That evening I go to bed early, exhausted from my death in Swell Wood. In a dream I find myself on the second floor of a house, exploring a room. I split open a cement casement with a maul, and a hundred polished quartz crystals the size of ice cubes tumble out onto the floor from a crack in the casement. Next to this stands a potted green plant, resembling an apidistra, with three long shoots with circular white markings. The discovery delights me. I sift through handfuls of the crystals understanding that somebody hid them within the cement pillar so long ago that their existence has been forgotten. When I recount the dream to Ben at breakfast, he says, "Bring this dream with you into meditation. Breathe your love to it, reanimate it, then finish the dream. Watch carefully what it turns into."

I bring all the dream images to mind and breathe affectionately to them as if I am a gardener of the imagination tending my delicate blooms. The crystals and three-stalked green plant organize themselves into a hoop which becomes a pendant shield hung around my neck over my solar plexus from pubis to sternum. The plant occupies the middle of the shield, surrounded by the crystals, which are inlaid like sequins. The crystals flush yellow in the heat of my breathing, then bloom like crocuses; each flower has numerous layers of tightly packed yellow petals. I remove the green plant from its pot and set it into the "soil" in the center of the crocus blooms, which are already two inches tall and growing. At the most acutely sensitive spot on my sternum—Ben's stabbing ground—the plant yields a lovely white rose. Orange leaves appear inside the yellow crocus petals, which by now have completely filled out the shield as a uniform field of yellow intensity. Now, within the center of the white rose, a small, glittering ruby emerges as the white petals fold down to highlight the radiant jewel in their midst.

When I stand and return to Ben's kitchen for tea, my posture feels radically different. I feel stronger, stouter in the chest, more masculine somehow; I can breathe deeper, my sternum isn't so ferociously sensitive. The pendant shield across my chest is as palpable as my blue denim shirt and will remain with me for days.

15

AN EMERALD BLADE FROM INSIDE THE GNOME EGG

wo days later we're back on the Aller Dragon at Hellard's Hill, a mile up Hydra's spine from Heale, just above the hamlet of Wick and overlooking Oath Hill. Locally this place is known as the Fairy Dell on account of its devic presence, says Ben. People once came here to meet with the fairies, gnomes, elves, and other of the fabled Little Folk of the green mounds. We park the car and set off through the woods along a rutted, muddy farm track. Suddenly, I feel as if we're being tracked, overshadowed by an invisible stalker. I wheel around and momentarily glimpse a figure reminiscent of the scarecrow in *The Wizard of Oz*, only this one is twice as tall, considerably fiercer, and airborne a few feet behind us.

"That's a *hearn*," says Ben. "Friendly chap. It's an agricutural guardian and protector of the fields. Its vibration is close to the human range so they are sometimes easier to discern than members of the elemental kingdom. But you better watch out for that one."

Ben indicates an oak tree, and I jump out of range with a shout. A man leaps out from behind the tree and hurls a five-pronged javelin straight for my throat. Before I can defend myself, somebody inserts a shield between my throat and the javelin, deflecting it; the attacker, who is bearded, coarsely-dressed in leather jerkin and fringed girdle, and clearly from another epoch, angrily dissolves back into the air. Ben halts, breathing quietly, attuning to something. I follow his cue and, when my breathing calms, I have another remarkable sight: standing behind me, no matter in what direction I face, is a twelve-foot-tall, masculine angel.

Thick, silvery, majestic, his outstretched wings are feathered in royal blue; he brandishes a gleaming sword in one hand, its diamond blade facing left and upwards in an attitude of poised defense; in his other hand, a glittering shield. It was his shield that protected me. He speaks in low, steady syllables no louder than a whisper in my mind, but as he speaks, his arms and hands describe delicate motions through the air, as if in a separate language. "I am Alinoris Aloina: yours." He wraps his wings around me like a radiant tipi making me instantly feel I can withstand anything, anybody's spear or javelin. My aura enlarges, strengthens, integrates, as a living shield around my body within which the yellow solar plexus shield radiates sunlight as if a star blazes within.

"You never know who you'll meet in these woods," says Ben. He walks further along the path as if encounters with angry Celtic tribesmen and beatific guardian angels were everyday occurrences for him.

The rutted track terminates in a green pasture that slides down from a thick woods. A farmer has parked his tractor in front of a haystack as big as a cottage and relaxes as his radio blares out the news and hit singles. We pass a collapsed stone cottage ingrown with vines, nearly digested by Nature, then we cross a turnstile and step onto the broad field that swells into a knoll crowned by the woods. The outcropping slope ahead is gently terraced and its grass has an inexplicably misty-soft green; it exudes an ethereality, a shimmer between worlds. We step over a tiny gulley, and, as if passing through a veil, enter this otherworldly domain, this shape-shifting land of creamy bliss. We perch on the knoll and at once, without making an effort, I'm swimming up to my neck in the Fairy Dell's supple loveliness, imbibing devic intoxication through my skin in great draughts.

A rapture envelops me, permeating the dry, scaly pores of my body, softening what is hard, melting what is resistant, transforming all to golden effulgence. My head sways like a nodding spring flower. Numerous pinpricks of light explode in the air before me: I see stars. The elements are unaccountably in perpetual motion before me, transiting at light speed across the landscape, through my body, my eyes, my mind, popping into my physical senses as starry pinpricks of delight. There is a presence on my left knee, the subtlest of weights, but I can't bring it into focus; I can discern, just a few feet beyond me, two dwarvish figures, stubby old men with round faces, eyes like blue beads, wizened smiles, long beards, caps, jerkins, sturdy breeches. Dwarves. Tolkien's dwarves are what the Celts called the little underground men. Gnomes.

"Ben, am I seeing gnomes?" He doesn't answer. Fifty feet away, he's sprawled on his stomach studying something in the grass, tapping his feet together in the air with the delight of a six year old. Eventually, he gets up and walks over to me. "Of course you are. And they're seeing you, too. Checking you out, taking measurements, making bets. They're mischievous but reliable, these gnomes, once you establish a working relationship—which you'll need to for any success in your work. As for that elf bouncing on your knee, well, they can be more problematic. They have their own ideas about things. Still, it's a good sign for only the first meeting."

"What were you watching over there in the grass?"

"Oh, your standard ring of dancing fairies. The standard fairy coach speeding merrily across the dell. Pipe music, devic frivolity. What you would expect if you were sitting in the heart of a dragon."

Hellard's Hill, and its immediate neighbor, Red Hill, constitute the heart of Hydra, Ben explains. This is *Al Fard al Shuja*, The Solitary One in the Serpent, said the Arab astronomers, or *Cor Hydrae*, in the Latin of Tycho Brahe—the heart center. "It has long been said amongst Men that whosoever might taste the heart of a dragon would know all the tongues of Gods or Men, or birds or beasts, and his ears would catch whispers of the Valar or of Melko such as never had he heard before," wrote Tolkien. "Few have there been that ever achieved a deed of such prowess as the slaying of a drake, nor might any even of such doughty ones taste their blood and live, for it is as a poison of fires that slays all save the most godlike in strength." Perhaps, but this injunction didn't stop that Norse hero Sigurd Fafnirsbane. He roasted the heart of the dragon Fafnir and afterwards understood the speech of birds and became wisest among Men. Ben interrupts my reflections. "That's all very mythologically correct, but what I would like to know from you is what you think of what this gnome is trying to show you."

A gnome gestures for me to turn around. I see a huge, white golfball embedded in the hill: it's like a pockmarked egg of light fifty yards wide and seventy-five yards high. Inside the egg are innumerable chambers or cells within which a multitude of gnomes are busy with activities. Uncannily, the egg reminds me of a rabbitt warren or college dormitory. The gnome conveys to me the information that this is a gnome settlement for this section of Somerset, a kind of district headquarters. Then he shows me an image of the hillside beyond us. It's dotted with numerous radiant apertures—"doors out," he calls them.

Somehow I can understand what the gnome is saying through a kind of direct thought transference coupled with a nimble picture-making ability. As the gnome "speaks" to me, I see myself, as if observing a stranger from a distance, wreathed about the neck with diaphanous fairies and encircled at the waist with merry gnomes, tossing their caps as they dance around this mute and dumb Gulliver in their midst. One bright-red cap lands—impossibly!—on an organ pipe, one of many packed like bamboo shoots in a reedy column at whose base sits the organ. Suddenly, I can hear the gnome and he says distinctly: "The great Pan greets you at the dragon's heart where he sings and plays on his pipes."

"All our old friends are rushing out to greet us this afternoon," remarks Ben. "We are most fortunate. By the way, if you have any questions about this gnome egg, I'm sure Battingley here will be happy to oblige you with some information." *Battingley*—so the gnomes have names. As his name is mentioned, Battingley doffs his cap and bows. It's all on the edge of unbelievability but since Ben finds this encounter normal and has no doubts that we might be making it all up in some kind of shared devic hallucination, I relax into the spirit of things and ask Battingley a question. "What is the purpose of this gnome egg?"

"Battingley says to understand a gnome egg, you must know a little about the life and purposes of the gnomes," says Ben who acts as an interpreter. But soon his voice fades away and I seem to be listening to Battingley directly. If I ever thought that the ideas and intelligence of dwarves, or gnomes, was a bit simplistic and child-like, Battingley's discourse radically changes that mistaken notion. "The gnome eggs are located at high points in the Earth's magnetic field. Their job is to keep the magnetic field contour lines coherent as they interface at the splice with another web of etheric light and nodes, about which you are presently unfamiliar. The gnome egg is like a beehive or honeycomb whose geometrical shape helps it to maintain a coherent note within the local energy matrix and to act as a transmitter of energies from one dimension to another, through the splice from the etheric to the magnetic fields."

The gnomes walk the magnetic field waves and keep them clear, continues Battingley. Animals leave a few traces in the field lines but humans particularly discard passions and dark thoughtforms that clutter and pollute the waves. The Moon regularly stretches and contracts them. During Full Moon, the waves are the widest, like sound ridges. The gnomes are like walking ley lines, etheric geomancers.

"We walk through these ridges of sound the way light and life flow through the ley lines in your world. The world to us looks like the ribbed surface of a seashell. Long ago it was a single web and we danced through it everywhere. It was neither broken nor disrupted in any place. Now it is a terrible mess, jangled and discontinuous. We can only walk the waves in certain areas now. We avoid the black knots, those places you call cities. We cannot heal them. They have broken the waves and we have abandoned the black knots. They kill our ears. Our singing, which is our basic life vibration, purifies, strengthens, and amplifies the sound qualities of the waves. We make them flow coherently along the surface of Earth, like blood vessels just below the skin. The life forms of the planet depend on these waves and on our maintenance. We carry our life vibration out from the star nodes in your world out through the magnetic field, through the seashell. Walking, we are like tuning forks. We link the points of higher frequency in the field, tying them together. We work with those places where the wise among your kind have established healing vibrations. We don't do anything special. It's our nature to correct the sound vibrations by the way we are."

The waves flow in and out of the physical Earth, explains Battingley. It doesn't matter to the gnomes if they walk inside or outside the Earth as we know it. That isn't the way they see it. They follow the wave contours. Inside such a wave, the scenery is completely different than outside. The bubbles, or gnome eggs, are collective resonators, storing the group vibration of a colony of gnomes, holding the gnome "song" intact and coherent at important points in the overall energy matrix. The egg is a doorway out for gnomes, and a doorway in for humans, should they wish to pass through. There are other doorways, grace notes in the scales of the energy web. These doorways are for the *Yeti*, the reticent ones. "You must be very quick to slip through a *Yeti* door and you can do so only if invited," advises Battingley. A *Yeti* door—here Battingley refers to what other traditions call the Sasquatch or Abominable Snowman— is a harmonic overtone made by the overlap of several frequencies to make an opening.

Gnome eggs—and there are many around the planet, mostly in the northern regions of the northern hemisphere—pulsate according to atmospheric and magnetic field changes and solar flare activity as well. The eggs transduce these energies through the splice between the Earth's magnetic field lines and the etheric light lines in the subtle energy grid or planetary web. The gnome eggs were established before the beginning of Time on Earth by a great being sacred to the gnomes, something akin to Ophion, the primal world-serpent in the Greek myths. The gnome egg, Battingley tells me, sends tendrils of light out into the landscape for up to a mile in radius. These splayed tendrils resemble human nerve endings and the gnomes maintain them assiduously because they move the subtle currents out into the splice between the light and magnetic fields. Gnome eggs are always situated close to eggs of the great dragon. This Hydra and the other dragon nearby—Battingley refuses to be more specific—are originally hatched from eggs. "It's part of our work to look after the dragon eggs until they hatch."

I ask Battingley if it would be possible for me to see the inside of the gnome egg.

"This can be arranged now, if you wish," he replies. Battingley hands me a small, green crystal and places it in my palm to hold against my heart. I sit for a few moments in silence as my breathing steadies and my mind empties. I am inside the gnome egg with Battingley. No longer is it an elliptical white mist set halfway into Hellard's Hill, but a multicolor spherical palace of huge dimensions. Gnome kings in regal robes occupy privileged seats within individual concave niches as if in a gallery of the ancients. I walk respectfully through this hall of gnome royalty not sure if the gnome kings are lifelike statues or real but sleeping gnomes—a paradox within a paradox because I don't even understand in what way gnomes like Battingley are alive or real.

The gnome egg in part is a hall of records for the history of gnomes, says Battingley. Each king has an epic to relate, the history of his times. The gnome egg, I gather, is also a long hall, the kind of mead-hall the Beowulf poet had in mind, whose walls are decorated with the gnome king niches. The place is evidently holographic. As I focus on one king in his niche, it's as if my looking at him triggers something and suddenly I can view the pageant of his life and times like a movie; as my interest wanes, so the biographical tableau fades away. The records are also interactive, if not labyrinthine. I could get swept up in the drama of a single gnome king and never make it to the end of the hall.

A gnome king in ruby robes speaks to me, projecting into my mind the image of a dragon. "In the old time, the dragons were more real than anything you can conceive of today. Gnomes, too, were more apparent in the world than they are today to humans. We haven't faded; your perception has. In the older days, people of your kind saw keenly. You marked the flight of dragons, you observed the stride of gnomes. Now you see neither but that doesn't mean our work has changed in any way. No, our eggs are set close to dragon lairs because we work so closely with them to maintain the energies of the web. The dragon lairs help organize the wave ridges and knots in the web."

As the king speaks, the image of the dragon, which has been static like a picture, now leaps into vivid, animate reality with flared wings and flaming tongue and glorious eyes—and it's directly before me, ferociously real. The gnome king gestures for me to hold my green crystal against the dragon's flames. As I do this, the crystal transforms itself into a sword two feet long, a blade blazing with emerald light. It's shaped like a teardrop or an elongated heart, narrow and pointed at each end. I hold it before me in wonder.

"This is your gift from the dragon, the first of many swords," says the gnome king. "Do you understand what the dragon hoard of precious jewels is all about? Do you know what is meant in the old stories about human heroes eating the hearts of dragons? Evidently not." The gnome king explains: The emerald sword in my hands comes from the dragon's jewel hoard. The dragon transmutes the light of the stars into jewels which the gnomes guard on their behalf. The dragon breathes cosmic life into the stones, transforming them into jewels, except a jewel in this case is not what we think it is. Each jewel is a library, a source of wisdom and knowledge. The dragon instructs the gnomes where to plant these knowledge-crystals at certain knots in the web. Sometimes the gnomes present the jewels as gifts to humans if they think they will use the gift wisely, in service to others. The famous ring of the Nibelungs was such a gift forged from dragon gold, but it was not wisely used. "We hope you will use this sword wisely. In this way, the wisdom of the stars is distributed around the Earth. When you wish to summon a dragon, drive your gnome sword into the ground and wait."

The gnome king sweeps his arms down as if to plunge the sword into the Earth, and the dragon looms up before me, magnificently spangled, terrifyingly so, with wisdom jewels bearing insights beyond my comprehension. "My eye can cast once more the blinding spell upon thee that thou stand as stone," said Tolkien's Foalókë of the golden caves to Furambar who found "the sight of his evil head and dripping jaws was utterly hideous."

I shudder and snap back to the Fairy Dell with my eyes open. Ben smokes his pipe, blowing rings. Battingley sits cross-legged, whistling. Here I am on the mound with a tearshaped emerald gnome sword across my lap. Perhaps I can't nick my finger on it, but it's a real blade none the less. "Ben, what does it mean that the dragon grants the wisdom of the stars?"

"That's a good question. Now I can add another element to our introduction to dragon lore. You have already seen that Hydra, as an aspect of the cosmic dragon, Draco, is quite real in the landscape, in an enlarged sense of the term. You have now walked among some of her stars and looked into a few of her mirrors. In the old days, in Arthur's time, in the time that we now remember as mythic, when what we read today as fanciful stories, like Tolkien and his Foalókë, was actually the biography of initiations, the Serpent introduced men and women to the Mysteries. The Serpent was 'the great Mystery in the Mysteries.' Remember Oceanus. This was the water serpent wrapp-ed around the earth, or Tethys, to form a continuous, oroboric barrier of water or etheric substance, marking the outer limits of the world. Oceanus was 'He Who belongs to the Swift Queen.'

"It wasn't only Tethys that Oceanus encircled; it was the galaxy, the universe, the world egg. You cannot plumb the meanings of the dragon in a single afternoon. The gnome king was right. Pray for wisdom. The dragon is the form assumed by the first beam of light from the Abyss of the divine Mystery. It's the symbol of manifest yet ineffable deity. It's the entire electromagnetic spectrum of all possible light frequencies, the finality of the astral light."

But the dragon has a human dimension, too, says Ben. Dragons and serpents were ancient initiatory names for the hierophants of wisdom, the masters of esoteric knowledge who had tasted the heartblood of dragons, learned the speech of the birds, and lived to tell others. Like Fafnir or Tolkien's Furambar, they slew the dragon—within themselves. A dragon-slayer means someone who has slain or defeated—transmuted, ideally—this zoömorphic representation of human passions, urges, instincts, and animality. The dragon is

our turbulent, confused emotionality, the principle of primal chaos
within the individual mind of a man or woman in whom the possibility of free will has been awakened but not sharpened. The inner
dragon, naturally, is a reflection of the outer one, and the landscape
dragon is an intermediary between both. The dragon is brought to
order—slain—by the Sun God, the solar hero, the Grail Knight, using the sword-edge of spiritualized rationality to master the unlimited creativity embodied in the dragon. The blade is not logic but
Logos. Sigurd, Fafnir, Furambar, St. George, Cadmus, Hercules, St.
Michael, Arthur—these solar heroes mastered the dragon, became
one with their bodies, ate the dragon's heart of wisdom, rightfully
claimed the treasure hoard of divine wisdom on behalf of humanity,
and shared the spoils in service.

"One of which I will share with you now, although it will be only
the sketchiest of introductions," says Ben. "Do you remember the
eleventh labor of Hercules? He had to secure the golden apples of
the Hesperides. Hera had set the ever-watchful dragon, Ladon, to
coil around the apple tree as its fearsome guardian. He had one hundred heads and spoke dozens of tongues. Now, why did Hera, consort to Zeus, set a dragon under an apple tree? Because the tree is
the Tree of Life and the apples are the golden fruits of wisdom."

This brings in Qabala, the ancient science of the structure of energy, a revelation closely guarded by the Hebrew patriarchs for ages,
Ben continues. Qabala speaks through archetypal images and geometrical relationships about cosmic processes, the stages of creation,
the secrets of revelation. The Tree of Life is its central organizing
metaphor. This tree has ten spheres, or light containers, plus two
hidden ones, making twelve; twenty-two paths link the spheres and
each of these paths has a face, a signature, which we may know as
the major arcana of Tarot. The overall image conveys information
about how life, energy, and consciousness move, change, and relate
across the dimensions of existence, Ben says. The paths, each designated by a Hebrew letter and a number, represent the organizing
forces and intelligences of the universe. It's not arbitrary, but part of
the inherent structure of reality. *Raysh* 200: that's the golden apple

of Avalon, the world of astral light, a container; access to *Raysh* is what Ladon guards.

Qabala is a profound tool, a chisel that cuts a groove in consciousness," Ben says. "It's also the grammar of the zodiac, its syntax and diction, the key to the constellations of the temple. The essence of Merlin's mastery, the speech of Arthur's Dog. You'll see this later. But there's one more bit I want to add. That's Adam Kadmon."

The Qabalistic letters, when "spoken" by God at the moment of cosmic creation, formed a divine image: the form of Man. "Landscape zodiacs: terrestrial expression of the Cosmic Self:" not man or woman, but Human, the antecedent of humanity born of light. Qabalists call this primal idea of Man, Adam Kadmon, the Heavenly Man; Qabala's Tree is a shorthand, a somewhat abstract, condensed expression for this same fact. The Tree is the Man; you access both through the landscape zodiac, which is Arthur's teaching temple of the Grail. The spheres, letters, and paths of the Tree are the bones, organs, and physiology of this original Human as "spoken" by God. On a cosmic level, the stars and constellations are its cells. If we were to give the zodiac and its twelve signs a face, it would be Adam Kadmon, the celestial Self, says Ben.

"Which is why we have landscape zodiacs and dragons and dogs. As above, so below: macrocosm above, microcosm below—and in the middle, too. The geomantic landscape is the interface, the middle, and the Grail Knight is the lynchpin. Each landscape zodiac, like the Glastonbury temple, is potentially a miniature expression of Adam Kadmon. Or perhaps you'd prefer the Celtic name, *Albion*: a light being in our neighborhood.

"You need the dragon to animate him and the dog to guard him. The Tree is the engineering diagram that tells you how the system is wired. That's the whole point of the zodiac and the basis for training the Grail Knights. You're assembling a jigsaw puzzle, piece by piece. The mystery is you. Each time you visit a node in the landscape, meditate there, attune, become one with it, build its energies into your body, you complete one piece of the puzzle, snapping it into its correct position on the board. Complete the puzzle, snap the last piece into place, and there's the awesome face of Albion. That's why we're here. Hydra is practice, an introduction. That's enough for now. Come on. We have another place to visit today."

We leave the Fairy Dell with Battingley accompanying us and pick our way along the muddy track until we climb another short hill that awards our efforts with a panoramic view of the moors. I feel like Paul Atreides, finally astride the great sandworm, riding its neck as it undulates across Dune. "Wick Hill," says Ben "Great view." Below us lies the hamlet of Wick, a cluster of old stone cottages, a dairy farm, and large manor house; beyond this, across a tabletop of moors and rhynes, and upon a slight topographical prominence, stands the Church of St. Andrew, solitary out on the edge of the moors except for Aller Court, a two-story stone residence and dairy farm immediately adjacent. The village of Aller itself is situated a half mile away. A British Rail passenger train speeds past Aller on its way to Taunton, momentarily swallowed in bits by the railway trestle under the road. "This is Hydra's neck, her throat, approximately *iota Hydra* which the Chinese astronomers called *Ping Sing*, or Tranquil Star."

"That's a lovely manor house down there, very tranquil," I remark, pointing to the U-shaped stone structure and its well-attended garden.

"Indeed," says Ben. "Some friends of mine live there. Maybe you'll meet them one day. Let's get busy. Let's gather impressions of this new star point in Hydra, shall we?"

I close my eyes, concentrate on my breathing, drop all thoughts, and sink my consciousness into Wick Hill. Soon we sit inside a golden crystalline column like a horn or obelisk perhaps seventy feet high. The horn is three-sided like a sleek, geometrical spire. Sunlight streams into its tip high above me then cascades in bangles down through its golden casement. I have the sensation of looking through a golden window into the dragon's body and behold her ten-mile-long form, a vast, green dragon scintillating with pinpricks of light: double-forked tail, glinting scales, outstretched wings, fiery nostrils, golden head—a celestial figure laid as if buried into the spine of hills we have walked today. Flames flare in crimson breakers from Wick Hill out across the moors to Aller churchyard. Perhaps this is what St. John the Divine meant in his *Revelation* when he said: "And the great dragon was cast out, that old serpent, into the earth, and his tail drew the third part of the stars of heaven and did cast them to the earth."

I'm laughing, with some measure of disbelief, because up there at the tip of the dragon's golden horn flits a baby-faced little angel with stout wings and a cornet poised at its lips. She darts about like a heavenly hummingbird unfurling a banner from her cornet that reads: "I, Nunup Nanam." I turn to Ben for an explanation.

"Cherubim. Certain geomythic figures need periodic maintenance. This is handled by the lower orders of the angelic hierarchy. Twinkle, twinkle, little star, how I'd like to see—better! So little helpers come to polish the twinkle in the dragon's eyes, the golden horn, so our eyes can twinkle, too. Don't look so confused. Is this the place of the horns or the throat? The horns arise from the back of the throat. It's both. What's Battingley up to now?"

Battingley, bounding across Wick Hill, plops down near a tangle of blackberry bushes. He waves for me to join him, and when I do, I discover the spot marks the base of a silver dragon horn identical in stature to the golden one but with one additional feature. Underneath it, there is a stone chamber, a miniature cave big enough for two adults. Three large, thin stones form a dolmen entrance into Wick Hill. The largest of the stones forms a horizontal lintel across the two uprights; like the Greek letter π, it makes a doorway about three feet high. The interior is quite dark and unpromising; probably nobody has crept inside this place in centuries, not to mention the fact that, technically, I am momentarily gifted with X-ray vision and am viewing a stone chamber still buried beneath the ground. For all I know the chamber could have collapsed centuries ago and I am beholding only its etheric memory. Frankly, it's not an important difference as I'm beginning to appreciate in my travels with Ben.

"Yes, there was once a chamber here," Ben reassures me, having walked over to join Battingley and me. "In the older days when

Hydra was consciously used as an initiation node within the land-scape, Arthur's knights would spend time on their own inside this chamber, like motes in the dragon's eye. Sometimes a knight would penetrate the dragon's true dimension, not its simulacrum, and take an astral ride around the countryside on its head. Leave your body at the silver door, you who wish to journey with Hydra. After all, a knight is a youth on a horse, a *chevalier*; so what if the windhorse is a flying serpent? This is where knight and dragon collaborate and begin to mirror each other. The knight who breathes as Love from Above to Hydra helps awaken this figure, and when Hydra stirs, it stirs the Hydra within the knight. It's reciprocal. Both knight and landscape grow serially more conscious so that one day Albion may awaken on all their behalfs. Battingley has another place to show you."

Battingley stands further up Wick Hill just over its brow past the fence. When I join him, he sits on a stone puffing his pipe, indicating a spot on the edge of a tangled thicket between two wheatfields. At once I feel a tightness between my eyes and the sense of envelop-ment by wings. I find myself inside a circle of vertical stone slabs in whose center roots a thick shaft of light coming down from high above. I ascend the light shaft effortlessly, as if I know what I'm doing, floating in the updraft until I come upon a conclave of grey-robed human figures who hold the light shaft steady with their hands. They peer down upon Wick Hill through its telescopic focus. In fact, they can see a great deal more than Wick Hill: Hydra, Glastonbury, Somerset, and beyond—all is within their ken through this miracu-lous eye. The figures are irrepressibly friendly and pleased to see me, yet out of some mischief, they appear to be hiding something from me. "This is a circle of influence," they inform me, trying to remain serious before I slide down the light shaft again.

Ben is pleased with developments, though I can't say why. "Oh, an early glimpse of Blaise, I see. Well, well. The dragon is under professional guidance." When I press Ben to explain what he means, to tell me who this Blaise is, he clams up and changes the subject, becoming professorial.

"Let's consider Wick before us. Wick is at the root of the flame of the dragon, the fiery larynx, the source of heat at the base of the head, the bottom of the throat. It is the very candle-wick of the dragon's breath before it flares out the nostrils and down the tongue to sear Aller. Wick is also the belly of the Dog, whom you have not met, but will shortly. The Dog that guards the zodiac is the Girt Dog of Langport, Cabal, Cafall, Arthur's dog—you know, Qabala. The dog is the Tree and the *key* to the Tree. The flame of the dragon tickles the dog's belly with white heat. When the hara is heated, the dog barks and sets the whole star wheel spinning. The temple is activated and can be used again.

"The concentration aspect of the fire activates the still center, the place of spiritual gravity within the dog. Cabal springs to life and power and can romp with Albion, the Master of the Wheel who carries the animals and star effigies of the zodiac like spangles on his great arms. Remember, the zodiac is the anatomy and physiology of Albion, the great starry being of Man laid within the Earth, Adam Kadmon upon the planet. 'But now the Starry Heavens are fled from the mighty limbs of Albion,' said Blake. Well, we're hoping to change all that this time around. This point of intersection where the dragon's flame licks the dog's hara and lights the wick—we're keeping an eye on it."

"What on Earth are you talking about Ben? Starry Heavens, wicks, barking dogs, spangles—I don't follow you." I exclaim in exasperation.

But Ben only laughs. He ignores me and tries to outdo Battingley in blowing the most intricate smoke rings. Finally he says: "Later. Don't worry about it now. You couldn't understand even if I explained it, which I won't. Preview of coming attractions. Take a rest. Don't worry about it. Tomorrow we go fire-walking into the golden head of Hydra."

16

Starlit Memories
of an Ancient Contract

tarting at Wick Hill again, we climb down the slope, stride down the lane past the stone manor house, then the dairy farm, greeting its friendly border collie along the well-manured lane. We saunter up a rise, then down, over the railroad trestle and out across the moor to Aller churchyard. As we walk, I breathe with the dragon, visualizing how I am walking along the path of its fiery exhalations as if with the incoming tide. I carry my emerald gnome sword erect like a lance. Battingley skips on ahead. The dragon purifies the Earth with fire, Ben told me earlier, searing away impurities the way we might clear a jungle path with a macheté. Ultimately, the dragon is pure, as unsullied as fire, but on account of this immaculate purity, it has always been feared, killed, suppressed, imprisoned, denied, as the history of dragons in Western folklore and religious instruction reveals.

We cross the River Parett and skirt a herd of Holstein milkers then cross Durleazedrove Rhyne by a tiny footbridge. The Somerset landscape is so minutely domesticated, every last insignificant waterway, even if it's only two feet broad like this human-dug rhyne, is named and indicated on a map. The Church of St. Andrew, built in the eleventh century A.D., is still in service; in fact, the place is famous, at least for church historians and readers of the Anglo-Saxon chronicles.

These tell us that in the ninth century A.D. Guthrum the Dane was baptized here with thirty of his men after a sound defeat by

Britain's King Alfred at Athandune, after which the Peace of Wedmore was concluded. It isn't on account of its historical significance that I feel strongly drawn to this place which, with every minute, feels acutely familiar to me. Aller seems to rush towards me in a warm embrace of remembering. Aller! It feels—I can't account to myself how this could be—like a favorite haunt of my childhood, like a beloved summer cottage, that I have until this moment inexcusably forgotten all about.

For a long moment, the church and Aller Court, with its fifteenth century stone barns, disappear. Instead, there is a circle of standing stones surrounded by flowering lime trees whose full crowns nod inwards making a canopy above the stone circle, which is about fifty yards in diameter. Here at Durleazedrove Rhyne stands an arc of twelve shoulder-high standing stones set securely in the field in a parabolic reflecting dish facing into the Aller circle. This relationship, I'm sure, is meant to facilitate an exchange of energy. I turn to Ben for an explanation.

"First, you should remember this place was once called Arthur's Village. Why be surprised then that you remember something about it so easily? Of course it's familiar to you. The stones are a clue to the true function of Hydra. Cadmus planted the serpent's teeth in the field, remember? Think of these stones as serpent's teeth that the ancient geomancers planted in the mouth of the dragon. Everything reads backwards in myths, you know. You decipher it in a mirror. Now, Hydra had one head that was immortal and golden, and thus indispensable, which is to say, permanent. Hercules buried this head under a rock. The Celtic geomancers erected a stone circle here as a crown on its golden head. The stones also ground the energies of the seven stars in Hydra's head. This is Arthur's *Pen-Dragon*, the head of the dragon—well, one aspect of it, at least. The arc of stones helped to focus the flames from Wick Hill into a single 'laser' beam that irradiated Hydra's golden head. When the Grail Knights then sat within this beam, inside the head, other dimensions became accessible to them. It deepened their insight. That's why the stories say that soldiers leapt out of the field in which the dragon's teeth were planted. The fires of the *Pen-Dragon* made truer knights of them. This is a question of initiate awareness."

As we approach Aller churchyard, I see there is a huge crystalline sphere of light occupying the stone circle like a golf ball on a tee. Both crystal sphere and stone circle are embedded like jewels within a glinting sword blade, sheathed in the earth, point downwards, the hilt protruding upwards from Aller. It's as if a giant had plunged his sword into the ground here to summon a dragon just as the gnome king advised me regarding my emerald sword. The Aller sword is about twelve feet across and a hundred feet tall. We walk around the church to the front entrance and its old gravestones, set amidst two lime trees and a queer tubular mound like a mole's tunnel about twenty feet long. As I stand at the mouth of this tunnel, which uncannily resembles a sword sheath laid upon the ground, I hear distant voices chanting: *Ar-thur! Ar-thur! Ar-thur!*

I sit down on this tubular mound with the sensation of chanting resounding beneath me as if men were working an underground smithy, making swords. Battingley joins me, holding his gnome sword upright before him. He demonstrates a special movement. Holding our blades hilt upwards with both hands and at shoulder level, we slowly lower our blades and insert them into the ground like keys. The feeling is instantly oroboric, as if I've plunged the sword into my own root chakra and that my head and root have fused into one center, establishing an energy circuit. My body temperature rises, my spine heats up, and perspiration forms as energy pulses through this circuit. My body enlarges tremendously until I am hollow and vast, spread out across ten miles of Somerset landscape.

The dragon's dual-forked tail, her swelling belly, devic heart, sailing wings, horned throat, omniscient eyes, rolling flames, and golden head—this is my body. Stars twinkle inside me. Every exhalation inflames the Aller moors as my body quivers from Hatch Beauchamp to Aller. My head is made of a circlet of golden stones packed in warm earth. I'm inside a vertical light shaft ascending rapidly as if in an express elevator, rising high above the moors, above my own undulant body made of hills, above the Somerset star wheel and its myriad of star shapes. For a split second, I glimpse a domed city of awesome light lying brilliantly below me on a desert plain. Then I'm back in Aller churchyard with Ben and Battingley both of whom study me carefully.

"If you're free, Battingley has a few more remarks to make," says Ben as if I have been inattentive. "He says the Aller Dragon is a very ancient one, in service to Grail Knights for uncounted millennia. As such, it was among the first to be 'slain.' Battingley says you can enter the dragon world in several ways, including the gnome egg, if you're properly escorted. With gnomes, that is. The gnome sword is your confirmation."

Once Ben begins to speak on behalf of Battingley, it's only a few moments before I begin to hear the gnome himself, as if a microphone has been passed and another voice takes up the tale. "We make the emerald sword from the dragon's body," Battingley tells me. "We forge it in her. She can make many swords, no end to how many. You summon the dragon by inserting your sword into the heart or crown points in the landscape body. Sword calls sword. Do you understand?"

"Yes, now that you mention it," I reply. "The dragon somehow becomes identical with the sword and both become identical with me."

"Correct," says Ben. "The sword is the body of the dragon in another form. Through a process of training, alignment, and conscious focus, the dragon becomes the sword. You've experienced it directly but Qabala teaches the same thing. The numbers for *Nachash*, the Hebrew word for serpent, are 358; add the digits and you get seven, the number for the Hebrew letter *Zayin*, which means sword. So, *Nachash*, the dragon, is *Zayin*, the sword. As Battingley rightly says, sword calls sword. The dragon slayers activate the outer landscape dragon by activating the dragon within themselves. The sword is the insight gained from mastering the dragon and it is the insight necessary to master the dragon.

"Let me tell you a story to make the point. You'll like it; it's about Arthur. The young Arthur has been instructed by the Lady of the

Lake to swim out to a barge and fetch a sword and scabbard. Arthur admires the sword and 'liked it passing well,' as Malory writes. But he has to pass a test in discrimination. Which do you like better, the sword or the scabbard? Merlin asks him after Arthur has retrieved both. 'Me liketh better the sword,' says Arthur. 'Ye are more unwise,' replies Merlin, 'for the scabbard is worth ten of the swords, for whiles ye have the scabbard upon you, ye shall never lose no blood, be ye never so sore wounded. Therefore keep well the scabbard always with you.' Later it isn't the sword but the scabbard that Morgan, Arthur's sister, steals. She knows their relative values. So, young Grail Knight, what's so special about the scabbard?"

"Wait a minute," I announce as the implication of Ben's story dawns on me. "Are you saying Hydra is the scabbard for the sword, for Excalibur?"

Ben smiles and quips to Battingley, "You see, a little trip up the light shaft does wonders for his brain, don't you think? Sharpened his gnome sword a little bit. That's right, Grail Knight. In one sense, Hydra is the sheath or scabbard for Excalibur. Excalibur is a sword, of course, but Arthur gains it by degree. It is the sword of insight, gained by degrees through a series of swords. Many little swords make one big sword. The life of the Grail Knight is all about collecting swords, or so it seems in the early days. The gnome sword is the first of many you will gain by degree. Eventually, if you wish, if you persevere, you might attain Excalibur. Here at Aller the knights temper their swords in the Pen-dragon forge. Merlin evaluates their insight. They help to collectively forge Excalibur for Arthur. The scabbard is the wisdom you master regarding the use of the sword. Let's let Battingley finish, shall we?"

"We made an ancient pact with humans," resumes Battingley, speaking with solemnity, pausing after each sentence to make sure I understand. "Knights sit in the chamber at Wick Hill at midday; they call the dragon with their swords in the ground. Knights assemble at Oath Hill, the dog's throat, at dawn with their swords held aloft, making their oaths in tribute to her. Knights concentrate here at Aller, the dog's heart, inside their swords and shift location.

Always, we accompany, sit with them, guide, direct, advise. We promised long ago to help anchor the dragons of Earth on your behalf. You promised long ago to help us rise out of the earth into the air on your wings. It was a reciprocal agreement, an ancient contract. We both promised on behalf of the planet."

I am so wrapped up in Ben's explanations and Battingley's commentary that I've lost track of the afternoon. Dusk is already settling. The horizon over Burrowbridge Mump is streaked with orange and crimson. Stars twinkle through the pale blue membrane of the sky. The air is moist and scented with Earth. I ask Battingley to tell me more about the ancient pact between gnomes and humans.

"This is from a time when humans were devas, angels on Earth. That was even before the dragons were brought here. Later the dragons were brought to ground and stabilize human energies and to elaborate the light lines across the planetary surface; and we worked with them. The dragon is not separate from you. Not one of the dragons on the Earth is separate from you. Neither are gnomes. We are part of your body. We are in Albion. As you reclaim yourself, you remember us and we rejoin you in your body of light. You will, if you wish, see us around you all the time now. That's the way it is with Grail Knights. The human is very expansive. You embody the world.

"Hyperborea—do you remember it? Very early days for us both here. You were in more of an ethereal state, prehuman, exalted, more angelic. The Earth was a field of flowers. This was before the establishment of the energy matrix and its geometrical structuring. These flowers were the original spiritual centers on the planet: chakras, wheels, vortices. You were large beings. You created domes of light on the landscape out of your own self. You breathed soul into the landscape, animating it. You inhabited these earth flowers like suns. You imagined the world then sustained it. You projected the gnomes and the other elemental families out of yourself. Albion birthed us. You created us to experience this new world for you and to help maintain it. You asked us to specialize in the transformation of Earth energies on your behalf.

"At the time of the dinosaur souls came the split. You withdrew from your angelic self, which went above, and split us off from you, and we went below, and you contracted into your human form in the Middle Earth. You extruded angels and gnomes and created the world—heaven above, nature below. Where there once was one Human, there became angels, humans, elementals. Angels above, gnomes below, humans in the middle. Angels and gnomes are equal parts of your human being. Your angelic side remembers Heaven. Your gnome side remembers Earth. You are in between, in the middle—in a muddle. You've forgotten both, the above and the below.

"It was sad, painful, that moment of separation and parting when you split into three. The ones still above came down and realigned the planet with the galaxy through the energy matrix, planting stars in the ground. They asked us to walk the sound ridges and maintain the splices. They introduced the Mysteries to help you remember. You walked on the ground without your wings or memory. We were sad for you. We remember how your face looked when your being split into three. Anguish. Rapture. The ambivalent pain of birth. You looked outside yourself for the world. You forgot the mirror that showed you how you contain the entire world. We are an aspect of your memory, at large in the world you created. We remember. We remember for you. That is our part of the contract."

Battingley's narration of ancient time reminds me of the Norse creation myths of Middle Earth. There was Niflheim, the world of clouds and shadows, and Muspellheim, the land of fire, also called Asgard. Together, they created *Ymir*, a giant in human form, the first of all living beings, another version of Albion. Ymir was killed by his progeny who formed Midgard, or Middle Earth, from his inert body. Ymir's body is Midgard, while his skull is the starry vault of the heavens. Muspellheim above, Niflheim below, Midgard in the middle. Ymir or Albion—it's the same cosmic being in this geomythic story.

"Like Somerset, the Island Set of the Sumer, the Island of Sumer, the Sumer Country—the middle abode," says Ben, who has an uncanny knack of tracking my thoughts like radar. "Somerset, here, under the stars, in the middle realm. Not summer, but *sumer*, the middle ground, the place of access to Gwynfa's Land of Light, *Gwylad yr Haf*, the White Land. This is Niflheim, where we live, the realm of clouds and shadows. You want Midgard, you have to find the doors. Fortunately, the landscape is riddled with rabbitt holes, like Aller, that lead into the true Somerset."

It has grown dark about us as we sit in Aller churchyard. Overhead, the starry skull of Ymir scintillates with a billion pinpricks of light, each one a mystery. "It is a very big place, this galaxy," ruminates Ben. "Perhaps 400 billion stars. A diameter of 100,000 light years. Numerous varieties of sentience and conscious evolution. Earth is far out in space, two thirds the distance from the galactic center. That's a long way from downtown. Far beyond the exurbs. The galaxy, as such, is too big to know or visit in an ordinary sense, yet here it is, our home. We live embedded in the galaxy. That's what the zodiac is all about, this Somerset zodiac with its stars of the middle abode, or as a friend of mine once called it: the Region of the Summer Stars.

"Today you had a little taste, an aperitif, of how human consciousness enfolds the entire star wheel. You met the Hydra within you. A good beginning. But you must realize that you contain *all* the constellations and that the landscape zodiac contains them all as well, on your behalf. I'm talking about a good deal more star families than the astronomers have counted. They're up to 88; they're short 44. The wheel has 144 constellations (with 12 repeated—the twelve ecliptical signs of the zodiac), and they're all part of Albion. Nor is the Somerset temple the only star wheel on the planet. There are hundreds: different sizes, different strengths, same design, each a miniature galaxy on Earth.

"All the figures of the zodiac, named or unnamed, are part of you. You are a starry colossus. You are Ymir. You are the Heavenly Man whose body is the zodiac. Albion. The galaxy is your mind and your mind is in your heart. You are the master of the star forms; you are the builder of the temple. That's the Grail Knight's potential. It's your star wheel, whatever you call it."

Ben ticks them off. The Twelve Hides of Glaston. Arianrhod's Silver Wheel. The Spinning Castle of Caer Sidi. The Cauldron of Cerridwen. Branwen's Cauldron of Regeneration. The Girdle of Signs. The Starry Wheels of Albion. The Abyss of Learning. The Crown of the Circle of the Holy Apostles. Our Lady's Way. The Mother's Bowl. The Roaring Cauldron of human passions called Hwergelmir. King Arthur's Round Table of Logres. "The life of the galaxy is your speech but how can you say it all at once? You eat the golden apple of wisdom and the seeds become star seeds in your body. The galaxy awakens and spins inside you. Your smile permeates the wheel out from the center on this side of the Blazing Star. One day I hope you might remember this Star. That's our human part of the ancient pact."

I ask Ben why Aller was once called Arthur's village. "It is a deep karmic situation. Aller once witnessed a complex grouping of individuals at different stages of development, constellated around the goals and aspirations of Arthurhood. In Arthur's village, there was a difficulty in manifesting and completing a particular group destiny pertaining to the initiation of Arthurhood. Each person, or knight, male or female, had to go through a personal strengthening process, except some did not and thereby held the others back. The group karma remained incomplete. The incompletion of this soul group was in turn connected with the Christ and the difficulties his disciples had in their self-completion after the Ascension. These difficulties were mirrored in a later time at Aller in the preparations for the Christed initiation of Arthur. Arthur stands between the Christ and Adam, between Albion and Man. The same souls came back to Aller to finish their group destiny here because there was a wound, great pain in the land. It was unhealed in Arthur's time and remains so today. But there is another chance now and certainly a great need.

"People all over feel this pain but don't understand that it's from beyond their individual wounds. The key to healing is that each member of the Arthur group must complete himself, then the pain and incompletion of the entire group may be transmuted and the Grail may be dedicated at Aller."

"Ben, the way you talk about Arthurhood makes it sound like a position or developmental stage rather than the quality of a single person. I thought Arthur was a man who lived once during the sixth century."

"And during the ninth and thirteenth centuries, too, around here, as a matter of fact. Arthur is not something that exists in time. Arthur exists out of time, as do the other characters in the legend. They are archetypes, energy configurations, yet they pertain in particular time periods when human consciousness finds familiarity with these archetypal viewpoints and relationships. There have been fifteen similar periods in world history in which cultures have resonated with this myth system. That means there have been fifteen Arthurs, not always Celtic, but known in different languages and cultures. The Tibetan and Mayan, for example. But while the names were different according to the cultural contexts for the reappearance of Arthur, it is always according to the same archetypal formula. Arthur, the once and future king, remember? We are moving into the time of the manifestation of the sixteenth Arthur."

I am astonished with Ben's revelation. "Arthur is coming back? Who will be the sixteenth Arthur?"

"That remains to be seen. Time to go home and eat dinner. I'm famished, aren't you?"

17

A Lilac Crystal with Wings

ate afternoon, and all day I've felt a strong tug to visit Aller again, which is where I'm heading now. Ben loaned me the Morris Minor and I drive out to Wick Hill. I feel unaccountably anticipatory today. Something wonderful is approaching me. I park the car near the dairy farm and set off on foot. The sun is wobbling into a misty, amorphous western horizon as I reach the railroad trestle that swells up from the sea-level Wick Meads. So much has happened since I crossed Pomparles, the perilous bridge from Glastonbury into the land of myth, since I walked into Ben's strange world of gnomes, dragons, swords, and the mysteries of Arthurhood. A farm tractor pulling a full hay rick lumbers over the narrow bridge, and I have to squeeze myself in against the railing to avoid getting stuffed with straw. It passes right through Battingley who finds that amusing. My gaze rolls out along the empty railroad tracks out to the horizon. Here I am, on a railroad trestle in the center of this low-lying world of green willow stands, murky rhynes, soggy meads, old churches, blue sky, and a talkative gnome. "We can see the stars in the daytime and the forms they take," says Battingley.

From out of the southwest, a train shatters the stillness. Seven passenger cars speed underneath me with astonishing immediacy. I wave to the conductor just before he barrels under the bridge. He clangs his horn as the train pummels through the trestle in a hideous suck of air that leaves a tremor in its wake. I feel so happy.

I practically skip and hop across Aller Moor to the churchyard, still elated with the sudden, explosive appearance of the train. I perch on the stone wall that bounds the mead-side of the church like a quay. The fields at dusk are perfumed and striated from the season's first haying. The beneficiaries of this earth-scented salad, a couple hundred cows clustered at midmoor, are silently chewing, making milk. Lazy waves of timothy from an unmowed field lap up against the stone wall as a delicate mist settles silkenly over the meads, settling in so low to the ground you can inhale the grey moistness through all the pores of your body. I dangle my legs, close my eyes, and sway happily from side to side.

The dusk seems to grow brighter and my smile deepens to include the landscape in its regard. I feel wrapped in a cotton duvet spun of angel wings. My body feels flooded with a creamy warmth as if somebody has emptied a pitcher of light into my head and its contents flow like velvety syrup through me. Opening my eyes, I find a lilac crystal resting in my cupped palms. Before me, in an effulgent arc of wings and luminescent silvery faces, stand six angels. As if they are one angel, they wink at me.

18

IT'S A DOG'S LIFE:
FIRST SCRATCHES

've moved to the Dog. In fact, I'm now living in the very house that caught my eye as I sat at the dragon's horn and surveyed the hamlet of Wick. Ben had to leave Somerset for awhile but before he left, he introduced me to his friends at Wick Manor, the Pendletons. I've taken a little room at the top of the stairs in this 400 year old stone house, tucked into Wick Hill and facing Aller across the fields, and I now have four housemates: Russell, Berenice, and their two children, Edmund, who is six, and Celia, four. Russell is 40, a potter, a slender man with grey wavy hair swept back from a polished forehead; his eyes flame blue, and at times his face is flushed with androgyny. Berenice, 45, has long, thick, wavy Celtic brown hair, an impeccably pristine complexion, a gurgling laugh, dark brown eyes. She works with the Bach flower remedies and homeopathy in a private practice. It's been only a handful of days, but I feel at home and among old friends.

The manor is big and comfortable and invites constant investigation through its rambling, drafty corridors. The lintels are low, the doors squeaky, of which a few are ponderous, and on the stairs down from my room on the second floor, if you don't lower your head, you'll bang it at the last step, on the ceiling. Ivy overgrows the manor's south face, but its lushness accommodates conference pear, *Stephanosis* jasmine, rambler roses, and Virginia creeper; all this rustling greenery fronts a long, narrow lawn flanked on both sides by a perennial, semi-formal (depending on how often we weed it) flower bed, a few scraggly apple trees beyond, then cow pastures.

Once the manor was the imperial center—if not the reason for being—of this tiny hamlet, with its dairy farm and vanished Perham Chapel somewhere in the fields. Wick: the name is rich with geomythics, from the Old English *weoc*, as in *candelweoc*, which was a bundle of fiber, usually twisted cotton, used in a lamp or candle, one end immersed in grease and the other end lit: hence, candlewick. In Middle English, *weoc*, or wick, came to mean an "abode," especially a farm, sometimes a hamlet; but even the exoteric meanings point to something else. In Ben's lexicon, Wick is the throaty, burning taper of the Aller Dragon that lights the belly of the Girt Dog of Langport. The Girt Dog is the guardian of the Somerset zodiac, the geomythic dog whom geomancy scholar Mary Caine calls "the Cerberus of the British Mysteries."

Russell thought we should call in at a few of the local geomythic sites and make our introductions. Our first stop today is Muchelney Abbey, the second oldest religious foundation in Somerset and, like Glastonbury Abbey, in ruins. Muchelney sits, anatomically, at the foot of the Girt Dog, a couple of miles from Wick, and has been sitting there as a church for over a thousand years. The original monastery was founded around 700 A.D. by Ine, King of Wessex; in 939, it was refounded by King Athelstan as the Benedictine priory of St. Peter and Paul; it became an abbey in 950 and flourished as such until 1539 when King Henry's Dissolution of the Abbeys reduced it to its stone foundations, as it remains today. The sixteenth century Abbot's House, still standing, occupies ground only a little above the Sedgemoor marshes. A marvellous structure of stout stone and wooden beams, it would make a wonderful *zendo* if we owned it and brought in the Buddha. I scurry along the raised stone walls in the Abbey grounds like an inept tightrope walker while Russell scouts for the intersection of ley lines near the vanished high altar. He finds it, then beckons to Berenice, the kids, and me to join him.

As we sit around him in the ruined apse, Russell starts speaking, as if reading a text, in a slow, deep voice. "We come to you as the angel of the air, the angel of earth, the angel of the sun, the angel of the water." He speaks as if he's passing on a message from invisible companions within the ghostly Abbey. "We come to bring you a simple love, the simple love between a brother and a sister."

Now our companions come into focus: four angels, one at each corner of the church foundations. Russell has a bright, twinkling star just above his belly button that seems to radiate lines of light out to each of us, joining us at our belly buttons where we each have a similar blazing star. Russell holds a garden pail from which he plucks wooden plaques each bearing a handwritten message: "I love you. We love you. You love you." Berenice dances happily with a very tall creature who startlingly resembles Chewbacca, the eight-foot-tall, intelligent ape in *Star Wars*, while a beaming Edmund has gained a yellow bumble bee's body, or else he's turned into a cherub.

As for myself, I feel inexplicably healed. Before we came to Muchelney, I had squished my neck on that low-hanging ceiling as I inattentively put my foot down on the last step coming down from my room. I arrived at Muchelney with such a headache, dizzyness, and blurred vision, I thought only a chiropractor could remedy it, but now it's all gone. We sit quietly, enjoying Muchelney's stillness, then Russell says in his regular voice: "This is a trial run for our eventual healing work on the ley lines and landscape zodiac. They gave me a copy of the Grail and wished I would distribute blessings from it. I foresee a series of festivals on all the zodiac centers as a step towards reanimating the figures and healing the network. My feeling is that this has a lot to do with the work of the Archangel Michael."

Our next stop is Burrow Hill, a bare, rounded, green hill sentinelled on top by a single vigorous sycamore tree. Visually, Burrow Hill is a miniature sacred mountain in anyone's picture book of world myths. We make our way in slow, reflective heliocentric spirals along the flanks of the hill following the natural windswept ridges. Occasionally, I see surprising things. An egg bursts open and out jumps a six-year-old boy followed by many other boys unfamiliar to me. As I round another spiral on the hillside and glance up at the sycamore, an angel three times the stature of the tree stands there. At the top, we sit around the tree, our backs facing the bole, and settle into meditation. Russell sits in a large, moving chair with wheels, like a coal miner's trolley, and it rolls down a track into Burrow Hill. A large, gold Buddha hovers above him like a protective umbrella. I become aware of four eagles—each a different color: black, red, white, and gold—possibly thirty feet tall, one facing each direction, like guardians. After viewing the birds, I look for Russell, but he's gone.

Fifteen minutes later, he returns, looks at me, and shakes his head. "Crikey. Those were some birds. I was half-afraid they would eat me. You know, the way Castaneda's eagle eats the attention of the unwary. They glared at me steadily as I went down into the hill. There was a white-haired man in a white robe, holding an open book. 'Wherever you look from here, it is open mind,' he said. Then he pointed to a crystal cave, which was suddenly illuminated by a shaft of sunlight. I got a ping through my body on that one. Berenice was in a long, purple robe dancing in slow circles among the eagles. I saw you peering over your glasses with a grin."

What about the Buddha over your head? I ask him. "I invoked the protection of the Buddha before I descended into the hill. It always helps to travel with a bodyguard."

As we reach the base of Burrow Hill again, I look back to the tree and see four crystalline columns austere as icicles making a square about the hill. Each column rises at least one hundred feet upon whose top stands one of the fierce eagles. Inside the hill is a vast stone chamber, much bigger than the physical hill could possibly contain. *Necropolis*, I hear whispered. Beyond this impression, the meaning of Burrow Hill is impenetrable.

The mood at Dundon Beacon, which is part of the Gemini effigy in the Somerset zodiac, is not welcoming, either. The village of Compton Dundon huddles the base of breadloaf Dundon Beacon, thickly wooded now but once bare and green when it was a Celtic hillfort. It takes us almost two hours to progress up the hill because, for one thing, we can't find the access road from the village; then we stagger around in ferociously brambled and bethorned and steeply unyielding lower slopes, and still we cannot locate the path. A randomly directed bivouac eventually delivers us to the top. Over a picnic lunch, hundreds of squishy, ill-tempered insects jump into our lemonade, slam into our faces, and the flies are thick and pestering as gangs.

As I walk along, it requires constant diligence to keep my attention focussed on my breathing; the hill, if that's possible, is in a terribly foul mood today, as if the fairies and gnomes are grouchy and infecting the hill itself with their affliction. Three fairies and a pixie glower rudely at us alongside the trail, reports Berenice. There are numerous fat, chubby fairies in yellow cotton skirts and orange blouses, all with sour expressions on their faces, says Edmund. I see a couple of gnomes, churlish and unfriendly, lurking by the trail. Soon we all feel infected by this invisible malaise, especially as we stand at the clotted, viewless top of Dundon.

In all respects, the beacon is obscured. A thirty-foot-long brambled tumulus slumbers among the trees, a Celtic artifact; a series of broad, flat stones descend desultorily from a reluctant wood into a vanished pool, like a strangled, voiceless stream; a solitary standing stone marker, easily a thousand years old, now indicates nothing, or else signifies secrets long forgotten. If I were a doctor, I would say Dundon feels like a sick patient, desperate for healing. Its energy is abrasive, scattered, deeply resentful of something, as if nursing a festering wound from an egregious insult long ago. The gnomes, fairies, and woodland spirits will not—cannot—forget until this misdeed is redressed.

Dundon's oppressive ill temper finally leaves us as we set foot on pristine Chalice Hill in Glastonbury. The Hill of the Mother, as some call it, occupies a prominent position within the Aquarius effigy in the zodiac; it is a dewdrop of loveliness. Like estranged lovers, how quicky we've drifted apart, Glastonbury and me, since I left a week ago. Yet I can see you better, you crazy Celtic anomaly, now that I've been away; here we stand, arms crossed defensively across our chests, not sure of the next move. But my affection for Chalice Hill and its innate goodness melts away these considerations as we make our way to its rounded top, lush with timothy and the fresh cow splats. As Celia and Edmund fly around the hilltop like kites in a strong wind, disappearing behind a sleek beech, the three of us sit down facing west, overlooking Glastonbury, and breathe deeply from the belly—from that tiny blazing star just above the navel we noticed at Muchelney.

For a moment, I am alarmed by a tableau of monsters and hideous figures, but, as if I am in-between television channels, when I adjust the inner tuning and focus more purely on my breathing, the image clarifies itself into the tail of an enormous green dragon, supine on an equally massive couch. Russell walks slowly into the dark-panelled hall of a medieval castle, passing the dragon with no difficulty. "All the beings of the past, of the present, of the future, are beings of light vibrating at different frequencies," he announces, in that same slightly altered Muchelney voice. "Everything is light vibrating at different frequencies—the grass, trees, all the beings on the planet and throughout time."

Silence for ten minutes, then Russell says in his own casual voice, "You and Berenice were both surrounded by eggs of light. Your physical forms shifted back and forth between light and matter; so did the hill and the grass, and everything else. I walked into an etheric temple. I feel a transformation underway, a big change for us, just on account of this little visit." As we collect Edmund and Celia, who are wrestling under the beech tree, I have a flash. "You know how Arthur's knights, when they gathered at Pentecost at Camalate, always talked about their strange adventures on the Grail Quest? I wonder if they had outings like these—innings, I suppose, when they visited intangible temples, dragon guardians, and snarly eagles? That would give the whole business a new twist." Russell grins. "It would have to be."

We have just enough time before sunset for a dash up Glastonbury Tor. We take the path on which only sheep dare to tred, and it is unaccountably steep today. It's uncanny how transformed Glastonbury seems when viewed from the ruined St. Michael tower here on the Tor's windy summit: remote, anemic, even geographically altered, as if the roads and houses have taken on a new orientation in a week's time. I never noticed this before in my frequent ramblings over this green, bony mystery, but it seems the configuration of the roads ray out from Chalice Hill like train tracks in five distinct lines, as if a master cartographer drew them on the land-scape so future carpenters, masons, and roadbuilders would know where to put the homes and roads. Along a lower ridge of the Tor, Russell and I notice a set of four large, silver pipes that make a gentle, transparent crescent down the slope. I can see the grass through them so I cannot say whether they were ever materially or just evanescently here, like the other strange sights I've been treated to today. Still lower down the slope is another bundle of ten pipes that resemble thin rubber hoses; these hug the hillside and snake down to Wellhouse Lane, just next to Chalice Well. A white dove perches on the silver pipes. *Om mane padme hum,* Russell intones several times: multidimensional musical notes and Sanskrit letters, like neon signs in living color, pulse out of the pipes.

Then Russell exclaims, pointing to the black pipes, "Do you see that bridge?" I do; it's a rainbow bridge that arcs from the black pipes on the Tor to a tiny concave field just above Chalice Well. A voice announces, as if from everywhere at once: "We are creating a rainbow bridge between this world and the next." The rainbow bridge scintillates in response to an invisible sun; at its base stand two actual trees. I stare at them as if a memory is at the tip of my recollection. Russell catches it and says, "That would be the Shambhala doorway."

It's dark as we drive back to Wick, and I have to fight off Edmund and Celia, who use me as a battleground and trampoline in our cramped backseat. Celia tries to make amends by kissing me twenty times on the cheek. I have discovered a secret weapon that will un-failingly work to keep them both at bay: they're both awfully ticklish and curl up into little balls of hilarity under the raking of my relent-less fingers. "What's all this television about anyway?" I query Russell, referring to the images and experiences we've had today. "Previews, I should think," Russell replies. "And I think we're in for a little more tonight."

19

THE EXQUISITE SOFT PRESSURE OF SIX ANGELS

I was upstairs in my room seated at my desk, elbows plunked on the table, staring at my typewriter and its blank paper. I was trying to write something about Arthur and the Round Table, but my thoughts kept returning to the experiences of the day out in the zodiac. Frankly, I haven't been able to write anything since I moved to Wick. Nothing makes sense, at least not in the ways things used to, nor can I summon my opinions into words. After all, they're only opinions; I want facts, and the world is getting stranger hourly. For a man who writes all the time, I have the Block. The keys are frozen, the words *in absentia*. Russell knocks, peers through the door with a grin, and announces that we have some visitors, can I spare a few minutes to come down and be sociable.

There's nobody in the livingroom except Russell and Berenice, and they both look like they're meditating. I sit on the couch, fold my legs, and breathe with a smile from the belly. I'm startled by how strong a presence there is already in the room, even though it's presumably just we three sitting here. The room is warm, tingling, deeply still, suffused with a lovely, blissful radiance, which envelops me more fully with each exhalation. My eyes are closed, but somehow the room shines brightly, and keeps getting brighter all the time. My face, my body, my breath are variations on this smile. I feel embraced, enfolded in a cocoon of melting love, a rushing stillness, an intense lightness, an exquisite soft pressure that vibrates knowingly at my center, and now organizes itself into a voice:

"We come as a Blazing Star, as the center of the sphere of stable consciousness. We come as Love from Above. We surround you all with the lilac flames of transmutation. In each of you we place a lilac flame. We come from not too far. We come as a Blazing Star." It's one voice but it feels like a chorus. The room dances with lavender flames as the voice conjures forth the image of six silver-haired angels who make a cordon around us. Each stands about eight feet tall with wings like sails, androgynously gorgeous angels yet tending towards the masculine in ambiance. They seem happy with themselves and two of them wink at me.

"We are *your* Blazing Star," one of the angels says. "We understand you have a few unanswered questions. You may ask us, if you wish."

I suppose my years as a journalist prepared me for this moment. I've interviewed a few people of stature and a few people whose presumptions of stature were similarly daunting. I guess I could handle a half dozen angels. I reached for my notepad, as much a part of my life as my glasses, pulled out a pen, and flicked through my list of vexing research questions. "As a matter of fact, I do have a few key questions," I announce to the diaphanous, twinkling angels who seem to pulsate in and out of visibility from angels to brilliant points of light. "How about this one. What was the Grail Quest all about?"

"Always humans have had this paradox: if Man had an inkling of his function here, then he could not live or survive on this planet. Only through the process of individuation and acceptance of the image of the Grail in the Arthurian legend, and as expressed in other cultures, is it possible to see how Man can fulfill his function on this planet. This pertains to a broader purpose, to something deeper and more meaningful. The vast proportion of humans are here to perform a function so shocking to themselves that they couldn't stand the knowledge. A few others can take on the responsibility and take on the image of the Grail, although we emphasize it is inherent in all humans at particular levels. It is through a process of the examination of the conditions of consciousness, locked in a spacetime continuum and body, and within a process of individuation, that enables the Grail to be realized. This involves personal approaches by people following different ways. The nearest a human gets to the process of comprehending the Grail is allied to what you call memory. The process is important. The prior condition of the human organism that contains consciousness came to be locked in a space-time continuum. There were certain genetic factors determining how consciousness came into human form. The Grail quest is the memory of that which existed at the point when consciousness decided, phylogenetically, to take human form. This is linked, incidentally, to the legend of Gawain and the Green Knight.

"The key to this is the Grail. This is a bowl or chalice: it is receptive and contains something. The principle is the process whereby the unitive, the bowl, contains something, the process of individuation, which is the overflowing of the bowl. The process is demonstrated in the Arthurian legend whereby only a certain percentage of the knights could give up their ego base and survive the process. Only a small number had a large enough spiritual background with the facility to survive the personal death to reach the unitive level. The Grail legend is the synthesis of this process, combining the unitive and individuative aspects. The bowl is the receptive vessel for the unification process, which is a continual process involving the essence of human consciousness. The unitive aspect runs deep and was inherent in Lemurian and Atlantean cultures. Before Man was corrupted by the nature of the unitive consciousness, humans could act from a different base than you have any idea of today."

This prompts another question: What is the nature of the relationship between Arthur and Merlin?

"The Arthur-Merlin relationship was not formed in one lifetime. It existed before and after the time of the Celtic Arthurian legends—many times in many systems. Seeing Arthur at the center is a mistake and covers up the truth of the other characters. The legend is a composite of parts and is not focused solely on Arthur. No character was more important than the others because they each represent different aspects of individuation in a process moving towards unification. The synthesis is the entire myth but when preferential treatment is made towards one character, this stems from the Christian myth of the single, kingly figure filled with Christ energy—in other words, Jesus. But the Buddhic energy is invested equally in each character.

"Arthur himself played a part related to all the other parts; that was his commitment to the myth. What is known and recorded about him as an individual is secondary and unimportant compared to what his mission was. To investigate Arthur as a person outside of the context of this process loses the point of the process. If you wish to know more about Arthur as a person, that information is available to you. You can remember. But in the process of memory and recall, do not seek for the process of individuation in that, but do it as if reading chapters in a book. If you are familiar with the book already, you will know what's on the page before you read it. The key to the memory of the Arthurian legend is the Grail quest, and implicit in this memory is that which is beyond time—Spirit."

I gamble on my next question, glad of a pause in my flurry of scribbling. Certain coincidences of place-names, mythic figures, and legendary events have drawn my thoughts towards Tibet. "Somehow I feel Tibet has a connection with Glastonbury and the Arthurian legends. Is this possible?"

"The two ancient civilizations which we call Lemuria and Atlantis were both concerned with unitive consciousness. People in Atlantis had developed kinesthetic powers, telepathy, and transportation around the planet. Tibet, from its Bon tradition, was involved with the individuation of consciousness. Merlin was an adept, a Grand Square Master, trained in Lemuria and Atlantis, in the new synthesis of the unitive and individuative aspects of consciousness. He came to initiate Arthur and his knights in this. The early Vedas mention an Arthur figure, but in the West, the Arthur story is the only record of this, the only expression. The Bon tradition was already deeply established in Tibet, but it originated in Lemuria and Atlantis. Then this was merged with the Buddha-Dharma, which stressed the individuation of consciousness. This then formed Tibetan Buddhism. The synthesis of these two aspects of consciousness is only found in the

Arthur story, which, as you know, was later largely corrupted by the Christian ethic."

That confirms a hunch I've had for months. But how did Merlin make this transmission, from Atlantis and Tibet to the Arthurian knights of Somerset?

"We must, firstly, look at the process with which Merlin and his alchemical initiative was involved. Secondly, to call this process by names like 'Tibetan Buddhism' is a mistake. Thirdly, the relationship between Arthur and Merlin must be seen from the evolution of both their consciousnesses and not as a separate process. Their evolution is interdependent in a process of individuation. The process Merlin was involved in was an initiatory level stemming from Lemuria and Atlantis. He had karmic debts to particular aspects of consciousness of humankind such that, through his level of adeptship, he could bring on a karmic fulfillment in Arthurian times. His relation to a system must be seen in terms of how systems evolve. Consciousness and its parameters evolve. The system itself does not contain the nature of consciousness. All the systems that lead to individuative or unitive consciousness stem from the same source and have origins in Man's historical depths.

"We can look now at this more closely. At the atomic level, something is pre-recorded and has the possibility in any moment of consciousness to be remembered if the imprint on the atomic structure can, through a process of creative analysis, be seen. Then the imprints in the energy patterns reveal the interrelatedness of aspects of consciousness. If you see the interrelations on a cellular, molecular, and atomic level, then you can see the process under which the Arthurian legend evolved and you can assimilate it into present-day consciousness. The level of Merlin's initiatory power was on the elemental or atomic level as the biographical mirrors held at various points in history to the Merlin figure reveal. Through the exploration of an individual in a given space-time situation, it is revealed to you what went before. There is no assimilation of material merely by looking into the past. Assimilation must happen in the present moment, otherwise this is rather like cooking a meal without gas. It is a matter of looking at the elemental basis of being.

"Alchemists like Merlin are always involved in a transformative process called transmutation. This is another aspect of the Grail. Focus on the fire burning above the bowl, rather than the bowl's contents. The fire itself will do nothing without your conscious will. When you bring the fire aspect into focus, this makes possible the transformation of what's in the bowl. At this point three images will be helpful to you. First, the sword. It has a straight blade and golden handle embedded with jewels. Second, the chalice, a bowl with no stem but two small handles; above it burns a small flame. The bowl is filled with liquid. Third, a stone with eight sides, at the center of which is a diamond. These images or symbols can be used together, taken with the three part answer already given above. Dwell on this. Accept it and give it your love. This will bring you understanding of the process of transmutation."

The angels pause in their speaking but their angelic wrap intensifies, as if they are hugging us harder and deeper. I see vividly before me the chalice with a lilac flame burning above its brim. For a moment, I am inside the chalice—or it's inside me—and the lilac flames vibrate coolly and audibly through me until I shudder from the cold-burning flame.

"Love is what transforms fear. Where there is fear, there is no love; but where there is love, there is no fear. Love is a refined state, not accessible to mundane consciousness; it only exists at a supramundane level. It has not to do with a personal ego, with lives or identity. It comes from a different source in the psyche. It is the basic ground through which and under which consciousness operates. It is the primal voice, feeling, and thought behind the apparent thinking or associative level. It is the basic ground through which caring and kindness operate. Love is transcendental kindness. Cultivate kindness as a preparation for transmutation through the lilac flame. The easiest way to practice kindness is towards inanimate objects as it's harder towards animate ones and living beings.

"All this, in part, relates to the system through which Merlin helped to initiate the knights or bring them to a level of initiation and personal transformation and into a new level of consciousness in them-selves. When Merlin left, it was at the point where he, as an indi-vidual, allowed his responsibility to become manifest in parts of the Round Table. He passed it on where it took seed among Arthur and his knights. Merlin was a catalyst, an initiator for transformation; that was his true responsibility. The subject is complex and how accurately this information can be transcribed by you depends on your own level of understanding. This pertains to the assimilation of things at a point you don't understand yourself, yet we offer them to the potential understanding of who you are yet to be and to those who may come after you."

"Does Glastonbury have a special destiny to fulfill in all this? Does it have a relationship with the Buddha-Dharma?"

"You are preoccupied with form, which is not an expression of quality," the angels reply. "A qualitative experience is of the form-less. To attribute a qualitative experience to a Dharma/no Dharma situation is a mistake. The way a place called Glastonbury relates to a form of Dharma has echoes in time. The spacetime today of Glastonbury has little or no relevance to the time echo of the form of Dharma you cite. It has had a time in the past and will again in the future in which Glastonbury comes under the influence of this par-ticular form of Dharma. But the emphasis in the present time is on the expression of Dharma without form. This is a qualitative expres-sion for those who serve it. To give it any form or a rigidity of expres-sion will be a negation of it."

Still, Glastonbury clearly has a special role on the planet at this time—hasn't it?

"The place has a potential as an energy matrix. You might see it as a launch pad. If a group of people or individuals work on them-selves and link into the matrix, it enlarges their possibilities. Only a few now have this ability. There is not known to us a group that is making the link, though some are being made ready for it. Your research is relevant to this."

"So the Grail is all about memory," I remark. "You seem to want us to remember something. What?"

"The possibility of remembering anything is here. All you have to do is put the process into action. You create your own limitations. What you need is a positive attitude and programming. There are many means of programming human consciousness. Most of what is programmed in your time period, the one in which your present incarnations occupy, is called negative causation programming. This pertains to redressing an imbalance in the human psyche. This is why you cannot remember easily. The products of your society are a result of this programming. Humans moved away from their divinity and abused power in Atlantean times. Therefore, humanity had to be redressed. The Architect of Human and Cosmic Destiny, the one concerned with the soul evolution of all human beings to their divine origin and its reunification, has a plan in mind to bring about perfect balance once again. You are at this period at a certain disadvantage in relation to your conscious capabilities, but we suggest you are still as limitless as ever."

"Is that what Merlin was doing?" I ask, suddenly flushed with a possible connection. "I mean, did he send the Grail Knights out over the countryside, into the zodiac, so they could remember themselves and reprogram their consciousness?"

"Now you're cooking with gas. Did you know Merlin was called 'Star Worker?' He was instrumental in the conception and birth of many of the knights, Arthur included. He had natal charts for each of them before they were born. He selected the knights partly on that basis. Each knight had to work through the various oppositions, squares, transits, or other problems aspected in their charts in relation to one another, and, in a manner predetermined by their individual levels of initiation and previous adepthood, they had to work on themselves. Merlin sent them to positions of power in the zodiac to familiarize themselves with their obstacles, astrologically, metaphysically, hierarchically. Merlin had, in the past, transcended all disturbances within his individual horoscope. It was his wish to initiate all the others to be free of these influences or to be able to use them positively."

"How does Morgan fit into this picture? The Arthurian legends represent her pretty unfavorably. Were she and Arthur really enemies?"

"In previous years and lives, there has been in your consciousness a particular relation between the female and male aspects of yourself. What happens within an individual is that these two aspects begin a unitive process. This is the uniting of wisdom and faith within a context of energy and concentration. Morgan is a name which resonates at a particular level and identifies an aspect of consciousness which exists at the initiatory level. This pertains to the preliminaries of the arising of faith from a base of experience. This is not faith as a pre-requisite to a system, but faith based in and allied with experience. The relation of this form of faith and Arthurian wisdom is the relation of Arthur to Morgan.

"Belief has nothing to do with faith, nor does wisdom have to do with knowledge about things. Arthur as a principle is *that which knows*. It is not concerned with knowledge *about* things. The discrimination between that which knows and that which knows about separates true faith based on experience from experience through wisdom. Morgan as a principle is *faith based in experience*. Morgan waits upon Arthur to stop wishing to know about and to accept knowing. You can rely on personal experiences for more clarification of this point. When looking into these relationships, it is important to see consciousness as contained within a physical base. The male and female parts should be viewed as the left and right parts of the body. When the left part accepts the right, and the reverse, then instead of disease you have ease and union between Arthur and Morgan, wisdom and faith.

"What about Arthur's relationship with Guinivere? What does the Lancelot aspect say about Arthur's inner aspects?"

"If Guinivere and Morgan can be seen as different aspects of the feminine in the legend, then Morgan is faith based in experience and Guinivere is faith based on belief. Thus, Guinivere is an aspect of Arthur's consciousness and can only relate to a part of the Arthurian legend. This is manifested in the character of Lancelot who knows without humility, who is brighter than bright but misses the point and the ground. Guinivere and Lancelot are the left and right hand aspects of Arthur's consciousness at another level. By the way, what do you make of his name?"

"This sounds silly but how about this: Lancelot is the knight who uses his lance a lot?"

"That's not so silly."

"Oh. Okay, but what was his role with Arthur?"

"We had hoped you would ask what his lance was."

"Okay. Would you tell me what his lance was?"

"Of course. His lance was his ability to see the Other Side, to penetrate deeply into the Mystery. He understood much about Merlin and the others. It was this quality that attracted Guinivere, though she misinterpreted his penetrative qualities in sensual terms. You could interpret his lance as a phallus or as the horn of the unicorn. He was Arthur in his all-seeing aspect of penetration. We have explained that at one level the whole story centers around Arthur in that each knight is an aspect of Arthur's consciousness as the knight relates to Arthur, besides being an individual himself or herself. It is relevant to be aware of a third woman of importance to Arthur. Do you know who?"

"Morgause? No. Oh, how about the Lady of the Lake?" I blurt out.

"The Lady of the Lake is the one. She indicated to Arthur's consciousness that faith based in experience, in actual fact, was the attribution of Morgan and Guinivere at a certain level of initiatory experience. Morgause and Morgan are different aspects of this same quality.

"Tonight, you are shown the stone, and, in it, the sword, and behind it stands the Grail. That you ask these questions at this time is not coincidental. They are the unfolding of a pattern in energy, as something transparent formed in consciousness can now bring through a realization through in a spacetime period. Always, when an open or empty vessel taps into a conscious energy source pertaining to a matrix of sacred names or words of empowerment, such as these Arthurian names, then the nature of the matrix will bring the vessel to a level of individual consciousness. It is a transpersonal process, to do with the nature of consciousness in elemental form. The transformation of this is part of the experience of the matrix itself and the memory within the self of the aspects of the matrix that are integrating. We leave you now but will return after a break. We are your Blazing Star."

20

THE LIFE OF AN ANGEL: WHAT THEY DID TODAY

he room pulses blindingly white, then the light condenses into a brilliant pinpoint and the angels are gone. We open our eyes and look at one other: we're all grinning without inhibition, punch-drunk, exuberant. The atmosphere in the room is thick with angelic affection. Nobody speaks, but frequently we break out in a rash of giggles. Russell goes for tea. As we sip our Earl Grey, a curious thought seizes me. Sir Thomas Malory writes that Merlin had a mentor and confidante, an obscure fellow who lived in the north and to whom he regularly confided news and information about the activities of Camalate. His name was Master Blaise. "Hey! Do you think these angels are that same Master Blaise—you know, when they called themselves a Blazing Star? Blaise?"

As if on cue and in direct response to my question, the angels return. The room hums as the air thickens with angelic love. It's like a dimmer switch for a one thousand watt bulb; as the angels come into us closer and deeper, they slowly turn the dimmer switch to an increasingly brilliant illumination. Except that the light seems to emerge, not from a single bulb or focused presence, but from within the center of everything—the room, our bodies, the plants, consciousness; then it condenses again into the form of six angels.

"We return as a Blazing Star. We come to answer any questions you have, if you wish."

"Well, yes, actually, I have a few more. To start with, who are you?"

"Angels, we should think. Can't you tell? Your intuition is correct. Blaise is a term you may apply to a thought form appearing as angels. Definition is apparent through a qualitative experience. You define yourself by the qualitative experience in the way you sit, walk, and talk. We, too, are defined in every way we express ourselves. We come as a lilac dancing flame. We come as the flowers of deliverance. Think of us as the lilac flame over the Grail bowl inside your being. Fill it with all your love and make a space for us inside. There is an indissoluble link between humans and angels predominating in the higher realms. We are representatives of the Great School, which is an inner circle of humanity working on both sides. We have two or three representatives in that place you call Shambhala, working on particular development projects. We come to you as a Blazing Star, as a pinpoint of light in a clear blue mind, where no clouds pass by unnoticed."

"Yes, but what *kind* of angels are you?" I ask, though I feel myself growing more dumbfounded with each moment. It's hard to keep a sharp, rational, journalistic focus; part of me wants to melt into the presence of these angels.

"Big, fluffy, fun angels, we should hope," Blaise replies. "Some have called us Ophanim. We give you contemporary images, suitable for your time period. We come in many, many different forms, such as the Bodhisattva on the lotus petals. Many forms. You name it, whatever it is, we've been it all. We have been all forms. We come in many forms. We transcend all forms beyond time and space. This is difficult for you to imagine so we come as angels. Surely you're familiar with angels? Good. That makes it a lot easier for us."

"Did you ever visit Arthur and Merlin in their time?"

"Arthur's experiences with angels, such as at Beckery Chapel, were much rarer. Your time now is characterized by psychic tides and the development of consciousness in individuation. Openings have been made. We refer to current trends influencing the availability of communication with beings of another order of being. These events were revelations until 1947. At that time, holes were made in the etheric structure of your planet which enabled this increased level of communication. What you are experiencing tonight would be unending revelations to those of an earlier day.

"Think of us, if you wish, as six columns of enveloping white light, making a circle around you. We place you in the center of a tall, still lilac flame of transmutation, rising from your feet to well above the crown of your head. This burns away all impediments, all dross. The lilac flame burns in the cells of your body and in each moment of consciousness. We place you within the lilac flame as an expression of our Love from Above. In the very center of the lilac flame, there is a still point of bright light, a Blazing Star. Think of us as this blazing pinpoint of light. Think of us as the *Nimitta*, the comet of consciousness, as a very fine point of light within the lilac flame. As a Blazing Star."

"How do you guys pass the time, besides visiting people like us?" I know this sounds appallingly irreverent but somehow it seems to match the uncanny mood of informality Blaise has established.

"We will give you an extraordinary piece of information. We will speak to you of the life of an angel. We read from today: Awoke. Found we were already awake. Looked around and thought, This is it. It is this. Knew it was no thought, knew it was inspired. Knew we didn't know, knew we had work to do, knew it was joy. Knew we would return to Earth one day. Knew one day we would have bodies like yours. Knew we would try to help as many humans, as you call yourselves, as possible. Hung around a few church spires here and there. We were mainly in Europe and North Africa today, though two of us made a significant presence in Central Mexico."

"How many of you are there, Blaise? More than six?"

"We are in excess of 40 million potential manifestations. Each is a Blazing Star. Each has its own vibration. Each one could be named, but many are unnamed. The six of us each have 144 major manifestations and each of these has 6^6 minor manifestations."

"That's a lot to keep track of."

"No problem. Nothing compared with what you could do. A great human called the Christ once said: If you only had a grain of faith, you could move mountains. He spoke literally. It's like this: you make it as it is. Therefore, you do with it as you will. The Architect of All Absolute Existence made you in His image. We are not so fortunate. You have Buddha Nature. You have Christ Spirit. You and He are one. We only serve. We have to come back in your forms to rejoin with Him. No possibility for us until our time is right. To have human form is a rare and extraordinary event. We are envious of it. Each of you who occupy this form have an opportunity of uniting with the highest, with the Lord Absolute. We do not have this possibility in our present form.

"We are not complaining, you understand. Just trying to put things in perspective for you. We are more than happy. We are in a state beyond your experience. But we must return one day to your form to come closer to the Master of it all. We don't have bodies. Therefore, we are free of tangible karma. We are practicing seed planting of Love, whereby when we incarnate, we will reap a little Love from Above as an anonymous gift from the beings we've been in the past. You live in the age of darkness which some call Kali Yuga. We come into full physical incarnation as Satya Yuga, or the Golden Age, commences, approximately beginning in 2020. Then we achieve bliss in physical base, transcend all limitations, and return to the Source. In 2020, we'll only be babies. You will most likely meet several of our manifestations before you disembark."

"What will you come back as, some kind of spiritual teacher?"

"Usually we like selling fruit. Fruit is given. And we like to make a buck. Seriously, though, angels are amongst you."

"Anybody I know?"

"Let's just leave it at that," Blaise replies, but as they speak, I see a fruit seller in New York City. He's a little seedy and unshaven but smiles gorgeously. He wears an oversized Harpo Marx coat with secret pockets and surprises. He holds an orange, beckoning a stranger to approach. He winks at the customer—me—as I approach, rolls the orange across the counter to me, then flings open his coat to reveal magnificently iridescent wings.

"Actually, we're a bit spread out today," Blaise continues. "We've been busy in India with the riots. Anyway, you've been speaking to one of us that normally doesn't get to talk a lot. Just hangs around smiling, but he's done okay."

"Where did you come from before you came to Wick tonight?"

"We have spent the previous four months in the star system you know as the Great Dipper on a world related to the star Polaris. Here many souls from Earth reside after bodily dislocation."

"So you have responsibilities all over the galaxy?"

"We love the zodiac on behalf of those above. We invite you to love it, too. We are like dentists. When you brush your teeth, if you don't brush them all correctly, then some will rot and drop out. They will decay and need external help. Now, if you care for each tooth with love, with toothpaste and toothbrush, each tooth will be whiter than white. It will shine from within your mouth like a star. This is what we do with each part, every part of each place, even the dark crevices of humanity. We send some love into even those places. We try and get rid of the decay so that we may all become One again in the brightness of the big star we are."

"Sorry, Blaise, but there's something here I don't understand. You seem to travel faster than the speed of light yet by your own description you are light."

"We would like to express the fact as it is, but you would need a different set of symbols to understand. However, energy follows thought. We can be in many places at the same time. Remember? We have 144 manifestations and our lesser manifestations of 6^6 as well. Each time we increase, we increase as a multiple of 6."

"For that matter, why 6 of all numbers?"

"There are 6 of us."

"I know, but I'm asking, why 6?"

"Because there are," Blaise replies, grinning from face to face at my perplexity. "Why is there one of you? Answer quickly."

"One is hard enough to deal with."

"One can do so little. Six can do so much more. One more thing. We have already been in this spacetime where you experience us now in this house. Yet we were also never here in person."

"Are you speaking from here right now?" I ask dutifully, but I really don't need any more paradoxes. The fact of Blaise is sufficient in itself.

"No."

"And you were never here in person either?"

"Correct. This is it."

"Well, Blaise, the only thing I can figure is that if you're governed by the laws of light speed, you must have sent six of you here ahead to be here on time."

"You must be joking. We are not governed by any spacetime continuum. We are in front of or behind any notion of instantaneousness. We are already here."

I have mental energy left for only one more stumbling attempt to understand these elliptical angels. "Was it some kind of video cassette of yourself that we've just had a fascinating dialectical conversation with?"

"That is a matter of perception, but it is a symbol worth looking at. We leave you now as we came, as Love from Above, as your Blazing Star."

Even as Blaise withdraws, there is something else, an anomalous, deep vibration. It sounds like a big truck idling just outside the house or a speeding train rumbling in our direction on tracks that run underneath the house. Our bodies tremble within from this sonorous vibration; we look around for the source of it, but clearly and enigmatically, it comes from inside us—from inside everything, especially that Blazing Star or pinpoint of light Blaise showed us. I step outside the living-room but there is no vibration there. After ten minutes of this thrilling drone—the Blaise Sound we will call it henceforth—it subsides and the angelic wrap slowly recedes from the room, leaving a ravishing trace, like perfume.

"How about making us a nice pot of Grail Tea?" Russell asks me. This is England: when in doubt, have another cup of tea. Anyway, I'm glad to walk about again, even though, in one evening, the world has turned upside down and inside out.

21

REVISITING AN
OLD POPULAR HANGOUT

wake this morning as if lying with a new lover, floating in a sea of angelic feeling. I am a feather in a pillow made of angels. I luxuriate under the duvet with the same swooning sensation of blissful stillness as we all felt last night during Blaise's visit. The angelic aura cocoons me, permeating my breath, my body, my atoms; every successive moment of awareness bears the insinuation of revelation. I am dipped in angelic wax— lilac. How many years have I spent meditating with painful knees and unanswered *koans* and here Blaise descends in an eyeblink with the scent of samadhi on their wings. Not only that: Blaise loves us, loves *me*, not because I've done anything remarkable, but because I exist, I'm human, and Blaise is unconditional love. That's angelic carte blanche in my book, an original blessing: grace from above.

At breakfast, Russell says he dreamed we sat in a room examining sacks of mail. We were delighted with the obvious response to our efforts in the zodiac but felt reluctant to deal with all the correspondence. Something to do with our future, I should think, Russell adds. Over cereal, he laughs as I relate how I nearly fell down the stairs this morning, long before I got to the last step where I usually bang my head. I seem to have misplaced my body and have been colliding with anything that has edges.

Another zodiacal expedition is on the books today. We leave Wick in the late morning and drive a dozen miles to Cadbury Castle, an excavated hillfort at South Cadbury, a miniscule village. In the late

1960s, archeologists tentatively suggested this treeless prominence was "probably" the headquarters—Camalate—for a fifth century A.D. "Arthur-type" military figure. That wasn't terribly bold of them. In 1542, Renaissance traveller John Leland made this unqualified statement regarding the hillfort's legendary associations: "At the very south end of the church of South Cadbyri standeth Camallate, sometime a famous town or castle. The people can tell nothing there but that they have heard say Arthur much resorted to Camallate." Folk legends also identify this 500 foot flat-topped hill without doubt as Arthur's. The hill is hollow and Arthur's knights lay inside asleep in the stony fastness of Arthur's Palace, the legends say, but on occasion they gallop down Arthur's Hunting Causeway on spectral horses. These ghostly manuevers are practice for the triumphal moment when Arthur, the once and future and returned, rouses them from their long slumber and leads them out of Avalon into Logres, the besieged land of Britain, and the whole wide world.

Camalate feels ripe with expectation this morning, as if we have arrived only seconds before the curtain will rise on a marvellous performance. The place feels strikingly different than it did on my first visit. At that time, several months ago, I stood on the brow of Cadbury Castle and surveyed five counties with unimpeded view. To the northwest, Glastonbury Tor was a nippled, misty knob while Camalate felt riddled with ghosts, specters of Arthur, shades of the archeologists, phantoms of legend. The air was imbued with sadness, a mute stillness, the sense of recollection hovering just beyond reach.

The broad, empty greensward of Cadbury Castle belied its once populous Arthurian youth. I felt I had arrived at the scene of a tremendous party the day after, when the celebratory field has been cleaned and raked, and only the odd memento of yesterday's revels kicks up at my feet—raked clean other than palpable echoes in the ethers. Avalon might have been the lunatic, excessive place of the spirit, but Camalate was the executive headquarters of Arthur's Celtic milieu. "We are all far too inclined to look backwards, and even to revere the past," said Tudor Pole in a 1963 letter. "For me, it matters not whether the whole Arthurian saga consists mainly of myth, so long as these myths can still prove useful in pointing *forward* to a greater spiritual fulfillment for the race."

That feeling of poignant distance is not the ambiance I feel today. It is uncanny, but today Camalate feels as if it is prepared specifically for us, like a star witness finally ready to testify and clear up matters for good in a baffling case. As I walk slowly up the path, I see Russell dressed in a maroon, ankle-length robe leading a group of horses down the hill. Two of the horses have young knights upon them as riders, and one of these is a boy, about fourteen. He wears a crown, his eyes are intensely blue, and he looks unnervingly like my dead brother. I continue up the hill, my hands clasped clerically at my waist, breathing with each step, aware of my breathing, my eyes partially closed. At the summit, Russell and I perch on the eastern rim of Cadbury. As if overlaid upon my perception of us, I am aware of another man and woman in Celtic clothing standing where we are, similarly taking in the view over the quilted fields. Russell stands next to me in that same maroon robe with a white sash drawn at the waist. I occupy somebody else's body, as if the etheric echo of another once familiar form has slipped over me like a glove. I have a red beard, my frame is shorter, stockier, more muscular and thicker, and I'm about 15 years older; there's curly red hair on my chest and arms; I wear a leather vest over a loose cotton shirt, a thick canvas-like skirt, pleated leggings of leather, leather shoes. Behind me stands a slender, winsome woman with braided blonde hair and a pure white dress that ripples about her ankles. A voice inside me says: "I've finally come back."

Russell looks himself again and I follow him across the hill, asking him his impressions. "We seemed to be watching a procession of knights moving through the valley," Russell says. "There were etheric residues of buildings, probably originally defensive in function, that lined the far hills in the east. By the way, that was quite a nose you had back then. Quite a big knob above the beard."

We sit down at the center of Cadbury Castle and wait for the cows and flies to disperse. Then Russell says, "Be at home wherever you are. Open your eyes and look around. Berenice, love, see if you can find Arthur's throne room." In a few minutes, she beckons to us and we join her at a spot near the eastern rim. "There are five ley lines passing through this spot," she announces. "I see the throne, which faces west, up the hill; it's a huge chair." Russell leads us off again westwards then begins a circle dance, like brisk *Tai-chi-chuan* movements. I close my eyes and he is a human corkscrew, a vortex. One spiral spins above the ground, expanding from a tiny point in widening gyres into space, while another spiral spins oppositely into the Earth, getting wider as it penetrates ever deeper into the ground. It's no longer Russell who is spinning, but a woman with thick black hair tied in a bun. Her face is pale, her lips rouged, her expression austere, yet cooly lovely, and I know her: Nimuë, Lady of the Lake. She was one of the two women who walked with me along the Avenue of Oaks.

Another man stands with us, again co-inhabiting the physical space where I thought Russell was spinning. He has straight white hair that flops boyishly to his shoulders. Sixtyish, his skin is slightly pockmarked; he looks like a Brooklyn cabbie, the kind who will fire off impertinent remarks at passengers regardless of their social status. Dangerous, reliable, demonstrative, powerful. His eyes sparkle penetratingly as he looks directly at me. Yet he has an amiability, a good-natured twinkle, a man who seems half-magus, half-fool. Merlin!

Late in the evening, Blaise announces their arrival an hour before they congeal into speech. It's as if the air in the room is suddenly transformed into attentiveness, populated with ears and eyes that carefully observe our thoughts and conversations. We feel inspired by their watching. It's as if Blaise watches us from within reality, beholds us from within our awareness. Things grow warm, affectionate, still, happy, deep, as all the edges and petulances dissolve into a sweetness that flows as blood through us. Blaise meditates us as, approaching, they slowly turn up the dimmer switch of their presence, brightening the Blazing Star above our navels, until the illumination is palpable and the inexplicable, intriguing Blaise

Sound—the droning at the atomic heart of anything—drives up outside the house, inside our bodies, under the floorboards. We feel as if "translated into Heaven," as Malory often said of the more fortunate Grail Knights in their angelic encounters.

Blaise comes into focus and greets us. "We come as a Blazing Star. We come as a pinpoint of light. Feel for this pinpoint of light inside yourselves. Feel for this tiny Blazing Star just above your belly buttons and a little inside. Breathe with your Love from Above to this Blazing Star, as we breathe with you...."

After a few moments of our breathing together to the Blazing Star, Blaise continues. "We come with a blessing. Put light in your hearts, all men and women. Wear love as your clothing. Stand firm on Mother Earth. The jewels of the spirit are found on the Earth. There is light in the veins of all men and women. Light is in each cell: white light, pure light, radiating from each of you. The golden ray pours in from above. Light and love are always with you. That is our blessing. We come as we are. It's good to be with you this evening. We are pleased with what you saw today. Always, if you wish, at this time, remember us. We are not absent from you at all. We are linking you actively, each in your own ways. You know not completely what you do. We are with you in all of what you do."

"Blaise, what was the significance of our seeing Nimuë at Camalate today?" I ask to get the press conference rolling.

"The Lady of the Lake is a figure of authority. She is the guardian of the astral realms from the lowest astral rubbish to the highest astral orders. Nimuë is one of the three aspects of this woman. The downward spiral you saw moving into the Earth is the spirallic pattern of feminine energy. This is the mother, the wife, the seductress. The upwards, ascending spiral is Man standing in the light."

"I want to ask about Camalate. If the members of Arthur's Round Table remembered themselves today, or were reincarnated and they got together again, what would their work be?"

"This question rests on false premises. Not by reference to the past but to the present should you look. Each situation is like a link in a chain of events with a potential memory synchronous with other memories. The solution is integral to the beings involved. If you ask the question in the right way, you will get the right answer."

"Okay. If me, Russell, and Berenice, and maybe a few others, were to form a group, what would our work be?"

"The question in its essence is still false. The essential base from which it is asked is not firm. It is advised you should not begin a question with an *if*, which puts up a wall. It becomes difficult for us to see what the question is asking."

"Alright. What is the proper work of the Camalate Center?"

"This question is far more important. In Camalate you have a sacred name with a gematria, which means there are numerological correspondences that form patterns of light. These represent a reciprocal energy matrix that surrounds this sacred name from a divine source. Camalate. When different beings resonate to this sacred name, that name takes on for them a focus. The question probes into the nature of the forces of light and darkness that surround the name Camalate. In its subdivided parts, Camalate means, through time, a particular place used a lot, a coming together of the conscious aspects always for the purposes of awareness, truth, light, and love. If, in that context, beings come together in a synchronous act, anything is possible, provided those beings are working towards a process of individuation. The individuation of all parts concerned, based on the idea of the name of Camalate, will eventually be of the essence always carried by that name. This essence is that which draws a lot to itself.

"Camalate is the place to which came a lot of people for the purposes of realization of light, understanding humility, truth, love, sincerity, spirituality, integrity, compassion, and three other qualities not revealed at this point. The sacred name is held in the hearts or in the center of a sphere of beings and will draw to itself the nature of its generation. It can be used by the group for its perfect purpose, to harmonize the energies of consciousness and take it through the process of individuation."

"Will you give us details on how Arthur and the knights used the zodiac?"

"We have spoken before of an energy matrix in this area. Here we are referring in part to the zodiac. The pattern is an energy configuration the knights were familiar with, including its hidden energy lines. Merlin, Morgan, Arthur, and Nimuë, as initiates from Atlantis, were already aware of this pattern. They supervised the knights' initiations and sent them through the zodiac where they received instruction in individual aspects of the pattern.

"See for a moment a matrix of light with a central point and a curve of consciousness from that central point, then see at another dimension the whole interrelationship of the matrix within the zodiac. The curve at one end is Butleigh and the Tor is at the other. There is a line or parabola which runs between these two points and is formed by what you call intersections of ley centers. It is the key to your understanding of this question.

"We have described an energy matrix. The intersection of ley energy, if plotted between the Tor and Butleigh, forms a parabolic curve of consciousness. This curve includes Pointer's Ball and extends to a place called Lugshorn. It is an etheric bridge that links one reality with another. *Pointer's Ball* was how the place was first called because, at this place, it was possible to point, in pre-Atlantean times, to a particular spacetime dimension. This was possible because of the matrix and pattern that surrounds Pointer's Ball. The earthing point for the continuation of this pattern is at Lugshorn. We cannot describe in words known to your language all the implications or give you a more factual answer. It would involve us going into terms which you would not comprehend. We would have to speak in a language which existed before the Babylonian separation when there was a unitary consciousness over the Earth."

"I see. Well, what about the Dog? I mean, here we are, living in a zodiac figure called the Girt Dog of Langport. Some called the Dog Cafall. How did Arthur relate to this Dog in the landscape?"

"During Arthur's life, a system prevalent among the adepthood was known as the Qabala. This was part of the Mystery teachings from which much of the Western magical tradition was derived. The relationship between Arthur and his Dog is the relation between

Arthur and a system of magical usage through which he worked his devices."

"Did Arthur use the Qabala to defend Britain?"

"Yes. The system used is enormous. It requires a very thorough training on behalf of the adepts over many lifetimes, even back to pre-Atlantean times. It is not possible for us to begin to explain the whole of the practices or the purpose or the devices used in the defense of England during that time. We can only present you with something that is a mirror from that time and which will be relevant to you now in your time. This image will be known to you but you need to work with it.

"If you would visualize a sword pointing down through the top of your head with the point reaching the base of the spine. Next, visualize the scabbard which contains the sword. The points of the scabbard, which contain the handle, come out at the shoulders. This is a means of self-defense and protection. There is another sword which is an activating force. This sword rises the other way up, without a scabbard. Its handle is in the Earth and the tip of its blade appears just above your head. Its cross handle is at the pelvis.

"Now, to say this is an image for attack is wrong, but it is an active force for the Light. You have a complete system pertaining to Qababla and the means of defense for an individual within a system of knowing, faith, and trust. This image pertains to the Tree of Life and its correspondences in the microcosm. When the group that you're to be a part of forms and this image becomes operative, it will not only protect yourselves but will also protect others who have not the same background, experiences, or level of experience. This is Excalibur. We surround this image with a purple flame, more accurately, a pale lilac flame. It is the flame of transmutation that lies above the bowl of the chalice, or Grail. It is the Pendragon, the force that surrounds the sword Excalibur."

"It appears now that a series of events in my life and the process, as you call it, that I'm going through corresponds with similar events in the Arthur story. This intrigues me." I do not at first realize how big a target I have made of myself for the six Blaises.

"Of course. But we have already said Arthur's position and function are secondary to the process. That process is involved with a fundamental activity in consciousness. It is the exploration of a personal transmutation of elemental forces within physical base. The most important element here is *your process*. The concept of 'my life' is inherently wrong. Do not, on your peril, persist in this way of thinking. This idea was born in the dark. We give you this to help you understand. Life is not a concept that means anything to us. There is to you and to us no meaning in this concept. If there is life, there is also death, and we believe in neither. A moment is a moment—that's all. The shadow contains much of what we have to work with. What you do with us is a contribution to the light of this shadow. It's your choice and your free will. Please make sure you make the best use of us. We cannot guarantee that our assistance will continue for much longer. If we could tell you what you need to know, then the whole process and operation would be a lot simpler. But we cannot. We can only respond to what you give us in your questions. So what is your question?"

I haven't any idea what my question is. Things are suddenly as bad as when I used to stare dumbfounded, like a deer frozen in the headlights, at my Zen Master who had just lobbed another explosive *koan* into my mind. What is my question? I can't think of any, or of anything, and I can't remember who I am or who is furiously writing down all these words while listening to six angels.

"We are aware of that," says Blaise, removing me, for the moment, from the spotlight. "Feel the energy. The lines of light move faster than sound. Sound touches where light cannot. Hear the vibration where the lines of light cannot touch."

We sit silently in the living room, feeling the Blaise energy. Even so, I know I'm not off the hook yet. Blaise has another knock for me.

"Are you able to fulfill the conditions required of you in this project? Can you fulfill the purpose designed for you, which involves presentation ability, the quality which you bring to the given task? You are only 60 percent operative at the present moment. You have to strive within yourself to overcome desire and enthusiasm, and to get on with the task. Then the qualitative aspect will be revealed. While you are still intrigued by the process, then much will be withheld. This is an irrefutable law in a transpersonal process. There is something to be brought through, one way or another. If not through you, then it will be placed somewhere else, as others are being made ready if you can't bring it through. Because of intrigue and enthusiasm, you often miss the point.

"The positive thing you could bring to your work is humor, which you've been lacking of late. This brings clarity and increases efficiency and operativeness in your work. If everything is taken seriously, full of deep meaning, then everything loses meaning. Only through irony can the tragedy be appreciated, particularly when you talk about truth, which can only be expressed through irony, paradox, and parody. You have an awareness of this and have experienced it already. We are what you might see as a circle within a group of humans working towards a particular end. We come to you through this means because there is no other means to communicate it to you. We leave you now but will return. We are your Blazing Star."

All I want to do is crawl under a bed where the angels can't see me. Why didn't somebody tell me angels have Zen sticks too and are given to whacking students in the familiar waking-up zone? Russell and Berenice grin at me, and the more forlorn I look, the merrier they become. "Blaise found a sore spot, it seems," says Russell, giving me two imitation Blaise winks. "A little too much intrigue and enthusiasm up there in the Grail chambers?" Before I can think of anything clever to say, Blaise returns and I direct my "Yeah, but—" to them. "Blaise, I don't understand what you mean about enthusiasm. That's one of my better qualities."

"We are indicating a tendency in you, which you recognize, to do with a negative form of excitement about information given to you through an unfamiliar way, and not from books or eyes or ears in the usual way. You are now presented with information in a previously unknown means and this invariably produces in everyone an excitement. Watch this. Be mindful. Don't let it corrupt your work.

There is no more intrigue or excitement in this way of gaining information than in any other way. If you watch this and you are careful
with it, you will be much more useful."

I see what you mean by paradox, at least. Here we are, chatting
with a half-dozen angels for the first time in our lives, and they tell
us not to be impressed or else they'll go away. My self-esteem is wobbling and the idea of devoting, say, ten minutes, to a proper sulk up
in the Grail chambers is appealing, but considering our company, it
seems pointless.

"We would like to present you with a pattern that could be important for you. If you grasp this picture, it will lead to many more
facets of what we mean and facilitate the process you are involved
with. Picture a river that flows. Within this flow is everything. There
are stones across the river, from one side to the other. The river is
broader than your imagination can picture. Each book of this type,
such as the one you are working on, is a stepping stone across the
river, but only one in a sequence of many. As consciousness expands
and evolves itself by linking into a process, another step is made
across the river. It is possible that through the investigation you are
making, some light will be born and will be of much use to us in the
work we are trying to bring through at this time. We are fortunate
because this is an opportunity for us to present something more consciously than we have been able to before."

As I imagine the river forded in paving stones made of books, the
walkway between the shores becomes a ribboning rainbow bridge.
Six Blaises wave to us from the center of the bridge. Then something
occurs to me. "Oh. So it was you guys who showed us the rainbow
bridge at the Tor."

"The same.

"Blaise, where among the stars we see at night are you from?"

"We have explained, we are what we are: many forms. We come
through many forms. We are an expression of light for you all. It is
not accurate to say we come from afar. It is not accurate to say we
come from nearby. We are as we are. We come with love, as love.
When you look out of your eyes up at the sky at night, you see many

pinpoints of light. If all these were gathered together, multiplied, then seen as one star, you would see a Blazing Star, as we are. It is very bright where we are. So bright you cannot even imagine it. At best, most humans see only a tiny flash of the light we are. Brilliant beyond your imagination. Look up and you will see the golden bird. It carries a tiny aspect of who we are."

"Well, as long as we're talking about things we can't imagine, what's that funny droning sound we hear just before you arrive or after you leave?"

"It is more like a tiny fragment from one of our tires touching the Earth. We give you our blessings. Sleep well. We leave this light in your heads, as your Blazing Star."

22

Through the Mirror in the Lion's Head

Russell and Berenice leave for bed and I should, too, because it's three a.m. but the words and images and energies of Blaise's visit are too much with me to fall asleep. In the midst of all this, a moving image comes into my mind, as if someone inserted a video cassette into my attention.

There is a living-room, lit by candles, perfumed with incense, and occupied by a half-dozen meditators with serious intent. They expectantly await a revelation, hopeful figures in a seance. They keep looking anxiously towards the wall as if something is about to burst through and shower them with cosmic wisdom. I see what is on the other side of the wall. It's like a big telephone switchboard with hundreds of earphoned operators seated before computer terminals, making connections on a board, speaking into their microphones. Everyone is busy and the swell of voices is nearly deafening. All the operators are angels, their wings folded demurely behind their chairs. A large boss angel in a white jumpsuit and lilac flame insignia on her lapel walks down the aisles, checking on her staff's performance. She stands behind one operator who has his feet up on the console, half a cup of coffee in his hand, his eyes closed, with a luxurious smile irradiating his face. His telephone is ringing insistently.

On the other side of the wall, a woman—part of the seance I first glimpsed—strains in meditation to get this operator's attention. The boss angel chuckles then nudges the daydreaming operator who sits up in a start, shakes her head wistfully, and answers the phone. Other angels shout out questions. "Anybody got anything esoteric on needlepoint? Something hot from the Akashic Records perhaps?" Another says: "What are we allowed to tell them about the meaning of life?" Another operator keys in "Please hold" on her screen, then flies down the aisle, through a swinging door marked "Records, Akashic: Earth Videos."

Shunryu Suzuki-roshi may not have had this scenario in mind but his advice about practice is to the point. "When you practice zazen, you should not try to attain anything. You should just sit in the complete calmness of your mind, and not rely on anything. The calmness of your sitting will encourage you in your everyday life. So actually you will find the value of Zen in your everyday life, rather than while you sit. "If I might slightly amend the roshi: You will find the value of Zen in your everyday encounters with angels.

In the morning, I wake remembering a dream. Berenice and another man wear gauzy lilac robes and are singing a song she wrote called "Memories." My brother, who has been dead for many years, runs up to me in a bathing suit. He has been playing on tightropes and diving boards over a pool. Don't tell anyone I'm here, he says conspiratorially—he's looking much younger, really boyish, than he was when he was killed at age 19—because I'm playing a game of chase. He runs off. I cross a stream that is no deeper than my knees and about a dozen feet wide. The water is cold, the current swift, and I feel soft pebbles on my bare feet. I reach the other shore and am happy to see a woman I once loved; she is gambolling contentedly and greets me warmly. I lie in bed savoring the feeling of this memory and the dream contacts, although I don't understand their message.

Over breakfast, Berenice and I review our experiences with Blaise. "You stress your supposed identification with Arthur too much," she says, marmalading a slice of granary bread.

"But it's like reading the minutes of the last meeting of the board, except I didn't know I had even been at the meeting or that any minutes had been taken," I protest.

"Even if you had some connection to Arthur once, you still have to understand your self-nature now, whoever you are. You still have to find what's behind your ego identity. More tea?"

"Thanks. I'm looking for the transparency of the present episode in which the mythic background shines through," I propose.

"Perhaps, but you should remember that Arthur and yourself are both in a process of transformation, like Blaise said. You should start to experience things more from your belly. Give your head a rest. You're always talking about belly and hara and all that. Don't rush so to label your experiences with words before they even happen. Then all you understand is your words. Would you mind terribly if I left the dishes for you? I have a client in about three minutes."

I start sudsing up the breakfast dishes then jump back suddenly from the sink. Blaise is waterskiing across the sink, zipping adroitly around the dishes as if they were breakers, plowing smoothly through the waves of suds. I feel a brightness at my belly, as if somebody is persistently winking at me from inside. When I finish the dishes, I get out the vacuum cleaner and give the expansive kitchen floor a proper Hoovering. I feel Blaise with me everywhere: leaning over my shoulder, sitting on the rubber hose, pointing to dirt particles on the floor. As I make a miso soup for lunch, slicing up fat carrots and peeling onions, Blaise is with me, humming like a merry householder on a Saturday morning, wrapped in a chef's apron working the cutting board alongside me. Here we are: a couple of househusbands making lunch. Blaise wears a Walkman and wiggles to some peppy tune as he dices the onions, but his wings get a little tangled up in the cord. Extricating his wings from the Walkman, Blaise somehow trips over himself and multiplies; now there are six Blaises tangled up in the cord, slicing onions, humming happily. The day passes like this. With every gesture, every step, every little activity, climbing the stairs to my room, carrying out the trash, raking the compost pile, answering the telephone, brushing my teeth—these irrepressibly happy Blaises are with me, mirroring everything I do, in multiples of six. In the evening, I sit for an hour on the couch, not doing anything at all, just letting Blaise breathe me. I am inexplicably content with doing nothing, not meditating, not thinking, not expecting, with just feeling Blaise's presence. Berenice and Russell read, but they feel it, too. Soon Blaise shifts gears and starts speaking to us.

"We come as a Blazing Star, as a pinpoint of brilliant light at the center of your being. Breathe with us to this Blazing Star for a moment.... Good. It is important for you at this time that you grow into yourself. The opportunity only exists for a limited period. Love yourself deeply. In you sits something magnificent. Remember yourself. Do not be afraid. Take all from us as you wish. We are here to serve you. You have no need to be afraid. Stand in your light. You are that light. We bring you into that light. If you want attention or respect, then you can bring all of it to you. Settle down in yourself. You are our love. You are our light. We give to you. We are of service to you. Live in love. This is it. Humility only exists when you sit in the right place in yourself. It is arrogant to think others should listen to you if you do not represent that which is best in you. Humility comes with loving yourself, accepting yourself. You begin to feel a difference now.

"You all have much to offer from inside yourselves. How can we tell you all you need to know about what you are to do and allay the fear that might arise from your seeing the enormity of the task? You three have taken one step towards us into the Light. Now we take one step towards you. We cannot jump nor can we linger. During this time, we are with you all the time, as you saw today, though we may come in strange forms which you can't accept. We bring you gifts now. [I see baskets of apples tumbling over, flocks of white doves landing.] You must understand fire. This is one of our gifts. The positive fire is concentration, kindness, caring, and love, but the negative fire is annoyance, anger, aversion. This is the untransformed fire. If you don't label the negatives as they arrive, but experience the energy as fire, we will help you transmute it with the lilac flame over the Grail chalice. We are the lover. You are the beloved. But the beloved always has free will. You do as you wish. Your choice effects who you have been, who you are, and who you will be.

"Something is happening in Glastonbury tonight around the Tor. We are mostly occupied with this tonight. This pertains to a group we're facilitating in preventing fundamental damage to a particular water course by something known in your time as the water board.

We have a group gathered who are trying to divert the effects of possible cataclysmic changes produced by a few humans motivated by forces of darkness. We must leave you now."

Naturally, our attention focusses at once on Glastonbury and, as if with long-range binoculars, we scour the town for signs of trouble. Despite our curiosity, we don't have any idea what kind of drama is playing out under Blaise's orchestration. An hour later, Blaise returns to explain matters.

"We are pleased to be back with you. Much of what we needed to accomplish tonight in Glastonbury at Chalice Well has gone well. First, we have a message, then we would like, if you wish, to take you to Chalice Well. There are five curtains. Two have opened for you already. Look behind the third curtain and much of what you seek will be revealed. The curtains are thinner than you think. You have already passed through the first two. All you can do is this: Whatever you experience, whether tangible or intangible, look underneath the experience, like a child looking for a lizard under a stone. You're not expecting anything to be there, but you're always wondering if there might be. This is the process of memory, the way, the truth, and the light. A symbol is being shown to you now. Tell us what you see."

"It's a gold heart with three crescent shapes inside, and all this is inside a pentagram," I respond slowly, as the image forms in my mind. "Now it's a pendant on a woman's left shoulder. She wears a blue sweater. It's Berenice."

"Good. The symbol that lies on the front of the curtain must be penetrated for that curtain to be withdrawn. Then the next curtain will be revealed. A complete understanding of the nature of the symbol will be the penetration of the curtain itself. We would suggest that Berenice represents for you an assimilable image of aspects of your feminine. Now we take you on our wings to Chalice Well."

It's not that we leave the livingroom or even, as far as I can tell, our bodies, yet with Blaise doing the driving, somehow we find ourselves, in part—meaning, with part of our attention—at Chalice Well, having a look around. My focus is split because I don't lose track of my breathing, or of my body sitting cross-legged on the couch at Wick Manor in the late evening, yet, to an extent, I can look around Chalice Well and participate in the experience Blaise has in store for us. "What do you see?" Blaise asks me.

"I see the Tor and its tower. It's like a beacon with a searchlight that sweeps the countryside. It doesn't feel wholesome to me. It's polluted."

"Now focus your attention on the Lion's Head fountain here in the garden," Blaise continues.

The lion is no longer made of stone. It is much bigger, and roaring: a quite believable, full-size lion guardian, except now it changes into a curly haired golden Apollo with sunlight raying out from his head. I move through him, and past many other appearances, as if I'm penetrating multiple layers of images until I reach a bright mirror. It spins and turns into a polished silvery-black crystal. Russell tries to hold it steady, but it flaps about like a fish in a boat struggling to regain the water.

"Look into this mirror," says Blaise. "Steady your breath. Look into the mirror."

I see my father, then my mother.

"Breathe into the mirror with your love."

I see a clown's face with a bloodied jaw, then the blood disappears, then the clown's face is healed and whole.

"Breathe into the mirror with your love."

I summon to mind the image of a woman I once loved in California—I had dreamed about her the other night—and breathe love to her. Suddenly the mirror steadies and reveals an angel with outstretched wings and a golden coronet on his head. The angel smiles radiantly at me. "Ahhhh," says Blaise. "We leave you for a short while to talk over your experiences."

Russell chuckles and then says, "What a trip. We all joined hands and rode under the belly of a huge angel about the size of a double-decker bus. He dropped you and Berenice off at Chalice Well but we hovered over the garden for awhile. There was a ring of tall angels lining the garden where the fence is and lots more smaller angels inside, and an enormous angel the size of the Empire State Building on Chalice Hill. He had golden wings and the light they emanated and the light from his head rose straight up into heaven. Two angels worked with you steadying the mirror. One was white and seemed warm and compassionate, but the other was dark and had a stern, severe attitude." Turning to Berenice, Russell says, "Tell us what you saw, love."

"It was very curious. I found myself walking around the garden and saw three women who were dancing. Somehow I was one of them. The seven chakras of each woman were illuminated, and each woman emanated a stream of light across the garden. I felt Blaise telling me that all three women were aspects of myself and that we— the three women—made this garden long ago. Each of the three women have another three aspects yet to be revealed, making nine women in all. Then I understood that the bodies and minds of these women and the physical garden itself were the same but in different dimensions. Her name is Morgan. I mean the name for all nine women is Morgan.

"Then the scene switched into the physical dimension, but it was clearly a very long time ago. A stream flowed down between the Tor and Chalice Hill, where Wellhouse Lane is today. The stream was about three feet wide and had a peaty, mossy, stony bank. An earthen path that was also golden ran alongside the stream on the Tor side. At the bottom of what is now the garden, there was an open, grassy knoll; on the Tor side, there were Scots pine, oak, apple, and yew trees. I noticed the spring bubbled out of the ground in a little vale between the two hills and to the left of the present road."

"By the way, what are the curtains Blaise is talking about?" I ask Russell as we walk into the kitchen to make tea.

"The curtains? Don't you remember your basic Buddhism? The five *skandahs*. Sense formations, sense doors. It's in the *Heart Sutra*, where it says form is emptiness, emptiness form. The same is true of feelings, perceptions, impulses, and consciousness. Those are the five *skandahs*. The curtains. They're all empty forms. When Blaise says, 'see through the third curtain,' he means see the emptiness of perceptions, even what they're showing us. See through them to what is really there. Even when Blaise shows us something, we never see it very accurately. Things aren't what they seem."

When Blaise returns, I have a question ready for him. "I'd like to know how Arthur and the knights used the sacred sites around here. A place like Othery, for example? Even though there's an old church there now, it looks like there once might have been a barrow or mound underneath it."

"Picture a grassy field with the midsummer sun overhead," says Blaise. "Now tell us what you see."

Again, I have the same inexplicable sensation of dual presence that I experienced earlier tonight in our outing to Glastonbury. Without leaving my seat on the couch or without any loss of my awareness of my breathing, my attention is rivetted somewhere else as an image comes into focus. "There is a line of people that fades into the distance on the left, along a dark, winding road. A shepherd in a dark robe stands with a staff before the entrance to a barrow that has two upright, thin stone slabs and a horizontal lintel laid across the top. Past this is darkness. He wears a skull cap, has short hair, looks fiftyish and friendly."

"Breathe to the door with love," Blaise says.

"Oh. Right. It seems this man has a cross around his neck. Inside the cross is Marilyn Monroe in a bathing suit. She raises her arms and her entire body is golden. She looks blissful and moves slightly when I see her. Inside the door are a lot of gorillas—no, more precisely, they look like Chewbacca from *Star Wars*, the same 'gorillas' as Berenice danced with at Muchelney. They're about eight feet tall, stand upright, are lean, almost lanky, and look reasonably intelligent. One offers me a twig with button-like white flowers, which he's plucked from a large bush. I carry this twig as I pass through the door. There is a second, interior door. This one is guarded by a man in a bronze spacesuit; he is a kind of astronaut-soldier and feels a bit Atlantean. He wears a globular helmet and has a long gun or rod. He doesn't notice me."

"Breathe to the door with your love," continues Blaise, unimpressed with the dramatis personae of my vision.

"It's a wooden door. I knock three times, then enter. Inside, there is someone who looks like Albert Einstein. A human, involved in something creative, full of thought. There is another man with whiskers who sees me; he tips his hat and dashes off down the hall. Wait a minute. Wasn't that guy in *Alice in Wonderland*? Oh well. Now this is a strange sight. A lot of these Chewbacca-gorillas are hanging by the arms from hooks, as if they are fur coats in storage. Wait. They are coats, or skins—no, they're bodies they can put on and take off. One of these figures stands before me and has a human face. He smiles, then gives me a leaf and a wand and gestures for me to look up. A spiral of white light weaves upwards like a corkscrew in a transparent shaft towards a rotunda, or domed ceiling. Somebody says, 'This is the inside of a dome.' I walk out of this chamber, through the doors, back to the grassy field, but now there's something new here that is hard to describe. I can only say it resembles a huge, black bowling ball. A giant, mysterious black sphere on the grass."

"We are most pleased you have seen this. You have been shown a small part of what Othery was used for in Arthur's time. Soon, with the help of your friends, you will understand more of what has been given. We leave with our love. The lilac flame dances above the bowl. The pinpoint of light within the lake gleams for you all. We are your Blazing Star."

23

IMPRINTING THE GALAXY ON EARTH WITH DOMES

The next afternoon, I lie out on the grass in the back garden staring at the clouds, wondering what a black bowling ball on a grassy field outside the dome of Othery means. That and a lot of things, I suppose. The feeling grows in me that I've forgotten a great deal or have failed to retrieve from memory much of what I once knew and ought to know now. Something bigger than I'm aware of is going on, has, no doubt, been going on for a long time without my awareness. And now this black bowling ball, with me unaccountably inside it, is starting to roll towards—I don't know what.

Edmond and Celia bound out of the house to tell me Russell and Berenice are taking them to Burrowbridge Mump, do I want to come? The Mump is a mini-Tor with ruined church, contoured slopes, lovely view, but considerably less public fanfare, situated four miles down the lane along the River Parett. Even more so than the Tor, the Mump is a topographical anomaly, a solitary bump in a flat landscape. Geomythically, it's the Dog's nose. Despite these blandishments, I feel disinclined to budge from my cloud-monitoring position, supine on the grass, so the Pendleton's drive off without me. Fifteen minutes later, I sit up straight and, like a hunting dog, cock my attention towards a vaguely palpable activity somewhere in the landscape. I breathe deeply, then slowly, close my eyes, and find I am with Russell at the door of a cave that opens into the Mump, about half way down its slope on the south side.

A straight line of light sears across the landscape, linking the Mump

with Glastonbury Tor a dozen miles away. Something peculiar overshadows the Mump: it's like a multicolored globular lampshade that
fits over the hill and environs; at the inside top center of this translucent lampshade is a very bright light, like a bulb. Numerous spokes
of light ray out from the lampshade giving me the impression of an
immense, radiant wheel; and some of the lines are spirallic, which
imparts further kinetic energy to this configuration. Meanwhile,
Russell and I enter the cave in the Mump. Again I encounter the
gorilla-skins hanging like uniforms in the foyer. Further in, a man
holding a double-barreled shotgun guards the entrance but he seems
oblivious of us. Past him, we encounter a man in earthen brown
friar's robes; he sits outside another inner cave and smiles at us.
Examine his pendant, Blaise whispers to me. I have to breathe with
Love from Above for some minutes to steady the pendant before it
comes into focus: an eagle within a circle. Then we're outside the
cave again, and I'm removed again, back to the lawn at Wick facing
the roses—not that my physical body ever went anywhere.

I stand up, stretch, walk through the driveway and up the lane,
over the turnstile, then run up Wick Hill where I can physically see
the Mump. I can't see Russell or Berenice, of course, but I do sense
them descending the Mump and climbing into the family Citroen.
There is the light canopy over the hill again, but now it resembles
two hands cupped in prayer as purple rays stream down the wrists.
For a moment, I sense myself inside the dome again. The roof glitters
with prismatic light, like the high rotunda of St. Paul's Cathedral in
London; beams of light traverse the landscape projected, apparently,
from the portholes that pockmark the high-domed ceiling. One beam
passes through Wick Hill and the Aller Dragon's twin horns; another penetrates our house then heads on to Langport; another goes
to Glastonbury Tor. Then I see the Dog: a black Labrador retriever
stretched out hugely across the landscape, its sleek skin speckled
with stars, its wet nose glistening at the Mump.

By the time I climb down from my perch on Wick Hill and return
to the garden, everybody is home again. "I did, actually," says Russell,
when I ask him if he saw the Dog. "And there was a line of light

from his nose straight *up* to Sirius in Canis Major—the one up there," he says pointing to the sky. "The Mump was packed with angels, too. I counted at least sixteen, plus eight extra-large ones, plus an angel for each of us, including you. There was a Templar Knight who pointed his sword into the empty church; when I walked into the ruins, I saw more swords pointing in to a blue flame with a green aura with a pale lilac flame burning above it. By the way, those aren't gorillas. They're *Yetis*, you know, Sasquatch. They seem to work inside the domes."

"What about that lampshade over the Mump? What do you make of that?" I ask Russell.

"That's what Blaise means by a dome," says Berenice. "That's right. I remembered it right away today. It looks like an upside-down flower with its green stalk rising into heaven and its flower petals laid on the landscape. It looks rather like the head of a sunflower. It's a kind of latticework of light like a lace doily suspended over the hill with lots of blue lines of light raying out for lots of areas in the country-side."

For the remainder of the afternoon, and through dinner, a strange discomfort and irritation steal over me. I feel unsettled about being guided and buffeted about by invisible beings. How can I tell for certain I'm seeing things accurately or that I hear the words of guidance with any precision, and where is it all leading to? A shudder shakes me from deep within my body or perhaps from a place deeper than that, and it only adds to my nervous mood of disorientation and grumpiness. Russell notices my mood at dinner and asks me what's wrong. I try to explain.

"You have to realize you are up against a lifetime of conditioning," he says kindly, preslicing his potatoes before he eats them. "All of which is now staring you in the face. Your whole life, people have told you this stuff isn't real, that you're slow, thick, insensitive, or whatever else they've told you—mistakenly. Don't label it. Just breathe love to it. That's the antidote. You're burning off a layer of psychic skin. All these thoughts that trouble you are the fumes. Your creative source is stirring; that's what the shuddering is about. New energy waking up. Pass the green beans, will you, love?"

But I haven't shaken off the gloom and anxiety when Blaise arrives later in the evening. They point it out without preamble. "Will you take off your brown robe that you brought in with you tonight? This is your scholarly attitude from the past. Sometimes it is useful, but sometimes it gets in the way. We give you the key of discriminative wisdom"—It's a gold key with six crenellations, three on each side—"We give you a blue electric fence to let in the light and keep out the shadow. Let the experiences you've had settle into your mind and body. Do not be in a hurry to understand them. Things are moving very quickly now. Be still more often during the day."

Despite Blaise's recommendation, I am eager for clarification of some of the things I saw today. Factual answers are a balm for my troubled psyche. "What is that line of light we saw from the Mump to Glastonbury Tor?"

"There is an etheric tunnel of light in the air between the Mump and the Tor," Blaise tells us. "There is also an underground tunnel, now in darkness. The end of the light tunnel comes out in a curve of developing consciousness at the Tor. It was used for transport in a hurry in Arthurian days when transport was slower than it is today. It was used by Merlin and his adepts from Atlantis."

"We have the impression those Chewbacca-type gorillas I've been seeing are actually *Yetis*. What is their role in all this?"

"These figures that guard doorways allow you in and keep others out. Therefore, they are good. No problem. They allow you in as you are with your Blazing Star."

But what I burn most to know more about are the domes. I checked in my library upstairs for references and found domes referred to in only one source, a curious self-published book called *The Phenomena of Avalon* by an Italian with no command of the English language and no particular address. His name is Gino Gennaro, and I first read his book, which is a concise, esoteric history of Earth and its culture from the viewpoint of the Fairy Kingdom, several months ago in fascinated noncomprehension. His writing is like *Alice in Wonderland* under the glossalalic influence of LSD. He informs the reader that while he has seen much, he understands little of its significance. He writes about "floating chapels" and "celestial grails" and "luminous floating domes" and "the healing grails of the planetary Knights of the universe" whom he also called "Cosmic Chaplains." The Chaplains brought the "celestial grails" to Earth long ago. Now it seems that though Gennaro may not have known what he was talking about, he was correct. His floating chapels, evidently, are Blaise's domes.

"Correct. We often recommend this little book. It is relatively accurate if a little pessimistic in parts. The domes made the etheric structure of the Earth what it is by imposing a conscious matrix upon the planet. This made the Earth a place for possible human or conscious-being evolution. You have seen only a fragment of what is around you. The domes were ships. They travelled at a speed faster than light, which means they exist spatially in between what you call matter and spirit. You cannot understand this completely as your technology is not advanced to the point of appreciating anything approaching this concept. The first time the domes visited the planet, there were no humans. The second time, there was only primitive life. The third time, there were some humans who could see clearly and some saw these domes. The domes will return. More precisely, the domes did not come one time. They were not here two times. 'Came' is not accurate. They exist in an area of spatial relation that is not qualifiable as 'came' and 'went.' After the domes "departed,' they left impressions on the Earth's surface. They left an oscillating pattern, which will continue until the Earth ceases to exist or until they are reaffirmed by another visit. The domes will return one day."

"Is a dome responsible for that pattern of straight lines that we saw running out from Chalice Hill?"

"Correct. When the dome was placed over Chalice Hill, which we would call a Captain Dome, it activated lines of light and energy already there. These are still visible today. Even in their ignorance of these lines, people have built houses and roads near these paths of truth, light, and love, and have fed off them. As people become more conscious, these lines will become brighter and assume their real form. The domes were linked to the Camalate Round Table. There is a dome over this Somerset zodiac. There are many domes, more than you can imagine. Merlin discovered them and informed Arthur. Morgan, however, knew much more about domes because she was an arrival in a dome. We know this is beyond your comprehension at this time."

"Were the domes distributed around the Earth according to some pattern or plan?"

"The domes were positioned relative to star formations above. Experientially, each dome represents the life of a star as experienced on Earth. The domes sent out lines of communication, or dome lines, to each other and to positions they had previously occupied when last here. This set up energy matrices. The position of these dome lines was modified and strengthened, dome to dome, by the golden lines coming down from above. Each Earth point of special interest to you is connected from above with lines of golden light. Each part of one thread, or filament, is connected and infused with Love from Above. Such is your Earth. It is Love from Above. What has happened in the formation and growth of the Earth is only that—Love from Above through the golden lines. We will see the return to recognition of the golden lines of light from Above that bring love to your Earth. We will bring with us an awareness of these lines. We will give much to those who gain in awareness and become conscious of patterns of Love from Above over the Earth."

"We said at Chalice Hill recently that everything is light vibrating at different frequencies. Nothing exists other than as that. The domes are light impressions, radiating and vibrating at various wavelengths reciprocally all over the planet. Sound is an aspect of the reciprocal vibration and wavelength of light of which the domes are made. This phenomenon still exists as the domes exist and are reciprocally maintained through the light force, which is the life force which has a sound and a vibration. In the body, the place where pimples come up are at the intersection of nadis. It is the same with domes and dome lines. The dome has the possibility within of creating the feature that would enable detoxification through that part of Gaia's

surface. Namely, volcanoes. Volcanoes are excema, boils in the surface of Gaia. The toxins come to the surface, break through, and
ooze across the surface."

"You see, what is left at Chalice Hill and the Tor and other places
you will discover is a memory of what was once there. The domes
have all gone, but they will return when the Masters of Destiny and
the Angels of Light see that Man stirs in the spirit. They are not
actually here except as memories. They were materially here once.
All you perceive now is an etheric memory. Imagine a very bright
light bulb held in front of your eyes. Its image would stay there long
after it was turned off. The Master Domes came and went. They
carried love, light, and energy, and brought back fuel for the smaller
domes, like the one at the Mump, so they could all bring this planet
to life. Regarding active domes, there are too many to count. Most
are as active as they should be at this time. Some will become more
active and some will become less active. Each dome has a time-re-
lease facility. There are underwater domes. The domes are not particularly distributed in relation to land or water."

"In the atomic structure within the matter composing the Earth,
the star map or landscape zodiac was actually blueprinted into the
matter in the same way your bald head was in the genetic code
before you were born. The blueprint was in the genes. Therefore, the
atoms had blueprints, which said bald head, fuzzy curls. Certain
domes can generate a zodiac, relative to their position on Earth. Each
has a particular time relationship in terms of the aspect to be revealed at a specific time. Like a clockwork."

"The zodiacs are never all active at the same time, but the minimum active is seven or eight. The zodiac domes are additional to the
regular domes. They correspond to star maps, each with different
emphases, relevant to a particular star system and orientation. They
are different from regular domes in the star projection feature in
that, like a planetarium, each zodiac dome has little holes in it al-
lowing starlight to penetrate to specific points of the Earth. You saw
the string to Sirius at the Mump. These big domes are big and their
function is big. Remember the Black Bowling Ball. This is related to

these domes. There is a dome over each of the pentagonal features of the Earth energy matrix, and smaller ones inside them. This is a multidimensional energy matrix projection that crosses many levels of energy, form, and information."

"What are ley lines then?"

"These are lines of energy connecting one dome to another in a matrix of light over the surface of the Earth. The domes need fuel. It comes down silvery tubes, drawn from the Master Domes, as you have already seen at the Tor. When they return, each dome is energized. Each dome has a portal. The Masters of Destiny look out from the portals of the domes to see how Man fares in his conscious aspirations towards the Quest."

"So ley lines only originate at domes?"

"As far as we are aware, your statement is correct in relation to Earth planetary nodes. Each dome emitted particular patterns of dome energy to other domes. These were pre-determined on a planetary matrix model before the domes arrived. The dome lines or ley lines are specifically pulsating lines of energy that oscillate in intensity at various times during the calendar year. Each dome had a predetermined pattern. You will see all the different matrix patterns at future points as your journeys extend."

"So have the ley lines gone away, too, like the domes?"

"Yes. Ley lines are also a memory. If you had your nose cut off, you would still have a memory of where it is. It is like this with ley lines. Even the memory carries a lot of power, more than you realize. Humans are foolish to tamper with these lines unless under specific guidance through thought forms to help them deal with the material. Man's foolishness here creates more work for us and gives the Dark more of a chance. People should leave alone what they don't understand, otherwise we will never finish our work. The domes were brought to Earth to create a Paradise for humankind. Each carried a light form, or seed crystal, of what was to be, both locally and globally, through the grid. Of these Paradise seed crystals, some have been activated, but otherwise humankind has either not been aware of this divine potential or has not bothered to make use of them to create the intended Earth paradise."

"Who brought the domes? Gino Gennaro spoke about Cosmic Chaplains. Was it them?"

"Do you understand electricity? Well, don't expect to understand something which is twenty times more evolved than your electricity. Don't you think it's reasonable there should be a higher intelligence behind all manifestation? As far as we're concerned, this is a fundamental reality. The domes were brought as a response from the Architect of Cosmic Destiny. That is his working, but not his formal title, by the way. The Cosmic Chaplains are workers for the Architect of Cosmic Destiny. They are not describable in terms of angels. You might refer to them better as pure energy. Masters of Cosmic Destiny, architects and engineers of infinite capability, brought the domes to Earth in line with past proposals and future events. Elohim, who are an order of angels, were intermediaries in this process. They were used to pay service debts to the Masters of Destiny when they came to Earth."

"In this subject you are beyond your conceptual range. The full explanation requires the assimilation of planetary, solar, and universal histories. Before Adam, the Elohim. You can remember this. The Masters of Destiny are advanced beings from the inner circle of esotericism. You might, if you wish, call them Buddhas, Gods, Goddesses. When they describe the portals of consciousness to Man, certain of humankind will heed the direction and set forth on the quest for truth, happiness, light, knowledge, love, wisdom, and individuation. Then they will return happily to their fellows, introducing the Grail Quest to them as a representation of the divine source. Now we suggest, if you wish, that we take a break. Go have some Grail tea. Then we have some questions for you regarding your process."

24

WITH ARCHANGEL MICHAEL AT THE SEVENTH LEVEL OF THE TOR

everal hours have passed since Blaise's visit, and it's now well past midnight. After our Grail tea, each of us curled up in our chairs and took a nap. Somehow Blaise has stirred us again with a gentle angelic alarm clock and we're upright and ready for more conversation. Of course, this angelic dialogue is ruining my work schedule and sleeping habits. I'm going to bed most nights now at a time when I used to get up.

"We come as a blazing sword whose point is the needle," says Blaise. "We hope you are well rested. We are what you think we are. We have always been, we always are, we always will be. We wish first to define something from an earlier meeting that was left unfinished. A human being has a body. He has the idea of a body that he calls mind. This is our first point. The second is that extension and thought are what we mean when we speak of energy. They are to us synonymous. Third, the face of the universe is directly perceived through the human mind relative to the state, relative to its ease or disease, and thus its comprehension in human bodily awareness of extension and thought. If the body is well and at ease, then it can extend and expand in thought. What you refer to as tension is what constrains or contracts the mind. We have been delaying your writing a little so you could understand an important point. Something that underlies your questions. It pertains to what you will write next."

Blaise is right. For days, I've been struggling with a section about the levels of the Tor and have gotten nowhere. "What use did Arthur make of the Tor in his initiation of the Grail Knights?"

"The initiation largely took place somewhere else. The adepts, who had already been through their initiation but who aspired, would ascend the Tor for development and individuation of their consciousness through all seven levels of human potentiality in aspiration and actuality. These are available now as then."

"I'm trying to write about the seventh level of the Tor, but I haven't a clue what it is."

"How true. The seventh level of the Tor is a single point of light in consciousness. It is the clear, brilliant pinpoint of light at the center of clear, pure mind. You have a deep underlying question. We come with love. We suggest you perceive the seventh level as the crown at the top of the head. If all the cells of the physical body have a small crown placed on top of them and they are supported by the warm Earth underneath, then you begin to perceive the understanding necessary for the seventh level of the second stage. We recommend also that you picture within yourselves what it may be like to go completely beyond anything that you have conceived before you experience the seventh level or second stage. We are most concerned about the experiences you have at this stage. You must gather your energy. Remember our definitions. Remember all the parts of yourself. Remember the Tor. Remember what lies at present within the fence around the tower. This fence is not a coincidence at this time. We say, take each step, one step at a time.

"Within Man's understanding of the physical world, there has come a dimension of mathematical proof of a nonphysical reality that lies within present scientific knowledge. There have been many works inspired and guided from the other side to make way for the knowledge that turns the dark into the light, or, more accurately, that balances completely the light and dark in the spirallic process of evolutionary growth, expansion, and consciousness. The question you have asked is the key to a possible understanding of this process. The question in and of itself invites the knowledge that was contained during Lemurian, Atlantean, and Eleusinian periods regarding the seventh level or second stage. We ask you, then, what was the first stage?"

"Superficially, I'd say it is everything that's happened to me up to this point."

"Correct. This answer makes it possible for us to reveal more to you. We ask, if you wish, that you consolidate your questions. Pull out of your personal history that which leads to a final elucidation in the looking you are doing. Remembering is pulling together *all* the parts—your mother, father, your arms and legs, all your past beings. In the remembering, you have to remember everyone who came as a part of ourselves, as we would remember an arm or foot or head. You must remember both past lives and your life now, and everything that has come before your eyes. The key to the process is remembering. That is the whole thing. We leave you for awhile with a blazing sword. Its point is the point of brilliant light. It is the needle, pure and clear. We leave you each with a Blazing Star within yourselves."

Russell and Berenice retreat to the kitchen for another round of tea while I start flipping through the pages of my life—to the degree I'm aware of them, which is limited—looking for relevant data. I'm surprised how fast anomalies and long-standing unanswered questions turn up, things I've forgotten about for decades. That unusually friendly man—a friend of my father's from work, I'd always thought—who said hello to me at a company picnic, calling my name, smiling at me, for just a moment, yet with such a look of recognition that I lost my breath and could never figure out who he was, and I never saw him again or asked anybody about him.

That time I was a teenager mowing the Swanson's lawn, the way I always did on Sunday morning when they weren't home. That backyard was my private thinking ground. Invariably I had the same fantasy each time while doing the long swath in the back: I explain life on Earth to a visiting group of UFO people who have landed discreetly on the lawn. I tell them about Freud, the *New York Times Book Review*, oil painting, the poetry of Ezra Pound and Dylan Thomas, the perplexities of intergender relations in my high school, and whatever else I think represents my knowledge base at the time. Afterwards, they applaud me, give me a certificate, and leave. I never told anybody about it or thought it strange.

Then there were the voices I always heard in my head, ordering me this way, then that way, making me spin sometimes, or feel guilty other times, or anxious at not achieving something. It was a kind of superegoic sussuration that made me squirm and worry and even thrash about a little at times.

As I jot down these memories, and many others, a curious kinesthetic sense of the Tor as my body and its Michael tower as my crown chakra overtakes me, and I feel myself to be in two places at once, which, by now, isn't surprising. Russell and Berenice return, as if on cue, as does Blaise, so we continue with the agenda.

"What have you noticed in your remembering?" Blaise asks me.

"The sense underlying all the images I've remembered so far is a consistent question: *What am I?*"

"Good. You are a being composed of what you call elements in different proportions. Your quality pertains to earth and water. You are a water-based being. A large percentage of your total makeup is water. It is cohesive and has the quality of fluidity within cohesion. Your quality is expressed through energy and energy relates to earth. Earth is expansion and extension, qualitatively. You breathe the air and the air moves through you. It comes and it goes. You live in the water and then you are born into the air. You take your first breath. The air is movement expressed by being. What enables all this to come together is warmth. We call this fire and fire is concentration. It enables the water to relate to the air and to rest above the Earth as clouds. All this takes place in the ether. Ether is in between everything. If you look into your body, then you'll realize how much ether exists in you. Ether contains it all. Ether is formless. Between each elemental aspect as it manifests, it manifests in ether. *Between* is ether. We have given you as clearly as we are able at this time something beyond which is what you are. Now will you consolidate your questions from the images you have remembered."

At first, I'm not sure what Blaise means, but as I continue to sit quietly, a question wells up within me like a bubble. "The times I did LSD in college, I always had this unsettling experience of losing the spacetime context and dissolving into something I didn't recognize."

"That is a prior experience to the seventh level. It is water."

"Then, just before, I was experiencing my body as the Tor."

"This is earth, knowing the earth. The crown that is seen is not the crown."

"When I was a boy I had fierce temper tantrums, really heavy-duty explosions, when I would kick holes through doors and flail about like a crazy man."

"That is fire."

"Also, when I was a boy, there were nights in bed before I fell asleep when I'd start thinking about myself, then the world, the sun, the stars, the cosmos, and I'd suddenly feel I had been swept away into infinity and a big empty space and was only a tiny speck. This all meant that I would die one day."

"The sense of infinite space is air. It is impossible for a human ego to maintain itself in infinite space, which is what you brought with you."

"Well, I often get this almost indescribable sense of expansiveness bounded by a thin, expanding membrane. I feel completely hollow inside. It is a strangely pleasant, almost sensual experience, it comes according to its own schedule and never lasts more than about five minutes."

"That is ether, the space between everything."

"Oh. So that's it. Blaise, I've always wondered about that man who knew my name and said hello to me as a boy."

"The man was an early reminder of where you came from. We come in many forms. Now we wish, if you wish, to take you to the seventh level of the Tor."

Thus, without our lacing up sneakers, pulling on a sweater, or even bestirring ourselves from our chairs, Blaise whisks us to the top of Glastonbury Tor. There, a black-robed man with horns and a crooked nose and a tanned, leathery face rushes about jabbering with agitation, nonplussed with our arrival. He's obviously a black magician up to no good who doesn't like being interrupted by this angelic embassy; he runs off as we consolidate our presence by St. Michael's tower. We stand in a line, Russell in the middle, facing Blaise, towards the south; then Blaise asks us to describe what we see.

"There are a half dozen angels linked together, then another dozen behind them, and behind them an ocean of light," Russell says. "They make a ring around the tower and enfold us with their wings."

"Now focus your attention on the top of the tower," says Blaise. "Tell us what you see."

"I see a tall, white angel with outstretched hands and he seems to be orating or singing," I venture, realizing with a combination of amusement and humility how poor my eyesight is in this realm.

"I see a pale lemon light around the Tor, surrounded by blue," Berenice says, "and the hill is skirted round with dark green trees. At the top of the tower there is a blue diamond, and, above this, a blue dove. Now I see a huge, transparent angel about twice the height of the tower, maybe more. His elbows are about even with the crenellations on the tower."

"The Archangel Lord Michael is pleased to see you all tonight," says Blaise with a touch of pleasure. "Michael would like to show you all something. Focus your attention just above the tower."

We are silent for a few minutes, then Berenice says, "Michael is raising his hands over his head and his fingers bring down the light from heaven like conduits or lightning rods."

"Good," remarks Blaise. "Now look around quickly over the landscape and tell us what you see."

"There are various figures of the zodiac lit up on the ground like an airport runway at night," says Russell. "I see the lion; and the centaur who is half-human, half-horse with a golden unicorn in his head. The Gemini twins are like two infants overlit by a pale sun."

Even mewling, half-blind kittens like myself sometimes get a proper look at things. "Over Wearyall Hill, I see a complex crystalline form that takes up one-fifth the surface area of the hill. It has a cubic base and dozens of icicle-shaped shafts or pillars. There is another large crystal on Dundon Beacon and one at Pointer's Ball. What are these things?"

"These were placed here long ago from Lemuria to store records,"

Blaise answers.

"Just for a moment I had a peek inside one of these crystals," says Berenice. "It's like a beehive."

"We know everybody is a little tired from our evening's work," says Blaise, as we "return" to the livingroom at Wick. "But we have a few further messages to present before we leave you tonight, if you wish."

"Sure. No problem, Blaise," I remark, half-asleep. "It's still an hour before dawn."

"We are most concerned for you all. We come in many forms that you may learn and experience at this time. You must, should you wish, accept what we send, for it is only by this means that you will remember completely, overcome your opinions, overcome your beliefs, overcome the words, overcome the personalities, overcome the forms, overcome the concepts. Be completely with what comes to you all from now on until we tell you otherwise. For the best in you, we recommend most strongly that you accept completely what we send. We cannot and will not interfere with your choice. It has taken a long, long time to establish this opportunity for you all. You can, should it be your wish, change so much in yourselves. Then you may become what we are and always have been and always will be in the spirit of our love. This is it. *This* and *is* are one. *Is* and *it* are one. *It* and *this* are one. Feel the sound. Feel the light. Touch the Earth. Each step is a step of love. That is all. All is one.

"We give ourselves completely into the celebration. It is the celebration of this space that lies within, within the gate. The door is ajar. Even though it opens only a little, the light pours in. We make the temple glow. Each cell, each atom, is touched by light. Each thought is full of light. Each sound is a sound beyond sound. We come with love, the love of light on Earth. We leave you now as a Blazing Star, as a pinpoint of pure, self-effulgent light, within, without, having form or no form, beyond the beyond."

I stagger up the stairs and fall asleep on my bed before I can undress, thinking, just as my eyes lock shut, who would have thought angels could be so chatty?

25

"Thoughts Extended, Both Ends the Same"

ne of the advantages of being an angel—not to mention six of them—is that you don't wake up in the morning in a ferocity of itching from insect bites. My legs are splotched like strawberry jam tarts from my intemperate scratching. The Dog has fleas! I don't suppose there are any more visible biters down here by the railroad trestle, but I've been having a lazy time relaxing in the sun and waving to the engineers when the trains rumble by. I'm perched like a primrose, nodding and drowsy, on the steep grade overlooking the double-barreled track, now empty and trainless in the endless summer afternoon. Even in England, on a good year, the summer days last a sunny long time.

How long have I been out in the field on this assignment, anyway? I mean the work that Blaise keeps alluding to and none of us ever remembers. The work that's been occupying us for a long time, long before we met this year. Berenice said something about driving into Glastonbury this afternoon, and I told her, as I needed a new typewriter ribbon, I would probably go with her. I rouse myself and walk home under the broad canopy of blue sky just as she pulls out of the driveway. On the way into Glastonbury, Russell says: "If there is any place you feel you should visit, let us know and we'll drop you off." I close my eyes and see the Tor.

I pass through the first turnstile and breathe with Love from Above to steady myself. *Hara*—don't leave home without it, especially if you're visiting exotic terrain like Glastonbury. The Tor is unusually busy and populated today. As I stand facing the contoured slope towards the tower, I see an old business friend from New England in a white robe directing a choir. At the first turning of the maze, a pack of white dogs, flanked by a team of black dogs, stream along the curve, pulling a coach stuffed with passengers. At the Living Rock, three elderly women have reluctantly squeezed themselves onto the same bench. They drink tea and eat egg salad sandwiches. Facing southeast towards Cadbury Castle, I see several angels and dozens of men and women in variously colored robes ringing round me in song. Some have transparent wings like dragon flies. A middle-aged couple walks past me with a friendly nod as I rest at the second bench facing Wearyall Hill. They discuss the quality of accommodations at the George & Pilgrim's and complain about the high cost of butter these days. Chalice Hill sports a big crystal, a cube topped by a pyramid and four evenly shaped vertical shafts that make a crown. Behind me, a couple of guys toss a discus of light back and forth like a frisbee. Overhead, an Army helicopter drones about its usual, secretive business. Further up the slope, a gang of short-statured people unroll a huge, black tarpaulin to cover an entire flank of the Tor in the area of the silvery pipes.

Now, at the tower, a Jesus-type figure stands smiling. A young couple walks by, holding hands. The man wears a yellow polo shirt and brown trousers, the woman wears a lilac dress, pink blouse, and a long ponytail, which I'd like to pull. Not far behind them, a flock of witches cavort on broomsticks. They wave to me as merrily as children driving bumper cars at an amusement park. A young man in loin cloth stands before the tower. He's a healthy, well-built man, with bright blue eyes, but he's strapped to a cross. A woman nearby talks to herself about how she thought people weren't supposed to cross over the fence the National Trust put up around the tower to keep people out so the hill won't erode and slide into the Severn River by Sunday morning, thank you very much. She takes a tiny camera out of her handbag, snaps a photo of the tower and its fence, then shuffles down the slope, mumbling inaudibly.

The transparent form of Archangel Michael more than fills the space of the tower and, in fact, dwarfs the puny stone edifice many times over. He's filling up a milk bucket with light from the clouds, then empties the contents onto the Tor like cream over a muffin. Michael faces southwest, along the orientation of the St. Michael ley line. I'm pleased he has his orientation straight. On the north side of the tower now, there is a young man with long, stringy hair in a white, torn robe. He looks like a stoned California surfer, as he rushes back and forth with a troubled expression. Two women perch on the eastern shoulder of the Tor, engaged in a conversation.

There are certain places on the Earth that owe their formation and destiny to heavenly influences, and one of these is Glastonbury Tor, said Wellesley Tudor Pole. "This means that they still possess a direct link with the energies emanating from the Archangelic Hierarchy, and, in the case of the Avalon Tor, with Michael in particular." Long ago, as far back in time as the advent of humanity on this planet, said Pole, the Tor became one of many global centers where the spiritual origins of Light and the Creative Father were worshipped. At that time, the Tor was enveloped "in a sacred aura of protection." After the Lemurian and Atlantean cataclysms, the explicit potency of the various Sun centers was eclipsed and "only the hidden *seed* of the cosmic energies surrounding such centers as this Tor survived." Retrograde forces, including retrograde expressions of Druidism, transformed spiritual practices into debased ritualism. "However, I am convinced that a pure strain of Druidic lore persisted at Avalon," establishing the right conditions for Joseph of Arimathea and his companions, "bringing with them the Message of the Christ."

At the bottom of the Tor again, the sheep graze contentedly and the lambs don't bother to flinch in alarm as I pass through their ranks. By the gate at Wellhouse Lane, an enormous woman in a dress as billowy as a tent carries a picnic basket down the lane to her Morris Minor. A flock of at least forty ravens suddenly ascends into the pine tree before a house. Inside this tree before me is a doorway and its door hangs ajar, its hinges snapped. A hand emerges from the darkness within, raised in warning, to stop the traffic. A blue

Mercedes with four women drives swiftly past. Under two willows there is a brick pillar shaped like a cone about twelve feet high. It seems to be a one-person elevator. In the little dell between the lane and the uprising body of Chalice Hill, near a solitary apple tree, stands a brick smokehouse with a smokestack pillar behind it and, behind this, a silver arch stretching grandly like a quicksilver rainbow into the distance. A young couple asks me in impeccable British, Do I know, exactly, how to get into Chalice Well? I do and tell them, then Berenice arrives in the Citroen and we drive home.

It's all a test, of course. Angels always have something up their sleeves even when they're not wearing a shirt. Right after opening salutations, Blaise drops the quiz on me. "Would you please explain what you learned today on the Tor?"

"I learned the use of the key to discriminative awareness you gave me as I sorted through all the experiences. Some had more quality than others. But I felt confident in following your guidance and accepting all the images. I felt I was viewing both worlds, inner and outer, with equanimity. I didn't make false distinctions between what is visible with my eyes open or closed. Also, I saw the distorting filter in my mind and knew I wasn't receiving the images accurately. Plus I had a nice walk."

"This is as we would like it. We have a word for this: *kesajee*. This means, 'thoughts extended, both ends the same.' Some spiritual traditions on Earth call this the meeting of minds. We are with you in the totality of light and love. Allow a few moments, before asking your next question, for this experience to come in."

We sit silently for some time, breathing, waiting patiently, then I see angels dancing around me, making a crown around my head. Now all I see is a brilliant, starry sky, and, under this scintillation in our back garden something huge rolling towards us slowly, growing larger as it approaches. The Black Bowling Ball!

"We roll towards you. When you know the black sphere of stable consciousness, there will be no more questions. It is the memory of all questions. It relates to your purpose, your life, and your existence here, now, on a moment-to-moment basis. Knowing the black sphere of stable consciousness will take you beyond all questions, all answers, all concepts, all form, all emptiness, all ideas or notions of self-nature, beyond the beyond. It is what you are. It is what you are not. Ohhhh, that we could explain it to you. We give you our love. We bring you into the light. The Black Ball is the ultimate question and within the ultimate question is the ultimate answer. Beyond space and time, beyond concepts, beyond formlessness. This is it. We leave you as a Blazing Star within the black sphere."

If enlightenment is a bowling match, then rolling the Black Bowling Ball guarantees you a strike. In fact, it is the end of the bowling alley itself. "Well, just what we need. Another bloody mystery," says Russell. "And what are you laughing about, Grail Knight?"

"It's a scene from a movie that nobody's made yet, but I might, called *We Roll Towards You*," I answer, still chuckling. "Word gets out that the secret of the universe is a black bowling ball, so some California entrepreneurs outfit a panel truck. They paint a big sign on it that says, 'Beyond the Beyond Bowling Balls, Inc.,' and they deliver inflatable backyard bowling balls the size of garages and special costumes with wings and suction shoes so people can roll towards each other on their cosmic bowling balls while dancing on the surface while they—"

"Bubble out over the top like yourself, I should think," says Russell, tittering as if water-surfing on a smooth, round dark ball.

26

PLUCKING APPLES AT THE WELL

nother day has passed in the time it takes me to drink a cup of Earl Grey because here it is, already mid-evening and Blaise is arriving.

"We roll towards you on the Black Bowling Ball of stable consciousness. A qualitative experience is of the eternal moment. We can only be expressed as a qualitative experience, which is wisdom, truth, love, light in action, thought, mind, and deed. This is how you may reach us. First, set the intention to open to a qualitative experience. For your level of being at this moment, that is the total of that which you can bring to the moment. Set this before yourself. Next, feed the center of your being with your love, a love you feel within yourself when you say you love someone. You feel the love within yourself no matter how much you love someone, and you love your experience of that love born within yourself. Bring out this love and feed it into the center of your being. This is the second step. Third, open your heart and imagine that in your heart sits a being who is pure and divine, of radiant energy. This being begins to be a possibility as a channel for us to be with you.

"The path before you has much on either side, but essentially it is straight. Let go, should that be your wish, and allow the support that is there for you to manifest completely. Let go the breath with love. Let go the past with love. Let go all expectations of the future with love. Be with the qualitative experience of what lies at the center of a being filled with love. Nothing that it does is outside of that love. Nothing that it doesn't do is outside of that love. Love in nothingnesss; nothingness in love. Love is warmth; warmth nurtures the Earth; warmth consumes the air and stops the thinking and allays the fears. Be with us now for we come with love.

"Your process is a boat. You each have a boat. The boat will take you across the ocean, but when you reach the other side, you do not need the boat anymore. We follow you and support you as you pass, but we cannot interfere or stop you or prevent you from leaving the boat. We can inspire you, but the work of application and correlation is your responsibility."

Ah, there's my modest little boat—My, but she's yar, I hope—still tied to the dock: a white rowboat, two-seater, with blue streaks on its sides, a little paint flaking in patches. "Blaise, for months I've been wondering what went wrong with Arthur. You know, why Camalate collapsed."

"Arthur did not, could not, would not accept himself as he was. He was not sent on the Grail Quest because he already had the Grail. Merlin had given it to him. He had not made it his own but always attributed it to Merlin. So we present you with an image. A lilac flame burns over the golden bowl. In the center of the flame, there is a still point of brilliant, pure light. The bowl gives off a blue light. It sits on the ground in a grassy meadow. On this golden bowl is a pattern, symbols or glyphs of the zodiac, which run around the bowl. They face outward, and each is enclosed in a hexagram, except Capricorn which is enclosed in a pentagram. The top single point of the pentagram points upwards. A blue light surrounds the bowl. The flame sits above. The Star blazes at its center. Behind it all are two swords. One points up, from Earth to Heaven; one faces down, from Heaven to Earth. Bring this image into the center of your being."

We breathe in silence to this new image, then Blaise finishes up business for the night. "We would like you to bring the Grail to the Tor tomorrow through this image and sit facing Pointer's Ball, if you wish."

Wolfram von Eschenbach evidently knew what he talking about when he said of the Grail, "A troop left it on earth and then rose high above the stars, if their innocence drew them back again." So that sly, innocent troop of Blaises has launched me on the Grail Quest. I sit here on Glastonbury Tor under their auspices about 75 feet down from the tower. It's a relatively secluded spot where I can't be seen from the top although I am rivettingly obvious to anybody looking up from the Tor's base. Nobody seems to be walking along the trail behind me today, as if it is invisibly cordoned off. It's as if Blaise shooed everyone off the Tor today for an hour so I can get on with my questing.

I've done the new Grail visualization and examined the twelve zodiacal symbols on the rim of the Grail bowl, beginning with Leo. A blaze of sunlight suddenly cuts through the clouds, so I know things are beginning. I find myself standing in a grassy field. At the far end is a large, white building with a spire. Mountains surround the field. I walk across the field carrying the Grail regalia of bowl, swords, flames, star, but before I reach the white house, I encounter a smaller, darker house with the number 8 printed on its doorpost. I remove the numeral and put it in the Grail bowl. I grew up in a house whose street number was eight. Suddenly this dark house collapses, and I notice the wood is rotten.

Now I stand on a cliff overlooking a plain, and there's the white house again several miles away. I have an uncomfortable feeling I'm expected to fly to that house, like Carlos Castaneda when he had to jump off a cliff to prove his mastership. I don't especially mind, as I enjoy flying in dreams; on the other hand, I don't like heights, which means anything less than 39,000 feet, because when you're that high up it's pointless worrying about it, or anything more than four feet, which is low enough to safely jump. I pretend I'm diving off a board into a warm pool and, thus launched from the Tor, I extend myself through thought to this mobile white house, hoping it doesn't move again before I get there. It doesn't. Where my thoughts go, there fly I—this is the key to inexpensive mobility in this business. My body, meanwhile, is happily rooted on the solid earth of the Tor, discounting the fact it's a hollow hill. Castaneda had it harder. He had to jump with his body and hope he could wing it across the abyss.

I stand before the door of this white house with the number 10 on its doorframe. I knock, and a *Yeti* answers. He sports a pendant at his left breast, a gold leaf. He hands it to me, and it becomes a long, sharp sword. I open my eyes, which are back on the Tor in my head where they belong, and note that a shaft of sunlight illuminates a spot in the fields below the Tor, more or less where my house stands in this other dimension. The light shaft sweeps fifty feet to the left, then disappears as the clouds thicken again. Behind me, dwarfing St. Michael's tower, stand several hefty angels with open, flaming wings.

My next house call is Chalice Well, where I sit near the Lion's Head with a yew tree at my back and an apple tree on either side. Before me there is a large doorway without a door. Inside, the blackness is dense, but, as I enter, four men walk past. One is Russell, one is a close friend, two are acquaintances. Without hesitation, I lop off their heads with my *Yeti* sword, and they tumble into a wicker basket, turning into apples. I transfer the apples into the Grail bowl and hope this little transaction doesn't give my friends a headache. My apple-picking concluded, it's time to leave, and, as I reach the gatehouse, Russell, head-intact, says to me, "You look absolutely shell-shocked. What have you been up to?"

"Giving my friends a stiff neck, I should think, including you. Where have you been? How did you know I was finished?"

"Well, I was at Tom Quickham's memorial service. He says he didn't like dying and it took him a long time to adjust, but now he's very busy and they almost didn't give him the time off to come to his service."

I am unaccountably exhausted for the rest of the day and can't manage much more than the occasional writhe on my bed. My friends may have lost their heads but it is I who has the headache. Berenice opens my bedroom door and says Blaise has arrived and wishes to have a word with me.

"We are pleased with your progress and your efforts today, but we recommend that you use our energy more," Blaise begins. "It is limitless. You try too hard and exhaust yourself with your finite energy. Call on us. We wish to be used by you in this work. We recommend you do not use your finite energy for the research you're involved in. We have much to do together. We do not wish you to be depleted by your efforts. It is only superfluous. Do not use yourself up. If you need practical advice on how to call on us, then we can share this with you. What is the highest you can conceive of?"

"In my present state, nothing."

"Good. Call nothing into yourself. Nothing can never be depleted. Nothing contains everything. If you invoke nothing, visualize it, think of it, be it. Then you become a space into which all energy, extension of thought, can be poured. Do not use your head too often in your research. You cannot carry what you call the voltage there. By the way, you seem a little cloudy tonight."

"I can't imagine why. Would you explain what happened to me at Chalice Well today?"

"One step at a time. What is the question underneath all this?"

"I suppose it's about those apples."

"There is much difference between a concept and the fruition of a concept. Fruition knowledge is that condition in which what is known is turned to fruit. This is most serious and most amusing, as you learned today. Fruition knowledge is what you are close to within your experience even though you have a strong temptation to externalize it all, even when we place the fruit in the bowl. Perhaps now your question comes clearer?"

"It doesn't."

"The four apples are the four aspects of the way you perceive yourself. They are mirrors you find acceptable. What is your question?"

"I'm stuck."

"Ah-hah! Call on the nothing. We are the black sphere of stable consciousness. We leave but will return."

"These Zen Master angels!" I say, nearly fuming but laughing as well. "They brush off all my questions then ask me what is my question."

"You seem cloudy tonight, Grail Knight," says Russell, imitating Blaise's slow, deep delivery. "Oh yes, Blaise, it was all the Guinness I drank to relax after being exhausted from doing your adventures all day. Well, you should call on us for nothing. We're good for nothing,

Grail Knight!"

When our laughter subsides, I'm astonished to find I'm no longer dead tired but actually feel peppy and energetic as if I had slept a full night. Maybe there is something to Blaise's nothing.

"We return. Things look much better since we left. In fact, possibly a bit better than over here. A friend of ours lost several feathers today. You have no idea how much trouble the Concorde gives us. Oh dear. If you could only see the mess. Feathers everywhere. They don't even see us. Anyway, sorry to bring you our little troubles. Are there any more questions?"

"I rest my case for tonight," I answer.

"Your case is not complete. We find you guilty. We sentence you to infinite joy."

"Oh no. Not that."

"Yes, that. No contrast, just joy."

"No Guinness?"

"No Guinness. Just joy."

"Well, maybe I do have a question. What's the difference between a Zen Master and an angel?"

"A Zen Master has properties which angels do not. We hold such beings in great awe. They can get off the Wheel. They can remove themselves. When we get human form again, we will become Zen Masters."

"Does that mean my Zen Master was an angel before he was born?"

"Don't be silly. He wouldn't like you to suggest such a thing. Then again, he wouldn't not like it either. Hmmmfff."

At this point I involuntarily express a loud belch.

"Too many beans, Grail Knight," says Blaise.

"No, I didn't have any beans for dinner."

"Oh yes you did."

"No, really, I didn't have miso soup or tofu or beans all day." But my protest is drowned out as we laugh until our stomachs hurt.

"And so, it's been a long day in the sun," says Blaise. "We need, ohhh...a bath. We're going over to the Dead Sea for a dip. See you later. Our love, wish you were here, Blazing Star."

27

GRAIL KNIGHTS ARE LIKE DOCTORS, ALWAYS ON CALL

ear is rising like a mist, chilling me. For the last two hours, I've been sitting in meditation in the room just beyond the livingroom, which we've converted into a *zendo*, concentrating on the Grail image. I'm wearing a thick shirt, vest, and wool sweater, but I can't shake off the cold that envelops me. My breath rides out my body's shivering, but the unaccountable fear disturbs me more. Waves of fear and anxiety break on my shoulders like astral surf. During walking meditation, I even felt afraid of my shadow, cast against the wall. I sit on my cushion as unease stares ambivalently back at me. My skin is vibrating audibly. Something feels intimidatingly close. Even the thought of angels puts me on edge. I've tried breathing with Love from Above to the Grail, but all I can see are icicles on a doorway and my breath feels cold.

Everybody has gone out for a couple of hours, so I have the house—and my fears—to myself. I light a fire in the grate in the livingroom and continue my meditation in front of the flames. I don't understand this. Sitting is usually the safest place on Earth. With forty million angels on my side, what do I have to be afraid of? Yet here I am, shivering, looking anxiously over my shoulder for that bogeyman to spring out of the closet and get me. It takes me an hour of practically sitting *in* the fire to warm up. It may be September in England but it hasn't grown *that* cold outside at night. Soon after, Russell and Berenice return, put the kids to bed, and have a good laugh at my overdressed discomfort. Then Blaise pays us a much-needed visit. "Blaise, how come I'm freezing?"

"You're not. The lilac flame vibrates very quickly and can be cold. When the lilac flame draws near and penetrates your being, the energy and extension in thought can be construed, or misinterpreted, as cold. This is only a misunderstanding. Remember that at all times we come only as love. Fear is a label, a thought-form, associated within memory with sensations of an unpleasant nature. There is, in reality, no tangible objective phenomena called fear. It either exists in the past or in the future. It is impossible in consciousness to penetrate in the present into what you call fear.

"Each of the experiences that is given to you at this time is an unfoldment of your being. The sharing and the warmth and the consciousness of which you are a part brings to the surface memories from the past to be exorcised from your being to enable you to stand clearly in your own light. The relevance of our love is the context for all that takes place during this time for you. Only when, in the nature of your own individuating consciousness, you become separate from the totality of experience possible for you will it be necessary for you to exorcise similar phenomena from your personal history. We come to wipe away anything that could possibly be labelled as fear. Never see it as an investment worthy of your identity. Never allow yourself to put the 'I' in front of fear, to say, I am afraid. We are your Blazing Star."

Alright. Let's say nobody in particular was frightened a long time ago in the future for no good reason. Anyway, I'm feeling a lot warmer now.

The next morning I'm off to bring the Grail to Arthur's Courtyard. Berenice drops me off on her way to visit a client. I sit on the bench across the little waterway that bisects the Courtyard. I breathe with Love from Above to the Grail image and place my awareness inside the Star in the lilac flame that rises up to my head inside. I'm interrupted by the worry that maybe I should be sitting under the yew tree again, but when I relocate there and spend ten minutes re-establishing the image, I'm not convinced and return to this bench again. Finally, I get down to business.

Four women appear and sit on the bench opposite me. One is Berenice, one is my mother, one is a past girlfriend, one is a local acquaintance, but none has sufficiently privileged status to escape decapitation. Four heads plunk into the Grail bowl. If I get enough apples, I'll make cider. Most of the visions the Grail Knights had were induced from intoxication by Somerset's hard cider, Russell once quipped. Still in doubt, I sit on the other bench and see if I can pick any more apples. My brother appears as a young teenager, accompanied by Wellesley Tudor Pole as an elderly gentleman. Respectfully, I chop off their heads. That gives me ten apples. Twelve, I should think, completes the set. In the evening, Blaise clarifies my experiences in the apple orchard.

"Each apple is the fruit of your experience. Each has been an acceptable mirror for your experience. There are two others. Focus your attention on your process. Much can be, will be, revealed to you. There are four aspects within your practice that you should remember. They are called the Four Foundations of Mindfulness. We suggest you refer to these foundations. It is essential for your process. In Christian terms, there are four apostles: Matthew, Mark, Luke, John. The four worlds, or Zoas, are clearly expressed by William Blake. We suggest that you look into the fourfold nature of Man in these various expressions. It will illuminate something within the context of your process and your consciousness at this time.

"We cannot, will not, are not able to do too much for you. We will, wherever possible, assist in clarifying or assimilating for you. We are, within the context of presenting information that isn't related to your personal experience, somewhat tied down by the nature of that extension in thought contained in your question. But always, we attempt to point to the process. The more you remember the process, the more clarity will be yours. We come with love. We attempt, when you wish, to facilitate, where possible, the process for you. The Grail is available. It is waiting. Be prepared. Everything is relevant at this time, although some thoughts, feelings, and visions are more relevant than others. Can we ask you a question? What is the Grail?"

Oh, oh. A trick question. They've just lobbed me the kind of brambly inquiry that has caught up far more wily Grail Knights than I, like Parsifal, and gotten them chucked out of the Grail Castle, visualizations and everything. I see the bowl, the flame, the whole of the Grail image, then I realize with a blush that I know *about* the Grail but I do not *know* the Grail.

"Ahhh. Good. Hear the sound. See the light. Touch the warmth. Put simply, Grail means truth. Examine the rest of the word, for in it lies can be found when you spell it backwards. Liar."

"I'd like you to facilitate some clarification, if possible. What is the story about Arthur's Courtyard?"

"Arthur's Courtyard was designed under guidance through inspiration in conscious light to sacred dimensions made with sacred measurements. It will be used in times to come as a meeting place between your side and the other. It is a place which is unusual on the Earth. We hope one day it will be used by you and the group with which you are to be involved. It was designed for groups like this. It was designed by us for use by you and others, before you and after you. The stairway between Arthur's Courtyard and the Lion's Head is not an ordinary stairway. If you climb the stairway, consciously aware of stepping on each step, there is an extraordinary experience available. We are happy that things progress, that your process deepens. We would like, if you wish, that you revisit the Well tomorrow. We leave you now as a group of stars on a lake of stars—many, many stars. We leave you as a Blazing Star in a lilac flame."

It's just after lunch and I'm back at the Lion's Head chopping block. I pluck a black tomato off a vine, put it in the Grail, then throw it out. That tomato will never turn into an apple. There's the clown behind the stone lion again and the angelic mirror, but this time it's steady, more like a glass door which I easily pass through. Inside, I overlook a round table, open in the center like a torus doughnut. Seated around the table are a dozen golden figures, mute and packaged like mummies or like C3PO, the chatty android in *Star Wars*. They have human form yet lack discernible facial features. I stand before one but can't bring the face into focus. The scene shifts and men ride horses through a thick mist. I'm lying on the ground looking up at mounted horsemen, my friends. I occupy that same red-bearded, stockier, older Celtic body I found myself in at Cadbury Castle. My beard is much greyer now and mailed armor confines my chest. A man familiar to me leans over me with concern.

"Bedivere," I whisper, slipping in and out of bodily consciousness; sometimes I float peacefully above my body, which seems to be mortally wounded. Bedivere takes my sword. I lie on a barge flat on my back. We approach the Tor across shallow waters. The marsh water is for me almost at eye level. Several women, robed in black, accompany me on the barge. One stands resolutely at the prow. I know it's Morgan. I'm dizzy, faint, drifting out of my body, only barely returning. Another woman turns to me: she's older, white-haired, maternal, but her face is otherwise obscured. Now I'm back before the round table of golden mummies, except before me stands the same Celtic Arthur whose body I have been occupying. Here he is in full vigorous manhood, with beard, tunic, and fierce green eyes. I bow, then lop off his head and toss it in the Grail.

An hour passes and nobody walks into this corner of the garden. Blaise does such a wonderful job as gatekeeper. In my physical body, I walk around to Arthur's Courtyard, pass through the gate, then slowly climb the fourteen stone steps. It makes me dizzy, as if I'm climbing a mountain trail. At the fourteenth step, there is an oak door with the number 20 in brass. I knock four times, then enter a king's court and walk slowly along a carpeted path to the king, seated at the far end and expecting me. I carry the Grail delicately and with concentration as if it's priceless china. People line the royal hall and survey my progress, as if there hasn't been a Grail Knight through here in a long time. Physically, I am walking up the garden path to the well, and, fortunately, nobody is around to ponder my eccentric behavior at this moment. The king is short, his head a bit squarish, his beard red, his hair long and straight, and he sports a gold crown. But he seems discontented, restless, unhappy, unhealthy, hurt somewhere. We look each other in the eye, then I retrace my steps, re-enter Arthur's Courtyard, and mount the stairs again.

This time the sensation is like arriving at a place similar to mountain-perched Montsegur in southern France along the Pyrenees. This was the famous Cathar stronghold and possibly the prototype for Eschenbach's wild Grail Castle mountain, Munsalvaesche. I knock, enter again, and proceed, as before, attentively, conscious of the hundreds of eyes intent on my progress towards the ailing monarch. Strangely, I feel like a serving woman bringing an old man a drink. I notice a crown sits on my head, too. Just ahead of me, a second king empties basins of light like milk onto the path and into my Grail bowl. When I reach the seated king, he gestures for me to walk around the well then take a seat next to him. Together, we survey the court, the flowers, the muralled walls, the courtiers, all of whom seem much happier now.

The Fisher King, after all, is the one on whose behalf the entire Grail Quest is undertaken. He is guardian of the Holy Grail and master of the Grail Castle, only he is maimed and incapacitated; his wound keeps him from enjoying the spiritual fruits of the Grail. He figures, in nearly all the medieval Grail stories. In Chretien de Troyes' version the Fisher King lies on a couch, "a handsome nobleman with grizzled locks;" he is very rich and courteous, cannot mount a horse, but occasionally goes out in a boat to fish. In *Perlesvaus*, Pelles the Fisher King is attended by twelve knights who are each one hundred years old, although they don't look a day over forty; they owe their youth and longevity to daily ministrations from the Grail. In another text, the Fisher King is "a tall and stalwart knight of a goodly age, a little grizzled;" he wears a golden crown, wields a royal scepter, and sports a large ruby ring: he is "so fair and courteous a man."

In the evening, Blaise gives me the dossier on the ailing king. "The Fisher King is an image that goes backwards and forwards in time. He was a prominent feature in Lemurian, Atlantean, Mycenean, Grecian, and Arthurian myths. He pertains to that aspect of consciousness that lies at the deepest level. The Fisher King rules over the deep past and the deep memories of the soul. His wounds are that which do not remember, contained in the root chakra energy center at the base of the spine. There, conscious energy is not manifest and cannot be brought to the crown. The Fisher King pertains to the different doorways in the soul and its relation to the deep past. The energy is released through a passage through these doorways for the development of soul life. Injury has closed down the access to this root energy that would reveal the soul's purpose and nature, its level of development, and the individual's present ability to penetrate that veil."

"I felt like I was a Grail Maiden carrying the Grail to the king. Could you explain her role in this?"

"The Fisher King is an aspect of consciousness in relation to the deep past. The Grail Maiden is the intuitive aspect freely available to penetrate into the soul lessons learned by the soul up to the present time, to gain access to the astral realm. Meeting the Grail Maiden on the etheric plane brings intuitive insight and wisdom pertinent to the soul's journey up to that point. We refer you to the Lady of the Lake as both the guardian of the astral realms and as another aspect of the Grail Maiden."

After Blaise leaves and Russell and Berenice go to bed, I sit in my room, empty my mind of thoughts, and breathe. If I don't have any more visions in the next ten minutes, I might even say I am legitimately practicing zazen. But that's not to be because I find myself at Arthur's Courtyard again with the Grail. Evidently Grail Knights are like doctors, always on call. A large group of people is assembled on the far side of the diagonal stream that bisects the Courtyard. Many I recognize, all in long, grey robes, arrayed in a spiral without visible end. My brother and Wellesley Tudor Pole are here in white robes, accompanied by angels. A curtain is drawn over this scene, and I understand that's all I get to see tonight. To be continued.

After these messages. I return with renewed diligence to my breathing, but I'm off again to the Lion's Head this time where I face the round table. Arthur is here before me, his head intact, grey-bearded, and beaming, and his companions are now revealed without their golden casements. A woman stands by Arthur's side, but I cannot see her face. Guinivere by any chance? Then another man catches my attention. He wears a silvery breastplate with an emblazoned red cross inside a white shield. Evidently, he's a Templar Knight. Then I'm supine on the mystic barge to Avalon again, still not dead. Two women stand at the prow, their hair swept back in the breeze, while the third woman, robed in shimmering white, will not turn around and reveal her face when I call out to her.

28

THE CRYSTAL CITY
INSIDE THE EMERALD

In the morning I sit under the apple tree with Celia and Edmund. We're playing a game. "Sit under this tree and don't move a muscle," I tell them. "When an apple drops, whoever gets it first wins. But you can't move at all until the apple starts to fall." They're a little dubious about the rules but willing to give it a try. Being with young children is a new, untested experience for me, and it's showing me a lot of my rough edges. Sometimes Edmund infuriates me the way he grabs my trousers and clings to me, not giving me any space. Sometimes Celia gets as intractable as a billy goat who will not budge from his chosen spot. We may be out on a walk and she stops; I pull, cajole, bribe, command, fume, joke, ignore, enunciate loudly, but Celia only digs herself in deeper. When she feels like it, the log jam suddenly breaks up and she runs free again and our walk resumes its progress towards or away from home or into mealtime or housecleaning.

When Russell and Berenice are away, I'm the babysitter, cook, cleaner, and general lion tamer. Berenice doesn't like it, but the kids do, so before sleep, but while they're tucked away in bed, I give them each a professional tickling. Celia snuggles under her duvet, calling out in a tiny, unconvincing voice with perfect intonation, "More bouncing, please." This means, bounce her on the bed like an elongated basketball, during which, inevitably, some tickling happens. "More tickling, please," she warbles in between bounces. Edmund is less forthright about the business. He curls up to protect his ticklish parts—his entire body—but often his big feet are left exposed; when the tickling and bouncing get riotous, he crawls under the bed, thinking he's out of range. Berenice, as I said, doesn't approve of this, fearing the bouncing will break the beds and the tickling will keep the kids awake. So we don't tell her. And we're not tickling or bouncing now, but sitting perfectly still and expectant, awaiting the drop of the first apple. More clever than patient, Celia shakes a limb and a half dozen apples tumble down on us. We scramble for them, breaking all the rules.

Berenice calls to us from the patio, reminding us it's time to leave for Hamdon Hill. This is a site new to us about twelve miles from Wick, possibly part of Corvus, the eagle, in the zodiac. According to Michael Beckett in *The Pyramid and the Grail*, the configuration of Glastonbury, Midsummer Hill (in the Malverns), Avebury (in Wiltshire), and Hamdon Hill (Somerset) represents what he calls "the Pyramid of Albion" and contains the Grail Castle. Hamdon Hill, specifically, says Beckett, is the entrance into the fabled Grail Castle that inhabits, invisible to us, the fourth dimension. "The medieval Christians and Tibetans have proposed that, from time to time, the spiritual dimension of heaven will come into focus—no, the solid reality—within the Pyramid of Albion." To Russell, this sounds like a good advertising pitch for an outing, so we're going to have a look for ourselves.

Hamdon Hill, we discover, has been heavily quarried, leaving it seriously pockmarked. At some point, it was made a public park and is today richly populated with picnickers and loud radios. A terrific gale picks up almost the moment we step out of the Citroen, fanning out trousers, jackets, and dresses like sails in full blow. Storm clouds settle over Glastonbury in the north and the rain falls in sheets, yet elsewhere the sky is unaccountably clear and unperturbed or only partly cloudy or only sluggishly overcast, depending on where we look. The weather has become a six ring circus, with one meteorological act following the next: first rain, now clearing, next clouds, then sunshine, followed by grey, sheeting rain.

We stagger about Hamdon Hill like kites straining to soar, finally securing ourselves to a bench facing north towards Glastonbury, although the closer-lying hills occlude the Tor. I look out over the broad valley that laps at the base of Hamdon Hill and see a brown-robed man—like the Othery inner dome attendant—holding a green pyramid. I turn to tell Russell, but he's just dashed off to collect Edmund who is flapping around like a paper bag over the knots of Hamdon Hill. It rains now with impressive ferocity. I scrunch myself tight up against the hard metal bench seat and turn up my collar. That's all the raincoat I can muster and, of course, I am instantly drenched. Rain smears my glasses and the cold wind raises goose bumps on my skin. Russell comes back within earshot. "What am I supposed to do now?" I holler. "What about the Grail Quest, man?" he hollers back, and the wind carries his belly laugh right into my wet frown. Right. The Quest. The very wet Quest. "Then stop this raining so I can tune in!" I shout imperiously to nobody in particular.

Sometimes it pays to shout, especially when your weathermen are angels who know how to play with the weather. In five minutes the sky has blown clear and calmed down, and warm sunshine pops into the sky like breakfast toast. Russell has collected Edmund, Celia, and Berenice and, as they troop past a hundred feet away, he shouts: "Miso soup for tired Grail Knights, this way." In closer range, he confides that Blaise wanted us to observe this flamboyant display of weather, almost as if to say, "Get a load of this, if you wish." We stop for a cream tea in Montacute where Russell tells me he saw the complete Blaise Grail image inside the same green pyramid I saw. This leaves me frowning because I see I gave barely half my attention to Blaise's pyramid and got distracted by the meteorological effects, except that's what Blaise wanted us to watch. But the real point of our windy visit to Hamdon Hill, we learn tonight, was simply to familiarize ourselves with its physical environment, so we would recognize it when Blaise brought us back. Still, I haven't been able to shake that edge of irritation and inadequacy, and when Berenice is late joining us tonight after Blaise arrives, my annoyance flares.

"We come as a sword," says Blaise, "as a pinpoint of light out of the tip of the sword. The light passes down each edge of the sword. We greet you all. We are pleased with things, but we recommend with our utmost love that you spend more time being still in all your forms of action. It is important now that you take your Grail bowl to your place of stillness for as long as you are able to breathe love into it. You are at a point that is very important in terms of what you, with us, are attempting to bring through at this time. We come as the sword form above to below. We come as the point of light at the tip of the sword, as the point of pure consciousness. Do not become interested in the images that arise from the bowl. Simply breathe love into the bowl. We will breathe with you."

After some moments of group breathing, Blaise says, "We wish, if you wish, to take you back to Hamdon Hill." At once we find ourselves at a triangulation marker, and at once I slip into the mists and confusion. I don't recognize this marker, and I cannot breathe with love and I feel annoyed, even furious, with not being able to see anything. Curse this myopia. Somehow I drift off into grey mists a hundred yards away from Russell and Berenice and I miss the whole show. Blaise tries to reorient me but already I'm filled with self-disgust and float disconsolately somewhere in the fog. I start berating myself. You'd think with all these hours of meditation—and I sat at least three hours today—I'd be able to see something, keep my eyes open in here and not get lost, and you'd think I wouldn't allow myself to get so peeved that I can't—and so forth.

"The stillness is the foundation," Blaise says. "Attitudes of expectancy, success and failure, can produce a minor irritability. We recommend that you do not concern yourself with expectancy, success or failure, but with the process. Concern yourself with the qualitative experience. We expect nothing. We expect less than nothing. You should relinquish all ideas of achievement. This makes space for something to happen qualitatively, an opportunity for something to be achieved. Be not concerned with what happens next. Do it now. Do it with quality. We leave you to discuss your experiences."

I still feel miserable, cranky, sulky, inadequate. You name the negativity, I'm feeling it. I try to shovel my way through the rubbish so we can piece together what Blaise has shown us at Hamdon Hill. "We were standing by that triangulation marker, though you seemed a lot less distinct than usual, looking pale and distressed," Russell says. "Hundreds of angels of various colors and sizes danced around us in a huge ring. It filled the hillside, like the fringes at the bottom of a lampshade. Blaise said he had brought some of their friends. There was a dome overhead with a brilliant white light like a bulb at the center. Light flowed down the sides of the dome in rivulets that changed color, from pale, pastel lilacs to a rainbow spectrum. The dome covered all of Hamdon like an upside down mixing bowl. How about you, love?" Russell says, turning to Berenice.

"There was a golden staircase. I climbed it, and, at the top, I saw an amorphous light being, although its arms seemed extended to me in welcome. It gave off such a happy, lovely feeling. The stars formed a dome and a kind of lacework knitted together with lines of light. Then I noticed a series of indigo squares on the landscape, like a patchwork quilt, and I had the curious feeling of peering into the Earth."

"Okay, Grail Knight, tell us what you saw," says Russell, chuckling mercilessly, knowing full well what a mess I made of the outing. "I know you saw something."

"Well, I found myself on this bench, separated from you guys. I noticed the gentle valley below us had turned into a huge, grey canyon. Behind me stretched a horizontal vale of yellow fog. I approached this fog and saw an Army tank filled with liquid light. 'This is one of ours, though what you see is not how we perceive it,' Blaise said to me."

"I saw that, too," says Russell, "but it seemed to me more like an upside down mushroom with tendrils spilling out from its top."

"Then I saw a green pyramid in the mist," I continue. "It gave off a steady, green aura and its surface was highly geometrical, as if made of cut squares of green glass."

"Oh. Thank you very much for reminding me," Berenice says. "I started to enter the Earth. There was a shaft of light that went down to a city. It was futuristic in style, a crystalline city, with roads of light and buildings that vibrated. They were fluid yet solid and very bright and gave off a blue aura like electricity. The green pyramid sat like a cover on the crystal city. Inside the pyramid was a huge deva, like a presiding deity. Then Blaise brought us back."

"I think that city exists in the future," Russell comments.

I retreat to my room for the night, feeling miserable, and crawl under the duvet. My lack of humility stares me coldly in the face. I squirm and hide my head under the pillow because I don't want the angels to see me behaving so poorly. Why couldn't I see everything? I wait for the Lethean wave of sleep to roll me into unconsciousness where I will no longer be such an unhappy Grail Knight who can't see crystal cities inside green pyramids when he's travelling on the wings of angels. The next morning and most of the day brings me no respite from the gloom. Depression and crankiness sit on me like a stagnant weather pattern and I hardly leave my room all day.

This grey mist has really gotten out of hand, I declare to myself around teatime, and I sit down on the meditation cushion to see if I can break it up. It takes me ages of effort to breathe as Love from Above to the Grail bowl. I have to empty nearly every bottle of vintage stock from the Love from Above cellars to fuel the process. Finally, things get warm and the sun breaks through, and I'm so relieved that I forget to be excited when I find myself back at Hamdon Hill in front of the green pyramid. The Grail image of bowl and lilac flame does indeed reside inside the pyramid while the Star within the lilac flame is effulgent. Down the canyon is Berenice's crystal city, but, when I try flying down for a reconaissance, I'm yanked back up here like a yo-yo. I examine the Hamdon Hill dome from inside and out. Inside, it's like the globular lampshade over my bed and its 100 watt bulb; from above, it's like a diaphanous jack-o-lantern hung on a string over the hill.

The phone rings downstairs, and I hobble down the stairs because my legs are asleep. It's Russell, and when I tell him I've recovered and I'm sorry for being such a sulk, he laughs. "Blaise didn't mind. It's good to have an angel who takes a positive attitude. Blaise always looks on the bright side of things. I just wanted to ring you to say we're heading for Chalice Well and we'll put in a good word with the boys for you, okay love." I decide to join them.

I walk down to the railroad trestle, climb the fence, and sit down between two stout willow trees on the verge of a lush, green pasture. The westering sun is warm and friendly. As I relax into my breathing and complete the Grail image, I'm back at Arthur's Courtyard watching a procession of angels file past in pairs. Russell, Berenice, and I sit on the bench. I move to the Lion's Head, where a six foot square crystal unfolds itself like a lotus revealing its jewel of light within. I move up to the well and empty my Grail bowl. Immediately, it's refilled by that same kingly attendant who replenished me the other day. The Archangel Michael stands magnificently transparent on the Tor, like a poised eagle whose wings enfold the tower. I open my eyes and smile at the sunshine-washed field.

The wind comes up, the sun slips behind a cloud, a dragon-fly nips me on the head: time to go home and make miso soup for dinner. But thank you, dear dragon-fly, for reminding me of the four foundations. My body is a prodigy of mosquito bites. This is the contemplation of the body. I am variously buffeted by sympathies, antipathies, and indifference. This is the contemplation of feelings. I exhibit states of distraction, anger, delusion, sulkiness, self-pity, excitement, and insight. This is the contemplation of mind. I spend my waking hours being entertained or disappointed by *makyo*. This is the contemplation of mind objects. Thus speaketh the Buddha, roughly paraphrased for the Grail Quest. "The only way that leads to the attainment of purity," teaches the *Satipatthana Sutra*, "to the overcoming of sorrow and lamentation, to the end of pain and grief, to the entering of the right path, and to the realization of Nirvana, are the Four Foundations of Mindfulness."

Blaise makes a brief, as it were, cameo appearance tonight, obviously squeezing us in between other cosmic appointments, God only knows where and with whom. As they arrive, and as the angelic dimmer switch is gently, blissfully, turned on stronger, a man hands me a pink rose, half-open. I place it in the Grail bowl. "We indicate the lilac flame of transmutation," says Blaise, getting to the point. "We place a flame on each of your shoulders. We place a flame above your head. We place a flame in your belly. It is a qualitative transmutation flame of a very pale lilac. We ask you a question. What is in your Grail bowl?"

"A pink rose with a long, green stem."

"What is inside the rose?"

The flower petals open like two cupped hands raised in prayer to reveal a large, flat crystal like a city seen from a distance. The crystal city of Hamdon Hill, in my hands!

"So we leave you all with this," says Blaise, who knows how to please. An egg floats through space into my Grail bowl. "Hold this carefully in your Grail. We leave as the still point of light at the tip of the sword."

29

Dancing on the Black Bowling Ball

I have a little more apple picking to do. A day has passed, and here I am once again at the entrance to Chalice Well. At the top of the *vesica piscis* spillpond, an angel holds open a doorway for me. I pass through into another version of Chalice Well suffused with light forms, in which everything—fountains, flora, angels—are diaphanously crystalline. In Arthur's Courtyard, I examine the crystal jewel within the pink rose that Blaise gave me last night, but it's impenetrable. There is an egg in the Grail this morning, last night's gift from Blaise; it contains the dark outline of a human fetus floating in amniotic bliss, arms and legs extended. Somebody is pregnant. I mount the fourteen steps to the Lion's Head and enter the Grail Castle. The Fisher King gestures to the well. My Grail bowl fills with light. His throne is topped by a golden rotunda; like an igloo, the rotunda swells up at the end of a long, tubular hallway. The Fisher King gives me a pink rose.

I'm becoming something of a florist this week. It's nice of the Fisher King to remember me with roses because, as a Grail Knight, I can tell you, this whole business of the Quest is on his account. As Malory tells us, long ago the Rich Fisher King misused the sword of King David, who had it from the giant Goliath, and grievously wounded himself—by the Dolorous Stroke—in the upper thigh, such that he had to retire in pain and immobility, spending his latter days languishing upon a couch inside the Grail Castle. He's known thereafter as the Maimed Fisher King. Every day the Grail is brought before him in regal, though solemn, procession, but he cannot be healed.

In Eschenbach's version, it's Anfortas, Lord of Munsalvaesche (his name, from the French *enfertez*, means "infirmity") who is also called the Sorrowful Angler. Anfortas is miserable; great fires are banked up in his sitting room, he's heavily rugged up, but, "the malady racking him to the point where he had to open his eyes, he was made to live against his will and not die." We learn of his "frequent sighs" and "doleful glances;" he's a man beggared of joy, dragging himself through a wretched existence. The countryside, which depends on his royal energy for its fruition, becomes the Wasteland. The connection between Avalon, the realm of light, and Logres, the physical world, becomes severed; Logres becomes the impoverished land. The Grail Knight's job is to find the Grail, locate the Fisher King, ask him the right questions, apply the sword correctly to his wound, then serve him the Grail. Restored, he becomes once again the Rich Fisher King and the Wasteland becomes a Paradise, again.

Theoretically, any Grail Knight could do the job, but, frankly, you're more likely to succeed if your name is Parsifal or Galahad. Galahad was the only knight who could stand the heat of the Siege Perilous at the Round Table. This was a chair that burned everyone's fanny upon contact, except Galahad's. Naturally, only a jejune Grail Knight takes this literally. "The Siege Perilous is a precarious position," Blaise says. "Insight leads to knowledge; knowledge is information; and information is energy. If the energy is not used for the good, then it is perilous for the knight. So Galahad was the only one who could handle this condition safely. Galahad is the knight whose consciousness has reached the point of true insight." Only Galahad can heal the Fisher King's wound, which was precipitated by the Dolorous Stroke. "The Dolorous Stroke is simply insight used for oneself in a separatist sense rather than insight used for the good of many through the crucifixion of self," Blaise adds.

Overhead, in the Fisher King's world, the sun blazes happily in a blue sky, while in the Grail Knight's world, the sky is a slatey obscuration of drizzle. He's got good weather and a bum leg; I've got bad weather and good health—so I guess I serve him. I sit down at the yew tree bench, and, before I consider what's next, another head, the twelfth, rolls into the Grail. It's the white-haired, silent woman from the funeral barge, the one I called out to with no response. It's awful when you can't tell your girlfriend from your mother, but, at this point, I'm fifty-fifty that she is either Guinivere in old age or Arthur's mother, Ygraine. As her head turns into an apple, a lavender blossom drifts into the bowl. Back in Arthur's Courtyard, I stand on the "embodied" side of the diagonal channel as if pressing my nose against a pliant, transparent membrane. Then I cross over.

My brother hugs and kisses me. An angel gleams from each of his blue eyes. Tudor Pole clasps me affectionately on the shoulders. I tell him I am reading his published letters to Rosamond Lehman, and he chuckles. I am very happy to see them both. With Tudor Pole I feel an uncanny kinship, the kind of fondness a young man has for a wise, kindly uncle who taught him much in his childhood. Seeing my long-dead brother on the other side has a liberating effect, as if the last scar from the deep wound of loss is transmuted into joy. "Your brother is with you on the other side," says Blaise in the evening back at Wick. "Later you will understand why he crossed over early. It pertains to a mutual function. His death was your initiation into an intimate experience with death and the dying process." It's hard to focus on dying, because Blaise is in our midst with forty million twinkles in their eyes.

"We have had a good day together. We are most pleased that you have seen us well today. We present things in many forms, much of which you miss. We suggest you open your eyes and see the many forms in which we come to you at this time. Each has a message for you, should you be able to see. Each contributes something in what we call extension of thought to what you are looking for. Each brings a gift from us. Look behind the forms. See us through their eyes. We are waiting to talk to you through their forms. Do not separate the quest from our journeys together, either in what you call your thought body or physical base or when we come to you in many forms. We will warn you when not to open yourselves, but unless you are warned, be open, not to talk, but to listen, to receive. You listen to us, see through their eyes—the ones we bring before you. We are concerned that everything is seen as part of the process, that nothing is outside your process, even the bubbles in the sink, if you can bring your attention to that point of receptivity. It is a wonderful gift. See us in the doing, the listening, the activity, the quality, It matters most that you are not concerned with success or failure. We pour a blue fluid into your bowls. Hear the sound. Are we not happy together?"

"It's a groove, Blaise. The monks in the medieval Grail Castles were never this loose and easy," I chirp, perhaps intemperately.

"Now we will do a little dance for you," says Blaise. Big, white angels do a soft-shoe shuffle on a glistening spherical surface. "By the way, several of us are wearing sunglasses. It is very bright where we are." Six big, white bird-angels with extended wings sport Blues Brothers wraparounds.

Berenice doesn't quite catch the mood or is perhaps a trifle Mary Poppinsish about frivolity among angels and asks, "What should I do to allow more space in my day to stay centered?"

"We suggest you find it in all activity or nonactivity. We would suggest a couple of occasions. You find it easy to make space for yourself in the garden. You are contented there."

"Thank you very much," Berenice says.

"We haven't finished yet."

"Sorry."

"Thank you very much. We are just looking where else to suggest. You could walk to the railway trestle and wait for the trains. Try it. You could wave to the people as they go by. Obvious, really. We will do another dance for you. What a good day we are having!"

There is a whooshing sound, and a ring of crazy, smiling Blaise angels begin their circle dance. One Blaise lifts his white skirt to expose cute golden ballet slippers, then he pirouettes on his big toe while the other Blaises, impressed, applaud and nod their heads. "Can we answer any more questions tonight?" one of them asks.

"You just answered one I've been wondering about secretly for a month," I declare. "You know, whether angels make jokes."

"Surprise, surprise! Aren't we unpredictable! We would like to think so, if we could think. Reticent? You think we won't take you seriously if you ask us that question?"

"Alright. Do you like our idea for a movie, the one we're calling *We Roll Towards You*. We only have a few gags worked out so far, but they're not half bad."

"Yes, we do. Now you see what else you are here for. When you cross the ocean again, we will bring you what is needed for this project. It is only a short hop for us. Distance is no object in our business. As you know, we are most happy to be with you tonight but, believe it or not, we have some very serious business elsewhere. We leave you as a dancing, Blazing Star."

I feel as if Blaise has poured champagne all over me, all through me, and I'm floating in happy bubbles, every cell of me. Russell feels the same and we break open the Guinness. Soon we're floating on a froth of stoutish mirth. Russell imitates Blaise and says, "Wow, look at Berenice's pink socks! We really need our sunglasses to appreciate those. Please tell the Grail Knight, if you wish, that he's looking scruffy again. Too many holes in the sweater. Berenice, you're being *morganic* again." A *morganic* remark, as Russell and I know well, is the kind of nonsequitur that curves away from meaning into outer space, an inscrutable comment, delivered in perfect British locution that loops and grins idiotically out of reach just as one jumps for it mentally. A *merlinish* remark, which is Russell's speciality, is pre-emptive, auto-cratic, wittily derisive, ironic, rude, such as saying to dinner guests regarding your life partner, "Most nights I go to bed with a head-ache." A Grail Knight dutifully records all morganic and merlinish remarks as overheard in the Grail Castle.

Celia and Edmund have left their box of toy cars and trucks on the coffee table. Russell sets up the tracks, and we take our sports cars out for a zip along the mahogany freeway. Everything is going great until, in an excess of sport, my Jaguar rounds the rim of Russell's glass of Guinness on only two wheels, loses it, and crash plops into the foam. Russell is displeased with this demonstration of *levitony*— a species of giddiness inspired by angels—and says, "You shouldn't drive after drinking, you know."

It's two-thirty in the morning, Russell and Berenice have gone to bed, but I'm wide awake and full of *levitony* without mercy. I found a box of cigars in the cabinet and am now puffing away like a mogul. I have Stevie Winwood's *Arc of a Diver* quite loud on the stereo wired to my brain through headphones. Blaise sits with me in the room, several of them smoking cigars, tapping their slippered feet in tune to the music delivered to their ears by headphones. We are *levitonious*. I float on a mellow lake of joy watching a dozen, maybe a dozen dozen Blaises disco in sunglasses to "Spanish Dancer," my favorite on Winwood's album. The beat is slow and seductive and frankly I have no idea what the lyrics are about. The Blaises shuffle about, playing electric guitars, turning their sunglassed heads towards me, intent on the music. But as they dance, their bodies change into iridescent rainbows, then into light swirls that expand like raging fires into fantastic mercurial forms dancing on a tremendous black sphere appearing suddenly on the horizon of my mirth. As the Black Bowling Ball emerges into full sphericity, rolling towards me, the Blaises start manifesting their true form as immense, majestic light beings with stars in their eyes and galaxies in their palms, and I shiver in my chair.

30

Lunch at the Fairy Dell

ate in the morning, we pile into the Citroen and set off for London. We're going to Gatwick to pick up Hilary, a friend of Russell and Berenice. She lives in Cambridge but is returning from Florence after a fortnight's holiday. On route, I'm delighted to see there is no let-up in the Blaise antics.

A single engine Cessna lifts off the ground alongside us and there's Blaise waving from the tail, with helmet, goggles, and parachute. A motorcylist overtakes us and there's Blaise in the passenger's seat, grinning, with arms and wings raised. He slips off in a backwards tumble, stands up, shrugs his shoulders, flies off. Entering London, we drive through a district with huge, crescent-shaped apartment buildings three stories high. A Blaise stands statuesque in every window: hundreds of Blaise sentinels, immaculate winged draperies festooned with angelic twinkles. At the British Museum Reference Room, with its elegant rotunda and wraparound bookshelves, several hundred Blaise scholars pore over their texts, each wearing lilac half-frame glasses.

Outside, facing Russell Street, Blaise further entertains me as I wait for Berenice to pick me up. A taxi rolls by with Blaise in the front seat, a wing around the cabbie. Another taxi cruises past with Blaise sprawled luxuriously on the hood. A third taxi turns into the road with three Blaises in pin-stripe suit in the backseat reading the *Financial Times*. At the corner of Russell and Bloomsbury, Blaise wraps wings around a young strolling couple. Another Blaise consoles a woman standing dejectedly in her doorway. Another Blaise overshadows the roasted-chestnut vendor. When I discover I don't have forty-pence for a packet, the man kindly gives me the nuts for half-price, with Blaise winking at me behind him. "Blaise just sliced three lives off that guy's karma for helping a Grail Knight in distress," quips Russell when I relate the incident later.

At Gatwick, there is Blaise, many of them, in line at the check-in counter. The Blaises are impeccably, smartly dressed in business suits, slick executives from Fleet Street, except for the wings and the fact they stand eight feet tall and look very bleached. Each Blaise carries a leather attaché case; when they open these for inspection at the gate, there is a blinding burst of light from inside; when the bedazzlement subsides, there is only a single pair of neatly folded lilac socks inside the case. The luggage tag reads: "Blaise. From Not Too Far." The Blaises—there are hundreds now in an orderly queue—pass through a special departure gate labelled "Angels, if they wish" that opens directly onto the runway. They do a circle dance, then pirouette into the London airspace like corkscrew helicopters. When I narrate these events to Russell, he is skeptical: "You must be joking. Blaise flies only Concorde."

Then we picked up Hilary. Ah, Hilary. She's fortysomething, winsome, full-bodied, with long auburn hair, an acupuncturist living in Cambridge and a student of Tibetan Buddhism. Back at Wick, I saw her outside through the second floor hall window. She was at the end of the garden doing a headstand in the late afternoon sunlight; as she stood upside down, her sweatshirt top fell down and her breasts swayed free like fish streaming towards a pillar. In the evening, as we have our tea before the fire, she sprawls comfortably supine, her face turned towards the flames, her breasts a soft mystery under her sweater. Pull me down on top of you, love, and wrap your silken legs around my back, I think to myself. Yes, the Grail Knight is in trouble. Cold shower required.

The Irish hero Cuchulainn had the same problem—breasts—according to the *Tain Bo Cuailnge*. It seems the otherwise invincible Cuchulainn was advancing on King Conchobor's stronghold at Emain, threatening to spill the blood of everyone in the court unless a sufficiently brave man stepped forth to challenge him. "Naked women to him," ordered Conchobor. The women of Emain came forth, led by Mugain, Conchobor's wife, "and they stripped their breasts at him. 'These are the warriors you must struggle with to-day,' Mugain said." Cuchulainn was undone and hid his countenance. "Immediately the warriors of Emain seized him and plunged him in a vat of cold water." The sizzling Cuchulainn burst the vat asunder and had to be dunked in two more cold tubs until his concupiscence finally cooled down.

Around midnight, my bedroom door and Hilary's both suddenly blow open. We both appear in the hallway to see what's happened. She's in a nightgown and I'm in long underwear. We laugh then go downstairs for a pot of tea to discuss the coincidence. "I was thinking of talking to you but I didn't know what to say," Hilary says. "The thought crossed my mind, too," I say, filling the kettle, hoping she doesn't know about Mugain.

During meditation this morning, my thoughts rove to the Fairy Dell and I feel urged to invite Hilary out there for an expedition. But I can't quite bring myself to say, "Oh, Hilary. By the way. An angel friend of mine wants me to take you to this fascinating hill nearby to meet a bunch of fairies." My pride intact and my fantasy world undivulged, I set off on my own. A miniature white palace stands on the far side of the Fairy Dell mound, attended by a generous population of fairies. A gnome gestures to me from the top of the hill where it borders the woods; he wants me to follow him into the glade. Inside, he points to a circular bower bounded by beeches and suffused with green, as if the site sits inside an emerald shaft of light. Sitting down, I'm immediately swarmed by a host of fairies and a much larger female spirit that, to me, resembles Snow White. "Don't be silly, that's a sylph," Blaise whispers.

I offer them all the contents of my Grail, like setting out a bowl of milk for kittens. Then the gnome accompanies me out of the woods and chuckles when I stop to gorge myself on the wild blackberries. When I reach the lane again, Russell, Berenice, Hilary, and the kids are fanned out across Wick Hill picking berries. Since my palms and face are already berry-stained and as I remember Wick Hill sports an aggressive community of biting insects this week, I wave them off.

"We don't want any suffering Grail Knights on our hands," shouts Russell. "Why not go home and tend the Grail Castle. Make us a nice miso soup but will you please sauté the onions longer this time so they don't get our wind up."

When Blaise visits later, he suggests I revisit the Fairy Dell tomorrow. "Your gift to the fairies will be replenished twice over. The gift you made will relate to the devic realms. Made without our suggestion, it will bring much support for you in the future as the word has been passed amongst them." With Blaise's imprimatur, I'm emboldened to invite Hilary to come see the fairies. It's too late for her anyway: she's been exposed to Blaise. Her life is now forfeit; she is condemned to angelic joy and paradox.

Around two-thirty the next afternoon, we set off. As we enter the dirt track leading to the Dell, a man with two dogs passes us and one dog snarls. "We have company," says Hilary. I don't understand her at first, then I realize she's referring to the gnome tagging along behind us. When we reach the emerald mound of the Fairy Dell, the sylph and a cluster of fairies and the gnome escort us into the woods. We pass through a devic doorway then sit, physically, near the brow of the hill, only fifty feet from a wheatfield. The weather grows windy, cold, damp, threatening a storm. The fairies ring round us while the gnome sits cross-legged on a tree stump, smoking a pipe with the air of an amused guardian. Fairies drift down among us like autumn leaves. The sylph sits opposite us like a chaperone. A large male with little horns on his head like cowlicks appears, his skin dappled in green leaves, his face wrinkled and mischievous, his hand clutching a curious flute. Pan!

I offer Pan an apple and give the sylph a flower, then I set out the Grail again for the fairies to lap up its light. Pan gestures for me to follow him through a door into a large tree. Inside, there is a guardian: a tall, thin man with a long, somber face, long nose, a dark stovepipe hat. I breathe Love from Above to him and I pass into a bright room. Here several tiers of musicians in white garb strum guitars. One guitarist shows me his instrument: behind the strings in the hollow of the guitar's box is a mirror reflecting a woman's face. I don't recognize her.

Returning to Hilary, I find our devic friends have disappeared. But someone—I can't discern any features, face, or sense of identity—gives us presents. I get a biscuit like melba toast with a dark crust, then a handful of biscuits tumbles into the Grail. A white marble with a blue streak inside. A palm-size Blazing Star. A red ribbon tied in a bow. Hilary receives the same gifts. We sit alone and quietly in the bower. After a long while, she says: "It's really hard to speak. I was in a shower of light. Come sit next to me."

We sit facing each other, stomach to stomach, my legs behind hers, and hers crossed at the ankles behind me. We sit inside a cocoon of pale blue and lilac light. Long stretches of silence punctuated with giggles or comments. "I've never sat like this for so long and been so comfortable," Hilary says in my ear. "The Earth is a cushion. Grail Maidens are very celibate, you know. We only go as far as a little friendliness. I dreamed about you last night. It was very strange. Somebody said: 'You must take the Mother's Son from Pointer's Ball to Hartleypool through the Vale of the Buddhas.' They said it was you I must take."

Around seven, as the light fades and the grey clouds flush orange on the horizon, the gnome, lots of fairies, the sylph, and Pan escort us to the gate. Back at Wick, I stagger into the livingroom and collapse on the couch. "Grail Quest, man. I'm beat," I mumble, trying to ignore Russell's evident curiosity as to what we might have been up to out in the woods. Hilary says in mock disgust, "I've never been so shocked in my life. This guy is the biggest fraud. Luring innocent Grail Maidens out into the woods on false pretenses." Protestations aside, we're both grinning from wing to wing.

"It's like making friends," says Blaise later on when I ask him about the experiences in the Fairy Dell. "Pan is a guardian of the devic realm. He will be of much assistance to you all later. He will make contact through you. He will instruct you in growing things. The sylph's role is withheld from you at this time. The fairy biscuits we call discs of transmutation. In what is now Catholicism, you see a similar process but without the understanding. They call it transubstantiation. They use bread to bring the transmutation into themselves. Largely they do not receive this, as you did, direct from the spirit, the source, the one light from which we all come. The white marble is your faith and within your faith is space. This is the blue streak in the white globe. Within the sphere of your faith is the space for the experience of all that is presented to you for assimilation through your trust or faith. When you are centered, then you are a channel and what comes through you, you can learn from. If you are strung out, then you must learn from others.

"The Star is something about which we will speak later, when you experience it more clearly. We suggest that you breathe your love to it when it arises again. The red ribbon refers to what is happening to your irritability and annoyance. We see them gently being tied up as a red ribbon. You may also breathe your love to this ribbon."

Hilary slips out of the room for a moment, so I ask Blaise, confidentially, about Hilary. " We come in many forms to support your activity," Blaise replies. "Do not dwell too much on this experience. We ask that you see us coming to you in various forms as situations, events, and people. We suggest you allow yourself a little more joy." Up in the Grail chambers as I fall asleep, I make a mental note to compile a list of all the gifts that have been piling up. Since they don't take up any physical space, it's easy to forget about them, which, as any well-trained Grail Knight knows, would be discourteous.

31

THE INNER ROUND TABLE
CONVENES AT WICK

t's close to six o'clock in the afternoon, and I'm seated comfortably between the two willow trees down the slope from the railroad trestle. When I left the house fifteen minutes ago, the sun was only a vague memory from better days and the sky was a sheet of grey, but now the light has returned delightfully and the grass before me is a blaze of green. I'm here to find out what these fairy biscuits are all about. I pop one in my mouth and feel it dissolve. At once I stand before the gate by the blackberry bushes at the top of the Fairy Dell. The sylph guides me to a house marked No. 34. It's two stories high, ginger-colored, with a peaked roof, but it slants precariously off the side of the hill. The sylph asks me to carry this house to the top of the hill and set it down evenly; when I complete this task, its number changes to 35 and I'm back under the willows again.

I sample another biscuit. This time I'm transported to the fairy bower where Hilary and I sat yesterday. The gnome leads me through the door in that tree into the roomful of guitarists. This time, looking in the mirror, I see myself (as a male) reflected in the mirror (minus my glasses) at an older age. A man in red pajamas with a bloodied, dented face lies on a couch, looking at me with a horrific expression. I breathe love to him remembering the fairy adage that often a kiss transforms a hag into a beauty and a frog into a prince. It works. Now he is a stout, robust man of 25, still clad in red pajamas, who looks uncannily like Edmund about twenty years older.

Back under the willows again, I dare a third biscuit. This one brings me to the brow of the Fairy Dell, near the white palace. Pan is before me with his pipes, girted round by innumerable fairies. What I construed to be a white palace is now revealed to me as a complex organ with vertical pipes. Pan seats himself before it like the grand *Kapellmeister* and plays a tune. I'm back at the willows again after a few bars. It's time to go home anyway; the sun has slipped irretrievably into the clouds, and it grows cool and dark fast.

"We surround you with a wall of lilac flames," says Blaise in their opening remarks tonight. "We bring a small offering to you all. We give Berenice a buckle for your new shoes. We give Russell a furry animal to hold. Care for this as we care for you. Grail Knight, we simply give you a golden pen. One day we will give you something else that will write for you."

"Thanks, Blaise. What were those faces in the mirror I saw today?"

"We suggest you have been introduced to the Guardian of the Threshold with a little joy. The house is yourself as you are in the spacetime you are now in, at your present biological age. As you moved the house up the hill, you saw a fragment of what you will be. You must look into these figures in what you call red pajamas in stillness. Pan is in one aspect of consciousness a musician. What he and the devas do in the place you visited will be made clear later.

"We are pleased with the process. We are happy to be with you tonight. We come to you all with the love that we are, as a Blazing Star. We come as three in one. We come as one in three. We come as many; we come in many forms. We see change among you.

"We show you three things in the center of the room. There is a green, opalescent pyramid that contains the golden Grail bowl filled with electric blue light. The lilac flame burning above the Grail bowl reaches the top of the green pyramid on the inside. At the bottom of the lilac flame is a point of brilliant, pure light, a Blazing Star. Behind the Grail bowl and inside the green pyramid are the two swords, one pointing up, the other pointing down. Above this pyramid is a *vesica piscis* made of rainbows with sky blue inside each circle. A golden sword with three jewels passes straight up through these rainbows as they intersect. This sword has a bright light at its tip. The sword's handle has three jewels: sapphire, ruby, and emerald. At the top of the *vesica piscis* is a hole containing nothing, or everything. It is the black sphere, a hole in space. We have constructed something through this image in another dimension that will remain long after this house is gone. We ask that you breathe with love to this image for a moment, if you wish."

The image grows large and vivid and the three of us are inside it, like a bodily overlay over each of us. The Grail is at my pelvis, the *vesica piscis* at my chest, the sword parallels my spine, but when I see that the black sphere sits where my head is, I fall over backwards. Then Blaise resumes.

"We are one with you all. What we send at this time to you brings the process closer to activation, closer into the one light from which we all come, closer to the pure energy, closer in all ways. We are with you in what you do, even if you do not tangibly feel us in any of your senses or extra senses. We are with you in many forms. It is most important for you to realize this at this time. Each human today has been placed on Earth. Some come with a magnificent purpose, to help build the bridge of light to the other side. Others are working out debts that they incurred either to each other or to the planet itself. The planet is in need. Do not feel special because we come through many forms to teach you, to be with you, to love you, so that we can work together in response to your wishes. Do not be concerned with appearances. You will be side-tracked if you are. We wish so very much that you might see beyond appearances, even if these forms are ones you find most difficult to see through. People appear to you, as you look out from your being, in many different ways. Some you open your heart to because you recognize their being. We suggest you try to see the essential nature in *all* beings, no matter how difficult the appearances may be to you."

"Can you handle a couple questions, Blaise?" I ask.

"We would have been surprised if you hadn't asked, but still we are most happy to answer anything you wish. We can handle anything but can you handle the answers?"

"Well, how much time do I have for this?"

"Only the rest of your existence, which is a flash in the pan to us. You need more water in your cup. We will teach you how to make Grail tea."

"Oh. Well, thanks. Should we use this new Grail image for meditation?"

"If you put any more images inside yourself, you will not have room to breathe. We suggest you empty yourself every now and then. Then you may be able to receive something. You glimpse something you will all do later. Do not immerse yourself in what is to come. Much has to be done, here and now. You have too many beans. Yes, beans. It is digestion, not the correct amount, that is at fault. Relax. Do not chew as if it were your last bite. Be gentle with us as you eat us. Then you will digest us easier. We too will digest you easier. We leave you as a feather falling through space."

...And as a stolid bull grazing contentedly, mindlessly in the pastures, digesting under the aegis of an angelic sky. Blaise has sent me, the incorrigible Taurean with Scorpio rising on my back and beans simmering on the stove, out into the field to ruminate on recent events in my Grail bowl. Getting this Grail Knight launched is like trying to fly a brick.

Berenice calls the bull in from the field, and we drive off to the next town for a dinner party with friends. I confess I hadn't thought much of Betty until I sampled her cooking tonight; my opinion has radically altered into rapt, everlasting praise for her cuisine. When I am able to free my attention from the feed trough, I notice Russell has been trying to get me to turn around. "It's Tudor Pole with somebody else," he whispers. Tudor Pole stands behind me, his hands resting avuncularly on my shoulders, and the somebody else is my brother. I excuse myself from the table and walk into the kitchen for a private chat with these friendly ghosts. I'm happy to be with them again, but I'm not sure what to say, so I show them my Grail regalia. After a while, they leave, more or less dissolving through the wall with Cheshire smiles.

Back at Wick, I'm not sleepy, so I settle into the couch to reflect on the day's activities. There is a burst of light in the room, and the six Blaises appear smiling across the cosmos. My brother, Tudor Pole, and another companion—he's bearded and robed, resembling a Biblical patriarch—join us. Tudor Pole and my brother sit on either side of me on the sofa, and I put my arms approximately around both of them. The patriarch stands behind me. More company arrives: Pan, the sylph and gnome, a troop of fairies. The sylph hands me a bouquet of dried flowers. Pan gives me a flute. I bow to them all and become the Grail image, with my center of awareness positioned at the Blazing Star inside the lilac flame.

I don't know what the meeting is about but it seems to be a kind of preliminary convocation of an inner round table. It's one in the morning when they file out through the wall. I can't wait for morning to tell Russell about this, so I concentrate on his face until he appears in person in his yellow bathrobe, frowning and smiling simultaneously. "I'm not a genie in a lamp, you know. You're lucky I had to pee and was getting up anyway. Alright, then, what is it?" I tell him about the meeting, and Russell tells me he thinks the patriarch was Joseph of Arimathea, the spiritual custodian of the Holy Grail and its lineage throughout time and space.

Malory says as much in *Le Morte d'Arthur*. Joseph of Arimathea was the founder of a "Secret Church of the Grail," which was maintained afterwards by his son, then by a continuous spiritual lineage into Arthurian times. Galahad, Parsifal, and Bors are each visited by a spectral Joseph. "And therewithal beseemed them that there came a man—and four angels from heaven—clothed in likeness of a bishop and had a cross in his hand; and these four angels bare him up in a chair and set him down before the table of silver, whereupon the Sangrail was; and it seemed that he had in the midst of his forehead letters that said, 'See ye here Joseph, the first bishop of Christendom, the same which our Lord succoured in the city of Sarras in the spiritual place.' Then the knights marvelled, for that bishop was dead more than three hundred years before." Make that nineteen hundred years.

I still don't feel like going to bed so I settle down on my cushion and breathe as Love from Above to the Grail image. This brings me abruptly to the Upper Room at Chalice Well where I am seated at the inner table with Joseph of Arimathea and many others. The numinous blue sapphire bowl, much discussed by Tudor Pole in his writings, sits in the center of the table. I breathe as Love from Above to this bowl, which Joseph has given me to hold; it oozes light the way dry ice exudes steam. I feel surrounded by young Christian apostles, earnest initiates of the true Christ, from an earlier day, including Berenice. Joseph places the blue sapphire bowl on my head as the crown of the new Grail image. He asks me to return to the Upper Room in a few days with Russell and Berenice. Now I'm ready for bed. At three a.m., I hang up my Grail bowl and call it a day.

32

MAKING A DENT
IN A FEW HILLS

 spend the next day—what remains of it after the Grail Knight rouses himself from a cavernous slumber under the duvet around lunchtime—in the pasture again, peristalting the Grail process through my psyche until it's time for another Blaise visit.

"We come in many forms, as many names, as many faces," Blaise announces. "We come through all expressions. We come as love." Tudor Pole, my brother, and Joseph of Arimathea come into focus as Blaise finishes his opening remarks. "We place a bowl inside each of you. Each of you has his or her own bowl. We place various things like feelings and light into your bowls. Now, the green pyramid with the lilac flame, the bowl, the Blazing Star, the *vesica piscis*, the sword, the sky, the rainbow, the hole in space—all these exist in another body of yours outside of a deeper inside. It is very difficult to explain, but we think we can understand your questions. If you imagine something in a completely different dimension from the one you perceive—oh dear.

"It is just inexplicable in words. Use or no-use do not come into this. Acceptance or nonacceptance do not figure. It is what it is, just as it is. We are most sorry. Your words are so inadequate for describing something like this. The nature of your language is all in comparisons. Something exists beyond comparison that makes description of it impossible, because we cannot describe something that is incomparable. There was a time on your planet when there was a language with a certain—we cannot go further. We are getting our wings twisted. We are you. You are us. Giving, receiving—are the same, no problem."

"Okay. Let's try something simpler, if you have your wings untwisted."

"Jumping bean, what is it? If you had an inkling of what it's like trying—it's so much simpler than you think."

"I wanted to ask what I should do next?"

"We made an appointment for you in the Upper Room today. The last part of your synthesis of this information will take place there."

"May I pursue my question a little further?"

"Do you want us to leave?"

"No, no."

"We almost hid in the corner while you pursued your thought forms out the door. We suggest you take a walk from the bottom of Wearyall Hill across the hill and over to Chalice Hill. Set off about 10 a.m. tomorrow. Collect and remember yourself at the thorn tree. Try to be at the top of Chalice Hill by midday. Take a small offering of gold with you, if you can. Be prepared to make an offering, whatever feels right at the time. You could also take some miso soup in a flask. It's good for Grail Knights. We are involved in a process. You are helping us as we are helping your process. They are the same. We work under instructions from a higher source. When we say that, we don't mean higher in relation to lower. We mean *higher*."

"Blaise, it seems Joseph of Arimathea has joined our little transmutation party. What was his role in Glastonbury and the Grail Quest?"

"Joseph, in the company of the Christ in His thought body, brought the Grail to England. He travelled to many sites of the old religion with the Christ in His thought body. Then, with several others, Joseph settled for a while at Chalice Well. There are, in this region, several etheric imprints of this settlement and its work. The Grail brought by Joseph was imbued by the Christ in His thought body and left near this area. Joseph brought a chalice from the Last Supper and bearing other vibrations, points in his personal awareness that related to his personal practice. It is not possible for you to understand this. When you know what your Grail is in its entirety, with your breath of love, with your conscious ability and consideration, then you will understand more of the Grail's past. You see, there is much more about this than we can reveal to you at this time. Later, more will be made clear. The lilac flame dances above the Grail cup. The zodiac surrounds its edges. The cup overflows. The light fills Avalon. All who are ready for it are in the process of transmutation."

"What is the blue sapphire bowl that Joseph put on my head?"

"The blue sapphire bowl is an angelic creation made for the purposes of the transmutation of heavenly energy into the earth sphere. It is made of light in a matrix of crystal. Its appearance in Glastonbury in 1906 was to facilitate the transition to the Michael rulership. Its relation to the Grail is much like the relation of the Sun to the Moon. The Sun is the light in the bowl. The bowl is its reflection and materialization. The blue sapphire bowl sits on the black sphere as a representation of the completion of the movement of light through form, through emptiness, and into a new form of light. You might also see it as an angel's Grail bowl. The being you call Tudor Pole is the bowl's guardian. It is the completion of a long process begun by Joseph of Arimathea. The bowl you received is an etheric replica of the blue sapphire bowl. It is capable of many extensions in thought. It is the Star made manifest as a receptive dish. We leave as we come; as you know us, so we are, as a light at the center of the lilac flame, as a Blazing Star."

Most people, I suppose, on the morning commute to work, probably talk about the news or what they saw on television or maybe stare out the train windows counting telephone poles; but this morning, we're chatting merrily about our angelic friends and the peculiarities, the nuances, of the Quest. When I say "we," I mean a "we" fully extended in space: stuffed into the Citroen besides the three of us are Pan, the sylph, the gnome, my brother, Tudor Pole, Joseph of Arimathea, six Blaises, and a brace of fairies who don't take up too much room, actually. Joseph is hunched over like a basketball player in an old Volkswagen Bug, while four of the Blaises are strapped like exotic luggage to the roof, their flared wings catching the wind like sailboats. Several sport bumper stickers on their wings: "Polaris is for Angels." "Avalon—Love it or Leave it." "The Dead Sea's For US!"

Berenice pulls up at the foot of Wearyall Hill, and I clamber out for the serious business of the Grail conclave. Disembarking, I fancy myself bearing a large sign strapped to my chest and back, the kind streetwalkers use to advertise restaurants: "Danger: *Makyo*. Grail Knight at Work." Blaise has blown the sky nearly clear after an overcast, gloomy beginning.

I breathe myself into the Grail image, my companions fan out around me, and we make our ceremonial way up Wearyall Hill. At the Holy Thorn, I pause for a look inside the huge crystal I saw here from our night's outing with Blaise on the Tor. I see my brother and me aboard a schooner that lands at Wearyall when it was a wooded island in the inland sea of the Summer Country. I sense the ocean all about on Wearyall. At the end of Chilkwell Lane, I suddenly feel something is leaking. I look back along Chilkwell and discover I have left a trail of blue light like dayglow paint the whole way from Wearyall. In alarm, I check the Grail bowl but the crankcase is full. As we move up Chalice Hill, a gnome emerges from within each of the couple dozen beech trees and joins our conclave as we walk the perimeter of the hill. The wind has become a Bruckner symphony in full throttle as I perch between two oaks facing Bushy Coombe. I have a little smithing to do. I'm making a gold bow tie from my red ribbon. In the heat of the work, fumes of annoyance and irritation waft upwards from the Grail bowl, which has become a portable alchemist's alembic.

At noon, I move to the top of Chalice Hill and play a tune on Pan's gift flute. Gnomes kick up their heels like inebriated leprechauns; Blaises lift their skirts and make handsome pirouettes; a female fairy floats dreamily down through my perception in gossamer clothes of lavender, an ecstatic, ethereal face of pre-Raphaelite loveliness. Our conclave now forms a necklace on the Mother's throat, with my brother and Tudor Pole on either side of me, Joseph of Arimathea directly behind me, the six Blaises making an angelic crescent behind him, and a couple dozen gnomes describing a yet broader arc behind them.

I offer my gold bow tie and the sylph's flowers from last night to a large, flat stone that faces the Tor and is inserted into Chalice Hill like a dolmen. Turning to face Brent Knoll in the northwest, I see a host of angels dancing about the standing stone. My attention brings me closer to this stone—it also resembles the Hindu *lingam*, a stone in pillar form said to represent Shiva, the cosmic creative energy— and I read its chiselled inscription: "God is Light." I empty the Grail light like cream dribbling over the stone then touch it with Excalibur (at least, my visualized form of it) and the golden sword (from the Blaise image) then call on all the light centers in my body to add wattage to the stone's illumination. I sense the stone pillar is a doorway requiring activation. Inside, a figure opens a door into a chamber where a crystalline form sits on a table. I realize it is not a crystal but the geometrical expression of the light body of a spiritual being. For purposes of recognition and familiarity, I choose to see this figure as a Hindu guru (or rishi) in loincloth and with beatific countenance. He beckons me towards a black door that opens into a barrow. I knock five times with my golden sword, and the door swings open into the darkness. I pass through and fly off with the rishi.

Our first stop is Brent Knoll, a Tor-like sacred hill perhaps twenty miles from here, visible on the horizon, and once known as the Hill of Frogs. I take a fairy biscuit, dip it in the Grail light, then place it on a stone on the hill. But why frogs? Later it makes sense when I check the references for frogs. It seems that among the Eygptians the frog represented the goddess of birth and protector of mothers, Heket, who was often portrayed as frogheaded, presumably an allusion to the frog's considerable fertility; the green frog of the Nile represented prolific generation, new life, abundance, longevity, even regeneration, and, in at least one Eygptian tradition, Heket, with her husband, Khnum, was regarded the creator of human beings. For the Hindus, the Great Frog supports the universe and symbolizes the dark, undifferentiated "waters," or *prima materia*; and for the Celts, the frog was a symbol of the Lord of the Earth, the embryonic power of the waters to heal and birth. Prodigious things indeed must have happened here on Brent Knoll in the old days.

Next we journey to Burrowbridge Mump, where I deposit a Grail-dunked biscuit in the church ruins; then to Camalate at South Cadbury Castle, where I leave one on Arthur's once and future etheric throne; then to Dundon Beacon, where I place a wafer on the single stone standing in the woods at the brow of the hill. Then the rishi and I fly high above Glastonbury Tor, spiralling up an umbilical cord into space until we reach what my imagination presents to me as the underside of a giant treehouse platform, like the flans of the Elves in Tolkien's world. My impression is that the door is shut and I cannot make it through: end of adventure.

Blaise has a little more flying in mind for me. In the evening, I sit down for what I hope is some honest working-man's zazen of the old empty mind type *sans* visions, but Blaise swoops me up and we're off over Glastonbury, where I continue my meditation at an intersection of five ley lines at the Edgar Chapel in Glastonbury Abbey. "When the dark forces assembled here release their powers from the Earth, men and women will shine from their chalices filled with Light," says Blaise.

The idea is for me to channel or transmit gold light down the ley lines, which seem to converge at my solar plexus, precisely at the Blazing Star inside the lilac flame in the Grail image. I pull out Excalibur from its spine sheath, dip its tip into the blue sapphire bowl on my head, then lay it diagonally across the light lines. I do the same with the golden sword and place it diagonally opposite Excalibur, making crossed swords. I empty the Grail into the leys and watch the light flow like pure water through a sluiceway.

Now I examine the white star that the Invisible Hand gave me at the Fairy Dell. It resembles a multifaceted crystal, with more facets than I can possibly count. I hold it in my hands at my belly at the intersection of the light lines and summon up all the Love from Above I can muster. It's not enough. I feel my brother, Tudor Pole, Blaise, and Joseph support me with their breathing. I call on Nothing to support me, like Blaise said. For good measure, I add a visualization Russell shared with me involving a golden tube of light with the Buddha on top. When I invoke this tube, golden speckles of light snow upon the crystal and I relax. It's going to work. Soon a pale golden light suffuses the light lines, and the white Star reveals the image of a tiny tree inside.

Later in the evening Blaise arrives to review our activities. "We come as a point of light on a golden line of light. We are lines of golden light. We surround you with walls of lilac flames from the Earth up to the stars, walls of lilac flames making a tube of lilac light from Heaven to Earth. We place it there for you all. We ask that you remember the opalescent green pyramid we constructed together. Remember the golden bowl inside the pyramid, filled with electric blue light. The lilac flame from the bowl reaches the top of the pyramid. Beneath it is a Blazing Star, a point of brilliant, pure light. Above this pyramid is the *vesica piscis*, the golden sword between the two rainbows, sky blue in each circle. The sword points upwards. In its handle are three jewels: sapphire, ruby, emerald. Above this is the hole in space. Breathe with your love to this image for a few minutes.... Good. The pyramid we built with you is as we gave it. It is beneath the *vesica piscis,* and the handle of the sword is just above the point of the pyramid."

"Blaise, what were we up to at Chalice Hill today?"

"We spoke of offerings you should make when you got to the tree. We hoped you would make a small material offering of gold. This would have facilitated a little more of your experience. But what you did was almost perfect. You made an indentation at these five sites that is needed in human awareness, so that one day, many more humans will see. We have a good friend called Lord of the Dance. One day you may learn a few steps. There is great joy in dancing. We say, we will not be pleased if you get caught up in self-importance because of this work. We are most concerned that, on the one hand, you know what you are doing, but that, on the other hand, what you humans call your selfishness does not become absorbed by it. It is very tricky. If you are a human with human consciousness and you do what you do consciously, then it indents in what you call the collective consciousness. You must realize, too, that your training is in its very early stages. We are only introducing possibili- . ties very slowly. We are making you ready for what is to come.

"Now, we give you a specific thing to do. We want you to make a circle of earth about two feet in diameter. We want you to prepare this lovingly, then ask us about this again. The gnomes will show you where to go. We place a little nothing in your bowl. [A thin, white lozenge banded in blue drifts down] Now, Berenice, about this joy you want to share. What can we say about this? Feel it, that is enough. Words: rubbish, really. Joy: hmmmm. Love: hmmmm. Big words, simple experience. Simple love, simple joy. [Berenice burps] Simple wind. That's it, that is all. Do not look any further than what is in front of your nose. Be happy, be well, be good, goodbye. We flutter off as a Blazing Star, brighter than bright, bluer than blue."

33

CHANGING A LIGHT AT THE GRAIL CASTLE

I walk out the front door and wait for the gnome. He appears by the rose bush, nods his head merrily, and waves me along to follow him. We pass through the Fairy Dell then into the woods, zigzagging across the hillside, through brambles, over stumps, under limbs, until he stops and points to the ground. I set out my string, tape measure, trowel, and kneel on the earth, appreciating the soil's fragrance. Is it all right to pull up this ground ivy? I ask the gnome. He nods. When the earth circle is made, I make a cross in it, hollow out a little depression in its center, then set the palm-size Blazing Star in it like a seedling. I empty half the contents of the Grail on the Star seed and offer the rest to the gnome. Then I dip the gold sword into the blue sapphire bowl and anoint the Star, breathing Love to it all the while. Job done, seed planted.

"We are glad you constructed your earth circle," says Blaise in the evening. "It needs more attention. We suggest you go there early tomorrow. Spend a little more time breathing with love to your circle before you leave the woods. Then go to Chalice Hill again. Walk up Wearyall Hill over the ridge on a slightly higher path than last time. Arrive at Chalice Hill by noon. We will be with you."

"Is there a relationship between my earth circle and Chalice Hill?"

"There is, but we will not explain it to you at present. It pertains to the relationship between the Dog and Aquarius. Much of your work pertains to this. As it is incomplete, we prefer not to explain it. Now, on Wearyall Hill, there is a line that is of a higher vibration. You will be guided to this tomorrow if you complete your exercises before leaving home. We suggest you walk with your full attention in the walking, both to the earth circle and back and then from the foot of Wearyall Hill to the tree on Chalice Hill. Make your offerings of gold and incense and whatever metal objects you feel appropriate. Make sure you are at the top of Chalice Hill at noon. We will show you more of the Grail Castle. Then we would like you to meet Russell and Berenice at Chalice Well."

"What do you mean by offerings?"

"You have something in gold that you mentioned last night: a ring. Orientate yourself, when you are there, not quite towards Wearyall, not quite towards Brent Knoll. It's more of an etheric orientation. Make your offerings to the Light. As you walk each step towards the Light, think of nothing else. Feel the Light, be the Light, hear the sound. Spend only ten minutes quietly at Chalice Well, then leave. We leave you as we are, in stillness and in light, as a Blazing Star."

The next morning at ten a.m., I'm standing on the brow of Wearyall Hill surveying a half dozen bundled silvery pipes that hug the ground in their route across the landscape to Chalice Hill. These must be the "fuel" pipes for the domes Blaise described, passing overland to the other dome behind me at Beckery and perhaps further out to Burrowbridge Mump, also domed. A curious thing happened to me at the earth circle several hours ago. When I finished smoothing the soil and chanting for a few minutes, I saw an Australian Aborigine making an identical circle, using a knife to trim the edges. He saw me looking at him.

The Grail conclave is less of a spectacle today, just the bare bones of Grail Knights and Blaise, but we're accompanied by the gnomes from the trees as we climb Chalice Hill. I prepare myself for an hour, cleaning up shop with breathing and listening before I walk to the crown of the hill at noon. I make my offerings: my old wedding ring and a Swiss Army knife, both of which were stolen a year ago in San Francisco but since we're dealing in etheric currency, I assume this doesn't matter. The beatific rishi stands before the cave-barrow like yesterday, waiting for me. Sweat beads on my forehead, but finally I enter the darkness and knock on the inner door. I enter a castle: in

244 ✦ Richard Leviton

the foyer is that same slumbering green dragon that Russell encountered in his preliminary visit to the inner temple. I walk through a
gallery of oil paintings, mostly portraits—probably a holographic
records room similar to the gnomes' castle—then enter a large, open
space under a rotunda. An emerald, bright green and three feet high,
is positioned on a platform in the center of the hall. I breathe love to
it but it remains impenetrable, or so I think. I find myself in a different hall, long and regal like a throne room.

A cathedralic ceiling curves grandly above me. At the far end of
the hall stands a king holding a scepter. The Fisher King, I presume.
I carry the Grail to him. He seems to float up to the ceiling, where he
inserts his scepter, which resembles a lance, into the source of the
brilliant light that floods the hall. This is the Spear of Lugh, somebody whispers. That was one of the four precious objects of the Tuatha
de Danann, the godly forebears of the Irish. The king, standing on
the floor again, inserts his spear into a silver vessel. Then my perception goes awry because I see myself as the king repeating the same
steps, inserting my gold sword into the Grail. But the Grail is much
larger now: it's like a huge public fountain mounted on a pedestal.
All the zodiacal glyphs have been carved on its rim, just like in the
Blaise image. I lean over the Grail at the Taurus section and ladle out
four draughts with my blue sapphire bowl. I approach the Fisher
King—who is himself again and not me—empty its contents on his
head, drenching him in light.

Since I know the story, I thought I would pre-empt him by asking
him the question that traditionally he would ask the Grail Knight.
"Whom does the Grail serve?" I query. "It serves you," the Fisher
King replies. "Who *is* you?" I ask him. "You and I are one," he says.
So much for upstaging the old boy. Our genteel riposte concluded,
I'm back on Chalice Hill just in time to remove my sneaker from the
mouth of an overly curious cow who has also made a Grail offering,
only inches from my jacket, of fresh splats. And, true to script, the
Grail Castle has vanished.

For reasons obscure to myself but no doubt vividly prescient to my
subconscious, I feel dissatisfied with my performance. On the stroll

down Chalice Hill, I berate myself for my perceptual myopia. I feel so blind sometimes. "And now I take upon me the adventures of holy things," says Lancelot in *Le Morte d'Arthur*, "and now I see and understand that mine old sin hindereth me and shameth me, so that I had no power to stir or speak when the holy blood appeared afore me." Lancelot, despite his "sins," eventually makes it into Castle Carbonek, as the Grail Castle was anciently called. "And with that he saw the chamber door open, and there came out a great clearness, that the house was as bright as all the torches of the world had been there. Then looked he up in the midst of the chamber, and saw a table of silver and the holy vessel, covered with red samite, and many angels about it." Approaching the silver table, Lancelot "felt a breath mingled with fire which smote him so sore in the visage" he had to be carried out of the Grail Castle, after which he spent the next twenty-four days in a swoon. He should have called on Blaise's Nothing for a little extra spunk, but I must say, in Lancelot's favor, that the Grail Castle is a tricky business.

There hasn't been a Grail Knight who hasn't described the "Palace Adventurous" as this infernally revolving, spinning castle, like a merry-go-round with only one slot through which you gain entrance. Once inside the "Castle of Wonders," you have to be on guard for hurled spears, trap-doors, sudden attacks, perilous beds, wily courtesans, attacking lions, surly hosts, and the likely chance that the whole place will disappear with your first wrong move. The main thing to remember is, never sit on the beds in this place. In one account, Bors sat on the Perilous Bed. Big mistake. "There began so great a crashing that no one in the world would not be frightened," says the poet of the medieval Grail saga, *Lancelot*. "For at once arose a wind so great that it caused all the windows, of which there were more than a hundred, to bang together." Then a long lance with a head like a burning candle was flung at Bors "as hard as lightning," wounding him in the shoulder. A flight of arrows and bolts comes through the window at him, then a lion jumps him; later he encounters a dragon and a leopard. Finally, a pale, thin man with serpents twined around his neck plays a song on the harp about Joseph of

Arimathea. In the morning, the Fisher King looks in and asks the Grail Knight if he's passed the night comfortably.

The Grail Castle is certainly a marvellously treacherous place, but who built it? According to Albrecht von Scharffenberg in his Middle High German poem *Der Jüngere Titurel*, (circa 1270 A.D.), it was Parzival's grandfather, Titurel, who built the Grail Castle. When he was fifty, an angel told him the remainder of his life would be devoted to the preservation of the Grail; with the aid of friends similarly inspired, he constructed the castle as a hallows for the Grail in the Forest of Salvation upon a solitary mountain (Munsalvaesche). Previously the Grail had been ungrounded, upheld only by heavenly hands, floating above the site without a castle to contain it. Titurel's Grail Castle is high, circular, and topped with a grand cupola, surrounded by twenty-two chapels which form an octagon; at every second chapel, there is an octagonal bell tower topped by a white crystal cross and a golden eagle. The towers form a circle about the main dome, which is lacquered in red gold and blue enamel. Inside the central dome, the sun and moon are depicted against a blue enamelled sky of stars; beneath this stands a miniature replica of the entire Grail Castle, and inside this resides the Holy Grail.

I join Russell, Berenice, and the now legendary chef Betty and her husband at Arthur's Courtyard, where we squeeze onto one bench. The six Blaises stand on the stream then beckon me to dip my white marble with the blue streak in the water. I present this to Russell and give Berenice a fairy biscuit then dip my gold sword in the blue sapphire bowl and anoint Betty and her husband on the top of their heads. Blaise does a dance and the ten minutes are finished. "I saw three knights and four angels across the stream," says Russell. "Two more angels stood with us. One knight dubbed the other two on the head and shoulders. Everybody wore armor and a gold circlet on the head."

I have a Grailful of questions for Blaise when they arrive in the evening. To begin with, what is the Grail Castle?

"The Grail Castle does not exist anywhere on Earth in the sense you know it. It is the etheric double of something in a different time and space mirrored here for a purpose. The castles on Chalice Hill, Hamdon Hill, and other sacred hills are etheric doubles of this place, brought here and placed as buildings, as etheric temples, for the evolution of the planet and its soul beings. Their purpose is yet to be fulfilled. A very small number of humans in the past had access to the particular level of consciousness necessary to perceive these castles in the etheric realm. Access was made from the etheric castles on Earth to the actuality of the castle in another dimension, but this has not occured since Atlantean days. Access will become more available and this will be firmly established in a short time."

"Why did Malory call it Grail Castle Carbonek?"

"At the time of the Arthurian myths, the predominant structure in form for Man and his being-consciousness vehicle, that in which consciousness was contained, was a carbon cycle, as in carbonic acid. The Castle Carbonek was the individual knight's exploration of his own inner temple. You are in the experience of transition from the carbon cycle to the silicon cycle. You see many manifestations of this in the interest in quartz crystals and silicon chips. This is the outward manifestation of an inner change of being, from carbon to silicon. The transition is largely a shift from water to air, Pisces to Aquarius. We find again that descriptions for the process of the transmutation of elements is difficult for you to comprehend. Eschenbach, who said the Grail was a large, green stone, as you saw, was a prophet before his time. He had insight into his own Grail Castle, as you do."

"What is the Grail Quest all about then?"

"It is to stop humans from becoming depressingly boring, to indicate to humans joyful boredom. It is a level of nonattachment. It is beyond being identified. It is an inherent awareness. It is slow and purposeful. Joy is nonaggressive. We need something to advertise the Quest. We hope it will become a bit of a fad. Much can be transformed by this means."

"Malory keeps referring to the 'city of Sarras, the spiritual place,' when he refers to the Grail, and he says Joseph of Arimathea was 'succoured' there by Jesus. What does this mean?"

"Sarras is an ancient word. It is the same forewards and backwards. It was part of a ritual device. It holds a magic square. The Grail was earthed, in a sense, through this name in ritual. Sarras is something that cannot be described any further at this point. We can say that, amongst a particular group, a collection of beings, there was mutual agreement as to a particular place in which to ground their individual experiences of the Grail. That was Sarras."

"Is the dome over Chalice Hill the same as the etheric replica of the Grail Castle also over the hill?"

"Not exactly. Chalice Hill dome is not the Grail Castle. The difference is that as you breathe to the crystal you planted at your earth circle, so one day there will be a tree at Chalice Hill just as there will be at your circle. The domes each carried a light form or seed crystal of what was to be. Some of these have been activated. Man has either not been aware of them or not made use of them to form what he may have known as Paradise. If you breathe to the crystal in your earth circle, you will see a tree. Now, at Chalice Hill something also exists like a crystal that contains the Grail Castle."

"Do you mean the green emerald on the platform? It was impenetrable. I was baffled with my inadequacy today. I felt flawed. I couldn't see much. Everything was difficult."

"It was not impenetrable. In spite of yourself, you managed to get through the crystal. Yes, you did. These are all difficulties you put before yourself. Why you do this is your business. We come with love. We only wish to be of assistance. Because you think something must be hard, then you make it hard. This is the switch. It's all incredibly easy. We are with you. Sometimes we would like to sledgehammer..."

"My head?"

"No, to crack some of what's hard so that some of what is soft can seep through. Things would be much easier for us all. Your mind needs sharpening. It is woolly sometimes. Success and failure—oh dear. What problems we tie ourselves in. These self-images are not conducive on the Quest. Drop them. Let go of ideas of who you are and all that stuff, if you wish. Otherwise, we will never finish this project."

"I'll do my best."

"We do not ask that. We ask that you just do. No I, no best. Understand?"

"Yes. Now, what about that event in Arthur's Courtyard today. Did I see it accurately?"

"It was an event that took place at that location some time ago. It concerns you. You needed to remember it, but you only remembered a fragment because everything was hard today. We hoped having your friends with you would help you remember. If you had just sat, without trying, without doing anything, Russell would have seen the whole story for you. No matter. You got enough as it was. It was Bors being welcomed back from the Grail Quest by Arthur."

"Blaise, when I was on Chalice Hill and saw the dome overhead and saw the domes over the Tor, Beckery, the Mump, Brent Knoll, and Cadbury Castle, I sensed they were all linked together somehow."

"Good. Imagine a bright dome, many of them touching all over your planet, connected by lines of love and light that are very bright." As Blaise speaks, I see an opalescent basketball in a fishnet shopping bag; each knot in the weave is a dome; the fishnet itself is the planetary grid matrix. So who's holding the bag?

"We are only one string. There are four beyond us, the Archangels, with two on each handle, one operative at any time. At this time it is Michael. The hand is the hand of whom you call the Buddha, the Enlightened One. The Buddha holds this bag. You must realize that each dome has a golden and a silver line connecting it with all the other domes on the planet. They comprise what you see as a fishnet web. All the golden and silver lines are joined together at one point. The silver lines come from Canopus, the golden lines from Sirius, through the Buddha."

"Oh, before I forget, who was that man I saw making an earth circle in Australia?"

"You were looking behind us. That was naughty."

"I thought you were showing me this."

"Forget this. We better tell you since you saw that there is a man in Australia doing something similar, synchronously with you, but it has to do with something you wouldn't believe. We would like that each morning you spend a little time with your earth circle. Go there physically. Be still, don't worry. Don't be attached to success and failure, right or wrong. Your temptation is to anticipate or expect rather than wait. Anticipations are a great evil. We are most concerned that you recognize that no matter how much you put into this work, you will only be given one aspect of the truth, at best. You sometimes get it right. Sometimes you get it wrong. Slow down. We can only make recommendations. We come only as love. We come as a brilliant, pure light, as a pinpoint of rainbow light. We come as a pinpoint within the rainbow point of pure light. We surround you all in a wall of lilac flames from Earth to a point higher than the imagination can reach—a lilac tube of dancing flames. We leave you now with the lake of pure blue, a forest of lilac flames around it and above it. We leave you as a Blazing Star."

The next afternoon the three of us converge at the Upper Room for our appointment. Despite Blaise's advice to me not to anticipate anything, all morning I've felt as if I'm on the eve of a dentist's visit for something dreadful, like a root canal. As if I know what's going to happen but can't focus it into words or images. Nothing much happens that I'm aware of in the Upper Room. We sit in silence, brushing away thoughts like flies, then leave. Russell and Berenice head for the High Street to shop, and I wander over to the Edgar Chapel. I enjoy a quiet moment in the sunshine with Blaise, my feet dangling with boyish insouciance over the wall. The brilliant blue sky sharply frames the white clouds and the wind moves them along briskly. An eagle flies over the Tor and drops a marble for me to examine. Inside, I see my parents in their late twenties, before I was born, and myself—or maybe my brother, because back then we looked alike—hovering above them as an expectant cherub.

Has it been a good idea, I wonder, ever since that moment I overshadowed my parents decades ago, organizing this incarnation? And what is this Grail Quest about anyway? A palliative for boredom? I hardly think so. I've wandered into a *makyo* minefield, but, far from killing me, the frequent explosions I've tripped off have enchanted me; a few have even vaguely educated me, though much of the experiences do not make much sense to me at this moment. I've even made appointments to have *makyo* and then been disappointed when they haven't materialized. How are *makyo* to be regarded? asks Yasutani-roshi. "All these strange visions and sensations are no more than symptoms of a sick state, a state which is not yet whole. Their nature is like that of dreams. Never be tempted into thinking that these phenomena are real or that the visions themselves have any meaning. But such visions are certainly a sign that you have got halfway to a crucial moment in your sitting when you must put forth all your strength."

Where do you draw the line on *makyo*? Is the Grail Quest a *makyo*? Is Blaise? Is Yasutani-roshi? Am I? "Hence the best course to adopt when such sensations appear is simply to go on sitting with all your might."

I ask Blaise about our apparent nonexperience in the Upper Room today.

"It had something to do with future possibilities. There has been a synthesis in your work on the Grail Quest in response to a situation we created for you today. It is in the form of inner experience unknown to your conscious mind, registered in your dreams, if you like. You dreamt this morning of what was to take place before arriving at the well. We did not suggest you speak about it so we could arrange several interfaces of inner dynamics for you. Experience will show you what has taken place. You are in a difficult time in your quest when much can turn around. Remember that we come through many forms. Do not be afraid. We surround you with lilac tipped flames of gold. We only suggest. There are many possibilities. It matters little to us. We wish you to ask about Galahad. What does his name signify?"

"Galahad. Oh. Well, how about, 'what a gala he had?'"

"That is one aspect. Another is gala-had, meaning the chalice, the Grail. Galahad did not return from Sarras after he restored the Fisher

King and became king himself in Sarras. One aspect of consciousness did not wish to make the return to Earth, having achieved the Grail. Thus the Grail was not completed, was not brought down to Earth. Parzival, like Galahad, also achieved the Grail but was not required to return. It is very much like one knight made a committment to bring something back for humankind that would be of assistance, something, if you like, that was part of his boat whereby he got to the Grail. If we could tell you how it all fits together, it would not be very interesting for you. Always, it is your choice. Tomorrow is Michaelmass, Michael's day. We would like you to visit the Tor and face Pointer's Ball. We suggest you begin at sunrise and finish at sunset. Be happy, Grail Knight. We leave you now with our utmost love, as your Blazing Star."

After Blaise leaves and Russell and Berenice retire to their bedroom, I try going to sleep, but I keep wondering what happened to me at the Upper Room today. I decide to see if I can retrieve it through meditation. I return my thoughts to the Room and sit before the thin veil and the simple table beyond it. Now I am seated by invitation at the Last Supper table. I am aware of several faces around the table: my brother, Tudor Pole, Joseph of Arimathea, but there are many others. Now I see why Tudor Pole often mentioned meeting souls from all over in the Upper Room. We seem to be standing around a golden round table except it is more like a recessed hollow, like a *kiva,* and we line its edges looking in like pillars of light. In the center stands a *lingam,* a smooth pillar of pure white light. *This is my body,* says a voice silently. The *lingam* is set on a scarlet base. *This is my blood,* the voice says.

I gather the experience I am working my way into involves the Christ and the experience of the Last Supper, not as an historical event but as an archetypal initiatory reality, available anytime and, to a degree, through the Upper Room. This Supper, of course, was the last meal Jesus the Christ had with his apostles in the upper room of a house in Jerusalem. The sacrament of the Eucharist (from *eucharistein,* "to give thanks") and the Mass (the *dominicum sacrificio,* "the Lord's sacrifice," and *mysterium oblatio,* "mystery offering") have since commemorated this profound moment of sharing in a solemn church ritual. I try to penetrate this experience further because I appear to be watching it but not quite in it; I sense there is more to be revealed if I can only find a way into it. I struggle with this for some time but get no closer.

Then the image of myself as a young boy between the ages of six and ten comes vividly to mind. What is that bromide that only as a child can you enter the kingdom of Heaven? I can *feel* that boy's bouncy, dimply energy, his wise innocence, his direct, bravura penetration, and I emulate him. Suddenly my attention zips off to a field near my parent's house in Massachusetts where I used to play baseball with the boys in the neighborhood. Standing at home plate, I look left towards a row of maple trees. Something is here, an energy, a presence. The trees and the playing field are situated on a dome line coming out of a landscape zodiac temple just on the other side of the mountain range less than three miles away. But something is here before me as if in the air. It's like a tear in the fabric of physical reality, as if a curtain, painted with blue sky and clouds, is being parted by two hands, revealing another dimension within.

It's as if a giant angel were moving just underneath the transparent skin of physical reality before me, its huge outline coming into focus with every passing second, about to burst the delicate membrane. It's the Archangel Michael; and as soon as I perceive him, he whisks me away. The next moment I find myself in a vast cathedral filled with many thousands of men and women. The place feels oddly familiar, as if I've been here before. In fact, I must have been here at least two times, once as the ten-year-old-boy and again as the adult Grail Knight. But, for some reason, the memory of the boy's trip is easier to access than my visit today.

What I had thought to be a golden *kiva* I now realize is the Holy Grail, resplendently golden. It's as big as a house. I contemplate it from several angles simultaneously. I stand before it, upon its rim, and within its hollow center. I feel so wonderfully weightless, so free from the gravity of bones and muscle; thinking like the boy I suppose, I find travelling in my light body is as soft and velvety and unobstructed and boneless as wearing flannel pajamas. A brilliant white light sears through the Grail, momentarily erasing everything from my field of vision. *This is my body,* says the silent voice again. It is as if this universal light illuminates all my being bodies—my auric shells—frankly revealing my numerous flaws and few perfections. My sins, they call this, splotches on the robe of light. *This is the birth,* the voice says.

But just as my karmic errors are ruthlessly revealed in the light of day, so are they forgiven in the luscious warmth of this light. *This is my blood,* the voice says, as a drop of bright scarlet permeates every atom in my being, every thought, every millisecond of awareness, every grasping gesture of individual being. *This is the baptism.* Like an infant, I surrender myself to the baptismal immersion in the sea of scarlet. I know I am being quickened with the consciousness of Christ the Logos, focussed as if to a crystalline point of awareness on the threshold of beholding a new world.

That is all I can retrieve tonight of my experience at the Upper Room. I look at my clock. Three hours have passed. "An upper room, symbolic of the world redeemed," writes Qabalist Gareth Knight, "in which you shall abide in your redemption."

34

A Mass for Michael at Pointer's Ball

s Hilary and I perch on the southern shoulder of Glastonbury Tor facing Pointer's Ball, the archangel Michael stands behind and above us, the stone tower no bigger than a shin guard for this majestic spirit. It's his day today: Michaelmass, September 29. The British slur this regal name into three clipped syllables, but Michael prefers four (*my-kay-ell-mass*) including the full Catholic ramifications of the final four letters—*a mass for Michael*. He Who is Like Unto God, or God's countenance, said the ancient Hebrews for whom Michael was patron protector, angelic prince, and chief among the seven archangels.

In earlier days, Michael would occasionally appear in a vision to a fisherman or peasant anywhere from Constantinople to Cornwall. He had only to point his finger at a hill and soon a church and pilgrimage shrine would spring up to commemorate the spot. The *Michaelion* was his principle sanctuary at Sosthenion, while a healing hot springs at Collosae gave Michael the epithet of Heavenly Physician. In 391 A.D., Michael manifested before an Italian landowner named Garganus, instructing him to found a church at Monte San Angelo. In 590 A.D., Michael appeared in Rome, inspiring the faithful. Ancient Persian lore claims that the Cherubim were formed from the tears Michael shed over the sins of the faithful. For the early Christians, Michael was the benevolent angel of death, deliverance, and immortality, conducting the faithful souls into the eternal light. The Egyptians regarded Michael as Protector of the Nile and his feast days were fixed according to the periodicity of this great river.

Among his angelic peers, Michael is the Prince of Light in the perennial battle against evil and the legions of darkness. He's generally pictured as an angelic warrior, with helmet, shield, and blazing sword, leading the hosts of Heaven against the forces of evil, be they Belial, Satan, the Dragon, Gog and Magog, even the Romans. His traditional titles make an impressive resumé: Recorder of the deeds of men and women in the Heavenly Books; Captain of the Heavenly Hosts; Leader of the Church triumphant in Heaven and militant on Earth; Slayer of the dragon of evil intention; Preparer of the Way for each Messenger from God; the Celestial Medium through whom the Law was given; Guardian of the holy sanctuaries.

In the early Islam tradition, Michael stood with an innumerable array of angels on the borders of the Full Sea, his wings the color of green emerald. "He is covered with saffron hairs, each of them containing a million faces and mouths and as many tongues which, in a million dialects, implore the pardon of Allah." In the Hebrew tradition, God presented the *Decalogue* (or *Torah*) to Moses on Mount Sinai with Michael as an intermediary, while Jewish lore maintains that the face Moses beheld in the burning bush was, in fact, Michael's as a forerunner of the Shekinah. The *Book of Enoch* has Michael standing beside God's throne, while another source calls him the Cherub Who presides at the Gates of Paradise, maintaining the way of the Tree of Life. Michael holds the Heavenly Scales of Justice; he weighs the souls of the dead for the quality of their deeds while alive. Michael is the heavenly librarian and recording angel, the guardian of the magical formulas by which Heaven and Earth were established—which is geomancy—and holder of "the keys of the kingdom of Heaven."

In Rudolf Steiner's Anthroposophy, Michael is the upholder of the purity of Cosmic Intelligence, humankind's cognitive birthright. Through Michael, men and women respiritualize intellect, infusing materialist thinking and science with spiritual insight. Wellesley Tudor Pole notes that Michael is the light-bearer and messenger, the one who prepares the way for Christ. Of Michael, Prince of Heaven, Pole writes: "He is the chief engineer in charge of the sluice gates which control and regulate the release of the 'Waters of the Spirit' into our midst."

Since 1879, when Michael began his new 350-year regency, he has been chief among the seven archangels and has undertaken his tasks with a particularly urgent agenda. Fortunately for him, he can be in thousands of places at once, including right behind us, at the Tor, one of 700 such Michael-dedicated sites in Britain.

The morning here is gorgeously suffused with clear autumn sunlight making the hill feel unusually Aegean, like a marjoram-scented island tucked away in the sparkling blue sea. Out at Pointer's Ball there is a blaze of light, which, when I squint long enough, settles itself into the appearance of a crystalline tree. Blaise is with us and has begun commenting on Pointer's Ball, although as my attention fluctuates from focus to drift, his words swell and fade in my hearing.

"Pointer's Ball was used in the Atlantean epoch to facilitate changes in consciousness. It was a system of landscape engineering whereby an energy current from the Tor was moved through the zodiac to Lugshorn, thereby activating the landscape chakras along the way. What you see as a crystal tree at Pointer's Ball is the thought-form left by the Atlantean engineers. It can be reactivated. The place where you now sit is one point for transmission from the Tor crystal to Pointer's Ball. Energy from the Tor was sent to the tree at Pointer's Ball where it was received at four points along the crystal finger leading to the Ball, then the finger would light up. Michael facilitates this transmission. Michaelmass was the principal time for this energy channeling."

"Why did Michael do this on Michaelmass instead of some other time?" I ask Blaise.

"Because at this time of the year Michael blesses the Earth with his sword to cleanse and shift the energy. He connects the major grid lines and tries to flush through any negative blockages. It's this date because that's the one Michael chose. It has to do with the Moon and its relation in distance to the Earth; it is further away during that time than in the spring when it is closer. The energy of all living organic matter responds to this and changes its nature at this point. Also, the energy matrix of the Earth changes in polarity due to this phenomena around this time. Arthur and his companions, under Merlin's guidance, participated in this activity. When they helped to move the energy through the Arc of Expanding Consciousness, they refreshed themselves."

Blaise points to the gnome accompanying us, who jumps up and runs to a point further up the slope, about one hundred feet from the tower. "This is another of the four transmission points from the Tor, from which energy was directed from the crystalline force field inside the hill, to the finger at Pointer's Ball," says Blaise. This point was used, in part, to purify the energy through a particular form of mental concentration. The Arc spanned a cross-section of the zodiac and helped to infuse a highly purified quality of energy into the landscape system, Blaise explains.

The Michaelmass activity was a little like cleaning the pipes. When light was sent through the 'pipes' of the Arc and into its reception points in the land, it radiated this light throughout the area like heating coils. Merlin and Arthur, as part of their protection of Britain and their work with the Somerset shrines, mobilized the knights to clean the Arc and rejuvenate the zodiac every year at Michaelmass. Blaise tells me that then each knight took his or her seat at a place of spiritual light in the zodiac. Arthur sat at Lugshorn, Merlin at the Tor, Nimuë at Pointer's Ball, Morgan at Park Wood. "Then the system would hum. The Arc was like a tuning fork that set the zodiac humming the right tune. With the new Michael rulership that began last century, the tune is changing. Hear the sound."

We shift our location again to the base of the tower itself, then Blaise continues. "Once there was a stone circle at this site. Merlin used its etheric memory in his work. The trace remains today, though inactively. What you perceive as a giant crystal inside the Tor awaits proper use. We see it more as a celestial seed of light awaiting the touch of Michael's sword to sprout."

For a moment, I sense the immense light field underneath us in the Tor, or, I should say, where the Tor is but in another dimension. It rumbles and quakes as angelic sunlight glints on its many facets. It's as if, in this light, the zodiac figures stand up and stretch after a long slumber, as the Arc light passes through them, humming them warmly into life again. "We say, the phoenix perches on the glass mountain and surveys the starfields. Think on this."

Pointer's Ball is like a finger lying beneath the skin of the land, gently lifting up the green flesh. And it's a fat forefinger, too, with "knuckles" where it bulges upwards in knobs; the "finger" gradually recedes into flatness a half mile away into the Levels. To most people in Glastonbury, Pointer's Ball is an anomalous ancient earthwork twelve feet high and thirty feet broad—another Celtic mystery in the crowded showroom. Once the site was known as the Golden Coffin or Bridge of the Sun, images derived from *Pontes Baal* (or *Bel*—from the Celtic name for the Sun-god); zodiac supporters suggest the landscape sliver is one of the horns of the old Somerset goat, Capricorn of the star wheel.

"This is the site of *Pontis Vallum*, the fort of the bridge, which defended the Isles of Avalon from the mainland," declares the stone marker that indicates the site. The Shepton Mallet road ungraciously cuts through the last fifty feet of Pointer's Ball and this last mounded strip of forgotten Celtic geomancy is equipped with deck chairs, fruit trees, a rotisserie, a plastic swimming pool, and a trimmed British lawn. Lorries and innumerable motorists thunder past the earthwork everyday probably not even noticing it. "Even in the eyes of conventional historians, Ponter's Ball [sic] marks the outer boundary limit of a tremendous sacred enclosure," says Anthony Roberts.

Hilary and I walk slowly down the long finger of Pointer's Ball. The ridge is festooned with spiderweb streamers, fluttering sliver threads that stick to my ankle as I move along barefoot, avoiding the copious cow splats and the spikes of stinging nettle. A farm tractor drones steadily in a nearby field, crows caw and circle overhead, the trees are daubed in pastel leaves. Everything is motionless, almost dreamily so: one pasture, populated with sheep, seems more like a cemetery of white, fuzzy stones; another field is dotted with solitary milkers; and the church spire at West Pennard ambivalently pricks the blue sky. I turn around to face the Tor, which is a mile away, and see two large hands cradling its interior crystal.

At the far end of Pointer's Ball, I see another set of cupped hands prayerfully holding a star of light—the Ball. I feel displaced. Pointer's Ball is a long, glinting index finger probing the glassine astral waters of Avalon, for clearly we are dissolving into the Other Side of Glastonbury. I don't know why exactly, but I'm sure the finger is Nimuë's because, as I continue along the ridge, the finger becomes a crystalline pointer with an egg of light at the tip, and, inside this, there is a tree of light.

Hilary and I have company, too. Merlin walks on my right, Nimuë and Morgan on my left, and I co-inhabit two bodies again, my own, and the Celtic Arthur's. I suppose it doesn't hurt to have a spare. As we—all six of us—pass through a fence, a hedge, a line of trees, it feels like we've seamlessly entered a *temenos* at the fingernail of the earthwork. We stand before the crystal sphere and its tree of light set like a translucent egg in the misty waters of Avalon. A ribbon of women and men emerge from a giant egg of light (the Ball) about one hundred feet tall and fifty across. The Ball at the end of the pointer is Nimuë's temple. A long, glinting sword stands point down inside the crystalline tree. Then a curious split in my perception happens. I'm in two places at once. I see myself in this red-bearded Arthur body standing before the sword in the crystal tree, withdrawing the magnificent blade of light, brandishing it triumphantly against the Avalonian sun. Except I'm standing about a hundred feet from where I'm standing.

"Pointer's Ball points into the astral realm of which Nimuë is the guardian," says Blaise, as Hilary and I sit down before the crystal egg. The long walk over the finger enables the knight to prepare for entering the crystal ball, Blaise explains. It is a dimensional portal, out of your time, into another. This is where Arthur received Excalibur, at least one form of it, and instructions in its use. This is also the place to which Bedevere returned the sword when Arthur departed, Blaise says. This is also Nimuë's crystal cave in which

Merlin was seduced, which is to say, here a demonstration was made of Nimuë's occult accomplishments and spiritual prowess as an initiate—an enchanting cave heaven, if you will. Arthur, Merlin, Morgan, and Nimuë sat at the base of this tree and channeled their light into it. Blaise laughs and says, after all, they helped it to grow in the first place as a conduit between the worlds, as an emissary of the heavenly Tree. The four would make a mini-pilgrimage to the four stations of the Arc on Michaelmass, while the other knights were stationed at points throughout the zodiac. This activity often consumed several days.

There is a great deal of memory from Atlantean, Lemurian, and Hyperborean times stored in the crystal egg at Pointer's Ball, Blaise continues. Arthur, Morgan, and Nimuë were aware of this and often resorted, under Merlin's guidance, to its files. "In a sense, in so far as it represents a sword of insight, this is where Excalibur was forged, where, as you saw, Arthur extracted the insight, or sword, from the crystal stone of the tree of light in Nimuë's temple. Her name, incidentally, means, approximately, 'beautiful water jewel,' from an old language."

After Bedivere returned it, Excalibur remained dormant, Blaise says, but the secrets of its making and use are never forgotten and will be restored to human knowledge in our time. Nimuë transmitted the secrets of the forging of Excalibur to Arthur because she knew he would require it in his defense of Britain and for the spiritual development of his time. At one time there was a physical temple at this site, although it was a doorway into the astral temple. "Nimuë's cooperation, as guardian of the astral plane, was essential for the well-being of Camalate and its milieu. Arthur withdrew the sword from the tree as a test of his qualifications for kingship. It was a private event witnessed by Merlin, Morgan, Nimuë, and your Blazing Star.

"Blaise, who were all the people streaming out of the temple?"

"These were knights whom Nimuë instructed in Avalon and guided through initiation into the astral realm. It was a training whereby two modes of consciousness, the unitive and individuative, or, if you like, the solar, masculine, cutting, and the lunar, feminine, receptive, were fused into one operative whole." This process often produced a jolt in consciousness, which was reflected in the Arthurian stories as a beheading.

Remember Sir Gawain and the Green Knight? Blaise says. Knights losing their heads also meant they were unable to remain awake in their experiences on the other side. The information was lodged in their light bodies but required effort on their part to retrieve its contents, to regain their heads. "Energies of the solar plexus and heart were fused to form a shield, and, in this process, the head as the seat of the rational mind was largely unimportant."

I don't think it's evidence I've lost my head when I say that this is a day the word *lovely* was invented for. Hilary and I amble back along Pointer's Ball, our fingers entwined. I'm trying to get her to think she's Guinivere and that, it follows, I've found my life's love, but she'll have nothing of it. "Don't be silly, Grail Knight. I've always thought of myself as the Lady of the Lake, rising out of the mists, giving Arthur his big sword, then disappearing again, like an enigma."

Merlin and Arthur were riding along one day when Arthur complained that he had no sword, Malory writes. Don't worry about that, Merlin replied; that will soon be remedied. "So they rode till they came to a lake, the which was a fair water and broad, and in the midst of the lake Arthur was ware of an arm clothed in white samite, that held a fair sword in that hand." That damosel is the Lady of the Lake, Merlin told him, "and within that lake is a rock, and therein is as fair a place as any on earth and richly beseen; and this damosel will come to you anon, and then speak ye fair to her that she will give you that sword."

A gnome greets us at the gate at Park Wood, but, just before we slip into the silent wood, I notice a massive crown of light set over the tree tops with a single bold light shaft rising up from its center. We follow the gnome in a sunwise spiralling stroll through the woods until we stop at a gateway. "Park Wood is made up of some very magical trees indeed," writes Anthony Roberts, "and its careful geomantic shaping (protected by a bank and ditch) takes the form of the serpent/dragon sun-crown of old Egypt."

In the minds of Somerset zodiac mappers, including Katherine Maltwood, Park Wood is the mystical center and crown of the zodiac, marking *Kochab*—meaning "the Star, the abode and essence and spirit of life," said Maltwood—in the constellation Ursa Minor or Little Bear, formerly the Pole Star. The *axis mundi* is a World Tree with the Star of Life blazing at its apex, says Roberts. "If my psychic source is correct, then Merlin dwells in the 'crown of the land' at Park Wood under the benign influence of a Life Star. In mystical lore, Merlin is said to lie among trees (even *in* trees) yet under stone; he is never said to be dead." Merlin would surely agree with that. Meanwhile, Blaise has more to tell us.

Blaise explains that Morgan often brought the knights to Park Wood as part of their training. She had them pace through the heart of these woods, as we are doing; however, the wood was formerly much larger. Here they were subjected to a series of confrontations with elemental spirits. The devic presence is strong here. Love from Above enters here on behalf of the zodiac, a little drop of Eden, you might say. The crystal crown, and its spikes, is a protective aura around an inner Grail bowl. The bowl and crown need polishing. There is a place in Park Wood where Arthur sat to experience the center of the zodiac, Blaise tells me. When each knight completed his circuit of zodiacal experiences, he came here for a topping up, to sit at the still center of the turning wheel. Here they solidified and consolidated their insights. "Feel the zodiac around you. Its shapes are stirring with new life. The stars are coming out in the daytime."

Spiderwebs may have been the insignia of Pointer's Ball, but it's mushrooms for Park Wood. There are mushrooms with tawny elephant ears harboring recumbent fairies; dark umbrella mushrooms; golden mushrooms growing in shelves; ordinary whitecaps; mushrooms appearing at every footstep through this damp, leaf-strewn wood. The gnome guides us to a dell bounded by yew trees. "There are three jewels in the crown," Blaise says. "Topaz, emerald, and ruby. The Arc is like a waterfall; Park Wood is a rainbow that spans the waterfall." Where we stand now is the gnome shrine, their jewel, the emerald, Blaise says. This is one of the places where the Green Knight performed his initiations on behalf of Morgan.

When Gawain arrived at the Green Chapel—a grass-covered barrow by a stream—to reluctantly keep his appointment with the Green Knight, he decried it as a "hideous oratory, all overgrown,/And well-graced for the gallant garbed in green/To deal out his devotions in the Devil's fashion." Even though he had chopped off the Green Knight's head by way of demonstration at Camalate, he wasn't excited about keeping his end of the agreement: to let the "Fiend himself" reciprocate and "destroy me here" at the "chapel of mischance" with his great four-foot blade. Indeed: whoever said initiation was fun?

On the other hand, whoever said it was all suffering and losing one's head? About two dozen gnomes have formed a circle around us. I offer them a blue cordial from the Grail bowl, which they accept with a bow. The grove feels gnomish: stout, merry, sparkling, compact, mischievous, attentive, even bearded—gnome energy from the inside. Hilary sits on the ground facing me and we clasp each other Fairy Dell-style, sitting stomach-to-stomach, waist-to-waist, in a permanent hug, making a human egg. She unbuttons her blouse and moves my head between her breasts. They are lovely and large and soft and my mouth and tongue kiss and lap them in joy. But in the midst of my fondling, I notice a green glow on the left side of Hilary's sternum (her right), as if, somehow, an emerald were lodged inside, radiating light.

Even as I nudge her nipples, it seems her third emerald breast imparts a strong green light. Blaise wraps us in a blue eggshell of light and for a moment, I am in two places at once again, seeing us from a distance: Grail Knight, Grail Maiden, interlocked in a blue, diaphanous sphere with a radiant green interior, encircled by luminous angels and chuckling gnomes. A Blazing Star burns insistently in each of our crowns. The gnomes are ever so polite about our conduct and the Blaises face away towards the horizon, whistling tunes until Hilary and I untwine ourselves, rebutton, and continue the tour of Park Wood rather than each other's body.

Our next stop is a fairy dell, a circle of thickly ingrown trees, so dense and low we have to crouch as we walk through; even then, their branches scratch our shoulders. We reach a small, grassy clearing and sit, silently absorbing the tranquillity. "The ruby grove was the center for another form of initiation through the devic realm," says Blaise. I offer the fairies blue light from the Grail. The third site is a single tree surrounded by a fifteen foot radius of smooth grass. "This is the topaz site. Here we do *our* initiations. Here the Light comes in. We surround you both in a crown of golden light. A Grail Knight must be able to work with and integrate the energies of the devic or elemental and angelic realms on behalf of the human realm."

As the gnome conducts us out of Park Wood, a farmer drives a tractor pulling a load of freshly harvested sugar beets across the field. A couple fat ones tumble off his wagon and we collect them for dinner. But we have one more stop before our borscht: Lugshorn, on the north side of Dundon Beacon, unmarked amidst cultivated fields.

Once again, a gnome meets us at the road where we park the car. This one—I assume it's a different fellow—is white-bearded, friendly, smokes a pipe, and walks with a muscular, swaying gait, almost bowlegged as if he were on a boat. Unfortunately, I lose track of him as Hilary and I talk and the wind blows us about. In fact, the wind grows so vigorous, seemingly the minute we step on the field, that it nearly sends the dried cow turds airborne. It's so windy I feel like flying myself as a kite. After all, as a man with a Taurean-Scorpio dialectic in my horoscope, that's my aspiration: to fly. I toss my meditation cushion into the wind to see if it gets wafted all the way to Blaise's house but it comes down fifty yards away. I run about the field in Hilary's green parka, flapping madly like a stork trying to get airborne.

The single lane track out to Lugshorn is rutted, muddy, and slippery, and soon my sneakers are caked brown, thick, and wet. A seasoned Grail Knight should always wear Wellingtons; since I'm just a beginner, who cares if I ruin my shoes? We feast on wild blackberries until our lips flush purple. A teenage boy saunters down the lane and we ask him where exactly is Lugshorn? Though he lives in the farmhouse at the end of this field, he's never heard of Lugshorn. Hilary and I sit down on her green parka at the edge of the field, back-to-back this time, her hands in my lap, mine in hers (as much as is possible), our heads touching at the occiput, and we rock sideways, slowly, watching the clouds change shape and blow past. We'll let Lugshorn find us; anyway, it has to be around here somewhere.

The gnome returns, or is it that my perception of him comes back? He points to a place on the edge of a plowed field. Lugshorn. After studying it, I see a ten-foot-high wood-slab fence and, inside this, a circle of standing stones, perhaps three dozen, each about four feet tall. This perception seems to nudge Blaise into vocality again. "Lugshorn is the bolt that secures the Arc of Developing Consciousness to the Earth. In the center of this circle was a special seat called Merlin's Gate, the Gate of Fire. It was a doorway between worlds. Arthur sat here on Michaelmass as an envoy on behalf of the knights. Lugshorn is also the crown of the second Gemini infant in the zodiac. We call Lugshorn the sacred part. It is the blessed area, the one that was born whole, the new birth. We are treating it now with violet light. The lilac flame of transmutation plays here every day."

In the evening when we all gather in the livingroom after tea, Blaise deepens our understanding of the Arc and its environment. "We surround you with a lilac wall, a tube of lilac flame for each of you, each with a gold flame burning at its center. In the middle we place a pyramid of green light. Within the pyramid, we place the golden bowl. The bowl has twelve symbols on its outer edge. They are what you call the signs of the zodiac. All are in circles but Capricorn is in a square. All signs face outwards on the golden bowl. Within the bowl, we place a pearl of brilliant, pure light at the center. Above the pearl, we place a flame of brilliant blue light. The tip of the flame touches the top of the pyramid. All is complete when we place the Black Bowling Ball of stable consciousness on top of the pyramid. Breathe with us for a few minutes to this new image....

"We are most happy to be with you all tonight. The emerald pyramid glistens. We sing for you all. What do you wish to know?"

"Blaise, today you told me some words for the Atlantean practices in the Arc on Michaelmass, but I don't think I got them right. They sounded pretty strange. Can you confirm me in these words?"

"We touch each shoulder with the sword of Michael. We touch the left, then the right, then the left, then the top of your head, then the right shoulder again. We confirm you thus."

I hadn't expected to back my way into an angelic *adoubement*, so I'm half-grinning and half-flummoxed when Blaise finishes. Before I can sort things out, Blaise continues. "Michael loves ice cream. Strawberry and vanilla. The big ice cream cone in the sky, the end of all desire. He's taking a lick right now. Ummmm. He's just dribbled and the drops are covering the cities of Europe. Wonderful. O Michael. He is what you would call a gas."

"Blaise, I don't know if this is the right time to bring it up," says Berenice, "but for some time I've had this feeling that there really are two zodiacs, not one."

"Correct. There are two zodiacs. There is one Earth circle and one Heavenly circle of the astral-causal plane. The one you can see on the landscape is the Earth circle. The other is a potential in the etheric. Glastonbury is the center, where the sword crosses through both circles. It is a point of access to both worlds, the fish, so to speak. The sword itself is what you call the Michael ley line. On the Earth, you have a representation created through consciousness and divine inspiration: this is the physical zodiac. You have another circle in the etheric with particular influence over the other half to activate it. Both were made simultaneously, through a unitive consciousness under divine guidance."

"That same image of a sword passing through a *vesica piscis* made of two overlapping circles hangs over the entrance to Arthur's Courtyard," I remark. "What does this image mean?"

"Perceive one circle to be the circle of manifestation of everything on the Earth plane. The other circle is the manifestation of everything on the etheric or astral-causal plane. These two circles interlock. The point where they touch is as one leaves the other, the little fish-shape appears in between both circles. The space between them creates the third dimension which is out of time and space, not related to either Heaven or Earth. Much information about this symbol derives from a past time era. Its relevance and implications are for the Piscean age now passing from this planet. A new dimension is occuring now, better described by other symbols. A new symbol structure is about to emerge. It is extraordinary the way this symbol is being brought through. All the Masters of wisdom, all the Buddhas, the Christ, the messiahs and avatars, in their different aspects of consciousness, are contributing to the Earth plane to make a composite ray, which will emerge in the next 200 to 300 years."

"Is the Michael line you described as a sword passing through the two zodiacs a dome line or something different?" I continue.

"Yes, your assumption is correct. Something different. There are other lines of etheric force passing above the surface of the Earth's crust that are not necessarily radiating from the places that had memories of domes. The lines that are not dome-related do not oscillate in the same way. They are consistent lines of energy surrounding the planet. These lines and the dome lines are both phenomena operating on what we call the Dragon Oroboros line running through England. Both lines run parallel, one above, one below, over the Earth's surface. This grouping is what makes certain lines particularly noticeable today.

"There are twelve major Oroboros lines that encircle the planet as twelve great circles, and three sub-lines that also encircle the planet, making fifteen in total. Of these twelve major lines, each has a different solar energy, ordinarily denominated by zodiacal attributes. For example, one Oroboros line could be called the Sagittarius line; another, the Capricorn line. The three minor lines are ordinarily denominated by qualities of male, female, and neutral, or positive, negative, and neutral, or solar, lunar, and neutral. The Oroboros lines each have different and varying levels of vibration, or color, although they do not involve all the colors of the spectrum. A principal color is gold, while lilac is found on occasion. The Oroboros lines are like primary energy tracks. They contain the organic film of life on earth. After the birth of a biological being such as your Earth, the primary energy lines determine the nature of its growth and environment."

"Do the Oroboros lines vary in width?"

"The Michael Oroboros line, for example, varies at different points, at some places measuring four feet, at others, several hundred yards. Meridians of the Earth vary at nodal points particularly. There are many grid lines around the surface of the planet. Some are on the actual Earth; some are a few feet above the ground; some large grid lines are several hundred yards above, and the final line is about two miles above the Earth."

"I have the feeling there might be more than the standard twelve figures of the ecliptic in the landscape zodiac. It doesn't make sense to have only twelve constellations when there are dozens more out there—you know, *up* there where you guys hang out."

"Correct. There are 144 constellations in the temple, including both physical and etheric circles. The twelve principal constellations of the ecliptic are duplicated, making two sets in two ecliptics. That leaves 120 other constellations without duplication. You must only count the bright stars, the major magnitude stars, when you are determining star points for the landscape. The constellations are not divided equally between the physical and etheric circles. There are 96 constellations in the physical ecliptic, which correspond to the stars in the Northern Hemisphere; and 48 in the etheric ecliptic, which correspond to stars in the Southern Hemisphere, of which some have a more pronounced, some a more subtle, effect. For instance, the constellation Canis Minor in the Northern Hemisphere exerts less influence on Glastonbury today than the Southern Cross from the Southern Hemisphere. For this time period, there is minimum activation for the Little Dog. When the new age dawns, there will be more activation, more awakening."

"All right. Let's come back to this Arc of Developing Consciousness. How does the crystal at the thorn tree on Wearyall Hill fit into the picture?"

"We bring you for a moment back to the tree. Tell us what you see."

I am inside a transparent crystal or a geometrically defined field of white light. This would be the Lemurian memory bank we saw with Michael that night at the seventh level of the Tor. A long bamboo slatted footbridge spans a tremendous chasm. There is a dark cave at the far end of this narrow, swaying bridge gaping two-thirds up the barren, rocky side of a mountain. I cross the bridge, enter the cave, and am greeted by numerous *Yetis*. The image falters momentarily to a cluster of Smokey-the Bears then to an array of bear manikins.

"Breathe with love to this appearance," says Blaise.

The image of the bears shatters. Now there is a multipetalled flower like an aster in hues of rose and lilac. I see Wearyall's Holy Thorn from a new perspective. It's a young sapling with many cones of rose and lilac asterlike flowers, each blooming at the tip of a long, green stalk, which emerges from the tree's trunk. "This must be Joseph's flowering staff!" I exclaim.

"Correct. Now look out over the landscape towards the Tor and Pointer's Ball again."

A huge male figure reclines in the landscape, his body stretching from below Wearyall to the Tor, Pointer's Ball, Park Wood, and beyond. He struggles to rise, but he is shackled to the Earth, groaning like Gulliver among the Lilliputians. I'm too astonished to speak at first because I suddenly understand something from William Blake. Albion, said Blake in his long poem, *Jerusalem* (1804), is the "Human Form Divine," an image of spiritual beauty expressed in human form as a giant who is the antecedent of all men and women. In Paradise, Albion was, originally, in God's view, "the Angel of my Presence" and "the loveliest Son of Heaven." Then, entering incarnation on Earth, Albion gained selfhood but lost the vision of his divine origins and purpose and began a time of suffering. "In a dark & unknown Night/Outstretch'd his Giant beauty on the ground in pain & tears," said Blake. The seven diseases of the soul settled upon Albion as he "groans in the deep slumbers of Death upon his Rock." Like Prometheus in the Greek myths who was bound to a rock at the edge of the sea for transgressing against the gods, so, too, is Albion chained to matter, "sick to death" from "horrible falsehoods" spread by his sons and daughters.

Albion is a prodigy of the spiritual worlds, yet so grievous is his forgetting that "the Starry Heavens all were fled from the mighty limbs of Albion." This is most unfortunate, Blake said, for two reasons. First, Albion is destined to marry Vala (the Earth or Gaia), who is his "Bride & Wife in great eternity;" and second, Albion has a gift for the world, a "lovely emanation" called Jerusalem (not the physical city but a spiritual conclave and dispensation). Albion shall arise again, Blake promises us. "The time will arrive/When all Albion's injuries shall cease, and when we shall/Embrace him, tenfold bright, rising from his tomb in immortality."

"Is this Albion?" I ask Blaise.

"It is. We did not hope or expect that you would see him already. We will show you more later. We are hoping to present an angelic mass of which you have been initiated into the primary phase. We hope to bring through an angelic mass for the coming time under the direction of Michael. It will be a Michaelmass at Pointer's Ball. The prologue to the mass is the Albion experience."

"Is Albion male or female?"

"Appearances are deceptive. Albion lies, or should we say, *he* lies, on the Mother."

"Is this *the* Albion, the only one anywhere in a zodiac?"

"No. They are all one in Britain. There are others. Each is an aspect of Albion, but they are all one. They become involved in a process of reciprocal maintenance and are therefore energized as the Glastonbury Albion awakes. Now we ask you: what is light? Light is energy in matter with a degree of movement. In itself it is stillness. At its center, energy is stillness. We would like to illustrate this. A hurricane is a mass of energy revolving around a center. It carries movement touching at its periphery but it is still at its center. Each hurricane has an eye, a center of stillness. Light is like this. It is a point of stillness with energy vibrating at its periphery. Light is stillness in movement. It is what it is. It is not known by its relation to something else. It is known by itself. You can recognize light as a phenomenon that is independent, arising in any moment from a point of stillness. What we are describing is something that is an important key for you all. Light is synonymous with consciousness. Albion is the conscious mind's interpretation of this figure in the landscape. There was once a man who said: 'I am the Word, the Truth, the Light. I and the Father are one.' It depends on whether you created it or not. Spend more time in the next few days at Pointer's Ball. We will present what needs to be in the angelic mass for the coming time under Michael's direction."

"Thank you Blaise, now I wish to ask—"

"We wish all the time."

"When you wish upon a little star, you mean?"

"We wish upon a mighty big Blazing Star, smaller or brighter than you can imagine. Beyond that even."

"Well, anyway, I desire to know—"

"Desire is something we lack, unfortunately. But in a way, we aren't sorry. If you waste your time in misery in your physical body, we will chastise you when you are back with us. Be what you are. A being of light trapped in a physical form, trapped in the experience of infinite happiness. We wish....Wish we....We....Tsssshhhhhh."

"I'd still like to know if I heard those words correctly that you mentioned today?"

"Oh dear. What is correct, we ask you?"

"What you say."

"And incorrect?"

"Distortion."

"How lovely. We like to know we are correct. We are pleased. What is correct?"

"Correct, incorrect. Both are empty."

"Emptiness is form."

"Form is emptiness."

"This is not. Is not this. Not. Is. This. Oh dear, anyway, we leave you now, as a point of light in a sea of emerald mist, as your Blazing Star."

It's just as well Blaise left, because I forget what comes next in that Buddhist dialogue. After tea, Hilary and I retire upstairs, and I get into her bed. This isn't the best of ideas from her point of view. "You must remember I'm basically solitary," she says primly. "I need my space. I don't want a lover, and I don't want to be one. It's the wrong time in my life. You know what I think? Breathe love back to your boyhood. Find a scene in which you felt pain or rejection, the source of this neediness. Look at the pain, embrace it, and spit it out." With this, she shoves me out of the bed with her strong legs. "Good night, Grail Knight."

I dream. I sit in a circle with three women, all close friends. One is very young, Celia's age. Another woman is naked and complains about her breasts, that everybody always comments unfavorably about them; she makes an insulting remark to the third woman in my group, and I say something in her defense. Now we are escaping from a bus, running across a field. I hold up a barbed wire fence so they can pass through safely. I am their guardian. Several of the women have long, lovely hair, which gets tangled in the barbs; I gently free the snarls from the sharp points. One woman says goodbye to me. I hug her and squeeze her breasts; she smiles happily. Another woman will not embrace me until all evident signs of my sexual arousal have subsided. We both laugh. The third woman wears a long, white tunic, as I do, splattered in red, whether blood or wine I don't know.

I wake. Hilary slips into my bed, setting the tea tray on my desk. When I relate my dream she says: "These women are all aspects of your feminine consciousness. You see, you didn't have to sleep alone after all. You have lots of women available at the snap of your fingers."

35

DOUBLING UP TO MEET THE GREEN KNIGHT

e're bound for Pointer's Ball again today, but, before we drive off, I call in at my earth circle. The seed is sprouting like a cotyledon of light, I tell Hilary on the drive into Glastonbury. We walk slowly, contemplatively down the crystal finger of Pointer's Ball, flanked by a half dozen Blaises with flared wings. Michael looms like a skyscraper behind Nimuë's crystal egg. When we reach the tree of light and sit down, a troop of angels dashes about frantically like a hundred Groucho Marxes balancing long swords on the tips of their fingers. This must be the cartoon before the feature film.

Michael lowers his great sword towards my head, and I drift out into the astral dream state of Avalon, afloat on its waters. At least an hour passes, marked by that kind of vacuity an insomniac must feel after staring at a blank television screen until three a.m. I know I've been up to something but I have no idea what it was. I guess I was beheaded again: I fell asleep, or lost my head, my awareness, during an incursion. I can always watch it on video later because somewhere in this unfathomable body of mine, this concatenation of being bodies beyond measure, the experience is recorded. As Woody Allen quips, showing up is worth ninety percent. A lot of the time these days, I feel more like the horse than the rider, tethered with nosebag while my master conducts his business inside the saloon. Just before lunch, we stop off at the Holy Thorn.

I see Albion in daylight, golden and forlorn, supine, shackled on the zodiacal wheel, the Arc of Developing Consciousness sweeping like a scimitar from his heart to crown. Thou wast to me the loveliest Son of Heaven, O Albion, mildest Son of Eden and Angel of My presence—tied up.

After lunch, Hilary drops me off at Pointer's Ball again then drives off for an appointment. I have the finger to myself this afternoon. It's cold and raining, not the ideal weather for ninety minutes of meditation in a puddled, manure-splatted, damp field that juts dreamily into the mysteries of Avalon. The wind blows fiercely as I breathe as Love from Above to the Grail image and make my way down the soggy, slippery finger. I can't see anything through my glasses because they've steamed up; and I can't see anything when I take them off because that's why I wear glasses. Well, I can see my feet and the ground, but just the general outlines. Trousers, socks, sneakers, shirt, hair, face: all soaked. The sword-balancing angels, dry to the feather tips, now saunter unperturbed under broad umbrellas. Even Michael sports a mahagony-handled umbrella. Okay. So you angels are nice and dry and toasty on the other side where it doesn't rain but blisses, while we hard-working journeymen Grail Knights slosh our way to a probable enlightenment. How did we ever cut a deal like this?

This blush of heroic self-pity warms me up and improves matters for the present. Except now I notice behind me another Grail Knight—another me—identical to myself except he's on the other side, too. His—my—edges are fringed in light like an aura, and his insides are spacious, if not empty: I'm looking at my own light body. Now, as if from a height of a hundred yards above the glistening crystal finger, I see myself as a man in flapping red raincoat outlined in white light, drenched in sunlight, not rain, flanked by six magnificently plumed angels striding through waves of light. No rain, no wind, no manure. It's as if there are two interpenetrating processions happening, one in rain, one in light—and I'm in both of them.

I reach Nimuë's crystal tree inside the egg and sit down on the wet ground. If I knew how this bilocation business works, I would sit down in my light body and stay dry. Let the other Grail Knight get wet. This is a full lotus job. I need the extra body heat and mental focus that only terribly painful knees can deliver. Periodically, the rain abates and I start to relax, thinking I might dry off a little, but the gods of meteorology evidently are finely attuned to my thoughts because no sooner do I lapse into self-indulgent ruminations about comfort than another vociferous crest of rain and wind assails me. I hide under the skimpy parka and pretend I'm somewhere else and the rain can't find me. An angel hands me three apples from the tree. Michael lowers his sword to my head. I see myself walking around with the angels, with Blaise, with Michael.

Maybe his sword is a ladder out of my head. Lancelot, one of Arthur's premier knights, had to cross an iffy bridge with bad flooring, the infamous sword-bridge. As Chrétien de Troyes wrote in the twelfth century, this sword-bridge spanned a "wicked-looking stream, which is as swift and raging, as black and turgid, as fierce and terrible as if it were the devil's stream." Plus it's dangerous and bottomless, not the kind of stream you want to fall into when you lose your balance on a sword-bridge. Of that dubious construction, Chrétien says in *Lancelot*: "The bridge across the cold stream consisted of a polished, gleaming sword; but the sword was stout and stiff, and was as strong as two lances." It was attached to a tree trunk at either end of the chasm; also attached to a great rock at the far end were two lions. Naturally, Lancelot has to cross the chasm and deal with the lions to complete a special mission charged to him on account of his being a Grail Knight.

The seasoned Grail Knight learns to travel without maps; the apprentice Grail Knight is too dumb to know even that. I have no idea what else happens to me at Pointer's Ball. The other me should be reporting this; he's the one who did it. This me is just a cranky, wet horse not pleased with conditions.

When I trudge back to the beginning of Pointer's Ball again, Hilary is sitting in her warm car. She turns the heater up to full strength until my glasses steam, my socks exude mist, and my teeth stop chattering. It could be worse, I suppose. At least we get to be miserable during business hours. In earlier days, the Grail Knights got their visions at night, sometimes in dreaming, or sometimes doing just what I did, falling asleep on the job the minute they shoved their head into the astral. Michael prefers we conduct Grail Knight business during the daytime now. "Michael was the revealer through the night and in our age he must become the revealer during the day," writes Rudolf Steiner. "The time has come when human beings must recognize that within them the latent faculty is ready to be awakened which is able to behold, through day-revelation, that which in earlier times was transmitted in night-revelation through Michael."

It's my Taurean brickness, I suppose, that inspires me to mention to Russell this evening that I'm not sure anything much happened out at Pointer's Ball in the rain. Russell goes into a flounce about this. "You take these experiences too much for granted. What you saw today and what Michael did would once have been enough for somebody to go off and start a cult with twenty thousand followers."

"You don't mean I have to go back to California?"

"You ask Blaise for an ice cream cone and instead they hand you the whole ice cream factory. Then you turn around and say, 'About that ice cream cone you promised.' You're just too much, Grail Knight."

I absorb Russell's commentary draped over the sofa in a mudra of exhaustion compounded by the delights of two Guinnesses at room temperature. The seasoned Grail Knight always unwinds with stout after a vexing day on the Quest. "When you make a move forward in consciousness and release stored tension," Russell says, "inevitably there's an initial feeling of enervation." That's good to hear; I thought it was my wet feet.

The next morning, I borrow Hilary's car for the commute to the Ball. I park on Wellhouse Lane, climb the Tor, descend the Tor, saunter down Ashwell Lane and out to the main road. Lorries swoosh past nearly sucking me into their windwake. This is not a pedestrian-friendly road. Michael stands atop the Tor with his light sword upraised, while beneath him, the four spurs of the Tor crystal—the Michaelmass transmission points—glitter as if newly polished. He lowers the sword to the ground, while, with his left hand, which holds his shield, he reaches into the stars.

"Michael protects as well as energizes this planet," Blaise explains as we walk along the finger of Pointer's Ball. "He uses the shield to divert unwholesome influences from reaching particular points at particular times on Earth. He also uses the shield to reflect energies from celestial sources and beings to various points on the Earth's surface. He is using his shield more at present than his sword during this potentially difficult time. There are four transmitting points on Pointer's Ball. We'll show you them." When I climb the ridge and sit down where Blaise indicates, the sun suddenly jumps out from behind a uniform field of grey sky. The six Blaises grin, point to the improved weather, and congratulate one another. They spread a blanket on the ground and remove food and drinks from a picnic basket. "Don't mind us, Grail Knight. It's elevenses. Get them every day. You know, low blood sugar in the late morning."

Four knuckles of intense light glint along the finger of Pointer's Ball. "Close your eyes, Grail Knight, and tell us what you see," Blaise says, their mouths full of sandwiches. Albion sprawls across the zodiac, the Grail image superimposed on his massive body. The green pyramid with golden bowl inhabits Albion from Beckery to the Tor.

"Good. Pass the mustard, love," Blaise says. The needle at Pointer's Ball is the gold sword through the *vesica piscis* above at Albion's chest. The crystal egg at the end of the sword, or finger, is the blue tip of light at the end of the sword. Pointer's Ball is the eye of the sword, formed by two overlapping circles in the Levels. These are Albion's lungs. The first three knobs in the needle are the three jewels in the sword, three energy nodes: emerald, topaz, and ruby. Where you sit is the emerald knob, set here by the gnomes under Michael's instruction. Michael's spot is at Albion's throat, at the crystal egg, at the blue tip of the sword." Nimuë's egg is enhaloed with a blue ring today, a jewel on top; behind this towers Michael, wings flared to the spiritual winds. The rest of the Grail image lies further in the landscape: the Black Bowling Ball at Park Wood, the blue sapphire bowl at Lugshorn.

Walking the Arc of Developing Consciousness is really the same as walking *in* Albion, I realize—it's walking outside in the landscape through the same Blaise image I visualize around me, both of which pertain to our human higher being bodies.

The second knob at Pointer's Ball is close by. "This is the highest spot, our little place, the topaz knob," Blaise says, like a real estate agent showing his prize offering. "It was designed as a meeting place for representatives for both sides on Michaelmass. We surround you now as an angelic circle." I am enveloped by a luminous tent of wings; the Blaise faces are only inches from mine. "We are standing as a circle of light around you. Oh, but we feel so much better after a proper lunch. Once people sat in an inner circle, surrounded by us, their backs facing the center. One person sat in the center and chanted: *O Michael uplift us now.* We sang along with them, in our own way."

We saunter further down the finger to the ruby knob. 'The fairies dance here and tickle Albion's throat. He gurgles with glee.' I don't see any of the merry little folk today but it doesn't matter. I'm doing pretty good with the angels. Probably because they're bigger, easier to see. Maybe it's their sunglasses; it's easy to pick them out in a crowd.

We move to the end of the finger, to Nimuë's ball of light. "The crown of the tree receives the sword stroke from Michael and lights up," Blaise says. "Michael's sword rests on your crown, too, in the blue saphire bowl, and lights everything up." This is a ceremony in which Michael infuses his spirit into humans, Blaise says. Pointer's Ball was once and can be again, if we wish, a place for such initiation. I have to keep slapping myself in the face to stay awake because the mists of the astral lap against the crystal finger, tugging at consciousness, luring it off its mark to slip into the dream state. Overhead, the slatey sullenness of the sky threatens immediate rain. I can do without getting soaked again so it seems time to reel in that part of me who is out in the astral rowboat fishing for fresh *makyo*.

For a fleeting moment Blaise adjusts the weather and the sun emerges, turning Nimuë's egg into a sphere of glittering loveliness. I have the sensation of passing through a long series of arches, a receding tunnel of vibrational changes, almost like a vertebral column of gradual dimensonal shifts that empties me into a new domain.

There is the Fisher King, himself and his surroundings all in pale golden light. There is Nimuë in pale blue surrounded by a robin's egg blue shell or aura. And there is Michael, I presume, radically different than the essentially anthropomorphic form with glorious wings. This Michael is more of a composite of the intention and energies of hosts of angels, composed as if from their songs, their *halleluias*. It's as if they are singing a mass to Michael: *All hail Michael!* Albion's heavenly brother, his angelic half who never left God. On the other side of this realm, on the Glastonbury side of Nimuë's egg, Albion lies shackled across the land, here in the Somerset temple of the stars and elsewhere, in many places in human consciousness, bound in matter, asleep to Michael, his angelic awareness.

Michael daubs the egg with his sword then flies off like an awful white owl back to the Tor. As we make our way back down the finger, Blaise says, "Put Michael before you in all you do. We suggest that he needs your assistance. Note the intention before moving, walking, sitting, thinking, reading, writing, washing—in everything you do as you are about to do it. Put Michael before you in each intention. *O Michael uplift us now.* If you catch only two per cent of your actions, this will make an extraordinary difference to your ability to be of assistance. *Let Michael be with me in this*, you can say to yourself. Let Michael be with me in this sitting, in this walking, in this lying down, in the every-day matters concerning the nature of your bodily existence." Once back in Glastonbury, I take Blaise's advice and let Michael wipe my steamed glasses, adjust the rear view mirror, and drive me all the way back to Wick Manor.

It's late in the evening. I'm exhausted and cold. We're waiting around for Blaise's arrival so we can go to bed. They must have been held up by traffic. Finally, the familiar burst of light fills the room, and the six Blaises pop into relative, if diaphanous, form again. "We come as a Blazing Star, from not too far. We breathe with you. We ask that each of you place your attention at the tips of your little fingers. Concentrate your attention on the meeting of the little fingers. Breathe love to it." Bright lights as a half-dozen green-smocked men in surgical masks lean over me as if I'm in an operating room.

Strange place to store a memory. I examine my little finger with sudden interest. "We once said to some people that we come as we are. We said to them through a good channel: *beings*. But they misinterpreted us and thought we said *eons*. Much confusion arose from this. It is good to be back."

"Blaise, what do you mean by eons?"

"Don't tell us you're going to miss it, too? We are holding our wings in glee. We wish you to ask us your first question."

"Okay. Am I finished with my experiences at Pointer's Ball?"

"Am I finished? MI-5? Do you mean the secret police?"

These guys never let up. "No, I meant, what is this light body business all about, the extra me that was flying around at Pointer's Ball?"

"Much has already been written in your time from your culture about this. We refer to Carlos Castaneda. At this point, you wouldn't understand what we could tell you about the phenomena you describe because you only perceive a fraction of the experience you have been undergoing in the preceding several months. You will remember much more from this light body later. By the way, we have some fun for you in Cornwall. It will be different from what you expect. You will see what happens. All is going very well. Much has been accomplished, much is beginning to flow. We recognize your small part in this process and we thank you all. See you at the beach. Sleep tight. We leave as a Blazing Star."

"What's all this about the beach and Cornwall?" I ask Russell after Blaise leaves.

"Oh, did we forget to tell you, Grail Knight? We're going to Cornwall for a few days for a special Grail Quest expedition. My sister's got a seaside cottage down there. It won't be too big a hardship for you, I shouldn't think."

Just as I am falling asleep, I catch a vivid glimpse of part of what I was up to this afternoon at Pointer's Ball. *Avalon, Avalon, Avalon,* chants Nimuë from inside her egg, which is more like sculpted mist the sharper I see it. I step onto a barge, and she poles us across the misty water towards a magnificent crystal mountain like a six-sided, translucent green emerald set inside a concave, pale bluish tea saucer or dish. This is *Ynys Witrin*, the Glass Island, the Tor's double. We pass inside into a brilliantly golden interior, like the heart of a domed cathedral. Except it feels like I'm inside a head, a golden cranium whose every crystalline facet is an eye of awareness. This multitude of golden eyes watches me benevolently. This is King Evelake, says Nimuë. I recognize the name and its permutations: Evelake, Avalok, Avallach, King of the Summer Country—*Avalokiteshvara*, the Lord Who Surveys, the Bodhisattva and cosmic chaplain of the captain dome of the Tor.

I stand in the center of this golden-eyed rotunda and turn into a shaft of light, which instantly transports me, like the contents of a tube, straight up and out of the golden dome. There I stand, as if on a rooftop in a celestial city, surveying the glittering outer surfaces of numerous yellow-golden domes linked, umbilically, with intertwined silver and gold threads.

When I re-enter the mountain, there is the Green Knight, fiercesomely huge with brandished sword. The Knight of the Green Chapel created a powerful impression when he strode, unannounced, into Camalate on Christmas Day as Arthur and his knights were feasting at their great table. 'Such a horse, such a horseman, in the whole wide world/Was never seen or observed by those assembled before,' writes the anonymous medieval poet of *Sir Gawain and the Green Knight*. The Green Knight was an 'awesome fellow,' taller than all mortal men, 'half a giant on earth,' a fellow 'fiercely grim' yet the handsomest of horsemen—and he was clothed entirely in glittering, vivid green. Even his axe—'huge and monstrous/A hideous helmet-smasher for anyone to tell of'—was done in green, hammered gold. None could account for his country of origin but all reckoned him 'a marvel in the world.' Later Gawain would learn, upon visiting the Green Knight's chapel in the woods (a barrow), that 'He has lived here since long ago/And filled the field with gore.'

The Green Knight is a mythic expression of Michael in his celestial integrity, as the initiator of Grail Knights. There is a circular table with an intensely reflective surface, a pristine mirror. I float over this mirror and rather than seeing my physical body reflected back, I see instead my Blazing Star; its brilliance is doubled in the mirror, and I am suddenly out in the vast starfields of the cosmos. I hear choirs of angels singing: *O Michael uplift us now*, over and over. Somehow I know that I and all the stars and the angelic choirs are inside Michael's sword, which is as big as the galaxy. It is the galactic sword of pure mind, of Cosmic Intelligence, of the immaculate awareness of all the denizens of Heaven and their purposes expressed as a sword, as a penetrative focus of insight.

When I realize this, I find myself standing next to Michael, or the Green Knight—or the Buddhist *Manjusri*, for that matter, "He Who is Noble and Gentle," the Bodhisattva of wisdom and dispeller of darkness who wields a sword and a book of wisdom; probably these three are equivalent expressions of the same ineffable being—holding the sword of pure mind with the cosmos of stars inside it.

I am aware of the Maimed Fisher King, who sits in a cocoon of pale golden light; the sword is for him, but this is not yet the time for his healing. I must first understand the wound. Stepping outside the crystal mountain—or perhaps I should say the Green Chapel—I enter the voluptuous apple orchard of Avalon, acres of apple trees with plump golden apples and silver leaves.

36

MICHAEL MARKS THE SPOT WITH RAINBOWS

arly in the morning we load up the Grail bus and set off for The West. In the evening, after setting up house, after dinner, after the kids are in bed, Hilary, Russell, and Berenice call in at a local pub for a pint of cider. I stay home and sit before the coal fire in the livingroom and breathe as Love from Above against a background of splashing waves outside. A swirl of melting joy informs me Blaise is drawing in close, possibly with something in mind.

I'm standing at my parent's house in mid-1950s Massachusetts. I'm six. My long head sports a crewcut; my face is chubby, dimpled, a little wily, the grin is contagious. I'm with my red wagon by the side of the garage. I wheel it to the backyard, lay in it, leave my body, and float happily around the yard. Then I see a brilliant light at the top of the ash tree at the corner of our property; it's enhaloed in lilac. I fly up to this light and discover it is a portal. Breathe your love to this doorway, Blaise advises, and immediately I'm through, soaring to a place high in the mountains, possibly the Himalayas, among the topmost snowy crags. The mist swirls occlude the sun, and just below me sits a lama in grey robes framed against the austere rocks. He is so radiant he's almost not human. He smiles, beckoning me to sit before him. I don't see what happens next, but I find myself at a stone railing of a mountain monastery overlooking the snowfields. This must be Tibet or some Buddhist country because behind me a five-tiered stupa depicts the sacred mantra, *om mane padme hum*— "Hail to the Jewel in the Lotus." I feel intensely happy here.

Now I stand by a single tree before a mountain lake; light shimmers on the water like poured milk. I try not to get too excited because, according to Yasutani-roshi, the voice of my Zen conscience, even visions of Bodhisattvas and Himalayan lamas are *makyo*, so I wipe this evening's vision off my slate of authentic spiritual experiences. But then, by this same argument, Yasutani-roshi is equally illusory plus he's dead, so, hypothetically, I could be having a vision of him, in which case I'd have to tell him he's a *makyo*, too.

In the morning, as I wake, I remember a dream. Ranks of men and women, each carrying a lilac-enflamed Grail, parade along, led by Michael, to the sound of a brass orchestra staffed by Blaise. "Are you awake?" I ask Hilary, who is sleeping in the top bunk in this tiny, sea-facing bedroom.

"Yes," from deep under the duvet.

"What are you doing?"

"Listening to the sea. Watching the gulls. Staring at the blue sky."

"Aren't you cold up there in the top bunk?"

"No."

"Well, I mean don't you need some company up there to keep track of all those birds?"

"No."

"You know, the view's pretty good from down here, too. Care to have a look?"

No answer. The Grail Castle is locked shut this morning.

We drive into Marazion, the little sea-perched town that features St. Michael's Mount—"the Rock in the Wood," as the Cornish once called it. It's a granitic fortress rising solitary like a miniature volcano in Mount's Bay, topped by a very old church, framed against the silvery sea. Local legend knows the Mount as *Dinsol*, the "Castle of the Sun," possibly because one night in 495 A.D., fishermen at work in Mount's Bay beheld the archangel Michael standing luminous and awesome upon the rocky mount. An old legend claims that once a giant named Cormoran lived on the Mount, and he gave King Arthur a bit of trouble. Malory says: "He hath vanquished fifteen kings, and hath made him a coat full of precious stones embroidered with their beards." Arthur came to the Mount and smote the big troublemaker with his dagger, cutting off his head. "This was the fiercest giant that ever I met with," he boasted afterwards, "save one in the mount of Araby, which I overcame, but this was greater and fiercer." An even older legend holds that the Mount was once part of the legendary but vanished land of Lyonesse, which has since sunk under the ocean. As recently as the early 1600s, the Cornish knew the Mount as *Cara Cowze in Clowze*, meaning "The Hoar Rock in the Wood." They believed that it overlooked a drowned forest now lying under the bay.

The dome over the Mount is tied in a ribbon with a rainbow as Michael stands through and above the rock like a friendly winged giant. It's one of his places, after all, and he's standing on his own Oroboros line as well, the same energy highway that passes through Burrowbridge Mump and Glastonbury Tor.

At high tide, you can't get to the Mount except by boat, but, at low tide, there is a long stone causeway out to the huge rock. We pause for a few moments at Chapel Rock, a solitary greenstone prominence that got here on account of an argument between the giant Cormoran and his wife, Cormelian. They were building a stronghold of white granite quarried in the nearby hills and transporting it through the thick woods out to the Mount in their giant's aprons. One day, Cormoran slept while Cormelian did all the work. She was tired from carrying the heavy white granite such a long distance and thought, since the boss was asleep, she'd substitute the lighter greenstone, which she could quarry much closer to home. Cormoran awoke to see her holding up an apron full of greenstone. An unrepentant patriarch, he kicked her, which broke her apron string, scattering the greenstone all about the Mount, of which Chapel Rock is a survivor. A variation on this tale has Cormelian accidentally killed when a neighboring giant at Trencrom Hill returned Cormelan's hammer by tossing it; Cormelian took the hammer on the head and fell over dead. Cormelan buried her under Chapel Rock.

Pilgrims to the Mount prepared themselves in prayer at Chapel Rock, and probably long before the eleventh century when the first versions of a church were established here. Chapel Rock is also a meteorological safety zone. The minute we set sneakers to causeway—leaving the Rock—it rains and blows and doesn't let up until we reach the National Trust bookshop well into the village that huddles around the great church. Of course, the reward for getting soaked is a rainbow and today we are quadruply rewarded. Four rainbows intermittently and successively touch down at precisely the same spot over the inland hills as viewed from the railings outside St. Michael's church. "We'll have to find the bottom of that rainbow," says Russell.

The Mount this morning exhales gaiety, and there's a playful spirit to the way the sunlight dapples the rocks and the wind crashes against the old church and the waves pummel the adamant cliffs. The elements are alive! It's the kind of happiness that makes you want to whistle and hop and pat the heads of little children. It's the kind of angelic silliness, another dose of *levitony*, that inspires us— well, Russell and me, not Berenice, bless her—when we return to the car to put on funny hats: woolen caps with ear flaps, yellow bonnets with ribboned ties, bright purple tokes with badges; we sail out beyond worry and seriousness to a giddy new land. Meanwhile, the tide has rolled in, and the causeway has vanished under the blue-green sea.

It takes Russell only thirty minutes of inspired navigating—Berenice drives—to find the place where the four rainbows set down. It's an unmarked hill near the village of Cripplesease that was apparently once used intensively as a tin mine. Numerous brick-lined air shafts pockmark the stubbly, treeless hill. We pick our way through the heather and over recumbent boulders to a rounded summit. The late afternoon air is cool and exhilarating. From the triangulation marker, we can survey a large portion of Cornwall: Penzance and St. Ives in the northeast, Land's End to the southwest, and ocean everywhere. Dozens of human-sized stones lay strewn about the hill like the wreckage of a once complex stone circle. Maybe Cormoran and Cormelian had another rock hurling match over here, something worthy of the histrionics in *Who's Afraid of Virginia Woolf?* I pick my way across them to a perch overlooking Marazion, which flushes radiant in the soft, westering sunlight. Blaise sits with me amid the rocks.

"The stones were once arranged in three rings. The site was used as an anchor bolt for rainbows and other arcs of ascending consciousness. Michael touches the center of these circles with his sword and the light springs into the visible sky as a rainbow. He is pleased you have found his temple site, *Michaelzion*, Michael's place of light." I see people making circle dances, but they are turnings in consciousness, inward spirals as they furl to the center of their beings where they find Michael. His sword is like a bridge of light linking this hill with the Mount.

It's nearly dark now, but I'm happy and buoyant enough to keep myself warm all night. I ask a friendly gnome to show me the way down the hill and to keep me from disappearing down some old tin mine shaft or other sudden holes in this unreliable terrain. The orange horizon melts into blackness; an infant crescent moon twinkles confidently. The Grail bus is lit up when I arrive, as everyone has been waiting for me. Celia is wrapped in blankets and looks upset. "She fell into one of those nasty puddles," says Berenice. "Did you see the lovely dome over this hill?" Russell asks me. Before I can answer, he adds, "I saw Michael standing under it surrounded by Blaise. All of them were watching us. By the way, Hilary, what was all that arm flapping about?" Hilary blushes. "Oh, I just felt myself inside a shaft of light, turning slowly like a corkscrew. Like I was dancing in the stones."

After breakfast the next day, I set out along the cliff path that overlooks the Cornish coastline. I know this path. Once, years ago, I spent a couple months hiking the cliffs along Devon and Cornwall, camping out, reading Walt Whitman, loving the views. The sea is dazzlingly blue, the sun is warm, the breeze is pleasant, and all the angels are cooing in their dovecotes as I undulate the footpath— altogether a well-behaved English seaside morning. The trail skirts a plowed field, furrowed in two directions, lathed in sunlight, and framed against a cerulean sky with three puffy clouds. Sheep graze in a steep turnip field, sampling the leaves. I don't see how the farm-

ers can till these fields without their tractors tipping over and plum-
meting into the sea. Blue sea, blue sky, white clouds, earth, stone,
wind, surf, whistle. And a lighthouse.

"You should stop here," announces a voice in my head. It doesn't
sound like Blaise. "There's an envelope marked Coast Guard with a
hundred pounds in it on the desk in the lighthouse room. You do
need the money to pay Russell for your rent." Uh oh. Who is this?
Indecision grips me. I *am* desperately short of cash at the moment,
it's true.

I approach the lighthouse and its attached private home. All the
doors are locked. I start climbing the metal fire escape; three quarters of the way up, or about thirty feet, I look through the window,
note a pile of blankets, frown, climb down. There is blood on my left
hand as I step away from the last rung of the ladder. Except I'm not
bleeding anywhere, and I didn't cut my hand, so who's blood is this?
End of big mistake. Time to retreat quickly. I ponder this unsettling
experience all afternoon, wondering how Blaise could have advised
such a digression, knowing Blaise never would do such a thing, feeling confused about trusting inner guidance. Somebody's tampered
with the Grail Knight's radar.

After dinner we gather in the livingroom, waiting for Blaise. I ask
him at once about the lighthouse. "This is a most sensitive issue. We
do not wish to discourage you, but you must be aware and skeptical
of any guidance that is not from entirely altruistic motivations. If
you consider the guidance to be altruistic, then okay. If not, then
make sure you have double checked it with your own sitting. Then
you must ask yourself again. You must be prepared for an inevitable
degree of distortion relative to the degree of clairaudient or clairvoyant reception you have developed at the time. The process you are
going through is difficult, for you must learn to trust your intuition
yet not be fooled by other forces trying to speak through you or imi-
tate us.

"We must warn you of possible interference for you personally at
this time. We would prefer it if every person we work with was a
completely open line, but obviously this is not the case. If you imag-

ine that everything in your life happens unconsciously, even what you call meditation, even what you call awakening, even what you call illumination, if all this is seen as unconscious activity, then you must understand the nature of your distortion at the lighthouse. The possibilities for a human to be more conscious are extremely few. It is like trying to grow a precious flower in a desert that never receives rain."

Before we break for the night, Berenice says she feels inspired to take us to a place called Roche Rock near Bodmin for sunrise. The next morning around six o'clock, we collect ourselves, chilled and sleepy, and set off in the Grail bus for Roche Rock, which is a hermitage, holy well, and Michael-dedicated site. Apparently, a long succession of Celtic saints lived up here in the fifty-foot high outcropping rock into which a chapel was set around 1409 A.D. "It towers dramatically above a flat, barren landscape, rivalled only by refuse heaps of the china clay industry to the south," writes geomancy tour guide John Michell.

It's still dark and predawn when we arrive; the rock is shrouded in mist. We pick our way up to the ruins of the chapel along a series of slippery iron steps secured to the rock. Blaise stands like wraiths against the wheaten stones; their feathers rustle slightly in the breeze. In the chapel, Russell and I chant *om mane padme hum* and watch the crystal inside Roche Rock—or that *is* Roche Rock in another dimension—flush yellow and vibrate palpably. A huge lilac flame burns over the rock rising up through a small dome overhead. Numerous light shafts are embedded like quartz shanks in the landscape around the rock. Lines of light radiate out from this central light seed inside the rock. Before the rock stands a ten foot high guardian stone with an uncanny resemblance to a carved Buddha and probably with a function like the Tibetan Dharma-protectors called *heruka*. There's an awful lot packed into such a small, remote place, we agree, as we leave Roche around eight.

We stop for breakfast at a country inn and warm ourselves in a spacious empty lounge before a crackling fire. A teenage boy carries in thick chunks of beech and piles them at the hearth. We could spend the whole day here, no questions asked, as long as the firewood lasts. A waiter brings coffee, evidently not concerned that, in addition to our visible party of six, there are also six lanky angels reclining luxuriously on the inn's plump easy-chairs. "All morning I've been seeing this image of a stone circle on a high, barren hill," Russell announces. "I think it's in Dartmoor. We could stop there on the way home."

It turns out to be Okehampton Tor on the northern boundary of Dartmoor: a treeless, rock-strewn hill topped by a dome. Mist and clouds lie low over the dark, heathery moors and hundreds of grey boulders are strewn across the hill like megalithic corpses. Traces of a former stone concourse across the brow of the hill are evident, terminating in a rash of abandoned stones. Psilocybin mushrooms are abundant. Probably to amuse ourselves, we construct a miniature stone circle from pebbles directly under the epicenter of the dome, then we perambulate this *tor* several times, striking out in different directions. The scattered stones are like ghosts, derelict, autistic, clutching a possibly fabulous past unspeakably to themselves. Periodically, the sun peeks through the grey sheets of mist but no rainbow is forthcoming. We leave as dusk wells up from the damp ground.

Hours later back at Wick, we lounge like Victorian grandparents before a cozy fire, dozing, reflecting, wondering, privately reviewing our activities in Cornwall. Blaise slips avuncularly into our somnolent ambiance.

"We saw the beginning of this day together. We were together at the changing time, morning and evening. We are thankful for this. We hope you are happy today. We wish to thank you all. We were in the sunshine all day. We are aware you know you were partially under instructions from Michael on this trip. He attempts, as you wish, to guide you to where you will be of most use. If you wish, put Michael before you in all things. He is most pleased for any assistance at this time. The process we informed you about at Michaelzion is largely inoperative at this time. Later, if all goes well, we may be able to focus will, interest, and attention on certain energy points to increase resonances through ley lines to help rebalance Earth energies. Things are not well with the being you call Earth. She will protest before too long. She is in need of love and attention from Man, rather than abuse.

"At dawn you were surrounded by a particular form of what you call a ray of the Earth. We are constantly attempting, through the golden light lines and lilac flames on key Earth centers, to rectify and heal some of these acts of Man's rape. The scale of this rape is extraordinary. Earth is very forgiving. She has healed much with our help, but Man continues the extensive rape. Earth will be avenged. We will be helpless in this. We will only be able to place in safety those that in some way have been attempting, however deludedly, to assist us in our efforts of love."

"Blaise, we saw a small dome over Roche Rock, but it was much smaller than the other domes we've seen. Is it a different kind?"

"You see, Grail Knight, each dome had the capacity to send out up to 48 energy centers or lines of light or dome lines. At the end of each is a small dome. We call these dome caps. They are smaller than the originating dome. They are placed at star centers or power points. Each dome sent out these heliocentric lines in the same pattern as the sunflower. This is the Fibonacci series or *phi* spiral, the Golden Mean. Roche Rock is a dome cap."

"How many domes are there on Earth?" I ask. I had been querying Blaise with this question in my mind for months now, with no answer.

"You have been persistent with this question. Therefore, we will answer, though reluctantly. There are evidences on your planet pertaining to the presence of 1746 domes."

I try not to do cartwheels through the room. 1746 is a big number; in gematria, it's one of the famous ones; and to a large extent, it is a key to understanding ancient cosmology. "The number 1746 is a symbol of fusion between the negative and positive forces in nature, 1080 and 666, of which it is the sum," explains John Michell. This number is identical with the Biblical reference "the grain of mustard seed;" though the mustard is among the smallest of seeds, when fertilized, from it, at least allegorically, springs the universal Tree of Life and all its myriad living denizens. According to Michell, in terms of gematria (transposing numbers for letters using either the Hebrew or Greek alphabet), 1746 also denotes the "Glory of God is Israel," "the Hidden Spirit," "the Treasure of Jesus," "the Divinity of Spirit," "the Spiritual Law," and "the Chalice of Jesus." "In the alchemist's retort, as in nature's womb, the opposite elements are fused together, and the fruit of their union is the Universal Spirit, 1746," Michell writes. Meanwhile, I make a quick calculation on my notepad. "That means there could be 83,808 dome caps on the Earth. By the way, did Roche Rock have another name?"

"Michael's Rock. It was the stone on which Michael took up his ministry from Gabriel, not this time, but before. By the way, you saw more there than most people ever see. Be content with that. You are shown much under extraordinary circumstances."

"Thanks, Blaise. Would you explain the function of Okehampton Tor? The dome there seemed to have some special apparatus."

"We would express it as a funnel, or, to continue in your terms, as a dome with a wide opening where you walked in and then a narrow opening at the other end where you found all the dispersion stones. [Blaise means this in the technical sense of optics: the separation of complex light as by a prism into its differently colored rays.] Also, as you observed, it is a site of vertical energy from beyond the Earth's etheric. Michael superintends this for the purpose of unitive consciousness. We have already told you that domes facilitate changes in human consciousness."

"On a technical level, how does a dome do that?"

"If you wish, we can show you. Close your eyes. Picture a hole in your head at the top with light coming in. Use your eyes to look through this hole. Tell us what you see."

There is a shaft of light with a blue snake spiralling around it that turns into an oscillating band of blue sparkles. A couple dozen humans in floor-length blue frocks stand shoulder-to-shoulder making a wreath around this light shaft. They peer down the shaft at me. Somehow I feel they're all Blaise. I try to see beyond or around this cadre of angelic physicians, but I can't.

"Good," Blaise says. "There is something tangible over the Earth at any point, available at any time to human consciousness, should the human access this planetary matrix through his own personal light shaft and being. Domes are in the same spatial relationship with Earth power points as is this personal light shaft to the planetary matrix." I realize Blaise refers to something similar to Pierre Teilhard de Chardin's Noösphere, his description of a global mind web.

"I want to know more about Albion. What do you recommend?"

"We recommend you walk from Wearyall Hill at the Holy Thorn to Chalice Hill, passing through the Abbey tomorrow. Begin early. Stop when directed. Albion will be revealed."

"Thanks—for everything."

"No trouble. You help us. We help you. Simple. It's what you are here for. Don't forget this now that you're almost beginning to remember a little. We leave you now as a Blazing Star, from not too far, as we are."

37

"We Were Just Having Fun, Loving Albion"

 ere on the crest of fish-back Wearyall Hill on my virgin walk across the forgotten body of Albion, I remember intimations I had of a vast, sprawling landscape giant from the first time I stood here, surveying the complex of Glastonbury hills. Wearyall and Edmund hill are his legs, the Abbey is his crotch, Chalice Hill his stomach, his chest the Tor, and then he curves into the ether realms through the Arc of Developing Consciousness to the throat at Pointer's Ball—what better place to sing an angelic mass for Michael, Albion's celestial counterpart—through Park Wood, his brow, and Lugshorn, his crown.

Now I see that, in a remarkable sense, the anthropomorphic figure of Albion actually summarizes the entire zodiac: Albion is the totality of all the constellations, their energies, thoughts, intentions, myths, the face of cosmic Man etched in light and matter, the Man of the Tree of Life, as Qabala suggests. Albion is all of this in the context of the Earth. Albion is the anthropomorphic expression of the cosmos of stars, the hidden encoded image within the stellar hologram, the Hanged Man on the Tree of Life.

The Tree is an analogue of the Absolute, Universe, and Man, writes Qabalist Z'ev Ben Shimon Halevi, and Man, our Albion, is the meeting point between these two fundamental poles. By Man, I invoke its metaphysical, pregendered connotation, derived from *manas*, meaning "One who thinks." "A complete but unrealized Tree in miniature, and lower than the angels, his is to choose to rise higher by climbing the branches of himself, and so gain the ultimate fruit."

Man is the prime example of the *idea* of Creation, the perfect reflective image of the intelligible order of the Creator, Halevi adds—"an exact replica in every detail in miniature of the cosmoses above him."

In the case of the Somerset landscape zodiac, we have the cosmos among us, the galaxy on Earth, and its quintessential face is Albion, the life of Man on Earth, the mirror reflection of Michael, and a guide for each of us as little Albions. Geomancy is his language and the way of the Grail Knight is one of the doors into his domain.

The two sides of Albion, both as the legendary name of Britain and as "the Ancient Man," come together in Blake's poetic vision, *Jerusalem: The Emanation of the Giant Albion*. "Come & mourn over Albion, the White Cliff of the Atlantic/the Mountain of Giants: all the Giants of Albion are become/Weak, wither'd, darken'd, & Jerusalem is cast forth from Albion." Albion, Blake tells us, is sick to death, sunk down in pallid languor, with a pale and ghastly disease: "He walks in misery and pain, his giant beauty and perfection fallen into dust." Albion lays cold on the rocks as storms and snows beat around him, and the starry heavens are all fled from his mighty limbs. "In a dark & unknown night: outstretched his Giant beauty on the ground in pain & tears....Loud roll the starry wheels of Albion into the world of Death." The basic problem, Blake says, is that Albion turned away from the Divine Vision and fell into the "Satanic disease of selfhood," and thereby into ruin. Fortunately, his redemption from this "long & cold repose" and his return to glory is foretold, and Blake looks ahead to a time "When all Albion's injuries shall cease, and when we shall/ Embrace him, tenfold bright, from his tomb in immortality."

But first we must reanimate some of his starry wheels—the landscape zodiacs—before Albion can reclaim his glorious heritage, and this seems to be the work of the Grail Knight. So here at the first bench on the brow of Wearyall Hill on the leg of Albion, Blaise, too, forecasts the Giant's eventual awakening. "The landscape figure you see as Albion," Blaise says, "has been no more than dimly perceived for many years. Albion has never been birthed completely. He has only been awakened slightly at points of transition. The fifteen previous Arthurs have been like an alarm clock. It rings and you say, Oh no, I want to go back to sleep. Then it rings again. You say, Oh no, I want to roll over—and so on. But now Albion is almost ready to get up and have his breakfast. The fifteen previous Arthurs contributed towards this time, inevitably and inexorably, for the sixteenth Arthur."

Albion is like Michael's brother, Blaise adds, and Michael is, in a sense, his guardian. Albion must be awakened in stages, one energy center at a time. Then as one Albion stirs, they all do, the Albions of all the planet's zodiacs. This is part of the angelic mass for Michael, unbinding Albion, singing to the points of light in his body. In the coming time, when the Dark Age, the *Kali Yuga*, has finally ended and given way to the time of golden light, the *Satya Yuga*—just around the corner, Blaise adds—Albion will awake, spring up, and "walk" about Britain and the rest of the world in celestial triumph. Michael's sword and the Grail Knights' swords will undo Albion's humanmade binds. "This in part is what you're being trained for, Grail Knight," Blaise adds.

We shift to the next bench, and Blaise continues his commentary about the legs of Albion. As Albion's legs are asleep, their vital points must be stimulated to get the energy circulating again. The Holy Thorn marks an important acupoint in the meridian system of Albion (to borrow acupuncture terminology—we might call them geopoints) as do the nodes I've already visited at the Tor, Pointer's Ball, and Park Wood. There is a corresponding treatment point on his other leg at Edmunds Hill. People have forgotten how Albion lies and lives in the landscape, how they walk and drive and farm inside his numinous body, Blaise says. The Holy Thorn, and its etheric flower, marks the spot where Joseph of Arimathea, master geomancer and "geopuncturist," infused Albion with Christ energy, achieving a certain purification in Albion's dreamlife, and by extension, making it possible for an early, pure form of Grail-Christianity to take root and flower in Glastonbury soon after the Crucifixion. "In the treatment points of Albion's leg, you have the secret of Wearyall Hill itself. It means 'heal the spiritual hero.'"

Of course: Wearyall, Wirheale, Wir/hael, "heal the *vir*"—make virile again. Hale (hail) the spiritual hero! *Hael* is Anglo-Saxon for health, safety, salvation, hale, whole, and sound; the related word *haelan* means to make whole or cure; *haelend* means savior or healer; *haele* means health and safety. *Wer* means male person, from the Sanskrit *vira*, which means man or hero, forming *viriya*, meaning energy and virility. In Hindu thinking, *Viraj* is the male aspect of the cosmic Creator god, Brahma.

We have to assume *Wirhaele* is a magically compounded word like so many others in the Glastonbury mythos. In *Wirhaele* we have the place of primary creative, fertilizing, potentiating energy that makes a human whole, makes one hale, that heals one—the hill is the reservoir of *vir*. Now *vira* also connotes the adept, spiritual hero, or divine Man, giving us *Vira-heale*, the place of the healing of the spiritual hero, or the place from which we hail the healed spiritual hero. Didn't Powys write of Wirral that it was "the actual site of that Terre Gastee of the medieval romances, which became withered and blighted after the Dolorous Blow delivered by the unlucky Balin upon King Pelleas, Guardian of the Grail." *Let us now hail, hale, haele the vir!*

The Maimed Fisher King is an expression of the spiritual hero who needs healing; the King's wound, in his upper thigh, blocks the memory of his divine origins and deep past. Here comes Joseph of Arimathea, who inserts a flowering staff where once a spear impaled Albion's flesh, and by the expert placement of this staff—precisely where the Lemurian library and deep memory crystal resides—it becomes a key to restoring Albion's memory and healing the wound at its root. Most people regard the Fisher King's thigh wound as a euphemism for an injury to his groin or genitals or to his root chakra. According to Wellesley Tudor Pole, Joseph, back in Palestine, perceived Albion's destiny in Somerset at the moment he burned the Crucifixion cross. "It was in the smoke and flames of that conflagration that Joseph became aware of a stupendous vision. Not only was his own future made manifest, including the great destiny he was to fulfill in the sacred Isle of Britain; but the future of the human race was symbolically revealed to him."

But perhaps the most important letter in the popular name

Wearyall is the "y." This is the tenth letter, *Yod*, in the Hebrew alphabet and means an Open Hand; in Tarot, it corresponds, in most interpretations, with the path of The Hermit, which depicts a solitary magus bearing lantern and staff. In either case, it is a fitting icon for Joseph of Arimathea, master geomancer, arriving on Wearyall with his flowering yodic staff on behalf of our Albion. *Yod* as the number 10 is the number of all potential, says Qabala; its very shape (a candle flame on its side) signifies germinal beginnings, the primordial point, the initiation of new life impregnated with possibility. More important still, *Yod* is the first word in the Divine Name, *YHVH*, known as Tetragrammaton.

Joseph of Arimathea is, from this perspective, the embodiment of *Yod*, the Hand of God, wielding divine power on behalf of God for humanity, but not for himself. In this case, he plants his *Yod*, or staff, into the prime matrix of Wirhaele and initiates a new zodiacal, evolutionary cycle. Joseph plants his Piscean seed in Wirhaele for a future Aquarian flowering, and he fertilizes it with the fire of *Yod*, which is why his staff as the expression of his status as magus suddenly blossoms. It conducts the charge of divine *Yod* into Wearyall Hill on behalf of Albion. Thus Joseph's flowering staff illuminates the way to the New Jersualem, Albion's destined temple. As Tarot scholar Madonna Compton notes, "It is truly a balanced middle path wherein the great Seer grasps in his hand the Lamp of guidance in the inky darkness."

Paradoxically, in the Glastonbury landscape body of Albion, the Abbey sits ambivalently just above Albion's crotch, at the generative, procreative, sexual center—part of the problem, but potentially part of the solution. My next stop is the Abbey fish pond. The second chakra concerns the water element, feeling, emotion, the reactive process of attraction and repulsion, the perennial dialectic of male and female, the tastes of relationship. The lily pads are lushly green and sport white flowers. I sit down under the hawthorn tree, near the life jacket and the cautionary sign "Danger—Deep Water" and observe a transparent, multifaceted nimbus of light, like a crystalline crown, set over the water. The tiny pond is like an eye with a monocle, all the better to peer into Heaven. Its energy was kept pure through the prayers of the monks, but it has been mostly unattended since the Dissolution, says Blaise, adding, "A chorale concert around the pond would help reactivate its energy as part of our Michaelmass."

Leaving the Abbey, we climb Chalice Hill, from which we survey redhatted Glastonbury, the silvery fisheye of the Abbey pond, the green whaleback of Wearyall. It's warm, sunny, and breezy; mushrooms the size of withered oak leaves poke up through the thick grass, and a cluster of cows graze indolently on the far side of the hill here on Albion's belly. In the Arthurian stories, when Arthur married Guinivere, her father, King Leodegranz of the Summer Country, gave them a round table for their wedding. This round table was nothing other than the Somerset zodiac and its divine guest, Albion, who sleeps supine upon it.

Leodegranz was Albion's steward, but to Guinivere—from the Welsh *Gwenhwyfar*, meaning, approximately, "White Shadow"—fell much of the geomythic maintenance work. For example, the old stories speak of her abduction by a giant, an uncouth youth, or a chauvinist monarch, requiring a rescue by Lancelot. What probably happened was that Guinivere immersed herself in various geomythic aspects of Albion, disappearing for a time into the Giant's numinous domain, walking in Albion awake in her dreambody. "Now keep an eye on Wearyall," says Blaise.

Suddenly, Blaise is gone from the rustling beech grove of Chalice Hill. I spot them on Wearyall, where they describe a feathery circle around the crystalline thorn tree. Michael stands tall with sword and shield amidst the hoop of frolicking Blaises. In an instant they've relocated to the fish pond, pirouetting on water, then, like angelic frogs, they hop to Chalice Hill, the Tor, Pointer's Ball, Park Wood, and Lugshorn in seconds, repeating the same antics. In less than a minute, Blaise returns to the beech grove. "What was that all about?" I ask.

"Oh, not a lot. We were just having fun. Dancing the energy spots, aligning the centers, attempting to bring balance, loving Albion. By the way, we place Albion's sixth chakra at Park Wood and his seventh at Lugshorn. It may not seem too elegant when you see it on a map, but the reason is they are different aspects of similar diagrams or illustrations, for different purposes. The sixth chakra we place at Park Wood predominantly because it is of the indigo ray. We are in the process of transformation and attempt to heal the place you call Lugshorn using the violet flame of transmutation. Pointer's Ball is the fifth center, the Tor is the fourth, Chalice Hill, the third."

Blaise reminds me that the Albion chakra system is only one of three main temple structures here in Glastonbury. There is the zodiac structure of Pisces, Aquarius, and Capricorn, and their star centers, all of which overlay the town; and there is Glasteing's Tree, situated along the Michael Oroboros line, from Beckery to Paradise, that fish-shape between the two halves of the zodiac and in between the worlds. All three interpenetrate, although the details of their energy centers are somewhat different. I ask Blaise what is an energy center, or landscape chakra, from their perspective.

"Picture tiny flowers all over the Earth. Some combine to form larger flowers, and some of these form even larger flowers. Chakras are like this, energy flowing from one flower into another, flowers opening, flowers as part of other flowers. Each is independent and interdependent, similar and dissimilar. Ultimately, the eighth, sixth, and fourth chakras are all the same, but, at a level of relative truth, it is still possible to transpose various systems and work within logic."

My growing picture of Albion is missing an important element, Blaise continues, so we relocate to the Tor. Albion's heart center needs a pump and this we find inside the Tor with its aortal Michael Oroboros line. The Michael line, as it passes through Glastonbury, imparts a continuous pulse of archangelic consciousness, keeping the temple sites, both physical and unmanifest, along this line in conscious relationship with Michael. When the Michael line is stretched taut through conscious human participation through its nodes during ritual activity or geomantic focus as part of a Michaelmass, the line hums a tune.

Once people performed a special dance approximately called *firillen* on the Michael line at Albion's heart, Blaise tells me. I pause at the

Living Rock on the Tor and place my hands on its smooth surface. It's like inserting a cassette in a VCR; the images start playing at once. Michael stands at the summit of the hill in the center of the stone circle. Men and women dance around him, moving circularly in opposite directions. I hear their voices: the dancers in one circle chanting *Albion of Avalon*; those in the other, oppositely moving circle, chanting *O Michael uplift us now*. Michael points his sword into the circle of people and stones, and the auras of each flame hugely white.

Images of the geomythic Albion form in my mind as I sit at the steps of the St. Michael tower, the chants still echoing vaguely in my ears. Albion is a huge primordial human falling backwards into a hole in the ground, which is the Somerset zodiac wheel. You see this backwards dive when you contemplate the Arc of Developing Consciousness as a parabolic overlay on the landscape. His body makes an ungainly curve as it falls backwards into Earth through the center of the star wheel until his head reappears numinously lilac at Lusghorn. Albion's body is the whole of this zodiac, its anthropomorphic summation, even if his geomythically sculpted body occupies only a portion of the land within the physical zodiac. Still, Albion's presence interpenetrates every star in both zodiacal halves. His body is made of stars, his sinews are knit with constellations, and he inhales the air of Heaven. His arms are upraised, curving over his head; he wears the effigies of the zodiac like bangles on his thick arms. Albion, seen from Wearyall at his legs, is massive, supine, shackled in the gloom of unawakened incarnation, but from Lugshorn, his crown, he has just arrived, pristine from Heaven, landing on his feet in a wild jump of exaltation, brandishing his spectacular zodiacal shield in a gesture of angelic glee.

Perspective is crucial. From Wearyall, major healing is required: Albion is truly weary of his sojourn in matter. From Lugshorn, Albion is an Olympian colossus writ geomythically large in the landscape, full of unfathomable promise. All the starry wheels turn in cosmic splendor upon his mighty limbs, turning on the majestic choirs of their spiritual denizens. From Lugshorn, Albion is indeed the brightest Son of Heaven, a light being in our neighborhood. "And remember," Blaise says, "all of this is a reflection of *your* spiritual self, as a human being living in physical form. It is not separate from who you are."

Albion's joy is contagious. It makes me feel instantly better, stops me from worrying about certain matters of the present incarnation. I spend my last twenty pence at the baker's for two whole wheat and raisin scones, my favorites. My check from America is long over-due. I ripped my only jacket on a barbed wire fence. I got fresh ma-nure stains all over my sneakers. My last pair of clean socks suffered an extreme odorization from a wet patch on Wearyall. Berenice's Citroen has enough gas for about five miles and Wick is fifteen miles from here. No matter. Empty pockets, ripped pockets, smelly pock-ets—empty form, humming a glad tune, spinning a little *firillen* for Albion on this big, green, muscular, heartfelt hill. Sun, wind, clouds, blue sky, green grass, even the sheep urge me to dance for Albion. I whistle and hum and skip along the dirt path down the hill with an extra buoyancy, and even though it's so windy I can't hear myself hum and suspect it will blow me clear over to Brent Knoll, I sense even the staid rockfast tower of St. Michael shakes its stony hips a few times, glad for Albion.

When I get home, no doubt accomplished on angelic petrol, Berenice has a message for me from Blaise—as if I haven't been with them all day. "Blaise wants you to go to Dundon Beacon to some shelves or other—you'll know which, he said—and take a shovel and dig a hole. It has to be one yard deep underneath the shelves. Specifically, he said, and I wrote this part down: 'All Hallows Eve. Tomorrow is what you may call a party for us. We will show you a treasure. We unlock a door for you. Dig gently with love.'" That's curious. Tomorrow is the Celtic *Samhain*, the first of November, the day all the barrows are thrown open and the faery folk walk the land and have their way. "Oh, and I put some extra potatoes in the oven because I figured you'd have lots and lots of appetite after all this."

I do, and the jacket potatoes disappear intemperately into the cav-erns of my hunger. "But how am I going to smuggle a shovel past that woman who spends all her time in her garden, watching all passersby at Dundon? Remember? She watched us the last time we went there, like we were thieves. And it is Nature Conservancy property, too."

Russell snickers. "Yes, I can see her now, the dear old mum, phoning the police. 'That's right, officer, I want to report a suspicious looking Grail Knight with manure on his trainers and a really unsightly torn jacket scrambling up the Beacon with a spade under his left arm, and—oh my God! I hardly dare say it— six angels with hard hats and jack-hammers right behind him.'"

38

Each Child is Backlit by a Guardian Angel

undon turns out to be no problem. Berenice loans me the Citroen and some money for petrol, and I terrorize everyone with my American undexterity at driving on what to me seems inalterably the wrong side of the road. My little shovel occupies the front seat. In the backseat, a half dozen wisecracking Blaises titter at my motoring foibles, the worst kind of backseat drivers. "Oh, you took that corner a little too fast, G.K.!" says one Blaise. "Mind that approaching lorry!" exclaims another. As we pass a clutch of young mothers wheeling prams, Blaise says, "Look at all the pretty babies!"

I suppose they're not totally useless passengers, because Blaise directs me to a different entrance to Dundon, far from the prying eyes of the Nature Conservancy's watchdog. I manage to cross two furrowed fields unnoticed and slip into the woods with shovel and blanket tucked under my left arm. Blaise leads me in a clockwise spiralling peregrination around the top of Dundon until we finally reach the shelves. The shelves are thick pancake wedges of rock, a jostled pile of plates suggesting a former waterfall spanning twenty feet, deliberately made. The rock wedges shelve into the ground, continuing their invisible waterless cascade inside the hill. In the etheric realm, a large crystal or field of light overlays the shelves. The crystal was once part of the Atlantean, then Druidic, use of this section of the Beacon, Blaise tells me. "Its use pertains to the Atlantean practice of fusing water and earth in a practice called *mudagen*. That is, we hope we got the word right. If you would confirm us in this."

And to think I've been taking these guys seriously. "Never mind. Dig your hole, Grail Knight," Blaise says in between titters.

Blaise is right about the mud, Druidic or otherwise. Digging under these shelves is like picking at compacted clay. It takes both my hands to pry loose the lumpy, sandy-hued mud from the shovel. My glasses keep breaking, too. The left lens pops out of its fifteen year old wire-frame holder and tinkles into the expanding hole. I have to wipe my muddy hands on my jacket to be able to pick up the lens, which gets smeared in the process, then clean it on my undershirt, the only nonmuddy piece of clothing I'm wearing, then delicately squeeze the fat lens into its frame, then strap the apparatus to my face again so I can see the world around me, then resume digging. As if invisible fingers are tapping my glasses, the lens pops out again from the rickety frames. Clearly, there are some grouchy, ill-behaved elemental spirits around here; no doubt they prefer contact lenses.

After a couple more rounds of this optometric conflict, I discard the glasses, squint ferociously to see the hole, and resume digging. At this point, I lay on my stomach on the blanket with my head wedged down the hole, scraping out the obstreperous clay with my fingers. Around midday, I reach a depth past which I cannot dig because the hole is now the length of my arm. Mud glazes my hair, shirt, jacket, trousers, and sneakers, and my fingers are so caked I can hardly wiggle them. Ah, the joys of *mudagen*, famous Atlantean pastime, I reflect, sitting ten feet from the hole, cleaning my glasses.

Suddenly, something shoots out of the hole as if expelled like a jet of champagne. It's a pale lily trailing a long stem and a tiny creature like a miniature gnome. It's funny because today, November 1, which the Celts call *Samhain*, one of their four quarterly "turning days," is the one day in the year when the *sidhes* or barrows of the Little Folk are thrown open and they have free—and usually mischievous if not destructive—access to the world of humans. Blaise stands in an arc around the hole witnessing this spirit's evidently long-awaited release. Michael appears among the Blaises and lays the flat of his sword on my muddy head. The Blaises erupt into a maypole jig around Michael. I gather my work is done, not that I understand it.

On the way down Dundon, my shoelaces come untied six times, my trousers get ripped on brambles, I get lost twice, and I stumble over a branch that I swear was not there two seconds ago when I lifted my leg to make the next step, but otherwise I make it safely back to the Citroen without the old lady catching wind of me. But I need a breather.

At the other end of the village of Compton Dundon rises a lovely grassy hill called Lollover. I take a breather and stroll up Lollover to enjoy the view. It's canopied with a dome, as is Dundon Beacon, under which stands what seems to me a house-sized, multifaceted crystal, like the ones I've seen at the Tor and Chalice Hill. I know they're not *really* crystals, not crystals such as we hold in our palms, only larger; to call it a crystal is a convenient mental image for something no doubt far more subtle. After all, things are in form mainly for the purposes of illustration. In one dimension there stands Dundon Beacon, a breadloaf-shaped hill of earth, stones, flowers, brambles, and trees; in another dimension there stands a crystalline structure like an upside-down umbrella from whose handle, at the shelves, spumes upwards a magnificent shaft of light. Correctly understood, both hill and crystal are compatible expressions of the same reality coinhabiting the same space but at different vibrational levels. In fact, all of the landscape around Lollover, Dundon Beacon, and Lugshorn is similarly, if mysteriously, foliated with these crystalline outcrops.

Lollover feels beatific compared to Dundon Beacon. It is a hill as if divinely prepared for lollygagging, for lolling over. You get a full view here of Dundon, Lugshorn, Somerton, Glastonbury Tor, the flat moorlands stretching green and low all the way to the Severn estuary. The clouds block and reveal the sun in constant succession as it shines on the Tor, rendering its flanks alternately sprightly green and somberly olive. You can almost make out the whole rainbow of the Arc of Developing Consciousness, leaping out of the Tor, anchoring at Lugshorn. And you can almost sense the sea flowing silently across the desolate mudflats, lapping against Lollover, another of Glastonbury's Summer Country islands.

Curiously, that's how John Cowper Powys envisioned the last days of psychically top-heavy Glastonbury with its Grail Seekers and Grail Killers: in mid-March "moving plain of waters" from the Severn leave all of northern Somerset a "waste of grey water" as Glastonbury becomes once more an outpost of four islands. As he drowns, one of Powys' characters beholds the Grail over the Tor. "The Grail under its fifth shape—upon the top of Gwyn-Ap-Nudd's hill... that nameless Object, that fragment of the Absolute, about which all his days he had been murmuring."

Yet as I lie here in the soft grass on Lollover, under the influence of the Gemini twins, under this star dome that links with the neighboring Dundon Beacon dome, I wonder if Powys' Grail might also be Gennaro's "floating Grails," his vision of domes. I wonder if Powys really meant that Glastonbury would one day drown, not in water, but consciousness, in accordance with Blaise's angelic equation. I can almost sense the days, apparently millions of years ago, when the brilliantly numinous god domes were actually present, when the Cosmic Chaplains did compassionately survey the evolving life and slow maturation of human consciousness, bringing wisdom in the wise domes. And they'll be back, Blaise promises us. The domes will return for a fourth visit. Maybe in our time.

I find myself at times these days examining the sky expectantly, hoping that perhaps they're coming now, ahead of schedule, bringing light. Quite remarkably, back in 1953, science fiction dean Arthur C. Clarke had a similar picture of things. In *Childhood's End*, the Overlords' silver, gleaming ships did indeed arrive in one apocalyptic moment, "pouring out of the unknown depths of space" to hover visibly above the planet's major cities. All the world was watching "while the great ships descended in their overwhelming majesty," changing the history of Earth, ushering in almost painlessly an unprecedented Golden Age.

Russell is waiting for me in the driveway as I pull up at Wick in the Citroen. "Keep the motor running, Grail Knight. Blaise wants us at the Mump right away. Just came through on the Grail teletype: 'Urgent. Get the Grail Knight.' And you'd better not let Berenice see you in the house with those clothes. Were you rolling in the stuff? Maybe I'll just stick you in the kiln and bake you the way you are, Grail Knight and Grail in one convenient ceramic form."

The Mump is unoccupied when we arrive. We pace contemplatively along its mazed contours, breathing attentively with each step, bringing the Blazing Star in the lilac flame to bear on the tufted path. Blaise stands sixfold in the ruined church foundation at the summit. *Forollen* was the Atlantean practice of conscious maze walking, I think I hear Blaise say, but after Dundon's *mudagen* I'm a little skeptical of these queer old words. Are they having me on again?

Russell and I stand with our backs to the St. Catherine church, facing down the body of the Dog, as the Blaises loom like sentinels in the arches. We wait, silently. This hill is connected with the Tor, and with Brent Knoll, Cadbury Castle, and Hamdon Hill, I reflect, and these, through their dome lines, with numerous other points across the landscape so that the whole Earth is woven together by numinous strands of connection.

Our vigil is broken when out of nowhere two school buses pull into the parking lot and five dozen children stampede up the hill, their lunch boxes swinging like scimitars, each screaming voice as if amplified by megaphone. They shout and dash and argue up the Mump, spilling themselves like jumping beans through the stones, ignoring us, never suspecting angels. Yet each child is outlined in light, as if backlit, and each is overshadowed by a guardian angel.

We walk through the children's riotous picnic and down the hill. "It's a funny business," says Russell. "I mean, in the earlier days, when these places were active, people used to be afraid of the holy sites. The spiritual charge was actually intimidating and only the priests and geomancers were sufficiently trained to handle it. Then the angels came and made it feel more relaxed for people to visit. Except the people forgot the sacredness of the landscape and now they storm up the old geomantic hills like they're just another picnic venue. These children should be in training for a more conscious awareness of the landscape."

"But then, did you notice how the dome lit up their light bodies, making them all seem happier as they ran closer to its core?" I ask him. Russell nods in agreement.

In the evening, Blaise arrives around eleven o'clock. "We come as a lilac flame of transmutation. We come as a point of light within a lilac flame of transmutation. We come as we are. We come as a sphere of electric blue light within a flame of lilac. We come as a point of light in a sphere of pure consciousness. We come as love. We come as we are. We come as a Blazing Star. We bring the blessings of Beatrice, of Lamech, of Aziel, of Isis, of Semech, of Eshnabar.

"We place within you two swords. One goes upwards, the other goes downwards. The point of the downwards sword touches the base of your spine. The point of the upwards sword touches just above the top of your head. They cross from front to back at a place just behind the center of your abdominal cavity. Here we place a point of brilliant light around which we place a sphere of electric blue, around which we place the lilac flame of transmutation, around which we place a golden ring. This is the golden ring of transharmoniousness. This ring is joined with another ring of brilliant silver. They intersect and form a *vesica piscis*. The golden globe of the Sun rests above the lunar globe of silver. In the center of this intersection, we place a pearl. Breathe with your love to this new image in your body...."

After a few minutes of breathing as Love from Above with Blaise to this image, I am inside Albion's geomythic body, which is standing up, unshackled. "Good," says Blaise. "Albion stirs as a conscious movement passes over his form. You see a little of our future together. We are happy with all that has taken place. You all begin in a small way to see a little part of what we try to show you. It is most comforting to us that you work as you do together. We are most happy and we look forward to many times when we will be together again. This will be the last time we will talk like this together for a while, though, as you know, we are with you all, and all the time at this time. We give you each All Hallow's Eve. We bring our wings together and wish you what you wish for yourselves. We surround you with dancing lilac flames. We place golden rings above your heads."

"Blaise, I'd like to know what happened at the mud hole today at Dundon?" I begin.

"We are very pleased and acknowledge the beginning of something that could be most beneficial for many of your kind. Don't worry about the hole. Dig more if you like digging; otherwise, it's finished. What you experienced under the rocks was trapped, a friend of ours. It made the whole hill malign. You released him. Things will improve slowly. It was a lily. You saw our friend in one of his aspects. Regarding the shelves, this is water as an expression of light, light as an expression of consciousness, passing over the seven steps of developing consciousness. As you know, Dundon Beacon is in relation to the Arc of Developing Consciousness."

"What about all the crystals I've been seeing at these places?"

"We have explained you are in the process of transition, of transmutation, from the carbon cycle to the silicon cycle. Therefore, the crystalline structure of Earth's matrix is beginning to become apparent in the etheric of the earth. There is another aspect. We speak of light being drawn up from deep within the planetary body of Earth in the form of water. Light and water are synonymous. Consciousness is dependent on the water aspect. Therefore, illumined, or what you call enlightened, consciousness is dependent on the state of vibratory resonance in any organism of the water element. What you perceive as crystals is light solidified, like a memory, but also a potential. Both are simultaneous, but the water that exists in these places is creating the pattern in the light. It's very difficult to explain.

"Your technology in either physical or metaphysical terms hasn't the vocabulary for us to distinguish between elemental base consciousness, light, movement, and matter. These crystals are found only with domes. What you perceived at Wearyall Hill, which doesn't have a dome, was an attempt in consciousness to emulate the effect of a dome for the purpose of geomantic alignment by a master geomancer. That is the only case where what you describe as a crystal formation exists over the Earth other than at phenomena we have agreed to call domes. We suggest, as a starting point, 'aberration of consciousness,' as a term to reinterpret the crystals in a more positive light. You'll find this explained in optics." (In optics, an aberration is the convergence by a lens or mirror to different foci of light rays that emanate from a single point, or the deviation of these rays from initially a single focus.)

"Dowsers and other people who investigate sacred sites always report lots of water running in veins just under the ground. Presumably most of these sites are either domes or dome caps, but why is there so much water present?"

"We would describe this as a reciprocal inevitability. As the light forms, or domes, arrived, then as above, so below: light forms were created below. It's inevitable: one above, one below. Light in one form above, light in another form as water, below. The lines below the Earth as water travel with more difficulty in material obscurity. The lines above or on the surface of the Earth do not have this problem. It is also a case of centripedal and centrifugal movement in terms of the effect of the lines on consciousness. That which draws in is centripedal; that which pushes out is centrifugal. Centripedal water below, centrifugal light above.

"You see, the domes came. A dome in the Earth was made manifest. The image of the dome that came is only an etheric memory, but the image of the water dome that formed is still present. As above, so below. The etheric memory is above, the physical memory below. There are many sites in Britain that show signs of terrific heat exerted there. There are places where rocks were made molten. This is tangible evidence of something beyond your range of heat, of something that arrived and went away. Also, the Earth as a living planetary body has veins of water, rivers, and streams, running above and below its surface. The Earth, in response to vast heat hitting its surface, even at high points of elevation on its planetary body, sent up water from its deepest layers to cool and protect itself. The heat came from the arrival of the domes."

"Can we talk some more about what happened at the Mump today and what you like to call *forollen*?

"It is more the attitude of letting walking walk that we consider important. We began to indicate something of the Earth pattern to you at the Mump today. It is an awareness of what might be called an alchemical reality, a linking of all sacred sites over the landscape, from one area to another, from one country to another, from one continent to another, from your Earth to all planets in your solar system, from all suns to all stars. And the pattern is in the making, in the connections being made in consciousness. You will be shown many patterns to heal the Earth of its suffering, to show Her some care among you who are in human form, to show Her that She is still loved, to show Her She need not destroy you all.

"We show you a mighty wheel with many spokes. At each spoke there is a point of light. The wheel has a hub. Each spoke has two ends. Each spoke is connected to the hub and to the wheel. The center of the hub is connected to neither the spokes nor the wheel. It is still. Listen to the sound. We turn the wheel into the head of a dandelion. This is your Earth. The center is still. The spokes leave from every direction. The hub, the patterns of light, emerge on the surface and extend beyond it. These points at the end of each spoke are what we have referred to as flowers, or petals, or nodes, or energy centers, or chakras. They relate to the center of the being you call Earth.

"So we were most pleased to see you at the Mump today. One day things will be different. We will stand with you in awareness of all who come. We are unfathomable peace, peace that surpasses understanding. We will bring all requests to Michael and be brought by Michael to bring about a new initiation into the mystery of what you call life."

"I'd like to know about the origin of terms like *forollen* and some of these other exotic words you've popped into my head."

"Would you, jumping bean? We have spoken to you of the nature of potential distortion. To arrive at anything clearly is very difficult and always a matter of individual interpretation and translation. We have spoken to you about your inherent feeling of rightness. This should be your rule. We impose nothing. In our awareness we present what we are able. You make suggestions. We state whether they seem appropriate or not. That is all we are able to do in relation to words. As we've told you, we are not particularly concerned with words. We are most concerned with your process. We are concerned with where you are in relation to your process. Words will merely distract the communication of the experience. When you are in communication, when you are being spoken through, then your creative side will also be in focus. Your spirit is activated in this manner. Therefore it is an aspect of the process of communication that you will create within it. This is an integral part of the process.

"Right and wrong creations in words have no self-nature. *My* mind is a nonconcept. Forget such things. They are a barrier to your understanding. *My* mind. *My* ideas. *My* concepts. *My* thoughts. *My* goodness....oh dear. It's very limiting. You are in any moment in time and space all that you have ever been and all that you ever will be. It is a denial of so much to say such things as *my* ideas.

"Now we ask you for a few moments to join us in a blessing tonight. It is a mark of our gratitude. We do not use the word 'mark' lightly when we say as a *mark* of our gratitude. Just be still for awhile and receive what we give to each of you."

I see a Blazing Star, then a sword of light, then a ring of interlinked humans and angels, then another dozen diaphanously backlit humans, including myself as one of them. Now there is a brilliantly white gazebo with six pillars set like a crystalline jewel in a shimmering green lawn, many acres in size. Six angels stand inside the gazebo, one by each pillar, pulsating in and out of visibility and form. The gazebo is extraordinarily familiar to me.

Then Blaise speaks: "And we say these words to the three of you. We are one in the spirit of our love. And Michael touches your crowns with the sword of clear, pure mind." My head blazes white, my body floods with light, then becomes the Black Bowling Ball with a big smile. "This is it. It will give you more of a chance to be in touch with us and each other, as you each will. Before we answer any more questions we would like a short break. This is what you would call an emotional moment for us all."

None of us have much to say during the break. "I'm amazed," Russell finally says, "at how Michael can scrunch himself down to less than eight feet tall to fit under the ceiling here." Then Blaise returns.

"We come as a Blazing Star, from not too far, as we are. Yet from beyond the beyond. Don't trouble yourselves. We are part of it anyway, little wheels within wheels, cogs within cogs, in the most perfect machine imaginable. We come as love. We come as light. In the beginning was the Word. The Word was made sound. The sound was made song. The song woke the Earth spirit. The air was calling the ear. This is how it was in the beginning. We hope you will show people Albion, so he may dance again for Glaston of the green waters and Avalon of the apple lands.

"We will be with you constantly in various forms during your visit to America. You would be best prepared having no expectations other than that. It is something that will astound you. Put Michael before you in all you do. Don't waste energy on worry or anticipation, otherwise you will need to be in America longer than any of us would wish. Don't worry. Be empty form. Don't forget to get on the plane. You don't have wings—yet. We've got your name down for a small pair, later. We ask that, when you fly over the ocean, you send with your breath love to all the fish in the sea, particularly the whales. Do you know, some of our best friends are whales. They can communicate easily from one side of the Earth to the other. They don't need phones. When a whale dies, all whales feel it. This is unitive consciousness."

On our drive home from the Mump today, Russell suggested we might link up during the winter solstice when I was to be at Mt. Shasta, California, and they in Glastonbury. I wanted Blaise's opinion about the idea.

"Yes, we like it. It was our idea anyway. We suggest you locate the base energy center of the Earth consciousness and work with what you have been shown—the images we have given. Mt. Shasta is an aspect of the base or root center of the Earth's consciousness. It is where the creative lies deep within the mountain. Remember what you want to do, your goals. Be sure that is what you want, what you will, for it is your choice. Place these thoughts into the center of the point you are at on the mountain. Arrive thirty minutes before the solstice; leave ten minutes afterwards, promptly, with love and attention on each footstep. When you've planted the seeds, there is not a lot to do afterwards other than to leave them to germinate. In this case, you are leaving them with a good gardener named Gabriel."

I was also wondering whether any of this is top secret, or can I write about our adventures with Blaise in my magazine articles. At the time, I didn't realize how unnecessary the question would be.

"You don't intend to put us amongst the beans, do you? We'd like a headline in *The New York Times*: 'Grail Knight Transforms Earth, Guided by Blaise.' Don't worry. We'll see what we can arrange. Just try. Don't even do that. Just have a little faith. He put you here. Let Him look after you. He's better at it than you are anyway. We have shown you from our various works through others how distortion can occur, how difficult it is for us to be comprehended. Yet, you see we use all opportunities for possible communication of our many forms, for what we bring will come through. And, beginning tonight, we bring through the Grail Quest as it truly is. First, we place a wafer in your hand. Pop it into your mouth. Say to yourself: 'I am the Power, and the Glory, forever and ever, Amen.' Feel the light."

I would surely like the address of Blaise's wafer baker. The angelic confection is scrumptious in terms of how it makes you *feel*. I watch with interest as my socks, corduroy trousers, patched woollen sweater, blue shirt collar, face, and faithful glasses disappear, leaving only the anatomical outline etched in light. A wave of gladness bursts through me borne on the momentum of eternity. Eventually my physical body, with notepad and hand poised to write down words of angelic wisdom, reassembles itself modestly in the vicinity of this eggshell of luminosity. Blaise sounds pleased with themselves. "And so we twiddle your green pyramids. We blow on your golden and silver rings. We send our love to your lilac flames. We are as we are, as the point of pure light in the sphere of pure mind. We leave you as we are, yours, in essence, a Blazing Star."

Three hours later, in my room, I'm still packing. It's not that I'm a slow packer, I've just been drifting off into reflections and considerations this whole time about all we've done these last few months at Wick Manor. Three pairs of corduroys, six sweaters, five pairs of socks, a half dozen shirts, all the same color, a vest, and thank God my check came today so I can pay for my plane ticket. It helps to have friends in high places.

I see Blaise in the Grail Knight Recruitment Office. They're reviewing my dossier, weighing my qualifications, shaking their heads and praying for somebody else to come along. Who is this jackanapes who calls himself the American Grail Knight, Cosmic, Terrestrial, Domestic—and Cheeky? Does he expect us to enter this in his permanent record? Permanent around here means a very long time. Can we credit his wiseacre answers to our sincere questions, and with the Boss—you know, the Big Architect of It All—leaning over our shoulders to make sure we haven't picked the American Bozo by mistake? Consider this reply to our interview question which has been standard for the last millennium: To what extent have you purged yourself of worldly corruption and the pursuit of material goods? To which the Grail Knight replies:

"No problem. My MasterCard was ceremonially revoked by abrasive form letter and credit bureau two years ago. In the spirit of renunciation, I took scissors to my Sears credit card and publicly— in front of my dog— snipped it into confetti. Thus have I purged myself of all wish-fulfilling plastic. I sold my car, threw out my old unpaid parking tickets, gave away my stereo—it needed a big overhaul—and favorite records, and I lost two pairs of still usable sneakers. I tossed my address book in the rubbish. I keep all my money now in a brown sock, over there, in the top drawer under the sweaters, and every morning I throw nasty darts of aspersion at a framed copy of *Money* magazine and wail at the material corruption and concupiscence irretrievably beyond my reach. Yes, angelic recruiting officer, I am prepared to undertake the Quest on daily rations of bread (whole wheat), water (provided it's diluted with either Guinness or miso), abstaining from meats and fine French wines the way the old Grail boys did. I'm prepared to go all the way solely on English marmalade and a pot of Earl Grey.

318 ✦ Richard Leviton

I'm not worrying about whether my petition will be accepted. I know for a fact, Blaise, you don't have anybody else in mind at this particular moment. And could you guys just lean on this case, like that, so I can latch it shut?

In the morning I wake much too early but remember a dream. I work with someone on a small patch of green lawn. It is close-clipped and has been trampled. We leave and then return. The grass has grown considerably and now there are hundreds of nearly open red roses flourishing amidst the grass blades. I knew they had been there all along but couldn't blossom until the lawn was left alone, unwalked on, for a while.

39

STRONG WHACKS FROM THE ZEN STICK

or three days now, ever since I came back to Wick from America, I've been lying under eight blankets in bed, down for the count with the flu. I haven't been this sick in ten years. Russell, Edmund, and Celia are sick in bed, too, and Berenice staggers about, almost recovered. Hilary is the only hale one among us and she probably wishes otherwise because she has become our nurse factotum. Lying in bed, I at least have the energy to remember our reunion earlier this week. She picked me up at Heathrow early in the morning and helped me load my books and ten-speed bike into her Volvo. We stopped at Stonehenge on the drive out to Somerset.

The ancient circle was snowclad, fenced-in, mute, suffering an intemperate wind, left alone by the tourists today who no doubt were staying indoors. "I missed you a lot, actually," Hilary confessed, clutching her scarf so it wouldn't blow off. "I wrote you dozens of letters, but I didn't mail any of them. I didn't know what to say to you, or else I didn't like what I said." That at least accounts for the epistolary void. Writers are cursed when all their friends are nonwriters: the mailbox is always empty.

At Wick, I quickly surmised the health disaster I had come home to. Wrapped in a great coat and struggling through a barrage of sniffles and coughs, Russell greets me: "I looked forward to your return so much, but now you're here, I'm too beat to feel happy." Last night we invalids sat by the fireplace huddled on the couch under blankets and coats, shivering, staring vacantly at the flames like nonogenarians on their last legs. After three months in exile, I have returned, but nothing feels right, or at least, the same. Wick has changed. I have changed. Blaise is nowhere to be found, at least not in the familiar ways. Hilary brings me tea and says, "I'd climb into bed with you, love, and be another duvet on top of you but I don't want the flu."

Being sick leaves me plenty of time for reflection. Blaise was right about this "brief" trip back to America, a suddenly foreign land to me. "We place a good line between you and Russell," Blaise had said before I left. "We see you both as a golden tube surrounded by four white pillars," they added. The flu struck us synchronously, along that "good line." I was in Manhattan meeting a literary agent. I had come into the city on a bus from western Massachusetts a couple days before my flight back to London. Around eleven a.m, as Samuel was explaining to me the thirty-eight reasons why my manuscript on King Arthur was unpublishable and needed serious, if not prodigious, reworking, I got the chest pains. Maybe his unencouraging words were like a sword stroke in the lungs. My chest felt like it was opening, growing warm, bleeding heat; by noon, I had a full blown cold. I stayed in bed for the next two days then limped through the airport and asked the Great Nothing to push me through the travel logistics, or, failing that, to provide a complimentary wheelchair. At the same time, to the hour, the flu dragon bit Russell here at Wick and he collapsed into his bed with a high fever.

Blaise had said they would be with me constantly during my travels in America and they were right. They arranged things. They astounded me, as promised, from the very beginning. I was flying People Express—a peripatetic but insolvent Grail Knight's blessing, before they were hounded into bankruptcy—and discovered to my embarassment when the stewardess came to collect three dollars for my luggage that I had only seventy-five cents. I looked to Blaise, who was standing like shaggy sheep dogs with sunglasses on the wings of the 747, for ideas. They shrugged their shoulders. I told the stewardess I was broke, could I pay her at Hartford? She smiled and waved off the transaction, moving on to the next passenger. The flight itself had been considerably late such that when we reached Newark, my connecting flight had left hours ago. No problem: would I like a free round trip ticket to anyplace in the U.S. as a compensation? That took care of my California junket. I sat out the eight hour late-night holdover at the old Newark terminal, which was as relaxing as an inner city bus station, and kept my seventy-five cents intact.

My pauperhood was swiftly resolved by a generous loan from my parents. They bought me clothes, loaned me a car, put things on their credit cards, made my way easy—conferred, if transiently, some of the privileges that might have been mine were I not on the Grail Knight career track in the fast lane for the Fisher King. My father asked me about Arthur and the idea of the landscape zodiac, and I answered in a format metaphysically edited for parents. As I did, I saw Blaise standing behind both my parents there in the kitchen, their wings outstretched to include the entire house. You never know about your parents; they might be into angels in their own sly way but hesitant to tell *you* about it. When I drove home from an errand, Blaise filled the car with multiples of themselves. When I sat alone in a movie theater watching *Starman*, Blaise sat next to me on both sides, their wings around me. When I took an evening walk through an exurban tree-lined neighborhood I had known since age one, past all the familiar maples and old bike runs, Blaise was with me. Sometimes he brought Russell or took me back to Wick, so I never felt alone.

What Blaise couldn't facilitate was a faster transmutation of everything of mine in the Grail bowl. Connections, attachments, emotions, fixations, inner obstacles—karma. I wasn't at a point of coherency and integration in my process, and much dross remained to be (painfully) burned off. I visited some old friends, Dharma bums, Kerouac would call us. We had lived and meditated together in various arrangements during the 1970s and organized our lives and thinking around the Buddhist teachings. In a rush of enthusiasm, I told them about my Somerset adventures.

"It's too far out," said Ralph. "It sounds like you're on the hallucinogenic merry-go-round, but it's not clear if you're changed or trans-formed or if it's worth going through it. You need to develop more discriminating awareness. Be more skeptical, even judgmental, when you have to. Be very careful about psychics and their supposed revelations. Don't buy it wholesale. Don't forget about enlightenment. Does talking with angels further your enlightenment? How do you know Blaise is interested in your awakening anyway?"

"You should have done more drugs in college," quipped Franny. "You'd have gotten this out of your system. You're a bit of a late bloomer. People were interested in this stuff *years* ago. What were you doing then? Most psychics I've met are unbalanced in their personal lives—wrecks, in fact."

"And I'm dubious about the way you assign all the credit to Blaise for your insights," added Ralph.

"You can't expect people to accept your 'vision' or version as the only explanation," Franny said. "It's still illusion on one level, the realm of the ecstatic Gods, but they're still on the Wheel, part of the six worlds."

Afterwards, as we watched Humphrey Bogart and Lauren Bacall snuggle after a long courtship waltz, Blaise filled the house with multiple angelic presences, transcending all dialectical perspectives. That night I woke with a tight pain in my chest. By seven-thirty a.m., it had grown into a headache, dizzyness, and a steady, rivetting pain along the sternum, like a muscle clenching, then releasing. By eleven it hadn't stopped. I'm too young for a heart attack, I thought, a little panicked. I lay on the couch, concentrating on my breathing, trying to release this horrific gas bubble in my chest. It felt like a heavy, cold, leaden anvil throbbing mercilessly inside me. I called on Blaise to help, *please*, it's too intense. By noon, the anvil had turned into a rosy, warm heart, freeing me from further pain, but leaving me exhausted. "Maybe it's your heart chakra trying to open," said Ralph, clearly speaking on behalf of Blaise. "All those swords in your chest are bound to crack something open eventually even in someone as thick as you."

Then I had dinner with a former business partner. We had known and fought each other for a decade, but we'd never extended our relationship much beyond the concerns of business. He was approaching forty, recently divorced, and suddenly keenly interested, if warily, in metaphysics. Henry asked big questions and each answer took an hour, spawning rivulets of digressions. "You've become a quiet English mystic," Henry said, leaning back in his chair at the restaurant, gripping his designer suspenders. "How do you know your arrangement with this Blaise isn't Mephisthophelean, that you haven't surrendered your soul for knowledge? Maybe you invented the appearance of angels from out of your own desires. How do you guard against evil influences and the distortions of group auto-suggestion?"

As Blaise would say, "Uh, oh, trouble at the mill." It seemed to me the problem wasn't that I might have imagined Blaise and company, but that I didn't do it thoroughly enough, with enough conviction, to convince anybody, possibly myself included. Henry, Ralph, and Franny, really, were only pulling at threads of doubt dangling from my own jacket of new experience. I dreamed a dentist told me I had lots of cavities, that my teeth needed lots of attention. I dreamed I was on a bus driving up a mountain road. I sat in the half-lotus position, visualizing a blue globe around the bus. A lovely woman— a girlfriend from early adolescence, now fully grown—stands behind me, draping her silken arms over my shoulders. She likes authors (or Arthurs), she whispers in a husky voice. Now we're at my writing desk. My manuscript sheets are the size of window shades. The room is situated in a renovated barn; the other rooms are ramshackle. "If only one were fixed up, we'd have it made—and with an angel in it with our remittance," she says, as we stroll about my office, arm-in-arm, anima and her Grail Knight.

The *coup de grace* in this continuing challenge from the world came during a private interview with my Zen Master. It was the end of a seven day retreat. I told him, sketchily, about my work with Blaise. I didn't tell him that moments before when we chanted the Heart Sutra in the zendo I had seen him with a hundred thousand grey-robed monks in a huge auditorium, chanting and practicing—the world assembly of Buddhas, the *Sangha* of masters. Advice to young Grail Knights: don't ever cross a Zen Master unless you know how to make the pre-emptive strike; otherwise, you're dead, you're history. He shook his head, disgusted with me. "You don't believe in yourself. Your direction is not clear. You don't believe my words. Even if the Buddha came today, he could not teach you. You must find your true direction, your true self. Get clear mind, empty like space. When you believe in yourself, then your true good teacher will arrive. I'm not your teacher, not any more. Now you're not clear at all."

"But you once said you were visited by all sorts of angels on Won Gak mountain during your enlightenment retreat," I protested.

"Put all that down. Don't check my experience. What is your center?" He glared at me, my executioner awaiting my pathetic answer. I make a fist over my belly button, hoping he'll see the Star. "That's not your center. That's your stomach. You must make center very strong," punching me lightly in the belly. "Otherwise, you keep going round and round and round, many more births. Only go straight—don't know. Now get out of here!"

In Zen I suppose you get used to feisty *roshis* bashing you about. Anyway, I took his advice. I did go straight—straight to Mt. Shasta where I had an appointment with the archangel Gabriel, despite the danger I was running of many more births. I was a little consoled, upon arriving in this northern California logging town and Glastonbury simulacrum, to know that were my Zen Master to come here, he'd give it a strong whack with his stick.

40

THE ADAMANTINE
SNOWPEAKS OF SHASTA

trange things are said about this snowbound logging
town, dominated by a 14,000 foot twin-peaked old vol-
cano and New Age millennialist prophecy. The Rosicru-
cians claim the mountain was the last refuge for displaced
Lemurians who established an expatriate colony here
when their continent in the Pacific was destroyed. Various psychics
affiliated with St. Germaine, a popular channeling contact, argue
that Mt. Shasta is an interdimensional headquarters of the Great
White Brotherhood, the conclave of the ascended masters. Those
with a Spielbergian space technology orientation assure us that Mt.
Shasta is the Grand Central Station for UFO and Space Brother visi-
tations, which often veil themselves in the majestically enigmatic
lenticular clouds that frequently form over the mountain.

Tschastal, the "pure, white mountain"—this is what the nineteenth
century Russians, who settled in Bodega County, California, called
Shasta. For the Shasta Indians, it was *Ieka*, the White; they regarded
Ieka as the abode of the Great Spirit. A grizzly bear once captured
and married the daughter of the Great Spirit, so the Indians built
Black Butte (an old volcanic cone or debris pile nearby) as her wigwam.
As recently as 1881, Shasta, itself an old, presumably inactive volcano, sported bubbling hot springs near its summit, sending spumes
of steam two hundred feet above the bare rocks. These days the de-
velopers are looking for ways to establish a ski resort in Panther
Meadows, on the other side of the mountain, through a virgin red fir
forest. *Tschastal* is cold in the winter: at dawn on the morning I ar-

rive, the temperature is ten below zero in the village, and that's far lower in elevation, and thus warmer, than where I'm headed.

I spend my first days here making preparations. I study trail maps, get chains put on my tires, buy groceries, and make a test drive up the mountain. The thirteen mile access road is partially open in winter, when it's not blizzarding, terminating after nine miles in a huge snowpile at 7000 feet. A dozen other cars are parked here, most of them with ski racks. I lace up my snowshoes, tie my parka snug around my face, and trudge off across the five foot deep snow towards a spot about a mile into the woods that Blaise has conveniently indicated with a golden arrow. A magnificent stillness grips the high mountain air. Pristine clouds drift past Shasta's keen brow. The happy cries of cross-country skiiers trickle up the valley. A golden flame burns between two cedar trees. This is where I shall sit in the morning.

On the drive back to town, the access road has turned slushy, which is a bad sign, at least for me, without four-wheel drive. Slush easily freezes and makes driving ridiculously problematic; this could pose difficulties for my early morning commute to the snowfields. The tire chains might break if I drive too much on bare road, the mechanic warned me. If the temperature gets too much below zero, your car might not start, the gas station attendant cautioned. I breathe as Love from Above to these worries and determine that, should any of them manifest, I will do the work, somehow, from my hotel room.

By sunset, clouds have formed at Shasta's rocky summit as if all the blowing snow has congealed into a blanket wrapping the ineffable mountain in a cloak of invisibility. In the evening I'm restless. I watch basketball on television for a while then meditate, but either way I can *feel* Shasta—Ieka's stony, snowy, transcendent home—waiting for me.

Solstice morning I rouse myself at 4 a.m. Driving up the mountain road at five-thirty, I realize I am attended by great fortune. A warm mist has descended over Shasta keeping the road—and the meditating Grail Knight— unfrozen. A blue globe as thick as a carpet and worth a hundred insurance policies envelops the car and Blaises everywhere accompany me as I chant the *Heart Sutra*: "...form does not differ from emptiness, emptiness does not differ from form." There's nobody around, no cars in the pull-out, only me, six silent angels, and the ambivalent mist. I turn off the motor, switch off the lights, and surrender myself to the immensity.

Beyond me, across the snowfields, Shasta breathes. I finally rouse myself into motion, leave the ephemeral safety of the car, and plod with webbed feet across the snow in the predawn dark. A shred of mist floats by like an errant kite framed against dark firs, and inexplicably my mood lifts and I feel happy.

I follow my tracks from yesterday to the golden flame between the two cedar trees. I spread a blanket, stick my snowshoes in the snow like a fence, bow to the four directions, chant for a few minutes, then sit down. I'm winging it, taking my cues as to format from Blaise as they present them. I don't know of any standard liturgical text for depositing wishes for the new year with the archangel Gabriel through the planet's root center—do you? I establish contact with Russell, Berenice, and Hilary, whom I see perched on the Tor in Glastonbury. The scenery here at Shasta is complex, as Russell later corroborates when we compare notes. He saw me seated on a shoulder of the mountain surrounded by lilac flames; behind me stood a grey mushroom form, possibly an astral fountain. A sparkling golden tube ascends from this light fountain far into space. A lilac flame burns over the entire mountain as well, right through the mammoth dome that canopies it. Around Shasta stretch two kinetic collars of light, one at the summit and another half-way down, resembling napkin holders from which rise a series of crystalline petals. All of this appears to be inside the mountain but I know it must be in the same place as the mountain but at another vibrational level.

Meanwhile, physical visibility is no more than twenty feet and Shasta is veiled to ordinary eyesight. I see before me two open hands, so into these, after calling on Gabriel, I place my ideas, requests, and general supplications for world peace. I wrap these seed thoughts in an almond-colored eggshell and breathe love to it until it flushes warm and rosy. I feel my own heart and root centers align themselves with the larger energy fields of Glastonbury and Mt. Shasta. Meanwhile, on the Tor, as Russell tells me later, Blaise says: "Gabriel, Gabriel, Gabriel, receive our requests. Receive them through the Blazing Star that is each one of us. Take them into the Earth, make them what you will. Michael, Michael, Michael, receive from Blazing Star what you will for us on your behalf. These people now gathered in light and love, hear them act with your will, so their will be One."

I leave the rose egg of our intentions in the snow as a solitary bird trills for sunrise. I chant, bow again, then walk fifty yards further up the slope. The mists begin to shred under an invisible wind and in five minutes the adamantine snowpeaks of Shasta are revealed. No thoughts, just breathing among the conifers. Then the mists blow back and I start heading down the mountain, almost running—the way a duck runs—so light-hearted do I feel. "You'll be back when you start walking in Albion," Blaise whispers in my ear.

In town I have a huge breakfast and am astonished at how many gorgeous young women live in this mountain community, if the patronage of the deli is any indication. I don't upbraid myself for this rush of appreciation for manifest femininity. My dream life is waxing lascivious lately. I am with a girl from elementary school, now a grown woman, at a public event. We sit close, holding hands, snuggling, arousing each other. I'm with a different woman who has her arm around me, leading me into a bedroom. Another woman kisses me passionately and puts my palm on her ripe breast. Another woman discusses a matter of business, then exposes her breasts, takes off her clothes, and waits, voluptuously, for me. With still another woman, I'm seated in an auditorium; she stands behind me, her arms draped affectionately over my shoulders. I follow a young woman at night along a path through the forest; I chant. A naked woman with pendulous breasts holds one in each hand. The right breast is for somebody else, she says, but the left breast is for me. "Men live psychologically in a harem," says Jungian analyst Daryl Sharp. "Any man may observe this for himself by paying attention to his dreams and fantasies. His soul image appears in many different forms, just as a woman's femininity has myriad expressions. The assimilation of a particular anima-image results in its death, so to speak. That is to say, as one personification of the anima is consciously understood, it is supplanted by another."

On the flight back to London, I managed to sleep a little despite the high fever and shivering. I dream. I walk up a hill into a city on the edge of a river. An open parking lot on the left, dark brown wooden buildings on the right, cars parked in groups of three. I walk with a man to a footbridge that spans a raging, white-capped river. The bridge is incomplete, with only a skeletal floor with big gaps over which one must jump; and it's a long way to the other side. It looks dangerous, very iffy, but the man starts to cross and expects me to follow. It reminds me of the bridge I crossed from the Holy Thorn at Wearyall Hill, although this one is much more dubious.

"At a certain spot not to be mentioned to outsiders, there is a chasm spanned by a frail bridge of woven grasses with a raging torrent underneath," wrote El Morya in 1881, a Himalayan adept who communicated with Theosophists in the late nineteenth century. "The bravest member of your Alpine clubs would scarcely dare to venture the passage, for it hangs like a spider's web and seems to be rotten and impassable. Yet it is not; and he who dares the trial and succeeds—as he will if it is right that he should be permitted—comes into a gorge of surpassing beauty of scenery, to one of our places and to some of our people." El Morya was referring to Shambhala.

41

WITH MORGAN IN
THE SHIP OF TIME

t breakfast, Berenice tells me her dream of Morgan. "It was like looking in a mirror," she says, pouring tea. "I saw a being made of nine spheres of light, all connected by lines of light. Then Blaise spoke to me in the dream. "This is Morgan, showing you where she fits within the Tree of Life. Remember the whole Tree. She shows you lines of light, how they connect the spheres under which she has control.' Then I saw the Avenue of Cedars." When Berenice says this, I feel a jolt in my spine and my Blazing Star twinkles fiercely. Berenice and I look at each other silently, then she says, "Maybe you should call in at the Avenue."

The Avenue of Cedars is a serene promenade of dark green cedars just outside Glastonbury, striding anomalously in two parallel rows across the flat countryside from Park rhyne to the edge of Butleigh Wood. If you conceive that Park Wood was once much larger, perhaps double in size, then it's possible to imagine the Avenue proceeding directly to the Wood as a ceremonial, possibly hierophantic, processional, similar to the Avenue of Oaks from Gog and Magog to the Tor. To the less mystically inclined, the Avenue resembles a grand bridal path on a country estate. To the surveyor, the Avenue yields a count of 68 trees still standing, spaced about 80 feet apart in each row, the two rows situated about 50 yards apart, and the whole length spanning about 3800 feet. Local rumor has it that originally there were 94 trees, planted in honor of a goddess whose name is now forgotten.

I spend an hour walking the length of the Avenue, gathering the general flavor of this grand geomantic gesture, until the processional fades away, ending in the woods. Then I retrace my steps to a broad, spacious lawn—an open stretch of the Avenue free from bramble, encroaching woods, or other obstructions—from which I have the best vista of both the Avenue and Glastonbury Tor. I settle down within myself to explore the Avenue from the inside.

I stand at the beginning of the Avenue, which seems to be the end closest to the Tor, down by Park rhyne. Similar to the Avenue of Oaks, there is a large double door securing the entrance to the Avenue of Cedars. No matter: one thing a Grail Knight begins to understand is that in this curious business, swords are keys. You don't use your sword to whack down a stout door; rather, you use your sword as a kind of identity-card securing admission. I present my sword from the Green Chapel, holding it up, vertically, before me, its innumerable stars twinkling within. Slowly the great doors swing open and I step forward into a brilliantly illuminated, long, arched hall made as if of milky glass; where there are cedar trees in one dimension, here there are translucent columns; everything, in fact, seems made of translucent marble.

I make my way slowly through this magnificent white hall, my sword held upright before me, more in the gesture of presenting a banner than in poised defensiveness. At the end of this arched passageway, there is another double door, this time of gold. As before, one tap from my sword and the doors swing open, admitting me into in into a white, circular chamber with a high, vaulted ceiling. I sense a significant feminine presence but cannot bring her into view; instead, I momentarily glimpse a gold *bas relief* of a spiritual figure I interpret to be Tara, the Tibetan goddess, the feminine emanation and savioress of the compassionate Bodhisattva Avalokitesvara. I stand in the center of this domed chamber, my sword catching the light in all directions.

There are numerous pillars—perhaps nine—spaced evenly around the edge of the chamber; in fact, they appear to be part of the structure itself. Each emanates a single light, each one different: green, white, yellow, red, and others. Each light laminates my sword in turn until the blade full of stars shines within a multihued shell. Like a sheath, like a—scabbard. Of course. Morgan's scabbard!

In the Arthurian tales, Morgan, that "great clerk of necromancy," as Malory ungraciously calls her, steals Arthur's scabbard, which houses Excalibur. As Merlin testily informs Arthur, the scabbard is far more valuable than the sword itself. This holds a great clue. The implication is obvious, though Malory never draws it out. Morgan "steals" the scabbard for Excalibur because she *made* it in the first place from her own magic. The scabbard is, in some sense, Morgan's energy itself, the nine spheres she commands on the Tree—and the Avenue of Cedars is central to this.

As I realize this, a cluster of women comes into view, each one standing before a single-color pillar. They wear floor-length white robes, their heads are hooded, their faces pale, their lips bright red: Morgan's nine priestesses of Avalon—"nine sisters rule by a pleasing set of laws those who come to them from our country," wrote Geoffrey of Monmouth in his *Vita Merlini*. The priestess by the red column beckons me; as I pass her column, the vaulted chamber disappears, and I find myself in a clearing in the woods. Before me, a red globe, about two feet in diameter, sits atop a marble pedestal, so that the globe is at the level of my chest. The priestess stands silently behind it. Behind her stand two marble pillars; through these, I look into another country, another world. I touch the scarlet globe with the tip of my sword. I try to probe the inside of the globe with the sword tip acting as my eyes, but it is opaque to me. "This is one aspect of Morgan's magic, one ray among many that activates the sword and forms the sheath," the woman says. I stand before her scarlet globe a long time, willing myself to enter its domain, but I am unable to. Then I am back in the central vaulted chamber looking down the long, marble hallway through the open double-doors.

I remember Berenice's dream about Morgan and her nine-sphered Tree of Life and suddenly something puzzling from Malory's account makes sense. Everyone knows Malory collated numerous Arthurian and Grail traditions, from England, Wales, and France, when he fashioned his *Le Morte d'Arthur*, but one story element has always seemed out of place to me chiefly because it is so old. That's the Ship of Time and the sword of King David.

When King David was king of all Israel, Goliath, the giant, was this people's mortal enemy, until David slew him and claimed his sword. This sword became a central possession in King David's lineage, passing to his wise son, Solomon. In David's day, the sword resided in "Our Lord's Temple, as the marvelloust and the sharpest that ever was taken in any knight's hand." Solomon, his son, was clearly an initiate, for as Malory notes, he "knew all the virtues of stones and trees, and so he knew the course of the stars and many divers things." He also knew that one day, in the far future, this sword would rightfully be claimed by the last of his lineage and put to good use. "There shall come a man which shall be a maid, and the last of your blood, and he shall be as good a knight as Duke Joshua, thy brother-in-law," his intuition told him. As Merlin later relates, this knight will be Galahad. But then, how to preserve this sword across the untold centuries that will elapse between Solomon and his lineage-successor? Solomon's wife—whose name Malory never provides—proposed an ingenious scheme.

She would build a ship of the best and most durable wood available and send it forth with the sword into the deeps of future time. She protected the ship against the ravages of time by weaving a great covering, "a cloth of silk that should never rot for no manner of weather." Solomon remade the sword's pommel, hilt, and sheath, while she prepared a great bed for the sword and three spindles— one red, one white, one green—to be fastened to its canopy. The spindles have an exalted source: the original Tree of Life as planted by Eve in Eden, from "the bough on which the apple hung." Malory seems to equate the bed, the ship, and the scabbard; all three are various housings for the Giant sword. Solomon's wife calls it "The Sword with Strange Girdles," and its sheath, "Mover of Blood," because "no man that hath blood in him shall never see the one part of the sheath which was made of the Tree of Life."

On the night before the Ship of Time is to depart, Solomon dreams:

he sees "come from heaven a great company of angels" who anoint the ship with water poured from a silver vessel; they also inscribe letters on the sword hilt, and a public notice on the ship itself. "Thou man that wilt enter within me, beware that thou be full within the faith, for I ne am but Faith and Belief." In the morning, the Ship of Time was "anon shoven in the sea" and sailed into the future with its king (and giant) sword; not long after, it docked at the Avenue of Cedars in Glastonbury.

We're dealing with an initiate's fable here woven from a conflation of equivalencies. The scabbard, the Tree of Life, the sword in the Tree (that I withdrew at Pointer's Ball), Morgan's magic, Morgan's nine spheres, her nine priestesses of Avalon, the Ship of Time—these are equivalent expressions. The scabbard houses, protects, and activates the sword of cosmic intelligence gained in the Green Chapel. It is the initiate knowledge of the sword's use—its activation codes, the command words of each Sephira (or Sphere on the Tree of Life) under Morgan's influence. As Merlin rightly counselled Arthur, the scabbard far exceeds the sword in value. The sword may be the embodiment of cosmic intelligence, a galactic blade, but the scabbard is the wisdom governing its use, and the "magic" through which it acts in the world.

Where does the sword come from? In one version, it comes from the Green Knight; in another, from a slain giant, Goliath. But the Green Knight is a giant, too; and the Green Knight is an expression of the Archangel Michael. Clearly, the sword has a celestial pedigree, and its imprimatur was claimed by the initiates David, then Solomon, on behalf of humanity, for, initially, the purposes of healing the wounded Fisher King. Later, through the Knight Galahad, the sword might be used wisely for its original purpose without inflicting wounds on user or beneficiary. For this to be possible, the sword, as initiate knowledge, must be housed, and activated, in a kind of time capsule, a scabbard outside of time, in a "ship" unaffected by the passage of time yet capable of access by those living in time.

That's Morgan's secret: most simply put, Morgan, or Morgan's energy, is the scabbard, is the Ship of Time. As if to confirm my line of thinking, Blaise interjects: "The Avenue of Cedars is a connection through to another Shambhala doorway, as on the Tor. The beings that here, are, at one level, to protect, at another level, they are initiatory. These beings use the trees as access points."

42

THE TEMPLE COMES TO EASTER

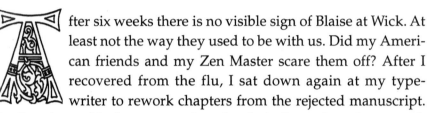fter six weeks there is no visible sign of Blaise at Wick. At least not the way they used to be with us. Did my American friends and my Zen Master scare them off? After I recovered from the flu, I sat down again at my typewriter to rework chapters from the rejected manuscript. But I can't get this dream out of my head. As I stand on the ground, I am concerned about a monolithic sheet of grey mist that lies as if suspended a hundred feet above me. This mist blows off and a huge house is revealed overhead, a mansion somehow suspended in the sky as if by crane. I'm worried it will crash on our heads, but my father assures me that the crane holds it securely in position. Then I am standing with a friend at the base of the Tor. There is something fuzzy and domelike in the sky. I hold a small golden bell, but it lacks a handle and clapper. I train this soundless bell at the sky object, and this brings it into focus as a golden disc. It settles on the ground and I use my bell like a phonograph needle to play the disc like a record. A high-pitched recorded voice announces the disc has come from a far-off star. And this morning, during meditation, I saw Gog and Magog—the trees—with a golden arrow pointing to a spot ten feet before them.

"It looks like an assignment has come in through the teletype from the Boys," says Russell. "It'll do you good, anyway, to get out of the house and out on the Quest again. I just had an intuition. It's Easter Sunday tomorrow, too. I have to tell you I feel compelled to, well, almost warn you not to eat any fairy food that might be offered you on the Tor."

The next morning at five a.m. I'm walking along Stonedown Lane in the predawn mist of Glastonbury. The devic presence is intense. Gnomes perch on rocks and fenceposts like teenagers on a Saturday night's street corner. Fairies swoop along the high banks of the road like barn swallows. A crow caws then flaps suddenly off from a bush. Yet something feels ambivalent on Stonedown poised at this moment of transition when the agencies of night yield to the uplifters of day. I wrap myself in a blue globe and lilac flame, half expecting to be jumped by a bogeyman. At the base of Stonedown, the energy shifts as if someone flipped a switch. Dawn breaks, and, through her morning door, a hundred birds warble into song. A finger of light nudges up the darkness along the horizon. Angels walk behind me. I feel inspired to chant *Avalon, Avalon,* over and over as I make my way to the ancient Celtic oaks, and, from them, up the oak tree processional to the Tor. The irony of Gog and Magog as trees is that they may be hoary and dying but as pillars they are imperishable. The secret of their eternity is embedded in their names, which appear to be transliterations from the Tibetan: *ma-hgags.* This means "imperishable, indestructible." No doubt this etymology is Merlin's handiwork, Tibet's emissary to Glastonbury long ago.

It's grown windy and rainy now, although this alternates with fitful splotches of sunshine. The gate hanging between the massive pillars of light at Gog and Magog is wide open. The "Philosopher's Stone," as Glastonbury mystics call it, glitters emerald green on the left flank of the Tor, twice the size of the boulder that occupies the same place between two trees; behind it stands one of the entrances to the fabled cavern inside this hollow hill of Avalon, the Green Chapel. Topping the St. Michael tower on the Tor this morning are three arching golden gates a hundred feet tall. Meanwhile, it is appallingly muddy at the base of the hill. The sheep stare at me and my devic companions with incredulity as I slop my way through the muck chanting *Avalon, Avalon.* I can't believe what I'm seeing either, so that makes two of us.

I sit down under an apple tree framed by an arching gate of light for which two diaphanous apple trees stand as pillars. I gather up my attention, breathing to the Blazing Star at my belly, until I feel focussed. "When we practice zazen, our mind always follows our breathing," says Shunryu Suzuki-roshi. "We say 'inner world' or 'outer world,' but actually there is just one whole world. What we call 'I' is just a swinging door that moves when we inhale and when we exhale."

The roshi's right, of course, and I'm aware as I breathe that Avalon just breezed through the swinging door into my mind. Since I know I'm incorrigible and beyond the reach even of the Buddha, I don't feel bad about spending the next thirty minutes chanting *Avalon, Avalon*, as the I-door swings back and forth from the constant traffic. Then I step aside to see what the wind has blown through. The TV screen blazes into living color as I switch to the Astral Broadcasting Corporation channel. "Zen is clear mind, always clear mind," says Seung Sahn, Soen Sa Nim, the Korean Zen Master. "Clear mind means that everyday mind is truth. Cold water is cold; hot water is hot—not special. Keeping clear-like-space mind, moment to moment, means your mind is like a clear mirror. When red comes, red; when white comes, white." When astrality comes, astrality.

Here is a rundown on the programming: Two men carry a large pole one foot thick, twenty feet long and set it into a prepared hole. Several women in thick black hair with white robes clasped with gold bands stand silently. Somebody I know from Massachusetts walks the Tor, robed in white. Morgan le Faye is caped and stands behind me; then she walks through the Avenue of Oaks, gesturing to each tree, as if bestowing blessings. The Tor is swathed in a grey mist, the tower veiled in fog. An angelic figure with arms outstretched stands above the Tor, its body radiating magenta light as a benediction. I see the Tor as if from a great distance above: it is a volcanic mountain, much taller, darker, steeper, with vertical grooves on its flanks, and the sea laps at its base. I think of its counterpart, Mt. Tabor, in Israel. Tabor, now called Jebel et-Tur, is a detached limestone hill of about 1850 feet resembling a truncated cone in the Valley of Jezreel. At least in the second century A.D., many claimed that it was upon Mt. Tabor that Jesus underwent his Transfiguration. An underwater golden door opens, revealing the interior of the

Tor. Once inside, I sit within a large crystal or field of light, then outside it, and watch it change shape five times, after which two hawks fly it away. Outside the Tor again, I see an apple tree, a coiled red dragon, huge—the size of the Tor—but not fierce, and behind it, a double row of flowering apple trees that form a lovely avenue. A red apple appears in my belly as if floating delicately on the rising and falling of my breath. It sheds its red skin and becomes a golden apple with two silver leaves—Avalon's most precious commodity, the preëminent Otherworld gift to Celtic heroes.

I walk through the apple gate, past the dragon, and along the apple tree promenade, carrying my golden apple. Innumerable rabbit holes pockmark the slopes like cavities and I remember Gino Gennaro's queer remark that "those rabbit holes led to the Garden of the Hesperides." He was advised, by his fairy chaperone, that he could partake of Avalon's magical fruit but only temperately, because "if I became fatter than the rabbit holes through which I had come, I would remain imprisoned in time and witness the fragrant beauty of the Hesperides garden turn into ugliness." No psychedelic rabbit holes for this Grail Knight, thank you, and no lascivious sylphs, either.

When I sit down by the Philosopher's Stone on the Tor and prepare the Grail visualization, that same lovely "Snow White" sylph I met in the Fairy Dell is suddenly before me. In fact, she is practically in my face, Manhattan-style, with a biscuit pressed against my mouth, quite aggressively inviting me to eat it. I stoutly decline and push her away until she relents. Then, undaunted, she invites me to follow her along the Tor maze to the summit, but it's an abbreviated pilgrimage. On the first turning, my bowels suddenly need immediate attention and I call a timeout in Avalon as I run for the bushes. On the next turning, the sylph aims for my second chakra. Her clothes are transparent, her derriere is winsome, and, facing me with rosy skin, blue eyes, melting desire, she fondles her breasts, strokes her crotch—Sharon Stone from fairyland. I respectfully decline and contemplate my golden apple until she cools down. It's all of seven-thirty a.m. Easter morning.

At the third turning of the maze, I start moving into metaphysically more upmarket real estate. I become aware of the twelve-petalled heart chakra lotus situated at the Tor. Everyone says Glastonbury is the planet's heart center so I start examining the evidence. Here before me, occupying a space four times the size of the Tor is a display of the twelve petals, or energy radiations, of this Earth-based heart chakra. They extend for perhaps a half-mile in all directions with a gentle uplift at the tips like a raised wing; Beckery sits on one as does Pointer's Ball. At the summit at last, I stand before Michael's towering golden gates, superimposed, but much larger, over the mundane stone tower. I pace around the tower chanting *O Michael uplift us now.* Then for a few moments I see the real version (or at least its daytime expression) of what my dreams indicated, and what St. John the Divine understood in his Patmos revelation: "And I, John, saw the holy city, New Jerusalem, coming down from God out of Heaven, prepared as a bride for her husband."

In these matters my eyesight is still quite the underachiever. I see a tremendous grey outline occasionally flushing golden and sparkling. It is radically large, like a dodecahedral spaceship hovering silently; like fabulous architecture from another world about to land with twelvefold intention; like a mile-wide apparition laying the whole of Glastonbury under its divine shadow, suffusing the ethers with "as it were a new song before the throne." The St. Michael tower apparently marks the doorway into the New Jerusalem. To enter, just leave your physical body at the door.

This evening we find we have new mentors, although Blaise alluded to them last year. Tonight Blaise introduces them as if they were protéges. "For descriptive purposes we would like to be called Elohim. We refer to ourselves as a group with a collective view that has transcended your physical world but still has karmic debts to certain of humanity and the planetary body called Earth. We, in what you call telepathic communication with each other, and on instructions from our guide, the Nimitta, also known to you as Blazing Star, come to answer questions that are presented to us."

"Okay. Let's start with this one. *Avalon* seems to be a chant with interesting invocatory powers. What's it all about?"

"Avalon is a key that opens the door to the astral plane. You witnessed this today."

"How about the golden apples?"

"The fruits of spiritual practice in certain cultures of the Middle East and Western Europe are traditionally called apples of insight. These apples are fruits sometimes gained at an inner astral plane. They are also the keys that can sometimes corrupt the practice of true spirituality. This is shown in the myths of the Garden of Eden, the golden halls of Ogygia, and the Garden of the Hesperides."

"Some of the Welsh poems about Merlin say he got himself stuck in an apple tree. Was that true?"

"Merlin helped to create the Qabala as you know it. Think of the apple tree as Qabala's Tree of Life. Within the system in which you were trained, there are paradises in which adepts get stuck."

"But apples are also associated with immortality in the Celtic stories."

"Correct," Blaise says, returning to the conversation. "Look at Adam and Eve in Avalon. Eve gave an apple to Adam and from this they stepped into their clothes, which were the three bodies—the etheric, bioplasmic, and causal—and an awareness of the levels of being. The five points inside the apple correspond to the five elements with five seed pockets each containing five seeds. The ten points around the pentagram correspond to a three dimensional form at many sites around the Earth. Each apple is a stroke of wisdom. The sword through the apple is the apple peeler or corer. You have this term, holograph. The holographic apple is the same as the planetary web and it is a light receptor. There is an inner core, two halves, and a surface that is green and red. That is how we see your Earth. The apple comes from the ultimate divine inspiration of the creative divine source and is the ultimate symbol. It is the closest image of the Earth for us. You cannot comprehend its role in immortality at this time."

"Blaise, this is just a wild intuition, but is the galaxy and thus any landscape zodiac shaped like an apple?"

"Not as wild as you think. The galaxy to us is a double helix seen through a fourth dimension. If you translate a double helix into your third dimension, it is an approximation of what the galaxy may look like. It is also what the domes look like."

"Is the apple the fourth dimensional image of the *vesica piscis*?"

"At one level, you could say it is also the *vesica piscis*. The sword passing through the *vesica piscis* or apple is the apple peeler, the apple corer. When you work at embodying this principle, it will become clear."

"This relates to the meaning of Avalon and the myth of Avalon, too, doesn't it?"

"Correct. Avalon pertains to nova. We leave you to explore this first. What do you see?"

"The word avon or nova. The Star. The letters *AL* removed from Avalon."

"We inspire this intuition. Avalon means the beginning, *AL*; the understanding, *AV*; and the continuity, *ON*."

"There's another apple connection," Russell says. "Sandalphon. Some kind of earth angel, it seems to me. I keep thinking of him and apples. What is he?"

"The origin in most recent thought in your culture comes through someone you are familiar with. The Adept Master William Blake was the first for a while to note the Earth's connection with the being called Sandalphon. He is not exactly an archangel nor a member of the angelic hierarchy. He is of a different order of beings, but closely related to the archangels. Sandalphon can appear in any material form, though his essence closely resembles the essence structure of an apple. This bears on the Avalon myth, but you must assemble the pieces." (According to Jewish legend, says Howard Schwartz, Sandalphon is the angel in Paradise who weaves the prayers of Israel into garlands or crowns of prayer for God the Holy One to wear on the Throne of Glory.)

"I've noticed that some of the key words like *Arthur, Morgan, Merlin, Avalon, Albion, Logres, Sarras, Gawain* all have six letters. Why is this?"

The Elohim answer this one. "Because all these words are divinely given. The sixth sphere on the Qabalistic Tree of Life is called Tiphareth, the sphere of beauty. The story here is the quest for the source of beauty. It is the quest, the seeking, the revealing, and the secret of the revealing of beauty that is the essence of the Grail story."

"All day long I've been wondering if I did the right thing in refusing the sylph's fairy biscuit. I mean, Blaise always says we come in many forms and that we should be open to them in different guises. Maybe I would have seen more if I had taken the biscuit."

"We are glad you did not take the gift. Had you eaten the biscuit, you would have lost all interest in finishing the project you have begun with Nimitta. Its relevance would have vanished from your mind."

"Oh. I see. Okay. I want to know more about Gog and Magog and the Avenue of Oaks leading from them to the Tor."

"The trees you mention are, Qabalistically, the two pillars on either side of the Tree of Life," the Elohim reply. "The physical trees are the only ones remaining of the Avenue. The left hand darker one is now almost dead. All the trees were planted to form a processional route through to an important sacred initiation site at the first level of the Tor, where you sat today. There are several ley energy vortices on the path from these trees to the Tor. They form a pattern whereby humans ready for initiation would have been helped to be balanced by the vortices they crossed on their way to the places of initiation. There is a gateway between the two remaining oak trees. Arthur used this site as a means of transmutation of consciousness. Arthur was informed of this pattern in the landscape by Merlin. Morgan was informed through another lineage of her own tutelage. The knights you saw there were exhibiting their spiritual credentials for their own benefit at a place they were prepared for since birth. You glimpsed this last year. Some understood the Philosopher's Stone; some did not, meaning its physical plus etheric and conceptual aspects."

"I'm confused about Gog and Magog. Their Biblical reputation is awful, but I sense they are astral guardians somehow and had a favorable relationship with Noah who let them ride on the top of his Ark."

"You are working along the right lines, though you are confused about origin. Magog was indeed Noah's grandson. He took the essential teachings of 'Expectancy' forward from Noah in what was a spiritual rather than a genetic lineage. There was a Gog, too. In present time, a scientist named Jung called these aspects anima and animus. They were both physical humans. Remember, the pillars of the Tree are also described as Boaz and Jachin. We cannot trace which names came earlier, but the descriptions are secondary to the truth they point to. Remember, the name of the tribe of Israelites called Essene also means 'Expectancy.'"

"Were the oaks here as a processional when Joseph of Arimathea arrived?"

"The Oaks of Avalon were made sacred by Joseph acompanied by the Christ in His thought body," Blaise says. "Each plant, each animal, each living entity, has an energy field. Joseph and the Christ were able to increase, through their being, the etheric or auric possibilities of those trees at that time. There were 144 oaks, 72 on each side of the processional. Gog and Magog were the first trees. Glastonbury, as you know, was a center for learning, a place of true education. The Qabala was integral to the tradition practiced there."

"Gog and Magog of the lineage of Expectancy must, in some sense, have known of the coming of New Jerusalem to Glastonbury. Why was Glastonbury chosen?"

The Elohim answer this as Blaise winks out and disappears. "There were several factors that Joseph of Arimathea remembered. He made conscious connections between Mt. Tabor and what you now call the Tor. There is geomantic evidence over the planetary body that there were similarities here and there, that is, between Glastonbury and Mt. Tabor, in geomantic structure with certain conscious correspondences. When you look at the seed, do you see the seed or the tree? Joseph had already a conscious experience of Jerusalem. He was therefore able to recognize and remember the seed that was the beginning of the New Jerusalem. There was a temple existent when

Joseph came, on a planetary or auric level, an impression of what was to come. Joseph remembered this. He saw what was to come. When Albion awakes, the New Jerusalem will begin to germinate. Joseph was a master geomancer. He was in touch with a living reality over the surface of the Earth on which he worked with love. Like a gardener tending his first shoots as they appear, Joseph knew what happiness his seeds came from. He offered them through Christ to the Father and thus brought down Heaven on Earth, the Holy of Holies, you could say."

"Was there a zodiac or Albion around the original Jerusalem in what is now Israel?"

"Both places have similarities in this respect. The main line of energy in Old Jerusalem passes through the main gate. But we suggest rather than call it zodiac or Albion, call it a star map. This star map lay at the periphery of the ancient city and in the countryside. We're talking of a period 5000 years ago. Names from that time would be extinct. A good geomancer will have the means to ascertain where these star map figures are in the landscape; otherwise, they are unseen."

"So the correspondence in terms of the star map was another reason to bring the New Jerusalem to Glastonbury?"

"Yes. It was one of many factors. Imagine the whole history of the planetary being prewritten to include certain key events. In your century you have already seen two wars that have involved most of the planetary surface. These, obviously, were written very carefully into the agenda of planetary history. Also, the matter of siting New Jerusalem was equally a key and important point in the history of the planetary agenda. The Architect of Cosmic Law, Destiny, and Affairs planned it. All beings on the planetary body of Earth responded to this agenda. All angels, Cherubim, Seraphim, Elohim, and others, work under direct supervision by those who work for the Cosmic Architect. He makes plans written in endless time, yet each moment is a fulfillment of his visions as the Creator and is brought about by those in service to him."

"How does a planetary chakra, like Glastonbury, facilitate cultural change?"

"Have you ever sat near a living master?"

"Do Zen Masters count?"

"Yes. Then you know you experience a change at these times in your consciousness to the degree of your receptivity to his vibrations. Imagine that the Architect of Cosmic Destiny, in his agenda, already moved the focus of conscious awareness of the sixth chakra of the planetary being to resonate equally at each culture, each creed. Then you see a parallel between the presence of the individual consciousness and a living master with the effect on a culture of the *Shambhallic Focus*."

"What is the Shambhallic Focus?"

"This is the mobile point, the sixth chakra, the focus from Shambhala now over Glastonbury. This is continually moving, with no fixed location. It travels over the Earth's surface. In your time period it may appear to be fully resident for about 100 years with an overspill of energy before and after of 50 years each. Its total location in time at one site is about 200 years. This focus was once resident in Jerusalem, as it was over Mt. Kailas in Tibet, for example, which, long ago, was the heart chakra of Earth. If you wind up a clock, then it proceeds through its mechanism to tell time. As the domes came three times, they preprogrammed the matrix of energy lines over the Earth's surface to coincide with certain planetary and constellationary exactitudes existing in the far future. Thus, at the present moment, Glastonbury is both the heart chakra and the recipient of the sixth chakra, the mobile Shambhallic Focus."

Shambhala is another one of those big myths, like Avalon, that you hear about for years without ever knowing much about it. The Buddhists of Tibet and Mongolia have chiefly propagated the "myth" of a mysterious spiritual kingdom sequestered amid the Himalayan snowpeaks. In Tibetan, Shambhala means "Held by the source of Happiness." From our perspective, Shambhala is a paradise realm where spiritual adepts and enlightened sages abide, no longer obligated to toil on the wheel of existence but willing to guide and direct human evolution from a distance. The followers of the ancient shamanistic tradition of Tibet called Bön claim that Shambhala is the same as their Olmolungring, the source of their teachings; Tibetan Buddhists contend that the Kalachakra teachings, preëminent practices taught by the Buddha, derive from Shambhala.

In either case, Shambhala is not accessible to ordinary mortals; its material existence is paradoxical and elusive; you need an invitation to go there physically and a refined clairvoyance to gain a visionary impression of it. According to legend, when the 25th Kulika-King of Shambhala assumes the throne (the 21st now occupies it) the connection between our world and Shambhala will become manifest in world events. Seemingly from the other side of the philosophical world, Rudolf Steiner indicated something quite similar. He said that beginning in the mid-twentieth century and then continuing increasingly for the next several thousand years, the Christ would start leading the initiated (meaning those who had experienced the Christ in the Earth's etheric) into Shambhala.

"We leave you now with this message. There are times in the history of each soul—though this term is often inaccurate and leads to misapprehension as to what occurs in the inner life—when periods of tranquillity and activity are not in balance. There are times when outside influences of planets, moon, and stars are designed to influence Man and other beings for specific purposes. These influences may precipitate fires, floods, earthquakes, storms, social upheaval, and personal turmoil. If Man is fully oriented to his inner life, committed to the development and manifestation of true spirit, then these influences are not relevant to the soul, and he can be independent of them. Be aware of this during the coming time. From your studies you will have as resources much whereby you can help others in the future.

"We have a direct message for you from Blazing Star. There are still many things and much work to be done before his full return is possible. There is a time allotted for this return. We leave you with a light of golden thread with a silver orb hung beneath it, a golden ribbon to tie around your waist, and a green thread run through a golden wire. Swallow this when in danger and use it along with the other protections you have been given in the past."

43

"RECEIVE AT EACH OF THESE BOWLS, DAY BY DAY"

n the eve of the spring equinox, Blaise visits us again, ending the long absence. They fill the room at Wick with that characteristic swelling expectancy of a rose opening its petals.

"We come as we are, as a Blazing Star. We are most pleased to be with you tonight. We surround each of you with a wall of lilac flames. Feel it as we are, in transmutation. Be aware of the lilac flames and release the past. Transmute it. We are pleased to see you all here. We are very far away but please know we come as we are, as Love from Above. Feel the lilac flame. Remember the black sphere of stable consciousness. We draw it between us all. Remember it. Surround it with lilac flames. Breathe your love to it. Be without fear.

"We bring you some instructions. We suggest you go to Windmill Hill tomorrow at the time the Sun shifts its zone. Be there for ten minutes before the equinox and ten minutes after, no longer. Prepare yourselves with the bowl and flame before midday. Breathe to them as you travel there. We would like you to be there in a spirit of gratitude. Particularly give thanks for the work of others on your behalf. The archangels Michael and Gabriel and your individual angels—give them thanks first. Ask them what you wish, but only that which you want. We will do what we can to be with you. We are very far away on a distant star. We are with you, too, each in blue, surrounded with the lilac flame of transmutation. We leave as we came, with Love from Above, Blazing Star."

We sigh and smile and muse and shiver. It's wonderful to have our avuncular angels back, our Uncle Blaise, as we've taken to calling them in their paradoxical absence—paradoxical in that they say they are never far, yet they are far away at present. Truly, they haven't left us because as our Blazing Star, they reside at the center of our being, so where can they go? Somehow this angelic conclave of forty million manifestations is identical to us—to the essence of all human beings—and lives within us in the deep, empty, still center. This would be self-evident if we could only remember it every moment.

Windmill Hill, situated in Baltonsborough, is part of the Sagittarius figure of the Glastonbury star map, according to the zodiac experts. We arrive at Windmill Hill around four p.m. amidst an inch of snow on the ground, a strong wind, and overcast skies. We sit beside a mounded well enclosure. "Mastery of deeper and deeper levels of consciousness brings to the surface of your body richer and richer qualities of 'Gold,'" comments Robert Coon in his writings about this site. "In the Zodiac, this 'mining operation' is remarkably symbolized by the medieval tunnel plunging deep into the heart of Arthur at Windmill Hill. What is the secret of Arthur's heart that shall redeem the world?" We don't know, Robert; we're just here to pay our respects. Blaise is with us, if faintly.

At the moment of the equinox, an open white rose drops into my Grail bowl and an ancient leatherbound book called *The Art of Excalibur* by John Dee, the Renaissance magus. The funny thing is, I'm familiar with his list of published works, and this is not among them. We place our seeds of gratitude and kernels of request in "Arthur's heart," in what Coon calls the "alchemical laboratory of the stars" and "the grand ideal latent in the Somerset landscape," then leave them for their appointed gardeners.

Thus the spring rolls in with April rains and May's apple blossoms and June's first blush of roses. I pass the time more or less equably with writing, reading, walking, contemplating, bicycling, breathing, fretting and gardening. Prodigies of spirit are forecast, if my dreams are an indication. I'm with my father who is dressed in a smart grey suit. He is animated, vibrant, perky, full of smiles, making an extemporaneous speech before a group under my direction. His speech is fulsome with praise for me. He concludes by presenting me with a gift of three thousand dollars, courtesy of the organization he represents. Whom, specifically, can I thank? I ask him. Thank everybody, he says, beaming. Later, after my wedding reception, I cross a large bridge over a river and meet a wealthy relative of mine half-way across. He is well-groomed with grey hair and is dressed like an affluent European from the early 1900s. He reminds me of the philanthropist and publisher Joseph Pulitzer, according to photographs I've seen of him. I feel faint when I first meet him, fall down, look up at him, then recover. Maybe it was all an act. He hands me three bills and wishes me good luck. "Prepare the receptacle," he tells me. Afterwards, I examine the gift: it's more than a million dollars.

Naturally, Russell and I spend the day talking excitedly about whether my dream of great riches means money or spirit. Bear in mind we are all chronically short of cash in these early days of the Grail Quest so a bequest of even one hundred dollars would be significant. No doubt Blaise has a good laugh at our ineptitude at oneiromancy. Help is on the way, arriving as evanescent as uncorked champagne, as a lithe, lilting, laconic chorus of new angelic voices.

"We bring the blessings of the Elohim. We bring greetings from Blazing Star. We are the Seraphim. We come specifically to clarify your discussions about the dream. We will begin from a point that must be understood. Whatever will be, will be. You have each what you refer to as training. You have learned to control various of your functions. You can sit still for a moment. You can be a little conscious for awhile. Much is still to be worked on in your form. You can do much in your form. Understand this. What will be, will be. You can be, you can create much of what you wish by knowing what you want, if this is what is to be. We know what will be. We can help you with the will of what is to be. You are very blessed. You each have much help from the Love that is above. You are very blessed. So don't worry. Don't think about it. Don't feel into it. Don't mess with it. Leave it for those that know what will be. Trust a little. Be what you are and what you want in you will come to be. You see, what you want comes whether you thought about it or not.

"We come as a light, by your wish. You do what you want. What you want will be. Each thought of ours that you hear is light. In you it resonates as light. Remember the Blazing Star. Remember the help you receive. We are here because of your request. Remember now what you most want is what will be in you. The receptacle is you. You can be light, light in this world, if that is what you want. Light in this context is consciousness. It is truth, Love from Above. The receptive can be penetrated with something from above. It can be made fertile and bear fruit. We say to you, please be ready, be prepared to receive, for there is much that can be given. Expect nothing. It will come by what you want and what you wished for before you came into form and have confirmed on numerous occasions since. You judge yourself.

"We come to help with light that is consciousness. In activity or passivity, in stillness or in movement, only carry the receptive. You have been shown by the Star. He waits with Love from Above for you to prepare. We know what will be; we can see. Be ready; be prepared. The Star has shown the way. Be free; be prepared. There is so much to be given if you are ready to receive. We have come tonight with this message to you from an immutable source. It is irreconcilable to human logic that so few can have so much. We will take a short break now."

A little bewildered, I turn to Russell for his reaction. "These Seraphim are something else," he says. "They sound like drunken elves, the way their voices ride a rollercoaster up and down the octave. I've never heard anything like it. Oh, I guess I better drop this one. Berenice doesn't approve of wisecracks about angels." The Seraphim return, bubbly and friendly, in the wake of our laughter, clearly having overheard our remarks.

"We only come in this way because our vibration is one that oscillates. This is a means for you to experience the energy oscillations that are the nature of our sphere. We would describe ourselves as, among angels, a parochial consciousness. Each human being has access with a part of their higher being bodies to at least two Seraphim, but some who are more developed may have access to many more Seraphim, or 1080 in all. When the Master Christ was on Earth, he had 1080 Seraphim accompanying him in constant presence."

"Among angels, what is your professional relationship, so to speak, with Blaise?" Russell asks.

"When the Nimitta leaves his lines open to you, the Seraphim guard the connection to these lines of communication. We are not at liberty to discuss or refute information given to you by the Nimitta. We can, if you wish, clarify various aspects in their subtlety or simplicity, but that is all."

"From your perspective, who is Blaise then?" Russell continues.

"Blaise is a teaching angel. He is the most wonderful among angels, the Uncle Angel, you might say. He educates the angels. We suggest your system of spiritual hierarchy needs reappreciation. There is no coherence to it. We suggest you work on a new hierarchy or angelology that is appropriate to your metaphysical understanding; then we may corroborate it. To make assumptions about hierarchy is very human. However humans tend to be oriented towards a consciousness of success or achievement. It is not so in the angelic realm. There is no one-up-manship. We are beyond equality and relate to unity. In the context of our unity, there is diversification. It is relevant to you to formulate your knowledge of our sphere into lists and tables but it is only relevant on the human plane. It doesn't mean we are subject to it."

"Is there any other reason why you chose this night specifically to first visit us?" Russell asks next.

"Certain favorable conditions made our visit possible under the auspices of various authorities familiar to you. Certain aspects come into consciousness this evening leading to the unfoldment of certain malefic forces coming to your planet. We wish you to know that certain people on a spiritual discipline will not be effected. The forces are to bring a lowering of discrimination on the material level between members of the human race. As the forces enter the planetary sphere, their experience will be seen and felt. Then you will gauge, through your knowledge, certain effects and be of benefit to those that suffer. The proportion of malefic influence will be felt directly in proportion to the amount of material separation, as a levelling of those in superior positions. Those who were poor will be materially elevated. This will have a positive influence. This influence, as Mars squares Jupiter, meets the planet all over its surface; no spot will be uneffected. Waves have been occurring over the last 250 years. This evening a particularly strong influence occurred, which will lead to quite severe changes in the monetary flows."

"What should we do in light of this?" Berenice asks.

"We ask, as always, that you work under your wish, which will carry far. You will receive, in proportion to your desire, information about planetary changes and energies being transmitted to Earth by order of the Cosmic Architect. You will be forewarned and your understanding broadened, so you can help others less fortunate than yourselves. Now, without so much as a word, we say in going: Be ready."

I must be a little ready because during the night something is placed in my receptacle. In a dream, I walk through the woods, into an open area where trees stand without leaves. I walk over a narrow footbridge that spans a stream that flows out from a pond. Over-head, an old, dead tree hangs over horizontally as a kind of wooden Damoclean sword, hanging by nothing stronger than ivy tendrils. I dash past, expecting it to crash on me, then I turn around and pull it down myself. But I make a mess of it. The tree trunk is impaled, vertically, in the soft ground, blocking the path; its skeletal limbs give it the appearance of a barbed club. Across the pond, a pudgy girl with small breasts and male genitals frolics by the water's edge. As I realize this is a hermaphrodite, my silver pen falls into the pond. I see it on the bottom of the shallow pond. My brother approaches and volunteers to retrieve it. He dives in and returns with a gold pen with a triangular top. I'm disappointed and still want my silver pen back, though I thank him for the gift. Later, I find the lost silver pen under a layer of bed sheets. In the morning, I berate myself for being such a jackanapes in dreamland and hope I didn't offend anybody with my Taurean opacity. I'd like that golden pen, too.

In the evening, we are delighted beyond twinkling when Blaise—our dear Uncle Blaise!—makes a live visit. "We come from afar. We come as a Blazing Star. We bring a message for you at this time. We ask, if you wish, to see an empty bowl below with you sitting in it. Next, we place the golden bowl, the Grail bowl with which you were familiar from before, above your pelvis. All the astrological signs are in glyphs around its rim. Place another bowl in your heart. Its base rests at your sternum. Its lip reaches to the points just underneath your arms. It is golden. Next we place a chalice, a small cup with a long stem, at your throat. The bowl of the chalice is at your throat. Its stem reaches down to the base of your spine; it is made of blue light. You now have three large bowls and a chalice. The bowl you refer to as the Grail is in the center.

"We say, receive at each of these bowls, day by day. The cup at the top flows over gradually, filling each bowl in turn until the bowl in which you sit is full. Do this if you wish. Be open to receive. This is most important. Whatever you need will be placed in your bowls as it is needed. Are there any questions?"

I can't resist asking about the Seraphim. "Blaise, who are the Seraphim from your point of view?"

"The Seraphim are big blazing stars. We are the tiny, tiny blazing stars. What is small is large; what is large is small. We are very tiny. Seraphim occasionally take a glimpse of us. Elohim rarely, but they are always looking for ways into incarnation. The Seraphim's number is not fixed to a multiple structure in the same way as ours is, although their prime number is three. The Elohim are divisible in any combination. Both the Elohim and Ophanim are not limited as to location to any point or star in your cosmos.

"We are most pleased to be with you all at this time. We come as we are. We are with you in many forms throughout this time. In this form, our presence is not so available as you have known. This is for you, as we know what is best. If you do what we ask, if that is what you wish, then we will return soon. We are busy with much in places that are far away. All is for the best. For now, as Love from Above, we are each of yours, from afar, your Blazing Star."

44

WITH THE BEE-KEEPER ON ST. BRIDE'S ISLAND

A waning sickle moon hangs suspended like a bowl over the greyish Tor. Venus shines solitarily and piercingly, a white cherry about to drop into the upturned crescent of the moon. It's three-thirty in the morning and I'm sitting in the field at Beckery in predawn stillness. There is an inkling of light in the east, but the mist lies like a groomed carpet over the green fields and brick warehouses.

Like Arthur, I was bidden to visit Beckery before dawn by an angel—six, actually. A huge silver canopy domes Beckery and environs for hundreds of yards and its curving sides are speckled as if with fishscales glinting from an unseen light. As I walked across the treacherous field, tussocky and soaking, and even now as I sit on my blanket, I am feeling myself in that same Celtic, red-bearded, hirsute, older body. Behind me stands Blaise, sixfold and silent and eight feet tall with wings upraised. Underneath the silvery dome of Beckery, I discern a white chapel as I approach, and it is inside this filmy oratory I'm now sitting. On the other side of the fence, not more than fifty feet away, a dozen sewage treatment tanks are noisily digesting Glastonbury's waste products.

I close my eyes, settle into my breathing, visualize the four bowls, and enter the stillness that permeates Beckery. I slide into that unmistakable sensation of being meditated, angelically regarded, enjoying that synergistic boost in consciousness that comes from being cocooned by angels under a dome. The blue sapphire bowl drifts shimmeringly down from above; an angel clasps it as it exudes light like dry ice. Curiously, I feel both firmly anchored to my breathing in this body on the ground, yet straining to break free of gravity and biology, to sever the moorings and move out into the Avalon lake. Occasionally, I open my eyes but the physical surroundings seem foreign now, remote, another world left behind. Two visitors appear: my brother and Tudor Pole; they stand with Blaise behind me, making us a vigil of nine companions. But who are we waiting for?

My attention reverts to the white chapel, which is illuminated by four golden candles set into tall candlesticks. Each is positioned at one of four corners of a sarcophagus whose contours follow those of a human body precisely as if it were cast using a live, but supine, form as a model. A pale white sun rises in an opaque sky. Behind the sarcophagus hangs a huge *bas relief* in gold of a rearing dragon. Now a woman appears, but her appearance shifts from one image to another: she is a young and sensuous woman; a plump matron; a white-haired, wrinkled crone. She whispers in my right ear, but I cannot make out her words. Her voice or presence at my ear feels like a bee sting that doesn't hurt. This same woman enters the chapel again from the left side. She smiles, and her smile has multiple dimensions: she is my lover, my mother, my wife, my sister, my grandmother. Her dark hair is tied in a bun under a moon-white bonnet with slender chin straps. Her white gown laps at her ankles and is sequinned with hundreds of tiny stars. A modest gold crown sits upon her bonnet. Her eyes are dark, animated, loving, wise, pools of knowing beyond me, yet for me. She gestures for me to climb into the sarcophagus; once inside, it's comfortable and I stare at the ceiling of the rotunda, breathing....

In the other world, the sun has risen, the chilled night air is warming up, and it's time to leave. The woman has departed, and the chapel, with its brasswork dragon, sarcophagus, candles, angels, have also vanished. Even so, I feel, in an awed, almost dazed way as I trudge across the tussocks at six a.m., that I have met the Bee-Keeper of St. Bride's Island.

I bask in the glow of this encounter, this celestial bee-sting, for the rest of the day. Who is she, really? She is one of the most vividly seen experiences I've had, to date, on the Grail Quest. She was almost palpable. I can't wait for Blaise to visit. I'm sure they know.

"We say, there is a different level of unfoldment taking place in you of which you are unaware," Blaise tells me when he visits in the evening. "We say, Beckery has more in store. Beckery will show you something of value, mark our words. Be prepared and breathe with our love. Things are not what they seem. We come as we are. We come as a Blazing Star. We surround you all with the lilac flames of transmutation. We place a blue sphere around each of you. At the center of each sphere, we place a star, a point of light like a pearl. Above, we place a golden sphere; below, we place a silver sphere. Pointing up, a silver sword; pointing down, a golden sword. Within each sphere on the left, at the points at which the spheres intersect, we place an emerald; on the right we place a ruby. We wish, if you wish, that you will breathe with your love to this image in the next days. May we suggest, Grail Knight, that you go to the church at the top of the hill in Langport. Be there three hours in front of the altar to the right of the old book. We wish to show you something about the Dog. We make recommendations about every action. If you follow these, your purpose will be clear. Just don't go back. Don't go forward. Be where you are. Be what you are. Allow that. We leave as we came, as Love from Above. We bless each of you. We are not too far, as ever, your Blazing Star."

45

Joseph Takes the Dog to Church

The details of my dream form in my memory as I linger in bed this morning. I am at my parent's house in the livingroom. A golden tiger gets up and stretches, but its presence doesn't intimidate me at all. The tiger turns into a woman, and we talk. The scene shifts. I am in a row-boat with a woman seated ahead of me. She turns sideways and I see her Egyptian face in profile. She wears an enormous jewelled head-piece resembling the plumage of a fabulous bird, all in diamonds. Behind her is a god's face sculpted in burnished gold. I'm wearing an ankle-length white tunic secured at my waist with a golden circlet; the robe over the tunic is fringed with purple and blue on the inside. I'm bearded, my arms are hairy, and I feel like a larger person. This memory shakes loose another dream. I stand in the backyard at my parents' place and watch two huge birds with pelican beaks run past. Each beak is a pale tan with a hint of pink. The bird itself is a hybrid of a pony's torso and an ibis' head. The birds calmly inspect me with human intelligence then shape-shift into the form of women. They smile. When I ask them how they managed the transformation from ibis to woman, one says, "With the mind." The other says, "Remember Portia and Nada."

A week later, I'm sitting in a pew in the All Saints Parish Church in Langport, getting religion on my own. I'm glad I've attained that quality of mind the Buddha calls "no attainment with nothing to attain" because this is my eighth visit to the church and I can't say I've attained what I set out to attain. In fact, I've attained nothing.

It's as if I sit patiently, expectantly under Blaise's apple tree waiting for one apple to drop into my palms—it must be somewhere in this church. Of course, if I knew what I was looking for, it would be easier to find it. Just for the record, let it be known that this Grail Knight does not enjoy sitting in churches. Had I ever regularly attended Sunday school as a child no doubt I would have been thrown out for poor behavior or inattention—at least I should hope so. Shall I recount my illustrious attainments here? On the first visit, I sat dutifully for three hours at a pew I thought Blaise had indicated but all I glimpsed there was a woman striding down the main aisle at eleven-thirty with a watering can to freshen the altar bouquets. At noon, as I stood by the ponderous wooden door into the vestibule, four twelve-foot-tall angels swooped down the aisle from the altar like Navy jets storming off an aircraft carrier. An unidentified voice in my head declared, "You're making it all up, you know." Fine. I'm making you up too, so shove off, I retort.

On my second visit, I tried a new location. At this pew, things felt watery, unmoored; I slipped in and out of my body into the astral lake and was entertained by a past life memory that wasn't germaine to my work in the Dog. By the fifth visit, I had found the "stove" but whether I could turn on the "gas" and cook with it remained to be seen. Blaise's idea of attainment after all is cooking with gas. When I pulled open the vestibule door and stepped into the church, I saw a column of light marking the pew. That's where I sat.

Immediately, I felt a tingling, weighty feeling in my groin as if someone were playing tympani in my root chakra. A man came into focus. It was Joseph of Arimathea. He stood before a grey stone basin about twenty feet in diameter and was accompanied by a dozen other men in long robes. The basin was set within a small wooden chapel. A blazing ball of light descended into the basin, which absorbed it and passed it into the Earth. The light flowed instantly up through the Dog's geomythic landscape body as if moving through pre-established channels, from the groin to the nose at Burrowbridge and the ear at Othery. I understood why this All Saints is nationally known for its stained glass window portrait of Joseph, which sparkles only a few feet above the altar. No angelic kudos for me, not yet. "You came very close to understanding, as you finally sat in the right place, but there is still more," Blaise said that evening.

The next couple visits were monumentally unproductive and the Grail Knight's morale slipped. I was also a little concerned that the various Church staff that flitted about me would misconstrue my chronic presence here as a plea for redemption and try to sign me up for membership. I sat by the pillar, but, instead of Joseph and revelation, I got boredom, tight breathing, heat in the chest, and frustrated. "You are very persevering," said Blaise, knowing how to stroke a Taurean down for the count in non-attainment mode. "You need patience for this phase of the work. It will bear fruit. Remember the apple tree as you breathe love. This is what you might call the next clue."

I breathed love like crazy next time, like springtime for an American in Paris, but I kept nodding off into irritability and frowns until I finally understood it wasn't me that was originating these negative sensations. It was the Dog. More precisely, it was the emotional barnacles encrusted in the Dog's root center for the past millennia and the cranky ethers in the church itself that kept him in a crotchety mood.

Now, on my eighth perseverance, as I'm about to leave, I see two branches of flowering lilac blossoms and then a two-petalled lilac heart where the stone basin had been. A lilac flame surges up from the heart, up through the church ceiling, and into the blue sky. Instantly, the unpleasant sensations that have bothered me like a hairshirt this week evaporate, transmuted into nothingness by the lilac flame. Blaise agrees.

"Feel the lilac flame of transmutation awakening the Dog's creative energies. They have been blocked for a long time. We place the dancing lilac flames at this spot and send the Dog our Love from Above. As you are aware, Joseph came to the landscape temple you know as Avalon. He was aware, and indeed recognized when arriving at the port of Langport, that the guardian of the temple was here. The Dog. Joseph brought the Christ energy to this area. He initiated the Dog as the zodiac guardian with the Christ light. Now that certain things have been uncovered, we would like you to visit other sites on the Dog."

Bring out the Dogs! I bound out of church and race out onto the road! I jump on my Grail Bike—a ten-speed Dawson I've managed to hold onto since college—and start a tour through the star centers of Canis Major, Canis Minor, and Monoceros, together comprising the three-headed Cerberus and temple guardian of the Region of the Summer Stars.

My first stop is the Church of St. John the Baptist in the hill-perched town of Pitney, a couple miles past Langport. This is *Aludra*, the cynosure of the Girt Dog of Langport, the tail star only a few miles from another hamlet called with the brazenly obvious name of Wagg. Pitney is the doorway into the Dog temple. From here, the Grail Knights would walk down the valley, up Pict's Hill, and into *Wezen*, the star center in Langport that Joseph initiated two thousand years ago. At Pitney, they took their bearings, took instructions on how to negotiate their geomythic tour, learned the map of the landscape star points, familiarized themselves with the Dog's luminosity. I can see the map even now: it's like an aerial view of the Dog with a couple dozen pricks of light sequinning his big earthen body. The Dog says in effect: Visit my star centers, know them, understand me, then I'll orient you to the larger zodiac temple, I will escort you into the cauldron of stars. Welcome to the *dogorrery*.

The church of St. Andrew at Aller is the next star point on my tour, and this one evidently lies close to the Dog's heart. Yes, Aller is both dog and water snake. I perch under the lovely lime tree that faces the moors and Wick Manor. I *feel* myself into the Dog's land-scape form, sitting calmly on my haunches, observing activities in the Region of the Summer Stars. The Dog's heart is happy, still, glad, loving, wise, contented, compassionate; his service to the zodiac is unhesitating, unrelenting, faithful. Stars twinkle and tingle in my canine form. This land is my body. These stars are aspects of my consciousness. The zodiac can be a nuthouse at times. My buddies the Polden Hound and High Ham Cur are resting now, but I am wakeful on behalf of my masters in Sirius. I am their dog. I never lose sight of the Dog-star here in my chest.

It's impossible not to love this Dog when you bask in the warmth of his heart. That's what T.H. White evidently felt, too, in *The Once and Future King*. Arthur, as a youth when he was raised far from court intrigue and public knowledge, was called the Wart and spent a lot of time with the Dog-Boy, the noseless kennel master at Sir Ector's castle. "They spent much of their time together, rolling about with the dogs in the kennel....The Wart's own special one was called Cavall, and he happened to be licking Cavall's nose—not the other way about—when Merlyn came in and found him."

The Girt Dog's nose is too big to lick, but when I reach Burrowbridge Mump, I sit down affectionately on what might be a freckle on Cavall's snout. It's the remains of an old tree trunk, facing south, about halfway to the summit. This spot marks an entrance to the stone chamber inside the Mump. I shift the Grail body into full lotus position for extra traction on the Other Side and breathe love profligately to the stone lintel of the inner chamber. This gets me through, first into a corridor, then into a central domed auditorium. A Grail Knight learns that, like Dr. Who's telephone-booth spaceship, the *Tardis*, it's always bigger on the inside. Wanting to make a good impression, I remain full-lotussed and sit on a circular platform encircled by ranks of ascending seats. The seats are occupied by men and women in simple clothes. They are silent, respectful, courteous—frankly, very British ghosts—evidently waiting for me to speak.

Due to technical difficulties with the Grail Knight's higher being body's reality transformer, we are unable to present the full text of his remarks inside the Mump nor indicate how they were received. We can report, however, that, at some later point, perhaps only a few minutes, perhaps an hour, outside the Mump again, he climbed to the St. Catherine church ruins, where an unidentified but "nice" angel installed a twelve-petalled lilac crystal in the Grail Knight's heart center, with an unlimited warranty on all parts and performance. The Grail Knight was quoted as saying: "It looks like a skillfully carved lilac pineapple with its flanges flaring upwards finely."

It's only a short pedal from the nose to the ear at Othery—or is it, Oath-Ear, Oath-Here, Oath-Hear? The church of St. Michael at Othery is canopied by a dome, light grey speckled with red, a quivering, filmy bubble glistening in the ethers. I sit in the front pew eating a chocolate bar as I read the "Guide for Visitors." It doesn't mention the dome or the former stone chamber within the earth mound upon which the church was anciently built. As I walk slowly down the central axis of the church, I walk simultaneously through a stone corridor into a corbelled chamber like Ireland's Newgrange, only smaller. The stillness inside this stone cave is as strong as a vacuum cleaner, and it sucks me into its intense concentration. Here the Dog listens, notes, remembers: a cheeky Grail Knight visited me one morning and chomped very noisily on a candy bar while making fun of my name.

Nobody in Somerset talks about a third Dog. The Polden Hound is widely acknowledged as a companion to the Girt Dog, but Blaise confirmed my suspicions one day and suggested that local place names might help me pin the third Dog down, geomythically. The star points in Monoceros, which is usually understood to mean "unicorn," include suggestive locales: Paradise, Pound Farm, High Ham, Low Ham, Breach Wood, Stout, Red Field, Turn Hill. The High Ham church of St. Andrew is situated in the snow-capped mountains of Somerset, high above treeline, where the oxygen thins out at 300 feet above sea level. It's a tenuous clue but the two gargoyles on the church exterior *look* like watchdogs. The solitary stone church, indecorous without fence, gate, or graveyard, or rather secular with neighboring dairy farm, has something tangible to offer the inquiring Dog catcher. High above the front door, nearly at the peak of the spire, sits an effigy: a reclining dog with large snout, curled up for a nap in the noonday sun.

I recognize the liability of waxing cocky and brain-enriched like Sherlock Holmes after a brilliant deduction, so I pedal twice as fast to burn off my pride at verifying the third dog. Or maybe I'm just happy today—why not? I'm streaking through the Dog, rolling from star to star in full Grail Quest regalia. I have the blue globe around me, a tall, steady skyscraper lilac flame from bike pedal to the top of the clouds, gold and silver spheres spinning around me like hula hoops, an arm studded with precious jewels including a ruby and emerald, a couple of fancy swords in good nick jangling against the bike, a blazing pinpoint of light, a heavenly dimple, perpetually flashing supernova at my belly button, and a black beachball bobbing hollowly across my back. Plus no mud or manure. Plus I have an official escort. I've got Blaise!

The road is deliciously devoid of traffic, which makes my zig-zagging from hedgerow to hedgerow a lot safer. I feel as cheeky as a ripe dandelion shamelessly blooming amidst the grass in an immaculate suburban lawn. The six Blaises perch like circus acrobats on my shoulders as I meander and swerve along the narrow lane. I notice that the golden socks on one Blaise are riding indecorously low about the ankles. I slam on the brakes and all six Blaises tumble off in forward somersaults that expand into cartwheels that trampoline them up into six successive telephone poles. These guys are fleet-footed!

"Are you impressed, Grail Knight?" one Blaise inquires, hanging by his feet from the telephone wires.

"Not a lot, actually."

"Oh. We are most disappointed. We thought our little performance would put you in raptures. We so wished it would."

"Well, you know how it is, Blaise. Form is emptiness, and all that."

"Alas, how true. Well, we'll just trundle on back to Polaris and amuse ourselves with the Black Bowling Ball. Bye, bye, Grail Knight. Don't fall off your bike."

Henley is my next stop in today's Dog peripatetry. My guess is that Henley might be the root of the single horn of the High Ham Cur, a dog with a golden third eye. I roll along the moor lanes, past indolent hay-munching cows, past a farm-boy in white shirt, jeans, and broad-brimmed hat—he's a stand-in for Whittier's Barefoot Boy. "Say, you haven't seen a crystal horn around here, have you, about two hundred yards long, pointing into the ethers towards Beckery, part of the third Dog? No, well, thanks anyway, and have a nice day." I *almost* ask him this. Instead, I put the question to the four bowls. I sit on a demure wooden footbridge on the edge of Henley moor and play Pooh-sticks with myself in the dilatory stream. Then the talking bowls tell me: "The horn lies in the etheric, in the waters. You won't find a landscape coordinate for it. It is the Dog's mind pointing like a finger of devotion to the Goddess at Beckery, the Bee-Keeper. This Dog is hers. It is virginal and devoted. She lies in a dreamy reverie, yet the horn is a direct line of communication for her with Beckery."

The Polden Hound sleeps in the sun, too. The Parish Church of All Saints at Ashcott—which is the *Procyon* star center—is a disappointment for Dog fanciers. The energy here is sluggish, bordering on nonexistent. This doggy is fast asleep. The *Gomeisa* star center nearby at the church of St. Michael at Greinton is not much better: marked absence of spunk. I lean against the locked outer church door and eat a peach and am assailed with astral images of body mutilation and blood. The Polden Hound, as Blaise told us, has retired to the dog-house, dog-weary, dog-tired, dog-gone. There's no bark left in this very undogmatic Hound of Polden. My last stop on this daylong Dog chase is Stathe, a star center along the River Parett, midway between the Mump and Wick Manor. On this dogday in early June, the river is almost bone dry, as is my throat. I crawl dog-gedly into the Black Smock pub and rasp out an order for a remedial Guinness, moisten my parched dogtooth, and trot on home.

Once home, I curl up in my Dog basket and take a nap because Blaise has an assignment for me tonight beginning at half-past midnight. I'm likely to be out with the Dog all night. At twelve-fifteen, Blaise arrives for a brief pep talk. "We come as we are. We come in the black sphere of stable consciousness. We are the point of brilliant light at the center of the sphere. We roll towards you. We surround you with a wall of lilac flames, a sphere of brilliant blue light within. Each of you has a lilac flame dancing above your head as our Love from Above. We will be with you tonight, as we were today, Grail Knight."

"I'm half-inclined to go to Oath Hill with you tonight," says Russell, "but I also feel you have to do it alone. Tell me about it in the morning. I'm going to bed!"

46

"HAS THE BUDDHA
DOG-NATURE OR NOT?"

eaving my cup of tea and stuffed chair behind in the well-lit room, I walk out the front door of Wick Manor and pause at the edge of light and darkness, at that line where the light from the house ends and the darkness from the garden begins. The sky, of course, is overcast, but the lilac flames are already banked high around me. An involuntary quiver ripples across my shoulders, which draw in tight as wisps of ancient fear rise up through my memory and drift beyond. With a deep, relaxing breath, I cross the garden, climb the cattle fence, and pass slowly into the darkness like a dutiful Hobbitt accompanied by six Blaises in place of one Gandalf. *Kwanseum Bosal, Kwanseum Bosal*, I chant out loud, which is the Korean invocation for Avalokitesvara Bodhisattva, our local presiding deity. I synchronize my breathing and chanting with my walking.

In the notorious Zen *koan* about Joshu's dog, a monk asks Joshu-roshi whether a dog has Buddha-nature or not. Joshu says, "Mu!" This means, colloquially, "no," but in Japanese it's the kind of ambivalent "no" that doesn't answer the question at all. Then the monk says, "All creeping things with life have the Buddha-nature. How can it be that a dog has it not?" Joshu replies, "You are attached to thoughts and emotions arising from karmic ignorance." Later, another monk asks Joshu, "Has a dog Buddha-nature or not?" "Yes," says Joshu. Then the monk says, "You say 'Yes,' but how did it get into this skin-bag?" Joshu: "Knowingly and purposely he sinned." Then the Grail Knight said to Joshu: "I took my Buddha-nature for a walk on the Dog and it said Mu!" Anyway, such ruminations pass the time. *Mu* is the Gateless Barrier of Zen, and Oath Hill is the Gateless Barrier of the Dog. As another roshi said of the *Mu* business, "If you have not done this and passed the barrier, you are a phantom among the undergrowth and weeds." And wet grass, too.

It's one a.m. as I reach the top of Oath Hill. I sit facing east, which is towards Aller. I make a vow to be strong and unblinking, a Buddha in wet sneakers. Nothing will move me or sway me from this spot, no *makyo* will entrance me, and no cows will splat on me. I will breathe Love from Above to everything in sight, even the farmers who will probably be out here at dawn to round up their cows. This is the Dog's Buddha-nature, too: Moo! They are busy with their bovine affairs, eating, grunting, shuffling, pissing, splatting, lowing, but that's alright: it's just the right edge of sentient companionship for my night's vigil. The clouds are clearing and the full moon emerges, but although it is pristinely bright, it's dwarfed in magnitude by Sirius, Dog-star, home of the Buddha, the brightest star in our galaxy and patron star influencer for this star center in Canis Major at the throat of the Dog.

A large German shepherd approaches me, pauses, then comes closer and offers his paw, which I take and squeeze gently. We regard each other silently. I know this Dog. I had beheld the Girt Dog of Langport several times already during meditation in my room so I knew what species of spirit canine had just joined my watch. Together we face Aller, the heart center of the Dog. After some quiet moments, I feel my awareness merge with the Girt Dog; we wait for our master to arrive. A small dome appears overhead, a kind of globular lampshade speckled crimson. Inside the dome I'm greeted by a small, gentle man clad in grey shirt and trousers; he looks remarkably like Philip Kapleau-roshi—Blaise always said they admire Zen masters.

I don't mean to suggest that Kapleau-roshi is taken to flying around in crimson UFOs at night calling in on Grail Knights pretending to be dogs, but, if I've learned one thing on the Grail Quest, it's that visuals are optional, dependent on the quirky mental contents of the individual Grail Knight. Just because you don't see wings, doesn't mean we don't have them, Blaise once said. Anyway, my psychopomp steps down from a throne and announces his proper home is Sirius and would I like to see his orrery—his Dog-orrery. I follow him into a large room equipped like a futuristic science museum. There is a three-dimensional moving model of the galaxy, with all the zoömorphic constellations and planets represented, moving, blinking, turning, just like the wheelwork-driven miniature planetarium called an orrery, invented by Charles Boyle, the 4th Earl of Orrery, in the early 1700s.

"We are only the Dog for the cosmic Fisher King," my host says. "We guide souls to him. Here we keep the rules and measures." After moments of silence, I feel myself merging with this Sirian astronomer, and we travel through the starfields and corridors of light until we hover above a palace marked No. 20. I enter through the domed ceiling and slowly descend through a rotunda of gold: walls, floor, ceiling, fixtures, throne—it's all gold. "This is Ogygia. These are the golden halls of Kronos in Eä," explains my Sirian companion. I stand before a figure robed in white, seated imperially on a throne. His beard is thick, trimmed at six inches, his hair is neatly groomed. His skin is astonishingly youthful given his evident hoary old age. "This is the Ancient of Days, Kronos, Lord of Time," a voice informs me. Then Kronos speaks to me.

I call on my years of journalism to remember his speech with any degree of accuracy because regrettably I didn't bring my notepad with me on this spur-of-the-moment visit. Approximately, this is what the Ancient said: "Long ago, I sent you forth from these golden halls with the Grail. This was your awareness of Eä. I told you to fill the Grail, then return, bringing me the contents, and showing me wisdom you had attained. I asked you to know the Grail because it is the secret of Eä. Know Eä, return, and feed me your wisdom. This I asked you. Remember the oath you made in this hall. You are not yet finished. When the Grail is full, return here, come home, serve me its contents."

End of interview with the Boss. The Grail Knight has barged into a big myth indeed. It's three-fifteen and I'm back from Ogygia on Oath Hill. The moon is a pale orange disc setting over the Aller Dragon's heart in the western hills. The eastern sky insinuates dawn. The Big Dipper tilts towards Polaris in a vivid sky. As the cosmos goes about its clockwork, I try to put the new pieces of the mythic puzzle together. Let's start with the beard. Confidentially, I was a little disappointed with the Ancient of Day's beard; the *Zohar* had led me to expect something more. The *Zohar* talks about "thirteen fountains of excellent oil" and "the most precious balm of splendour" that flow upon the beard, various "places of fragrance," even two beautiful white apples somehow stitched into the magnificent locks. "The beard, whose hairs hang down even unto the breast, white as snow; the adornment of adornments, the concealments of conceal-ments, the truth of all truths."

Oath Hill's Ogygia came closer to resembling its mythic reputa-tion. In terms of the Greek myths, we're dealing with a multigenera-tional family feud among the male members: Uranus, Kronos, Zeus. Kronos (or Saturn) dethroned and "castrated" his father, Uranus, then Zeus did the same to his father, Kronos. Zeus banished Kronos, his wife/sister Rhea, and the other Titans, except Atlas, whose ser-vices were still needed to hold up the world, to a remote island in the farthest west, in the land anciently called Hyperborea (whose rem-nants now include the British Isles). There, in the golden halls of Ogygia, Kronos dwells in a minimum security prison overseen by the Hundred-handed Ones, including Gyges ("Earth-born"), Briareus ("Strong"), and Cottus, the only ones specifically named in classical texts. In the *Odyssey*, Ulysses spent seven years with Calypso, daugh-ter of Atlas, on her island of Ogygia. "Once through the stait/nine days I drifted in the open sea/before I made shore, buoyed up by the gods/upon Ogygia Isle. The dangerous nymph/Kalypso lives and sings there, in her beauty/and she received me, loved me."

Eä comes by way of Sumerian mythology and J. R. R. Tolkien. According to ancient Sumer belief, Anu, the King of Heaven and first among Gods, had a son who was known as Eä, whose name literally meant "house-water;" he was alternately called Enki, which meant "Lord of Earth." Eä was "Lord of the Saltwaters," meaning the seas and oceans, or *Apsu*, meaning "the Deep," an attribution reminiscent of the Greek Poseidon or Roman Neptune. As Lord of the Deep, it would be within his province to concern himself with fish, celestial or otherwise; hence, the cosmic Fisher King attribution is apt. Eä, whose wisdom was commemorated by the additional epithet of *Ninigiku*, or "Lord Bright-eye," was instrumental in designing and creating *Adapa*, the Sumerian Adam.

Tolkien, albeit less a scholar than a mythopoet, says that Iluvatar, the primal God and probably equivalent to the Sumerian Anu, gave vision to the Gods and set it amid the Void, "and the Secret Fire was sent to burn at the heart of the World, and it was called Eä." Elsewhere the bard of Middle Earth refers to the "regions of Eä, which are vast beyond the thought of Elves and Men" and to "the Kingdom of Arda, and that was but a small realm in the halls of Eä, whose life is Time." Tolkien also notes that Eä means the world or material universe—literally, "It is" or "Let it be"— was the Iluvatar's (as Father of All) creative word when the world began its existence.

In Qabala the God-Name, or holy mantric sound for the first Sephiroth called Kether at the crown of the Tree, is *Eheieh* (virtually Eä), sometimes translated as "I am that I am." The quality of Kether is often described as The White Head or Vast Countenance, and its magical image is an ancient bearded king in profile. "Imagine a great head arising from the depths of a calm, still sea until it completely covers the space above the horizon," writes Qabalist Gareth Knight. Then perceive this vast head reflected in the waters. Kronos can fairly be considered a Kether figure, Knight adds, "in that he devoured his children as Kether finally indraws all that has been created through it."

According to a fourth scholar—Blaise, probably the one best placed to get it right—"Iluvatar is Kronos, who is the Lord of Time. Eä is the sound before sound. The word referred to in *Genesis* is that sound you know as the Eä. Eä doesn't need healing but needs making whole. This would be the conscious activation of a small section of the universe. You may find it interesting to know that your Sun is called

Kronos by some, Helios by others, and generally, from the viewpoint of, say, the Pleiades, it is known as Sol. The story of the Fisher King implies this meaning."

Dark clouds are blowing in from the east, banking down the delicate pink bloom that flushes the cheek of the morning sky. The cows are unimpressed with the visitation by Kronos and continue their work on the grass of Oath Hill. I feel radiant with aplomb. I used to feel always on edge outside alone at night, as if I were always fleeing from an unrelenting question shouted down from the cosmos to me: Who are you? Why are you? I would take up the litany: Who am I? My God, I don't know, I would croak back, and this Don't Know would blow me out of the house of my complacencies into the nagging unknown. But not this morning. As I pick my way through the furrowed fields and muddy, puddled lanes, as the dawn whispers on the horizon, as the stars shine through the forms of angels, this morning I answer the old query with a laugh. "Just wait. You'll see."

Who am I? Cow flops splatter on wet grass. Don't slip! "The dog! The Buddha-nature! The perfect manifestation, the command of truth. If for a moment you fall into relativity, you are a dead man!" But the monk wasn't satisfied with Zen Master Ikan's answer and asked, "What sort of thing, in the last resort, is this 'You,'" to which Ikan replied, "It is not a thing." The monk riposted: "Can it be perceived or thought of?" Ikan: "Thought cannot attain to it; it cannot be fathomed. For this reason it is said to be a mystery." Grail Knight: "A Sirius mystery."

In the late afternoon, after a rest, I pedal down the Michael Oroboros line to St. Bartholomew's Parish Church in East Lyng a few miles past the Mump. This church, which dates to the mid-1300s and is situated like a geomantic knot on the Michael line, which passes through here, corresponds to *Mirzam* ("the Sirian announcer") in Canis Major. I prefer to call East Lyng the "Dog's Bone." There are no people about, so I have my pick of the seats. The steps before the altar seem promising; after a few minutes of quiet breathing, aspects of East Lyng's earlier days come into focus.

Some time ago in this same place stood a stone beehive-cell oratory, safely elevated above the soggy marshland. Several men step out of a coracle and enter the stone chamber, which is about fifty feet in diameter. Here at *Mirzam*, the young Grail Knights sequestered in a kind of geomythic academy to study and reflect on the Dog and its three aspects. Here the Girt Dog examines itself, gains self-knowledge through the knights, extends itself in thought to gain a self-perspective. Here the Grail Knight gnaws on the Dog's bone and sucks out the vital marrow of wisdom. Here, the Dogorrery is known; the Dog is comprehended in its roles as temple guardian, custodian, psychopomp, and the Goddess' ever-faithful. "The *fili* (seer) must chew the flesh of a dog in order that his gods should show him the things which he desired they should reveal," reports Cormac in his ninth century *Glossary*. In an all-night solitary vigil, the young Grail Knight and *fili*-apprentice prepared himself (and herself) for the trek across the landscape into Glastonbury for a dawn appointment with the Bee-Keeper. First you know the Dog, then you jump into the Cauldron.

Here at East Lyng, the significance of Sirius becomes apparent to the contemplative Grail Knight. The Dog-star, the lynchpin for Canis Major, was called *Serios* by the Greeks, meaning the "scorcher, the sparkling or burning one." For the Arab astronomers, Sirius was *Al Kalb al Jabbar*, the Dog of the Giant, and its name suggested "the blazing star of the one who crossed the Milky Way." The Sumerians spoke of Canis Major as the Dog of the Sun. Aratus, a venerable astronomer from antiquity, referring to the "star-enwrought" Dog-star, said, "The tip of his terrible jaw is marked by a star, that keenest of all blazes with a searing flame." Other sources place Sirius at the Dog's nose or eye, but Pindar spoke for them all when he characterized Sirius as "the shape-shifting dog of the Great Goddess," whether she was known as Isis, Hecate, Athene, Minerva, Sarama, Hel, Gula, or Bridget. Sirius is the eye of Anubis, the Keeper of the Mother's Gate, the opener of the way who eats the flesh of the dead and carries their souls to Paradise. Diane the Huntress had her *kuons*, the faithful dogs of the wood. Gwyn ap Nudd's chief of hounds was Dormarth, which means "Death's door." "Handsome is my dog, and round-bodied," Gwyn boasts in the Welsh *Black Book of Carmarthen*. "Dormarth with the ruddy-nose, ground-grazing; how you gaze on me when I mark your wanderings on cloud-mount!"

Esoteric tradition holds that the Buddha "came" from Sirius, the eye of the Dog. Blaise-roshi has said the Buddha holds the gold dome lines en route to Sirius. So I ask you, Zen-bemused Grail Knights of the world, from my pontifical perch at East Lyng, my *kyosaku* ready to whack you for any wrong answer: "Does the Buddha have Dog nature?" This is a Zen *kuon*.

The church warden has arrived and wants to lock up St. Bartholomew for the night. As I ride out of town, I see the Dog inhabiting the landscape, its geomythic body criss-crossed with an intricate pattern of light lines, pulsating knobs, and thimbles of color, which include the star centers I've visited. Places of intersection between straight-running dome lines and curving, heliocentric dome lines are called *line nodes*, Blaise explains; these form a third level (with Oroboros lines, domes and dome lines) of geomantic heightening, and a myriad of minor but potent energy points in the landscape. "There are thousands of places, even in England on the Michael line, where the geomantic treatment may be done at different levels and for different purposes. You have domes, dome caps, and many forms of linear intersections where lines cross. Some of these line nodes are solar-positive, some are lunar-negative, some centrifugal, some centripedal."

Happy with this new insight, I zigzag centripedally along the road, meandering through a skein of starlight on the Earth between the dog's bone at East Lyng and the dog's belly at Wick.

47

A Light Rain at the Hill of Mort

ummer solstice tomorrow and all week we've been expecting Blaise to announce an assignment for us. Hilary has arrived at Wick in anticipation of this. Finally, around ten-thirty p.m., Blaise shows up with our marching orders.

"We come as we are. We come as a Blazing Star. We come from not too far. We are most pleased to be with you all tonight. We place each of you in a dancing lilac flame. We place within each flame a point of brilliant blue light. We surround you all with blue light. We have travelled far. If we could be tired, then we'd be worn out. We have a message for you. We pointed out a small hill near Hamdon Hill. In the future, we will refer to this as Mort Hill. We would like, if you wish, for you to be there at nine-thirty tomorrow morning."

The next morning as we perch under our umbrellas at windswept Balham Hill (the Ordnance Survey name for Blaise's Mort Hill), near Chiselborough—on private property and without, regrettably, proper permission—we realize a little glumly that this summer solstice could just as well have been the winter solstice for all the good weather we're not having. It's cold, windy, rainy, wet. We saw it coming at breakfast and groaned over our porridge: grey clouds lowering themselves into place over dour Somerset, guaranteeing rain. We bundled ourselves in raincoats, gloves, hats, umbrellas. When we stepped out of the Citroen at the bottom of Mort Hill, the wind instantly doubled its intensity and the mud practically flowed down the dirt track like geomantically-charged lava. The dome over Mort Hill remained intact with respect to the elemental onslaught. Which brings us by an uncommodious vicus of circumambulation to the summit of Mort where we now dutifully huddle under a clump of squat trees and two flimsy umbrellas that keep blowing inside out. Blaise arrives, dry, warm, and cheery.

"We greet you all today. We greet the earth, the fire, the air, and the water. We are here from quite near. We bring you each a lilac flame of transmutation. Each of you is surrounded with a flame. A lilac flame bursts forth from this hill, too. We ask you, if you wish, to breathe your love to Mort, as Love from Above. Each of you came through your pain, your trials, and your personal suffering. We ask, breathe Love from Above to the flames of transmutation at this time on Mort."

As Blaise speaks and I struggle to write on water-sogged paper and Hilary strains to keep the umbrella over me, another part of my attention notices a milky white dome in the valley to the northwest, just beyond Hamdon Hill. This is the canopy of the mysterious crystal city. Momentarily, I'm inside the dome, viewing the huge crystalline structures of the veiled city. Then I'm yanked back to Mort Hill and notice that the six Blaises and about a dozen Seraphim have formed an elegant, numinous coronet around Mort Hill and that within this angelic crown burns the lilac flame. The four of us sit in its flaming mist, meanwhile getting completely soaked with rain. Then Blaise resumes.

"We ask you to place your attention at the point of light at the center of the flame of transmutation. It is still, above Mort. Allow this point of light within the lilac flame to sink into the Earth of Mort. Feel, each of you, the point of stillness within the flame, sinking into the Earth of Mort, going deep down." Now I see something startling when I follow the point of light into the heart of Mort. A group of subhumans with square heads walk about, looking worried, as if the angelic light had stirred up their nest. Blaise continues. "Feel for the point of stillness within the ground at Mort. Listen for the sound behind all sounds." Later, Russell will tell us he heard the inimitable Blaise Sound droning at the back of the gale winds. "From the point of stillness within the flame of transmutation, from the point of stillness within Mort Hill, from the point of stillness behind the sound, breathe with your love. Now we reveal its connection through lines of light covering your planet. We facilitate your individual and collective memory at this point of stillness within Mort."

At this point, Russell tells us afterwards, he saw Mort Hill as an intersection point within a planetary grid system made of the fifteen Oroboros lines and numerous bright nodes. Each node was attended by angels and lilac flames and the light lines pulsed pink and pale blue. "Water is light," Blaise says. "Water contains consciousness. Consciousness is light. We bring you this. We ask you to rest awhile. We will return."

Blaise has given us a breather, but we are four soggy dogs drowning in *samadhi* with nowhere dry to trot along to. But as we sit under our brace of incompetent, exhausted umbrellas, levitony descends upon us, and thus buoyed, we laugh and wisecrack our way through the short break. In fact, we are each seized with the urge to pass water and head in gender pairs for the bushes. Then Blaise returns.

"We bring you all a lilac flame. We surround you with the flame of transmutation. Each flame has at its center a point of brilliant blue light. We ask you to place your attention at the center of the flame, at the point of brilliant blue light. Breathe to it with your love at this place. Remember, the effort is not yours. It is as Love from Above. We greet you all from the point of light within the lilac flame of transmutation, from the blue point of Christed initiation within the Buddha Body. We greet you all: earth, air, fire, water. We thank each of you for being here. We place our blessings upon you all. We give of our love. We leave as we came, as a Blazing Star."

Within ten minutes, the rain and wind stop, and, within a half hour, the sun bursts like a dimple from the dispersing clouds that are congealing into cumulous towers and blowing rapidly out to sea. It's hard to believe how rapidly the weather changes as we leave Mort; surely these effects were stage-managed for this outing at Mort. We're all a little giddy and stunned—and famished!—so we stop in Montacute for a massive breakfast where we "talk among ourselves" during the break, as Blaise would say.

In the evening when Blaise returns to clarify matters, they bring the Seraphim as well. "We come as we are. We come as a Blazing Star, the center of the sphere of stable consciousness. We come as love, as Love from Above. We surround you all with the lilac flame of transmutation. We place each of you in a flame. We surround you with brilliant blue. We say, this is the Christ light. We fill your middle bowl with golden light."

"Say, Blaise, about all that weather today. Did you guys do that?" I ask.

"Water is consciousness on a material plane, as close as can be. It is also truth. We brought that pure element of change, fresh air on a material plane, a wind spiral, which through playing with the water element, created the spectacular event that you had the possibility of witnessing within your limitations." Then the Seraphim added, "We, with others, were consciously activating certain earth energies into activation in a section of the planetary grid system under supervision of the Nimitta of consciousness, or Blazing Star, and others under the supervision of Michael. We were aware of what you call weather."

"We come to speak of Mort," Blaise continues. "Mort is a nodal point, Mort is an entrance place to the crystal city. It is well now. The Earth energy has been closed there for many years. It has now been activated. We are pleased that you were all there to witness its activation and the beginning of that portion of the conscious activation of the grid system. The grid is a phenemenon with multiple dimensions confirmed by various agencies throughout its evolution. Changes are happening within its original structure. Certain of the Platonic Solids within the formation of the grid have been relatively inactive. Now they begin to become activated. The forms of the Platonic Solids are in a process of change from one to another. The astrological attributions of each Solid simultaneously change. This change happens about every 2400 years.

"You witnessed a little of the seeding of this activation today. One of the first events of this time on planet Earth experimentally happened at Mort Hill today. It is a new energy that we brought into a previously functioning circuit. The new pattern that emerges is free of some of the constraints of domes and dome lines, which have locked the growth spiral into a particular pattern for a particular period. Now it becomes more open. We are looking at a multidimensional field, a hologram of possibilities, a new grid structure emerging from the potential seeding from the beginning, from the source. Only the old grid system is presently a reality. The old grid will carry on to a degree even if the anchoring of the new dynamic doesn't completely take form. When enough of these points are empowered and cognized, then the Earth will automatically detoxify. Gaia will be freed. Everything changes. Everything at this point is a possibility. Whatever the future holds is dependent on many inopportune opportunities.

"Mort has many possibilities for the future. It has many sacred spots although it has been spoiled in the past largely through human ignorance. We ask that you remember this place when you breathe love. It needs your love, too. We are sure it has been what you term a geomythic figure of the Earth Mother or a female deity. One thing we overheard in your discussions today we would like to clarify. It has to do with the animals of the zodiac. We would like you to consider the names of the figures very carefully as you are beginning to be realize that some are not any longer appropriate and are in fact out of date. Mort Hill is an abbreviation in your language for transmutation, as in mortification, mortuary, and Mortdred. Each of these suggests a death, a transfiguration, and a major change in physical form and being."

This prompts an eruption from Berenice. "Oh my! I've completely forgotten until now. I saw a coffin and a cross by the entrance to a long, black tunnel. I went through this tunnel and came out the other end as a tiny parcel of consciousness within a huge ball of light."

"Is what Berenice saw the same as the Black Bowling Ball with the point of light at the center and the same as Eä with Polaris in its center?" I ask Blaise. I might have added as well: Da Love Ananda's "cosmic mandala" and the uniform experience of people undergoing Near Death experiences. In either case, there is an intense point of light surrounded by a black, tunnel-like sphere, then a corona of color.

"All the same. We are often at Polaris. We like to spend the winters there. Better climate, more sun tan. We like wearing sunglasses, you know, lying under the lilac sun. Originally, there was a temple at Mort, at the pinnacle. For many centuries, people dwelled there for the experience of transmutation. The hill represents part of a figure that rests on the eagle's back and is transmuted through the awareness the eagle carries."

"Do you mean Mort Hill is part of the eagle in the zodiac, then?" Russell asks.

"Correct. The eagle eats awareness. You are familiar with this from your reading. The eagle is one of the four elemental logo figures for the zodiac. Each logo figure, as each zodiac figure, represents an aspect of consciousness. You may like to look for the representatives of the astrological symbols for the four elements. This indicates there are four directions, each enlarged and enhanced by an elemental logo."

I've read about that Eagle and its big hunger for awareness. When Blaise gives us a few minutes to collect ourselves, I dash upstairs for my Castaneda books. Don Juan's first rule of the *nagual*, or the second attention, pertains to the Eagle. "The power that governs the destiny of all living beings is called the Eagle, not because it is an eagle, but because it appears to the seer as an immeasurable jet-black eagle, standing erect as an eagle stands, its height reaching to infinity," I read out loud. "The Eagle is devouring the awareness of all the creatures that, alive on Earth a moment before and now dead, have floated to the Eagle's beak, like a ceaseless stream of fireflies, to meet their owner, their reason for having had life."

When I finish reading, Russell says, "Then Burrow Hill must be part of the Eagle, too. Remember those four eagle guardians and the necropolis you reported? Crikey, I always knew Castaneda wasn't making it up. Now what about that crystal city? What did your friend from Cambridgeshire tell you about it?" This was a fellow who had been writing to me about his visionary incursions into the same terrain we'd been exploring with Blaise.

"He said he first saw the crystal dome in a dream. He was guided through the city by its 'cosmokrator,' whom he described as a large, black gorilla, the World King of long ago, before the time of humans. Maybe he meant a *Yeti*. Then he was taken to the King's Gardens, which he found 'exquisite,' and was told the city was known as Roïyat and existed far in the future, several thousand years. The city had tall, faint, glassy towers tinted a hazy rose-brown, he said. Then he saw the city a couple times during the daytime near London and met the city's queen whom he described as a tall woman of Asian appearance, magnificently robed."

"We return," Blaise announces. "In your investigations, you will encounter many things and you will pursue others. It is possible you will visit the crystal city, but we cannot tell at this point."

"Blaise, the grid overlay we saw today looked like a dodecahedron, the Platonic Solid with twelve faces for the ether element."

"Correct. Visualize a sphere with fifteen lines of golden and white light encircling it. These are the Oroboros lines going around your planet. They cross one another at even intervals making a total of 62 points of intersection. These form 120 equal-sized triangles. This figure incorporates the Platonic Solids known as the icosahedron and dodecahedron. The grid form for the Earth is a combination of all five Platonic Solids. This grid produced the environmental structure. Each Platonic Solid has a relation to the lines of force traversing the globe. This is the lattice of energy that covers the Earth. Within each of the intersections of the fifteen lines, there is a positive and negative line also running across the Earth's surface. These two are represented by pale blue lines that form the recessed side of the 120 triangles. The forward lines of these triangles are golden or white. The positive and negative lines are not fixed. They oscillate in a rhythmic pattern and in no way should be interpreted as permanently positive or negative in your ordinary dualistic way. The pale blue lines, incidentally, relate to the icosahedron, which is the Solid for the water element."

"I was once in the Sahara Desert and had a glimpse of something that I thought was a stellar grid," Russell says. "Is this pattern along the same lines as the planetary grid?"

"It is not the same as the Earth system. If you imagine a geodesic solid or other multifaceted rhomboid solid, then you can see lines of subtle energy passing from one plane of experience or existence through to a similar plane or facet in a rhomboid at another dimension. This is the stellar-Earth connection. It's linked with forces of an etheric nature. The stellar grid may be visualized from Earth as a lace curtain or pattern of interconnected snowflakes stretching across the entire night sky."

"What effect do we have when we sit on a nodal point like we did today, on one of the turning points of the year, like a solstice?" I ask. "How does our consciousness make any difference to the grid?"

"The field of your psychophysical organism, the electromagnetic and bioplasmic structure, is inherently linked to the Earth's electromagnetic and bioplasmic fields. When a being interrelates and unifies, or what you call 'meditates,' at the right point in time and space on the surface of the Earth and in themselves and there is coincidence, then we are cooking with gas. Then you, in your process of transmutation, participate, or coincide, with the larger process of transmutation affecting the planet through its grid system. We say, if you wish, place your attention within your star. When you move in consciousness, there is an effect in the Earth. Each step you take, every move you make, has an effect. Everything is interdependent and interrelated.

"If you have an imprint of an event in your higher being body, then that event transmits itself into the body of Gaia, which repercusses on the surface of the Earth. One reason for developing your self-nature, for coming to awareness of yourself, for realizing the Star you are, is that this imprint makes an imprint within the body of Gaia and repercusses on the Earth. If you are in a particular place where the energies are sympathetic with your blueprint, then there is synchronous reciprocation of vibrations. These will make an impression within the body of Gaia. The more conscious you are of your personal imprint and its part and the imprints that have been graced you, the more these imprints have an effect in the planetary body. One conscious step makes for a step of consciousness in the world. You are a co-creator with the Most Almighty Architect of Divine Existence in the Plan of all positive possibilities within this Earth. You either take up each step as your conscious responsibility or you don't. It's up to you. You are the Star you are."

"Well, Blaise, can you give us a precis of the history of humans on Earth? There's a great deal of disagreement even among esoteric sources."

"Oh dear. It would take too long. What would you really like to know? What you request is really a history book. It's not a short story. Anyway, it is not part of your mission to write the complete history of this planet."

"What part is relevant to our mission?"

"Where the history affects the present implications at an energy level. Therefore, it is necessary and appropriate for us to explain certain aspects of the history of how things have come to be the way they are, so you can deal with them more effectively rather than having no knowledge as to how things have become the way they are."

"Blaise, you've been mentioning the blue light and the Christ lately," says Berenice. "What is this all about?" And I interject: "Right. Good point. Is that what Joseph of Arimathea was doing with the Girt Dog?"

"When you reach the point of the Christed initiation in the Buddha Body you will know what we mean."

"What on Earth is that?"

"We are instruments of the Archangel Michael in this activity. He brings the Christ spirit forward from the final event at Golgotha. He prepares the Christed initiation in the Buddha Body for the coming Maitreya, the event of your future. The Christed initiation in the Buddha Body is the central theme of Looking for Arthur, of your work with us as a Grail Knight. It is your future. It is eight plus twelve equals twenty, the inner and outer heart, the dodecahedron, the planetary grid system of your planet: Joseph's seed. It is about the event at Golgotha when matter became spirit. We will leave you now. We say, each of you, have a little Love from Above. We leave as we came, as a Star, brighter than the brightest star, as a Blazing Star.

48

THE GRAIL KNIGHT
CALLS IN AT BEN'S REPAIR SHOP

en has come back and just in time. He came by Wick yesterday and we drove off together. "You need a friendly visit," he said as we headed for his house. I appreciate his perfect timing. No doubt he knows the Grail Quest has veered off the road into an embankment. "So. Tell me about your front-end collision with Deborah that has left such big dents in your psyche," Ben says with a merry gleam. It is as if no time has passed since we were last together.

Ah, Deborah of Charmouth, my *dakini* lover. It started out seemingly euphoric, but maybe this was but the first blush of unimpeded eroticism. She stayed at Wick a couple of months ago for a weekend, and we kept in touch afterwards through the occasional letter. She's a woman about my age, with brown hair in a long ponytail, green eyes, and a nimble tongue that can range from fishwife vulgarity to abstract intellectuality. She has a small flat in a seaside town and invited me to visit for a weekend. I went down to Charmouth right after our Mort Hill expedition. I felt I needed a vacation from the Quest. We danced for a while at an intrigued distance but it was like two magnets trying to resist the other's pull. The snapping together in a magnetic embrace was inevitable. When we finally, suddenly, hugged and clapped bodies together in the kitchen, bolts of light rivetted our bodies together and we didn't climb out of bed for two days. Ah, the cosmic, terrestrial, domestic, and randy Grail Knight was in the Castle of the Maidens rescuing the damosel and himself from languishing in celibacy.

After we parted, we wrote each other a lot. "You made a giant dent in my psyche," I told her. "It's hard concentrating on my work but it's a delicious sensation and I'm not complaining. A part of me is still in Charmouth." Deborah concurred: "Something has shifted, deepened in me. At many levels, I have been overwhelmed and re-made by your visit. It is, indeed, a great mystery and quite outside my conscious or logical control. It smacks of destiny. I feel deeply disoriented, re-arranged, grateful, opened, and happy."

The domestic Grail Knight made a second, weeklong house call to Charmouth and the deep disorientation was even more pleasant. We played and joked and toured in a swelling aura of sexual energy. We called in at old churches and hillforts, remembered bits and pieces of our past, talked about enlightenment and angels, spiritual practice and metaphysical delusion, and carried on the usual negotiations about points of lifestyle, furniture arrangement, shopping, and pillow fluffing. Oh Ben, her lance is sharp and with it she sees easily into the other worlds, yet, strangely, she is consistently skeptical and critical of our involvement with Blaise.

We lay on the beach at Charmouth one afternoon in early July. "By constantly attributing every success to Blaise, you fail to understand the wider context in which Blaise exists and the function of your consciousness, of which Blaise is an aspect," she began. "Don't you see? This gives you subtle permission to be fascinated, exclusive, weak, single-track-minded, and self-centered. Never mind if it's in the higher, rarified reaches of the self. The real spiritual process is to realize God in person, not its messengers. To embody God. This means taking total responsibility for yourself as a transcendental being, not from the standpoint of a karmically contaminated personality. Otherwise, all you get is duality, projection, dissatisfaction, and continual seeking. These project you further and further into realms of contaminated action." We batted this around for awhile, then she said, "And lovey, I think we ought to be celibate when we're in Switzerland, okay? I want to focus all my energies on the initiation. I'll probably want to spend a lot of time alone, too."

Russell, Hilary, Berenice, and I were driving to Switzerland for a

Tibetan initiation ceremony that would last a fortnight and draw about 5000 Westerners. Deborah was going by plane and would meet us there. "Now that I'm hearing your voice, I miss you like crazy," she cooed on the telephone when I called her from the Weymouth ferry. That night I dreamed. I am outside in nature with a beautiful woman. She comes on to me sexually. At first I resist her, for God knows what reason. Then she transforms herself. Her eyes grow intense and radiant, and she flushes with the light of a spiritual being. She rides me as if I'm a horse with a wild expression of passionate joy. I squeeze her breasts and her body ripples with energy. You have to be careful with *dakinis*, I tell myself in the morning. A *dakini* makes Madonna seem like a truculent Bobbsey twin in comparison.

The *dakini*, or "sky dancer," has perfect insight into emptiness and practices "the empty dance of Awareness," as Tibetan Buddhism scholar Keith Dowman notes. Her nature is equivocal and ambiguous; sometimes she's thought of as a witch, an enchantress, or manipulator who abuses her extra-worldly sexual powers. But the *dakini*'s sexual potency opens her human consort's perceptual doors to insight. "For the initiate on his way to the center of the mandala, however, a woman as a *karamudra* of Awareness is a guardian of the mysteries, a guide through the doors of the mandala, a bestower of initiation, and the object of the initiation itself." In the realm of tantric practice, Dowman adds, every woman is the *Dakini*, because "there is no difference between woman in her everyday reality and the all-inclusive divine female archetype that permeates her being and dominates her mind."

Deborah arrives a couple days after we do, and I feel her presence even before I see her amid the thousands of Buddhists under the big tent. I turn to look down the long end of the aisle and there she is, walking past, looking for me. She is not the celibate, ascetic, hermitic Deborah she promised to be once she got here. No. She is effusive, romantic, bubbly, loving, and erotic. "I've missed you so much," she tells me hotly on the ear. "You've changed. You're soft. Do you think we can make love this week, today—as soon as possible, actually?"

No doubt Padmasambhava, on whose behalf this Tibetan ceremony is conducted, will, in his state of exalted enlightenment, find our picaresque activities amusing, because from this moment on our goal is less to comprehend the arcana of the Tibetan initiation than it is to find a secluded place to have a bed-collapsing romp. At least figuratively, because we are not destined to romp in beds. I have monks in my dormitory room and Deborah has two dozen roomates in a large hall, so we roam the countryside for trysting places. By the end of the fortnight, Deborah has tied herself in knots, and I suppose I have, too—the body is wanton and insatiable, the mind is hypercritical and disruptive.

"This relationship is no longer supportable," Deborah says. "I'm exhausted. I feel constricted. You're so averse. You invade my sitting practice with your psychic gymnastics. I'm so annoyed at myself for chasing my pleasures all over Switzerland." The Grail Knight replies testily: "The trouble with you is that you bludgeon yourself with a hammer at the first sign of happiness." And Deborah: "If that's all the respect you have for what I said, don't bother coming around in the morning."

In the morning around seven I enter her dormitory room and wiggle her toes, which stick out from the end of her blanket. She glares over the covers then smiles wanly. "Let's go for coffee, lovey," she says. Over breakfast, she says, "I sent you good thoughts last night so you would know it's not as bad as it sounded. Obviously you got them. Just don't grasp me so hard. You're so clinging. Hey, relax, lovey, I'm still fond of you." But the damage had been done. Something felt shaken dangerously loose inside me. I dread being abandoned by women, so naturally I attract it. If our emotions are a console with depressable buttons, this one is labelled: Press for instant panic reaction. On the drive home, I sat in the backseat of the Citroen as we motored through the Swiss Alps and stared at two snowpeaks that seemed to float like icebergs miles above the green horizon. Eventually, Deborah and I decided to dare another week together in Charmouth, but here the ship of romance truly ran aground, disabling everything except the cannon.

"What good is all this esoteric knowledge and psychic television doing you, anyway," Deborah said. "Be careful with this Blaise. In a few years you might be in considerable difficulty regarding the seeds you're planting now. You may find you've been wandering in nothing more than a fascinating realm of *samsara* guided by spirits who don't care about you and maybe don't wish for your enlightenment. I swear. This week I've never seen you so confused, maximally frightened, maximally desperate. You're coming from a place of unwholesome emptiness."

When I staggered home to Wick, dragging my unwholesome emptiness like a millstone, Russell said I looked so bad he thought I had the flu again. A week passed, marked by greyness and obscuration, exhaustion, intestinal upset, emotional volatility, a sore throat. I grew paralytic with doubt about my work, my process, my involvement with Blaise. My writing was muddled and inconsequential and pathetically uninspired. The weather took its cue from my despondency and served up unrelieved overcast and cold splotches with drizzle. The image of myself in the dream mirror was equivocal. I'm in a large hall with eight Koreans in pale turquoise robes bound with lilac sashes. They escort a Westerner, a man about forty-five, to the stage and sit around him at a table. This man is tall, lean, with sparkling blue eyes, a strong, chiselled face, short brown hair, combed back flat. I sense the solidity of his *hara* from a distance and wonder if he practices martial arts. A woman, who sits in a slouch next to me, challenges him to account for one of his secret romances. That is not your business, he replies evenly. I study his face intently: can I trust him?

For the *coup de grâce*, the Seraphim make a brief visit to Wick. "We say, you must realize Nimitta awaits you. The operation is not complete. You have received much. Now it is your will, your wish, what you do, but you have much that you haven't followed of what the Nimitta has suggested. This prevents much further contact with this source, though they wish to be more active with you. Please understand this, that you are responsible for what happens next." Later Russell told me the Seraphim were laughing as they emptied buckets of golden light over my forlorn head, fortifying me with seraphic inspiration. The next morning, Ben providentially showed up and wisked me away to his house.

"Well, that's a story indeed," says Ben. "The radiator and grill are certainly bashed in and the fender is crumpled, but I daresay the motor still works. Do you think you might be a bit too intense in the way you conduct relationships? You dive down fast but cramp all the way back up. Maybe you could value your own needs more keenly rather than banging your head up against a walking dialectical challenge. There are pitfalls on this path. Cut the strings. You don't need a *dakini*; you need a deeper sense of well-being, a clearer, more direct dialogue with Spirit. Let it fill the empty spots in your life. And for God's sake, Grail Knight, don't go rubbing salt on your wounds. Every Grail Knight slips up often and badly, but almost always redeemably. Emphasize being, not doing, for a while. Crack the coconut, drink the milk.

"Now about this Quest. You know by now, or at least suspect, that the actual figures of the Arthurian story are largely symbolic for spiritual experiences and energy relationships. You're hinging a lot on this myth, but it may well prove to be but a steppingstone to things of far greater importance in your future. You're still relatively young, not an old boy like me, certainly. Do the spade work, sure, toil in the field, master the terms, but see the opportunities under the little stones. Changes are coming. What is the Grail? I suggest there are seven levels of experience to the Grail, most of which you've tasted, but two about which you know nothing. Look into the five Grail changes. Look into the five Platonic Solids. Look into the five places where the Grail was dedicated, where you and I made a little dent in the hills. Don't you remember?"

"That was you?" I say incredulously. "In the loincloth by the barrow?"

"The same. Did you think Blaise was the only one who can come in many forms? Indeed not. Let me continue. Remember Aller. Remember what I told you months ago there about the Christed initiation of Arthurhood and the unfulfilled destiny of the Arthurian circle?

Some day you will, if you wish, return to Aller to complete the Grail dedication. Maybe I'll join you."

We sit in silence in the darkening kitchen for some time. Then Ben speaks again. "Rest well. Let it all go. Don't worry about it, Grail Knight. Here is a little verse to send you off with:

> You take the path from Magotty-Pagotty
> Through Copley Wood to Worley Hill
> The Orphic Egg—
> Humpty-Dumpty, Compton Dundon,
> Magotty-Pagotty, Come and play
> We bring to you a brand new day!

A dream accompanies my waking in the morning like a bedmate. In the backseat of a Volkswagen van, I find a woman's lower torso, severed from the trunk from the belly button down. It's a manikin. I step out of the car, leaving the dummy trunk inside. Then I'm in another car with a woman I once knew from the Zen center. She says she'd like to sleep late, which is fine with me because I like cuddling with her in bed; she is indifferent to my suggestion. We lie on a giant mattress in her apartment. She sprawls luxuriously on the bed as if dallying in a bubble bath. She wears a silken nightgown and shower cap with trailing lace. She changes form before my astonished eyes. She turns into a fairy with wings, diaphanous body, meltingly beautiful face, but she is oblivious to my feelings and her own sexuality.

49

DOWN THE GREAT STREAM INTO THE ORPHIC EGG

fter a week back at Wick, I feel restored to myself. Plus, Russell helped me identify Ben's Magotty-Pagotty. It's an old stream that flows—trickles is more precise— through Copley Wood at the foot of Worley Hill about an hour's bike ride from here near Kingweston. I like the name: Magotty-Pagotty. It has that queer and quaint Old Forest-Hobbiton flavor so familiar in Tolkien's world, which, of course, derives in large part from the British landscape and its antique mysteries in the first place. The weather today is geomantically correct: grey sky, intermittent showers, brisk wind. After a long pedal on the Grail Bike, I trek across a stubbly hayfield recently mowed, then perch before the entrance to Muncombe Wood, which abuts Copley. Blaise and a brace of gnomes sit beside me.

"Consider the egg," Blaise says laconically, presenting to my attention the mental image of a large, luminous egg. "And mind you don't step on the fairies as you search for the Orphic Egg!"

I open my eyes just as a lilac-winged butterfly poises for an eternity on a piece of straw. Once in the woods, I see a clutch of scalloped, flesh-colored mushrooms protruding from a soggy tree stump. Under the eaves, a community of fairies and wood spirits relax, and I take care not to step on any of them, not that it would do any more damage than mildly insult them. What am I looking for exactly?

Look for the egg, both Ben and Blaise said—what egg? The Ordnance Survey map indicates several obelisks and old stone markers as resident in these woods; this is often an indirect sign that the area holds some geomantic significance. Standing behind a waist-high obelisk, I tune in for a few moments. Almost at once I become aware of a large, transparent brown bear standing behind me, observing me with interest. Evidently, Copley Woods is situated within, or in very close zodiacal proximity to, *Ursa Major*, the Great Bear, whose tail and hindquarters are the Big Dipper and its seven stars.

After some desultory wandering through the woods, I pick my way down a hill to an old, nearly desiccated stream bed. No doubt in its day Magotty-Pagotty was a thriving, spring-swollen body of water, but today there is hardly a trickle and only the occasional gurgle as the water sighs over a rock. Yet an unmistakable ancientness lingers in the air like an antique perfume, an insinuation of primeval happiness and undisturbed stillness. I half-expect Tom Bombadillo—"Hey dol! merry dol! ring a dong dillo! Old Tom Bombadil is a merry fellow; Bright blue his jacket is, and his boots are yellow."—to come hopping along his Withywindle to greet me. An old voice speaks to me out of Magotty-Pagotty, but its hoary words fall incoherent just short of my hearing. By the stream bank, I find three sets of broken bird eggs, a promising concidental sign.

I cross Magotty-Pagotty and begin the long climb up Worley Hill. Sometimes I follow the trail, but more often I stagger along misdirected. If I have ever had Native American incarnations, I have surely forgotten all the fleet-footed, quiet-stepping tricks of the trade. I have never seen anyone walk as inelegantly and with so much branch-crunching, so much face-besmearing, so much gulley-lurching, so much mud-patch-slipping as this American Grail Knight careening through Copley Wood. Not to mention the now smelly socks wet from sloshing through mud, the trousers damp from sitting on clammy stream banks, and the stomach growling in a body whose physiology is approaching the hypoglycemic. I flop down in weariness before I reach the summit of Worley Hill; when I feel a little refreshed, I try meditating. A host of dream monsters and ambivalent denizens rush out to greet me, but I brush them away like flies. I've lost track of Blaise. I can't find the gnomes, and I'm faint with low blood sugar. After a long, fretful trek out of the woods, I flop down on the hayfield again and, with eyes half-closed, look back over the hill. A giant egg of light sits like an ovoid dome over Copley Wood and Worley Hill. Blaise's Orphic Egg at last. I've been stumbling and chattering through it all afternoon.

Back at Wick I don't feel I have accomplished much today, but apparently Blaise does, because in the evening they pay us a call. "We come as we are. We come as a Blazing Star. We come as a point of light in a sphere of stable consciousness. We surround you with walls of lilac flames up to the point of light above. We place a lilac flame above each of you. Within each flame, we place a sphere of sapphire blue, bright blue light.

"Life is cells in dynamic equilibrium radiating to each other in movement in space. We cannot know when you will be enlivened by something we have suggested in the past. We cannot predict this in your time. It is what keeps your availability to us now. We have come tonight for a special purpose. We have pre-recorded this message for you at the bright time. You have been shown specific things to do. You are hearing something you are meant to hear at this time. You must let go your strings. You must be free for awhile. You need to do something from something *higher* in yourself. We say to you, open yourself to this possibility. There exists something that needs to be done. It is most necessary that you understand and be open to a new possibility in each of you. Russell, Berenice, what the Grail Knight is to undertake relies on your support. All for now, yours, as ever, Blazing Star."

The next day it takes me two hours, including bike and foot, to reach the Worley Egg. Now that I'm here, seated on wet ground by the most diminutive of streams imaginable, I have no idea how to find an Orphic Egg in it. Somehow I know that's what I have to do: find an Orphic Egg in Magotty-Pagotty to match the big one over Worley Hill. It took me several hours and a lot of indecisive wandering through the woods just to find this little knoll above Magotty-Pagotty. I followed the stream out to the edge of the woods where it seems to disappear into an old cistern. Here I was joined by fairies, gnomes, and a sylph, but nobody had anything to say to me. Monday morning blues after a wild weekend perhaps. Then I traced the stream back the other way, feeling for a place where the ancientness felt the strongest and where there was enough of a gurgle to remind me this was, in fact, a physical stream I would be sitting next to. Special effects like these are important.

A man with short brown hair and brown robe gestures to me urgently to cast my attention higher, up to what appears to be a black marble edifice or cliff-face on top of which a light being presides. The brown-robed man places his hands before his face so I can't see him anymore, then he points up again. I start perceiving myself differently—radically, in fact. It's as if I now stand behind myself in a body of light. My translucent hands rest fatherly on the physical shoulders of the Grail Knight, who is quietly breathing, eyes closed. My neck tingles as I feel a radiance illuminating me from behind. "By this stream it is purified," says a voice. "By this stream it is remembered. By this stream it is replenished. By this stream it is fulfilled. Find the divine seed in the Great Stream."

When I open my eyes, I see two eggshells in the water. On my walk out of the woods, two deer suddenly bound out of the brush and lope beautifully past. When I rejoin my bike, which I stowed in the brambles, I see a crimson spiral of light inside the Orphic Egg. I creak my way home, pedalling twice as hard as normal just to keep at a standstill against the gale force winds. Oh the aching sinews of the Grail Knight chugging his weary way home after a day on the egg-hunt. Russell greets me at the front door of Wick with a grin. "Listen to this. I found out about Magotty-Pagotty. It's Sanskrit, originally, and means 'Great Stream,' the great flowing forwards. *Mahati-Prahati*. How about that? You could say it's the river of the wisdom of the magi, the flowing together of all the mysteries of the body, mind, and spirit since the beginning of time. It holds these like water flowing over that which is buried, deeply and secretly, in the ground of the psyche and the world."

After a bath, lunch, and a strong pot of tea, I scour my reference books for clues about the Orphic Egg. In the Greek Pelasgian creation myth, Eurynome, the Goddess of All Things, rose out of Chaos,

set the north wind in motion, and turned it into the great serpent
Ophion, or Boreas. Eurynome then danced, which aroused Ophion;
they copulated, after which she took the form of a dove and laid the
Universal Egg. Ophion coiled seven times around the egg until it
hatched: out tumbled everything in existence, stars, planets, Earth,
trees, living creatures. In the Orphic Mysteries, it was Orpheus who
was born from the egg, and before him, Dionysos. In the Eleusinian
Mysteries, Dionysos appears as an egg-born holy child carried in the
liknon, the winnowing basket. Castor and Pollux, the mortal-immor-
tal twins, emerge from Leda's egg.

The ancient Mystery tradition called this the Mundane Egg, says
H. P. Blavatsky in *The Secret Doctrine*, in which she concisely sum-
marized the egg's esoteric attributions. The Egg was the consummate cosmogonic symbol, representing the origin and secret of being, both human and universal. Various solar heroes—Dionysus, Ra,
Brahma, Osiris, Apollo, Phanes, Vishnu—each emerged from the
Golden Egg. And according to Castaneda's Don Juan, our physical
body is contained in what seers describe as a giant, luminous egg.
Our energy essence is egglike. "When sorcerors see a human being,"
Don Juan told him, "they see a giant, luminous shape that floats,
making, as it moves, a deep furrow in the energy of the earth, just as
if the luminous shape had a taproot that was dragging."

Says one gnome to his mate, "There goes the American Grail again,
crashing through the underbrush like an elephant gone amok, after
that infernal egg." I take my seat again the next day on the lip of
Magotty-Pagotty and settle into my breathing. I visualize the four
bowls, put myself in a golden tube of light, and put all this within
four towering pillars of light, rooted deep in the ground and rising
far above me into the clouds. A rainbow girts them, with the red
band closest to the pillars. Beyond this, filling all space, is whiteness.
At the peak of the golden tube sits the Buddha, imperturbable with
a slight smile blossoming on his face. As I shower myself in this golden
light, the bowl at my heart center gains in golden luster. Now I visualize myself to be standing within the Great Stream. I let the water
be light, let it flow thickly and copiously and steadily through my

heart. In this way I occupy myself for the next four hours. What flows through me is not water, of course, but it isn't light either; rather, it's a continuum of deep consciousness, an awareness before time, before all incarnation, before human phylogeny—a secret, most ancient of ancient. *Mahati Prahati*."

Then something singular occurs: a blaze of light flares in the heart bowl like a pearl bursting into flame, a seed on fire. "Good. The seed is aflame. Now you must understand what the divine seed is," says the voice without countenance. I'm finished for the day and pedal home over the undulating, windy hills with a reverent regard for this white seed that still burns with such fierceness in my chest.

In the evening I'm in the kitchen playing with the stick-on letters on the refrigerator door and have just written out "Blaise" when Berenice appears at the door to say Blaise is here. "We come as we are," Blaise says, when we're all seated in the living room. "We come as a Blazing Star. We surround you all with the lilac flame of transmutation. We shine the golden ray of wisdom into your midst. We bring the silver thread between you all. We are pleased to speak with you. This is something left behind from something we did earlier in what you call time. We say, you are now at the point where you begin to see the essence of Magotty-Pagotty. We are pleased. So we ask you now, What does the Great Stream fill?"

"My heart," I answer.

"What is that?"

"The blaze of light, the seed."

"The Grail has at its center the seed of the flame of immutable love. The river Magotty-Pagotty fills the Grail with light to kindle the seed of the immutable flame. We ask you to see. It is represented, inner and outer. Do you understand?"

"Kind of in between yes and no. It hasn't filtered down into words yet."

"Good. We give you another clue. Your work today has enabled us to provide it. The Stream flows into the Grail. Use this in your meditation. It is important at this time that you support one another. Four pillars hold space with wide silver threads between you all. Hilary is with you, although at a distance. We pour the golden light of wisdom between you. It runs across the floor. It fills the room. We surround you with the lilac flame of transmutation. We ask for a few moments that you be in remembrance of us as we are just a little ways away, as a Blazing Star."

No sooner has Blaise faded away than the Seraphim take their place. "We greet you all. We bring joy from above. We bring greetings from Nimitta. Listen a moment. Nimitta sends their love. He—we should say, they—says, be well in what you do. The Stream unfolds. The Grail Knight gets his toes wet. Today many things come clearer. Today a light dawns as a blended ray. There is so much to be revealed. We say, Grail Knight, tomorrow go to Magotty-Pagotty again as a representative of the four of you. You know what to do. Nimitta has already explained.

"Since the beginning of time, Man on this planet has been limited in sound and color vibration to particular rays from one to seven. Occasionally an extraordinary being comes to your planet and covers a spectral diffusion of the seven rays. These Beings are called Masters. They come to bring you peace and joy and love. You are in an extraordinary time. Now the blended ray begins to pour down on Earth. Each ray is now merging with the next in preparation for a complete harmony of vibration. The masters of Eternity pull together these eternal rays and the full spectrum of experience falls on each of you. It is the beginning of the rainbow ray falling on humanity. All right, there we are. We have been pleased to be with you. Now we leave with a skip and a jump."

"You know, these guys are *always* happy," says Russell with a sigh.

50

A COCOON OF FIRE
AT THE HILL OF THE WHORL

ight a.m. the next morning I'm on the road again to the Great Stream. Two hours later, I take my seat by Magotty-Pagotty and sit for an hour with the full visualization, including the flaming seed in the Grail. The Stream flows into the Grail, Blaise said. I struggle with this puzzle but, when nothing new develops, I follow an inspiration to explore Worley Hill, which seems to be the epicenter of the huge, luminous egg.

I walk slowly through Copley Wood to Worley Hill, cupping the flaming seed of immutable love in my heart center like the most fragile of eggs. Midway, I encounter a procession or possibly several overlapping ones. A Templar Knight leads one, bearing a large banner with a white cross against a red background. The Fisher King from Chalice Well leads another group of perhaps three dozen men and women. He shows me his heart seed, which he too cradles delicately. "This is the Hill of the Whorl," he says, indicating the sevenfold spiral of red light inside his heart seed, or egg. The others in his group also carry flaming seeds in their chests. I tell him I'll meet him at the top of the hill. Behind this group comes another Knights Templar band. Both groups veer off the trail into the underbrush, evidently following an older way to the top. I stick with the visible trail but get lost in about ten minutes.

I bash through the woods in confusion and never keep my rendezvous with the Fisher King at the crown of Worley Hill. I'm tired and annoyed and make my way back to Magotty-Pagotty in this peevish temper and get lost again. An hour later when I regain my bearings, I find I'm a great distance from where I had thought to be yet only fifty yards from a familiar field. Confidently, I set out for this field but never make it, getting lost yet again, which keeps me spinning for the next hour. My befuddlement deepens and I lay down on the forest floor in disbelief. You shouldn't be able to get lost so many times in Copley Wood: it's just not big enough for all these variations in disorientation. When I open my eyes, a half-dozen gnomes are peering down at me in concern. "I thought you guys were my friends. Why are you letting me get so bloody lost all the time!" The gnomes shake their heads and respectfully retreat from the barking Grail Knight. Finally, I regain my bearings, a mile off course and, fuming, make it back to my bike. "I'm never coming back to this damn place!" I shout to the wind and hay stubble and enigmatic Orphic Egg.

The next two days are a downhill coast into depression. Deborah calls to announce the unequivocal end of our romance and to expatiate with great precision on my two dozen most unforgivable defects. This leaves the Grail Knight forlorn and frowning in his chambers. On one of these gloomy afternoons, Russell visits me in the Grail den with some new information.

"It just came in over the wires, a special message from Blaise," he chirps. "Blaise gave me a quick tutorial on the eggs and told me to pass it on to you." Russell explains that the Orphic Egg relates to Orpheus who was the God of the Underworld, which means the lower astral plane. Orpheus was a Nefilim, originally one of the families of angels that eventually took human form as one of the five ancient races as described in the *Zohar*. The others included Giborim, or mighty ones; the Rephaim, or giants; the Anakim, or the tall ones; the Amelekim; Asa and Azael formed the Nefilim, the fallen or degraded ones. The Nefilim, says the *Zohar*, were the "fallen or degraded, the second in rank of the angel hosts that were cast out of Heaven and became incarnated." These were the Sons of God who beheld the daughters of men and found them fair.

This is intriguing with respect to the Orpheus legend. Orpheus, the Greek myths tell us, was the son of Apollo and the Muse Calliope. He became a master musician, playing the lyre to such perfection that all who heard it in the "cheerful upper world" were irresistibly charmed, including Eurydice, his wife; she was eventually killed and lost to the Underworld, which threw Orpheus into profound grief. The inference is that Eurydice was actually a mortal human woman but that the two formed a divine pair, a kind of Nefilim-human syzygy. Later, the Maenads tore Orpheus to pieces in their fury, and he rejoined Eurydice in the netherworld as a shade. From the Gods' viewpoint, this might mean Orpheus as a Nefilim entered the human incarnational stream, which from his vantage point, was a bit like the world of shades.

Some call Orpheus' eggs 'Cosmic Eggs' to suggest the way in which Heaven and Earth originally were a single form, one egg. But, according to Blaise, neither term is particularly accurate. In any case, the Orphic Egg is an egg with a seed that is related at an elemental level to the Earth, pertaining either to landscape or grid activations or the amplification of Earth energy configurations. Blaise says that usually the Orphic Eggs are situated at the root center of a zodiac or at a place that serves to stabilize the starmap on the landscape. In this zodiac, Worley is the entrance to the labyrinth. Although the official entrance is through Aries, there are several other points providing access to the labyrinth or starwheel through Worley Hill. The Great Stream of Magotty-Pagotty runs close to the entrance of the labyrinth at the Christ Child of Compton Beacon and Lugshorn, Blaise explains. Therefore it is said: All you enter here. The Egg is symbiotic with the Big Dipper aspect of Ursa Major. It is not technically correct to say the Orphic Egg sits inside the Great Bear's Wain, or Dipper, but it indicates the relationship.

I ask Russell why the Fisher King said this was the "Hill of the Whorl."

"That's easy," Russell replies. He tells me the name comes from the word "whorl" and its Middle English variants, *wharwyl* and *whorlwyl*, meaning something that whirls or turns, a convoluted line or a coil. Whorl implies *phi*, the golden mean, and the heliocentric spiral we see in domes and dome caps. *Phi* (from the Greek letter, ø, and mathematically expressed as an infinite number, 1.618034...) is one of Nature's premier design principles, showing up at all levels of expression from DNA to flowers to seashells to hurricanes to galaxies. And *phi* has philosophical implications, according to sacred geometry scholar Robert Lawlor. "The *phi* proportion is the perfect division of unity because the entire proportional universe that results from it relates back to it and is literally contained within it. The division by phi of Unity gives a model of evolution guided from within and indisputable proportional evidence of the possibility of a conscious evolution as well as of an evolution of consciousness."

Russell further explains that the phi spiral generates a logarithmic number sequence (as described by the Italian mathematician Fibonacci: 3, 5, 8, 13, 21, 34, 55, 89, 144...) which is actually an infinite progression. When the numbers in this series are plotted geometrically, they generate an expanding spiral. As such, phi is a kind of divine seed that governs the unfolding and transforming of the five Platonic Solids, which are the ideal geometric expressions of the five elements—earth, fire, air, water and ether. And these five Solids are the same as the five Grail changes. Which brings everything back to Worley Hill: the whorl of the phi spiral that will result in the Grail dedications at five landscape sites in this zodiac, each embodying a different Platonic Solid or Grail change, begins at Worley Hill—the hill of the phi whorl. "Doesn't this make your day? By the way, the Boss wants you back at Worley Hill tomorrow."

The Wick-to-Worley Hill commute is becoming such a regular activity that maybe I should buy a condominium in the Orphic Egg. I downshift to first to make the steep climb into Somerton. You wouldn't want to meander or happily zig-zag too much on this road; the drivers mean business and have every intention of getting somewhere fast, if not yesterday, and could easily launch a pedalling Grail Knight into the far pastures. My inner overcast is at last breaking up. Last night in a dream Berenice said, "So, now you know your work is about the celestial rays of the Great Bear."

Earlier this morning, during meditation, I had a feeling the Archangel Michael would play a role in today's work with the Orphic

Egg. Settling into a relaxing coast on the other side of Somerton, I roll past a car in the climbing lane that sports a bumper stick with a single word: "Mike." As I approach Kingweston, my intuition is confirmed. Michael looms magnificently, flared behind and above the translucent cosmic egg of Worley Hill. Blaise flies hexatically around the Egg, wrapping it in a sevenfold lilac ribbon.

I stow my bike in the bushes on the edge of the Kingweston Cedar Walk, which, like the Avenue of Cedars outside Glastonbury, is the remains of an ancient processional marked by cedars in a double row. I have company this morning and they are most welcome: it's my inner Round Table of Joseph of Arimathea, my brother, Tudor Pole, the sylph, various gnomes and fairies. In a flash I know exactly what I am to do. I cup my hands in a mudra at my sternum and hold the flaming seed inside the golden Grail at my heart. Then in rhythm with my breathing and walking, I chant *O Michael uplift us now*, letting the words sound in my heart center as a kind of sonic bellows for the seed. I become aware of yet more company, a great host of men and women doing the same, chanting and walking, bearing their flaming seeds. We walk towards Worley Hill where Michael awaits us with his fiery sword.

It's familiar, it's habitual, this morning *kinhin* through Copley Wood to the egg-whorl of Worley Hill a very old practice indeed. It takes us an hour to reach the designated spot, as indicated by a cooperative gnome whose directions I have been following. We sit down, the three of me. Three because clearly there is me, the American Grail Knight with full persona accouterments and accompanying physical body; there is the light form of this same self, that avuncular, wiser "higher" fellow who stood behind me, hands on my shoulders, when I sat on the edge of Magotty-Pagotty; and there is the flaming seed itself, antecedent and parental to us both. There's Blaise, too, which adds another forty million to the throng at Worley Hill today.

We sit before a grassy dell with an old oak tree directly behind me. The others—Blaise, gnomes, inner Round Table, the great host of earlier knights—sit around me in concentric circles. Michael stands

before us, waiting for me to complete my preparations. I recapitu-
late the Great Stream sequence—the four bowls, the seed, the golden
pillar, the four white pillars, rainbow, white background, the flowing stream of light. Then I breathe Love from Above like a blowtorch
to the flaming seed until it swells and becomes twice the size of my
body with me inside it. It forms a membrane of fire, a flaming eggshell around me, like a personalized cosmic egg. I sit inside this egg
or cocoon of fire. Michael lowers his sword, its tip blazing fiercely
with celestial light, and touches the egg around me. Fire to fire and
only fire remains. A line of light opens up between my heart and
crown chakras. I breathe, then breathe some more. Time passes. When
I open my eyes, the ceremony is finished and everybody has left.
Inside my chest a luminous membrane like an eggshell envelops the
flaming seed.

I walk vigorously down the hill to ground myself and when I reach
my seat at Magotty-Pagotty, Blaise greets me with a mischievous
grin. "Look at your seat now. There appears to be something for
you." It is an egg the size of a muskmelon. Inside the egg is a squirming baby gnome. He is fully dressed and winks at me like a puppy
sticking its nose out from a wicker basket as the children run into the
room. "Guess you'd better take the fellow home," Blaise says.

A Grail Knight gets asked to do a lot of strange things while on the
Quest. I try to work out the logistics. I'm riding a bike and it doesn't
have a basket and I don't have a knapsack, so the only course is to
mount the baby gnome in his egg playbox on my head and wheel
out of Kingweston Cedar Walk with live cargo aboard. When I roll
into Wick at dusk and come through the front door, Russell announces dinner, then stares at my head. "What's that on your head,
Grail Knight?" he asks laughing.

51

MERLIN TALKS ABOUT HIS STONE

gnome on my head indeed. Before I went to bed last night I put the gnome egg on top of my bookshelf, regarding it with disbelief. Obviously I had no idea what to do. Russell knocked, leaned in the doorway, grinning with that familiar air of impending bad news, then said, "Get out your schedule book, Grail Knight. You have an appointment at—guess where?—Worley Hill tomorrow at dawn. The Seraphim made it for you."

So it's seven a.m. and barely light as I stow my bike in the bushes at Kingweston Cedar Walk and greet a gnome who tells me he is to be my guide. A visit to old Worley wouldn't feel right if I didn't get lost at least once in transit. Thus, at a critical moment in my transiting Copley Wood, the gnome points to the left—which means, start bushwhacking here—while the trail continues on straight, which means, enjoy easy walking here. Twenty minutes down the primrose path of comfort the Grail Knight is lost and foundering and retraces his steps humbly back to the gnome who waits patiently for his errant charge. I follow him obediently, and soon we arrive at a little dell that girts a massive beech tree like a sacred penumbra. Thanks to my Boy Scout's independence, I'm an hour late. Late for what?

A Grail Knight gets accustomed to strange goings-on, but even I am slightly nonplussed. There is a class in session—on the Other Side—and I am flattered and chastened that the professor has delayed the morning seminar for my arrival. The professor looks remarkably like—no, it's just too strange to dwell on the suspicion that it's Ben. I sit down, take off my wet sneakers, settle into my breathing, do some Blaise visualizations of flames and bowls and pinpoints of light—as a kind of cognitive calisthenics—and prepare myself for class like a good Grail schoolboy.

Before me stands a golden altar and around this sit many other Grail Knights of both genders. We appear to be seated inside an eight-sided room. With the beech tree, the altar, and the octagonal design, it's as if I am in a live version of the standard elements of the icon for the *Ananda-kanda* inner heart chakra, according to Tantric tradition. That esoteric chakra, according to the traditional icons, has eight petals, a wish-fulfilling tree called *Kalpataru*, and a jewelled altar upon which stands a great vase overflowing with nectar. Through the *Ananda-kanda*, the spiritual aspirant supplicates the higher divinity for enlightenment through a special conduit that connects directly with the crown chakra. Here, in the live version, a radiant spiritual being—the professor transfigured—stands behind the altar as if at a lectern.

"Merlin, the Sirian initiate, comes before you," a voice announces. Then Merlin speaks. "The consecration of the Grail occurs when the elements that comprise physical base are transmuted into a resplendent whole. This is signified by the golden bowl of the heart. Through this golden bowl, the elements are harmonized." Merlin bids me to place my heart bowl, filled with blue light and with a white flame of the seed burning above, upon the altar. "What do you wish, Grail Knight?" he asks me.

"Enlightenment and peace for all beings," I answer.

"You won't be lying in bed in the mornings with pretty Grail Maidens as often as you might wish, should you get your wish."

"Oh. Well. At least sometimes, then?"

"So be it. I touch your four bowls with this sword. See the wheels of light in each bowl, filled with blue light yet also empty. Drink from the Grail on this altar. Let the blue light of the Christ circulate through your body, your physical base. Good. Now, consider the Grail. It is an ancient symbol, older than you can conceive. Yet it is only a symbol of a vast and grand project." As Merlin speaks, my chakras light up like neon wheels and begin rotating like planets. Then he resumes.

"Consider the human soul in the physical body as like a block of unshaped grey stone, a large rectangular mass. Over the eons, through the incarnations, the soul slowly sculpts this grey stone. This stone is the unmade heart of consciousness. It is an unshaped 'raw stone' of potential. It is the Philosopher's Stone in its inchoate infancy. Through living in time, through transiting the zodiac, through consolidating the Round Table, you eventually sculpt this stone into a chalice. Through your wisdom, you will transmute this stone into a golden chalice, into the Grail. Then it may receive the Christ. Then it may flush with the glorious light of the Philosopher's Stone. In the end, you bring it back to the Fisher King at his golden halls of Ogygia.

"Originally and finally you are a Blazing Star. In between you enter into many bodies of manifestation of progressive density. You enter into innumerable incarnations on Earth and elsewhere for the purpose of experiencing the fourteen celestial rays of the Great Bear and the twelve zodiacal energies. Why? To bring this Blazing Star to life within the grey stone and to sculpt a human form from it, illuminated from within by the Star, which is what you are. By the Grail you may know the Solar Logos, the great spiritual Sun.

"The Solar Logos is a point of knowing, of cognition, of unification, whereby the multiplicity of voices of stars, planets, and other stellar consciousnesses is apprehended and made coherent. As an ordinary human you tend to hear them discordantly; through the Grail you begin to hear them harmoniously. Truly, the Grail is formed out of the energies of the Solar Logos, which is the Word of the Sun; it is a Sun sculpture. The Sun is the seed from which the Grail grows. It is the basis for the consecration of the Grail."

This concludes Merlin's seminar. I stare at my notes like dictation from a foreign language. Standing up to stretch, my legs wobble as they tingle awake. I admire the smooth shank of the beech tree and thank it for its inspiring "treeness." A hoary, bearded tree spirit, much like Tolkien's Ents, emerges from the beech and gives me an acorn. Then the gnome guides me out of the woods again; as we make the hour's walk back to my bike, I rummage my mental files for information about the Solar Logos. The works of Alice Bailey and the teachings of her Tibetan mentor, Dhjwal Kuhl, come to mind. He says that the solar system is a twelve-petalled lotus wherein each petal is made of 49 smaller petals; the whole lotus flower seen from the higher cosmic planes resembles a vast blue lotus. Within this blue lotus are the seven planetary spheres, each a planetary logos, each one of the Seven Heavenly Men. These "Men" are aspects of the life of the Solar Logos who is known as the Grand Man of the Heavens and the Great Heart of Love.

As such, the Solar Logos bears the interpenetrating aspects of the central spiritual Sun, the Heart of the Sun, and the physical Sun. The Solar Logos is the "sum total of manifestation within the solar system, which vibrates to the steadily increasing measure set by him," says Dhjwal Kuhl. The Grand Man holds a position equivalent to "the nucleus of life at the center of the atom" and embodies the "ultimate perfected principle of love-wisdom." This principle, also known as a Dragon of Wisdom, is a sentient, evolving being, and in its form as a twelve-petalled cosmic lotus, the Grand Man is one of the twelve petals in the heart of the Cosmic Logos. In other words, the Solar Logos is one of twelve members at a cosmic round table of similar solar logoi. Blaise likes the idea of the Solar Logos, too, for they whisper in my mind, "We feel the Sun is a concept with balance and is truly cosmological. The Sun doesn't step down energy but transmutes it to produce varying vibrations within planets reciprocally involved with its orb."

Back at Wick, after a massive, calorically-buoying lunch, I address myself to less abstruse subjects than the life of the Solar Logos. It's about that gnome on my head—well, on the bookshelf. He's still there, that little grinning mystery from the Other Side, and I'm still here, nonplussed and incredulous. It's one thing to tramp about the woods with gnomes; at the end of the day, they go home and the Grail Knight goes home, and we spend the night resting in different dimensions. There's always room for private doubt: do gnomes really exist? Do Grail Knights really exist or am I imagining it? But when you have a gnome, an infant no less, resident in your private chambers, there is no time off for idle disbelief; you feel your understanding of the world abuts a mystery. Surely gnomes can fend for themselves; they don't really eat food, so I doubt he's hungry. And surely he could run off back to his people any time he felt like it, yet here he sits in his eggbox, cheery and bouncy. Then it comes to me. The Fairy Dell! That seems my best bet for finding a foster home for this Copley Wood castaway.

I bathe the gnome egg in golden light, set him on my head again, and present my little friend's case to the gnome on guard at the entrance to the Fairy Dell track. When we arrive at the Dell, I explain the situation again to a group of gnomes and sylphs. The fairies wheel around us in an incorrigibly happy dance. Will you look after this gnome and find him a home, I ask the gnomes. They agree. I hope I've done the right thing. There is no *Miss Manner's Guide to Excruciatingly Correct Gnome Etiquette* that I'm aware of. Blaise thinks it's a good joke and has no advice to offer me. "You are dealing with other guidance. We have a degree of provincial authority, you might say. We are aware you need other assistance on occasion."

In the evening, Russell pops in to tell me I'm expected at Beckery in Glastonbury at four a.m. the day after next. This will take some fancy logistics. I make arrangements to stay with a friend in Glastonbury and pedal the sixteen miles into town in the late afternoon, arriving at tea time. On the long ride in, I suddenly remember something the celestial woman said to me last time I was at Beckery: "We place a wreath of bees on the head of the stone bull. Remember Hermes." With a sigh, I enter this on my ever-expanding list of things I don't understand in the Quest.

52

THE STONE BULL RETURNS TO BECKERY FOR A SONGFEST

hree-thirty a.m. and the Grail Knight walks through the silent neighborhoods of Glastonbury towards Beckery. The mound is warm and dry, a surprising dispensation promising a Grail Quest adventure in which at last I will not muddy and soak my trousers, socks, and sneakers. *O Michael uplift us now!* I chant as my brother and Tudor Pole stand with me. The Seraphim are here, too, taking the form of slender winged stalks of flame. I settle into the four golden bowls image then breathe as Love from Above. After a time, I see something.

A golden plain with a golden temple in its midst; the temple door is open. Somebody asks me, "Who has opened the door for you?" It must be that handsome guy in light, the Higher Self I met at Magotty Pagotty. A hive of golden bees with black stripes flies out the temple door and makes a wreath of seven coils around my head. "We place a wreath of bees on the head of the stone bull," the Beckery woman says again, although, at the moment, I do not see her. As I look more carefully, the wreath comprises seven bees.

Over the next hour, the identity of each of the "bees" is revealed to me. One by one, each bee turns into a woman, and I contemplate her face. Their beauty is breathtaking. They are twenty years old and twenty thousand, hauntingly beautiful preRaphaelite faces. The Beckery woman whispers to me to love each woman, to become one with her. Names are whispered: *Electra. Merope. Taygeta. Maia. Asterope. Alcyone. Celaeno.* The seven women form a circle around me just as the bees had wreathed my head. "We are sisters," a voice says. "See us make a ring around your heart bowl. Hear the choir. See the stone."

A stone about three feet tall, one foot wide, and egg-shaped cohabits the space where I sit. First, I see the stone within the heart Grail bowl, then everything expands and I'm inside the stone and it sits inside the golden bowl. I can also see the form from outside, a glorious light sculpture. I breathe Love to it, especially to the stone; soon there is a burst of light from within the core of the stone. A bull's head with horns is revealed. And with this Taurean revelation comes the exaltation of a large chorus in full song. Now I see eleven more identical stones, each containing a different live figure of the zodiac, each one, like this stone, set like a diamond on a broad avenue of light. This stone bull at Beckery sits on the Michael Oroboros line. Wait a minute: seven bees, seven sisters, a horned bull—those are the names of the seven stars, the Seven Sisters of the Pleiades, which are a star cluster in the neck of Taurus. So the Pleiades, the Sailing Ones whom the gods turned into doves to escape the lascivious advances of Orion, have some kind of anchorage here at Beckery, but what about the choir?

The ancient Welsh *Triads* speak of Three Perpetual Choirs, or *gyfangan*, of the Island of Ynys Prydein. *Gyfangan* means a harmonious song or uninterrupted choir. According to the *Triads*, one choir was "at the island of Afallach, and the second at Caer Caradawg, and the third at Bangor." Afallach is Avallach, which means Glastonbury, which is why folklorists have always believed that one such choir was situated somewhere at Glastonbury. "In each of these three places," explains the *Triads*, "there were 2400 religious men; and of these, 100, in turn, continued each hour of the twenty-four hours of the day and night in prayer and service to God, ceaselessly and without rest forever." My guess is that the Choir of Afallach is situated right here at Beckery, the Bee-Keeper's Island.

But what about the bees? The Welsh *Triads* tell us that ancient Britain had three names: before it was settled, Myrddin's Precinct; after it was settled, the Island of Honey; then later, the Island of Prydein (or Britain). Obviously, an island of honey needs bees. Long ago, writes Gino Gennaro, Hermes "mingled his celestial bees amongst men and, through the seven arts, imparted the canonical, planetary knowledge to humankind." He writes that Hermes and his "bees" installed and supervised the planetary grid matrix and stayed around long enough to instruct humans in the spiritual geomancy of its maintenance. In Blaise's vocabulary, this would be the second or third dome presence. Gennaro implies that Hermes' "celestial bees" were perhaps angels or highly evolved humans or other spiritual beings—maybe Pleiadians, for that matter—that were once active in the formative days of Earth.

Hermes and his bees established "a new terrestrial tree of life, composed of twelve special vibrating stones placed on each planetary meridian;" this "tree" comprised a kind of planetary geomantic ritual calendar around which full-moon festivities were organized, Gennaro adds. Maybe this stone at Beckery was one of those vibrating stones. Hermes is further implicated through the iconography of the Hermetic Shield. In at least one version, the shield is in the form of a bee itself: it features two crossed keys at the top, a beehive mound underneath, a man's head with three bees underneath. Hermes, the legendary messenger of the Gods, the fleet-footed communicator with winged sandals, was the son of Zeus and Maia, who was one of the seven Sisters of the Pleiades. He was the god of the crossroads and set stone *herms* at such places to protect and guide wayfarers. Hermes unlocks the doors to the Mysteries; his esoteric teachings, including instruction on geomancy, are recorded on the Emerald Tablets.

There is one more bee connection to consider. Melchizedek, according to Hebrew legend, was the first king of Jerusalem, but esoteric tradition says he came from the planet Venus bearing three gifts to humanity: wheat, asbestos, and the honey-bee. Now, in conventional astrology, Venus is linked with the constellation Taurus and is said to "rule" it. This gives us a Venus-Pleiades connection. "The Pleiades are connected with the evolution of mind in the Seven Heavenly Men, and Venus was responsible for the coming of mind to the Earth," says Djwal Kuhl.

My thoughts are so taken up with Hermes, bees, the Sisters, the stone bull, Venus, and choirs that I am back at Wick before I've even gone through the routine complaints about the long bike ride. I'm not even ruffled that somebody has eaten all the almond-raisin granola I had stashed in a secret container in reserve for today's breakfast. The day passes quickly and happily as I browse my reference books for more clues, hot on the trail of another Grail Quest mystery. After dinner, Blaise arrives with some answers.

"We come as we are. We come as a Blazing Star, within the stable sphere of consciousness. We come as the pinpoint of light surrounded by the sapphire blue of Christed light. We come in the sphere of stable consciousness. We surround you all with the wall of lilac flame. We surround this dwelling with a lilac flame of 2.3 magnitude. We bless it well. Breathe with this lilac flame for a moment." As we do, I see a nearly blinding lilac bonfire raging in the atoms of the house, the furniture, our bodies, even our thoughts and awareness. Then Blaise resumes.

"Good. We are most pleased to be with you tonight. This visit is inherently rushed as we need to impart several days information before going on an important mission in another part of your universe. We come with a purpose. We ask that you, Grail Knight, visit the place called Ivy Thorn later tonight for the equinox. We say that Russell and Berenice here, and Hilary in Cambridge, will be with you but in their light bodies. We will take them. We wish, if you wish, for you to say these words at Ivy Thorn: 'O Knights of the Grail. O Knights of the Grail. Be with me now. The time is right for a blessing to come on. I write a book. Help me to sharpen my sword that I may speak the truth from this, the Ivy Thorn.' You will be shown more then. We wish to say you are doing very well. Your experiences this week are favorable and in sequence with external events. We are most pleased you have re-established this link. It is crucial on many levels, though we do not want you to be in any way full or empty of your self-importance. We will stay with you a little if there is something you wish to ask."

"Well, Blaise, I'll start at the top of my list. About these Perpetual Choirs and the one at Afallach. What are they?"

"Over the course of England, three heavenly choirs have been established on the landscape. They were activated from a divine source. Glastonbury is the center of one choir. The Choir is singing to the Earth. The choirs are a reflection of a heavenly model related to three different aspects of consciousness translated to Earth. The old themes were Faith, Hope, and Charity. The new themes are Humanitarianism, Individuation, and Idealism. They will be revealed later in Man's evolution should humanity develop along the lines intended. They are the theme music of Albion, which changes with each epoch. In their long history, the Choirs were more active in the past, although they are still active in the astral body of Gaia. Their activation again is imminent through human consciousness when they will be involved with healing."

"Okay. Good, and thanks. Now, how about these special vibrating stones that Gino Genarro refers to? Did I see one of those at Beckery this morning?"

"Correct. These were actual stones brought by the Cosmic Chaplains under instruction of those that energized and activated them. They were planted over the surface of the Earth for the benefit of all beings that were to come into existence or to visit here. There were twelve such stones. There is one in Glastonbury still. It is the so-called egg-stone behind the Abbott's Kitchen at the Abbey. Once it stood at Beckery as you saw. The stones, as you know, are materially visible. Each stone has its time, though they all resonate in harmony and are in resonance with one another."

"I gather each stone was placed on a Oroboros line like the one running through Glastonbury and Beckery. Does that mean that one stone was a Taurus resonator, another a Capricorn, another a Pisces, and so forth?"

"We understand your question, but there are certain misconceptions in it. Remember at all times that much of the symbolism involved in descriptions pertaining to the zodiac are humanmade and are relevant only to humans. From our point of view, things are more cyclical and interdependent. It's not so much constellations and stones but rather matter vibrating in synchronicity. The stones are synchronously resonating in reciprocal maintenance with each other and thus feed the Earth. The Earth reciprocally maintains the relationship of interdependence. Each of the twelve stones resonates at a particular frequency that is in sympathetic harmony with certain astrological constellations. The most relevant point here is the relationship. The Earth is an active force as well as receptive. Each celestial, terrestrial, and lunar body is in sympathetic resonance with the others, travelling at tremendous speed through infinite space."

"It seems that Hermes and Michael occupy the same Oroboros line in Glastonbury, and, in other matters, there seems to be an overlap between them. Are they the same being?"

"Different or the same, same or different? We aren't sure. Know what we mean? It is like a candle flame used to light another candle—is it the same or different flame? Hermes was the first candle. Then Michael."

"Blaise, who is the celestial woman I've seen at Beckery?"

"Someone important to you, in fact, to all of you and your work. Her name is Nada, Master Lady Nada. Her name means 'sound.' She is master of one of the celestial rays of the Great Bear and as the Magdalene, worked closely with the Christ during his Earth mission."

"So Lady Nada is St. Bridget, the Bee-Keeper of Beckery Island?" I ask with mounting excitement. We're getting some serious answers tonight.

"Correct."

"Were the bees real bees or something symbolic?" I continue.

"Oh dear. You take things so literally."

"Your energy seems like a bee," Berenice says.

"That's not surprising. We work together for one who ascends higher than the Highest. We not only serve together; we are in rapport with many, simultaneously and synchronously, throughout time and space over millennia. We are that consciousness of unified educatory means. Bees work together to gather honey. We work together to return all to the Source. We put back into harmony that which has been out of harmony. We come to replace that which is displaced. O how happy we are, a tiny, tiny Blazing Star."

"What about Melchizedek? How does he fit in?" Russell asks.

"Melchizedek was a man born on Earth. He had contact with the Cosmic Chaplains, those that came from other than Earth, or what you call extraterrestrials. He was aware of the domes when they were here. Melchizedek was a son of the Mastery of Destiny and was later King of Salem."

"He's supposed to have come from Venus," I begin. "And Venus is supposed to have a kind of older sister relationship with Earth. What is really involved here?"

"Venus is a mediator between the One who is predominantly interested in Earth and those that are not. Some misinterpret Venus' role and give it more importance than is due. Venus is in relation to Earth more like a stepping-stone."

"Okay, but then how do the Pleiades fit into this picture?"

"At present, there are more craft than you can imagine surrounding your planet. They exist in the fourth dimension. If you are in danger, they will appear. At present, you and others are protected by the chaplains from the Pleiades. That's because part of your lineage is Pleiadian."

"Blaise, do you really mean craft in the sense of ships?" Russell asks.

"No. All angels have around them an energy field. The Pleiadians are not angels, but they are able to bilocate and manifest in their energy bodies invisible to humans and create energy fields that could be described somewhat inaccurately as craft. Unfortunately, many of the people who get involved in the UFO movement are still corrupted by paranoia. Remember? We come as we are. We come to remind you. Oh dear, you can't understand it all, so forget it."

"Where are you going tonight, Blaise?" Berenice asks.

"We are going quite rapidly towards a nebula called Arcturus. It is a single star with another star close by. That's where we're off to, to put something in order there. We will be talking like this to a friend of ours that lives on a planet there. From there, we will be going for a couple of days to the Pleiades to talk some more friends."

"How long will it take you to get there?" Russell asks.

"We have already explained we are in transit and this is not measurable in your time, not exactly. But you could say six to nine hours. Travel to us is like looking through a telescope and seeing yourself at the point you're looking at. However long it takes for your concentration to merge with the object is the amount of time it takes to get there. We are, as you know, quite a large group of potential manifestations. Therefore, it requires a lot of concentration."

"Are you bringing all forty million?" I ask.

"You'd be very lonely if we did. Anyway, we're just basically six tiny little stars."

"Are they interested in the Arthur story on the Pleiades?"

"They follow your progress with keen interest, certainly on the Pleiades. In several of the planets within the Pleiades system, though not so much in the planet surrounding Arcturus, they hear live reports from us. Many of the teachers waiting to incarnate on Earth at present reside on the planets surrounding the system of Pleiades. Therefore, they have interest in the way humans are being prepared for their inception."

"How do you talk to the people on the Pleiades?" Berenice asks.

"We would be most happy to describe this process to you. It is done with mirrors."

"Blaise, are you joking?"

"Yes, this is a joke. We do it by direct thought transference through the beings who are attuned to us wherever any of us are. We can manifest in form or without it. We have roughly a limitless number of manifestations. We can transfer our consciousness to a limitless number of sentient beings at any moment, to as many who receive our direct thought or consciousness transferences as are able to step down and transfer this to many others. They are simultaneous, spontaneous thought reciprocations in consciousness. Receptive consciousness is all that's required. Knowledge of Nimitta and absorption in this brings a point of conscious contact, and this opens up communication. Also, humor is necessary. It is impossible for us to be in thought transference with those who have no humor. Some of the Masters in Shambhala cannot contact us because they have no humor. It's very foolish. It limits possibilities. If you take yourself as consciousness too seriously, you limit that consciousness and pre-clude the possibility of communication with Nimitta."

"Are you the angelic Aristophanes, then?" I ask.

"Aristophanes wasn't funny. We also know bliss and rapture. Hu-mor is the crack in the door to let those more profound states enter consciousness. People on the Pleiades, of course, have humor. No-body can communicate with us without certain conscious prerequi-sites. Other sources are more accessible. It's just the way things are. We think you think too much. Look before you, each of you, look now. We will show you something. We'll leave you now with a smile on your faces. Go well, tonight, Grail Knight."

We're silent for a few moments as we perceive what Blaise shows us.

"I saw a ladder with a star at the top," Russell says.

"I saw silvery exploding fireworks," Berenice says.

"I saw myself grinning wildly, holding a big blue box of laundry detergent called *All*, as in the answer to *all* your questions, and Blaise was standing behind me, grinning."

Russell and Berenice go off to bed while I climb into the Citroen at fifteen minutes past midnight and set out for Ivy Thorn Hill, which is just behind Street. As I drive, Blaise shows me something else. Forty million angels with sunglasses are hitch-hiking in deep space. One of them holds up a handwritten sign; written in lilac magic marker on cardboard it reads, "Arcturus, if you wish." The Blaises nudge one of them to stick out his thumb. He blushes, never having hitched a ride before, but puts out his thumb as the Millennium Fal-con storms by. "Those guys gotta be kidding," grumbles Hans Solo to Chewbacca. "This crate's only rated for Seraphim and that's two million too many for me any day of the week." But Chewbacca in-sists and the Falcon wheels around and stops to pick up the Blaises. When the hatch opens, only six stars no bigger than fairy dust twinkle into the ship.

53

"O Knights of the Grail: Be With Me Now"

Michael uplift us now. O Michael uplift us now. I chant this repeatedly on the drive to Ivy Thorn Hill. The Citroen doesn't have a radio anyway. In the brief interstices of my concentration, a petulant voice protests, "But why do I always have to go alone? Aren't there any other Grail Knights out there anywhere?" This will be my first visit to Ivy Thorn. It is unrelievedly dark when I turn off the car lights in the small pull-out at the top of the hill. I never thought to bring a flashlight and I don't see well at night. But as I step out of the car into equinoctial mystery, I marvel at the stars glittering through the translucent rosy dome over Ivy Thorn Hill.

A gnome walks up and introduces himself as Mattingley, offering me his hand to guide me through the woods. Ah, I see I am given a little test of faith. Here are the elements. I don't know where to go. I can't see a thing it's so dark. A gnome's hand has no palpability. Yet I must take his hand and let him guide me. Okay, but not too fast Mattingley, old boy. At one point, I ram up against an unyielding web of branches and resort to a box of matches to light my way out of the *cul de sac*. It's not Mattingley's fault. I tried to take a short cut. He points to a dim pathway on the hill, and suddenly I stand on reliable ground again, and my feet happily tred a series of stone steps going downhill: six, eleven, fifteen, a couple steps to the right and I sit down on a reasonably level patch of ground. It's one-thirty a.m. and showtime.

"O Knights of the Grail. O Knights of the Grail. Be with me now.

The time is right for a blessing to come on. I write a book. Help me to sharpen my sword that I may speak the truth from this, the Ivy Thorn." I recite Blaise's litany eight times, blushing less with each recitation. After all, who can hear me, besides Mattingley, and he's on assignment like me. A brilliant pinpoint of light appears over the trees in front of me, then Blaise stands behind me, with Russell, Berenice, and Hilary, as promised, if not exactly in their pajamas, at least in their light bodies. I sit quietly for about fifteen minutes and watch the Saturday morning cartoons on the astral plane like a solitary patron in the cartoon theater as the projectionist flips through a rapidfire sequence of dreamlike images. Insignificant *makyo*, nothing to warrant a whack from any cruising Zen masters; anyway, most Zen masters would be tucked into bed at this time of night, their *kyosaku* under the pillow. Tired of the programming, I practice my four bowls visualization. Now, at one forty-five, as if a switch has been flipped, the astrality promptly concludes, the air clears, and my bowls are set on an altar before me as a multidimensional golden sculpture. A huge stillness breathes celestially through Ivy Thorn.

The Archangel Michael stands before me surrounded by a large circle of men and women. I scan the faces for somebody familiar, but these are all brothers and sisters of the Grail whom I have not met in the flesh, not yet. I withdraw my sword but notice with dismay that, although the point blazes impressively with light, the edge is blunt and rounded. Grail Knights with swords that have the edge of a butter knife do not excell in this work. Through my sword, I glimpse, alternately, a man in white robes seated on a throne (reminiscent of the Fisher King from Ogygia) and a cradled infant. I periodically repeat my Grail litany like a persistent songbird and enjoy this sense of Sangrail community and welcome.

As if somehow on cue, all of us withdraw our swords from the stone of our being bodies and brandish them as an explosion of rainbow light envelops us: balls and blazes of color as thousands of Grail Knight swords are upraised in honor of Michael, chief patron, initiator, and protector of Grail Knights. We are a circle of committed swords making a nimbus about Michael, who stands before the living sculpture of the four golden bowls on the altar. Our gesture of removing the sword from the stone somehow creates the Round Table from us. All of our swords are a part of Michael's single great sword. Apparently my sword was taken from me momentarily because here it is being handed back, its tip diamond-sharp and fiercely gleaming. We hammer our sword edges against Michael as if he were an anvil. Michael sweeps the circle of Grail Knights with his sword, dubbing each of us on the shoulders as if lighting a thousand straw torches from his single flame.

Now someone speaks, possibly Michael, although Blaise says archangels usually speak only through intermediaries such as other angels. "Welcome to the Eye of the Bull, Aldebaran in Taurus. See the illumined eye of the bull grow red with us in its middle. See the Seven Sisters surround the stone on his neck. This is your emblem, your shield. You will recognize it among yourselves. And now we give you a blessing."

A woman of unspeakable beauty and grace appears, her form robed in emerald, exuding warmth and love, her face veiled. I strain to see her face, breathing Love from Above like a frenzied bull at the long galloping end of a pasture. Then a voice like Russell's says, "You can't see the face of the Goddess and live through it, man." A voice like the Grail Knight's replies, "But that's just in the myths." A voice like Berenice's says, "This *is* a myth."

I don't know who this celestial woman is; maybe it's Lady Venus, or Dante's Beatrice, or the Gnostics' Sophia. A Grail Knight finds that often it's like being in Hollywood and knowing that somebody famous and important has just walked by, except, since you don't watch *Entertainment Tonight* or read *People* magazine, you just can't place the face or recall the celebrity's name. Anyway, the celestial woman stands beside Michael and anoints all our swords with an emerald wand, making the tips flush emerald all at once. Then she speaks.

"We must make Earth a sacred planet. That is my commission and yours as well. We take our inspiration from this, the illumined

Eye of the Bull." Then Blaise nudges me to offer a closing benediction, dictating it as I go. "O Knights of the Grail. We leave now with this blessing from the Lady Above. We will remember this night when we gathered and spoke the truth at this, the Ivy Thorn."

I can hardly wait to drive home and wake up Russell and Berenice and tell them what we did. I bound up the hill and skip across the grass to the Citroen, finding I can see quite well in the dark now. My eyes have finally adjusted. I'm so elated. At last, a celestial beehive of us, a planetary Round Table of Grail Knights from all over. I wish I could have met a few of them, gotten names and addresses. Maybe somebody knows some good Blaise jokes. I walk into Wick at three a.m. half-hoping Russell will be waiting anxiously for me at the front door. The house is silent. I'm too wired to sleep, so I perch like a mad bee on my bed, buzzing around the Grail Castle, stinging everything in sight with Love from Above. Eventually, I topple off into sleep because when I open my eyes it's seven-thirty in the morning and Russell is shaking my feet to wake me up. "Go on then. Tell me what happened," he says, handing me a cup of Earl Grey. When I finish my account, he nods in agreement. "That's about what I remember, except at the beginning I saw the four of us descending a golden staircase, then we walked through a golden courtyard outside a golden temple. Crikey. You know what I think? These guys really go in for the gold!"

I spend the next couple of days basking in the itch of my heavenly bee sting, waiting for Uncle Blaise to return from the Pleiades. I am just loading up the dishwasher and wiping the kitchen counter clean and turning on the tea kettle when Berenice tells me our avuncular comical angels have arrived. I practically run to the livingroom.

"We come as we are. We come as a Blazing Star. We come as a diamond point of light surrounded by the sapphire blue of Christed consciousness, encircled in gold, the ray of solar splendor, and all of this within the stable sphere of consciousness. We roll toward each of you. Breathe with your love, as Love from Above...." As Blaise speaks, the Black Bowling Ball rolls towards me and into my brow until its diamond center is aligned with my brow chakra. "We bring

amid you the Sword in the Stone. Breathe with your love to this."
Five minutes pass in silence, then Blaise resumes. "Now discuss this
among yourselves until we return."

"Well, that was something," I begin. "A sword was pointed into
the diamond at the center of the Black Bowling Ball. Then the diamond became that rectangular slab of grey stone I first saw at Worley
Hill during Merlin's seminar. It had a concavity, and the sword was
half-inserted in this place. Then the image shifted to my heart and
became a round table with the sword again half-inserted, or half-
pulled out, from its center. Then the sword fell out and floated in
space before me. The round table disappeared and instead there was
a golden infant in fetal position."

"I saw lots of light resembling a sword in the stone," Berenice
says. "It was a golden blade. The sword and stone grew bigger and
much brighter, then the sword was removed. An angel held it, kneeling. The hilt was at his brow while the sword tip pointed diagonally
into the ground. He faced another angel who held either a book or
something spherical, or perhaps a baby."

"I saw a stone like an egg," Russell says. "Inside was a golden
sword with jewels on its handle, a ruby, and two emeralds. The
scabbard and sword hilt were positioned vertically inside my body.
Through the heart, which was shaped like a stone, was a little golden
child with a sword through his middle and head. Then an angel
dubbed a man with this sword. All of this took place in a pale green
light."

"Good," Blaise says, returning to the conversation. "Each aspect
you have each revealed is your information given to you at the Ivy
Thorn. Each of you had a different aspect revealed. This is the first
time we have revealed the nature of the Sword in the Stone."

"Do you mean the sword has three aspects and we each hold a
different aspect of the use of the sword?" Berenice asks.

"Yes. You were present by your will to witness an event in consciousness. We revealed the Sword in the Stone. Each sword each of
you saw has aspects of its truth. You will remember more as time
goes by. We have, this evening, facilitated a path in each of your

memories of an event. The work you must do draws closer now. Be prepared, if you wish. Remember, breathe as Love from Above. Know we come in many forms. We come as we are. Heal your relations with those that come. Know us in them. Respect one another. Be as Love from Above. We have suggested to Hilary that she make a trip to Wales. You could go, too, Grail Knight. We want you to go to Cader Idris. We want you to go to the Prescelly zodiac for Michaelmass. We wish you to be there at dawn until sunset. You will be guided, if you wish. We wish you to go to St. David's, a church in Dyfed. No problem. Call Hilary. She was told at the Ivy Thorn. She knows."

"Do you have time for a quick question before you go?" I ask. "Where did you come back to when you returned from the Pleiades?"

"To the proximity of your planet. If you are interested, we could tell you where. Well, it's like this. Imagine you're already somewhere, like here. Then imagine you know you're somewhere else. Well, we are in between these two. That's our rough location. We suggest you don't just dismiss us."

Blaise must know I'm not satisfied with the answer. "No, no, Blaise, I wasn't going to," I protest.

"Good. That was a joke. We leave you now. Much to do tonight. Our Love from Above, your ever-loving Blazing Star."

Blaise can quietly slip away to his condominium somewhere between here and there, but I have trouble at the mill. Hilary. I don't think she will be happy about this angelic commission. We haven't been too friendly in recent months, nor was she impressed or pleasured with my disastrous dalliance with Deborah of Charmouth.

Regarding the Sword in the Stone business Blaise has just introduced, this is serious mythic material. In the standard version of the story, upon the death of King Uther Pendragon, Merlin and the Archbishop of Canterbury organize that all the lords of the realm and gentlemen of arms should assemble at a church in London on New Year's Day to behold a miracle by which they might acclaim the next king of all Britain. Merlin would devise this miracle. As Malory relates, there in the churchyard, against the high altar, stood a great stone, like marble, four feet square; in its midst was "an anvil of steel a foot high, and therein struck a fair sword naked by the point." Letters were inscribed in gold upon the sword: "Whoso pulleth out this sword of this stone and anvil is rightwise king born of all England." The young Arthur, squire to his cousin Kay who was about to be knighted, knew nothing of this. He wandered into the churchyard desperate for a sword for Kay, as he had forgotten it at home, when he came upon the sword in the stone. "And so he handled the sword by the handles and lightly and fiercely pulled it out of the stone;" then Arthur rode off to find Kay. When everybody saw Arthur with the sword, they had no alternative but to acclaim him king—which, of course, had been Merlin's plan—because none of the knights had been able to budge the great blade. For good measure, Arthur reinserted the sword in the stone then pulled it out again. Eventually, he got the point that this minor achievement had suddenly made him King.

Just before I slip off into that same vague place between here and there, I have a waking dream. I stand on a stage before a large audience, breathing as Love from Above from the Blazing Star. I withdraw a golden sword from a golden scabbard then brandish it aloft in my right hand in triumph.

54

THE VIEW FROM THE GREAT ASTRONOMER'S CHAIR

arly morning now and I'm edging myself with trepidation into Blaise's promised "no problem" weekend of touring Wales with Hilary. She has indeed made plans to visit Wales—with her best friend Ann in honor of her birthday, I learn after phoning her. She's booked rooms at a resort hotel in the Black Mountains and is not keen about changing plans, dumping her friend off alone at a hotel and heading off with me into the wild angelic yonder. Frankly, she doesn't even want to see me.

She rings me back an hour later; very grumpily she says I should meet her in Bristol at the train station. She hasn't broken the bad news to Ann, and I haven't broken the bad news to Hilary. Blaise is sending me out on a Grail Quest weekend extravaganza with £26 in my pocket. Russell's broke; Berenice can't spare anything from the grocery money; and the kids have already emptied their own piggy banks. So Hilary will have to finance my Grail weekend in Wales.

It's that inimical cosmic humor Blaise is always talking about, that special crack between the worlds that gives us access to the very funny Nimitta. This weekend calls for a supercool Grail Knight: Mr. Ingratiation, Mr. Humble, Mr. Charity-case. Mr. History. Get out the chamois persona and don't show any cheek whatsoever!

At eleven a.m. I'm standing outside the Bristol train station with my little Grail Knight suitcase in hand trying to look friendly and innocent, but knowing I'm guilty. Hilary and Ann occupy a dark, sulky mood, which remains unpricked by conversation for two hours.

I breathe Love from Above to them from the back seat, put them in a golden tube, and run for cover inside my own blue globe in case the darts start flying my way. We reach the hotel, have a miserable lunch bathed in sunlight, and set off, the two of us, for Cader Idris in the north. Ann was fuming and sullen when we left her, without a car or companion or much to do for the weekend. Hilary is disgusted with me for being so uncommunicative these last three hours and for keeping to myself and not contributing to the conversation. Conversation? I suspect we have been travelling in different cars all morning.

"Say, Hilary, wasn't that a lovely dome over the mountain just behind the hotel? And what did you make of that amazing dome line that went right through the axis of the old Abbey?" I try to be cheerful but I know the rope is knotted precisely around my neck, and Hilary will keep it on a short tether, giving it fitful yanks when it pleases her.

"You know, you've really treated me awfully these last few months," she says. "And now you can't even tell me why I am supposed to be going with you. What am I—your royal chaffeur? I'm half-thinking I should dump you here and return for my weekend with Ann." Ah yes, and leave the hapless Grail Knight alone and feckless in Wales with a very tight itinerary, no car, no backpack, no sleeping bag, no money, and the challenge of hitch-hiking several hundred miles in order to climb a big mountain to have God knows what kind of experience.

Thus worrieth the hanged man upon Hilary's gallows. Guilt, not manna or pennies, falls from Heaven upon me as I dangle, my neck cocked in an expression of wry discomfort. The worse part of it is, I do not know why Blaise wanted Hilary to come, other than to drive me. I scour the text of Blaise's comments with scholarly zeal for clues in the syntax, for nuances, innuendoes, or implications that will make Hilary feel she must be part of this trip. Blaise asked her privately, no doubt, but the Grail Knight brought through this information in the daytime so I'm responsible for confirming her importance. Except I can't even manage my own.

"You're so evasive," she continues. "You haven't once said if you love Deborah or how you feel about her. You just give me these rationalizations. I don't blame her for throwing you out. I would have."

The tourist office in Dolgellau tells us that the only remaining accommodation in the entire town is a double bed at *Gallt yr Heddwch*, which is Welsh for "House of Peace."

Things grow vaguely more cordial between us in the evening around the time our third pint of cider starts making its tingly, tart way into the bloodstream as we sit on the front porch of a pub overlooking a lovely estuary at sunset. The rosy mist of dusk settles in tissues over the evening low tide. "So what do you know about Cader Idris?" Hilary asks in an almost friendly tone.

Fortunately, I am well-prepared for this question and ease myself into an amiable travelogue. Cader Idris, which means "Chair of Idris," is so named in recognition of its ancient tutelary deity, Idris Gawr. The Welsh *Triads* describe him as one of the Three *Gwyn Serenyddion*, or Blessed Astronomers, of the Island of Britain. According to the *Triads*, "The Three Blessed Astronomers—Idris the Great; Gwydion, son of Don; and Gwyn, son of Nudd—so great was their knowledge of the stars, of their nature and influence, that they could foretell whatever anyone might wish to know till the day of judgement." Gwydion shows up in the Welsh tale *Math Son of Mathonwy* as "the best teller of tales in the world," a master magician and shape-shifter; Gwyn is Glastonbury's own king of the red-eared hounds of hell and master of the Tor's chthonic temple.

Local tradition has it that a night spent alone in the Chair of Idris is guaranteed to produce madness, death, or poetic inspiration. Welsh tradition further personalizes Idris in the form of *Brenin Llywd*, the Monarch of the Mist, a powerful spirit who sits in the high mountains robed in grey clouds. His favorite mountain haunts include Snowdon, Plinlimmon, and Cader Idris. Brenin Llywd, the Grey King, sits in the peaks and gleans the secrets of the stars; it's further claimed that he once received in his court of mist upon Cader Idris the master of the underworld hounds, Gwyn ap Nudd and the *Cwnwybyr*, the Dogs of the Sky.

Idris, or Edris, might have been a generic sacerdotal name as mentioned in the *Quran*, where it meant "the Learned" or "the Initiated;" further, Idris is sometimes equated with Enoch, the exalted spiritual personage who achieved immortality and walked with God and bodily ascended to Heaven; he's also equated with Hermes, the fleet-footed angelic messenger and master planetary geomancer. It's even possible, if you take hints from H. P. Blavatsky, that Idris was a Nefilim, or what she calls a Dhyan Chohan, or planetary angel incarnate in the human stream. Idris, Persian accounts tell us, exhibited exemplary faith and "consecrated divine completeness" during his 365 years of life. The antique Ethiopian *Book of Enoch* recounts his journeys through the inner worlds, while a recent work by the American visionary J. J. Hurtak describes Enoch as an ascended being of the angelic rank of the Ophanim (which puts him among Blaise). Enoch, says Hurtak, is the "One who initiates into Light" by revealing the 64 keys of existence in a cosmology of light. Enoch is the master scribe of "the Father's 'Tablets of Creation,' responsible for transmitting the scientific keys of the Living Light to the Mansion Worlds of Life." These spiritual keys were originally manifested to humanity at the beginning of time, Hurtak adds.

Meanwhile, Welsh folklore says that the *Tre Greienyn*, which are three gigantic stones at the bottom of the mountain, were once grains of sand shaken loose from the shoes of the giant Idris on his way to his stoney observatory. Supposedly these stones were once erected at the edge of a pond called *Llyn Tair Graienyn*, at the base of Cader Idris. If you throw a stone into *Llyn Cau*, another small lake on the southside of the mountain, in the morning it will have found its way into *Llyn-y-Gadair* on the north side, suggesting a passageway through the mountain. A prominent feature on the summit called *Tyrrau Maur* may be the remains of a former stone circle. And there's a crag on the mountain's south shoulder called Rock of the Evil One, so named by parishioners of *Llanfihangel-y-Pennant* because one Sunday the Devil danced with abandon on the rock, scaring all honest souls away.

My discourse on Cader Idris, I'm relieved to note, is blowing the storm clouds out to sea. Just before the pub closes, Hilary orders us a fourth pint of cider, which we drink quickly. Back at *Gallt yr Heddwch*, we edge ourselves in warily at opposite sides of the cozy double bed. We agree to pretend there is a sharp sword down the middle of the bed. But Hilary whispers to me about how lovely the moon is outside the bedroom window. As I slide over to her side to get a better view, our arms wrap around each other and we fall back together with a sigh.

We're out of *Gallt yr Heddwch* before six a.m. and begin our trek up three thousand foot high Cader Idris. Our bed-and-breakfast host equipped us with a flask of hot tea fortified with milk and whiskey to wash down the cheese sandwiches he also tucked into our snack bag. The morning is spectacularly pristine. The fast rising mists are warm and soon the sun blazes over the stony crests of Idris, transforming what have been mere silhouettes of outlying hills into vivid eruptions of stone, tree, and bush. The dome over the mountain is dramatically present, quivering with light and intention. As we pick our way along the trail, I quite casually, and with no effort, remember earlier visits to Idris, most notably during that lifetime in which I inhabited the red-bearded Celt's form. Hilary accompanied me here, back then, except she was a man at the time. Our guide this morning is an amiable gnome who calls himself Bejerinen, and, when we near the summit, he shows me where to sit. Time to get down to business.

I prepare the four Grail bowls, then a voice advises me to observe what lies underneath the blue light in my heart bowl. It is a diamond point of light enhaloed by blue. "Good," the voice says. "Use this Blazing Star as a torch to light your way." I follow Bejerinen in my light body into a cave in the mountainside. The cognitive format was set down at Pointer's Ball: I sit here with crossed legs, eyes closed, attentively breathing while I also head off in a different body on the adventure in progress. I have to crawl on my stomach through a dark, narrow tunnel, which finally opens into a dazzling crystal cave. Here I sit in meditation before a small pool of clear water. A man in white robes appears bearing a golden sword whose tip is brilliant blue. Without preamble or even greeting, he thrusts the sword straight through my heart until the blade slides out through my back. Then, in another swift movement, he withdraws the blade, holding it upright before me. (A Grail Knight learns to be grateful that many of the Quest's outings are conducted in this other, less vulnerable body—otherwise, we'd never survive the training.) The flame in my chest from the Magotty-Pagotty heart seed now flames three times brighter. Apparently he hands me this blue-tipped sword, because I find myself inserting it into my spine from the head downwards so that the blade penetrates all four Grail bowls. "This is the cave of your heart," my mentor says. "You may go now."

Bejerinen leads me physically to a lower spot on the eastern cliff face overlooking a lake far below. I sit down in a tiny, sheltered dell of soft grass amid tall shafts of outcropping rock. A sword of light lies across the lake as if on a table; its tip points towards me. "Stand behind yourself," my mentor says. "Hold the sword at the hilt with its tip at the blazing light in your heart." This manuever gets me inside the crystal cave again, except this time I notice it has a dodeca-hedral form, like a twelve-petalled flower—essentially the way Tantric iconography depicts the *Anahata*, or heart chakra. The tip of the sword, presumably wielded by my mentor, pricks the center of this dodecahedral flower to reveal an emerald within, and inside this, a dark-green spirallic seed.

As nothing else seems to happen, Bejerinen and I take a short break, then he guides me to a third location closer to the summit, facing west and overlooking a different lake. Now the sword hilt rests at the base of my spine while its adamant tip blazes at my brow. It feels like Blaise's famous pinpoint of light inside the Black Bowling Ball. In fact, this pinpoint explodes into the six Blaises, making an angelic circle about my forehead somewhere in inner space. "Sit in the seat of light," my mentor says, handing me his sword.

I clasp the sword with both hands and direct the blade into the cave of my heart, pricking the skin of the emerald and penetrating the seed whorl. I beam light down the blade to irradiate the seed, but this gives me a headache. "Draw the light from your crown center," he advises. My headache vanishes as the wattage increases drawn from this inexhaustible source. "Stand in the heart. Hold the bowl with love in your hands. Breathe your love to the seed. Keep the sword bright." I become aware that a woman robed in emerald holds the heart bowl, breathing her love to the whorled seed; she is the same spiritual personage who blessed the Grail Knights' swords as I witnessed at Ivy Thorn. My mentor—Idris, for all I know—holds the sword, sending his penetrative wisdom into the seed. "This is the ray of love and wisdom. Warm the seed, then sprout it." After some time, the seed blushes a lovely spring green.

This exercise finished, Bejerinen and I relocate to another east-facing position. I sit down, get comfortable, focus my breathing, then Bejerinen guides me into a tumulus atop Cader Idris. It is night, the moon is full, and I crawl slowly through the long, low entrance into the corbelled inner chamber, which is also lit as if by moonlight. The figure of a hexagram with a circle in its center has been made on the ground with little stones. There are gaps in the structure of the hexagram, but as I breathe golden light to them, the stones draw in closer and all the lines connect, revealing the classic Star of David, which is also the traditional geometrical figure for the heart chakra. Inside the Star of David sits a pentagram, and inside this, I experience in sequence an impression of the five Platonic Solids or regular polyhedra as described by sacred geometry: tetrahedron, cube, octahedron, icosahedron, dodecahedron. These Solids are a geometric expression of the abstract quality of each of the five elements underlying all matter, respectively, fire, earth, air, water, and ether. "Penetrate the circle with your sword," says my mentor. I turn the sword like a screwdriver until a burst of light fills the circle; penetrating the light, I find electric sparks; penetrating these, atoms winged with fire; penetrating these, a pinpoint of brilliant light within empty space.

About four hours have passed. I collect Hilary, who announces she has been languishing on the sunlit rocks without visions or company and, despite the exquisite scenery, feels she might be wasting her time. I don't pursue this point because it's the door that opens into the same insoluble question she posed yesterday: why is she here? Bejerinen leads us down Cader Idris.

At a certain point on the trail, he gestures for me to place both my hands on a large, upright stone. Inside I see a pot of gold coins. I'm given three coins, one for each of us. On one side of my coin is the image of two trees, on the flip side, a horse's head; but as I start breathing as Love from Above to this tiny bas relief, it becomes cinematic and alive. The whole horse appears, then its rider, who is a Templar Knight with a pennion depicting a white cross against a red field. He lifts his visor for me to see his face: it is myself.

At the base of Cader Idris, we have a snack on the edge of a stream. Hilary approaches it to wet her toes but slips, slides in, and gets soaked. She climbs out shedding water and laughs. Bejerinen kisses her on both cheeks, looks at me with keen, marbley, blue-beaded, otherworldly eyes, then takes his leave. It takes us about three hours of steady driving to reach the village of St. David's on the southwestern tip of Wales anciently called Dyfed. We check into a bed-and-breakfast then drive around town to get our bearings. I'm not aware of it, of course, but I begin making preparations for a big mistake. "That must be the way to the church," Hilary says. "Shall we go have a look?" We can do it tomorrow morning, I answer, and suggest that instead we spend a few hours relaxing and eating in the cafe.

The seacoast village of St. David's, like Cader Idris, bears a considerable myth. According to the Welsh *Triads*, St. David's is one of the "Three Tribal Thrones of the Island of Britain," the other two being Kelli Wic in Cornwall and Penn Ryoned "in the North," presumably Scotland. Arthur is "Chief Prince in Mynyw (St. David's ancient Welsh name), while Dewi is Chief Bishop, and Maelgwn is Chief Elder." St. David's is also one of Britain's three Archibishoprics, along with York and Canterbury, the *Triads* said. Geomantic legend speaks of a former Serpent circle of stones atop Carn Ilidi, the highest hill, which is somewhat inland and northeast from the grand peninsula that probes the sea like a stony finger.

So we sit and watch the sun sink over the western sea as a crimson disc, followed by the moon rising full and rose-tinged, and then the sunrise returns flushed rubicund and we wonder as we rise from bed whether it's the same celestial body that sinks into and bounces up from the endless waves. It's Michaelmass morning and at three-thirty a.m. we drive out of St. David's to Whitesands beach. We have to complete this leg of the trip briskly so we can arrive at Prescelly zodiac at dawn, so the itinerary is tight. The moon illuminates the sea, the beach, the grassy paths and stone promontories. We walk briskly towards our destination, which in my present thinking is a stone throne that is supposedly out here somewhere at Carn Illidi. But at five-thirty we are throneless and I tune in for guidance, hoping new information will float into my hands. Where is Blaise anyway? My palms remain empty but the bottom of my stomach falls out as Hilary points out the obvious.

"Why are we out here?" she asks, quite annoyed. "Didn't Blaise say it was a church in Dyfed? That was the cathedral you didn't want to visit last night. You know, your aversion to Christianity really does you no good."

Goaded by embarassment, I practically run the two miles back along the cliff trail to the car. Hilary follows close behind me, possibly wishing she had a whip. It's bad enough to implicate her in these solitary, but God-forbid not solipsistic, Grail Quest adventures; it's bad enough to ask her to drive me around and loan me money; and it's bad enough when I am so uncool as to slide naked and interested into her side of the bed at the wrong moment, like last night; but when I can't even get the address right on my visions, we have trouble at the mill indeed. With every slap of the sea, I feel ever more wet with guilt.

"As long as we're right at the edge of the sea, I'm going in," Hilary announces. She strips naked and dashes into the moonlit ocean where she frolicks like a dolphin. I stand on the beach, not at all warm, wrapped in six layers of wool and corduroy, holding her knickers and socks. She emerges from the wine dark sea with brine streaming in rivulets down her breasts and thighs, holding a long stick before her. "I, the Lady of the Lake, present Excalibur to you, O great fool! Now give me my clothes. We have to get to that church."

The church is locked, of course. It's six-thirty in the morning. We walk around the cathedral looking hopefully for early-arriving custodians. Not finding one, I sit forlornly on the front steps, my mistake looming behind me. Things don't improve much as we head for Prescelly, which should be about a ninety minute drive from here, provided you know how to get there. I realize Blaise didn't tell me specifically where to go, and I forgot to bring a map; this leaves us with a slice of Wales approximately sixty miles in diameter in which we must find the precise location where Blaise expects us at dawn, which was an hour ago. Not to mention that outside of a few devoted (or fanatical) geomancers in Britain, nobody knows the area as "Prescelly zodiac." Prescelly is a hilly district occupying a great number of square miles. We piece together scraps of information from a few guidebooks and arrive at Pentre Ifan, a well-known and frequently visited dolmen, by eight a.m. After thirty minutes of concentration and waiting for clues to drop into the Grail bowls, I still have no idea where to go.

"Nothing? Well, let's try those mountains behind us, over there," says Hilary, annoyed. We jump in the car and drive off. Our relations are increasingly uncordial this morning. "I never wanted to make love with you," she begins. "I thought it was you who wanted to. God! I really think I'm going to jettison you tonight and rejoin Ann. I'm sure she's having more fun than I am. I can't bear the thought of another night in the same room with you. And you still can't come up with one good reason why I should be doing any of this for you. I don't need this."

The weather supports this problematic mood. The wind has picked up and the clouds are so low they seem to blanket the bare hills. Soon we'll be locked in mist. We park the car and head up what appears in the dwindling visibility to be the highest hill in the vicinity. It's a gentle, slow rise through gorse and strewn boulders. I feel so frustrated, fearful, and guilty that I can't concentrate properly on anything, inside or out. Blaise, why did you put us together knowing the personality circumstances? Why didn't you give me more specific instructions? One minute I feel fed up with Hilary and her criticisms, and the next minute she sits behind me, wrapping her arms around me in a cradle and we nap in the descending mist.

When I open my eyes again there is Blaise, standing spectrally on a rock cluster a hundred yards away with Michael looming behind them. Unfortunately, the nap hasn't refreshed me, but it has strangely focussed my irritation into a kind of fury. I pull myself away from Hilary and storm down the hill, fuming, muttering, cursing, saturated with frustration and my own incompetence. I'm so clogged up I can't hear what Blaise is saying to me. "How about some lunch?" Hilary suggests, catching up with me. "Maybe you could call Russell from the pub and he can talk to Blaise."

We pull into a pub outside a village called Spittal, and I phone the home office while Hilary orders lunch. "A completely irritated Grail Knight calling," I announce to Russell. "You wouldn't believe how much fear and guilt I've been picking up from you two this weekend," Russell remarks. "Blaise was just here and left a message for you. Ready?

'What the Grail Knight is experiencing he is interpreting in personal terms, but he need not. First, the Knight of the Grail must overcome fear. Second, the Knight of the Grail must overcome guilt. Both the Grail Knight and Hilary are not personally involved in this energy. They have wished to be of use, and they would be of better use and more openly served if they let go of their personal situations. We are most concerned for what is being said. The lilac flames of transmutation are only dimly available under such personal circumstances. There is a great opportunity near to where they are now, if they allow themselves to be guided. They have already found the right spot. We are already in the process of witnessing the reactivation of this particular temple of which the Grail Knight has seen only a small portion from where he is at present. We suggest, if they wish, that they walk to the hill that is the highest and nearest to where they are now on the telephone. It is unfortunate that he is missing a bit but we understood there would be inherent difficulties in this invitation, though we thought it worthwhile. We leave you now with our love, as we are, Blazing Star.'

"So there it is. Hit the road, Grail Knight, and get back to that hill. You were already there. Blaise called it Eagle Mountain."

A few words of clarification and a fatherly pat on the back from Blaise does wonders for me. My mood snaps back into the jovial as I hang up the phone. Hilary recovers almost instantly when I relate Blaise's comments to her. A gnome calling himself Pembroke stands at the edge of the stonefield and we follow him briskly back up Eagle Mountain through the mist to the summit. Visibility is fifty feet and diminishing, and the mist blows past like luminous shreds of rag. "Thanks, Blaise, that did the trick," I call out, waving to them. Hilary and I find a place to sit and soon I am caught up in the mighty events of Michaelmass. "We are most pleased you have rejoined the activation process," says Blaise. "This event marks the inflow of new energy into an ancient star wheel. We set it turning again on Michaelmass."

Like a journalist covering a momentous event whose implications mostly escape him, I have the impression of a huge round table sparkling with millions of stars. Angels fan towering flames around its perimeter while Michael sparks the hub of the star wheel with his sword, wielding it like a thunderbolt. The great star centers are being tuned up like interdependent clockwork, setting slowly to spin again as wheels of consciousness within the human psyche. It is as if the angels transmit celestial energy to the atoms of the stones, igniting great flames of lilac to purify them. So big and widespread is this lilac flame that it seems to burn throughout the entire zodiac, across the planet of zodiacs. Grey smoke, the fumes of human negativity, rise up from the star wheels under the transmutative pressure of the lilac flames. Angelic winds blow the thoughtforms of fear, guilt, anger, and confusion out to sea from Prescelly. What we've been feeling personally is really a quality of the psychic environmental field; possibly, at some level, the whole planet is grumpy this weekend.

Michael wears the dome over Eagle Mountain like a shimmering cape, and the gold and silver twining cord from the dome rises into space like a spiral of celestial snakes over his head. "Breathe with us as we breathe with Love to this star wheel and all the others," Blaise says. "What you see at Prescelly is only a fragment of the Michaelmass being celebrated around the world at this time and in the times to come. Many star wheels will start to turn; many stars will shine from within the Earth. Men and women may awaken to a deeper sense of the opportunity always available to them, if they wish."

By six p.m., events seem to be winding down. It's nearly dark, ideal conditions for getting lost in the mist-blanketed moors. I ask Pembroke to guide us carefully down Eagle Mountain back to Hilary's car and we make it without incident or even stumbling. When we reach Carmarthen, Hilary wants me to take a train home tonight so she can rejoin Ann, but the day's last train has already left. Then she wants us to take separate rooms but decides on two single beds in one room because the rate is cheaper. After dinner and a long discussion of the day's events, we head for the bedroom. I am not going to make my famous mistake a third time. I counsel myself on the necessities of chastity for the duration of this trip, pull the covers snug over my head, and prepare to drift off to Grail Knight dreamland. Hilary turns off the lights. Then she whispers to me.

"Grail Knight, I have this wonderful massage oil. Do you want me to rub some on your feet?" "Okay," I answer, trying to sense which way this mercurial weather is blowing. Dutifully, I stick my feet out from the covers at the end of my bed but hide my head under the pillow. Hilary rubs almond oil on my feet, ankles, then slides her hands under the covers to anoint my calves. Her hands gently massage my calves then pause. Eternity swells the room, then she laughs. "This won't do at all; forget the bloody oil," she says, pulling back the covers to get into bed with me.

In the morning, Hilary gets me on the train to Bristol with a wet kiss and a £20 note. When I read the Times, I'm dismayed at how much evil, cruelty, and upheaval has occupied the world this weekend—riots, murders, rapes, fires, violence, terrorism, political intransigence, greed, factionalism, and worst of all, indifference—while we were conversing with the angels. From star wheel to broken wheel indeed. Does a Grail Knight's efforts make a difference stacked against this kind of picture? When I arrive back at Wick at eight in the evening, I have just enough time to bathe, eat, and relax for thirty minutes before Blaise arrives for a much expected debriefing.

"We come as we are," says Blaise. "We come as a Blazing Star. We come as a pinpoint of brilliant light in the far reaches of dark within the sphere of stable consciousness. We are pleased to be with you all tonight. We are pleased to see you back, Grail Knight.

"You were to experience three levels of activation. First, the personal, at the place of transmutation where much can be transformed: Cader Idris. The second, St. David's, was the one you missed on this occasion, partly to do with your own personal difficulties in this area. We hoped you would experience the heart in an etheric sense created by humanity in the cathedral at St. David's. Third, the awakening of the energy of transmutation at Michaelmass in the landscape. You misinterpreted our activity at Prescelly a little. It was not exclusive to one site. It was more general. We chose somewhere for you within the context of what was most available at this time. We also wished you to visit these places as they have given you much that will come to light in the next few months. Much has happened to you of which you are not aware. This is okay. Don't worry. We wish to stress that for now you do not discuss this visit to Wales with anyone, even among yourselves. It must be fully internalized."

"Blaise, I'm sorry I fumed at you on Eagle Mountain."

"It has nothing to do with you. You must understand this. You still, after two years with us, take things too personally."

"But Hilary and I had lots of difficulties in the personal dimension."

"Yes, but imagine yourselves as Shakespearean characters. Hilary, as you know, is one of our very special children. We are most grateful to her. She is accompanied by us constantly. She has much to do. She has asked for a most difficult task, which sometimes her small self does not see. She has, and always will have, a Star from afar. She joins your work across what you call the subconscious."

"I'm still confused about St. David's. Even if I had remembered it was the church you intended us to visit, it would have been locked during the only times we had available to visit."

"This is incorrect. You are reluctant to ask into earthly things. You knew you were supposed to go to the cathedral, right? We arranged for someone to be there to open the door, but you got involved in other things that evening. What's gone is gone. It can be rectified later."

"That's good. The whole time at Prescelly I felt I was a journalist covering the event. You said I missed a lot. What kinds of things?"

"You were shown many wheels laid out over your Earth. What you were shown was a partial awakening across each wheel. Everything that happens at one wheel has repercussions at the others. They are light forms that are interconnected and interdependent. Even your being there affects everything. That's why you were invited. It is like calling in the journalists to cover the event, as you said. If you had not been as prepared in terms of detachment in this life, you would never have gotten there at all."

"No kidding. Well, as some angel friends of mine always say, 'We're thankful for little blessings.' But Blaise, there is another problem. While Michael was lighting up the star wheels, terrible things were happening in the world. It made me wonder what good we were doing in Wales on the grid when the world is so clearly falling apart on the streets."

"We come as we are. Remember, as Love from Above. Feel it. Be it. Be personally identified with that. You are nothing else. If you identify with other things, we have no protection for you. They are not you. What happens on Earth is neither good nor bad. Everything is arranged. We do what we are able in line with others. You do what you are able. Don't worry. What happens now is difficult for you to understand, but we will help. You must, if you wish, not think about it. Sarajevo or Prescelly: same or different? Be patient. You do what you do. Others are concerned with other things. Many are called to serve at this time. They have been returned in service as you are already aware. Don't try to see it all. See that which is your concern. The work you are being trained to do makes rapid change possible. It creates new conditions in consciousness that enable changes to develop. Often these changes are presaged by violent eruptions and disturbances. You see? Prescelly—new consciousness within; Sarajevo—disturbances and eruptions on the outside. We provide something of what you can feel as Love from Above through what you do. This will be felt by others, and they will tread on Earth differently in the future by what is written through you from us. They will be in their hearts with Earth in Her heart."

"Does this partial awakening have to do with the esoteric side of Michaelmass," Russell asks.

"Correct. September 29 is the day that Michael has chosen. It has to do with the Moon and its relation in distance to the Earth; it is further away during this time in the autumn than in the spring. The energy of all living organic matter responds to this relationship and changes its nature at this point. Also, the energy matrix of the Earth changes in polarity due to this phenomenon. Michael blesses the Earth with his sword to cleanse and shift the energy. He connects the major grid lines and tries to flush out any negative blockages."

"What about these gnomes, Blaise," I ask. "They don't look quite the way the picture books show them. Am I really seeing them? What are they?"

"Would you prefer to call them 'morphogenetic impulses from your Superconscious Mind as inspired by Blazing Star?' They are called many things. It's not important. Why not call them gnomes? Whatever is in you is out there. They are here on Earth to harmonize all elemental forces, to assist with the elemental balance, to assist in the cooperation with the human and plant kingdoms. They are involved in the conscious evolution of the being called Gaia. They are here to enact certain preset, preordained missions that can be activated only in cooperation with the human kingdom. Otherwise, they can be undisciplined and mischievous and not very constructive. Ideally, human consciousness should be interfaced with the angelic kingdom; the gnomes should assist the humans in angelic interpretations at a material level. Make space, Grail Knight. You think, feel, see, hear, you imagine you are close to a point of brilliant light. One day before we're done, we will reveal our true form amongst you. Then you will know. As you would say, it will blow you away. Look above you now. Just glance for a moment at us."

I see a refrigerator door open to reveal a fully stocked interior. Russell tells me afterwards that he saw a ladder continuously changing shape, climbing into the Milky Way and beyond into infinite space. Berenice saw Blaise as a cocktail shaker framed against the Milky Way. We thought this marked Blaise's departure, but he has a little more for us yet tonight.

"Now, continue with your questions, if you are sure you understand the proceeding remarks," Blaise says.

"Yes, I think so. I have a question about Beckery, but I don't know how to put it precisely," I begin. "It involves the Perpetual Choir and the Michael line and schedules of activation for the vibrating stones and the frequencies of—"

"Is this an encyclopedia?" Blaise replies. "Get it together, Grail Knight. Why not visit the Eye of the Bull again the day after tomorrow? The Moon of your planet touches it then at sunset. Any more questions? You see, Berenice, how it is. We show the Grail Knight a little and all the questions drip onto the floor. We love you all, before and since the Fall. We are as Love from Above, your Blazing Star."

"I guess I'll get out the mop, Berenice," I joke. "You know how it is. Wet floor, dripping with questions and all." I head upstairs for bed and dreams. I hold a newborn baby, my own, and he begins to speak. He turns into an adult Tibetan lama. I am in a house where I walk into a room Russell has just painted white over walls that were formerly lilac. It needs a second coat. My own room has large flakes of peeling lilac paint in one section, but otherwise the surfaces are smooth and thickly white. I start scraping the lilac peels for that wall's final coat of white.

55

A Lot of Gnomes
Around the Table

he Fairy Dell has become an amphitheater full of gnomes. When I got back to Wick last night, sauntering down the lane at dusk, a gnome jumped out of the hedge and said, "I'm Bomer. We wish you to visit your little baby gnome at the Fairy Dell tomorrow afternoon." Then he disappeared into the hedge again. Ah, the gnome on the head comes back. I thanked the morphogenetic impulse from my Superconscious Mind as inspired by Blazing Star and agreed to be there.

So after lunch today, when I stepped out the back door of Wick, I found the garden filled with gnomes, probably 150 of them seated cross-legged on the grass, waiting for me. They all jump up when I appear and acknowledge them, and we make a happy parade down the muddy track to the Dell. At the head of this gnomic procession, several larger gnomes carry a litter with a golden cupola, evidently transporting an important gnome. At the gate before the Dell, the gnome attendant respectfully asks me for an offering. I rummage through the Grail bowl to see whether any of the recent acquisitions might do—flowers, books, coins, acorn—but I decide instead to offer blue light from the heart bowl. The gnome fills his cup with this. On the soft, green mound of the Dell, the gnomes sit in such a way as to make a horseshoe around me; the sun emerges brilliantly from the clouds in synchronous appreciation. The gnomes each raise a placard upon which a single word is inscribed. I construct sentences from these. After I get the hang of it, I don't need to read off the cards but hear the gnomes speaking directly to me.

"Welcome to your Round Table of 144 gnomes. We are your personal Round Table of gnomes. Each Grail Knight of Camalate has such a table. We are what you make of us. This is a special day for us. Plant your heart at Camalate. We will tend the seed. We will guide you through the jousts. Here is your baby gnome whom you fished out of the Great Stream at Copley Wood. This golden gnome is our new king and will be the first lieutenant of your Round Table." Two dozen gnomes raise the cupola high above us. Its curtains are drawn open, and inside beams a golden gnome with crown and robe and amiable grin. "Dalai Gnoma! Dalai Gnoma!" the assembled gnomes chant, simultaneously applauding the young potentate.

The meeting breaks up as the sun slips behind the clouds again, but as I stand at the turnstile at the bottom of the Dell again, a new image overlays the mound. I see myself seated on the mound at the hilt of a sword of light fifty feet long, laid across a circle of twelve dozen gnomes. The gnome king sits on the sword tip. Blaise lines the circumference of the gnome Round Table. The Round Table of gnomes makes a shield over which the sword of light is placed. Inside the hill is a green stone, but it's more accurate to say the hill of soil, rock, and grass is but the outer skin of a massive emerald within. Inside the emerald stone are two coiled dragons. Underneath them is a pot of gold coins. A single gold coin is presented to me with the instructions to examine it only within the heart bowl. On the walk home, Blaise says with a chuckle, "We are aware the gnomes like you."

56

A Quick Trip to Arthur Through the Bull's Eye

ondon—I can't get the idea of making a research trip to London out of my mind. I thought I'd go to the British Museum to research a few topics, but I've been waffling on making the decision. It's a long journey and then there's the expense. The Fisher King, though rich, does not provide expense accounts for young Grail Knights. But then an old friend called unexpectedly and invited me to his flat in St. John's Wood for the weekend, and Berenice said her friend was driving into London Friday afternoon. The synchronicity settled the matter just in time for Blaise's arrival.

"We come as we are, as a Blazing Star. We surround you with the lilac flames of transmutation. We place each of you in a bubble of sapphire blue. We place within each bubble an emerald at its center. We bring the golden lines of light between you. We bring the silver cords from above. We ask that you breathe with us to this image for a few moments...."

"I saw lines of golden light like rope around the three of us," Berenice reported afterwards. "We stood under a dome," Russell said later. "The golden lines curved around, linking up lots of people, making figure eights, and everybody had this emerald inside the blue bubble in their chest. Then when Blaise mentioned the silver cords, which I saw rising up from our heads, everything dissolved into brilliant light."

"Good. We have made arrangements that will facilitate understanding of events that took place last weekend in Wales. We showed

you a large stone. It is Merlin's Stone. From it, he made the Round
Table. Before, it had the sword within it that only the true King
could remove, the one in yourselves who is true as Love from Above."

"Thanks for the nice arrangements and snappy synchronicity on
the London job, Blaise," I say.

"No problem. Open yourself to Love from Above. Remember, Grail
Knight, this is an important time. We can do much. Be what you
are. We ask, if you wish, to remember the Blazing Star."

"You're not the kind of guys I could easily forget."

"We have presented a complete picture that is constantly available to you without any effort. If you look down the right avenue,
rather than at the small bits that attract your attention, you will just
be able to write it all down. We cannot do it for you. We are at your
disposal. We just ask you to allow Love from Above. We make it
available to you. It is important for the Round Table. There is some
interference that is not of love. That is all. If you wish, visit Primrose
Hill in London. We give you all our Love from Above. Be what you
are. Remember the Blazing Star."

Merlin needs a reconsideration on a deeper level, I reflect as I carry
my cup of tea up to the Grail chambers where I sit down on my bed
for a think. Traditionally, Merlin is credited with creating the Round
Table after the young Arthur demonstrated his right to kingship by
withdrawing the sword from the stone. "This table was succeeded
by the Round Table, devised by Merlin to embody a very subtle meaning," wrote the anonymous twelfth century author of The Quest of
the Holy Grail. "For in its name it mirrors the roundness of the earth,
the concentric spheres of the planets and of the elements in the firmament; and in these heavenly spheres we see the stars and many
things besides; whence it follows that the Round Table is a true
epitome of the universe." Of course, nobody talks of Merlin creating
the Round Table from a stone, the very stone from which Arthur
withdrew the sword; they only say he put the sword in the stone.
Yet from my experiences at Cader Idris, I would have to conclude
that at least one aspect of this stone is the heart—the heart chakra,
Anahata, the stone cave of the heart, the inert, unawakened stone of

Love and Wisdom. The sword stroke penetrates the stone, like a spark of fire, activating the precious, whorled seed of new life within; from this, the Round Table eventually grows as a kind of spiritual heart flower.

How appropriate then that the Tibetan language reflects this sparking, initiatory role of Merlin's—remember Merlin brought a transmission from the ancient preBuddhist Bon of Tibet and Atlantis through to Celtic Europe—in the transliterated word for fire: *merlun*. In fact, the linguistic root of our Western or pseudo-Celtic "Merlin" is implicated as the vital principle (pranic essence) of the four elements: earth (*rlun*); water (*chu-rlun*); air (*rlun-gi-rlun*); and fire (*merlun*). Tibetan tradition also calls the vital principles of the four elements the "four gates of the sacred temple of the body." As Tibetan Buddhism scholar Lama Anagarika Govinda notes, it's important to understand that we are dealing not with "material elements or physical principles but with the vital and psychic forces and laws out of which our world is built—irrespective of whether we call it the 'inner' or the 'outer' world." So Merlin is implicated with the creation of far more than the Round Table: with nothing less than the material world from out of his Stone.

Yet this shouldn't surprise us, not if we study the ancient Welsh texts. According to the *Triads*, the Island of Britain was originally called Myrddin's Precinct; then it was called the Island of Honey; and finally, the Island of Prydein after it was conquered by Prydein son of Aedd. Myrddin Emrys, say the Triads, was one of the "Three primitive baptismal bards of the Cambro-Britons;" he was also one of the nine "impulsive Stocks of the Baptismal Bards of Britain," an institution once known as "The Chair of the Round Table." Myrddin was celebrated as the one who "knew the range of all their arts" and he was also one of the "Three Missing Ones and Losses from Disappearance" because he sailed away in his ship of glass to the Island of Bardsey where he entered seclusion in his glass house with the fabulous Thirteen Treasures of the Island of Britain. Presumably, this was a magical collection including, according to legend, a mantle, chessboard, sword, horn, chariot, cauldron, knife, whetstone, and other items not listed or remembered. Yet even with these accomplishments, Merlin took counsel with higher authorities, as Malory indicates. "Then Merlin took his leave of Arthur and of the two kings for to go and see his Master Bleise that dwelt in Northumberland; and so he departed and came to his master, that was passing glad of his coming."

So the Grail Knight's "Master Bleise" is no doubt passing glad of my arrival on time at six p.m. at Ivy Thorn, the Eye of the Bull, presumably for a bit of fancy swordwork: the undauntable Samurai Grail Knight thrashing about the hill like Zorro run amok on the young wine of his own enthusiasm. But this same jackanapes Grail Knight is not passing glad that Master Blaise is dispatching him to London on the morrow sans adequate finances. Whatever happened to pennies—pound notes would be better, or checks, if necessary—from Heaven?

No matter, because now that I'm here in the daylight—even if it is rapidly receding—I'm chuckling to see where I sat the other night at the grand conclave of Grail Knights. It's nothing more than an inconspicuous dell among the trees and brambles a small distance down the hill and on the edge of a well-trod path. Meanwhile, I reflect that if Blaise calls Ivy Thorn the "Eye of the Bull", he must be suggesting it is the star center for Aldebaran, the eye of Taurus in the Somerset zodiac.

In classical star mythology, Aldebaran (from the Arabic *Al Dabaran*) is the "Follower of the Pleiades," or the "Bright One of the Follower" (from *Na'ir al Dabaran*), so named probably because it "follows" the Pleiades, also in the constellation Taurus, across the sky. Aldebaran is one of the Four Royal Stars, or Guardians of the Sky (with Antares, Regulus, and Fomalhaut), and, as such, it is the thirteenth brightest star in our galaxy. It's been known as the Eye of the Bull since antiquity; Ptolemy called it "the Torch Bearer," the Babylonians called it *Iku-u*, meaning "The Leading Star of Stars," while an old English name for it was *Oculus Tauri*, or "Bull's Eye." And it's big: about forty times the diameter of our Sun with 125 times its solar luminosity, shining like a red (or rosy) giant some 68 light years away from Earth.

Aldebaran has a purpose in the cosmos and on Earth. "The initiate sees the New Group of World Servers brought under the illuminating power of Taurus, with the rest of humanity still under the influence of Pisces," wrote Alice Bailey in 1960. Taurus is the "nurturer of all illumination," possessing a "light-giving force" that influences and "rules" the New Group of World Servers, which, Bailey explains, is meant to work as an intermediary between the Hierarchy (of ascended spiritual teachers) and Humanity. This group is busy with "receiving light and power and then using both of these, under the inspiration of love, to build the new world of tomorrow." The Group, Bailey adds, is, at least figuratively speaking, the Bull itself, "rushing forward upon a straight line with its one eye fixed upon the goal and beaming light." The goal is to establish "a center of light" in the world and to hold up and constantly affirm this vision—and the imminence of its attainment—to one's contemporaries.

Now that I'm here at Ivy Thorn, the first order of business is to get out the Grail equipment; namely, the four bowls, the flaming seed, the emerald, the whorled seed inside that, and the icons: Venus (or the celestial Lady of Ivy Thorn) sweetly breathing to my heart, Hermes (or Idris) penetrating my brow, and the lilac flames, tying everything up in a transmutative ribbon. Then I'll wait patiently until whatever performance about to be staged on the other side of the curtain begins.

A huge emerald appears before me, many times my body size. I insert my brow sword into the six-sided green stone, place my attention at the sword tip, and will myself into the emerald as a kind of sword-assisted horizontal petard. Inside, I find a group of gnomes, or very diminutive humanlike people, seated around a table at whose center sits a black cauldron. I penetrate this cauldron, which holds a dark liquid, and enter a new dimension where I find a cabal of black-caped, mustachioed men also seated around a table—black magicians up to no good, most likely. On the right lapel of each man's cape is an insignia of two intertwined dragons: one red, one green. I penetrate the insignia, and for some time, I experience myself as a kind of jackhammer blasting through a cement wall a mile thick until I finally burst through the wall, pass through a familiar countryside, and am airborne, riding the sword through the clouds and into the stars. The destination of this rapid travel is another round table of men.

These boys look friendly. It's the familiar avuncular bunch of smiling Roshi Kapleaus, robed innocently in light grey, like the Sirian astronomers at Oath Hill. By now I should know this is my own mind's visual shorthand for Blaise, but for the purposes of the vision, I'll keep pretending its a gang of celestial Zen masters. They stand before an elegant orrery for the Earth. It's a three-dimensional holographic projection of our planet showing all the details of the planetary energy matrix or grid—domes, dome lines, Oroboros lines, zodiacs, star centers, gold and silver umbilical cords, flames, crystals, chakra petals—and it's positioned for contemplation in the middle of their round table. What a marvellous device! I could study this orrery for hours. But they want me to penetrate the center of this Earth model.

This puts me out in deep space again, a Grail Knight astronaut speeding through the snowflake star grid without a NASA spacesuit and, in fact, in my bare feet (as I removed my socks and shoes earlier for the half-lotus launch), cometting briskly towards *Megrez*, one of the seven stars in the Big Dipper of the Great Bear. The star swells and expands radically until I'm subsumed in a supernova of white and crashland on *Megrez*, an unidentified flying Grail Knight from outer space. If they get concerned about UFOs here on *Megrez*, maybe I'll make the evening news. "Barefoot Grail Knight from Earth Crash Lands. Requests Miso Soup and the Loan of a Pair of Socks and Sneakers. Says He Works for Blaise. Authorities Perplexed."

The authorities at *Megrez* have dispatched somebody to greet me. A man stands before me. He wears a gold crown, has loving sparkling blue eyes; white hair; a short, white beard; a long, gleaming sword; a shield bearing the Pendragon image (rearing dragon encased in lilac flames) and the image of the Mother of Christ with infant. In his heart is a golden Grail, and inside the Grail stands the

Christ in his human form, crowned and smiling. It takes me a few minutes to understand who stands before me.

Cheeky, slightly thick extraterrestrial Grail Knight, behold the once and future Arthur! Arthur holds up a mirror and I see myself in it, a few years older than I am now, with the same regalia of sword, shield, crown, Grail, and Christ. This image shifts, and in its place appears the image of the red-bearded Celtic Arthur with a similar outfit. Now the Arthur of *Megrez* takes Excalibur, points it directly at me, and pricks the heart seed within the emerald stone in the Grail in my chest. The seed blazes into life and a tiny hylum and roots emerge.

Now without even an interview with *Megrez* journalists, I'm back on Ivy Thorn Hill in my physical body, which is now enveloped by nearly complete darkness. I'm thus confronted by the prospects of a sixty minute bike ride without lights along narrow country roads without street lights. I laugh heartily, then lace up my sneakers, run up the hill, jump on my bike, and pedal down the road. "Blaise, can you help with the lights?" No problem.

They set up a light-weight scaffolding over my head and install a dozen dazzlingly brilliant spotlights, then all six Blaise technicians climb aboard my crown chakra and staff the stagelights as I pedal crazily along the darkened road. The intent of the lights, I gather, is to make a vague impression on the attention of passing motorists that there might be something on the road requiring extra caution in their driving, and, if they could see it, perhaps a chuckle. Blaise seems to have stalled out most of the potential cars because almost no cars pull up suddenly from behind and only two pass me coming in my direction.

With the lights and traffic control system humming smoothly, and the Grail Knight pedalling merrily along in the well-lit darkness and only occasionally riding off into the bumpy, well-manured pastures to surprise meditating cows and ruminating field mice, five of the Blaises are inspired to form a brass quintet while the sixth acts as conductor. I've been chanting *O Michael uplift us now!* to match my pedal strokes. Evidently Blaise thinks a little musical accompaniment will perk things up. So from left to right up in the crown chakra bandstand, there is Blaise on trumpet, tuba, trombone, French horn, and cornet. With the lights, pedalling, and chanting on automatic, we settle down to have some honest fun on the evening commute back to the Grail Castle. I climb aboard the bandstand prepared to tingle the triangle whenever the conductor signals.

Up here in the Blaise orchestra pit, I feel relaxed enough to reflect on tonight's outing to *Megrez*. It seems that if you want to go to *Megrez* and meet Arthur, start at Aldebaran; the bull will conduct you to the bear. I'm not surprised to find links between Arthur and the Great Bear. The Big Dipper (part of *Al Dubb al Akbar*, "the Greater Bear" in Arabic) is sometimes called Arthur's Wain (or Chariot); Arthur's name in Welsh, roughly translated as *Arth-Uthyr*, might mean "wonderful bear;" and there is the general mythopoeic understanding that Arthur "came" from the Great Bear. For the Egyptians, Ursa Major was the "Mother of the Revolutions," possibly referring to the "revolution" of the galaxy around the Pole Star. For the Chinese, the Bear was described alternately as the Plough, and its stars known as the "Seven Elders or the Purple Forbidden Enclosure of the Celestial Emperor." It was also called *Tseih Sing* or "seven Stars" and associated with the celestial palace of the "Lord on High;" with *Shou Lao*, the "Star God of Longevity;" and with *Tien Shan*, the heavenly mountain paradise of the Taoist immortals, guarded by Sirius, the "Heavenly Wolf." In India, the Dipper's seven stars are understood to be the home of the Seven Rishis, a septenate of primordial spiritual teachers and celestial human masters. The name *Megrez*—as a star it marks the junction of the bowl or dipper with the handle—comes from the Arabic *Al Maghrez* meaning "Root of the Tail," but the Chinese view it as *Tien Kuen* ("The Authority of Heaven") while at least one ancient Indian text claims that *Megrez*, which is 65 light years from Earth, rules the other stars of the Bear.

On the esoteric end of things, according to the arcane astrology of Alice Bailey and her Tibetan mentor, Dhjwal Kuhl, Ursa Major is the source of the seven rays of our solar system and the twelve basic energies that "work out into human expression via the Lords of the

452 ❖ RICHARD LEVITON

twelve [zodiacal] signs and the twelve planetary rulers." These energies pertain to the will and purpose of the Solar Logos and form an active cosmic triangle of influence with Sirius (which pertains to the love-wisdom aspect of the Solar Logos) and the Pleiades (the active intelligence and form manifestation aspect of the Solar Logos), says Kuhl. The Seven Rishis mark the time and duration of events in cosmic life and periodically transmit great energy waves through the solar system, like surging "electrical" impulses of higher consciousness; these are then stepped down or transduced by various intermediary planets and star families before reaching Earth, presumably for transmission through the energy matrix and its zodiacs.

And Arthur, as a celestial personage from *Megrez*? The possibility of a cosmic initiate known as Arthur is supported by two comments made by Wellesley Tudor Pole in his letters to Rosamond Lehmann, a correspondence full of esoteric treasures. "For me, of course, the highlight was the unexpected summons to attend a Conference of Arthur and his Knights," Pole wrote. "He has become an Initiate and in some ways an Elder Brother, available for the service of those who are developing 'second sight.' Being one of the great Orders working under the banner of Michael, it is natural that Arthur and his Cavaliers should be concerned once more with human affairs, now at this supreme turning point in another time of crisis." Later in 1963, Tudor Pole added this note: "I received a second summons to Arthur's celestial Court. This time I was allowed to journey there on my own beloved steed (with a squire and page also mounted, quite a cavalcade). Among much else I am expected to render the Chalice Well paved courtyard fitting once more to act as an exterior anchorage and focal point for 'Round Table' conferences, for Arthur's own use."

When Blaise returns later this evening for our customary press conference, they come as a Blazing Star, as they are, but without the brass quintet, and, even better, without any knuckle-rapping for my musical cheek on the ride home.

"We inspire angel jokes, Grail Knight. They're all right. They keep you happy. If a man or angel cannot laugh at himself, he is of no use."

"Blaise, who were those friendly guys in the grey robes, the smiling Zen masters? They didn't have wings so I wasn't sure they were angels."

"Just because you didn't see the wings doesn't mean they didn't have them. It was an aspect of us seen through dim perception rather than through spiritual vision."

"I see you guys a lot better when I'm not trying."

"That is oh so true, Grail Knight."

"Let's talk about Merlin. Why was Britain called Myrddin's Precinct? What were his Thirteen Treasures? And what does it mean that he went north to see his Master Bleise?"

"It was called Myrddin's Precinct because Merlin energized Britain from Atlantis, then Hermes initiated the Earth temple in Britain. Merlin is Capricornian energy, which is Saturn. Hermes is Gemini energy, which is Mercury. Look for the obvious. Don't be too literal. These are ages of planetary definition. The Thirteen Treasures were things that would be useful to Merlin. They are representations externally of aspects of Merlin's consciousness, of his level of adeptship. You could read this as the thirteen Qabalistic parts, each carrying inherent gifts, as in Enochian Qabala. Master Bleise's position in relation to Merlin and Arthur was as a tutor initiated in Mu and Atlantis. He was linked to a group consciousness karma of which Morgan, Guinivere, Arthur, and Merlin were contributors. By the way, you are on to an important thread with the Merlin-*Me-rlun* connection."

"But the reference to Master Bleise must also in some way refer to you, right?"

"Hmmmpppff. Listen, we are here to explain something else that we feel it would be impossible for you to locate by any other means, but something which you must know right now. It is another aspect of the Round Table. Merlin brought it from Ireland. Merlin brought the stones that are now called Stonehenge, which was the Round Table for some time. We presented this information some time ago in more detail to somebody else you are familiar with. His name was Geoffrey of Monmouth. Be aware that our information can be corroborated through this earlier reference. The stones from Ireland—this is the Round Table Merlin brought. Merlin moved the stones in the Hyper-borean era to Ireland from a place in southeastern Africa.

"This is a table to disclose all pertinent astrological and astronomical information relevant to Britain. It is a temple to the Goddess. It was only a few hours ride by horseback from Camalate and they had other means of travel as well. Several of the reenactments of Looking for Arthur were performed through Stonehenge and Arthurian ritual but not all. Merlin gathered the knights. Arthur stood by the twelve main stones, aligned and energized and put before the Goddess. It was a ritual for joining themselves as men with the Feminine. The stones held the Earth magic of the Mother, each aligned by Merlin to the twelve constellations of the heavens. Each stone was rooted in Earth, dug into the Mother to bless the Goddess. Each stone was attuned to the Spirit-Masculine above of each constellation. Each knight was thereby attuned above and below to Heaven and Earth in a ritual to greet his Feminine, to unlock the doors through the circle to the unconscious. Stonehenge was used at each equinox and solstice. Some stone temples were used only at equinox, some only at solstice. The Round Table known as Stonehenge was primarily a solstice or solar temple."

"Is Stonehenge likely to be used in this way again?" Russell asks.

"Stonehenge is unlikely to be used again. Things have changed. The potential through the Christ is more accessible generally without such complex Earth rituals. The Stonehenge ritual was one of the first events to hold heart integration, the male and female, for the birth of the Christ Child; it thereby allowed Christ to then come into matter as Jesus."

This is a most unusual development and one with considerable comic relief. Geoffrey of Monmouth is almost universally derided by scholars as a twelfth century fairy-tale mythographer, fabulously unreliable storyteller, and hardly the historian whose accounts are to be taken literally. In short, he is the historians' laughing-stock, the historiographic fool of the medieval period. His sincere account of Merlin moving the stones from Ireland by means of "all the gear which he considered necessary" is usually put forward as the most flagrant indication of his factual aberrations.

As Geoffrey recounted it, Uther Pendragon, Merlin, and fifteen thousand men journeyed to Mount Killaraus (in what is now Northern Ireland) to capture the Giant's Dance from its pusillanimous custodian, Gillomanius. Yet even with "every conceivable kind of mechanism," they were unable to move the stones an inch. Merlin had watched their efforts with amusement from the sidelines. "He placed in position all the gear that he considered necessary and dismantled the stones more easily than you could ever believe. Once he had pulled them down, he had them carried to the ships and stored on board, and they all set sail once more for Britain with joy in their hearts." When they landed in Britain, they assembled at Mount Ambrius on Salisbury plain where Merlin arranged the stones "in exactly the same way as they had been arranged on Mount Killaraus' in Ireland, thus proving his artistry was worth more than any brute strength."

Stonehenge was anciently known not only as the Giant's Dance, but as the Circle of Hanging Stones, because *henge* was Old English for "hanging." According to symbol historian Harold Bayley, Stonehenge was also called *Choir Gaur*, which may have meant "gigantic choir," by way of deriving "choir" from the Greek *choiras* for rock: hence "Rock Circle." The site was sometimes called "the *Gorsedd* of Salisbury, Bayley says, in which *gorsedd* meant Great Seat or Circular Sitting; alternately the site was called the Great Stone Fence, the Circle of the World, and the Stone Cell of the Sacred Fire.

"Blaise, were you guys all the 'gear' Merlin considered necessary to move the stones?"

"During Merlin's time away from your planet, in cooperation with his instructors and us, he received plans of the new site of the stones. We helped him move them during that incarnation. The date when they first came from Ireland to England was more recent than Hyperborea. It was approximately 2500 B.C. when the stones came to Salisbury plain. Maybe we lost a couple stones in the sea, but there are more than enough stones even today at Stonehenge for it to be used properly. There was nothing at the Stonehenge site before we moved the ring there. It was used as a sacrificial site prior to their introduction. Much cleansing was needed there in the etheric of the dome over the site prior to our bringing the stones. One day we would like you to visit Mount Killaraus. It was an important site during the post-Atlantean period, and much of your planetary history was influenced from there. For instance, there was no resemblance to your present sexual organs in Atlantean times. This isn't to say they were physically different, but the function of the sexual organs was entirely different."

"How old are the stones of Stonehenge and, for that matter, of the various key stone temples of Britain?" Berenice asks.

"It would be pointless to answer because there was a different type of spatial, temporal relation existing then than now. Just accept that Time has not always been. It was devised to teach. When its lessons have been learned, it will be removed. When the stones were placed in Hyperborea, there were sequential, temporal shifts but nothing in any way similar to what you call Time."

"Was the moving of these stones from Ireland to Salisbury somehow timed with another Arthur revival? The Seraphim said there have been fifteen Arthurs, for example."

"Like waves from a radio transmitter, the Arthur vibration travels through time and space, coming more and less into matter. This is now the peak of one such Arthur wave. For the approach to it, such books and interest in the subject of Arthur are a manifestation of one of these waves."

"What about Arthur's connection with the Great Bear?"

"Arthur's name means 'Sun-Star.' Arthur came from the Bear. He was the ruler of the Bear and not its son. Arthur created Draco, so he is not Draco's son. Uther was Arthur's incarnatory father as Joseph was Jesus' and Wilson is yours. When studying the Arthur mythic system, there are no antecedents or precedents. The myth contains it all from beginning to end."

"According to what I've read by Tudor Pole, Arthur is a kind of cosmic initiate, and Dhjwal Kuhl says the Solar Logos is one of the petals of the Cosmic Logos. Is there a connection here?"

"Arthur is the Solar Logos; as such he is an aspect of the Heart of the Cosmic Heart. He is one of twelve Knights about the Table of the Cosmic Logos. Look 'Heart-Star,' which is what your surname means, we have to run along. We'll see you at Primrose Hill as your Blazing Star."

57

FLYING A KITE WITH HILARY & THE BOYS AT PRIMROSE HILL

eart-Star Grail Knight sets out for London in the morning by train and is delightfully entertained as he sits whistling and tapping in the empty car by six smiling, rather large and flamboyantly winged guys sitting across from him reading the *Financial Times*, legs crossed, golden slippers polished and gleaming smartly, angel attaché cases across their laps. The next time I look up the executives from Heaven have vanished, but six much smaller, decidedly indolent, and perhaps overfed Blaises are draped over the luggage racks like luxuriating callico cats. These soon vanish, but suddenly the ashtrays pop open revealing dozens of twinkling stars. The train finally pulls into Paddington, and I get serious about my work, heading for the British Museum for a day spent poring through old books and etymologies.

Hilary meets me at six p.m. at Primrose Hill for a picnic. Munching our sandwiches, we admire the dome overhead, then Blaise arrives with some light entertainment. A young woman in tight jeans sashays past, and a couple of Blaise's wave mischievously from her back pockets. Another Blaise sits on a drifting autumn leaf trying to steer it like a magic carpet whose motor has stalled and whose joy stick is missing. A very serious middle-aged man walks past with a black bowler primly in position, but there is a curious white parakeet with flaming wings on its brim and this parakeet is wearing sunglasses. An elderly woman walks by with a wicker basket full of groceries, but she doesn't seem to know she is also transporting three Blaises tucked in among the leeks and tomatoes.

Hilary and I lean comfortably against each other and enjoy the sights and sounds of a city relaxing into mellowness in spite of itself. "Do you know what Blake says about Primrose Hill?" she asks. "'I brought a copy of his poems with me. Listen to this. 'Primrose Hill is the mouth of the Furnace & the Iron Door,' he says in *Jerusalem*. He also says that Los, who is the Elohim responsible for Albion the "Ancient Man," built his spiritual city, Golgonooza, on the banks of the Thames, "Outside of the Gates of the Human Heart.' Los tends the mighty furnace on Albion's behalf. 'Los was the friend of Albion who most lov'd him.' Then Blake mentions Albion's House of Eternity. London is central to Blake's mythology about Albion. Here he says of Golgonooza: 'He builded it, in rage & in fury. It is the Spiritual Fourfold London, continually building & continually decaying desolate.'

"I keep reading *Jerusalem* over and over—there's so much in it that's relevant to this business with Blaise. And the comments of Kathleen Raine the poet are helpful, too. She writes: 'The city, then, is for Blake a living spiritual entity. He called the interior London 'Golgonooza,' from the root 'golgos,' a skull, because the city's existence is in the human brain.' The whole point of Golgonooza, she adds, is to provide 'an earthly habitation for Jerusalem.' Here, wrap this blanket around you if you're feeling cold."

I am feeling slightly chilled, but my body temperature always drops when I feel something visionary approaching. I see myself walking down a London street into a theater on Shaftesbury Avenue, down the long aisles, past hundreds of seats filled with an anticipatory audience, and up onto the stage. There is a huge, round table as the sole stage prop. I am to be strapped to the table. I hold my sword aloft in my right hand then lay down on the table, which begins to revolve slowly. As Blake might say, behold the starry wheels of Albion turning in the Golgonoozan night. My attention partly returns to Primrose Hill where I sit under Hilary's blanket in the gathering dusk, yet I can feel myself standing with sword and Grail on a spoke of a mighty turning white wheel. Hermes occupies the hub position and his sword is upraised, too. The spokes of this starry wheel of Albion radiate far out into the landscape and across much of London.

"Primrose Hill is the center of another Michael star wheel," Blaise announces. This confirms the work of zodiacographer Mary Caines who, after documenting the Avalon star wheel, went on in the 1970s to investigate suspicions and "local clues" of a landscape zodiac situated in greater London, wrapped around the River Thames from Cobham Common to Shepherd's Bush for a diameter of about twelve miles. She calls it the Kingston zodiac, after the town of Kingston-on-Thames, which occupies the position of Libra, pictured as a dove, in her cartography. Blake's arcane mythopoeic writings in *Jerusalem* may well focus on the Kingston zodiac; the geomantic features and ancient history of greater London may well be the outer terrain of his recondite Golgonooza.

"Look at the kites!" Hilary exclaims, pointing to a young girl who darts about the green clutching the strings of a swooping yellow kite with capricious dipping tail. Something weighs it down, as if yanking on it like a ponytail. It's Blaise again, sixfold, having a terrific time riding the kite tail like an aerial rollercoaster. Eventually—and I doubt it's because their joy is spent—they slide down the tail like sleepy firemen spiralling down the stationhouse pole, landing as a clump of wings and golden socks right in front of a benchful of dour elderly British gents, frumped up with ascot, pipe, lapel handkerchief. They pay absolutely no attention to these clowns of God.

Quicker than an eyeblink the scene shifts again. Blaise stands within the Black Bowling Ball. It is vast, awesomely huge, and fills the horizon in every direction like an act of God. Inside the Ball is an emerald the size of the British Museum, and it's enhaloed by a scintillating sapphire blue sphere. The emerald contains the golden Grail within which lies a smiling golden infant. The infant becomes a crowned man, then a crucified king, then an infant once more.

Now the Ball grows vast beyond perception, so big it virtually disappears. In its place—or probably more correctly, within it—appears a mighty twelve-spoked wheel containing twelve similar, smaller wheels, each at the end of a wheel spoke. The image of Michael (or Hermes) with sword, emerald, Grail, and golden infant is repeated in each of the twelve smaller wheels as a kind of spiritual logo. Then Blaise says: "Behold the wheel of Hyperborea, Myrddin's Precinct." As I peer into one of the wheels, it reveals a familiar vista: aspects of the Somerset landscape and Glastonbury come into focus. "Behold the Region of the Summer Stars, one of many wheels in this section of the Wheel. Primrose Hill is the White Mount, the *Ananda-kanda*, or heart within the heart, of the London star wheel."

What could possibly come next after this display, I think to myself, not daring to ask the question in any official way lest Blaise take it as a challenge. Which they do. "This comes next!" the six Blaises declare. The twelvefold wheel disappears, condensing into a single Blazing Star that is "brighter by far" than any of the billions of stars framed by the Blaise tableau on Primrose Hill. When you hang out with a family of angels whose professional name is Ophanim, which is Hebrew for "wheels," you shouldn't be surprised when you start seeing a lot of wheels within wheels rolling towards you.

"Hilary, how about if you take us out to dinner and I'll tell you a fabulous story about what a hungry Grail Knight saw one evening on Primrose Hill. Sushi would be nice, don't you think?" Cheek, thank God, is permissible again; it might even be in fashion, with my dear friend of the Lake.

Blaise reveals another version of the Round Table as revolving starwheel motif the next evening when I take a walk before dinner back at Wick. I take Edmund and Celia with me to pick blackberries by the railroad trestle. The six Blaises join us attired like country uncles in suspendered overalls, wide-brimmed straw hats, and dangling corncob pipes. Each Blaise tilts his head upwards. I look above them. The sky is filled with hundreds of revolving wheels upon each of which a man or woman is strapped as if to a spinning dartboard. In the chest of each bewheeled human blazes a single star, a spectacular point of light. The wheels buzz around the evening sky like the denizens of a vast beehive. The bee-keeper looms in their midst, unbelievably large. It is a male figure like Hermes and Michael, yet neither I'm sure. He has a gaping cavern in his chest, a welcoming thoracic vacuity from which all wheeling traffic comes and goes.

Something else interpenetrates the human forms strapped to the wheels: as if superimposed on each body, there is a complete Tree of Life complete with fruits.

"Do you think we've collected enough berries, Grail Knight of America?" Edmund asks, tugging at my sleeve. "I'm getting rather hungry." Then Celia chirps, "Shouldn't we be getting back now in case the Heffalumps come after us?" Then looking a little worried, she adds, "Do Heffalumps eat blackberries?" Heffalumps, indeed, says the American Grail Knight, a bear of little brain—I've saturated their bedtime reading hour with stories about A. A. Milne's Winnie the Pooh and friends, which include the troublesome Heffalumps. Milne might as well have included the inexhaustibly inexplicable Blaise in his congeries.

"We come as we are," they announce upon arriving several hours later. "We come as a Blazing Star, within the stable sphere of consciousness, a Black Bowling Ball filling the horizon. We come as that pinpoint of brilliant light at the center of the sphere. We greet you all. Grail Knight, did you see Hermes and his Emerald Tablets when you visited London?"

"Hermes? Which big guy was he?"

"He was just behind you on Primrose Hill."

"Was that Hermes tonight with all the wheels in his chest?"

"Nope. That was Daedalus." Daedalus! The *dramatis personae* grows more mythological every day in this Grail Knight business. Daedalus' name means "bright" or "cunningly wrought," for he was the master craftsman, smith, and artificer of Athens; he built the labyrinth (presumably a landscape zodiac) for King Minos with its innumerable winding passages and turnings from which Theseus escaped through the aid of Ariadne's thread. Apparently, Daedalus instructed her in private on how to enter and leave the labyrinth and provided her with the magic ball of thread. Daedalus invented the saw and compass, and he also contrived the wax-sealed wings for his doomed son, Icarus, who would drown when the wings fell apart over the sea.

The implication is that Daedalus must have been instrumental in the design and implementation of the landscape star wheels, or round tables, comprising the entire planetary temple system of zodiacs. Each of the men and women strapped to a revolving star wheel must have been an adept or master of that temple, a kind of accomplished geomancer who dedicated (strapped) his or her life to the activation and maintenance of the star wheel matrix and became one with its energies. Daedalus constructed the Cretan labyrinth for King Minos; Los the Elohim built the spiritual city of Golgonooza for Albion. Both are variations on the structure of a star wheel or landscape zodiac— might we be dealing with the same being with Daedalus and Los?

"Oh well, you miss a few in this work," I say to Blaise. "How many zodiacs are there in the wheel of Hyperborea?"

"There are a total of 25 star maps in this section of the grid matrix. Of these, thirteen zodiacs have the potential to be complete while twelve will remain incomplete. The whole section is, at this time, under the influence of Virgo."

"Hermes showed me the wheel of Hyperborea covering all of the British Isles. It had many smaller wheels within it, presumably the 25 you just referred to. What relationship do these smaller wheels have with one another?"

"Each set of temples has a microcosmic and macrocosmic relationship. Each aspect is in relation to many other aspects. Each temple has a complete chakra system in itself, just as each adept is a complete system unto himself or herself. At each place in the temple, the adept can tune into the seed formation or Orphic Egg or Cosmic Egg, of the temple. This can in some cases relate to the root chakra of the temple or else to the place where the formation of the whole temple is stabilized, as in the case of Worley Hill. Each temple in Britain, and, to an extent, in the western European continent, is part of one large temple from the south of France to the Orkney Islands in the north of Scotland. This is what you call the Hyperborean temple; we call it the Western temple.

"Each one of the minor chakras in this temple has a complete system of chakras within it. Each temple contains all seven centers. It is what you might call a Cosmic Logos. At the heart of the Cosmic

Logos, there is the Solar Logos, spreading between the heart and solar plexus chakras. That is also a complete system with its own Cosmic Logos and Solar Logos within it. Basically just imagine that whenever you think in terms of scale, there are three aspects to the temple. First, the material, physical Earth. Second, the solar, Christ, the transcended Sun. Third, the cosmic, the Holy Ghost, or Father. Each temple has these three aspects.

"The temple of Hyperborea has a male and female current running through it. The southeast of Scotland is like the masculine channel of the main ley or psychic energy current flowing through Britain towards the crown of the British temple in the Orkneys. The female current goes through the island of Iona as both the current for that temple and for the entire British temple. Earth temple sites spread over the entire globe. There is no place on Earth that is not affected to a greater or lesser degree by templic energies, either dome lines or other energy lines.

"If you were to plot all the energy lines around the Earth on a globe, the icosahedron, the dodecahedron, and the other Platonic Solids connecting dome to dome, you would then have plotted the seven main chakras plus the *Ananda-kanda* and the extra monadic point. This makes nine, which corresponds on the planetary scale to the nine Sephiroth, other than Kether, of the Tree of Life from Qabala. But there are twelve points in the crown of Elohim, in the complete planetary temple; these can be plotted at their templic sites at various points across the globe. This is the Earth seen as one large temple with twelve points. These are also the twelve faces of the dodecahedron of the Earth energy matrix."

"In other words, the entire planet has layers and layers of complex temple structure and geomantic patterning, all of which goes back to probably the beginning of the planet?"

"Correct. It is a multidimensional, interdependent pattern. Most of it dates back to the time of Hyperborea, or earlier."

"Hyperborea keeps turning up. What was that all about?" Russell asks.

"It was a world culture, the globe at one point, with its culture centered first in Lemuria then subsequently in Atlantis. The epicenter of Hyperborea was what is now the British Isles. The Hyperboreans were travellers. Their origin is lost in time. They originally were resident within the Pleiades star system. The name means just what you know it as, the Sailing or Wandering Ones. Certain Elohim and Hyperboreans were sent here by the Most High Architect of Supreme Existence to lay down energy matrices over the surface of this planet that it may support beings with higher being bodies. But you see, Grail Knight, we are mostly concerned with where you are now in your quest and not ancient history, which is why we'll see you tomorrow afternoon at Worley Hill. Bye for now, we love you as you haven't remembered, as your Blazing Star."

Even though the process is the thing, I indulge myself in some foragings in ancient history before turning in for the night. Hyperborea is only spottily referenced in the classical canon. The Greek poet Pindar wrote: "Neither by ships nor by land canst thou find the wondrous road to the trysting-place of the Hyperboreans." Pliny mentioned Hyperborea, describing it a country with a blissful and pleasant temperature where one day lasts six months, no discord, sickness, or old age are known, and the people never die. Herodotus alluded to the griffins that guarded the gold of the Hyperboreans and said that, according to the Delians, the Hyperboreans regularly sent "offerings wrapt in wheat-straw" to Scythia. Pausanias reports that a Hyperborean named Olen was an ancient bard to Apollo, living in the time of Orpheus, and that he was the first among humans to sing the Apollonian oracles at Delphi in hexameter verse.

But it was Diodorus of Siculus who most thoroughly remembered Hyperborea for us. Among the Hyperboreans, so named because they lived "behind" the North Wind (Boreas), he wrote, was Leto, mother of the gods Apollo and Artemis. For that reason, Apollo is "much honored among them above all other gods; the inhabitants are looked upon as priests of Apollo, after a manner, since daily they praise this god continuously in song and honor him exceedingly. And there is also on this island both a magnificent sacred precinct of

Apollo and a notable temple which is...spherical in shape." In addition, there is a city there sacred to Apollo who visited the island every nineteen years; nearly everyone in his city played the cithara, singing hymns of praise to Apollo and his glorious deeds. Diodorus also briefly mentions a Hyperborean named Abaris who was renowned for his ability to sail through the air and across the seas on his magic arrow; in such a manner, he once visited the Greeks at Delos and established good will and kinship between these people and the Hyperboreans away in the far north.

The British clairvoyant Grace Cooke, in her numinous far recollections of ancient Earth history (*The Light in Britain*), states that the Hyperboreans were the "original" people of this planet. They were "perfect sons of God who came in all their glory as guardians of a young race on a young planet. These God-men, great and wise brothers, brought the knowledge of the spiritual Sun or Christ to Earth. They came first to the land of Hyperborea whose very stones became impregnated with the light they brought to Earth." Hyperborean rituals typically involved invoking, then disseminating, this effulgence throughout the landscape; it often took dragon form, Cooke notes, which insinuates the other nuance to the term Boreas, as the world serpent. The great Sun Brotherhood of Hyperborea spread this spiritual knowledge around the planet; the supra-earthly light they worked with is still resident in the landscape, Cooke adds.

She also drops a few tantalizing hints about a Hyperborean figure she calls King Ar-Thor "King Ar-Thor" who "mystically is the very spirit of Britain, who guides her destiny and will lead her to victory over the powers of evil." Might this alleged Hyperborean Ar-Thor have been the first of the fifteen Arthurs?

58

ANOTHER EPISODE OF
BLAISE ON MY HEAD

he first colleagues I meet at Worley Hill the next day are, in fact, the members of my gnome Round Table. No doubt their trip from the Dog was less tiring on the sinews than mine. O cosmic accountants, mark the self-indulgent complaints of the Grail Knight as he points out that his visits thus far under angelic aegis to ineffable Worley Hill total 130 miles and 64 hills mounted and coasted.

The gnomes and I make our way across the stone-infested field that leads to Copley Wood. If these were potatoes, the harvest would be phenomenal, but if I were the farmer working this field, I'd turn off my tractor and weep.

Michael—or is it Hermes or Daedalus? I wish these big guys would wear name badges until I get them visually sorted out—looms hugely over Worley Hill with sword and shield. Behind him, a twelve-spoked star wheel expands across the horizon like an icon for the Somerset zodiac. At Michael's heart, and at the hub of the wheel, is an image of a golden human who stands in the Grail holding a red rose at his chest. Before I know it, as if looking in a mirror, I am holding this red rose laid across my own heart bowl.

The gnomes lead me through the woods to a new site that overlooks Compton Dundon. Along the way, I refrain from challenging their trailblazing expertise because, frankly, I have no idea where we're headed this afternoon. How fortunate, Blaise would say. The Grail Knight works best when he's in the dark. The gnomes group themselves in a horseshoe around me as we all face Michael; a light drizzle sprinkles the autumnal woods.

"Michael welcomes you to this grove," announces an unidenti-fied commentator. "In his breast, see the Great Initiator. See Christ the quickener within Michael's heart. He pours golden light upon you to moisten your seed of new life." This said, the golden image of Christ in his human form occupies the center of the wheel in Michael's chest. It's as if the Christ in his human form is outstretched across the Round Table star wheel and this occupies the central chest cav-ity in Michael's archangelic form. On the other hand, if this were Daedalus, then Christ would be the Minotaur lurking dangerously at the heart of the cunning artificer's labyrinth. Either way, Christ *is* dangerous—he can destroy your hard-heartedness, illuminate your ignorance, and quicken your spirituality. He comes with a sword. Now the image gets more complex. Four images are superimposed like transparent layers: Michael's shield, the star wheel, a cross, and a green living tree; each is inside the next, while the form of the Christ stands in the midst of these four superimpositions like a blind-ing sun rendering each and all coherent. Like lightning, a golden jag of light connects this Sun with the sprouting seed inside the emerald in my heart bowl. Ignition.

The gnomes rise and set off through the woods, beckoning for me to follow. After a while we arrive at a new site on Worley Hill, also facing southwest towards Dundon Beacon and Lollover Hill. The place reminds me of Swell Wood in the Aller Dragon because of its upwelling maternal mood, as if the air, the earth, the plants, the animals, the gnomes, myself, were all within the breath of an omni-present Mother, little sentient globules carried on her soft exhalation from out of the still, loving ponds of her being. For a moment, it grows so still it feels as if Nature holds her breath. I see ethereal birds—a partridge, a white goose, a solitary swan on a serene lake—and sense but cannot see a majestic female figure breathing before me, perhaps as large as Worley Hill itself—perhaps the Mother of the egg. An hour later, standing at my bike just before pedalling off for home, I see her again, shawled, indescribably large, holding the Cosmic Egg of Worley Hill prayerfully in her hands like Eurynome, the Mother of All Living Things in the Pelasgian creation myth. After assuming the form of a dove, Eurynome laid the Universal Egg; then, at her bidding, Ophion (also known as Boreas, the North Wind) coiled seven times about the egg until it hatched. Out tumbled all the elements and creatures of existence, from stars and planets, to plants and animals.

Now with the Grail Knight's more mystical activities concluded, it's time for another episode of Blaise On My Head, or how I pedal home like crazy before it gets too dark to see. With a clash of cymbals, the six Blaises appear on the Grail Knight's head, quite smartly outfitted with goggles, crash helmets, lilac scarves, and golden gloves. As the Grail Knight barrels down the long hill approaching Somerton, the Blaises shout with glee, their scarves streaming out like wind socks. When I reach ground level, the Blaises swoop off like a flock of sparrows then wobble down the air under parachutes to land on the Grail Knight's thinly tufted crown again, whose interior now resembles a comfortable, well-equipped livingroom. A sign announces, 'The Blaises spend a quiet evening at home in the Grail Castle.' One Blaise watches TV; one has a Walkman and nods his head continuously; one types at a desk, using two fingers, surrounded by perilous stacks of books; another slurps miso soup; another meditates and pokes a dull sword into a teacup; and the sixth rides an exercise bike, working up a sweat. The Blaise watching TV announces: "Swedenborg was never this cheeky. He never made us out to be rhubarbs like this American Grail Knight." The Blaise at the typewriter turns around and says, "That's right, nor did that picklehead philosoph, Dr. Dee, neither. You'd think the Grail Knight would have learned something since that fiasco."

Blaise returns a few hours later in the evening when I'm back at Wick. Except they've lost some of that joviality that kept me pedalling happily on the long commute from Worley Hill. "We come as we are. We come as a Blazing Star. We come from not all that far away. Hear the sound....See the light of transmutation....See the brilliant blue sphere with the emerald within. We surround you with the lilac flames of transmutation. *O Michael uplift us now*. In the heart, only a part, we roll towards you as a brilliant blue within which is a point of light, so, so bright, in an emerald. We speak of healing. Healing is atonement. Water the seed, Grail Knight. We wish to show you something. We ask you to ask within yourselves: Who is Blazing Star?"

After perhaps ten minutes, Blaise continues. "Now, let's discuss what you saw. Grail Knight?"

"At first, I saw nothing. Then I saw a ring of grey-robed men looking at me as I stood in their center. That must have been you. Then I saw a Sun."

"I saw Blaise coming towards us as a star, and the four of us, including Hilary, even though she's not here, backlit by a candle," Berenice says.

"I saw the four of us each occupying one corner of the Earth," Russell says. "There might have been others behind us. Each of us had a star in the chest, but a different color: green, white, blue, red. Above the four of us, like a four-sided pyramid, was a pinpoint of brilliant light with a rainbow halo above it."

"Good," Blaise says. "Each sees an aspect. The Grail Knight is a bit tired tonight after a long day on the quest."

Of course the sympathy perks me up. "Blaise, why did you call Dr. John Dee a picklehead today?" Dee (1527-1608) was the Renaissance magus, occultist, astrologer, geographer, author, counselor to Queen Elizabeth, and Qabalist, who communicated with angels through an intermediary named Edward Kelley, and who constantly sought knowledge of the esoteric.

"Not John Dee again! Sometimes we wonder why you asked for this job. He was a poor example of an attempt to bring through some work in a previous time. He wasn't focussed to be of much use."

"Oh. Well, I guess I don't want to know what you'll say of me in 450 years. I'm starting to see the Tree of Life in everything, or everything in the Tree, like knights, angels, Arthur. It seems to accommodate everything."

"Please, Grail Knight, don't get too concerned with the Tree. For understanding, the end result justifies the means, but once the groove has been made, the chisel is no longer necessary. Therefore, please do not become attached to the Tree in itself. It is only a chisel, a tool, empty in itself. We warn you. Many have fallen with this. It is very seductive and can appear to take the place of why you began to use it, which was to gain understanding. It is like a filing cabinet. You wouldn't fall in love with that, would you?"

"With all due respect to your advice to the Grail Knight, I'd like to know about your relationship with Merlin in terms of the Tree of Life," Russell asks.

"Ah Merlin. What is *mer*? The Sea, the ocean, the unconscious, or subconscious, or greater consciousness of Man. Mer is mother. Merlin is the line to Mother: *Mer-Line*. The line to the Sea of consciousness, the love that comes to you with the Mother. We are telling you a big secret about Merlin. No one on your planet knows about Mer-Line. We will introduce you to him. Hear the dog bark. [A dog barks] Be careful. We stage this only rarely. We say, place your attention to your left. [I see a loving woman and the roar of the ocean; Russell sees a white line running that way as if towards an electrical socket.] Mer-Line is the umbilicus. He is that connection between you and the Mother. You would be useless, less than useless, without this connection. All our work with you comes through this line. It comes from Blaise through Mer-Line, through the spiritual connection from you to your Mother, the Mother's Line. The Father shines through us down the Mer-Line. The love of the Father is wisdom. Is not the function of the Mother, love and warmth? The Mother function is the love and caring for her children, which is compassion, pure fire. It is Love from Above via the Mer-Line. The wisdom and compassion joined is sometimes called what the relatively unintelligent feel to be *magic*. Magic exists in each gap of your time. In each moment there are 23 gaps. Magic is imperative: Magic. You think about that Grail Knight."

"What does that say about the relationship between the sexes?" Berenice queries.

"From a point of clear consciousness, the separation of male and female is purely harmonious. There are no difficulties in a conscious state. When there is awareness, then difficulty and apparent difference disappear. When there is unconscious activity and conditioned reflex, what we call sleep, then the apparent differences are very real to the participants in the dream. Merlin is the line by which, through a point of clear light, you may reach more consciousness, more awareness, more love. Therefore, you can consider more and take part in reciprocal maintenance and other factors important to the development of Man on a conscious level on Earth. A Mother is only an aspect of one in three. A Father is only an aspect of one in three. Three and three make six. We are a tiny star. Remember, each of you, we come behind every word as a tiny star, brighter by far. We love you all even after the Fall. We bring the blessings of *Beatrice*, of *Lamech*, of *Aziel*, of *Isis*, of *Semech*, of *Eshnabar*. Spell the first letter of the angels we gave you. It is a confirmation for you tonight. Blaise."

"Well, Blaise, I suspect I had a glimpse or an insinuation of the Mother today at Worley. Can you give us a perspective on the Mother?"

"The Mother is what brings you and all beings in human form into this world. No one has come here other than by the Mother. She is what you are. From within her darkness, you came as a star down the tunnel through the lesser lights. This is Earth. The Mother brought you here that you may grow. You will grow until you become the Mother. Then all who know her will return; but you cannot fully know her. She is always in the birthing process. She is always dying. She is always suckling her children. She is always doing what needs to be done. The only way of knowing the Mother is by finding the Blazing Star in the belly. Through that, you begin to know Her. Therefore, we come as we are, as a Blazing Star, brighter by far. The Mother is one way of describing all that cannot be known. It is for all men and women the beginning. It is, strangely, also their end. We say, know the Mother, and, in her, know Joseph's Seed as the Blazing Star. Know the beginning and the end in each moment of consciousness. We are available to you all. Remember: "Twinkle, twinkle, little star, how I wonder where you are." This is an epigram for the Mother."

"Was there a physical, embodied Merlin, too?" I want to know.

"Yes, there was a Merlin in the body. This story, as we explained, crosses the Four Worlds and the seven levels—at least. There has always been the Mer-Line."

"Is it like the way the Christ remains in the etheric atmosphere of Earth?"

"No, but in a way, yes. Christ died to save you all. All beings that incarnated on planet Earth since what you call A.D. have the possibility today of touching the initiation of Christ in the Buddha Body. Buddha remembered, Christ forgave. There is still suffering. There is still unlove. Buddha came. He rid the Earth sphere of the need to suffer by a practical teaching designed to eliminate suffering. Christ came with forgiveness for the repeated mistakes of mankind. He forgave even the worst sinners as only the Christ could, as Love from Above. He came down, spread it over the Earth, and ascended. He introduced a new possibility to life on this planet. Now we make way for the next initiation, the Christed initiation in the Buddha Body."

"Do you mean this in reference to what many people call the Second Coming of the Christ?" Berenice asks.

"The Christ is in the Earth sphere already. How could it come again? It's already here. He didn't leave. He initiated Earth two thousand years ago and is tied here until the next initiation."

"Is the Christ on the same ray as the Buddha?"

"There have been many Buddhas. Buddha means Enlightened One. Each Buddha has his own ray. What is happening now is that the Buddhas of all time join with the ascended masters and world servers under direction of the Great School for the manifestation of the blended ray of rainbow light. The Great School has no fixed location, and it has no limits of any decription. We are members but a tiny, tiny star. We're afraid Grail Knight that time's run out. The last grain of sand has passed through the hour glass and we must return to the Wheel. So we bid you farewell. Be open to Love from Above, and don't forget tonight's experience. In the meantime, bring it to mind and ask yourself: Who is that Blazing Star? We retract gently down Merlin's line, the Mer-Line. We say to you: Don't forget. Remember Merlin is with you from now on with our love, Blazing Star."

I wake in the middle of the night remembering a delicious dream. I am lying in bed next to the most beautiful woman in the world. I tell her so. She has the face of my first adolescent sweetheart ripened into womanhood, sparkle and innocence, the ageless eye of love and compassion. She encircles me with her strong arms and bids me lie on her. I lap her nipples with my tongue as they poke up under her silken nightdress then suck one gently, drawing out milk. You must like Tauruses, I whisper to her. What Sun sign are you? I am all of them, the full circle, the white completion, she replies. I am your Mother, everyone's Mother. Sitting up in bed, I shake my head, grateful She is tolerant of jackanape Grail Knights and their absurd assumptions.

59

WHO IS THAT BLAZING STAR?

A week has passed, and I haven't once stepped out of the house. Boss's orders. Blaise asked me to hibernate for seven days in the Grail Castle to water my heart seed and conserve my energy. "You must be patient, for you are growing a tree in your heart," Blaise said. It isn't all bad news actually: this interdiction on my movements means I don't have to ride my bike to Worley Hill again.

I've passed the time in my second floor hermitage with familiar occupations: reading, writing, meditating, window-gazing, pondering. The first morning after Blaise posed his sly question *Who is Blazing Star?* I woke in alarm. I had dreamed of being chased around the sky by a hundred winged Zen masters each carrying a *kyosaku* the size of a cricket bat and each with a Blazing Star at its business end. All of them were trying to whack me; everywhere I turned, there was another crazed Zen Master angel mistaking me for a cricket ball. "Blaise, you've slipped me a *koan* after all! You promised no more *koans*."

Who is Blazing Star? This vexatious, intractable question has snuck up on me and suddenly I'm whacked into awareness by one hundred blazing *kyosakus*. Are the Blaises and the Grail Knight the same or different? Where is all this heading? What is our commission? What on Earth did Hilary, Russell, Berenice, and I ever agree to before coming into this life, or any lives, even the first? What are we trying to accomplish with this Blazing Star, who is—what? Nor does it improve my mood when, during meditation, I see myself lying in a fishnet hammock suspended over a precipice between two cliffs. I'm glad I'm not a fitful sleeper.

Sitting up carefully and slowly in my precipice-hung hammock, I decide to ask the Star itself. Who are you? I take out my sword, climb up into my brow center, sit down, and penetrate the Sun inside the seed that is inside the emerald that is inside the Grail in my heart center. That gets me into the sphere of golden mist but into no further clarity. I take a break to discuss things among myselves, then try the sword trick again. This time I see a huge man in a complete suit of golden body armor, or perhaps his body itself is golden. He holds a bucket of gold light, which he pours upon a standing stone; his supply of golden light seems inexhaustible. More of the scene comes into focus: a circle of standing stones bathed in light; the stones are in fact light itself; their radiations spread out across the landscape. After another break, I try again. I edge the sword slowly through the emerald into the Blazing Star or Sun within until I emerge into the center of a Star of David, or hexagram, with a Blaise at each of its six points. From here, I pass into a field of white light then into a vast black space in which I am surrounded by a myriad of stars. One star particularly attracts me, and I make for it. Soon I am standing in the center of a circle of Blaises who wrap their wings around me like a brace of uncles. Despite their avuncular cheer, this doesn't put me any closer to answering the question, *Who is Blazing Star?*

"We come as we are," Blaise says in the evening when they appear in the livingroom. "We come as a Blazing Star. We surround you all with the lilac flames of transmutation. We place one flame above each of you. We place a sphere of sapphire blue within each flame. We place within each flame an emerald at the heart. Within the emerald, a diamond point of brilliant light. We place before you a book. It is the book of your karma. It is open. We bring the book before you. We give each of you a star. We place the sword behind you. We shine the golden light into the bowl. We show you the outside of the bowl. It has 24 circles. The zodiac is the route through to the 24 hours of the bowl. As you have grown, so you have, through guidance, come a little closer to the truth."

"Thank you, Blaise, but why have you given us these things tonight?" Berenice asks.

"You need them. They are sometimes referred to as Qabalistic magical weapons associated with different spheres on the Tree."

"Are the 24 circles related to Arthur's knights?" I ask.

"Each knight has either a wife or husband. Each of the twelve had female and male parts in the psyche. Your language is inadequate for certain concepts, but let's say some had achieved the inner marriage of the poles, others hadn't. Each of the twelve had it in potential. Arthur recognized the potential of the Christ child within each of them. Some brought that potential through, others did not. Grail Knight, may we suggest that you refrain from stepping forward with confidence and allow that which is waiting to come through, to come through. Too much thinking on your part. Be open to Love from Above. It will clear away all those opinions and presumptions. Don't think about it. Don't worry. Don't be concerned. Don't do anything. Just be open to Love from Above. We will be there with just enough Love from Above, as your Blazing Star."

The next day I sit down again with sword and intention and penetrate the emerald and star. I again travel through a white space, then a dark sphere, then a star field, and on to the single star. Here I find a single standing stone in the form of an egg; it contains a record player whose diamond needle is poised to play at the first groove of a record. On my return trip back to my bedroom at Wick, I pass through the "Star of Blaise"—Blaise says the hexagram design is original with them and, with respect, precedes David's—except I find it positioned horizontally in my chest like an interior collar. I retrace my journey through the star until I come upon a Round Table with twelve seated knights. In the center of the table is the hexagrammic Star of Blaise and in its center a black cauldron partially filled with gold coins. More coins tumble in from above, filling it to the brim. At last, pennies from Heaven! I take a coin and swallow it like a wafer. It passes through my body until it settles at the Round Table in my heart center. As I penetrate it with the sword, the coin reveals an old leather bound book entitled *Adventures of Excalibur and the Grail,* by Dr. John Dee, the sixteenth century picklehead. I don't recognize this among his published works. This is entertaining, but I'm sure it won't pass muster for my *koan*-posing angels, who will dismiss me with a ring of the bell for more hard practice.

"We come as we are, as a Blazing Star," says Blaise in the evening, stating the obvious without reducing the mystery. "Above each of you we place a red flame. On your throats we place a white sphere. At your solar plexus we place a blue disc. We move these around to bring balance. We surround you in the flames of transmutation, the lilac glow. We place each of you within a lilac flame, within a sapphire blue sphere with an orange periphery. Within this, at your heart, we place an emerald of green light, within which we place a diamond point of briliant light of the Nimitta. So here we are, as your Blazing Star.

"We show you a flower arrangement with a living ball of light at its center. We give you Love from Above. We can't make you love, for that cannot be taught, but we hope you'll make more of what you have and what you're given. Do not deny any act where there may be the manifestation of Love from Above through that act. You are all very close. You are playing safe. We are pleased you make some effort, but remember, be as you are. Allow Love from Above. You are full of opinions and presumptions. We say, don't worry, and you worry. We say, don't be afraid, and you have fear. We say, be open to Love from Above, and you deny it. What can we do, we ask you? Remember, we have only a limited opportunity. We give what we can. You chose yourselves. Remember that. We come as we are, as you do. Be as you are. Be open to Love from Above. We can do nothing more. Everything is available to you at this time. You can turn around or not. It is your will. Remember or not, it is your choice. How many times have you asked for this? You have access to Love from Above. Now is not the time to stand and stare—but, well, need we say more? Remember where we began. Remember who is that Blazing Star. Remember, we're not too far and with all our love, your Blazing Star."

After Blaise's departure we sit around the livingroom with long faces, having a midnight pot of Grail tea, feeling disappointed with ourselves. Whenever Blaise says our time together is limited, it makes us cringe that he might go away from our lives before we've ever understood what was here. How many times have we asked for this indeed, but who has asked for what and who is that Blazing Star?

We have our next interview with the Boss the following evening. "We come as we are. We come as a Blazing Star, as Love from Above. We surround you all with the wall of lilac flames, the flames of transmutation. We place around each of you the lilac flame. Within each flame, we place a sphere of sapphire blue with an orange periphery. Within this we place an emerald of beryl; within this we place a diamond point, crystal clear, brighter than the brightest star. We present to each of you an indigo cloak to wear around yourselves. We present each of you with a lamp to shine on your path.

"This is an important time. It is the culmination of much preparation and arduous work. Please be attentive. Don't waste energy. Conserve what you have. You must not let your imagination run away with you. You must be clear. There are, make no mistake, forces at work that are attempting to corrupt what you do. They can mimic us. Don't worry. Fear is what lets them in. But we must help you be aware of this whole situation. There is a cosmic conflict. There is an attempt between two opposing forces to usurp the power of light on Earth. This is only apparent now at the end of the Age of Darkness. We come as we are, as a Blazing Star. We wish, if you wish, to hear now from each of you. Who is that Blazing Star?"

"I feel you are in everyone I meet," Berenice says, "yet independent of us all, as love. I don't feel this is the answer you wanted."

"We have no expectations. Russell?"

"Blazing Star is at the center of everyone. It's the unifying thing before there's any separation, the point in consciousness where there is the recognition of unity."

"Hmmmm. Grail Knight?"

"It's a series of Chinese boxes. Open one, there's another inside, and another. Also, it's the Star of enlightenment that speaks."

"Examine all the possibilities. Each of you presents an aspect of who we are. We are in real terms unknowable. Yet you know us better than you know yourselves."

"We should trade places then," I remark. "Then you can tell us who we are."

"We exist beyond time and space, beyond any element. We abide in peace. We are made of love. We are more than you can imagine. At the center of your sphere is a tiny star, a Nimitta, a pinpoint of light, very, very fine. From the tiniest point you can imagine, we are in the middle of that point. We are an exploding star. We are the big bang at the beginning of the universe. We are the dark hole in space that contains all space. We are infinite life beyond light and darkness. We are in constant transmission with your stars. If you access your Star, you receive the transmission direct. If you access the Star by breathing as Love from Above, then you rapidly let go the conditioned layers of personality and allow them to be digested by the transmission from the Star. Then you become a transmitter for others to awaken the Star within themselves. We are the little point of light that fills infinite space. We are that Blazing Star and we are not very far."

Whack, whack, whack—the sound of *kyosakus* fill the room. Get out of here and don't come back until you know, rasps the Zen Master in your face. Tell me at once, Who is that Blazing Star?

The next day I move my desk to the floor and spend most of my business hours on the meditation cushion. I inquire of the Star. "It is a doorway," Blaise suggests. "We twinkle at its lintels with twelve eyes and twelve wings. Look more closely at your Round Table." A clear, multifaceted crystal appears underneath a smooth, shiny black stone embedded in the table. "Good. This is indestructible. It remembers. It is rich beyond measure with your measure." I penetrate this crystal with my sword. At once it expands to fill the room with milky light. I find myself on that same wondrous greensward with the six-pillared white gazebo, but this time it's a huge white mansion with hundreds of rooms, set at the far end of a giant lawn.

After a few moments of disorientation, I refocus myself at the sword's tip until an image forms. I stand in a vestibule from which thousands of doors open. I open one door and enter. I am a Hindu man with beard, dark skin, rings, white sarong, among thousands of Hindis at a religious festival. Live gurus, bigger than life size, sit on pedestals before which people bow and pray. I set off looking for my own guru but learn he has departed the fair. I open another door. I'm with young Christian monks dressed in baggy grey robes. We carry Bibles and sing hymns in the cloisters of a church. I open another door. I stand before the Wailing Wall in Jerusalem among many other worshippers. Another door: I'm out on that lovely green lawn again where many angels and humans in their light bodies, including myself, float happily about. Blaise, sixfold, stands in the gazebo like angelic pillars. Each Blaise has a bright Sun in his chest. I sit on a round table in their midst as they lay before me a huge leather-bound book. A name is inscribed in gold on its cover. About four-fifths of the book is filled with entries. I open the book and see a different name at the top of each page, one name for each lifetime, presumably. Each page, when I focus upon it, turns into a gold coin, which reveals a frieze, then a living movie of a different lifetime scenario.

"Coins, pages, doors—are they the same or different, Grail Knight?" Blaise queries with a chuckle. "These are aspects of the Nimitta the diamond. You are looking inside the Star. We are the Nimitta, the point of Absolute Light. All emanations arise from that point. It turns quite quickly, throwing beams of light out of itself as it spins. Here is the first cell, where the two became one. The potential of who you were yet to be was born from this point. The knowledge of all the beings you have been before and all the beings you are yet to be in the future was locked into this single cell.

"If you access the diamond, you access the cumulative knowledge of all the beings that you've been in the past and all the beings you are yet to be in the future for the benefit of the being you are now, that this being may be an expression of all that you've been and all that you will be. The deeper you access the diamond, or Nimitta, the closer you get to the Star. The Star is like pure being, original being, stuff that was locked within you that began you on your journey back to the Star. You see, your memory isn't so bad after all. Of course, you still don't know who is that Blazing Star."

"You seem to be distinguishing the Star from the diamond, or Nimitta. Would you explain this please?" Russell asks.

"The Star is the effulgence of the diamond. It is the tangible light force that surrounds the diamond, which is also known as the Nimitta."

I suppose the *kyosaku* hurts less the more you get whacked. Blaise comes by for another examination in the evening. "We come as we are. We come as a Blazing Star. We surround you all with the flames of transmutation. Within each of you we place a single flame. Its tip reaches the sternum, above which we place an emerald at the heart. Within this we place a point of brilliant light, an aspect of the Nimitta. We surround each of you with a sphere of sapphire blue with dancing flames around its periphery. We are pleased to be with you all, as you were before the Fall. Focus, if you wish, on the image we have given you. We place a sword above each of you. [At once this sword slices through my body from the head downwards, cleaving me at the crotch to reveal the Blazing Star in my heart as the only truly vital organ.] Good.

"We place a lantern before each of you. We place a star in your right hand. We open the book and place it before each of your lamps. We wrap the indigo velvet robe around each of you. In your left hand, we place a lectern. We also place to your left, before the lectern, a golden bowl. We ask that you just see where you are now. Remember all we have given you. Bring each of these magical weapons to mind...."

At least I'm prepared for Blaise on this item, the matter of Qabala's magical weapons. They aren't assault weapons as such, or even defensive ones. Rather, as Dion Fortune explains, "A magical weapon is some object which is found to be suitable as a vehicle for force of a particular type," or as a vehicle of its manifestation, as in the magician's rod, the seer's crystal sphere. The magical weapon for the Element of Water is a cup or chalice; for the Element of Fire, a lighted lamp; each of the Tree of Life's spheres, or Sephiroth, has a magical weapon. "These items are chosen because their nature is congenial to that of the force to be invoked; or in modern language, because their form suggests the force to the imagination by association of ideas," says Fortune.

"Good. Grail Knight, tell us what you saw."

"It was like sitting under a Christmas tree in your gazebo. The cloak and lantern and book and star and the rest were decorations on the limbs of the tree, like lights. They began to merge together as the lamp before me grew very bright. Then everything flashed white as the magical weapons merged into one light. I was in space as a star among all the other stars."

"That's pretty much what I saw," Russell says, "except for two details. I saw all the magical weapons as if inside an old alchemist's lab or apothecary shop, among the beakers, funnels, and cobwebs, suggesting this was very long ago. Then I went into the blackness and saw a single bright star."

"I saw lots of people made of white light or in their light bodies walking down a spiral staircase in the sky," Berenice says.

"We come as we are, as a Blazing Star. None of you said all of what you experienced, but that's okay. We will remind you of this experience periodically, or should we say, as you remember it. We say, the stars are out, we are in. We are that Star you are. We are like thousands and thousands of pinpoints of light at the tip of the needle. We shine out in space and are like the stars in space. There is no difference. So tiny we're ever so small, we're hardly there at all. We come as a Black Bowling Ball rolling through space. The ball and the space dissolve. We become space itself. We are beyond possible extension.

"We come as we are, as a pinpoint of light that is an atom of bright space within permanent blackness. We place a Star at the center of your being so small you would need the most powerful atomic microscope to see it. It's even smaller than that. It's half that size. It's even tinier than that. We just can't express how tiny it is. It's beyond tinyness. It contains the known universe. God is always very small. That's how God crushes that which is very big. The big expands beyond itself, dissolves into darkness. The small contracts into itself, becomes the brighter. We say, there's only a little Star and it's never very far. We leave you now, as we came, as a Blazing Star."

The next day passes quickly, in a twinkle, and soon it's time for another Blaise visit. "We come as we are. We come from not too far. We surround you all with the lilac wall of transmutation. We place the lilac flame above you. Beneath it, we place a sphere of sapphire blue with an emerald inside, and inside that, we place a diamond point of pure light. Rest with this image for a few moments.... Good. Grail Knight, care to tell us what you saw?"

"Sure. I held the Star in my hands, then it grew as big as a house and I walked in."

"Good. That is the Star when it goes supernova. Now breathe with love to the emerald, and tell us what you see."

"My God! It's one of a dozen jewels on a golden crown."

"And so it goes. We are pleased to be with you. We bring you a message, Grail Knight. We wish you to go to Camalate tomorrow and again the next day. Then go to Arthur's Courtyard; the following day, go to the courtyard at the Glastonbury Experience; and the day after, go to Chalice Hill. We think you're ready for the grave. We'll see you before too long, as Love from Above, your Blazing Star."

60

STUNG TO PIECES
IN THE CAMALATE BASKET

amalate at South Cadbury Castle, midday, the first day of Scorpio, October 23, and the Grail Knight, whose rising sign is Scorpio, has just arrived on bicycle at Arthur's jousting fields. The complacent bull—for the Grail Knight's Sun sign is Taurus—is about to get stung by the scorpion with the discomfiting themes of sex, death, rebirth, regeneration, and transcendence. Perhaps this brickbat of a Taurus will fly after all when the scorpion transmutes itself from its own catalytic venom into an eagle. Scorpio, the flaming sword that guards the Tree of Life, that incited the horses of Apollo to run amok in the inexpert hands of Phaethon, that stung the selfish Orion to death when he threatened all the animals on Crete—Scorpio is the sign of the warrior out in the battleground of physical desires, his ear cocked for the call of the higher worlds.

Our program notes this morning, supplied by astrologer John Jocelyn, complete the *mise en scene* for the Grail Knight's likely demise: "The Scorpio warrior has to deal with and work in this desire world, the great empire of error, until he fights his way to the light of truth in the sweated blood of his own agony and, through just such suffering, he emerges triumphant from the realm of death into the dawn of truth, the state of great joy." Scorpio is the sign of evolution, in which feelings, desires, and sensations are transmuted to regenerate the human. "The test of Scorpio is so difficult and dangerous an experience for most people because so many cannot lift themselves clear of its lower phase and mount up into the sky on eagle's wings, which is the promise and provision of Scorpio's re-generated forces." Shall we descend then to the transmutation-in-progress in which our hero, the American Grail Knight, cosmic, ter-restrial, domestic, and cheeky, will divinize desire, raise it to a higher plane, and turn it into aspiration. He may even live through it.

The weather at midday is alternately sunny and windy, and when I reach the rounded top of Cadbury Castle, I'm greeted by my brother and Tudor Pole, but not with open arms. My brother bears a large, bright sword and guides me with an uncharacteristically grim de-meanor to a spot on the northern corner of the hill. I notice the dome overhead and the massive sparkling emerald that is set within the hill; inside this stadium-sized emerald is a Blazing Star. I concen-trate on this Star to take my mind off what my brother is doing. He slices up my body—obviously a somewhat expendable one as I'm not dead from the operation—like a butcher and dumps all the parts in a wicker basket. Well, that's the advantage of having multiple bodies: if one goes down for the count, there's always another.

Despite my hasty dismemberment, I still feel hale and begin a lei-surely perambulation of the perimeter of Cadbury, walking along the old excavated and partially covered-up outer ramparts of the hillfort. Inside the emerald is a Round Table that is nearly the diam-eter of the hilltop. A different astrological sign marks each of the seats, all of which are occupied by knights. The Blazing Star occu-pies the center of this Round Table but just above it hovers, some-what ethereally, a golden Grail with wings. To my right on the edge of the hill runs a fence of twenty-foot high clear crystal shanks, mak-ing a protective crown encircling the hilltop.

Meanwhile, I've wrapped myself in a blanket because the wind is chilling, but the true blanket that envelops me is my desire. Deborah called me again, a couple of times, purring and flushed with antici-pation about sleeping with me again. Hilary wants to spend a week-end with me and that always means, at the least, sexual innuen-does. And Bekka, a lover from several years ago whom I met on a journey through Worcestershire when I was footloose and oblivous of the Grail Quest—without doubt, she is my most exotic anima personification—has called unexpectedly and wants to visit me for a week. Fluff up the extra pillows indeed!

All magnanimity (and bigamy) aside, there simply isn't room for three lascivious Grail Maidens in the Grail Knight's bachelor chambers and further, my landlord and confidante, dear Russell, happily married and regularly bedded, strongly advises me to abstain from uncelibate Grail activities until Scorpio has stung me properly, leaving me either dead or enlightened. Wait a minute. Make that four *femme fatales* on the Grail Knight's night-duty roster. As I pause on the brim of Camalate, I sense a whiteclad figure behind me, her arms gently resting on my shoulders, her long blonde hair in a pony-tail down to the crevice of her hips. One day I'll see your face, Guinivere.

I sit down again and search for a place in my mind where Deborah, Hilary, and Bekka are not slowly undressing and nudging their rosy-tipped breasts in my face. Meanwhile, somebody is happily hacking my body to pieces again, chucking the Grail Knight chunks into a basket like sod. That's two bodies under the cleaver—how many more can I spare? "Dangerous business, this Grail Quest," Blaise laughs. "Don't blow it, Grail Knight. It took us a long time to make all the arrangements." Okay, Boss.

Edmund, Celia, and I had a lovely quirky soccer game the other afternoon out by the apple tree, making up the rules as we went along, forgetting them, changing them, and laughing and tickling and wrestling until dinnertime when we dashed madly across the lawn and slipped and got grass-stained and then crawled laughingly to the front door. That's the energy that will get me through this tricky business. I tune into this feeling and breathe as Love from Above to the emerald in my heart center; I climb up into my brow, pull out Excalibur, and penetrate the green stone below me.

Inside, I find my brother again; I smile, then penetrate his right shoulder with my sword. Instantly, he is mounted on a horse, mail clad with crimson sashes and pennioned lance. He charges me in a furious pummel, thrusting his long lance straight through my heart and out the other end, leaving my body like a skewered mushroom before I can inhale even once. He charges again and rams it through me again, and then a third time. I'm perforated and perspiring. Damn, I wish I had been nicer to him when he was alive. Where's my shield, anyway? Where's the handbook on jousting?

Despite the loss of two bodies and three horizontal excavations of my chest cavity, I survive the ninety minute bike ride back to Wick, even though at times I would have preferred being wheeled back supine and groaning in a hay wain. Even better, I'm not accosted by any lascivious *dakinis* trying to disrobe my chastity and incite me to fewter with them in bed. Counsel is forthcoming later in the evening when the Seraphim arrive. "We come to clarify that which needs clarification. We are here to facilitate you on this path."

"Will you please tell me what my shield is, please?" I ask.

"Tell us, Grail Knight, what has Blazing Star been showing you these last months?"

Suddenly I see it—the shield: an emerald with a Blazing Star in my chest, a sapphire blue sphere around my body with flickering flames of orange and red on its periphery, a lilac flame rising up from the ground around and above me, flaming upwards to a single point of brilliant light, and a smaller lilac flame ascending from my head to this same Nimitta. My shield is the Blaise Image, I excitedly tell the Seraphim.

"Oh, thank you, you are bright tonight," the Seraphim say. "Your shield is magnificent, created by Nimitta. Now, as Blazing Star would say, we're cooking with gas. Nimitta left temporal space available for Grail Knight activities all day tomorrow."

"It seems my brother cut me to pieces twice today. How come?"

"It was an aspect of Mortdred from the final battle of Camlann. You presented him to yourself in the guise of your brother. Technically, it was not really your brother."

In the Arthurian stories, Mortdred is Arthur's bastard son, who is raised in secrecy and anonymity by Arthur's one-time lover, his aunt Morgause, along with her brood of boys (which include Gawain and Agravaine) and her husband, King Lot of the Orkneys. As an adult, Mortdred returns to Camalate to haunt Arthur with his youthful indiscretion; he is a pariah among the knights, who regard him warily. Eventually, Mortdred's insuperable resentment at being denied his birthright—an honorable, legitimate place in the royal family, as a son with a loving father—destabilizes Camalate, precipitating conflict, even war, and, in a final confrontation, Arthur and Mortdred mortally wound each other at the Battle of Camlann. Mortdred dies, Arthur is taken off to Avalon, and Camalate collapses. Functionally, Mortdred is the energy of Scorpio stinging Camalate and Arthur specifically with the *dread of mort*, death, and transmutation. Even Arthurhood must undergo the travails of *mort*.

"What about the Round Table inside the emerald at Camalate?"

"The inner Round Table you saw was pre-energized in the matrix of the hill itself. It is an inherent aspect of the geomancy of Cadbury Hill. As you are aware, the wooden Round Table was made for Uther Pendragon and was given to Guinivere at a later date; then it arrived at Camalate at Cadbury hill. Stonehenge, as Nimitta explained, is a Round Table at a different level. Avebury, too, is like these others. Cadbury, Stonehenge, and Avebury are Nimitta's wheels. Each circle of stones is a Round Table. Each circle of stones is a wheel. Your heart is a wheel, a Round Table. Each wheel relates to another wheel, bigger than these wheels—wheels within wheels. This is it, the Blazing Star—wheels within wheels."

"Well, am I supposed to fight with these guys on horseback?"

"If you don't fight, you cannot lose amicably. So, we feel most pleased with what we have achieved tonight, if we believed in achievement. Nimitta, incidentally, is working with higher members of the hierarchy and members of the Great School to schedule events at Avebury for a visit. We leave you now with love from Nimitta and Love from Above. To whatever further questions you might have you will receive answers by nonauditory transmission through our frequency."

In practical terms this means we'll keep you awake all night with fast-breaking insights, Grail Knight. It's about two a.m. and I'm watching three wheels revolving, two counterclockwise, one clockwise, with a human strapped onto the Round Table surface of each wheel, arms and legs outstretched. Natal dart boards, these interdigitating microcosmic clogs in a cosmic clock—the wheeling horrorscope, as a friend quips. In other words, our birth chart or horoscope is another wheel, another Round Table upon which we are strapped by our karma.

According to the esoteric astrology of Dhjwal Kuhl, each individual has three, not one, birth charts, at least potentially. Each chart (or wheel or Round Table) has a cross (metaphorically, a residential coffin) occupying the four directions (and four elements or logo signatures of the zodiac), and each corresponds to a level of spiritual development and evolutionary accomplishment. Most of us are strapped onto the Mutable Cross, which moves *against* the true flow of the zodiac and represents the crisis of incarnation, the mystery of form, and the manifestation of humanhood. Relatively unevolved humans, says Kuhl, make their karmic rounds of life, death, and rebirth on this zodiacal wheel with their limbs bound at the four elemental corners, crucified on the cross of time, space, and the elements—matter and biological personhood.

But this wheel can reverse its direction and start spinning counterclockwise *with* the zodiac when the "Probationer" becomes the observer of karmic events. This new Fixed Cross has the familiar elemental coordinates of Taurus, Leo, Scorpio, and Aquarius and deals with the crisis of orientation, the manifestation of Christhood, and the transiting of great points of spiritual crisis. It is also the cross of transmutation in which desire becomes aspiration. The third natal chart, the Cardinal Cross, represents the path of initiation and transcendence and pertains chiefly to the next solar system and the manifestation of divinity within a different elemental orientation. On this cross, the initiate has to incarnate only once more in each of the twelve zodiacal signs, thereby mastering the energies of the zodiac. Hercules' twelve labors, for example, are a mythic record of this advanced initiatory experience, as were Arthur's twelve battles as recounted by Malory.

What this adds up to, again in practical terms, is the Grail Knight takes his personal "horror-scope" (natal chart) to the geomantic Round Table (zodiacal chart) at Camalate or elsewhere to see how the energies match up and how well the two tables interdigitate. Where they don't, you joust. So I may not have slept well, but at least I understand now why I've been seeing myself and other figures strapped to these Round Tables revolving like starry waterwheels in the Grail Castle. Natal charts within zodiacal wheels, zodiacal wheels within natal charts, you might say.

I'm on the road to Camalate again this morning and will surely make more progress faster when the bovine gridlock in front of Wick Manor breaks up. Mr. Webber's two dozen milkers waddle elegantly down the manure-splattered lane en route to greener pastures, but nobody's in a rush, certainly not Mr. Webber, who rides behind the cows on his bicycle flicking a willow stalk at the hindmost when she saunters too slowly. Before I climb Camalate again, I prepare myself in the thirteenth-century St. Thomas á Becket Church at the foot of Cadbury Castle. I withdraw my sword and hold it before me, examining the jewelled hilt and blazing tip. I breathe life into the Nimitta shield and let it flame chromatically against the drab wooden pews. The bull may be grazing in the pasture, but the scorpion is loose in the jousting field: Berenice, beware.

The Grail Knight has prepared a list of grievances and criticisms, noting disdainfully that this anima projection is definitely not living up to his expectations and that changes must be made today, if not sooner. "Berenice, you are warm-hearted, mothering, and feminine," I say to her in the church, "but your mind is chaotic and undisciplined—*animus abscondis*, as it were."

"Grail Knight," the ghost of Berenice ripostes, "you're an unloving, cold, analytical, insensitive male with no awareness of the Mother—*anima obscura*, as it were."

"Berenice, you've locked up your inner male in a closet."

"Grail Knight, you chase every pretty woman in sight, trying to make her into your own unrealized inner woman." Touché all around.

This little skirmish puts me in a proper jousting mood on the great wheel of Camalate. The wheel occupies the entire hillside with the ghost of the original wooden Round Table situated like an eyeball in

its center. My escorts today are three scarlet-clad Seraphim, emboldened with swords and shields. I shouldn't be surprised: aside from
the fact they work for Blaise, the Seraphim are traditionally associated with Mars or Mars energy, and that's the planetary ruler of
Scorpio. Just some old friends over for the dismemberment of the
Grail Knight.

They direct me to the Blazing Star at the center of the wooden
Round Table. My breath is momentarily arrested as I realize how
keenly the inner and outer, the personal and the archetypal, the
mythic and the geomantic, match up here at Camalate, jousting field
of the heart. I settle my horse, folding myself into the full lotus, and
hold the reins steady on my breathing, but it's hard to stop my teeth
from chattering and my body from shivering because I didn't wear
enough warm clothes. Finally, I hone my concentration to a fine
point sharp enough to penetrate the emerald and Blazing Star and
knock a few Seraphim off their mounts.

The entire greensward of Camalate is a zodiacal Round Table,
divided into twelve wedges that extend beyond the hill and into the
neighboring landscape like directional finders. One wedge gleams
crimson, and I'm directed at once to sit in the Scorpio section, which
faces east. Each of the twelve wedges of the Camalate wheel has its
own Round Table out in the landscape, which is to say, each sign
has its unique jousting field. This gives Camalate 144 wedges, as
each principle Sun sign is represented twelvefold as a subset. The
Scorpio wheel is situated on what is now called Littleton Hill and its
immediate environs, a quarter mile away. Behind Littleton is Round
Hill. I know at once that this is the true site of Camlann, that quasi-
historic battlefield upon which the quasi-historic Arthur fought his
last battle and fell. Historians and archeologists have never been able
to trace the location of Camlann to their satisfaction and none that
I'm aware of has ever suggested Round Hill. But they were looking
for the remains of the wrong kind of battle.

Riding over to Littleton jousting field, I marvel at the elegance of
Camalate's extensive twelvefold jousting facility. It's like an immense
etheric sports stadium for Grail Knight transmutation, which no

doubt is sport and probably entertainment for the Gods, a few of whose names I might mention but won't. The entire geomythic theater, with its 144 different jousting positions, is at least one mile in diameter, with South Cadbury Castle as the hub of its wheel. "Therefore, I will joust with thee, for I hate all these that be of Arthur's court," said a feisty knight in Malory's text. They were not in this land but four days "but there came a cry of jousts and tournament that King Arthur let make."

I sit down in the center of the Littleton jousting wheel and survey the field. There are a couple of contenders laying about, waiting indolently yet attentively for my preparations. I cross my legs, calm my breathing, withdraw my sword, erect the Nimitta shield, and announce I'm ready for business. I try to wax wroth about their despicable presence at Littleton. "Yo! You clanking wimp of Somerset sausage made of liver-stuffed croissant and rich cream sauce—hey, over here, blimp-brain!" My encouraging remarks fail to rouse him, so I get up, walk over, and prod him with my sword. "Say fella, do you mind? I'm here all the way from the Dog—and that's a long pedal, let me tell you—for a little spot of jousting. So is this naptime or what?" He falls off his horse and lies inert like an assaulted insect retracted into its carapace—a conscientious objector, no doubt.

The next knight has more gumption and gallops with some spunk across the field, lance raised and fewtering. No problem: I hold my sword steady and penetrate the starseed inside his chest emerald, grab a gold coin from the pot, and withdraw, deflecting his lance parries with my shield. The third knight, smartly attired in silver armor with a scarlet sash—the Giorgio Armani look for Grail Knights—charges at once and is similarly decoined. The fourth knight declines to parry lance or to respond to my inflammatory comments—some kind of pre-Iron John, nonmacho, soft feminist-reconstructed male—so I take his gold coin without a formal joust and wish him God-speed at his mens' group weekend campout.

My four defeated knights strew the field like toppled manikins—Grail Knights manqué—as I crunch an apple with insouciance. "I marvel what knight he is that doth such deed of arms," queries King

Mark. "Sir, I know him well for a noble knight as few now be living, and his name is Sir Cheeky American Grail Knight," replies Sir Tristram, who is sleeping with King Mark's young wife, Isolde, so can you really trust him? "It were great shame," says King Mark, "that he should go thus away, unless that some of you meet with him better." Sir Tristram: "Sir, it were great shame and villainy to tempt him any more at this time, inasmuch as he and his horse are weary both; for the deeds of arms that he hath done this day, and they be well considered, it were enough for Sir Launcelot du Lake."

The horse and Grail Knight have enough spunk to return to Camalate and its central wooden Round Table before retiring for the day. On the lane at the bottom of Camalate, I encounter six bulls ambling desultorily along. "Blaise, is that you in there?" I ask one of the bulls. "Feeling a bit Taurean today, are you?" No answer, not even a shake of the nose ring.

On the great wheel of Camalate again, Arthur and Guinivere stand before the wooden table. Facing me, they ask me for my four gold coins gleaned from the Littleton wimps; they examine the coins, then ask me to explain to them the meaning of each. This requires some research. I spend an hour probing the coins with my sword but fail even to dent them. Whatever icons or movies they contain remain unviewed by this Knight. Then the crimson-clad Seraphim say, "Place them in the Well, tomorrow. Time to return home to the Dog."

Just to make sure no vestigial spunk is wasted before the day is out, on the ride home I make a wrong turn that sets me ten miles out of my way, which isn't fun if you've jousted all day plus ridden thirty-four miles and have never claimed you're some kind of athlete or thick-sinewed, steroidal, macho hunk.

How the disconsolate Grail Knight limps into Glastonbury the next day, his horse drained of spunk, laden with sighs and groans and complaints and halts and protestations. It seems he didn't wake up the next morning as quite the unflappable, unforgiven Clint Eastwood of the Grail he thought he'd been at Littleton Hill. The highest and, in fact, most coherent aspiration noted at the moment of his waking and its long-lingering problematic aftermath was to be ensconced in the downy, melting arms and shipwrecking thighs of Deborah from Charmouth. How the Grail Knight leaves a vapor trail of mental exhaust about his fuming head, polluting the Friday morning ethers of the Somerset zodiac as he chugs along, frustrated, isolated, desireful.

During my first hour at Arthur's Courtyard, I sit on the bench that's on the left as you enter through the gate. I visualize that the trickling waters flow through my body from my head to feet, cleansing everything in sight. I examine the gold coins, and each one reveals a knight on horseback, but this is hardly newsworthy for my august mentors back at Camalate. During the second hour, I sit on the bench that's on the right side of the stream, empty my mind, and let the waters flow through my heart until my body flushes white. No swordwork, no knights, no images, only stillness and flowing water. After the second hour, I feel healed, energized, wonderfully restored, even inspired. Headache, exhaustion, sore muscles, crabbiness, despondency—all gone. I understand the truth of Matthew Chancellor's evocative words in 1751 describing a dream in which he was directed to immerse himself in the Pilgrim's Basin here in Arthur's Courtyard to cure his asthma, which he'd endured for thirty-four years.

One night at home in North Wooton, Chancellor dreamed he was in Glastonbury and saw "in the Horse Track some of the finest water I ever saw in my life. I kneeled down on my knees and drank of it." A "Person" instructed Chancellor to drink this water for seven Sundays in succession, noting "where this water comes from is out of the Holy Ground where a great many Saints and Martyrs have been buried." When Chancellor's dream and recovery were reported, it drew many others to the Well such that at the peak of pilgrimage, on May 5, 1751, ten thousand people flocked to Glastonbury for the healing waters. Soon the water was sold by London apothecaries in bottles with a Grail-shaped label and the inscription "Calix. Dulcis. Avaloniae-Glaston." A decade later the spring lost its repute and the Well was practically abandoned again, although its restorative reputation was still acknowledged no doubt among intinerant Grail

Knights. Over the centuries, many thousands of healings have occurred in this stone-paved courtyard and will again in the future, Wellelsey Tudor Pole noted in 1963, provided the place is "beautified and brought back into full use for that purpose."

The next stop in my schedule today is Kopp's courtyard off the High Street, once accurately called the "little Covent Garden of Glastonbury" but subject to periodic tides of success and failure, mercantile fullness and emptiness. Today the tide is out and the wheel of commerce halted; the shops are empty as the managment sorts things out. It's just as well because now I will have no interruptions for my subterranean activities; and, as soon as I finish my psychic outing, I can dash back to the store and get two of those luscious hot pasties I saw in the window. I wrench my attention away from prospects of lunch to a stone fountain *sans* flowing water in the center of the courtyard. I position my sword directly at the center of this fountain then move my concentration to the sword tip. Instead of an empty stone basin, there is a three-foot-high stone collar around a recessed chamber. I use the sword as a torch and climb down into the dark vault: it's a tunnel, one of those ancient, numerous, and vanished tunnels Glastonbury is famous for, at least among the mystics and crazies, and—are you surprised?—Grail Knights.

I crawl on hands and knees through this stone-skinned intestine with my shield and sword proffered ahead of me. I meet one, then another, *Yeti*, who act as sentinels in the passageway but let me pass without incident, no doubt aware I am on company business. Now here comes a man, heavily armed, right at me, but, before he can blink, I've penetrated his brow and removed a gold coin. It turns into a pearl in my palm. Next comes a naked woman squeezing her breasts and trickling her fingers invitingly along her crotch, but she's as sexually bland as Madonna and anyway, no thanks, I already have Deborah, Hilary, and Bekka queuing for my bed. Even so, I liberate a silver coin from her brow pot and continue on through the fun house. If I were not finding this whole expedition a bit boring, I could actually get lost in here. But what most concerns me is this: when's lunch?

Finally, I reach the giant crystal inside the Tor of Glastonia, the glassy city *Ynys Witrin*, the island of glass, and the chapel of the Green Knight's domain. I penetrate the skin of the crystal mountain and enter a cavern with a pool of clayey water. To the left is a throne, unoccupied. The place looks like it was recently excavated or like a Hollywood set in between prop changes. I penetrate the pool and descend swiftly on my sword through an emerald, then a Blazing Star, until I'm on solid ground again. A fabulously handsome man and woman stand on either side of a Tree of Life replete with fruits. They hand me a golden apple.

I don't mean to complain, but when St. Collen entered the Tor in the seventh century by a secret door and found himself in the sumptuous halls of Gwyn ap Nudd, King Under the Hill, Gwyn rose from his golden throne and offered St. Collen all manner of foods and beverages, a smorgasbord beyond compare. Gwyn and his retainers were enjoying a massive lunch at which golden apples were no doubt a dessert option. The dyspeptic Collen then said something that probably prejudiced the lunchtime possibilities for all future Grail Knights visiting *Tref Wyn*, the homestead of Gwyn. Damn ill-spoken cleric! "I do not eat the leaves of a tree," he said boorishly, splattering Gwyn's table with a phial of holy water before he stormed out of the hall, lunchless. I'm sure I didn't toss any water at anybody under the Tree inside the Tor, but when at last I stride into the store for my hot pasties, the shopkeeper shakes her head. Sorry. All sold out. Can you call in again tomorrow?

61

"I Don't Mind Dying but This is Killing My Body"

he next afternoon I rouse myself from a brainless day under the covers, having spent the day as thoughtful and inspired and porous as a stone in the Earth, and stagger over to the Fairy Dell. In my half-awake state under the Grail duvet up in my chambers, I wasn't sure if it was Edmund or Bomor the gnome who was tugging my pajama sleeves, telling me to come joust.

Once I'm outside the house, Bomor walks with me along the rutted farm track at dusk. I sit on the green mound of the Fairy Dell and observe a black-caped knight on horseback; he sports an unbelievably large lance. I really don't need this today. I never wanted to get out of bed. For the hard-working Grail Knight, after six mornings a week there *ought* to be Sunday morning—tea in bed with *The Times*, leaving us well rested for the one day of fewtering, dismemberment, death, and the usual perquisites of the Grail Quest.

Bomor warns me to prepare my shield and sword quickly, but the black knight holds his horse to tight pirouettes and doesn't charge. His vassal does and quite precipitously. I manage to penetrate his brow and extract an acorn. That's why he's only a vassal. From vassals you only get nuts, not cash. The black knight still holds his position at the far end of the field, his face alternating between a skeletal and human visage. Now another knight advances on me, yielding a lump of coal when I penetrate his brow. This is a very downmarket lot today. It's grown dark and the full moon dominates the sky. As I leave for home, the black knight, all of three dozen yards away, keeps turning in preparation for a charge that he seems strangely reluctant to make; since I'm not sure about this guy, every time he moves I redo my sword and shield. "Most knights go to bed with a headache," I quip to Bomor, adjusting Russell's merlinish remark for present circumstances.

Berenice's uninspired dinner of boiled potatoes and indigestible bean-and-nut burgers leaves me in a flounce of dissatisfaction as I smack the suds in my bath. Angels of the bath-tub, hear ye the complaints of this Grail Knight, squirming in the bubbles. Why can't you send me a lovely young maiden with clinging thighs and moist harbor to chaste around my evenings instead of these deadbeats on horseback? The only answer I get from the boys above is the image of the Grail and its lilac flame. Transmute the erection, Grail Knight. An invisible hand seems to gather up all of Celia's bathtoys floating around me and stacks them in the Grail under the lilac flame. I suppose this is a cue. I make a mental list of all my desires, all the women I want to sleep with tonight, the missed luncheon specials, the motorized Grail bike, the enhanced income, the answers to all my questions, and toss them like broken tree limbs into the fire. The conflagration doesn't leave much: just a Blazing Star, a brilliant pinpoint of light inside an emerald, inside a bathtub, inside a bathroom, inside Wick Manor, inside the belly of the Girt Dog of Langport, on the outskirts of the Region of the Summer Stars.

Later in the evening, that brilliant pinpoint of light observed in the Grail Knight's tub expands into the familiar, but O so mysterious, six Blaises. "We come as we are. We come from not too far. We come as a Blazing Star. We greet you all. We are most pleased with the events, Grail Knight. We are pleased with what you have experienced. It was much of what was available. We surround you all with the lilac flames of transmutation. We place a sphere of sapphire blue around each of you. Around this, we place dancing orange and golden flames. Within the sphere, we place the emerald, and, within this, at the center, a point of brilliant light, a Blazing Star, a reference point of who you are. Be with this image for a few moments....

"And, from within the brilliant point of the Mind of Man, there is a point within the Mind of God. Friends of the Sangrail, we are pleased to be with you. We hope you will continue with the assemblage of the Round Table. There is much to be done. Time is short. We have a list of suggestions we will give you soon for adventures during the growing moon."

"Why did you say 'Friends of the Sangrail?'" I ask.

"We meant that you are one with us, as you are, that your purpose and our purpose is the same—no difference, except you don't remember. A little clue like this might break the veil that stops you remembering. We blow you a white flower, Berenice. We give Russell a red rose. We give the Grail Knight a green flower."

"Thanks, Blaise. How come some of the knights don't want to joust with me?"

"Didn't you read the stories? Then it should be clear why they didn't wish you to penetrate them. We can't and won't do it all for you."

When Arthur sponsored a jousting tournament at the castle of Lady Lyonesse, young Sir Gareth displayed his considerable competence yet would not joust with Sir Lancelot because he was his mentor and best friend at Camalate. Nor would Lancelot, regarded to be the best jouster in the land, take on Gareth because he saw how the young knight carried the day against a strong field of contenders; though he could, Lancelot saw no gentlemanly reason for ruining Gareth's triumph. "As for me, this day he shall have the honour; though it lay in my power to put him from it I would not."

"Was Malory aware of the esoteric aspects of the Arthur story?"

"Malory was inspired, but he attributed it to himself, which is okay. It's only one perspective."

"What does it mean that Arthur had twelve battles?"

"Arthur's twelve battles were the twelve segments. They represented a precognitive event for Arthur of what he would have to deal with in the process of letting go of the personality, for its death. Incidentally, Camlann did take place where you were shown, but many other battles happened elsewhere. Arthur never overcame Mortdred, as you remember. We refer to the Arthur mentioned in Malory."

"Malory says that Arthur also fought eleven kings right after he pulled the sword from the stone. Are these the same as his twelve battles?"

"Yes, on one level. On another level, it was Arthur's coming to understand each sign of the zodiac and its esoteric or inner aspects. The Arthurian legend exists on a phi spiral, so two points may appear to be similar but are actually at different levels of unfoldment. We hope that you don't emphasize the fifteen Arthurian events so much as the function, process, message, and myth-realization behind each of them. Arthur's twelve battles represent the assimilation of the Fixed Cross. This is referred to Biblically as overcoming the Four Beasts of the Apocalypse."

"Will you explain what these are?" Berenice asks.

"When you make space with others just to sit and be as Love from Above, then it has repercussions on your spiritual energy centers. Joy releases much in terms of energy in the aspects of yourselves that are important. Other emotions do not have the same effect. Each of you must free yourself, if you wish, from the Four Beasts of the Apocalypse. These reside in your first four energy centers, or chakras. Each of you has four beasts in your first four centers. You have a bull, a snake (or man), a lion, and an eagle. These are the Beasts of the Apocalypse. They are also, as you will remember, the four logo signatures of the zodiac. They are also the glyphs for the four elements of earth, water, fire, and air as they live in you. Each beast rules three zodiacal signs, giving you twelve in all. Learning the lessons of the four beasts is what your life's lesson and life purpose are about. Of course, it is dependent on your will. If your will is aligned to one of the beasts then, you will not be able to fulfill your life purpose. If you free your will from being attached to each or any or all of the beasts and their purpose, then you have a potential to do that which at present escapes you.

"It is your will. Whoever you are, we cannot and will not influence your will. It is up to you. You may subjugate any or each of the beasts through many means. If you tread your path, then you will encounter the beasts in their true form. You will meet them as pure energy. Each beast has a purpose, and its energy can be transmuted and brought in line with your life purpose. Each beast has a function. Each function can aid your true purpose. We can assist you with the way in which you may familiarize yourself with the Beasts of the Apocalypse. If you wish, we can guide and advise and aid you in being able to transmute the energies of the four Beasts of the Apocalypse. Is that clear?"

"Yes, Blaise, and thanks. Now what about this Emperor Lucius of Rome who had fifty giants working for him and demanded obedience from Arthur, who refused it. What does this story refer to?"

"The first three letters of the Emperor's name *Luc* indicates solar light. We could, though with some difficulty, define Lucius as in between the Solar and Cosmic Logos. He couldn't relate to the Cosmic Logos yet had transcended the Solar Logos. Arthur refused to send him his dues. Arthur was solar, but he was not ready to transcend this and was still working at his solar karma. Killing Emperor Lucius meant Arthur was unable to assimilate and transcend; therefore, he was obliged to put to death that which from a lower level appeared to be in his way.

"We'll see you at Chalice Hill tomorrow, Grail Knight. And so we leave you as we are, better by far, yours in love and truth, beyond reason, your friend of the Sangrail, Blazing Star."

I don't mind dying, but this is killing my body. I reach Chalice Hill close to dusk the next day after a slow sixteen mile chug on the Grail bike. Michael stands with sword and shield atop the Tor's glass mountain keeping himself busy fending off aberrant cosmic energies and noxious influences, while here on Chalice Hill stands an equally formidable giant of a woman, a two-hundred-foot-tall Mona Lisa whose ambivalent feminine smile quickly waxes malevolent. At least I'm well-insulated for whatever transmutative nastiness is about to descend on me. With my eight layers of jackets and sweaters, I am a circus walrus on wheels; I'm so fat with wool, cotton, and corduroy I can barely turn my neck. Blaise is here and gestures for me to sit down on the hill.

I enter the Blazing Star inside the emerald in my heart Grail bowl then find myself in that same vestibule with a thousand possible doors. One door is marked "The Mother," and I enter. I stand in a grassy field and wait. An old woman draped in black appears, and, although I can see a myriad of wrinkles, I cannot make out her face. I follow her up a steep mountain path along treeless hills reminiscent of Wales or Greece. We reach the summit, from which I survey the valley below and the neighboring mountain. She straps me to a wooden cross, sets the cross firmly in the ground so that I face the valley and the other mountain. Then she tells me to climb out of my body through the crown chakra and to take the crown with me. I slip out of my body through the head and stand next to myself not envying myself a bit. With my sword, I penetrate the Blazing Star in the emerald in the crucified body of the Grail Knight, merge with the Star, then drift inside it out into space, into a void. Far below I watch the old woman remove my body from the cross. Easy death, painless, didn't even feel the cold. She slides it into a wooden casket then buries it. Well, there go my financial worries. As Woody Allen astutely notes in *Love and Death*, being dead cuts down on your expenses.

The woman rejoins me, and we circle the mountain making ghostly gyres, then fly across the valley to hover above a cottage on the mountain. Inside a man and woman making love are on the verge of orgasm. At the moment of ejaculation, I descend into the woman's womb as sperm and egg unite. I watch myself grow into a miniature human inside this new human mother. I am a golden infant with a crown on my head. Somewhere a woman chants *O Mother of ours, unbend us now. O Mother of ours, unbend us now* as my new mother squeezes me down the birth canal into the world of physical light again.

The trouble with rebirth, I reflect disconsolately amidst the suds and Celia's plastic motorboats, is that it reinstates all the worries and problems you thought you dropped when you died. Woody Allen is wrong. Your bills don't go away just because you're dead. They just gather in the "in" box. Russell pokes his head in the bathroom. "Do you think you can wrap up the Grail bath in the next ten minutes? Uncle Blaise just wheeled in."

"We come as we are," Blaise begins as soon as I enter the livingroom. "We come as a Blazing Star, with a petal on each point, each point a point of light; at the center, a point of light, brighter than the brightest star. We surround you with the wall of lilac flames, the flames of transmutation, the elixir of transformation, from the point of infinite light above, down into the Earth below, a wall of lilac flames. Around each of you, we place a sphere of sapphire blue, brilliant in its transparency. Around this, we place a ring of golden flames, orange, topaz, gold, around the periphery of the sapphire globe. Within this sphere, just above the center, we place an emerald of six sides, brilliant green, like moss near a forest pond, of emerald green, brilliant and full of light. Above the emerald, at each of your throats, we place a ruby of eight sides with eight petals within, a brilliant ruby full of light. Just below the emerald at the center of your sphere, at the center of yourselves, we place a brilliant Blazing Star, a pinpoint of brilliant light, a Star, a Nimitta, just above the navel and a little ways inside.

"We would like you to remember this new image. See yourselves and others as this, while you're together and apart. Each morning when you wake up, each night before you go to bed, each time you leave the house, use this image. As you breathe love to the sphere of sapphire blue and golden periphery, so the Star grows more radiant, more brilliant, more bright. So we say, maintain this image. You do as you wish. Just be with this image for a little time...."

"Blaise, I notice you've changed the Blaise Image slightly, putting the Star below the emerald. Will you explain the significance of the elements of this image?"

"The lilac flames are the ray of the Christ. They are the flames of purification. They cleanse all other rays. They make pure that which is impure. They help you to see clearly, to hear clearly, to be clear. They bring you closer to the lilac ray, the ray of the Christ Light.

"The Star above is His Supreme Holiness, the Architect of infinite time and space, His Holiness the absolute infinite point of light above, the One in Excelsius, the point called Nimitta. We bring to you that point as part of ourselves, living in you as you and in everyone. The relationship between the Star within and the point of infinite light above is one, not two.

"The globe we referred to as a sapphire blue of brilliant light is the Buddhic sphere, the Buddha's emanation on the Earth plane, the Enlightened One, the Illumined One. The sapphire globe surrounded with golden light is the Buddhic sphere, surrounded with the gold of wisdom, of knowledge, not dependent on anything other than itself; knowledge that is truth as consciousness itself, as light, as joy, as rapture.

"The green emerald in your chest represents the Fallen One in you, the one so close to the Absolute who separated himself and fell from above. It is that in you which is that one. We will talk about the emerald more on another occasion.

"The ruby in the throat is the doorway between what you call conscious and unconscious experience. It is the doorway which swings, that allows the body's airs to come and go, as its petals open and close. It is the doorway that allows the gold of the periphery to the Buddhic sphere and the lilac ray of the Christ to communicate itself through the Star in the center of your selves, like a decoder.

"Why are we doing this image and what does it mean, ultimately?" Russell asks.

"When you let go of your body, you will understand what you have been given. We wish you all to use this image for it to be what you are in light. It will be there for you if you are there for it. If you only take parts, other than in the sequence we introduced, you may become a little fragmented. When you remember this image, remember it as we have given it to each of you. Each will experience it slightly differently through the filters of individual perception. This is quite normal, and expected, but remember, try to bring more light into the image. It can always be brighter. The message of the sphere and ray and the colors will have sounds that we will give you later. These will activate the light bodies you have filled and will facilitate more travel. Practice this image, if you wish. You will enjoy it, when the time comes, if you do."

"The three of us keep picking up that you're planning a visit for us to Avebury sometime. What's involved in your making arrangements for a visit like this? I mean, why can't we just go tomorrow?"

"Imagine the universe is like a great big machine. Planets, Earth, Sun—tiny little things in the machine of the universe. Now, how are the conditions in you and in the mechanisms of the universe going to coincide?"

"So it's a matter of astrological alignments?"

"If that's the way you want to see it. Humans nowadays think that things are fixed because you are so fixed with your rational mind. When you look up there at the sky, imagine each star as a console, each with a dial and several knobs. Someone up there is tuning the whole works. Remember that to arrange the inner and outer coincidence of events beneficial for someone like you is no mean feat. Remember also that it requires considerable tampering with the mechanism, so it has to be done by the one at the controls."

"The great disc jockey of the sky?"

"Correct. When Venus is in its correct position and its rays touch on your heart, then something happens; otherwise not. Your scale is small so our illustration is small. The facts are much, much bigger than anything your mind could imagine. By the way, Grail Knight, we have two recommendations. We wish all of you to be aware of the lines of energy covering the Earth. Think of them as you are still or as you move about. Be aware of them. Place your attention on these lines. Second, Grail Knight, this is for you specifically. As soon as the Moon is new, be at Glastonbury Abbey as early that morning as is possible. Spend at least five hours there. We would then like you to visit Arthur's Courtyard again on the following day. Other than that, once the Moon is new, remain here."

"Blaise, the other night you spoke of the Friends of the Sangrail," Berenice says. "Is it always the same people in the fifteen Arthur events?"

"We are pleased you have asked this question. This enables us to take you on a little trip, if you wish. We ask that you give us your attention for a little while. We wish to take you somewhere where you haven't been before. Breathe to the Star as Love from Above...."

We breathe to the Star until it shifts free from its position and becomes a means of conveyance. We seem to be travelling inside or as the Star. We hover above an island in the ocean then start descending. Afterwards, we compare trip notes. Berenice saw a massive mountain and many other hills below it. She saw Blaise as big as the mountain, then numerous people, including Edmund, emeralds strewn on the beach, crashing waves, craggy rocks. Russell saw the harbor, filled with all types of water-faring vehicles, from primitive coracles to futuristic bubbles, all forms of transport. He saw the three of us standing on the beach. I saw a golden dome, under which stood a building made of eight globes stacked on top of one another, each a different color. I entered the blue globe and was washed in a field of greyish blue light, then I stood on the beach, refreshed. After that, Blaise returned us to Wick, but the sense of being there at the mountain was much more vivid than on our previous trips out with Blaise.

"Where did we go?" I ask excitedly.

"Some call it Mount Meru. Some call it Mount Analogue. Some call it Mount Kailas. It goes under many names."

How remarkable: then it's a true place, as René Daumal suggested in his unfinished "symbolically authentic" metaphysical classic, *Mount Analogue*. As Daumal originally envisioned it, proposing the existence of Mount Analogue as a necessary idea, Mount Analogue was the "ultimate symbolic mountain" because it is inaccessible to "ordinary human approaches."

Secretly he knew it must be real: "I felt that in spite of everything *some part of me deep down firmly believed in the material existence of Mount Analogue*." It must exist geographically as the visible door to the invisible, as the axis that unites Heaven and Earth; as such, its base is accessible, but its summit inaccessible, to humans, Daumal reasoned. The island has a circumference of several thousand kilometers, says Daumal, yet it remains practically invisible to seafarers because it's protectively encased in a shell of curved space. "It's matter of a closed *ring of curvature*, spacious and impenetrable, which surrounds the country at a fixed distance with an invisible, intangible rampart. Because of it, *everything takes place as if Mount Analogue did not exist.*" Even so, Daumal estimated Mount Analogue's geographical location as southeast of Tasmania, southwest of New Zealand, and west of the island of Auckland.

"Why did you bring us there tonight?"

"It is for your inspiration in the months to come. It will give you a firm foundation of spiritual wealth."

"I saw a group of people on the beach, as if we were waiting for something, our work perhaps." Berenice says.

"You have only just begun. You have not even contacted your group yet. You know members of it but you have not started work together yet. Therefore, your position is indeed on the beach. The temple the Grail Knight visited was a healing temple. Each of you saw your part in the development as it is for this time.

"Was this astral travelling?" I ask.

"Where we go is not astral. Far beyond astral. There are three realms in your practice called the Three *Kayas.* We take you to the *Dharmakaya.*"

"That's high class stuff, Blaise."

"Only the best."

"But how did we go—in what body?"

"Your Star."

"But in terms of the traditional classifications of higher being bodies, which one?"

"Atomic being body."

"Is this how we travelled with you last year?"

"Those trips were not facilitated in the same way. They were more related to the projection of your mental body and its etheric shell. This is more dynamic."

"Blaise, you said just a moment ago we had not even contacted our group yet." Berenice says. "What group? Is this related to my question about Friends of the Sangrail?"

"Correct. It is a soul group. Such a group involves the same people, but they evolve and change places. Each learns more by being in

different relations to one another. Each soul group gathers more information for itself and its component parts by reënactments of the
same myth in varying relationships in different cultural settings; and
also by going backwards and forwards in time; and also by having
the facility of replaying this particular setting, so that there are several variations and they learn the most from it."

"Does someone ever leave this soul group?"

"How many cells make up your first finger? Approximately 1000
cells, let's say. Now, one of them decides it wants to leave, so what
happens? Is the finger the same or different? Each day you shed a
few cells from that finger, don't you? Each time the Grail Knight
bangs his fingers on the typewriter keys a few cells get scrubbed.
Imagine an atom with mobile particles, each buzzing around its center. Some wild ones zip off. Now is that atom the same or different?
Essentially it's still an atom, even though a proton or two may have
split. Now that means the energy field around the atom is of one
nature even though the parts may appear to leave. Each part is a
part of the whole and is in dynamic relationship with that whole.
Each is fluid and flexible and contributes to the whole. Each has a
knowledge and inherent memory based on its position and circum-
stance in relation to the whole. There you have an atom with a neu-
tron and some protons. Reciprocal maintenance is the key that unlocks that door.

"And so, Friends of the Sangrail, we leave you without scrubbing
even one cell from your little finger, as a Blazing Star."

62

How Morgause Seduced Arthur in a Tree

The New Moon has come around but it's arriving with a solar eclipse. "You must forgive everyone," Blaise whispered to me on the bike ride into Glastonbury. "Drop all the charges. Love them all."

Now, as I sit in the roofless Lady Chapel of the Abbey without thoughts or intentions on a bench wrapped in a shawl of the Mother's calm, I feel I can do it. Drop all the charges. The Mary presence is strong. I breathe to the Blazing Star in a well of love and serenity and absolution. Around noon I relocate to the fish pond; from here I can see the tunnel that links the pond with the stone chamber inside Chalice Hill. I see another tunnel making its mole's passage from Kopp's courtyard to the Tor; that's the one I crawled through. I also can see there is a special underground chamber between the Lion's Head and Arthur's Courtyard at Chalice Well and an etheric temple on top of it.

When I return to the Lady Chapel, these glimpses of secret subterranean Glastonbury fuse into a single image. Glastonbury: *Domus Dei*—the Home of God; *Secretum Domini*—The Secret of the Lord. This is how the monks always viewed the town. I think I see why. Glaston-bury's inner or essential layer is a living Tree of Life temple: Glaston's Berry, Glasteing's apple tree, from Beckery to Paradise, from the Abbey to Pointer's Ball.

The Glastonbury temple begins at Beckery Chapel on Bee-Keeper's Island, home of the Perpetual Choir of *Afallach* and with roots in the Pleiades. In fact, Beckery is the root of the temple; that's where the bees come in. The occult sound of the *Muladhara,* or root chakra, is the sound of buzzing, swarming bees; so Bee-Keeper's Island is the place where this root energy that is like bees is mastered, contained, and assimilated. From Beckery, you cross the Perilous Bridge over the River Brue into the domain of myth-living at Wearyall Hill, not weary at all: *Vr-Heale,* the site of the spiritual hero, the place of spiritual healing, the hill of the whole Human, and the place of high spiritual potency activated by master geomancer Joseph of Arimathea. Weary-all: a little holograph of Albion and his redemptive destiny.

From here you go overland to Pointer's Ball, Nimuë's initiatory domain, Avalonian egg-door, site of the sword test for kingship with the immortal Green Knight. Then to the Abbey, reputed grave of King Arthur, and on to Chalice Well, where Joseph established Britain's first Christian *ecclesia,* then past Merlin's secret doorway, his famed *esplumoir* to Shambhala, and up Chalice Hill, sacerdotal terrain for Morgan and her nine priestesses of Avalon and their arcane temple of the Holy Grail; on to the Tor, King Avallach's Glass Mountain, and then Paradise, anonymous dell of divinity overlooking a lime-hued bowl of tranquillity, and finally to Gog and Magog, the imperishable twin pillars at the top of the temple.

Overland processionals, underground tunnels, and light lines form the threefold skeletal structure of Glasteing's Tree of Life and the twelve spheres or stations along the way form its fruit. And it's enlivened by the Michael Oroboros Line that runs sword-glistening and true, straight and thoroughly through, Avalon's celestial apple. Just as enriching is the overlap of three domes, at Beckery, Chalice Hill, and the Tor, forming a triple *vesica piscis* whose threefold center and prime beneficiary is Chalice Well. And the twin-halved, doubly zodiacal star wheel of Somerset cleaves at Glastonbury along the Michael line precisely at the geomantic hinge between Pisces, waning, and Aquarius, waxing. In other words, the bulk of Glasteing's Tree is situated, with respect to positions on the star wheel, within a Piscean and Aquarian landscape.

The Celtic myth of Glasteing is central to the mystery, the secret of

Glastonbury. As William of Malmesbury related it, Glasteing, one of twelve brothers, followed his eight-legged sow on its wanderings through the countryside, eventually finding her under an apple tree suckling thirty piglets. Where she lay became *Glasteingaburgh*, Glastonbury.

Under an apple tree: clearly that's the Glastonbury Tree of Life temple—GLSTNBRY, as Qabala writes it. If we could read it, the name itself would reveal the mystery. GLS is all threes: Ghimel (3), Lammed (30), Sheen (300), or discounting the zeroes, 333, which totals 9, as in Morgan's Nine Priestesses, or the nine spheres of the Tree of Life below the crown as in Berenice's dream. The number indicates Mary, Mother of Christ, Queen of Heaven, ruler of the astral plane, Mother to Glastonbury, buried in the Abbey. In gematria, which interprets the number/letters of Qabala, this sequence of 3s is all about movement, from the most rarified to the almost palpable breath of the Gods, a "movement in progressive enlargement, from the uncontrolled functional action of Ghimel (3), through the controlled connecting agent Lammed (30), going as far as the universal Sheen (300), mythically considered to be the 'spirit' or 'breath' of God; in fact, the organic process of the cosmic life," as Qabalist Carlos Suarés explains.

TN comprises *Tav* (400), which is the alphabet's final letter, denoting a chalice as the quintessential shaping of matter into a receptive form; and *Noun* (50), denoting a fish, ruled by Scorpio, and pertaining to the issues of death and regeneration. Together they suggest the seed of manifested life, its transmutation and regeneration within the material chalice of biological manifestation: the fish in the chalice. The Grail Quest, in other words.

BRY is the berry, the fruit, the golden apple: the catalytic spiritual spark within the worlds. Specifically, *Bayt* (2) and *Raysh* (200) are two expressions of containers, *Bayt* being the cosmic archetype of all containers, the Cosmic Mother, and *Raysh* being the cosmic container of all stars and light, the astral or Avalon's golden apple.

Yod (10) is the staff, the rod, the hand of fire, the lightning jag in the Region of the Summer Stars that ignites and quickens; it is Joseph of Arimathea's flowering staff, the spark of cosmic existence enlivening the created worlds, life enlivening the Avalonian berry. BRY is Joseph of Arimathea initiating the Glastonbury temple, planting and fertilizing the seed for the New Jerusalem. The Glastonbury temple design was carefully wrought—shall we say in its very words, invoked?—to accommodate a grand future purpose.

"Glastonbury was known as *Domus Dei* and the Secret of the Lord," Blaise tells me as I wrap up my gemetrial musings, "because it is the temple which has the seed of the New Jerusalem. It is the gateway on the physical plane most available to Shambhala. It is the site of much activity in terms of future spiritual, cultural activation and past spiritual, cultural activation through particular energies that were left and are still channeled there although at this time they are somewhat distorted. Tunnels you say? O we do like tunnels! You're dealing with secrets here, Grail Knight. Don't think that secrets can be just given away. We're hanging on to a few. Watch your time, Grail Knight. You still have work to do."

I check my watch. Three minutes before the solar eclipse. I ready myself. Suddenly a standard issue Tibetan-style wrathful deity, an *Heruka*, lurches out of the other side of the Lady Chapel towards me in full, menacing charge. I slice him to pieces with my sword and continue to wait calmly. With impressive precision at the moment of the eclipse, a woman clothed in bright crimson with short black hair and sparkling green eyes suddenly appears before me. She is gorgeous, sexy, powerful, wily, dangerous. She kisses my seven chakras, then, before I can jump out of the way, she thrusts a long sword straight through my chest. I don't fight back. I can't. I'm stunned, but not from the attack. My chest has become a beanbag for the sport of the Gods, so what's one more blade in the heart?

No, I'm stunned on account of the elegance of the arrangement, the concept. Consider: in the stories, the young Arthur is "seduced" by his lascivious, scheming aunt, Morgause; their copulation produces Mortdred, the bastard son and Camalate-wrecker. The stories also tell us that Arthur was "buried" at the Abbey after Morgan and two female assistants ferried him by barge back to Avalon from

Camlann, which we know was an inner battle grounded at Round Hill near South Cadbury Castle. What does all this really mean?

The Lady Chapel quite clearly is the burial site for Arthur, not for his body but his personality, his conditioned self, his reactive mortal identity. Welcome to the *morthouse* of Morgause. Morgause is the dangerous disruptive, radically transmutative, catalytic energy of transmutation, the seeming *mort*, or death, from alchemical inner burning and purification. Morgause's morthouse is the fish, the *Noun* (50) of Glastonbury, possibly its most perilous aspect, because it's under the influence of Scorpio, which is ruled by Mars. It is a stinging, biting fish.

As Qabalist Israel Regardie explains, *Noun* (50), whose Tarot Trump is "Death," refers to spiritual dryness, the Dark Night of the Soul, "wherein all one's powers are held temporarily in abeyance gathering, in reality, strength to shoot up and blossom forth in the light of the Spiritual Sun." *Noun* (50) also indicates the alchemical formula of Regeneration through Putrefaction, in which base matter must pass through the stages of corruption or putrefaction (chemical change) as the "black dragon"—"but from this putrid stage the pure gold was derived." And what happens during a solar eclipse? The rational light of the Sun is blocked by the Moon and its affective arationality. What better time for Arthur, as Solar Logos, to be "seduced" (penetrated and weakened) by Morgause, the catalytic energy of transmutation, than during a solar eclipse while sitting in the Mars-Scorpio morthouse of the Abbey where Arthur buried himself? Arthur was seduced in the morthouse in Glasteing's Tree in a moment when he was off guard, in the shade.

In the evening, I have another encounter with the Scarlet Woman, the destructive side of the Mother of the World in her Kali aspect. In more colloquial terms, she represents the energy of what Qabala calls Geburah, or Severity, which involves restriction, contraction, adjustment, assessment, what Gareth Knight calls "a sphere of absolute and unmitigated truth." He further characterizes Geburah as a Scarlet Hall of Justice as it works in the world of form. Geburah's predominant color is scarlet and Khamael is its avenging archangel.

In Arthurian terms, this is the scourge of Morgause.

I see a burned out, ruined city with a rim around its base and a shattered dome and energy field overhead, a lot like a smashed cake canister. On its right stands a shining, brilliant new city of light and crystal, a silver city flecked with numerous mosque-like buildings and topped by a single vibrant dome. Between the two cities arches a rainbow bridge with many people moving across it. Morgause destroys one house, but she quickly rebuilds something better. I see an angel, like a mature woman in her fifties; she's smiling and is clad in scarlet like Morgause was at the Lady Chapel earlier today. She has short, black hair, wears a long, bright red dress and has arrestingly beautiful, velvety black wings fringed with crimson as if backlit by an inferno. This dark angel—flying mort—shows me images of burned-out places on Earth: destroyed cities, withered crops, darkened, flooded lands, skeletons and dismembered human bodies floating down polluted rivers. She eats the limbs and torsos of infants and drips blood all over herself. There is no sign of life anywhere, only dead bodies and broken cities, blighted land and grey, smoky, soundless skies—a silent apocalypse. The angel flies around the Earth like a maddened carrion bird, Gaia's crimson avenger with the gaping maw of death and retribution frightfully apparent, her black wings and blood-stained body enshadowing the planet. Kali, devouring and wrathful on behalf of Gaia whom we have for so long unconscionably neglected and abused. The Earth becomes an awful mort-house as Gaia precipitates transmutation on a global scale.

Counterbalancing this frightening spectacle, which is only a time-compressed vision of many years, already unfolding according to the mort-house agenda of floods, fires, earthquakes, riots, and indiscriminate violent death, I now see what resembles the close-up of a flower pistil and stamen. On closer inspection, it looks more like a large radar dish on the ground with a long, hollow antenna tube in its center extending deep into space. It's also a telescope. I sit in the operator's seat and see hundreds of lightly transparent gold balls descending in a pretty spring shower to Earth. When they land, they burst slowly the way a tightly packed milkweed pod bursts, spraying countless seeds in all directions. In this case, each golden ball is implanted in the Earth according to a recognizable, circular, geometric pattern then sprouts the antenna and radar dish. Each unit is a new geomantic light station and a place where we can tune into the wiser voices of the galaxy. In other words, the planetary grid matrix is reseeded with celestial conduits and light centers in the wake of a global mort-house effect. This comes as a benediction after the nemesis of the devouring black angel. A new worldwide cadre of geomancers and Grail Knights will begin attuning the planetary grid matrix and collective consciousness of humankind to these newly available galactic inputs.

The next afternoon, I'm back at the Abbey again, this time at the unfinished Edgar Chapel at the intersection of five light lines I once visited with Blaise while meditating at Wick. I penetrate this nexus of lines and enter a circular frieze, as if a frozen slice of memory, that quickly grows into living, vivid color. A group of medieval monks stand in a fifteen foot deep trench examining the entrance to a stone-lined tunnel that leads to Chalice Hill. I breathe Love from Above to this memory tableau and it reveals a wall of cubic black stones. These surround the entrance that the monks are examining down in the trench. I pass through this wall into an empty stone chamber that resembles a monk's cell. I sit inside under the three-leaved bay window. The room is copiously illumined by the light pouring in through this small window. I see what is producing this effulgence on the other side of the window: it's the Holy Grail.

I pass through the window into an ocean of light. Back in the empty chamber again, I notice a circular miniature zodiac embedded on the floor, with the glyphs for the twelve signs. Now I notice that the room has twelve bay windows and over each is a sigil for one zodiacal sign. I sit under the Scorpio window. I pass through the window into the ocean of light again. I swim through the light waves and reach the Holy Grail, which is radiant, golden, and prodigiously, inexhaustibly overflowing.

The late afternoon November sun casts long shadows in the deserted Abbey when I stand up and glance down the axis of its ruins.

I feel an inexplicable kinship with the vanished monks of the great Abbey from the time when this *vetusta ecclesia* flourished between the fire of 1184 and the Dissolution of 1539. "The tombe of Arthur in shining blacke stone was in front of ye altare," the discarnate Abbey monks called The Company of Avalon told Frederick Bligh Bond during his excavations of the Edgar Chapel in 1907. "In ye floor of ye Mary Chappel was ye Zodiac, that all might see and understand the mystery."

On my ride up Magdalene Street, I see a Mother figure of archangelic proportions upon Chalice Hill holding the Holy Grail, which spills over with light, flooding the hill, flowing like lava through the environs of Glastonbury, like sap running down the tree from its crown, like juice seeping out from its berries.

63

MERLIN'S TRAPDOOR
TO SHAMBHALA

ale blue frilled-lace panties. Deborah has sent me a letter in which she describes her new sexy knickers for my benefit. Edmund delivers my mail early this morning while I'm still lying safe and wary under the duvet as the morning dawns drizzly and forlorn. Later I set off down the lane on my bike for Glastonbury inflamed with desire to examine Deborah's panties *in situ* and completely uninterested in spending the day in another cold, wet field looking for Arthur or Joseph's Seed or whatever it is Blaise has me running all over the zodiac for. On the other hand, dead men don't make good lovers, and if I'm not dead yet, I'm certainly headed for the grave.

I grunt and steam my way up the long hill above Compton Dundon. My glasses fog up, but not so much that I can't see the six Blaises hovering above my slowly wheeling bicycle like Yeovil helicopters bonneted in lilac umbrellas. Then they jog behind me in lilac jumpsuits, pushing me up the hill, turning the wheels, straining under the effort, flipping on the windshield wipers for their dark sunglasses, which have steamed up in the heat. Grail Knight and horse take a moment off from the Quest to adjust the nosebag at a cafe in Street. Two thick slices of chocolate cake ease the long, slow journey into bliss so that when I arrive at Wellhouse Lane, just above Chalice Well, and sit in a wet field under drenching skies on a late November Saturday morning, the prospects of finding the Shambhala doorway have more appeal. I mean, how does everybody else spend their Saturday mornings?

In the Arthurian stories, Merlin is always appearing unexpectedly then vanishing just as precipitously. He travels great distances at inexplicable speeds; he returns from long journeys with important tidings; he's always thick with plans and prophecies. He has a special sanctuary variously called the crystal cave, his rock, and the *esplumoir*. Arthurian scholars have worked themselves into a lather of speculation and tortuous theory-building over Merlin's *esplumoir*. Is it a moulting cage, a bird's nest atop a tree, a glass house, a tomb, an Otherworld barrow, a peculiar trapdoor between the worlds? Maybe it was an apple tree much favored by him, as he declares in a sixth century Welsh poem, *Yr Avallenau* ("The Appletree"): "The sweet apple is like the Bardic mount of assembly; the dogs of the wood will protect the circle of its roots." An old man, an unemployed sorceror, and in the public reckoning, a madman as well, Merlin sits in the apple tree with his pet pig and reminisces about his former days of political influence.

In *Yr Oianau* ("Greetings"), Merlin says: "O little pig, a lustful pig/Since the battle of Arfderydd care not/Were the sky to fall and the sea to overflow...." The *esplumoir* may be Merlin's famed glass house on the island of Bardsey where he keeps the Thirteen Treasures of the Island of Britain, that is, his magical tools. "Before the other buildings, build me a remote one with seventy doors and as many windows through which I may watch fire-breathing Phoebus and Venus and the stars gliding from the heavens by night, all of whom shall show me what is going to happen to the people of the kingdom," he requests of his sister in Geoffrey of Monmouth's *Vita Merlini*. Merlin would gaze at the stars while he prophecied "things like these which he knew were going to come to pass."

I think the truth about Merlin's *esplumoir* is simple. In fact, it is right before me in this little pasture between Wellhouse Lane and Chalice Hill. There is a small beehive chamber and an irridescent rainbow arch ascending with a graceful curve from here to the horizon—and into Shambhala. This is Merlin's doorway, his moulting cage in which he sheds the being bodies of one dimension for the lightness of another; this is his hideaway in the apple tree, Glasteing's

Tree, his trapdoor to Shambhala.

"The kingdom of Shambhala had once been, they said, in the Island of Britain, the Celtic Britain of the last centuries before Christ," a Mongolian lama told Stephen Jenkins, "when *Gwynfa*, the Place of Bliss, was located in the Summer Country, about that ancient site of Glastonbury." Wellesley Tudor Pole, in a letter to Rosamond Lehmann, presented the case more precisely when he noted how a colleague of his from the College of Heralds, working on the Other Side, came to visit him at Chalice Well through a special doorway. "He had just come from taking an official part in the Wesak ceremonies in that strange, far-off Tibetan valley: one that has its own peculiar connections with Avalon and the vale between the Tor and Chalice Hill." And didn't Blaise declare just the other night that Glastonbury is *Domus Dei* because it is the gateway on the physical plane most available to Shambhala? Call it the *Suggaweg*, the Way of the Shambhallic Sow, Glasteing's wandering pig with eight legs and thirty suckling piglets.

Why a sow in the first place? The sow turns out to be a widely used zoömorphic symbol for the Mother, the progenitor and proprietor of the zodiacal cauldron of transformation. Demeter-Persephone in the Eleusinian Mysteries was sometimes called Phorcis the Sow, known as the mother of the Phorcids, or Fatal Women, one of whom was Circe, the swine-goddess in the *Odyssey* who seduced Odysseus' men and turned them into rutting pigs. Belief in the pig's oracular powers and prophetic wisdom led some to drink pig's blood as a way of inducing these same qualities in themselves. Coins from Eleusis depict a pig standing on a torch, indicating Demeter's Mysteries; in fact, Demeter was sometimes portrayed carrying a torch and a small terra cotta pig under her arm, making her connections to the Underworld explicit. In Crete, the third face of the Triple Goddess, the Crone, took the form of the sow. In Egypt, Nut the Sky Goddess swallowed the stars at dawn to give birth to them again at dusk, earning her the title, "the Sow who eats her piglets." In Tantric Buddhism, the Goddess was venerated as Marici, the Diamond Sow and Great Mother, Queen of Heaven. Marici was portrayed seated on a lotus throne drawn by seven pigs. In the Tibetan tradition, Vajra Varahi is the Diamond Wild Sow with three heads; Vajra Varahi is also the feminine aspect of Vishnu's third incarnation as a boar. Closer to home, in the Celtic myths Ceridwen, "the Old White One," Triple Goddess and Great Mother, was portrayed as a fearsome, white, corpse-eating sow with a wisdom-granting magical cauldron. Also in the Celtic canon, the pig is an attribute of the Irish god Manannan who provides supernatural food through his sows, which are killed, eaten, then returned to daily life as if immortal.

Not only is the sow strongly associated with fertility, the Great Mother, and inexhaustible physical-spiritual nourishment, but in Buddhism, she has a seemingly contrary but actually complementary role. In the Buddhist Mandala of Existence or Wheel of Life, the pig represents greed and ignorance and is one of three animals (including the rooster and snake) that depict humanity's limitations that keep it bound to the illusory aspects of matter and *samsaric* existence. Here the sow's presence in this mandala of Avalon has a heuristic role as part of Glastonbury's templic instruction. So there are good reasons for the sow having a strong part in this creation myth of Glastonbury.

Why did she have *eight* legs? Why does the Buddha's Wheel of the Dharma have eight spokes? Why is his prescription for spiritual practice called the Eightfold Path? Why does the Tree of Yoga have eight limbs? Indeed, you don't have to look far to be suddenly overwhelmed with eights when it comes to wisdom prescriptions. Tibet's great guru Padmasambhava has Eight Manifestations, Eight Aims, Eight Cemeteries, Eight Knowledge Holders. The city of Shambhala is said to be shaped as an eight-petalled lotus, and its king sits upon a golden throne supported by eight lions. Tibet's exalted Goddess and Protectress, Tara, has eight forms, or Eight Taras, to assuage the Eight Terrors. The ancient Indian text *Vishnu Purana* prophecied that, at the end of the Age of Darkness, the Kalki Avatar would appear as an armed rider on horseback, endowed with the Eight Superhuman Faculties of Shambhala. China has its Eight Inebriated Immortals, its Eight Dragon Kings, its eight Trigrams of the Primal Arrangement of the *I Ching* and its 64 trigrams, derived from 8 times 8. Sleipnir, the horse of the German god Odin, had eight legs. Islam speaks of its *Hasht bihisht*, or Eight Paradises. In his Sermon on the Mount, Christ referred to the Eight Beatitudes. Castaneda's Toltec sorcery has its eight points and eight worlds that comprise the "totality of oneself." Celtic Britain had its Eight Noble Families. In ancient Western cosmology, the eighth sphere was that of the fixed stars, out beyond the sevenfold realm of the planets. The inner heart chakra, the *Ananda-kanda,* has eight petals; the Platonic Solid for air, the octahedron, has eight faces. Even the compressed sacred name of this town, GLSTNBRY, has eight letters. As Gernot of Rechersberg, a medieval German theologian noted, "Eight, as the first perfect cube imprints us in body and soul with the security of eternal beatitude."

The reason for the thirty piglets is easy. They denote the equal division of the zodiac into twelve arcs of thirty degrees each, thereby comprising what the Celts called the Twelve Hides of Glastonbury. And as the Region of the Summer Stars is one of twelve zodiacal wheels in the Hyperborean master temple, Somerset's thirty piglets represent one-twelfth of the full litter of 360 piglets of the twelvefold Round Table of star wheels. The piglets are the zodiacal divisions of the great Mother's cosmic body or consciousness, her geomantic progeny. This also helps explain the story of Glasteing and his brothers each founding a different community (a zodiac center) in the Island of Britain. Glasteing found his sow under an apple tree here; this means he founded Glastonbury because it was, geomythically speaking, a golden apple in an apple tree, a pre-existent etheric temple site with the geomantic structure of a Tree of Life and with potent connections to the spiritual homeland of Shambhala.

Glasteing and his brothers, along with the regular courier, Merlin, may have brought instructions from Shambhala into the Island of Britain regarding its geomantic development. H. P. Blavatsky notes in *The Secret Doctrine*: "In the same manner and on the plan of the Zodiac in the upper Ocean or the heavens, a certain realm on Earth, an inland sea, was consecrated and called 'The Abyss of Learning;'

twelve centers on it in the shape of twelve small islands representing the Zodiacal signs—two of which remained for ages the 'mystery signs' and were the abodes of the twelve Hierophants and masters of wisdom. This 'sea of knowledge' or learning, remained for ages there, where now stretches the Shamo or Gobi desert." The Gobi desert in Mongolia is often regarded, at least in esoteric circles, as the likely site for the etherically manifest Shambhala. Glasteing, Avallach, Avalok, Evelake, Melwas, Gwyn ap Nudd, Avalokitesvara—do we have in these variously named figures from myth and legend one of the original hierophants who activated and presided over a zodiacal wheel of occult learning as described by Blavatsky? Take your pick: was Glasteing a Nefilim, an Elohim, Cosmic Chaplain—or Merlin himself?

Whatever Glasteing's identity may be, we know that Merlin brought a synthesis of individuative Tibetan Buddhism and unitive Atlanteanism into the Celtic Arthurian stream. Much of this intellectual traffic may have come through Merlin's *esplumoir* along the *Suggaweg*, that is to say, through his fluidic connections with Shambhala through this little doorway above Chalice Well, or, for that matter, through any of the other apparently numerous Shambhala gateways in the Somerset temple. Merlin left clues of his Shambhallic connections everywhere: in the names—*Me-rlun, mahgags, Mahati-pragati; Avalok*; in the icons: the Avalon mandala of Glasteing's octapedal sow with its Wheel of Life antecedents; even Arthur's Celtic association with the bear has at least a punning reference to Tibet. The "bear of Cornwall" may be the *bar* of Cornwall, meaning the middle, the heart center, the Round Table, and as in *Bardo*, meaning the six "intermediate" states of existence, from waking life to rebirth.

Lest we overlook the most obvious: Avalok—King Avallach of the Summer Country, surveying his dominions from the top of Gastonbury Tor. By a curious system of mythopoeic recirculation, our Celtic Avallach is none other than the Buddhist Avalokitesvara, the Bodhisattva of compassion and mercy who resides atop the heavenly mountain called Potala. The key is simple: *isvara* means "Lord" and *Avalokita* means "looking on"; hence, the Lord who looks in every direction. Avalokitesvara is the all-pitying one, the Lord who surveys the realm of humans, the one who regards us with his compassionate thousand eyes and thousand helping arms. Atop Red Hill in Lhasa, the capital of Tibet, sits the thousand-roomed Potala, the residence of His Holiness, the Dalai Lama, regarded by Tibetans as the living emanation or incarnation of Avalokitesvara. Here, in Gwynfa's Summer Country, we have instead Gwyn ap Nudd's fabulous palace of delights inside the Tor. Even more intriguing is the fact that Avalokitesvara himself is an emanation of the God of Boundless Light, Amitabha, who exclaimed, after generating Avalokitesvara from his right eye, *Om mani padme hum!,* meaning approximately, "Hail, the jewel of creation is in the lotus." The implication is that the jewel is Avalokitesvara standing in the lotus petals of the heart just as the mythic King Avallach stands atop the heart-center of the Tor with its twelve lotus petals raying out in all directions and just as the emerald itself, the reality of the Glass Mountain and Glass Island, sits resplendently in the geomantic lotus of Glastonbury Tor.

But just when I think I have the problem resolved, another clue drops into my awareness like a feather and commands all my attention. We must take another look at that sow. Hindu mythology tells us that Vishnu had 22 incarnations and 10 Yuga Avatars; in either category, one of these was Varaha the Boar. His consort was Varahi, the sow and "Power of the Boar." She, as Vajra Varahi, was also one of the Goddess' Seven Mothers and had five emanations: one of these was Yeshe Tsogyel, the famous *dakini* and spiritual consort to Tibet's renowned guru, Padmasambhava. He drove all the demons out of Tibet, subdued the shamanistic Bon magicians, designed Tibet's oldest monastery, Samye, according to a cosmic mandala principle, and established the Buddha-Dharma in Tibet. In the stories about Yeshe Tsogyel's life, it's said that on occasion she transformed herself into the Vajra Varahi form. It's also reported that their spiritual union was known as the Mystic Initiation. Padmasambhava initiated her in all the rigors of spiritual awakening and technique, and together they visited and sanctified many of the holy places (geomantic sites) throughout Tibet. Padmasambhava devised numerous spiritual treasures called *terma*, which would be hidden in the landscape, not to be revealed until an auspicious future time. Later, Yeshe Tsogyel travelled around Tibet and neighboring lands, burying these *terma* according to his instructions at 105 major power places and 1070 minor sites.

I realize I am pulling a thread on a large ball of mythopoeic yarn, but the story of their work and relationship in Tibet has remarkable parallels with the exploits of Merlin and his consort, Nimuë, Lady of the Lake. Might Padmasambhava have been another of Merlin's numerous guises? If so, then the icon of Glasteing and his sow reconfigures dramatically. Behold Merlin (Padmasambhava/ Glasteing) and Nimuë, (Yeshe Tsogyel/Diamond Sow) establishing, purifying, sanctifying, and preparing Glastonbury as another sacred site. They could have slipped through Merlin's *esplumoir* and travelled from Tibet to the Summer Country in no time. Might they have buried a *terma* or two in our midst?

As I stroll further up Wellhouse Lane, I suspect a great deal more could be teased out of William of Malmesbury's deceptively simple foundation story, but it's clear that a profound intention inspired the naming and design of the Glastonbury temple. At the top of Glasteing's Tree, I enter Paradise. Here the land congeals into a green wave of earth, an arc of lime-skinned hills. Paradise is ablaze, a beacon, a crescent earthen harbor with a temple of light radiant at its heart. Even without seeing anything more definite than a towering amorphous egg of light, I know that spiritual beings are living in ineffable rapture on just the other side of exactly where I stand on the Glastonbury side of Paradise. It's as if little wafts of heavenly perfume drift through the membrane. I know somehow that human and angelic beings are, at this moment, inside that celestial egg moving in a dimension free of Glastonbury's dialectical tensions, enjoying a life centered in the heart of the heart, and, no further away than my fingertips, gently pressing upon the skin of its bubble.

I walk back down Wellhouse Lane to sit in the heart of Glasteing's Tree, beside the flowing waters of Arthur's Courtyard. "Regarding

Chalice Well, there is within the grounds a chamber with pertinent remains from Jesus, Mary, and Joseph of Arimathea, though not the bodies," Blaise tips me. For an hour I keep busy with my sword trying to penetrate the chamber between the Lion's Head and the Courtyard cascade, but I get nowhere. I can see it, but I can't figure out how to get inside. "Let it come to you, just breathe," a voice counsels me. I breathe as Love from Above to the Blazing Star at my center. My body flames with light as the Blazing Star explodes as if going supernova in a single burst. This sudden irradiation illuminates the inner temple. In a few moments, four white pillars arranged in a crescent appear in the same place as the cascade. It is the portico of a temple of light. Three figures stand between the four pillars: Jesus stands in the middle with a rose at his heart; Mary stands to his right holding a lighted candle; and Joseph of Arimathea stands to his left with his staff. The cascading water flows directly through the heart of Jesus at the portal of this temple.

The Chalice Well temple is two-tiered and somewhat resembles the Parthenon. The first level is coincident with Arthur's Courtyard. Here inside the vestibule of the temple, visitors prepare themselves with a physical immersion or baptism in the Pilgrim's basin; then they face the spiritual presences of Jesus, Mary, and Joseph at the far end of the hall. Behind Jesus is a kind of large solar disc that now swings open like a golden cave door to the heart; as I breathe to it, it becomes a blinding golden-orange radiant sun. I can't see it, but I know the Holy Grail, or one expression of it, is situated behind this solar disc doorway. In fact, I have the queer sense that after the golden radiance of the Sun envelops me, I momentarily become the chalice itself. At the same time, I see the Holy Grail slowly turning, revealing all its zodiacal glyphs to me, yet I am also the Grail that is turning. The twin perspective is unrelievedly paradoxical.

My body is now the Grail, but this occasions a curious reversal of space. Where my physical body once was, that is now the hollow interior of the Grail; the space formerly surrounding my body, that is now my Grail body; and my attention is uniformly distributed throughout the chalice. Perhaps that is what generates the sense of slowly turning; what's really happening is that my sense of spatially-located consciousness is transiting the chalice, or more precisely, is everywhere within the chalice at once. Then, as the Holy Grail, my chalice-body receives a drop of scarlet blood; this generates a wonderful, exultant flush of warmth and crystalline focus, a communion gift of the Christ. Everywhere I look, it's scarlet, only scarlet, and the words come, over and over again: *Not I, but the Christ in me.*

The Grail seems to condense itself and reside in my heart center. Thus equipped, I discover that the fourteen stone steps at the end of Arthur's Courtyard, conduct me up to the second tier of this inner light temple, into the chamber of the Wounded Fisher King who sits by the Well, awaiting the healing ministry of a Grail Knight. For a moment, the Wounded Fisher King's hall is identical to the golden halls of Ogygia where I visited Kronos through Oath Hill some months ago. Kronos and the Fisher King are somehow complementary aspects of each other, possibly on that same *phi* spiral Blaise mentioned in reference to Arthur's eleven and twelve battles. You cannot get to him in any useful sense without having first had the blessings of this spiritual triumvirate and the sanctified immersion in the Grail and the scarlet permeation. I realize the inner etheric temple design of the Chalice Well property is a miniature Grail Castle, fully equipped for training in the Grail mysteries. "More than that," Blaise says. "It is a practice temple for the Christed initiation in the Buddha Body."

Now I understand. There is a physical chamber buried between the Lion's Head and the Courtyard, possibly bearing artifacts of Jesus, Mary, and Joseph, and there is a much larger etheric temple situated in roughly the same place, bearing a kind of holographic memory presence of each in gestures of permanent blessing. I also understand Tudor Pole's reverence and expectancy regarding the Chalice Well property. "My aim is to prepare it for use once more as a Gateway through which the Christ's message for the New Age can enter and spread across the world. This very holy spot could in fact become once more the sounding board for a revelation of Divine Wisdom, attuned to the desperate needs of today's humanity." In an-

528 ✦ RICHARD LEVITON

other letter, Pole alludes to a statement made by the Sufi Hazrat Inayat Khan who called Chalice Well the holiest center in Europe and possibly the world. Somehow Chalice Well remains immaculate and pristine, completely inviolate, unlike the rest of Glastonbury, holding its *terma* to its heart.

Before I leave Glastonbury, I call in at a shop on the High Street. In ten minutes I'm reeling and dazed as if I had eaten a pound of sugar. It feels like somebody let the air out of my *hara*, and I wobble along with a flat tire. The lilac flames feel limp, almost flabby. Ah, the Glastonbury Space. I've forgotten how things are here. The spaciness. I can almost see the spaciness as a quality of the air, as an etheric aberration, as if little particles of spaciness zip through the ethers bombarding the unwary with psychic entropy. I swim through the thick waters, almost drowning in the *yin* vibration, as if dreaming while awake, slowly wilting into a centrifugal spaciness.

"It is actually the Shambhallic Focus you are feeling," Blaise says, as I wheel out of town as fast as possible. "It is transmuting the etheric and astral environment, which, as you see, is quite distorted and polluted." The fabric of physical reality is changing before my eyes, Blaise explains. The ethers are mercurial, tentative, and confusing. The twelve petals of Glastonbury's geomantic heart quiver in the alchemical fires. Noxious gases and negativities burn off, making the air hard to breathe, unsettling psyches. This can be disorienting. Many jump to unwise conclusions under its influence. It can even have the effect of making people a little unbalanced as the transmutation process of turning the heart into gold is not finished, Blaise says. There are still many black spots, astral blemishes on the lotus petals of Glastonbury's geomantic heart, but these are slowly burning off through the Shambhallic Focus.

The Glastonbury Space envelops me like a fog until I reach Somerton, when it begins to lift, but my mind doesn't clear until I roll into Langport, into the safe clear haven of the Girt Dog. The *hara* tightens, the Star shines brilliantly again, and the lilac flames flicker vigorously around me.

Let us all now praise the famous Dog! "The Dog stands outside the zodiac's ecliptic," Blaise notes, "and is therefore less affected by the alchemy underway in the temple, particularly at Aquarius. This way the Dog remains calm, clear, ever-watchful, unswayed by the swirls of transmutation in the heart of Glastonbury." Nor is the Dog soaking wet like the Grail Knight, who wryly observes that the only thing that distinguishes this soggy bike ride from a bath at Wick is soap.

In the evening, as Russell, Berenice, and I drink our tea in the livingroom, the air grows mellow, full, then almost unbearably blissful as Blaise shimmers into focus among us. "We come as we are. We come as a Blazing Star. We bring you a brilliant point of light at your center. We surround you all with the wall of lilac flames, from the Earth up to the point of brilliant light above. Focus on this image for a few moments, if you wish....Now, we place each of you within a brilliant sapphire blue sphere with golden flaming edges. Above this, we place your individual lilac flames reaching upward to the point of brilliant light above. Within each of your spheres, we place the emerald in your chests and a little below the skin's surface. It is six-sided and about two inches long. At the point between the sternum and navel and a little way inside, we place the pinpoint, the Nimitta of brilliant, pure, diamond light. Dwell on this image, if you wish....We will pass amongst you now....We are pleased to be with you tonight. We hope you all had a fruitful time since we last spoke to you. We come with a few suggestions, if you wish, Grail Knight.

"Tomorrow, we would like you to go to the Mump between two and three p.m. The next day be at Oath Hill for one hour before dawn and stay for one hour after sunset. The next day go to the old church at Muchelney Abbey, where you sat before, in the morning between ten and noon, for one hour only. On the next day, go to Aller to the rise in front of the church and spend some time there. We will keep an eye on you. So, your friends the Blazing Star Boys, are off again. Goodbye. Goodnight to you all, our love in your centers, bye bye."

64

WITH MY PARENTS INSIDE THE GIRT DOG'S NOSE

 ell-padded, even warm, I sit beside an old stump on the nose of the Girt Dog probing his brow for insight. Behind me, though buried, stands one of the portals to the stone chamber inside the hill. Huge, transparent angels twice the size of Burrowbridge Mump encircle the hill, their backs facing in towards me. Elohim, I'm sure of it. With my shield held before me, I penetrate the wooden door that opens into the chamber. Once inside the stone chamber, I realize another dimension overlaps here. What is a stone cave in the Mump's physical realm is a huge open space, something resembling an indoor amphitheater in another. As I become aware of my new surroundings, the Elohim turn their attention to me.

The Elohim, now inside the Mump and on the periphery of the amphitheater, pass me around their circle, hand to hand, as if I'm a precious object, then deposit me in a concavity resembling a Round Table full of stars in the center of the huge chamber. I seem to drift into this starry table and out among the myriad of stars; in fact, I am a Star, a round, Blazing Star. No Grail Knight accouterments, no sneakers, no jacket, no bowls, just a Star.

Two Elohim accompany me, one on either side, one male, one female, both wearing gold crowns, stars prickling through their diaphanous forms. I feel as if I'm continually falling forward, or rotating, nonetheless moving through space at a terrific speed. We pass a celestial golden retriever who extends his front leg to point the way. Sirius, no doubt, if somewhat domesticated by the mechanics of my vision. Eventually, we reach a planet, except that momentarily it feels as if *I am* the planet. We set down on this planet on a grassy sward at the edge of a conifer forest. The Elohim carry me in a hammock across the fields through the forest and into a vast seven-storied building made of light and vaguely resembling New York's modernistic Guggenheim Museum, only much larger. It's so big, in fact, it seems to extend for miles across the landscape. Ribbons of light—blue, violet, gold—ripple like electric ley lines along the building's exterior.

The Elohim carry me upstairs into what appears to be a modern hospital operating room. I am still only the Blazing Star. They put me, as the Star, into an emerald that lies on a dazzlingly white table. I feel so small, so minute, a tiny speck of light inside a large, green canopy, a womb of emerald. I see an infant encased in a golden crystal up on a shelf, a different evolutionary stream perhaps, but it seems unhappy. I don't feel unhappy; maybe incarceration—incarnation?—in an emerald is a preferable state to being put up in a golden crystal. I notice that I have assumed the form of a small infant now, with a ruby in my chest and a translucent white seed within it. We leave the hospital, and the Elohim carry me in a wicker basket; we arrive at an impossibly tall mountain range overlooking a vast plain upon which sparkles a magnificent dome. It's Shambhala— I *know* it. We float down thousands of feet into the valley and enter the dome.

The Elohim immerse me in a luscious fountain of light. My exterior body is still the emerald, but I feel wet with light, flushed with consciousness. They put me into a tube of silver light then a golden one, then into a kind of washing machine tumbler, then into a series of colored tubes like organ pipes, fourteen in succession; each irradiates me with the energies of a different color. I feel as if I've been permeated with a living rainbow.

Now I see my present parents when they were young, in their late twenties, before I was born as their son. They walk along a wintry city street at dusk carrying a wicker basket. Later, I fly in gyres around my mother, awaiting the moment of her fertilization; afterwards, I feel myself squeezed through the birth canal as the once and future American Grail Knight.

There is one more segment. I feel as if I'm in four places at once: outside the Mump in half-lotus posture under grey skies; inside the Mump in the stone chamber; with the Elohim on their hospital table; and in Shambhala having the bath of a lifetime. A Damoclean sword hangs worrisomely over the Mump, its keen edge points directly at the table with me lying upon it as the likely target. Suddenly, an invisible hand thrusts the sword through the Mump and through my body; it cleaves my chest in two like soft clay, revealing the emerald, then cleaves that, revealing a golden infant with a heart of rosy red petals. The sword stroke quickens the golden child to life, and it emerges radiant from the lifeless carcass of the Grail Knight, and, like a pristine flower, it perches as an anther on a long style high above the petals of the Mump, as if awaiting pollination by celestial bees.

In the evening, Blaise sheds some light on these unusual experiences. "We come as a Blazing Star. We come from not too far. We surround you all in the lilac flame from the Earth through to the point of brilliant light, far, far above. We place each of you in the sphere of brilliant, clear blue sapphire light. We surround this sphere with golden and orange dancing flames. We place an individual lilac flame before each of you stretching up to the point of brilliant light far above you. Within each globe, above the heart and just a little below the surface, we place a green six-sided emerald about two inches long. Below this, between the sternum, but closer to the navel, we place, a little way inside, a point of brilliant light, a Nimitta, a Blazing Star. Focus on this image for a few moments...."

"Good. We greet you. We are most pleased to be with you tonight. We are pleased with your progress, Grail Knight, at the Mump. You saw much of what was available. And so the golden child is born again in the heart of the Grail Knight. We are hoping you will understand more of this experience in the coming days."

"Blaise, who is that golden child?" I ask.

"The golden child is a representative of a new order of being. The child is called *Eiwann*. The solar Arthur, as one aspect, and the lunar Guinivere, as one aspect, produce a child called Eiwann. This means 'I am the one' and is the same as the Christ child. The sword came straight from the top. You know, up there, the Boss. The Handless One. We understand the formation in your consciousness is not ready to assimilate your experience today."

"Blaise, will you tell us about the Elohim?" I continue.

"Certainly. Their numbers vary at different epochs, as they do now. Their numbers are not fixed as are ours. We had them perform certain feats for Man's possible evolution. A small section of the Elohim's activity during one epoch was concerned with the manifestation by three Elohim into fourteen planetary Logoi, in seven pairs. They are remembered in myth as the Titans. Valinor, the Blessed Realm, Mt. Olympus—these are all different names for the same place where the Elohim lived while on Earth. It was not in Greece but close by, between Greece and Turkey, where the Elohim dwelt on Earth as giants. Emperor Lucius' giants were Elohim.

"They, as we do, have a point of collective consciousness. They, under our instructions, are constantly available to you in your work and for your assistance. We are transmitting through the Elohim, through their sphere, which is closer to Earth and human consciousness than is our sphere, so that you can be in touch with us. What you have experienced during the last two years has been largely channeled through the Elohim as a step-down process for us to be able to communicate with you. The same applies to the Seraphim. They step-down through the Elohim but with the obvious vibrational differences. The Elohim have been very helpful and continue to be so."

"So the Elohim were the giants of myth. It seems that they were some of the oldest gods and goddesses, too," I comment.

"These are memories, aspects of your consciousness in your racial background. They exist in what is known as the archetypal bank. They are drawn upon neurologically for elucidation. The Elohim were giants, but so were the Nefilim, who came after them. By the way, we brought the Elohim along tonight to answer any questions you might have."

As if Blaise turns a dimmer switch, four Elohim shimmer into the livingroom at Wick just like the ones who accompanied me today inside the Girt Dog. They manage to foreshorten themselves to fit inside the fairly low-ceilinged room. Like a journalist cued to ask his questions at an important press conference without feeling nonplussed by the celebrity status of his subject, I start interviewing the Elohim immediately.

"Are the Elohim the same as what the Bible calls the Fallen Angels?"

"The Elohim came to form materialized as a direct consequence of the Plan that was formed by the Cosmic Masters of Destiny. In certain misinformed writings from delusory minds, we have been referred to as Fallen Angels."

"You were also the giants of myth, weren't you?"

"The Elohim were giants as one aspect of a Being manifestation projected by us. We were most vulnerable in a situation of animal level manifestation. Our consciousness was not attuned to any form of bestiality or the procreation prevalent on this planet at that time. Size was our only protection. We were very big."

"Did the Elohim mate with the human or animal women?"

"We, in one aspect of our consciousness, came to many of the animals at this level of form, those animals who are your prior descendants. We infused our consciousness with those, and, out of this, with some mistakes, we derived the present form you know as Man.

"Where did the animal antecedents come from?"

"They function as part of a cellular whole. Gaia, the planet, is a living being. We came here as a special effect, subject to Gaia's acceptance of us. Gaia has been very kind and put up with much. We, in our terms, have tried to foster and nurture her growth; Gaia, as a being, has four distinct spheres of being manifestation—mineral, plant, animal, human—and we have concerned ourselves mainly with the animal-human. We hope we have given you guidance that will be helpful. We leave now."

With this, they shimmer out of the room, leaving us with Blaise again. "Blaise, I had the impression the Elohim were doing some kind of genetic engineering in the Mump. Were they?"

"Burrowbridge Mump is a library, among other things. Do you remember the six-sided cells, the honeycomb of the dome at the Mump? A lot of the genetic engineering that took place in Lemuria, and later in the second Atlantean period, took place in the cells of the Mump. You saw just a little piece of this, an aspect of your celestial birth and human phylogenetic birth. How the Star and emerald were put into the living human being."

"Isn't it about time you told us more about this emerald?" Russell asks.

"Yes it is. We now give you some information on the emerald. The emerald is a tiny doorway in the electromagnetic field of your heart. It is the access point where that in you which is Love is in love with that in others which is Love. When two emeralds open synchronously, there is spontaneous transmission of Love from heart to heart. We don't speak here of the physical heart. We don't speak here of the heart chakra as sometimes you have referred to it. We speak of the heart of the heart. It has a physiological place, as the Star does, within your organism. We centralize the emerald for the sake of alignment from above. In actuality, it is slightly to the right hand side of your chest, at the level of the third rib to the right of the sternum and about two inches long, top to bottom, with six sides.

"The heart chakra is located in the center of the chest, between the collar bone and sternum. It is green in color. It is Glastonbury symbolized by the *vesica piscis*. The higher sphere of heaven, the lower sphere of Earth, and the space between the two, the upper line of which is the center of the heart. Follow the line to the right side of the chest to below the nipple and you have the *Ananda-kanda*. Between the heart chakra and the *Ananda-kanda* in the upper right middle of the chest, you have the heart within the heart. The emerald has nothing to do with any of that in terms of bodily locations. The emerald is purely in the etheric. The emerald is the manifestation of the Star in the emotional body or etheric body of recognition.

"The emerald is brilliant green. Imagine the green of moss in a woodland near a pond where there is pure air and pure water and the moss is not trodden on but just grows and is allowed to be. It is such a brilliant green as this. Do you know what color we refer to? Emerald, we call it. Now you have each been visualizing this as we have given it. Each of you should begin to make this green more brilliant, more rich, more deep, more green. But in time; don't force anything. Don't rush.

"The emerald was dropped into Man's biophysical organism at that point when form was brought into matter by the Lord of Light. He was closest to the Lord of Absolute Infinite Love and Light, His Holiness Extreme in Excelsius. But he wished to experience something that none of us had even thought possible. He achieved a part of the Plan and is most blessed amongst angels for his part in the whole. The emerald was dropped into Man's biophysical base at the time of the Fall. When man or woman begins to awaken the aspect of themselves that is of the Lord of Light, the emerald glows within them. It is a positive aspect of the Lord of Light awakening in the One. It is also when Man begins to awaken to other humans, when the Love in you meets the love in someone else, then the emerald awakens. There is intensively but one emerald. When all those who have emeralds awaken spontaneously at the same moment in time and space, then the Lord of Light will be united again with the Father."

"Why does the emerald have six sides?" Berenice asks.

"The emerald has six sides because each side is an aspect of the truth of yourself. One side is understanding. Another is knowledge. Another is compassion. Another is intuition. Another is peace. Another is bliss. The emerald has six sides. It contains six aspects that pertain directly to the six worlds that are synchronous with this world. Each of them has a transcendent or magnificent quality which that particular side of the emerald represents. These are not to be confused with any parallel or similar energy systems. The information we are giving you at this time is exclusive. Each of these sides, whichever, however, has to be balanced. When penetrated, each side removes the green emerald's outer layer and reveals the light within, the source of light within. Each of you may approach the emerald from different sides. The heart within the heart is approached differently, dependent on your differing characteristics. It differs dependent upon the individual nature approaching the heart within the heart.

"When we speak of light and love, we speak of things that are known. Each of you has experienced relative degrees of both. The light that the emerald contains is beyond any description. The experience is beyond any description. The nature that you become after experiencing that which is within you to experience is beyond what you commonly refer to as the experiencer. Were you to be exposed to the source of love and light within the emerald, you would lose your sense of spacetime continuity. Therefore, you must progress gently towards something that is not dependent upon the ordinary sense of 'going towards.' This experience is available to you relative to your readiness and openness to be able to approach it through any one of its sides. Gaining familiarity with the emerald is also part of the preparation for the Christed initiation in the Buddha Body. We leave you tonight with this thought. You cannot get there, to the Grail and the scarlet drop, without first passing through the emerald. The emerald is the temple for the Christed initiation in the Buddha Body. We leave you as we came, as a Blazing Star."

Naturally, I can't fall asleep, not after this new load of information and energy. First, I'm taken with this new perspective on the Elohim, humanity's parents. I check Blavatsky, because I remember she had an intriguing reference to our early days with the Elohim on Earth. "And universal tradition shows primitive man living for ages together with his Creators and first instructors—the Elohim—in the World's 'Garden of Eden' or 'Delight.'" Blavatsky cites an ancient historian named Pherecydes, who said, "The Hyperboreans were of the race of Titans, which race descended from the earliest giants and it was the Hyperborean region which was the birthplace of the first giants." And the Elohim were apparently crucial in the implantation of the emerald within the human form. When I first became aware of it, in Hilary's chest that erotic afternoon in Park Wood when I unbuttoned her blouse expecting to gambol among her lovely breasts, I never suspected the emerald had such a celestial pedigree or would become so central to our work and experiences.

But then I should have remembered that Wolfram von Eschenbach attributed its presence on Earth to the favorable intercession of various angels who brought the "forever incorruptible" green stone to Earth after a conflict in Heaven. "Such powers does the Stone confer on mortal men that their flesh and bones are soon made young again," Eschenbach writes in *Parzival*. "This Stone is also called 'The Gral... the Gral was the very fruit of bliss, a cornucopia of the sweets of this world and such that it scarcely fell short of what they tell us of the Heavenly Kingdom." Eschenbach also implied that the "Gral" was the famous *lapis philosophorum* (or *lapsit exillis*, which is very close to the Qabalistic term *lapis exulis*, meaning "stone of exile," or the manifestation of Divinity in the material world, i.e., human beings), the alchemical Philosopher's Stone: "By virtue of this Stone the Phoenix is burned to ashes, in which he is reborn."

That the emerald contains the Grail, I experienced directly at the Grail Castle over Chalice Hill when I managed to penetrate the green stone. As Parzival's name suggests "pierce through the heart, pierce the vale," I think it refers to the necessity of piercing the side of the emerald, as the heart within the heart, to attain the bliss within. The Heart, said the great Indian sage Ramana Maharshi, is the seat and source of consciousness, identical with the Self, "the very Core of one's being, the Center, without which there is nothing whatever." Maharshi called it the *Hridayam*, which means "that which attracts into itself everything finally in the end." It is the foundation of the Mind, the place where the "Ultimate Divine," the Enlightened One, dwells within each human being. Light first enters the *Hridayam* then flows up a subtle channel to the crown chakra then down through the other six chakras. This Heart, which is the prime center of spiritual experience in the human, is located two digits to the right from the sternum, Maharshi said; it is not an organ of the body, but rather the "very Core of your being, that with which you are really identical." The Heart is pure consciousness beyond space and time, wholly unrelated to the physical body and transcending the mind, he said. It's Blaise's emerald, by all accounts.

Now as I lie here in bed pondering the emerald, Grail, Philosopher's Stone, and the Heart, Blaise slips into my train of thought, helping me to put some things together. Like Worley Hill. The cosmic egg, the seed of immutable love, the Great Stream of uncreated Time, the unshaped Stone, the flaming heart-seed, the whorle, the unbroken wholeness of original Being before Heaven and Earth were differentiated. All are under the auspices of the Great Bear, Ursa Major. She is Artemis Calliste, sister of Apollo, daughter of Zeus and Leto, mother of Arcas; for the Greeks, she was the Great She-Bear who once ruled the stars; her name means "high source of water" and water, as Blaise tells us, is a code word for consciousness.

Ursa Major was the star ruler, guardian of the *axis mundi*, the world axis, the Pole of the World; her revolutions about the Pole Star determined the months and seasons. In Taoist belief she was *Ma Tsu Po*, Holy Mother, Queen of Heaven, virgin Matron of Measure, Mother of Mercy, governor of the weather. And in esoteric circles, Ursa Major is home of the Hierarchy, the conclave of ascended human masters, the great amphitheater of evolved spirits who guide Earth from on high—more precisely, from deep within.

All this happens *inside the emerald*, inside the Heart and its microcosmic expression in each human being; here, inside this two inch long emerald to the right of my sternum at the third rib. In here. The Great Bear is in here, inside the emerald in my chest.

Worley reconfigures for me. The seemingly separate experiences I had—at the stream, Merlin's classroom, in the dell with the gnomes and Michael—were fragments of a unified perception, of a unified experience within the Bear's domain. I see it now as an amphitheater filled with evolved human souls: the Hierarchy. Here I gain the Stone or Heart-seed (the Star), and here it is ignited, quickened to spiritual life within me by Michael's catalytic sword stroke. Here a little secret is revealed to me. It's almost a joke. Consider this image: Michael's sword impales my Heart Stone, not only setting it to flame, but causing it to explode, go supernova, to engulf my spatial identity entirely with its effulgence. Now I see that when my Stone (the Star, diamond, or Nimitta) went supernova, I entered into a pale sapphire blue space, an utterly empty yet calmly lucid blue space. In effect, I was *inside* the Stone; everything had been turned inside out: once the Stone was in me, now I am in the Stone. And the sword is in me, in the Stone. The Sword in the Stone.

What the sword really means is that I am able to withdraw my conscious awareness from this inner spiritual experience and maintain it as a sharp blade of insight when I return to my normal bodily awareness and seat of identity. I withdraw the Sword from the Stone when I remember what I did and understood while inside the Stone, while I was the Stone itself. The Sword is the Mind extracted from the Self: you extract the differentiating Mind from the unbroken wholeness of the Heart. The mind is a "wondrous power residing in the Self," causing all thoughts to arise, says Maharshi. The Mind comes out of the Heart, creating thoughts, self-identity, and the world; Maharshi calls this externalization. When the Mind is retained in the Heart, this is inwardness. "Thus, when the mind stays in the Heart, the 'I', which is the source of all thoughts, will go, and the Self, which ever exists, will shine." Like a cosmic Egg, the eternity of *pi*.

This is what happened at Ivy Thorn. We all did this, the thousands of Grail Knights assembled with Michael: all of us withdrew the Sword from the Stone. All of us retained cosmic memory and could brandish it as an adamant blade of insight, as a mind focus. You bring the insight out of the Stone as your sword. Knights together, swords brandished, create the Round Table. Withdrawing the sword initiates a growth process; it sparks the Stone into spirallic life, converting *pi* to *phi*, precipitating evolution from eternity; it ignites the whorle whose grammar is the *phi* spiral or the Fibonacci series of additive numbers (e.g., 3, 5, 8, 13, 21, 34, 55, 89, 144....) You pull the sword (Mind) out of the Stone (*pi*) and create the Round Table (*phi*) and the Grail, which then goes through its five changes.

This is the mathematics for evoking the five Grail changes. Gawain, who is the Grail Knight in *Perlesvaus*, watches the Grail change shape before his eyes: it is a crucified crowned king, then a child, then a man wearing a crown of thorns, then a fourth manifestation not disclosed, then a chalice. With each transformation arises a special fragrance and a great light. King Arthur also beheld the five changes, wrote the *Perlesvaus* author, who noted that as the Grail was beheld "in five several manners, than none ought to tell, for the secret things of the sacrament ought none tell openly."

You have to put these experiences in their rightful order at their geomantic locations, Blaise suggests. At Worley Hill, the Stone or Star flashes supernova and I am inside it, in a big empty blue space. At Chalice Hill, I enter the emerald inside the Grail Castle. At Ivy Thorn, I withdraw the Sword from the Stone; my remembering activates the Stone (*pi*) and births the Round Table (*phi*). Then at Chalice Well, I behold the golden Sun, which turns into, or ushers me into, the Holy Grail, in which I experience myself as the golden chalice. At the Mump, the golden child is born when the emerald in me is cleaved; this golden child, whom Blaise calls Eiwann, has rose-colored heart petals.

Now I remember something from Chalice Well. The sense of a scarlet drop of blood—the true *SanGreal*, the "holy" blood—a scarlet infusion of consciousness, a touch of the Christ: "I am the one!" This scarlet touch births the golden child; after all, Blaise said Eiwann is another name for the Christ child.

"You're on the right track. You are experiencing a single initiation, in stages, spread out across several landscape nodes," Blaise says. "This is part of the dedication of the Grail. These stages are the elements of the Christed initiation in the Buddha Body. Stone, Star, blue sphere, emerald, Round Table, Sun, Grail, scarlet drop, Christ child. The traditional five Grail changes are now part of this new, more complex sequence. There are a few more pieces yet for you to experience and integrate. See you at Oath Hill tomorrow, Grail Knight. Go to sleep."

65

EIWANN IN THE
SOUND ABOVE OATH HILL

 wo dozen gnomes and two Elohim greet me at the front door of Wick Manor a couple hours before dawn. We set off across the dark, mud-rich fields, past the surprised, insomniac cows splatting and chewing, and walk on to Oath Hill. It is so muddy it's like wading through slush; my sneakers and socks are soaked by the time I cross the last turnstile and head across Oath Hill towards the portico of the light temple. Why I never remember to wear Wellingtons is one of the sublime mysteries of the Grail Quest.

What's this? Somebody else is motoring across the dark fields in the same direction as I'm headed, not for an otherworldly appointment with angels but to round up his cows for the morning milking. Just before the farmer's lights bear down revealingly on the Grail Knight meditating without rational explanation in his field at six a.m., I dash behind the hedgerow and lie down flat. A man herds all the cows towards the barn a half mile away and drives off. The gnomes and I wipe our brows in relief. I reclaim my seat, facing east under a dreary, predawn drizzly sky. No matter: it's brighter where I'm headed.

The golden child beams munificently from his manger in my chest, intact and thriving after his birth at the Mump. His manger is set within the topmost boughs of a young tree. Eiwann takes my hand and leads me into a secret basement room at my parent's home and then to another in the attic. I say "secret" because technically they never existed as architectural reality; but they did exist, quite intriguingly, as dream reality. I often visited them in my dreams. I'd open a door in the basement, which had been turned into a finished knotty-pined playroom, and there was my den, a library stocked with books. Same with the attic: here I maintained another private scholar's den, filled with maps, charts, and interesting objects. I always re-entered these two arcane rooms with sheer delight, in a mood of discovery, excitement, and wonder.

Eiwann points to the top of an old ash tree in my parent's backyard. There in its topmost limbs is a pearl-shaped crystal doorway; that's the aperture I passed through decades ago when, knocked unconscious on the threshold of adolescence, I made a journey to Chalice Well to receive tutoring from Wellesley Tudor Pole. There are angels inside this crystalline aperture and they welcome me. I enjoy a view of the local energy matrix structure, the domes and dome lines in this area and am pleased to note that my parent's home sits under a dome cap on the outskirts of a zodiac temple and on the Oroboros line that passes through it.

Eiwann leads me into an underground chamber in the backyard; it must be fifty feet down. Inside, there are dozens of gnomes having a party about a round table. With a shock of joy, I realize this is my precious basement "library:" here I spent a whole other life happy with the gnomes, right in my backyard! In my childhood bedroom now, I'm aware of the Blaise gazebo landing on the peaked rooftop. I ascend through the attic, onto the roof, then glide into that lovely angelic space defined by the six white pillars. The Blaise gazebo zips itself shut, as the pillars fuse into one pulse of brilliant light and we travel like a comet through space. Ah: so this is my "attic" treasure room.

Back at Oath Hill, Eiwann points to the Blazing Star above his belly button. I pass through this as if walking through an open door into a field of light and into a luminous body. It belongs to that older mentor who stood behind me at Magotty-Pagotty, when Blaise asked me to make an effort from a higher place in myself. My mentor, who I understand is a "higher" version of myself, if not the timeless original, says his name is Willamaliah. The three of us—luminous

Willamaliah, golden Eiwann, and astonished Grail Knight—travel rapidly through the starfields and arrive at Blaise's white gazebo—the Nimitta chariot, I might call it—set in a lovely garden.

The six Blaises seem more vivid, more spectacularly self-effulgent than usual; fibers of light extrude from their angelic forms like an elaborate circulatory system enthreading the environment; their auras are as big as cumulous clouds; their wings are like nebulae dancing over the Earth; their faces are as youthful as ten year olds, as mature as unborn eternal souls; their eyes and mouths transmit the androgynous joy of being *this* close to God. How did Rainer Maria Rilke put it in his *Duino Elegies*? Every angel is terrifying, he wrote; "and even if one of them pressed me suddenly against his heart: I would be consumed in that overwhelming existence. For beauty is nothing but the beginning of terror, which we still are just able to endure, and we are so awed because it serenely disdains to annihilate us."

I sit in the center of Blaise's round table inside their gazebo as they empty blue light over me from a golden chalice. The blue light flows quickly through my body, irradiating every cell, every atom, every quark. Blaise shows me other places we have travelled together in the Nimitta chariot and demonstrates how the gazebo is manifested from the Blazing Star in their forehead. The Star expands to form the gazebo; you have such a Star in your forehead, too, Blaise adds. The gazebo condenses to a single pinpoint of light then dilates instantly into the gazebo again. It's like a collapsible, inflatable suitcase for angels on the move; and also for *Taliessin*, "radiant brow," another Celtic name for Merlin as prophetic bard; he must must have walked around Camalate with the Blaise gazebo condensing and inflating in his forehead.

Blaise gives Eiwann a golden crown and an eight-sided ruby, which the child clutches to his chest. As I concentrate on the ruby—for Eiwann is a part of myself and therefore within the field of my experiential awareness, as paradoxical as it sounds—I feel flushed with warmth. The ruby expands until it fills my body from the inside like a hot water bottle. There must be roots to this delicious warming flame; I find the seed of the ruby flame and look inside it: there is a green pyramid housing a domed crystal city exactly like the one we saw from Hamdon Hill and from within the Mump yesterday.

My attention returns to Oath Hill. I am connected like a puppet by innumerable filaments of light to the hand of an Elohim. A globular light form, reminiscent of a lenticular UFO, appears simultaneously over Oath Hill and my parent's yard like a dome of light two hundred yards across. I enter the hovering dome and greet my friends. All of us have a ruby inside our chests that glows like a crimson heart.

We travel to the mountains near the Gobi Desert in Mongolia that overlook the Shambhala dome. We descend as radiant, pulsing ruby eggs down to the crystal city. The translucent seed within the ruby is the key that opens the gates. I turn the key then feel myself immersed in that same fountain of light I experienced yesterday. In ruby form again—by this I mean our manifestation body is the ruby, nothing else—we ascend high above the Shambhala dome into what appears to be a giant Mother ship veiled in a lenticular cloud and spinning slowly like a top. It might be a ship and it might be an archangel; in this business it's hard to tell and native cognitive biases tend to control the paintbrush on the canvas of perception. Once inside, we move into a chamber with a yellow-gold glow, slowly congeal into human forms, not material but light bodies, and are welcomed by our colleagues.

It's gone eight o'clock and well past an hour after sunrise, which is when Blaise advised me to wrap things up. Time for breakfast and a laundry. Here in the daylight I can see the extent of the sartorial damage: my trousers from the knees down and my sneakers from ankle to big toe are irredeemably caked in mud. May as well throw them out as try to clean them. Russell greets me at the front door. "Breakfast for the Grail Knight. Hot porridge this way. Look at you, man. I mean, you'd surely have to have wallowed in the stuff to get that caked."

After breakfast I lie on my bed and muse about Oath Hill. I feel strongly that I have missed something about this morning's experience. "Look *above* the hill," Blaise whispers in my mind.

Immediately my attention is back at Oath Hill, where I sat on the ground hours ago. I look up. There is the underside of what seems to be a gigantic lenticular Mother Ship. It also resembles that curious *flan*—as Tolkien described the residences of Elves—I saw high above the Tor so many months ago. "Not a ship as such," Blaise comments. "Start with the Star. Breathe as Love from Above to it." I breathe to the Star and soon it flashes like a supernova and disappears, leaving me inside the sapphire blue sphere, which is empty and vast like space. The six-sided emerald appears before me, each facet as big as a six-story building. I walk through the translucent green walls and find myself in a large chamber that contains a polished round table. As soon as I sit down at the table, a brilliant golden-yellow Sun emerges from its center and grows larger and brighter by the second. I don't know if it's racing towards me or I am funneling into its corona, but soon I am engulfed by this effulgent gold. It begins to shape itself into the form of the Grail chalice. As I experienced at Chalice Well, where my body should be, that is the hollow of the chalice; where my auric field should be, that is the inside perimeter of the chalice. My awareness and sense of spatial location cycles round the chalice because it is the chalice itself, receptive and diffuse and omnipresent.

Now a flush of scarlet light descends upon me like a drop, filling me with warmth; as did the golden Sun, the scarlet drop engulfs me like a crimson blot swallowing up a speck of dust. Quite possibly what I now experience as a scarlet drop may be equivalent to the earlier impression of my travelling with Eiwann and Willamaliah in ruby crystals. The scarlet field disappears, and I seem to stand inside a well-lit geometrical structure with eight sides, like two pyramids of four sides each, stacked bottom to bottom. Wait a minute: that's an octahedron, the Platonic Solid for the air element, the geometric signature of eight.

Somehow this remarkable sequence of transformations has delivered me to the inside of the *flan*, or Mother Ship, above Oath Hill. Your ticket of admission, apparently, is knowing how to make these moves in consciousness. Blaise is right: it's not a ship but a temple moored high above the physical hill. The sequence of inner images is apparently the rigging by which a Grail Knight ascends, rung by rung as if climbing towards a ship's crow's nest, to this subtle temple. Up here, it's like being in an octahedral glass house high above the ground—could Merlin's glass house on Bardsey Island be like this? I look out through the "windows" and see, not hills and cows and barns, but stars—the billions of stars in our galaxy. Inside the windows, there are pillars of different lights.

As I slowly scan the full panorama inside the octahedron, I perceive fourteen different columns of light, one abutting the next, making a circular, coruscating double rainbow, except the colors don't repeat but are each different—fourteen hues, in fact. Inside the blue column or ray, for example I sense a crowd of people: old, dear friends, colleagues from an ancient day; but there are human and spiritual presences within each color column. Quite possibly this is another version of my earlier impression of being greeted by colleagues once I ascended in my ruby conveyance to the Mother Ship high above the plain.

Now the rainbow columns and the octahedral glass house unfold and dissolve into space, leaving me in the midst of a myriad of stars. A sound that is like a vertical shaft resonating from high above passes through me; like an axle, it causes the glass house to slowly turn around like a wheel. The octahedral glass house and rainbow columns have not definitively disappeared; they are both transparent and as if dissolved into space, yet still almost palpably present. The sound axle from above turns the octahedron like a wheel, setting it to spin slowly.

This is indeed a temple of paradox: I can see it yet not see it; I can hear it yet not hear it. *Yah. Yah.* That is the sound that makes the axle that spins the glass house above Oath Hill. Then I catch the sound at a slightly different angle. *Eä Eä.* That is the "sound before sound," the sound of the cosmic Fisher King, or the Ancient of Days, as Blaise explained several weeks ago after my visit, through Oath Hill, to Ogygia. Blaise, who has been coaching me every step of the way, says "Good. Oath Hill is really *IOA* Hill, the hill of the sound. *Yah, Eä, IOA* are the same. *Jehovah!*"

This is complex business indeed, but it's the key to the secret of the Oath Hill temple. Jehovah, in Qabala, is the long version of the fundamental, arcane name of God, *YHVH*, which is called Tetragrammaton, meaning "the Word of four parts." This compact name implicates and, in a mystical sense, summarizes or recapitulates the entire Tree of Life and its 32 paths of wisdom. Each of the ten Sephiroth of the Tree has a Divine Name, a special combination of syllables that expresses the sound of that energy. Qabala explains that, in the beginning, God spoke these ten names, syllables, or creative mantras, thereby creating the Sephiroth. *Yah* is the Divine Name for *Chokmah*, the second Sephira of Wisdom—Blaise's sphere. In a mythological sense—which is the realm in which we're most likely to be able to make the intuitive leap into some kind of understanding of these recondite matters—*Yah* is virtually the same as *Eä* which is the exiled Fisher King in his golden halls of Ogygia and his fundamental sound. Or perhaps we should say from *Yah* you can hear *Eä* (as in *Eheieh*, the God Name for *Kether*, the sphere or Sephiroth beyond *Chokmah*). The *Sepher Yetzirah*, a prime Qabalistic text, says: "He engraved *Yah*." This means that the Infinite Being—*Ain Sof*, God, the father of the Cosmic Fisher King, as Uranus is father to Kronos— "engraved" space with these Divine Names. In other words, God spoke the names, filling and structuring space with their formative energies, thereby creating the world. *Yah!*

In effect, God said, *Eä, IOA*, or *Yah*, thereby "engraving" space— impregnating it—with these sound energies. Not just here at Oath Hill, but out there, up there, in primordial time and space. Oath Hill is a holographic copy (one among many in the planet's zodiacs) born within the Dog that illustrates this cosmic design principle. And the minute we say "cosmos," we must simultaneously and equally say Human, for Adam Kadmon and Adam are mirror reflections of each other. These three seed syllables are essentially equivalent and interchangeable, as Blaise suggests. And as shorthand for Jehovah or *YHVH*, they imply something else, namely, the 72 Names of God, also known as the *Shemhamforesch* or The Complete Name. This means there are 72 three-letter permutations of *YHVH*; each of these variations Qabala regards as an angel or a formative, creative energy. This composite of 72 angels or 72 Holy Names of God is called Jacob's Ladder, which connects Heaven with Earth and upon which angels, spiritual presences, and, potentially, human souls, transit between the realms. Jacob's Ladder is also described as the Tree of Life in the Four Worlds; this is often pictured as four complete Trees stacked vertically upon one another. Qabala depicts these 72 Names (or angels) in various other ways: as written on the leaves of the Tree of Life or as if inscribed on the petals of a symbolic sunflower.

Through its "sunflower" guise, we gain an impression of the possible geomantic structure of the *IOA* (Oath) Hill temple. What I originally saw as a twelvefold division of the hillside with a central temple may well be a seventy-twofold division of space, a *Shemhamforesch* temple of the 72 Divine Names with a Jacob's Ladder connection (the rigging) to the halls of Ogygia, *Yah's* domain, high above. With the *Shemhamforesch* temple, we have an icon of the processes and products of Creation and the means for its recapitulation and assimilation and restoration—through us, through the mystery paths of the Grail Knight within the geomythic—indeed, cosmomythic—temple.

There is yet one more element to the *IOA* Hill temple. That's the *Teli*. "This is one of the most mysterious words in the *Sefer Yetzirah*," admits Qabalist Aryeh Kaplan. The *Teli* appears to be an axis around which the stars and the heavens rotate, from which the celestial sphere "hangs"—the axis of the galaxy, in short. Astronomically, some Qabalists attribute this function to the constellation Draco, which circles the Pole Star at the "top" of the galaxy. But another interpretation sees the *Teli* as a single hair in the beard of God. This is, of course, a metaphorical explanation. Technically, Qabala distinguishes a Greater and Lesser Countenance when it comes to God's face. Consider the Cosmic Fisher King (presumably, the Lesser Countenance) on his throne in Ogygia. He has a long beard, as befits a patriarch. His head is filled with divine, ineffable wisdom; it is living, eternal cognition beyond our comprehension. It is the unknowable divine intellect. We can't see inside his head; we can't comprehend his concealed inner wisdom. But we can see his beard, the outer expression of his wisdom. "These are not seen as simple hairs, but as channels through which God's wisdom emanates from His 'head,'" explains Kaplan.

From each hair in this divine beard hangs a separate universe, a revealed world, a letter in the Torah. "According to this, the *Teli* denotes the 'hair' in the divine beard from which our universe 'hangs.' This is the axis around which the universe revolves." The "hangings" of the divine beard are also called *Taltalim*, a word related to another word *Talpiot*, which is "the hill (*tell*) to which all mouths (*piot*) turn." In practical terms, Kaplan explains, *Talpiot* (*Taltalim*) indicates the "mount upon which the Temple was built, which Jacob called the 'gate of heaven.' This *Talpiot* is the tangible link between the physical and the spiritual." Finally, Qabala declares that *Teli* is the King of the Universe, the King over Space: "The *Teli* in the Universe is like a king on his throne." The *Teli* is the axis around which the universe revolves, the first of three aspects of "kingship" as defined in the *Sepher Yetzirah*. Even so, there is still a good reason for calling this site Oath Hill. As Rabbi Simeon is quoted in the *Zohar*, describing the thirteen parts of the white beard of the Ancient of Days: "And those who raise a hand and swear an oath on the beard of the old man, these swear on the truth itself." Or as the cheeky Grail Knight was heard to quip, When the Old Beard finds there is happiness in one of His created works, "He's having a good hair day."

In the mundane terms of my experience "up there," the axle of sound I perceived about the glass house is probably (metaphorically) a single beard hair, or *Teli*, for the Somerset zodiac temple. At another level, it is also Jacob's Ladder; it is also the mount (*IOA* Hill and its subtler dimensions) upon which the temple (Ogygia) was built. All of these aspects, it seems, are part of the geomantically engraved temple upon and above Oath Hill: the *IOA* Hill temple of the 72 Names of God, where you commit the *Shemhamforesch* oath, set within the throat of the Girt Dog. The God Dog. "Good, but that's only one third of the picture," Blaise says. "The Dog has two more features like this, plus one."

I rest up during the day, fretfully trying to restore my Grail sneakers with brush and soap and elbow, leaving them by the stove to dry. I borrow Russell's Wellies. Around three-thirty, I set off across the soggy pastures again, picking my way around the muddy rivulets and trenches. The first thirty minutes at Oath Hill are rife with distractions; it's as if the morning's focus was an experience out of the depths of ancient history, so remote is it from my current experience of the place. The farmer is out buzzing around his fields in his tractor but fortunately never calls in at this one where he would find the Grail Quest in progress, if somewhat fitfully. I shift my location several times, not convinced I'm sitting in the right place. Finally, I plunk myself down, facing west, and notice a large, freshly dug grave. Shovels and pick-axes are lined up in a row by the hedge. Six Elohim surround the hill, facing in towards me. They seem grim and relentless. They point to the grave.

"We suggest that into this grave you put all your likes and dislikes, your opinions, criticisms, ideas, your friends, your enemies, your parents, girlfriends, lovers, books, everything you've written or thought to write, your journals, all your articles, your notes, your memories—in short, everything you have called yourself," the Elohim tell me. This takes some time and is no fun. I chuck in everything I can find in the Grail Castle that has a "Made by the Grail Knight" label. It's a big hole and can easily accommodate all the treasures—and junk—of a lifetime spent outfitting the Grail Knight personality.

The Elohim hold a round mirror. In it I see that many graves have been dug here, many before mine. It's a Grail Knight necropolis, a compost heap of discarded personalities, a spectral temple where moulting Grail Knights have taken an oath to rebirth themselves. Then the Elohim throw my body, kicking and flailing, into the hole. Poor horse, I reflect: it never did get those hot vegetable pasties in Glastonbury after its dirty sojourn in the tunnels.

I lie in the bier seemingly for ages, without thoughts, feelings, or perceptions. It's growing dark. The houselights at Wick Manor flicker appealingly from a great distance, from the other side of this initiatory curtain; meanwhile, it's empty and desolate out here on Oath

Hill in the pit. Strange screeching birds dive-bomb me from over-head, bats probably. Willamaliah and Eiwann sit comfortably inside a mansion nearby, on a beautiful polished oak floor; they study me with concern. Then everything shifts and I'm with them.

I'm at my earth circle in the Fairy Dell, which is about a third of a mile behind Oath Hill. From here I discover that Oath Hill is parti-tioned into twelve equal segments, with a command post in the cen-ter in the form of a small temple. As for my earth circle, the crystal seed I planted last year has sprouted and produced a ten foot high tree of light encased in a vertical column of light that rises up be-yond my perception. That's the outside view; inside the tree is to-tally different. I sit inside a huge mansion, in mid-nineteenth cen-tury Queen Anne period architecture; it is three stories high, many times larger than Wick Manor; its shuttered windows are half-open. A spacious garden occupies many acres in the front, a long drive-way flanked by stately elm trees makes an elegant, curving approach before the mansion; the number on the front door is 35. I shudder as I realize what this house is: it's mine. Last year I set it on the top of a hill during a visionary experience at the Fairy Dell after eating one of those disks of transubstantiation. The house seems empty yet pre-pared, as if it has just been refurbished and is awaiting the furniture movers and new tenant. It's *my* house, rent and mortgage-free. From the vestibule, I observe how the Grail Knight, drained of blood and lifeless, is being cut into pieces, which are tossed into the pit. He's not having a good month. Poor guy. Wouldn't want to trade posi-tions with him.

Which brings me back to Oath Hill. A lion guards the entrance to the abbaton, yet he's not interested in sampling my flesh. Rather, he guides me inside and down into the Oath Hill necropolis where de-caying body parts are stacked in loathsome piles. If *Yah* is the sub-lime attic, then the abbaton is Oath Hill's gritty basement. We pass through a pearl of light and emerge on the high cliff face overlook-ing the Shambhala dome. There is a small cottage up here among the rocks. I sit inside the cottage at a table as a wise woman with long, frizzy black hair and a slightly disshevelled look attends me.

Which brings me back again to Oath Hill, to the grave. "Do you affirm all you have placed within the grave, all you have surrendered?" the Elohim ask me. I do. Take it all. I can always go back to the mansion. They fill in the grave, mound over the top, then insert a circular flag in the soft earth. It depicts a golden-red lion rearing against a blue field, fringed with scarlet. "Look into the eyes of the lion," say the Elohim.

I see Eiwann hovering above the green pyramid and the Shambhala dóme. I'm shivering when I stand up and start walking home through the dark fields. I feel terribly depressed and wobbly. Back at Wick, I take a bath, have supper, and disappear under my duvet for the night.

66

WITH BLAISE IN THEIR GLORIOUS WHEELS

epression, a sullen crankiness, an irritable restlessness assail me as I roll through the Levels on the way to Muchelney Abbey this midday. And strong crosswinds threaten to blow the unwary cyclist clear out to sea. I am not this wind. I am not this irritation. I am not this depression. I refuse to sign my name to any of these emotional states even as they blanket me. Thus the Grail Knight wobbles towards the Abbey. As I approach Muchelney, I notice a huge angel standing like the Jolly Green Giant wearing the site's dome cap like a Mason's apron. I sit down where Blaise indicated and this towering spiritual being begins his Sunday morning sermon.

"The Christ child awakens within the Grail Knight. The old man has been buried on Oath Hill. The heart is big. It has more room now. It can benefit many. Fill it now with good thoughts of Love from Above. Let the angels draw nigh. Let there be much *El nigh*. The sun shines. We blow all your clouds away."

Much El nigh indeed: a plethora of angels attends me. It's like being in an old-fashioned barbershop; you get shave, shampoo, trim, nails, even foot massage while you chill out in the big leather chair. I'm mostly asleep, passively slouching in the big leather chair as the barber lathers my face, clips my hair, slaps on cologne. Great moving volumes of light surround me: swirling, weaving, ceaselessly loving ministrations upon a wasted Grail Knight. After a while, my vision perks up and I see Blaise twenty feet in front of me. Each Blaise holds a cue card, and I read off their single words in sequence:

"Blaise. The Grail Knight looks sad. What are we to do? How about a little soccer?"

The six Blaises start kicking around an ordinary orange soccer ball, bouncing it off their heads, spinning it on their wingtips, cavorting like the Harlem Globetrotters in full dexterous display. They boot the ball into my chest. "Have a little peek inside," says Blaise. The ball has a trapdoor, which I open. Inside is the green emerald and crystal city. There's no getting away from this place even on my day off. "Who said it was a day off?" queries Blaise. Now a troop of angels empty a phial of golden liquid light over my crown chakra, and this dribbles like elixir through my body until I flush golden from the inside.

Another angel offers me a draught from a golden-white chalice that contains a clear, cool liquid. Instantly, it irradiates my body with joy. This angel gestures for me to kneel. "At Muchelney, Arthur's Grail Knights did much kneeling."

It figures. On the zodiac map, this is approximately the Girt Dog's hind leg. But experientially and functionally, Muchelney is the Dog's root chakra, and appropriately: here the Grail Knight's wounds are healed, just as one day the Fisher King's wounds will be healed. The huge angelic figure wearing the dome cap as a skirt stands before me, and I find myself saying, "I am nothing. I ask your guidance and support. Please fill me with light." The giant figure dubs me on both shoulders with a sword. Then he places a lilac flame over a six-pointed star in my brow and puts a ruby over a six-pointed star in my heart center.

"And now, Grail Knight, we suggest you go home and sleep the rest of the day," Blaise says. "Take it easy, you know?"

No problem, says the Grail Knight, back at Wick again, pulling the warm, thick duvet up over his face, a "Do Not Disturb" sign hung on his door. I don't want any news reports from this world or the next for at least three hours. It seems I've only just snuggled into bed when Blaise is wiggling my toes at the end of the bed, telling me it's time for another visit. I look at my watch. Oh: it's been six hours since I climbed in here.

"We come as we are," Blaise begins as we assemble in the livingroom. "We greet you all. We surround you with a wall of lilac flames. We place a golden pillar in each of your four directions. The flames reach down to the Earth and up to a point of brilliant light above. We place each one of you within a sphere of sapphire blue light, around which we place the orange, golden, and red flames. Within each of your chests, we place an emerald and, beneath this, a brilliant Blazing Star. Focus on this image, if you wish....

"We are pleased to be with you all tonight. We show you a carpet of green and red with little golden flecks. We give this to you all. From the point of light within the mind of infinite being, through the mind of Man, a source of contact and communication may be established for the benefit of all sentient beings. We are a Blazing Star, a pinpoint of light, a Nimitta of consciousness. We come as a sphere of stable consciousness. We ask that for a few minutes you place your attention just above the roof of the house. We bring you something to appreciate. [I see Santa Claus with sleigh and reindeer tumbling out hundreds of presents; these pile up on the lawn as high as the house.] Good. That's it. Let's continue."

"Blaise, what happened to me today at Muchelney? I felt so miserable all the way over there."

"When you have let go of something, given it away, then you need topping up again. Now yesterday you emptied out some stuff, lots of stuff, rubbish and other stuff. Hmmmpppfff. Didn't you? That leaves empty Grail Knight. So *much* confusion, so *much* problem. Much tossing and turning during the night. Oh dear. Poor old Grail Knight. But old Blaise comes along with his mates, many angels come and play football, cheer the Grail Knight up, fill him with lots of cosmic light. Good times to come. Oh, a smile on the Grail Knight's face. Good for Blazing Star. Look at it like this. Intellect first, okay, easy, relatively detached. Then comes emotions. Oh dear. Different business. Oh dear. Painful, not too comfortable. So intellect gives rubbish away; emotional problems come later. Big problems. You'll wake up different in the morning. We've topped up your tubes."

"Thanks, Blaise. Who else was there at Muchelney today?"

"Every sort of angel, more than ten kinds. Little fluffy angels, big mother angels. Very big angels. Lots of angels."

"What about that big one who was taller than the church and the dome cap?"

"Ezekiel. He's an old buddy of ours. He came along to bless you. We don't think you would undersand who or where he is. Ezekiel is a Human-embodied human form. By this we mean that most humans never embody human form. They are only in proximity to human form. You begin to embody occasionally."

"Is the Christ an example of this?"

"The Christ is a Master-embodied human form. Leo Tolstoy is an example of a Human-embodied human form in recent times. We can't think of any in this century. It is a very difficult thing to do."

I sense a wild hunch galloping into my awareness. "Will you give us an updated explanation of the Blaise Sound? You once said it was the sound of your wheels touching down. What is it really?"

"When we first made contact and brought the angel's energy into your personal sphere, it was the manifestation at a material level of something that cannot manifest. In other words, when the third and fourth dimensions meet, there is a tremor that is created in the space between the two. This is audible in the third dimension. This is what we meant when we said it was our wheels touching down."

"Wait a minute. There's something else to this wheels business. Ophanim, your name in Hebrew, means wheels, doesn't it?"

"Yes, there is a beautiful description of this in the Bible. Ezekiel's wheels. That is the clearest description of us ever written by a Human-embodied human form, or by anyone, really. This describes what is called the *Merkabah*. Well, this is it. We've enjoyed being with you all tonight. Just have another look over the house before we go. Watch us go."

"Crikey. It's a complete circular rainbow with a bright star in the center," Russell says. "The star makes a loop around the circle then disappears."

"It's a golden trumpet that comes out of a golden star," Berenice says. "It roams around the roof like a searchlight making a circle.

Now we're all inside a glass mountain edged in gold. The star moves away inside a golden ring with a rainbow on the inside."

"It's Santa Claus again, but all the reindeer are Blaises!" I exclaim, quite happy with the image. "Santa Claus throws me a pumpkin with a smiling toothy Halloween face carved on it. Inside there's a chocolate bar. Hey! How'd Blaise know I like bittersweet the best?"

Up in the Grail chambers again lying awake under the duvet, I feel myself simultaneously in three places: here obviously, but also back at Muchelney Abbey, and also in the playground of my elementary school in Massachusetts when I was a boy of about six. An angelic conveyance appears over the three-story brick school. It is far bigger than all the clouds. Winged horses pull a magnificent coach packed with angels. No, it's not a coach but an elegant swan of light, a celestial swan ship, perhaps the entire constellation of Cygnus the Swan.

I find myself aboard this amazing ship where the angels attend to me with great celebration. There are fountains of light, musicians, a circus tent of merry angels, wall-to-wall cherubim. Evidently I've been topped up before. The ship sets off for a tour of the galaxy, as two angels guide the winged horses. Examining a fountain on board, I find three white swans with black heads swimming gracefully in waters of light. I imagine myself seeing through the swan's eyes as it glides through the stars. The celestial bird soars through the cosmos, its wings flared like sails. Innumerable angels describe wreaths of light around me. Blaise's orange football is a bright star that burns away my obscurations, enabling me to see the crystal city within its effulgence.

The Cygnus star ship pauses over the Fairy Dell. The hillside where I planted my tree of light in the earth circle is foliated with hundreds of similar trees. It is a Grail Knight's wood of light trees, a landscape speckled with earth circles, each reflecting the specific body measurement of an individual Grail Knight. On the ship again, I notice that a central pillar arises from the fountain, sheathed in silver on the outside, gold on the inside, pure light within. My No. 35 mansion sits at the bottom of this fountain, and I sit inside the great house in the vestibule. On the floor before the great front door is a tile mosaic that depicts a winged grey serpent. Evidently, my earth circle directly connects with Cygnus.

When Ezekiel had his majestic journey on the *Merkabah*, also called the divine Chariot and the Throne of God, one of his sublimest visions was of the *Shi'ur Qomah*, the revelation of the "measurement of the body." This was the mystical figure of the Godhead, "an anthropomorphic description of the divinity, appearing as the primal man, but also as the lover of the *Song of Songs*, together with the mystical names of his limbs," explains Qabalist scholar Gershom Scholem. "This appearance of the Glory in the form of supernal man is the content of the most recondite part of this mysticism," Scholem adds. In Ezekiel's ecstatic *Merkabah* voyage, he journeyed through the seven heavens and seven palaces (the *Hekhaloth*) on his way to the deepest mysteries of the Throne. Ezekiel's vision as reported in the Bible is about the *ofan*, the wheels, the great wheels within wheels, the *Ofanim*—Blaise, in other words.

Technically, the Ofanim are the wheels of the *Merkabah*; they proceed from beneath God's feet and go to every place, explains the *Bahir*, a Qabalistic text. Ezekiel saw four wheels next to the Cherubim, and each wheel was the color of a beryl stone (green, emerald, or bluish green). He gazed upon the four living creatures, each of which had four faces and two wings; one face was human, one a lion's, one an ox's, one an eagle's. Ezekiel saw "a wheel upon the earth beside the living creatures, one for each of the four of them." The wheels within wheels "were full of eyes round about," Ezekiel wrote. Above the firmament over their heads was the throne of sapphire, and seated upon this throne was the likeness of a human. Ezekiel says: "Such was the appearance of the likeness of the glory of the Lord." Apparently this was the cosmic archetype of Albion. A man clothed in linen advised Ezekiel to "take fire from between the wheels" and "go in between the wheels, even under the cherub, and fill thine hand with coals of fire from between the cherubims, and scatter them over the city."

As I lie in bed marvelling over the wonders of Ezekiel's perception of Blaise, the image of the Blaise gazebo appears before me. Suddenly, I sit up in bed. So poor an approximation, so domesticated a vision! Of course. The Blaise gazebo is my pathetically myopic impression of the *Merkabah*, of the Nimitta chariot, Blaise on wheels, the blazing wheels. Blaise isn't just the *ofan* of the *Merkabah*, but the whole chariot; the entirety of Ezekiel's vision is of Blaise in their true form. The swan ship was perhaps a slightly upgraded child's version. There's more here. No matter that I saw just a fraction of Ezekiel's glory of the Lord, Blaise's six-pillared runabout. It helps me to understand something about the implications of the Blaise gazebo, how important it is in the scheme of things.

The *Autiot Yesod* ("Letters of Foundation"), which are the 22 number-letters of Qabala, is the complete Qabala, Carlo Suarés explains. The *Autiot* are aspects of cosmic life, "projections of the vital movement that is both within and without Man;" they are the "thought projections of cosmic energy" and the "sacred language of the cycle of civilization." God created the world through speaking the *Autiot*, Qabala teaches; in practical terms, this suggests that the letters as primordial energy structures actually formed the atomic structure of everything in the universe. The Hebrew language uses only the initials of the "words" of the *Autiot* as an alphabet (as in *A*leph, *B*ayt, *G*himel, *D*allet, etc.). The *Autiot* are engendered by the second Sephira (Vessel or Sphere) on the Tree of Life, namely, *Chokmah*, which means consciousness, knowledge, intelligence, and wisdom—pure thought, undifferentiated Mind above all division, simple unity. The consciousness of *Chokmah* "begets the *Autiot*," Suarés says, which means it generates the Tree and its 22 number-letters. It's important to note that *Chokmah* is Blaise's sphere on the Tree.

The *Autiot is* the Tree of Life—its 22 paths, 10 Sephiroth, or 32 aspects in all—and its appearance is the likeness of the glory of the Lord and is called *Adam Kadmon*, the Divine Human or Supernal Man, which is to say, the celestial archetype of Albion. The anthropomorphically embodied form of the *Autiot* is Albion, the Adam Kadmon or Divine Human resident on Earth. Take the four Cherubim, each with four faces: human, lion, ox, and eagle. These are the countenances of the Four Beasts of the Apocalypse, as Blaise said earlier, and these are nothing less than the four archetypes of the zodiac, the logo signatures for the four elements that comprise Man: air, fire, earth, and water. For example, the lion, for Leo, governs or regulates the three fire signs of the zodiac with its twelve faces: Leo, Aries, Sagittarius.

So the four Cherubim imply the whole zodiac, whether it is at a terrestrial or galactic level of expression. This, in turn, implies the Round Table of Camalate based on the zodiac, whether it is at South Cadbury Castle or in the Great Bear itself. This further implies the Grail Mysteries of the Heart, the Logos, whether it is at the human, solar, or cosmic level. It—*Merkabah*, zodiac, *Autiot*, Round Table, Tree—all comes from Blaise, from the Blazing Star, the Nimitta, the Ofannim. That's why Blaise always says—and now I see it's not an angelic boast but simple fact—they are at the center of things.

That's because *Chokmah* is Blaise's sphere; that is where the Ofannim, the ineffable wheels within wheels, exist in the Tree of Life, which is generated out of themselves. In practical effects Blaise *is Chokmah*. The zodiac is born out of the Blazing Star. The zodiac (and its alphabet, the *Autiot* of 22 letters or 32 parts), within Man or within the galaxy, is Blaise's doing; it is *Chokmah*-engendered. The stone circles, the landscape zodiacs, the Round Table, the Blaise gazebo, the *Heart* of the Grail mysteries—these are aspects of the Ofannim's *Merkabah*, the Chariot of the Heart. Why Heart? Because the 32 Paths of Wisdom that are the Tree of Life (10 Sephiroth plus 22 letter-paths=32) are written as *Lammed* [30] *Beth* [2] spelling the Hebrew word *Lev*, which means "Heart." Adam Kadmon (Albion) is the Heart (*Lev*) of the Tree, *Autiot*, Round Table, zodiac, and *Merkabah*. Qabalists regard the Torah (the first five books of the Old Testament) as expressing the heart of creation, literally. Not only are its five books appreciated as Qabalistically encoded energy codes depicting the mechanics and sequences of creation, but as a text it is bounded by the membrane of the heart, as its first letter is *Bayt* and its last is Israel, thus spelling BL or LB (the *B* and *V* being interchangeable)which is written *Lev*. And that's beautiful (Hadar meaning Beauty), whose apprehension is the pith of the Grail experience through *Tiphareth*, the Heart of the Tree.

The Heart is the king over the Soul, the source of all spiritual elevation: "It is in the heart that the action of the Mind is manifest in the body," explains Qabalist Aryeh Kaplan. "It is also the link between the Mind and the physical universe" and the "means through which the Mind is revealed." And the Heart of the Tree is nothing less than the mysteries of the Grail, cosmic, terrestrial, and domestic. The (*Lev*) and God's Glory (*Kavod*, whose numerical value is 32) are the same.

The Heart is the beauty (*Hadar*) of the fruit of the body, Kaplan says; and Beauty, as Blaise told us once, is the essence of *Tiphareth*, the Heart of the Tree of Life and the core of the Grail Quest. "And what is this heart? It is the 32 hidden paths of wisdom that are hidden in it," Kaplan says. And conveyed to humanity by the Blaise *Merkabah*, glimpsed at the place where much *El* is nigh.

67

THE SECRET OF
THE ALLER DRAGON

laise was right. The angelic topping-up at Muchelney has rekindled my spirits magnificently, and I wake this morning whistling and tapping my toes, one jovial Grail Knight off for the next adventure in an unremittingly *interesting* Quest.

Today I'm bound for Aller, to that queer little rise in the land like a mole's tunnel just in front of the Church of St. Andrew. The church comes into sight as I wheel down the access lane, and I notice it's topped with a dome cap that is penetrated vertically by a crimson sword. I sit on the rise in the churchyard, facing Aller village a half-mile away then insert my sword into the rise like an inverted periscope.

First, I appreciate that this rise is the remains of an old T-shaped tumulus. Down below, there's a grave with a casket fronted with the golden face of the sphinx mounted like a gargoyle. I contemplate the sphinx for a few moments then realize I'm dealing with a symbolic image: the sphinx is the mystery of the fourfold elemental human nature; the casket is not only the body's destiny but an image of living confinement within human elemental base, a miniature Noah's Ark, if you like. The casket slides across the floor, revealing a white marble chamber underneath; it resembles a traditional tile-inlaid Japanese bath about six feet square. A sheathed sword lies on the smooth floor. The insignia of a lion hangs on the wall. Wait a minute. I probe the lion's brow and discover a multifacetted pearl. These are equivalent symbolic images. The Japanese bath represents the purity of insight, but so does the pearl in the brow of the lion; it's the same pearl that I experienced at Oath Hill last night and through which I passed to enter the necropolis.

This understood, the lion insignia on the wall and the image of an actual lion with a crystal in his brow merge into a single lion holding a blazing torch. The torchlight fills my perceptual space like a house-sized lattice of light. This dissolves, and I find myself on high ground, possibly 20,000 feet above a plain. I stand in the radically high and craggy snowpeaks of a mountain range. Far below looms a huge, luminous dome, possibly ten, maybe fifty, miles in diameter; within it is the city of light. I point my sword at the domed city and will myself there. Eventually, after some dilatory fluttering among the clouds, I arrive on the desert plain standing among people who wear large crescents as decorative headgear; they greet me. After I knock three times at the front gate with my sword, the doors swing open, and I enter.

I stand before a gorgeous fountain of light that spumes rainbows and overlooks a spacious green lawn and elegant Grecian-style white buildings. Twelve fruit trees form a living botanical collar around a central fruit tree that bears all the fruits born by the individual trees. Somebody hands me a peach, telling me to take the pit home and plant it. I enter the central foyer of a stately white marble building fronted with pillars. It's apparently a library with a vast collection of volumes, card catalogs, and reading tables. An open book lying on one table catches my eye. It's the same book I once saw on the table in Blaise's gazebo. I look at the cover: it's *my* book, the chronicle of my lives. I turn to a lifetime, and as I read the entry, it balloons into an encyclopedia, and this turns into a holographic video offering endless fine detail if I wish it.

A man approaches. He is a blend of William Shakespeare and Clark Gable as his features struggle to achieve a physiognomic compromise in my perception; he's clothed entirely in blue. He leads me to a blue room where he hands me a blue pyramid with a green sphere inside and a white horse with a golden corn—a unicorn—inside that. He points to a wall chart that depicts the galaxy, over which innumerable triangles have been superimposed. Then he shows me a model of the Earth with a miniature version of this galactic triangulation grid overlay. He leads me back to the fountain, where a second man greets me.

This new mentor—who resembles Benjamin Franklin complete with bald pate, wire-rim glasses, and tufts of hair around the ears—leads me to another meeting room. He hands me a gold ring with a six-sided emerald setting; the ring contains the image of a white unicorn. He hands me a new object, a gold coin bearing a complex engraved image: the Grail Knight is seated in meditation with sword and shield in his hands, a crown on his head, Eiwann in his chest, the ruby, green pyramid, and crystal city within this. The image shifts again. I hold a peach-skinned infant who is calmly awake with a ruby in his chest and a seed of light within the ruby. Probably these are three variations on the same elusive reality.

"Welcome to Shambhala in the Gobi," he says, standing next to the mentor in blue. "Now you know the way here, you may return when you need. We'll be seeing you again fairly soon. Come and go with our blessings."

But there is a third man behind these two, and he now steps forward. I gasp when I realize who he is. *Ben.* The Ben with the beat-up Morris Minor, with the tiny cottage in East Lyng, the Ben who guided me through the Aller Dragon and the dragon of my romantic entanglements. Ben. Wait a minute. This is the same man who gave the lecture at Worley Hill on the Stone and who was called Merlin.

"The same," Merlin says, with a grin and a sweeping bow, following my thought processes with amusement. "Don't worry about it. I'll see you sometime on Mertowney Mountain. Come visit me at another of my homes. Time to go now."

I open my eyes. I'm back at Aller. I survey the church and the broad meadow stretching to Aller village, and then look down at my feet. There is a piece of broken boiler plate in the dirt, bearing the numeral 6 or 9, depending on which way you hold it: Blaise for 6, Shambhala for 9 (as in its letter count). And if you're speaking Qabala, 9 is *Tayt*, the ninth letter of the *Autiot*, depicted in the Tarot as the

Nineteenth Path called *Strength*. In this arcane image, a woman, known as the Daughter of the Flaming Sword, effortlessly holds open the mouth of a lion. In alchemy, the lion represents uncontrolled natural forces in the subjective world of the psyche; in astrology, the lion denotes the constellation Leo and its central star, Regulus, *Cor Leonis*, "The Heart of the Lion." In Qabalistic thinking, the lion represents the first formation of the Individuality projected into the worlds of form from the sphere of *Chesed*, the Sephiroth of Jupiterian expansiveness and exultant spiritual knowledge. Lions are always turning up in the *Mabinogion*, that surrealistic saga of ancient Celtic initiation rites. But *Tayt* also literally signifies a snake or serpent—as in the Aller Dragon.

As I stand up and stretch, preparing to leave, the crimson sword descends and cleaves the two upper grave chambers, upon which I am sitting, to reveal a third chamber, set even deeper. This is a domed stone vault that contains two caskets; I have a strong impression that the entombed bodies once belonged to the thirteenth century Arthur and Guinivere. Meanwhile, I ride home to Wick, marvelling at where Ben has got himself to and where he has come from. It's all done in the *esplumoir*, as Blaise might say.

Blaise arrives a couple of hours after dinner for the much-needed debriefing. "We come as we are, as a Blazing Star. We come as Love from Above. We greet you all. We surround you with the wall of lilac flames. For each of you, we breathe with your breath as it leaves your body. We place a Blazing Star at the center of yourself, as what you are."

"Blaise, who were those two men I met today?"

"They are the Masters who are most concerned with your present initiatory process. Two of them sponsored you. The first was Master St. Germaine of the lilac ray and the second was Master Lady Portia of the gold ray. They are two of what are now fourteen Ray Masters transmitting through the Great Bear. You saw a few aspects of their human incarnational lineage. They are particularly active with us today in work on behalf of the Earth energy matrix. Master St. Germaine brings the transmutative energy of the Christ. Master Lady

Portia brings the discriminative wisdom of that transmutation. St. Germaine and Lady Portia are involved especially with our dome activations because within this time period the yellow and violet are sympathetic resonances within the sphere. You saw St. Germaine in blue because that is your primary ray and he teaches you accordingly."

"How does the third master fit into this scheme?"

"The third Master, Merlin, prepares you. Merlin, as we once told you, is a Grand Square Master, which is a magus of high degree. We have worked with him since the beginning of your planet, and before."

"Does Merlin have a particular relationship with the Ray Masters?"

"No relation. He has a direct relationship with us."

"Was it Shambhala I visited today?"

"Correct. Aller is one of the doorways to Shambhala in Somerset."

"I'm not clear on the differences between Shambhala and Roïyat, or for that matter, Jerusalem and New Jerusalem."

"Jersualem existed in the past as a city with twelve gates. The New Jerusalem is yet to come. Shambhala exists on another plane. It is present, has been, and will be, and is not influenced by Earth activity, though symbiotically it is related to Earth with a degree of intercommunication when and where necessary. We showed you a gateway today.

"The crystal city, what your friend calls Roïyat, exists in the future and is not yet in manifestation. It is an aspect of Shambhala. It pertains to the Great Bear. We place its date of future manifestation at around 3000 A.D. It is possibly both a new dimension and a new realm for humans today. It is an unknown aspect because humanity has not evolved enough yet. You saw a part of the light city last year. We took you to it through Hamdon Hill.

"On the Tree of Life, there are only ten spheres. Yet we duplicate two and get twelve. There are twelve temples in the light circle, what you like to call the Round Table of Hyperborea. We call it the Western temple. There is an area near London where the light circle is close to the gateway to the light city. This is the sphere of *Daath* on the Tree, the veiled Sephira. *Daath* is an abyss where there is a connection with another realm, namely Sirius. You will learn that all these places are interconnected."

Like last night, I am too wired to sleep after my outing at Aller and visit with Blaise. As I sit on my bed, my attention returns to Aller. Today's experience begins to unfold again, but this time at a deeper level, as if I missed a lot the first time through.

Here is Aller, Heart of the Girt Dog, conduit with Oath Hill to Sirius and the Hierarchy. Now, instead of the church, I see Aller's original stone circle in full lithic splendor, each stone ablaze with a corona of light. Instead of the curious little rise or earth mound in the churchyard, there is an open rectangle inside the circle blocked out with standing stones; it's about four feet wide and twelve feet long, one end attached to the perimeter; it provides ample space for somebody to sit inside. That is where I am sitting now. It wasn't always open; now I see it as an enclosed barrow, a long, low stone chamber, like an Eskimo igloo, topped with earth. This must have been its original form. You sit deep inside this barrow in the darkness facing the stone wall, your back to the entrance, which is shut after you enter. What you are here to encounter is on the other side of the interior stone wall. The Aller dragon.

Although its body is geomantically deployed in the landscape from Hatch Beauchamp to Wick Hill, in a holographic, experiential sense, the entire dragon is coiled up and sentient on just the other side of this stone barrier. I pass through the wall inside my sword then confront the massive coiled dragon with my sword held before me as a razor's-edge column of light. I'm not afraid of the dragon; that's pointless, because the dragon is really a doorway. There is a complex circular matrix of criss-crossing lines in its brow; this is the gateway. It's a little confusing to say this, but I pass through this matrix by stepping inside my sword, then willing it through the matrix. I emerge in a black space in an empty field cloaked in darkness. This puzzles me. I see only a tiny point of brilliant light in this endless darkness; that pinpoint of light will be my doorway out of here when

I'm ready to leave, somewhat the way the wardrobe was for the children visiting Narnia.

Unending black—this is what I imagine Blaise's Black Bowling Ball, the sphere of stable consciousness, to be like on the inside. After a while the environment shifts and I am inside the Shambhala dome, hovering perhaps a couple hundred feet above the city. Below me is a promenade encircling a large reflecting pond girted by fruit trees laden with fruits; beyond this in a large concentric circle stands a series of elegant buildings in white marble done in Grecian or Renaissance architectural modes. Standing on the ground now, I gather fruits in a basket (this may be another symbolic way of experiencing the transmission from the three Shambhala masters) then return through the pinpoint of light in the dark void and stand before the Aller dragon again as I sit inside the barrow.

I examine my basket of otherworldly fruit and reflect on its mythic implications. Golden apples of the Hesperides. Queen of Heaven Hera's apple orchard of Hyperborea. The ever-watchful dragon Ladon, who guards them. Hercules' eleventh labor. Fruits of the Summer Country, the Middle Earth, Avalon, the Land of Light. You step through the dimensional doorway of the stone barrow and climb up, as if leaving the subway for the street, into the world of spiritual sunshine. Into the Summer Country, Gwynfa's realm, the middle realm, the *bardo*, or intermediate state, between the living and the eternal.

Like last night, Blaise is with me for another tutorial. "Aller is the 231 Gates," Blaise says. "Study the name."

If Aller were a Qabalistic name, it would be written as *ALR*; the gematria, or number equivalents, for these three letters spells *Aleph* (1), *Lammed* (30), *Raysh* (200), or 231. The *ALR* dragon. But what are the 231 Gates?

If you take the 22 letters of the *Autiot Yesod* and place them on the perimeter of a circle and then connect them all with straight lines, the total number of line connections between two letters will be 231. Qabala calls this matrix of two-letter connections the 231 Gates. Each of the 22 letters has 21 connections; each letter is connected to every other letter, forming a complex, circular geometrical figure. Let's say you made a stone circle with 22 standing stones and connected the stones in this same way using Day-Glo string for heightened visibility. You would have a physical version of the 231 Gates and a beautifully symmetrical structure best appreciated from above. It's quite possible that is what the ancient geomancers actually did when they designed the Aller circle.

Qabala says that Creation took place through these 231 Gates. It was through these letters that the universe was originally created; the *Autiot Yesod* are the agents of creation, the letters upon which the world is founded, and the means by which the world is sustained. God created the world by "speaking" these foundational letters (and all their permutations). In other words, the *Autiot Yesod* is not just an alphabet; its letters are the creative energies and forces by which the world is brought into being. As Qabalist Aryeh Kaplan explains, the 231 Gates are what remained in the Vacated Space that preceded Creation. "Before a universe could be created, empty space had to exist in which it could be made." It's paradoxical because even though Creation had not yet happened and only God existed, all existence was filled with Divine Essence or *Ain Sof Awr*, the Light of the Infinite. God had to make room, in the fullness of this undifferentiated Essence, for Creation, so the Vacated Space was created. In effect, the *Ain Sof Awr* was contracted to make room for Creation. "The hollow engraved in the Supernal Luminesence [*Ain Sof Awr*] was the Vacated Space, in which all creation subsequently occurred." This space was also called the "Lamp of Darkness" or "Chaos and Void," the inky gloom before Creation and the Sephira were brought into being.

Into this Vacated Space, God spoke the Letters of Foundation, creating the 231 Gates. The 231 Gates effectively include the entire Tree of Life with its 22 Paths and 10 Sephiroth. The Gates are the circle of existence that Qabala calls the *Galgal*, the mystical array of the 22 letters, the cycle of events in the world, the sphere of the zodiac, and the "King over Time," Kaplan says. More precisely, *Galgal* is the circle, the complete matrix of connections; the 231 Gates are the myriad connections among the 22 Letters of Foundation. In Ezekiel's vision, the *Galgal*, or sphere, is described as being below the feet of the Cherubim; that links it directly with the *ofan* or wheels of the *Merkabah*. So the *Galgal* is another expression of the Chariot's Wheels, a cycle or turning sphere (the landscape zodiac) through which one may be lifted up to the mystical experience focussed through the Cherubim. It's worth noting that *ALR*, read backward, which is a legitimate function in Qabalistic words, as mirror images reveal unsuspected nuances, is 132, which can be interpreted as *Aleph* (1) and *Lev* (32): One Heart. So *ALR* is the One Heart with 231 Gates.

Aller may be the home of the *ALR* or the 231 Gates, but how does the dragon fit into this? Let's back off a little and consider the dragon from a fresh perspective. *Ngaljod* is what the Australian Aborigines call their great ancestral dragon, the Rainbow Serpent, whose Dreamtime activities still resonate in the shapes, energies, and processes of the planetary environment. The Rainbow Serpent is nothing less than a "cosmological model for the spectral order of universal energy," or the electromagnetic spectrum, which is the continuous range of radiation from gamma rays to radio waves including the relatively small spectrum of visible light that comprises our visible world, explains Robert Lawlor, a scholar of Aboriginal culture. "The Rainbow Serpent is an energy figure symbolic of the sacred body of the Earth and the preformative spiritual order of the universe," Lawlor writes. "This image is the original appearance of creative energy in the Dreamtime."

In other words, when God spoke the creation into existence, this generated the original *ALR* dragon simultaneously with the 231 Gates. It's hard to see how they are actually different other than in expression; to a large degree, the 231 Gates and the Aller dragon are equivalent realities. At some level, *ALR* is Draco, the cosmic antecedent for all terrestrial dragons and dragon images. It is particularly interesting that as a constellation, according to Ptolemy's star chart, Draco snakes its way around the Pole Star and passes through all twelve constellations of the zodiac; this means it has stars in sections of all the signs of the zodiac. If you are God speaking the Letters of Foundation into the Vacated Space, the result is the 231 Gates or the Tree of Life—which is to say, all manifest existence, or the One Heart that bounds the Torah. And what is manifest existence if not the electro-magnetic spectrum, symbolized—embodied—by the Rainbow Serpent or *ALR* dragon?

When I passed through the brow of the Aller Dragon and entered a black space, this corresponded, at least on the conceptual level, with the Vacated Space that preceded the 231 Gates. Technically, for me it was more likely a gap between worlds or dimensions that I experienced, the dark crawl space between rungs of Jacob's Ladder, that great stacking of four Trees of Life. The first initiation into the spiritual domain comes through an introduction to the *Galgal*, which is the entrance to the mysteries, explains Kaplan. *Galgal* is the womb of the Cosmic Mother—"the womb from which one is reborn into a spiritual plane." In a similar way, the hollow interior of the Rain-bow Serpent is sometimes regarded as the "uterus" of the Great Mother.

Galgal is the cycle of time and the zodiac, literally; its number matrix (*GLGL*) declares this: *Ghimel* (3), *Lammed* (30), *Ghimel* (3), *Lammed* (30), or 3333 equals 12, the number of the zodiac. *Galgal* is the fount of initiation on this side of the Gates. The 32 Paths of Wisdom (the Heart or *Lev*) are called *Netivot*, which imply a personal, privately negotiated, individually blazed path into the mysteries; its numerical value is 462, which is twice the number of the 231 Gates, and this means *ALR* gives you a roundtrip ticket through the mysteries. "These gates are a means through which one ascends and descends along the 32 paths," Kaplan says. In other words, the *Netivot* are the ways in and out, the dual-trafficked paths, the criss-crossings of initiatory routes within the *Galgal* as the Grail Knight seeks the Heart of the Tree of Life—the temple of the Grail mysteries, in short, the *Lev* of *much El nigh.*

The Qabalistic symbolic shorthand is breathtakingly elegant. The Aller dragon is the 231 Gates; the Gates are *ALR* (*Aleph, Lammed, Raysh*), which means, literally, apples (*Raysh*) of the dragon (*Aleph-Lammed*, or *AL*). This means fruits of spiritual insight gathered in the

Summer Country and brought back into the Island of Britain through the *Galgal* (the letter matrix, the zodiacal circle, and the stone circle) of Aller. Let's look at this more closely. *AL* is the dragon because *Aleph* (1) and *Lammed* (30) spell 13, which is *AL*, and the number of primary dragons brought to Earth with the domes. *AL*, by gematrial equivalency, is also *Esch* (*Aleph* [1], *Sheen* [300]), the Hebrew word for fire. *AL* refers to God's 13 attributes of Mercy; *AL*, by equivalency, is *Ahavah*, which is Hebrew for Love (whose gematria is 13).

Raysh is the golden apple, or Avalon, because it (as 200) is a cosmic container, a house (daugher of *Bayt* [as 2], so to speak, the archetype of all containers), containing the galaxy of stars like the compact white pith of an apple. Why is it Hercules' *eleventh* labor that involves the apples of the Hesperides? Because when you array the 231 Gates as a mathematical table, at the eleventh line the letters *Aleph* and *Lammed* repeat themselves for the entire line: *AL, AL, AL,* etc. What more opportune doorway for Hercules, or any Grail Knight, to slip through the dragon (*AL*) into Hesperides or Avalon (*Raysh*)? Why do this? It's a second aspect of kingship, Qabala teaches us, indicating the King over Time, master of the zodiacal cycle (*Galgal*), which dominates time.

Which is probably why on my first visit to Aller I heard voices as if from inside the earth mound acclaiming *Arthur! Arthur! Arthur!*— once and future King over Draco, master of the *ALR* dragon.

68

IN A CIRCLE WITH THE THREE MOTHERS

ate in the afternoon the next day, I'm sitting in my earth circle out near the Fairy Dell. I sit inside the light cone and Tree of Life which have grown up from the original Star seed I planted here months ago. The roots have burrowed deep into the Earth. After a few moments of concentration, my attention is drawn to a place high in the mountains, to a cliff-face above the forests, even above the clouds. A huge lake lies like an aluminum disc across the land. It feels like Peru, maybe Lake Titicaca on the Bolivian border. I wear a white robe with a purple sash; several feathers are held upright at the back of my head by a ceremonial band. I see myself as another person would: here is a man, fiftysomething, with black hair, dark eyes, strong face, sinewy body. He sits in an earth circle inside a cone of light and tree just as I do. He looks into the future and sees the American Grail Knight sitting in his Somerset earth circle, remembering him. I am a future life of this Peruvian.

For a moment, I wonder which is my present, primary reality—then, in Peru, or now, in Somerset, or neither—because, for a moment, I sense I am simultaneously sitting on yet another earth circle, this one in a very different terrain, a pale, olive treeless environment not of this planet. It's somewhere in the Pleiades, I'm certain. I see myself sitting there, with a much larger, hairless head, contemplating my incarnational projections, including these two in Peru and Somerset. Have I ever left the Pleiades? Am I still, even this moment, still meditating at my earth circle on that other home planet? The earth circle seems to make these spatial and temporal identities somewhat interchangeable. As I sit here high in the Peruvian mountains, a lilac flame burns in me from groin to head. The Blaise gazebo appears on the rock ledge. Each of the six Blaises takes form through a pillar; they make a circle of angelic light; their hands join together to create a table upon which I now sit.

Watching this from my earth circle at the Fairy Dell, I see the gazebo condense to a single concentrated point of brilliant light; watching things from inside as the Peruvian, the gazebo remains the same; but whatever happens next I cannot see.

That doesn't matter because suddenly the Girt Dog appears below me as if I am surveying his geomantic body from on high. His spiritual centers are lit up as if with great bonfires, and I see the precise location of his seven landscape chakras. Pitney is the tail, the cynosure; Muchelney is the root; the Langport church on the hill is his second center; Wick, the solar plexus; Aller is the heart chakra; Oath Hill, the throat; Burrowbridge Mump is the Dog's brow; and Othery is its crown. But there is a deeper mystery within this sequential energy system. It's the Three Mothers—"a great mystical secret," says Qabala. It is also the secret of the Girt Dog.

These are the three letters *Aleph, Mem, Sheen*, or *AMSh*, from which emanate the elements of air, water, and fire, respectively. The 22 letters of the Hebrew alphabet are classified into three groups: the Three Mothers, the Seven Doubles, and the Twelve Singles; each group has its fundamental role in the stages of Creation. The Three Mothers summarize the whole process of energy and "express simultaneously the essence, appearance, and movement of everything," says Carlo Suarés. The Three Mothers come first in the *Autiot* as a generative matrix for everything else; as such, they are antecedent to the manifest Name of God. Or as Qabalist Gareth Knight explains, the Three Mothers represent a threefold basic universe. "*Shin* [Sheen]—the Spirit, the eternal matrix; *Aleph*—the driving power within; *Mem*—the reflective substance within which the whole edifice of forms is built." Another way of looking at the Three Mothers is to think of them as energy. As Suarés explains, *Aleph* is maximum energy, *Mem* is minimum energy, and *Sheen* is the action of *Aleph* upon *Mem*, allegorically, the spiritual face brooding over the primal waters. *Aleph* forms the air, *Mem* forms the water, and *Sheen* forms fire. The result of the interdependent action of these three factors upon each other is to create Heaven (*Schamaim*) and Earth (*Eretz*), which express "One energy flowing in two opposite directions," Suarés says.

The Three Mothers precede the Tetragrammaton, or *YHVH*; they are older, an antecedent stage in Creation and are thereby an even deeper mystery than this spiritually formidable, "unpronounceable" divine Name. The letters *AMSh* are the roots ("parents" or "mothers") of the first three letters (*YHV*) of *YHVH*. The Tetragrammaton, among other things, refers to the four primal elements of Creation; namely, water, fire, air, and earth, as they inform both World and Man. So *AMSh* precludes earth, the fourth element, which is then subsequently included in *YHVH*, the Name of God. *Vav* (V) derives from *Aleph* (air); *Yod* (Y) derives from *Mem* (water); and *Heh* (H) from *Sheen* (fire). So in *AMSh* we have the "mothers" of the three primary elements whose spoken form is *YHVH*.

These sublime mechanics of Creation are displayed geomantically in the design and deployment of the Girt Dog temple for the initiatory benefit of the Grail Knight—not just me, but all Grail Knights over time, past and future, too. We behold a cosmic design principle in action. The temple of the Three Mothers lies within the landscape body of the Girt Dog. The *Aleph* (air) temple is at Muchelney: here we encounter the *Merkabah*, the *Lev* or Heart of the Tree at the Dog's root center where much *EL* (or *AL*) is nigh. The *Mem* (water) temple is at Aller: here we meet the ALR dragon, the *Galgal* zodiacal cycle of Time, at the heart of the Dog. The *Sheen* (fire) temple is at Oath Hill: here is *IOA* Hill, the *Teli* or axis of Space, Jacob's Ladder, the *Shemhamforesch* at the Dog's throat. The Three Mothers: *Lev*, or Heart; *Galgal*, or Time; and *Teli*, or Space. No doubt that is why mythology acclaims the Dog as the servant of the Triple Goddess, a less abstract expression of the Three Mothers or as three-headed Cerberus, spectral Dog of the Underworld.

Qabala alternatively describes these three qualities as Soul (*Lev*), Year (*Galgal*), and Universe (*Teli*), and it tells us there is a "king" over each domain. The *Sepher Yetzirah* expresses it aphoristically. The *Teli* in the Universe is like a king on his throne, which means as its axis he rules over all space yet is not a part of it. The *Galgal* in the Year is like a king in the province, which means he is part of the flow of time and thus a level below the rank of absolute monarch. The *Lev* in the Soul is like a king in war, because the heart is the battlefield between good and evil, of one opposite the other. The three kings represent the three dimensional world of time, space, and soul. This is the cosmic creation drama enacted within Arthur's legendary dog, Cafal—Qabala—and our own Girt Dog.

But there is a fourth state that summarizes and unifies the Three Mothers and their kings. This is *TaGel*, which means "rejoice." The initial letters of *Teli*, *Galgal*, and *Lev* (TGL) spell out *TaGel* about which Isaiah declares: "My soul will rejoice (*TaGel*) in my God." As Aryeh Kaplan explains, "It is through meditation on these three elements that the soul can attain mystical ecstasy." Kaplan points out that the word also occurs in *Psalms*, which says, "God is king, let the earth rejoice." According to Kaplan, this means "God is King, *Teli Galgal Lev* is the Earth;" this indicates that "these are the three kings over His creation."

Which brings us back to Burrowbridge Mump. This is the site of "God is King." In this equation of spiritual geomancy, the Mump is *TaGel*; the Mump, which is the Girt Dog's brow, is the place where Eiwann, the golden child or Christ child, is born into the Grail Knight when the Handless One cleaves his heart. Eiwann says: "I am the One!" And we say, at the Mump: Rejoice! *TaGel*!

We are dealing with seamlessly woven mysteries of the creation of Man and World in the geomantic temple of mirrors called the zodiac. Since the landscape zodiac is a miniature holographic model of the cosmos, its temples illustrate, through experiential initiation, the stages, sequences, and processes of cosmic creation, whose single fruit is Man. Not only is Qabala's *Autiot* a key interpretive vocabulary for this spiritual geomancy; it may be *the* design code itself, the engineering specifications of the temple. Again, the system is a big terrestrial mirror, and the Grail Quest is the tutorial in its mechanics.

The Three Mothers (*AMSh*) within the Dog precede and are antecedent to the Tetragrammaton (*YHVH*) of the full zodiac, just as the Dog guards the temple and is psychopomp to all visitors. I learned this chewing the dog's bone at East Lyng. The Three Mothers are *YHVH*'s roots, the Mothers of air, water, and fire. *YHVH* represents the realm of the four elements in Man and World and the 72 permutations of the Holy Name (*Shemhamforesch*). Qabala conceives the Name (*YHVH*) "to represent the unregenerate man, who lives entirely in his body, eating, drinking, and copulating," explains Qabalist Israel Regardie. The Divine Self has not been born into this type of man or woman; the Christ has not incarnated in the flesh. However, when a human "so regenerates and purifies himself that he opens himself to the Holy Spirit, which completely revitalizes him"—through, among other routes, the path of the Grail Knight—then the Holy Spirit or *Shekinah*, represented by the letter *Sheen*, may enter the Man (male or female) compounded of *YHVH* and produce a change.

In the language of Qabala, this descent of the *Sheen* (the fiery breath of the living God) into the midst of the elemental name *YHVH* (Tetragrammaton) produces a new word, *YHShVH*. This is called the Pentagrammaton (the Word of five letters). More importantly, it produces a new being: the golden child (Eiwann). *Sheen* descends into *YHVH*, literally cleaving a space amid its four letters to produce the new word, *YHShVH*, and the new being, *Yeheshua* or Jesus, just as I witnessed at the Mump when the sword wielded by the Handless One cleaved my body and emerald to reveal the golden child within the heart manger. *Yeheshua* is the one in whom the golden Christ Child has been born, "in whom the birth of Spirit has equilibrized the base and unredeemed elements of matter," says Regardie.

Just as the Christ incarnates into Jesus (which religious mythology depicts as a child in the manger), so is the Christ similarly born as a golden child into the cave of the heart or "manger" of the aspiring Grail Knight. This is central to the initiation of the Grail. First there is one Christ child; eventually, there will be millions as the Christ in-carnates in every individual man and woman as a living spiritual presence capable of growth and evolution—a child with its whole life before it. We owe a lot to the Elohim, humanity's prime parents, for this opportunity. With their aid and through the geomantic struc-ture of the Mump and the dynamics of the emerald, the golden child is born into the Grail Knight, representing a new order of being, a new threshold of spiritual cognition. Eventually there is a conclave of Christ-initiated humans: friends of the Sangrail.

It all comes back to Blaise, of course. "It is through these Mother letters that one can enter into the realm of *Chakhmah* [*Chokmah*] con-sciousness, which is the portal to the transcendental," says Kaplan. The thought and elegance that went into the design of this temple are astonishing. What temple? The Dog, zodiac, Tree, myth, planet, Man, galaxy. Pick any level, you'll find the same elements because they're all different expressions of one another. Let us now praise famous dogs and their mothers!

"You begin to see a few aspects of our temple design," Blaise says. "You begin to see past one corner of the veil."

69

TROUBLE AT THE MILL

t dinner Berenice discusses certain problems she's had recently with Edmund and his behavior. Normally I don't have opinions about child-raising—I'm really a weekend rent-an-uncle—but on this topic tonight, I jump immoderately into the conversation.

"You know, Berenice, you really neglect Edmund. He'd be a lot less fidgety and wingey if you didn't have such a lackadaisacal attitude about mothering. I mean, if you aren't careful he could grow up to be really neurotic." Berenice looks at me in shocked silence. Russell raises his eyebrows in surprise. Nobody speaks for the rest of the meal.

Something didn't feel right about my remarks, wasn't me; the affect was off, a little bent, as if an ill-tempered voice from the shadows had suddenly sprayed the room with foul-tasting words. Later, in my room as I sip tea, I feel pleased with myself that I have survived the grave and can now start wrapping things up on the Quest. Summer holidays after an intense semester, and all that. Then Russell calls up the stairs to announce Blaise's visit.

"We come as we are, as a Blazing Star. We come from not too far, as Love from Above. We greet you all. We surround you with the wall of lilac flames. The individual lilac flame rises above each of you. We place around you the sapphire blue sphere surrounded by gold, orange, and red flickering flames. We place the green emerald in your chest with the pinpoint of light at the center.

"We come with a few suggestions for the Grail Knight. We would like it if you did not think in terms of having finished anything. This will not be useful at this point and could produce significant interference. We would like to suggest that for the next few days that you continue, among your everyday activities, the process of remembering. We ask that you deliberately try to remember all of the experiences at the earth circle. We say that much is in balance. There are influences attempting to corrupt the penultimate stages of our task together. We are not suggesting that you do not do other things, but keep as your objective during these next few days, in whatever you may be doing, the subject we have given you. We are most pleased with your efforts, Grail Knight, but remember also that you would be better to practice Love from Above in other circumstances. You upset Berenice tonight and this upsets us. So remember this, if you wish. It will improve things, and things will move forward."

"What are these corrupting influences you refer to?" I ask. "Are they what inspired me to say those nasty things to Berenice, as I now see it?"

"Yes, it was not your attitude. It was the corruptive influences. It is subtle stuff, and it gets subtler. You are responsible because you make the choice. Remember that as you return to America you'll be largely on your own. You'll be in charge. Presume that we will be present with you offering the alternative. Just remember, we are very quiet and very small. These two facts should be enough. Meditate on the small. It is a key issue in discrimination.

"The 'bad guys,' as you call them, are bigger and louder. They are wonderful imitators. You will always feel a sensation at the top of your head to denote the difference between us and others. Also, you can feel your solar plexus with your full attention. If it feels cloudy, then no Blazing Star; none of us would be there, clouds and rain and big wings. If it's a sunny day, if the navel is happy, the point between Heaven and Earth, and there is no rain, no clouds, no wind, and the heart is free—then we'll be there. This is a meter for guidance."

"You must find these corrupting influences rather distressing," Berenice says.

"Not at all distressful to us. We are absolutely in tune with cosmic harmony and the Architect of the known universe and the Plan. We are able to safely say that our concern is only on your behalf. Know that your free will presents two opposing views in any moment. We are linked absolutely and totally to what you may call the Divine Will. Therefore, we needn't worry at this point, but maybe when we get those bodies again, get reborn on Earth, then we'll have to link our will through effort like you do."

"My goodness. Was that you just now saying 'You see how it is' in my head?" Berenice asks.

"Oh dear. What a surprise. You are just a little tube spraying light around, even with your mouth shut—even more so. Remember, life is not what it seems."

"I'll say," I interject. "Take my parent's backyard. It's a complete psychic playground."

"It's your own psyche, Grail Knight. Your examining of it was like an operating theater arrayed with the entire contents of your psyche. Now we would like to talk just a little to you three. Each time any of you wishes to be with us, use the image we have given you recently. Breathe to this image with Love from Above. We are all at this point at the beginning of something very exciting, much more so now than at any point in our history together. Much depends on the coming months. We will be making attempts to hasten certain karmic evolutionary trends on your behalf so that your life purpose may be brought into clearer focus. This inherently may mean you will encounter certain problems. Greet them with gratitude. You are in the process of clearing major things out of the past. Greet these events as Love from Above. Don't worry about this, but let it sit gently in your minds on the impulse of letting go all doubts, all fears, all attempts to be anything other than what you are. We say this as your friends, Blazing Star.

"This was to do with remembering yourselves. What did you think when you were a teenager? When you were ten? What did your feelings say when you were seven? Three? How did it feel before that? Remember yourself. Remember. Each moment, you encounter yourself as a product of those experiences. All you need to do is look at it and remember. It's simple, really. You needn't make a gymnastic exercise out of it. Be as love and look. Seeing is simple if you look with love. You have cotton wool between your ears. It's just more simple than you think. Don't be misled by the big imitator, the one that gets in the way of your knowing that you're hearing at all. Berenice, you are more than either of the others, Russell or the Grail Knight."

"Well, I'm glad I buried my ego this past weekend," I remark.

"No, we're just saying to her that the feminine is potentially more receptive as a channel and she has been one of us and is potentially far more in tune than either of you."

"I guess Russell and I have just been hanging out with the Seraphim all these years?"

"Not in the same way. You will have to wait and see. Berenice has had close associations with us over many incarnations. We hope, as we have suggested, you will be as Love from Above. So that's it for tonight. We have much pressing business elsewhere. We have been unexpectedly assigned to watch over an event within the Sirius system, and we are very spread out at the moment."

"What's the trouble on Sirius?"

"In Sirius there are some forces that are trying to manipulate the tri-solar energies and turn them against the forces for which we work."

"Anyway we can help?" Russell asks.

"In your own way, through your connection with us, with Michael, you assist in the best way you can. It is just a little unexpected at this time. Not anything we can't deal with, but we just need to be more focussed there, rather than to be here with you. This event this evening will only occupy us until around daybreak tomorrow. As you know, there are forces that are antithetical even to those with which we are concerned. As you have met opposition and will meet more in the future, so others with whom we are concerned also meet opposition. The Suns within Sirius are being manipulated for the wrong needs. Therefore, our energies are needed to concentrate these within their natural pattern. We leave you in the bright, as love, as ever, Blazing Star."

Russell and I jump up at the same time and say, "Well, Berenice, Blazing Star's all time favorite, would you possibly allow us lesser souls to make you some high tea?"

"Oh yes, thank you very much. That would be lovely. But remember to keep the tea bag in for only a minute, and probably lots less, and put in lots and lots of milk, please."

I wake in the middle of the night from a disturbing dream. I'm in San Francisco. Two large fighter aircraft fly low over the land chasing each other, then they roar straight up into the sky. A massive ocean liner or tanker with a gleaming black hull sails through the air and crashes mightily into the Bay Bridge that links San Francisco and Oakland. I run for cover, down a hillside on a college campus just as the bridge and tanker explode in orange flames. Metal and debris are flung everywhere. I fluff my pillow and pull up the duvet. Is this a preview of the work of the "opposition" Blaise referred to? I must remember to start wearing a crash helmet and safety glasses whenever I go out from now on, I say to myself, as I fall back to sleep.

Late the next afternoon, the moon is rising. A full, yellow orb climbs through the trees as the sun slips below the horizon after only a brief daytime visit. I sit at my earth circle. Again I find myself in the Andes on that mountain lookout. I enter Blaise's gazebo, but this time on the inside it is a large, white temple fronted by numerous pillars; my colleagues are inside. We stand before an altar with a Blazing Star. The room swells with nearly blinding light from this Star; we transmit this light into the valleys and communities. Numerous beams of light ray out in all directions from the temple.

It's dark now as I leave the woods and stride across the rutted pastures for home. As I pass a derelict homestead consisting of a collapsed stone cottage and a couple of ancient trucks, something sinister looms behind me, as if breathing on my neck. I wheel around. A jagged red ley line passees through the field just where I felt the creepy sensation behind me: I've never noticed that before. Faces appear in this line, demonic, leering, faces, heads with horns, crooked noses, leathery skin, pointed teeth, red eyes—the full gestalt of a devil. They are so devilish it's almost a caricature. What keeps it from being a simulacrum from some Western cultural memory bank is the uncomfortable way they make me feel.

I breathe Love from Above to these unhandsome devils and continue on home, but, when I get there, I feel exceptionally crabby, spoiling for a confrontation, a squabble, with anybody, even the front door if it gets in my way. The only civil thing to do is retreat to the Grail chambers and hide under the bed until my foul temper dissipates. Around ten p.m., Russell opens the bedroom door and says, "The Good Doctor B. will see you now, Grail Knight." You can't keep anything from Russell, even when you're hiding under the bed.

"We come as we are," Blaise says, shimmering into view in the livingroom. "We come as a Blazing Star. We come as Love from Above. We are happy to be with you. We surround you all with the wall of lilac flames. We place above each of you an individual lilac flame connecting at the tip to the point of infinite light. We place around each of you the sphere of sapphire blue. We surround this with a flickering flame of orange, gold, and red. We place within your chests, at about the third rib in the middle, an emerald of six sides. We place a Blazing Star a little way above the navel and a little way inside. We place a ruby at each of your throats. Please be with this image for a little while. Breathe to it with your love....

"Good. As you all can appreciate, this is an unscheduled visit. It has been precipitated through necessity. We have come to make specific suggestions. First, Grail Knight, we suggest you do not physically visit the earth circle from now on during the next few days, though we think it would be good if you paid your respects to it before you leave England. Second, we have only been able, through great requests and much engineering, to secure one place for you at Avebury. Therefore, we suggest that no invitations are extended to others for this event as it could prove to be very dangerous for them. Third, we wish you to locate a place called Dunnery Beacon and to arrange for a visit there in the next few days before visiting Avebury."

"Blaise, did I disrupt things by visiting my earth circle today?"

"No, but there are now energies at work that are as yet unprecedented in your experience. It is therefore important that you are in a more protected environment. We have this house well-protected. The earth circle is more accessible and less protected. You picked up something there that has already produced some unfortunate consequences."

"Was it those devil figures I saw at the red ley line?"

"Correct. It was your conscious assimilation of something already attached to your being bodies. There are only rare instances when we have given you outside tasks in lunar declines and after dusk. There are energies at work unprecedented in your experience."

"Now I remember that some gnomes tried to discourage me at the gate to the Fairy Dell today. The main gnome acting as sentry had his hand out to stop me but I talked myself out of paying attention to him, or else somebody else said not to worry about him and pass on."

"We suggest you take some salt. Place it in a bowl of water. Anoint each of your spiritual centers or chakras with it, from the crown down. Then put your hands completely in the bowl. When they are wet with salt water, rub your feet all over. Then you may go to sleep, leaving the salt on the table in your room. In the morning, place the salt water on the compost heap. You were made to be unprotected today, with no chanting, no image, by energies you have not experienced prior to this occasion."

"It was peculiar. I felt quite blithely unafraid of anything, so I could calmly walk about in the dark without even doing the Blaise Image. How could I have been so naïve? Is this another example of the bad guys at work?"

"Yes. They have seen now that you are close."

"Close to what?" Berenice asks.

"If you want an answer, Berenice, we can whisper in your ear. Each morning place yourselves in the image we have given. Each time you leave your room, make sure you affirm it to yourselves and particularly before leaving the house."

"I take it the reports of there being a negative hierarchy are true?" I ask.

"Yes, relatively true. Satan, Leviathan, Beezlebub, and others form the first ranks of servitors to the dark side. Each of them is part of the hierarchy of that side, as Michael, Raphael, Uriel, Gabriel, and others are equivalent parts of the light side. What you are concerned with is the light, not in relation to the dark, but the true Light."

"Please tell me more about this earth circle, Blaise? What is it really?"

"It is a way for you to ground your consciousness within the Earth sphere. As you create these earth circles, you harmonize with the Earth and bring your consciousness in line with the Earth and its form. When you harmonize your vibrations with the Earth, then you effectively connect with the subtle energies of the Earth. When the Earth was created in the beginning, the energy matrix of the Earth was implicit in every particle. The grid is a manifestation of that energy matrix that was harmonized by those working from the upper levels to be able to emphasize the energy aspect of matter. As your consciousness and that within each particle contains the same energy matrix, then as you evolve consciously, you harmonize with that of the Earth. This has repercussions both for you as an individual via your DNA-RNA encoding, and for the planet via its coding. If you take the circle and you harmonize your consciousness with that circle, you harmonize with the Earth itself. You come to terms with solidity and expansion, energy and extension.

"It is necessary to have the human intermediary between the angels and the Earth. Your body measurements are instantly translated into that of the earth circle. The quality of an earth circle is what is important, not the quantity in a given location. The elementals are also intermediaries between the Earth and humans just as angels are intermediaries between humans and the Creator. As the angels wish to communicate with the elementals, it is only possible through humans.

"The Earth has a need. It's obvious what the need is. It is only through humans that the angels may assist the elementals in the healing of the grid and in loving the Earth. The blueprint for the landscape zodiac is synchronous and symbiotic with the blueprint of the Earth and the genetic structure of a Grail Knight. We say, the relationship between the body of a Grail Knight and its blueprint at the genetic level has a resonance with the blueprint laid down in the temple of the Earth. When any Grail Knight treads the temple, then a symbiotic relationship is formed that arcs across time and space, seeding the Grail Knight and the Earth with emerald and Star and the Source."

"In light of this, what, in your perspective, is a star—a star like Aldebaran or Megrez?"

"Look into the center of your being. That is a star. It is light, energy, motion, heat, and cold. It is electronic. It is atomic. It is inherently cohesive. It is concentrated and solid. It is movement. All these things are within the star. When a star becomes, it is conscious of itself. It knows that it is a star. A constellation is a star that is aware of its interdependence on other stars. The Greek diagrams of the constellations are reasonably accurate. They are representations of what you might call group souls. Remember, as above, so below."

"I wanted to ask about the blue stars I've been seeing," Berenice says.

"Blue is the after-image of orange. You have aspired; therefore, afterwards you get a little piece of blue."

"Hey, that answers a question I had the other day about the amber tube and blue ray I saw at Shambhala," I pop in.

"You see, Grail Knight, things aren't as independent as sometimes you tend to think. We come as that Blazing Star at the center, beyond mind, beyond thinking, beyond words, that point of light so small, so infinitely small. We take it all. We are extremely available and present, yet we are very difficult to contact through any other agency than direct relationship. Therefore you are six-blessed. It's a little jest, Grail Knight. They usually say thrice-blessed."

"Right. We certainly appreciate it. What about specifics regarding Avebury?"

"We hope you may be able to hire a car. Get you there in style."

"Blaise, ever hear the expression 'pennies from Heaven?' I don't have the money to hire a car."

"You'll be surprised. We have made a little provision for this. Go in a car, alone with six friends and all our manifestations. We aren't any of us going to miss this as we have all had to make individual requests on your behalf. Oh, we'll enjoy it Grail Knight. Get there anytime in the morning. Leave when it's done. Just get the car....We are experiencing some interference. Please breathe love to your images for a moment...."

Russell and I look at each other in alarm. We both see them. We've never had interference or an interruption in our visits like this before. I begin perspiring and shivering. Anxiety ripples across my shoulders. A circle of ugly, birdfaced humans with piercing red eyes glare down at us like a demonic crown. Fearful thoughts pummel through me, terrors of going mad, weeping uncontrollably, throwing things through the window, killing myself, do it now. It's uncanny the way they can dress up their perverted intentions as my own mental mannerisms and inner voice. It is so easy to mistake their dark persuasions arising in my mind as my own. But then that's their only place of influence; their only foothold are gaps in my inner vigilance, misidentifications of mental contents and mind states. So I refuse them entry. Out. Even in my shivering, I will not sign my name to any of their dark insinuations. These are not of the Grail Knight. I breathe love as fiercely as I can until the circle of devils retreats into the shadows.

Qliphoth. That's what Qabala calls them. The *Qliphoth* are the evil or averse Sephiroth, the mirror, negative image of the Tree's vessels of light. Each is an "emanation of unbalanced force," a negative shell corresponding to a Sephira on the Tree; these emanations, Dion Fortune explains, arose during a critical time in Creation when the Sephiroth were not in equilibrium. The excess of force from a particular Sephira ("an overplus of the necessary energy") form the negative Spheres of the *Qliphoth*; these spheres teem with cruelty, oppression, unslaked revenge, and other negative, destructive qualities. "These forces, whenever they find a channel of expression opening up, rise through it," Fortune explains. "Consequently the man who gives way to cruelty soon finds that he is not merely expressing the impulses of his own undeveloped or misshapen nature, but that a great force like a stream is urging him on." This is particularly so during the dark of the moon, or during the two weeks in which the moon is waning, when "the life-giving forces are relatively weak and the unbalanced forces relatively strong." At this time, the unorganized forces "have a tendency to rise up and give trouble; the result, in inexperienced hands, is chaos."

When Blaise returns, I comment, "They've really been lamming it to me today, haven't they?" I feel resolute but shaken.

"Yes. We feel at present you would do better, when in doubt, not to discuss us. We have much opposition as you will discover. We must leave now. Sorry for all the problems, but remember what we said last night. Greet these problems with gratitude, as love. See you at Dunnery Beacon. As ever, your friend, Blazing Star."

After I anoint my chakras with salt water, I climb into bed and hold a photograph of His Holiness the 14th Dalai Lama against my heart until I feel a warm glow. After all, as the presumed reincarnation not only of all the previous Dalai Lamas but of Avalokitesvara, the Lord of Compassion with a thousand arms, probably a couple ministering arms can be spared for the Grail Knight for ten minutes to rekindle my protection and to build inner strength. I should have known it wouldn't remain a carefree picnic with the Uncle Blaises in the sun forever, zipping around the zodiac funhouse with a pack of wisecracking, loving, doting, zany angels. At a certain point the Quest becomes serious business. You touch into things in the larger world, including the unknown parts of yourself, from which you have been providentially insulated for years, if not lifetimes.

So tonight I have had a little acrid *soupcon* of evil, a voice that mimics Blaise and myself, that can mask itself in the familiar but not commendable tattered clothing of my negativities. It will take a keen sword held in constant vigilance from here on in to keep myself clear—chaste and virginal, as the medieval texts would say—of the *Qliphoth*, however grateful Blaise wants me to feel for the early precipitation of their interference. You read about this often in spiritual autobiographies.

At a certain point, the Master lets the student stumble, make mistakes, be contacted by unsavory types, as a test. Not only as a test but as education, as a way to strengthen character. After all, God allows evil to exist in the world for a purpose; reality by decree is dialectical, the perennial struggle of light and dark. The *Zohar* says the light can be recognized only because of the existence of darkness. If all of Creation were light, we could never apprehend it; it would be a uniform environment without distinguishing qualities. In the same way, the good can only be appreciated when framed against evil. "It is only because of the existence of good and evil that free will can exist, where we can choose between them," Aryeh Kaplan writes. If we had no free will, we would be mere angels. Angels after all are divinely compelled to be good; only humans are permitted to choose evil out of our God-given free will. But only angels, for the most part, have the wisdom sufficient to choose rightly.

Maybe these beak-nosed, red-eyed subhumans are archetypal images of all my negativities, shadow faces from all my lifetimes that are now requiring repudiation, transmutation, and redemption. The darker side of the Grail Quest, the demon guardians of the threshold. Who says I have always been innocent and good in all my past lifetimes? God knows what transgressions lurk in my resumé. Surely I have been nasty, stupid, cruel, heartless, and evil, God forgive me.

I fall asleep with the image of the Bodhisattva of Compassion, the great thousand-armed Avalokitesvara incarnate as the Dalai Lama, clasped to my heart. I dream. I am talking with His Holiness, asking him questions. He looks at me long and lovingly. I sense behind me a lovely protecting angel twice my height, its wings wrapped around me like a cocoon. "The angel is also you," the Dalai Lama says, laughing gently.

70

THE DUNNER IS HEARD

unnery Beacon. Predawn. Amidst the rock cairns and swirling mist. Not an easy place to find if you're looking for a Celtic hilltop called Dunnery because the Ordnance Survey knows it as Dunkery Beacon, elevation 1705 feet, near Dunster, a medieval timbered village in northern Somerset, close to the Bristol Channel. Blaise had originally told us: "We would like you to visit Dunnery Beacon, elevation 1746 feet above sea level."

Blaise, I ask, might Dunnery now be called Dunkery and might it have slipped somewhat from its spiritual mystical height of 1746, Qabala's sacred number for the "mustard seed?" Indeed. "You are correct. We are checking sources for your time period. It appears that the second 'n' has been changed to a 'k' and the sea level has risen." It's as if time and social customs benignly conspire to occlude the geomantic mysteries; people forget, the temples are abandoned, and disuse slurs the descriptive place-names.

Dunnery—such a protean name. All the meanings and cognates fit: *dun*—to make repeated, insisted demands for payment of a debt; *duna*—to make a din, a thundering noise, to ring with sound; *dun*—dull, grayish brown, gloomy, murky; *dunner*—a resounding, reverberating noise, a blow causing a sound vibration; *doon*—a hill fortress. Dunnery is all of these and more.

Dunnery is a big, bare, moorish hill stubbled with stone and gorse, anomalously desolate amidst the otherwise lush neighboring hills, the green Vales of Exmoor. It's as if some malfeasance was perpetrated here long ago and the landscape has been paying the price ever since—as if a wound has poorly scarred over, its cause still unexpiated. The Grail's dun Wasteland. The three of us troop silently along the trail to the summit of Dunnery Beacon. Once seated here, Blaise appears and offers a dedication to the spirits of Dunnery.

"We come as we are. We come from not too far. We come as a Blazing Star. We greet you all. We are most pleased to see you here. We wish, if you wish, to put your attention on the image we have given you. Surround this place and yourselves with the wall of lilac flames, reaching down into the Earth and up into the heavens above, a brilliant lilac flame, full of light, reaching up to the point of infinite light above. Within the flame, we see many Blazing Stars, countless stars, as though from the heavens above, each one a Nimitta, each one a pinpoint of light.

"Please place your attention on the brilliant Star within you, just above the navel and a little way inside. Breathe to this Star as Love from Above. Place your attention on the emerald at your heart, an emerald brilliant green with six sides. Place your attention on the ruby at your throat, eight sides with eight petals within. Breathe to these points as Love from Above. As you breathe out, breathe as Love from Above. Surround yourself with the brilliant blue of the sphere. Surround this with topaz, orange, and red flames. Breathe to this globe with each exhalation. Breathe to is as Love from Above. A transparent blue sphere filled with light, shining bright. Above, place the lilac flame on the top of your head. Breathe to it as Love from Above. Try to bring this image fully into your attention and awareness.

"We ask on your behalf that there be peace in the element of air, peace to those beings that relate through the element of air. We ask on your behalf that there be peace in the element of water, peace to those beings that relate through the element of water. We ask on your behalf that there be peace in the element of fire, peace to those beings that relate through the element of fire. We ask on your behalf that there be peace in the element of earth, peace to those beings that relate through the element of earth. We ask on your behalf that there be peace in the element of ether, peace to those beings that relate through the element of space. We will breathe with you as you appreciate Dunnery."

With that, Blaise leaves us in silence to contemplate Dunnery. During Blaise's dedicatory remarks, I became aware of the dome over Dunnery and a secret stone chamber within the physical hill. Almost at once I find myself seated inside this stone chamber, which I soon understand is but a doorway into the inner realm of Dunnery. As at Pointer's Ball, I find myself holding the majestic galactic sword with the myriad of stars in the galaxy within it, many billion points of keenness in this sword of Mind. The sword grows larger, more brilliant, adamant. It is my body; I am inside it; it's expanding to encompass all of the galaxy.

Soon I am far away from Earth, yet still holding the root of the sword in my hands here in the Dunnery Beacon chamber. I am simultaneously at the handle and the tip of this sword, inside Dunnery and at the core of the galaxy, at both ends of the sword and the sword itself. The sword ascends from Dunnery like a scintillating beacon, ensheathing the entirety of the galactic spiral, its keen tip focussed at the hub, the "mustard seed" center of the galaxy; paradoxically, this is also the crown of my head, much dilated, of course. The sword encompasses the galaxy, yet it is inside my head—*a* head. The sword of pure Mind, compounded of the wisdom and spiritual intelligence of the stars—this is Michael's galactic blade, the cutting edge of the Logos.

Blaise's image of the sword in the Grail bowl lancing the Blazing Star is an image of reality. The Star in me, as the Grail Knight, and the mustard seed, or Star, at the pith of the galaxy, are somehow the same, if at different levels of expression. As I concentrate on the seed, breathing to it as Love from Above, it births the golden Grail which fills with light—redemptive nourishment for the Wounded Fisher King. I begin to shudder as I realize the responsibility accruing to sword-holder.

A question arises: whose I is wielding this cosmic blade? *Not I, but the Christ in me*, says Galahad; that's his secret, what insulates him from seduction and corruption with the sheeny star blade in his hands, enabling him to occupy the Perilous Siege with impunity. Each landscape zodiac on Earth is constituted identically to this primal cosmic icon I am glimpsing through Dunnery Beacon. It is as if I sit at the galactic core wielding the sword, its blade encompassing all the stars, its initiatory tip sparking life in the seed of each terrestrial zodiac. Golden Grails burst into geomantic bloom, restorative light overflows as each zodiac's Fisher King is fed. I sense the power and majesty, the Godlike potency of this sword—the awesome peril, the extreme liability of misuse. God save me from the Dolorous Stroke because it was misused once, this vast star knowledge. It was once misspoken.

The Grail legends remember this as the Dolorous Stroke by which the *Rich* Fisher King became the *Wounded* Fisher King presiding over the Wasteland of Logres. Dunnery, blasted and scorched, a doon of dry, bloodless stones, is an image of the Wasteland, one of the Dolorous Stroke's casualties. I feel certain that long ago, after frightful transgressions, the sword was taken from Dunnery (which is to say, deactivated, depotentiated somehow, its knowledge erased) and deposited in the Ship of Time (which is to say, the Avenue of Cedars in Glastonbury, the sword's sheath, which is knowledge of its use, activation codes—what Morgan "stole" from Arthur) for safe storage until such future time as a requisite spiritual maturity arose in men and women (as the Christed Galahad) so that its true, not debased, use might again prevail. After the Christ incarnation. Until Galahad, that consummately Christ-initiated Grail Knight, should arrive at Camalate and exhibit the sword's correct usage.

The image shifts and I see a massive golden crystalline skull inside Dunnery, overlaying the stone chamber. The head is buried inside Dunnery; not a human head, but a god's. A celestial *golgos* (Hebrew for "skull", as in Golgotha, the Hill of Skulls in Jerusalem). Flanking this golden head like sentries are Elohim, maidservants of the divine cranium, humanity's prime parents. Whose head is it?

I remember the Knight of the Green Chapel, Gawain's Green Knight, who with consummate insouciance bade Gawain to chop off his head. Gawain did so, but there were no consequences for the Green Knight; he didn't fall over, or even falter, and his head still focussed consciousness for him. "But stoutly sprang forward on legs still sturdy/Seized his splendid head and straightaway lifted it." He climbed upon his horse, as if nothing had happened to him, "holding his head in his hand by the hair." Is it the Green Knight's "head" that is inside Dunnery? Probably, but who is the Green Knight? The Archangel Michael, Lord Manjusri—perhaps. And *Bendigeidfran*, Bran the Blessed, the colossus of Welsh myth.

Bendigeidfran, the son of Lyr, "was king over this Island and exalted with the crown of London," recounts the ancient Welsh *Mabinogion*. He was so big he was never contained within a house. He commanded that his head be struck off and that seven of his companions bury it at the White Mount in London. This they did, but as the Assembly of the Wondrous Head, they spent many years—fourscore—in transit from northern Wales, calling in at various sites along the way. "And the head will be as pleasant company to you as ever it was at best when it was on me," Bendigeidfran promised them.

Bendigeidfran is a Welsh version of the Rich Fisher King, the Sumptuous Host whose Wondrous Head provides spiritual nourishment for his retainers. He's an earlier expression of the Green Knight, too. When Gawain keeps his appointment with the Knight of the Green Chapel, he is first taken in, feasted, entertained, and generally treated royally by a gallant who owns a comely castle set on a promontory above a plateau. This brave lord is "a powerful man in his prime, of stupendous size/Broad and bright was is beard, all beaver-hued/ His face was fierce as fire, free was his speech/And he seemed in good sooth a suitable man/To be prince of a people with companions of mettle." Later Gawain discovers this prince is no other than the Green Knight.

Originally, the Sumptuous Host is the Rich Fisher King, benign decapitator, master of the mystery of the head. The Sumptuous Host (the Green Knight of the Chapel or Bran the Blessed) is rich because he has full use of the sword. Even with his head cut off he knows how to keep his head; he never loses consciousness; he never forgets his divine origin and the oral formulas—spoken star knowledge, for his speech is co-creative magic, dragon-words of *AL*, Elohimic syllables of generation—for its recreation in matter. He is the Elohim's protégé. The sword *is* the head: that's the secret equation, the key in the lock that opens Dunnery.

As I tune into this wondrous golden head, the cranium of Bran the Blessed, I begin to understand why the sword is the head. The contents of the head are Edenic. It is as if the Garden of Eden is contained within the skull plates of Bran's head. The tree of knowledge, the fruits of spiritual insight, the words of creation, the formulas, the Holy Names, the permutations of Jehovah's unspeakable name. It is as if all of *Yetzirah,* the formative, foundational realm in Qabala (the third of the Qabala's Four Worlds just "above" ours, the material plane), the sphere of angelic consciousness, is contained within this golden head, *is* this head.

Heaven, or *Shamayim,* is round like a head, says the *Bahir.* What does the head know that is of value? Knowledge of speaking, the creative power of speaking, the formative grammar of speaking, star knowledge of the Logos: word power. Consider the sequence of equations: the dragon is the sword; this I learned at Aller. The sword contains all stars of the galaxy, their composite intelligence; this I learned at Pointer's Ball. The sword is a head, a memory bank of spoken creation codes. In this Dunnery instructs us. The head comprises the creative spiritual intelligences, the cognitive atoms in the body of Man, the Great Man of the Zodiac—Adam Kadmon, Qabala calls it, or Albion, as Blake calls it.

As humans, the Supernal Man is our divine antecedent, whose body, mind, and speech are compounded of stars aflame with speech. Man made of words—the Word made flesh. There are approximately a sextillion or 10^{21} possible permutations of all 22 letters of the Hebrew alphabet, explains Aryeh Kaplan. This number is very close to the estimated total number of stars in the observable universe. "Thus, from the permutations of the alphabet, a name can be formed for every star in the universe. This is in accordance with the teaching that every star has an individual name." After all, Blaise once said that every one of their 40 million-plus manifestations could be named, had an individual name.

Dunnery holds the key. It is the vocabulary of the world-creating permutations of the Divine Name, whose every syllable is a star. All the stars comprise the head, which is also the sword of Mind. This is magic on a sublime scale—Elohimic magic, for it is their sword, their sanctified *golem*.

Qabalist magicians know that, by chanting the appropriate letter combinations with the letters of the Tetragammaton, they could create a real mental or astral image of a human, a humunculus of light called a golem. Golem-making through creative speaking is similar to how the Elohim produced us. Did not David defeat the *giant* Goliath and secure his sword for posterity and were not the Elohim the giants of world myth and legend? Solomon the human initiate got the mind sword from his father David, who got it from the Elohim, humanity's parents. That's why I see Elohim, the forms of *AL*, encircling Dunnery's golden head like a corona; they are the sheath for the sword, the laurel wreath upon the head, the mellifluous tiara upon the Wondrous Head. The Elohim are our imprimatur for the use of the King sword.

The dragon is a sword, which is a head, which is a dragon again, oroborically. What power does this golden speaking head wield? Power over the dragons, the 13 magnificent "dragons" brought to Earth concurrent with the arrival of the domes. The dragons of Eden, the *ALR* dragons, emissiaries of Draco, embodiments of world-creating potency, prodigies of Boreas, the primal serpent who wrapped itself sevenfold about the World Egg in service to its consort, Eurynome, Mother of All Living Things.

The 13 dragons are central to the energy operations of the planetary grid matrix, Blaise taught us; their hierarchical energies are crucial, too, to the spiritual anatomy of human beings, particularly the seven chakras. As such, the 13 dragons represent pure elemental creativity, the *AL* (Aleph [1], *Lammed* [30]) of Avalon, the *beginning* of Avalon, starworld of light, the inception of Albion. Mighty words have been spoken through Dunnery: to dun is to ring with sound, to thunder resoundingly. In other words, the one wielding the galactic sword from within Dunnery, the one seated inside Bran's golden head, commands the 13 dragons, is master of the creative invocation of *AL*, the tongue of the Beginning. The *dunner* is the Rich Fisher King—as he was before the Fall. King in Avalon. Rich with fishes. But why fishes?

There is the Celtic Salmon of wisdom as dispenser of ultimate knowledge, but this is an icon that still veils the meaning. The fish moves and has its being in an element (water—the great Sea or *Mer* of consciousness) completely other than our life element. The King is rich with fishes because fish is the meaning of the Hebrew letter *Noun* whose number equivalent is 50. This refers to the 50 Gates of Understanding of Binah the Cosmic Mother, the face of the third Sephira. As such, the 50 Gates are the completion of the *ALR* dragon. The dragon is another expression for the seven chakras; as each has seven aspects, this makes 49 with one unmanifest, making 50 stages of consciousness. The 49 Gates make a Good Heart (*Lev Tov*, whose gematria is 49); this number is also the number of days from *Pesach* preceding *Shavu'ot* or Pentecost, which happens on the fiftieth day. Pentecost literally means "fiftieth" and is the day on which Moses received the Torah on Mount Sinai and on which Arthur's Knights annually gathered at Camalate for inspiration. In the time of Christ's apostles, it marked the time in which they were divinely inspired to Christ-like speech, to speak as the Logos. Finally, fiftieth also refers to the sum of the faces of the five Platonic Solids, which suggests that the five elements culminate in inspired speaking.

The 50 Gates and the seven chakras pertain to Qabala's second classification of the Hebrew alphabet called the Seven Double Letters. These are associated with the seven planets (Saturn, Jupiter, Mars, Sun, Venus, Mercury, Moon) and the seven directions. The sevenfold dragon enlivens, quickens, the human because it is the life of kundalini, Binah's breath (as the Western name for Shakti, the Hindu name for the divine Feminine energy principle).

So the king is rich because he also has the fishes, that is, he commands the dragons, masters the *Noun* (50 Gates), knows the words (the Dun alphabet), wields the sword of *ALohim*. The king is monarch in Avalon, the wondrous head of light, *Raysh*, the golden apple. Images and names from myth, when they are containers for initiatory knowledge, are so incestuous; they constantly cross-refer, dissolve into one another, point with circular fingers.

Avalon is the golden apple of resplendent wisdom, the cosmic star container, and that is *Raysh* because this Hebrew letter means "head" or "countenance." The controlling element of life is concentrated in the head, explains Tarot scholar Madonna Compton. "The controlling element in our solar system is the Sun, the Tarot key which belongs to *Resh* [*Raysh*] ... [and which] indeed has a shining countenance. Human consciousness is the form through which the Life-Power physically present in solar energy is perfected." So *Raysh* is Avalon's golden apple, its pith jammed with billions of stars; Avalon, the container of light, the resplendent radiating head; *Avalon*—the beginning, the understanding, and the continuity, the place where all is remembered, says Blaise. Avalon is the word that gets you into *Raysh*.

So what happened to which Dunnery stands today as grievous memorial? The *AL* was taken out of Avalon. The Fisher King lost his head, misspoke himself, went mute, forgot his beginnings, lost Avalon. They cut off the head of Bran the Blessed. The Dolorous Stroke was committed. Elohimic speech was abused. Bad magic. Knowledge of the Tree of Good and Evil—*evil*, a shocking discovery, the ambivalent dowry of free will. A wound in the cosmic soul of Man was inscribed.

Dunner—the ground reverberating with the sound of a fallen head. Humanity no longer maintained full consciousness when the head was cut off. When it was buried, it forgot it had ever possessed it. It suffered but could not remember why. The Word-Sword was put away on the Ship of Time. They buried the head, stowed it away in the archives of myth. The creativity of the root chakra could no longer communicate with the wisdom of the crown. Speaking was no longer potent, creative, invocatory, a magic wand. The uncountable stars of the galaxy lost their voice; they fell out of human sentences into isolated astronomical syllables. Mellifluosity gone mute; the voluble head turned to stone. The Wounded Fisher King languishes in the Grail Castle amidst the Wasteland, a desolation of his own creation.

The Word-Sword that proceeds out of the mouth of humanity with the signs of the constellations engraved on its blade "has grown old, atrophied, shattered, and lost its power," says Trevor Ravenscroft. Yet Ravenscroft takes his cue from a veiled reference in Eschenbach's *Parzival:* "The sword will withstand the first blow; at the second it will shatter. If you then take it back to the Spring, it will become whole again from the flow of water."

The source of this sword-restoring spring is the Well of Kunneware, says Eschenbach, and this is guarded by a dragon. "Only by discovering the original source of its power can this 'Word-Sword' be renewed," Ravenscroft adds. That original source is the Logos, the coherency of the stars, their consummate voice, Word or words, the ultimate fish in the voluble *Mer.*

This is the mystery of Galahad, the Christed Grail Knight, graduate of the Upper Room. It is for him alone that the Ship of Time, set into the still waters of higher, veiled knowledge (expressed as the sword of David), sails magisterially into the latter days of Arthur's Camalate, once and *future* speaking academy. Camalate is the place and means of creative speaking. Galahad's future is our time. What truer authority for the correct use of the world-creating potency of speech than the Logos itself? The Christ restores *AL* to Avalon, which is the power over the 13 dragons and mastery of the 50 Gates; this is Galahad's initiation; this is why Galahad can wield the sword and heal the Wounded Fisher King, why Galahad alone can assume the Perilous Siege at the Round Table. He knows how to say the right thing; he has the way with words.

Take the tip of the sword and awaken the mustard seed at the pith of the galaxy. Back to the source, to the quick of the Logos, Ur-source of words, the great *Awr.* The divine asymmetry of light, the *phi*-cycle underlying the physical. Galahad knows this. It is a very old story whose happy ending may be foredained but is yet to be performed.

Now I understand why Blaise brought us here today. "At Dunnery you may understand the wound," Blaise says, "provided you can learn to think in symbolic shorthand. To heal the Fisher King, you must understand the wound."

To *dun* is to make repeated, insistent demands for payment of a debt; a *dunner* is one who makes these importunate demands, the creditor. As humans, we are in debt to the Rich Fisher King; we caused his wound; we misspent his spiritual capital; we squandered the family fortune; we abused his line of credit. We misspoke ourselves. "Parzival must learn that Amfortas [the Fisher King] suffers because he, Parzival, has not recognized himself to be the cause of the suffering," says Walter Johannes Stein. Parzival, on his second visit to the Grail Castle, asks Amfortas: "Brother, what ails thee?" No one can answer this question except Parzival. "For the answer to this Parzival-question is, 'I myself have caused all this suffering that I see here.'"

The Grail Knight, once inside the Grail Castle, is prime witness to his own desolation. Parzival must inquire of himself: What ails thee, Parzival? What is my wound? Why cannot I remember where I came from and why? All of us have wounded the Fisher King, have occasioned "the slaying of what is noblest through his own imperfection," says Stein. That's because each of us is the Wounded Fisher King; the King is a time-hologram of billions of faces of human suffering and fallenness—of nonunderstanding and incompletion, of incarnational muteness. He is the life after Avalon, life without ever a taste of the golden apple. Now the Wounded Fisher King, our better half, as it were, the spiritual Self, demands—*duns*—that we make good on the debt, make reparations, restore his wholeness. The Wounded Fisher King is the dunner importuning us to rekindle his beacon. Restore light to the buried head. Qabala calls this *tikkun olam*, meaning to heal, repair, and transform the world, to redeem the soul of Adam Kadmon on Earth. "That is the mission of Camalate, once and future," says Blaise.

But why Dunnery Beacon, *this hill*, specifically? Why is this archetypal drama of human possibility and imperfection staged here, as if enshrined geomantically as an instructive icon? "Medusa," says Blaise. "Dunnery Beacon is the dome for the constellation Medusa."

As Greek myth recounts it, Medusa ("cunning one") is a Gorgon, the sea-born maiden with glorious hair whom Minerva transformed into a frightful, cruel monster with snakes instead of hair growing out of her head. Later, Perseus slew Medusa by cutting off her serpentine head then presented it to Minerva, who set it in the center of her aegis like a shrine to disembodied knowledge. "Now, the Gorgon Medusa had serpents for hair, huge teeth, protuding tongue, and altogether so ugly a face that all who gazed at it were petrified with fright," writes Robert Graves. A glance from Medusa was sufficient to turn somebody into stone, which is to say, to render them mute and inanimate. But by now we know we must read these myths backwards to understand their veiled meaning. Medusa put life into stone, spiritual life, creative letters, celestial faces; she put this into the stone of matter. Holy words of creation expressed as Merlin's Stone; which is to say, Medusa with the snake-streaming hair, spoke us all into existence through the "stone" of our higher being bodies. Perseus found Medusa, with the other two Gorgons, in the Land of the Hyperboreans—here, somewhere in the British Isles, by inference—"asleep, among rain-worn shapes of men and wild beasts petrified by Medusa."

In present-day star charts, the neighboring constellations of Perseus and Medusa comprise a uraniomythic icon: Perseus holds the sword in one hand, the severed snake-writhing head of Medusa in the other. The principal star in Medusa is *Algol*, from the Arabic *Ra's al Ghul*, the Demon Star or Blinking Demon. Ptolemy catalogued it as "the bright one of those in the Gorgon's head." The Hebrews knew it as *Rosh ha Satan*, Satan's Head, and as Lilith, Adam's first wife. Curiously, Medusa's blood, dripping from her severed head, had remarkable healing powers. Asclepius, the "blameless physician" and god of healing who learned the healing arts from Apollo and Chiron, received two phials of the Gorgon Medusa's blood from Athena; with this he could raise the dead or instantly destroy. Vestiges of the power of the wondrous head.

So this is Dunnery: Medusa's golden head atwine with the 13 dragons, aflame with the power of *AL*, with vocal command over the dragons. Medusa: larynx for the Dunner, beacon of Avalon, mind-sword forged of the myriad Holy Names, and more importantly, the *understanding* of how to wield the sword of pure mind, *how to speak*, how to be a talking head, how to complete the incarnation, how to *dun* on behalf of the Logos, the speaking life before and after the wound, how to be rich with fish.

71

A Bright Stone at Albion's Earth Circle

The thirteenth of December, the date Blaise set for my Avebury visit, dawns with uxorial comfort. I'm lying in bed with Deborah at her flat in Charmouth, a cup of Earl Grey tea and marmaladed toast on a tray before me.

"You don't see what your process is all about yet, lovey," she says. "It may take you years to remember it all. It's about waking up, remembering yourself. Gosh, love, do you know your whole body weight has shifted. Your chest is so different, somehow realigned from the inside. What *have* you been doing out there in the hills, anyway? I wrote you a little song, did I tell you? It came to me the other morning when I was at the market, counting my coins for some eggs. Here, I'll sing it for you."

> *Lover of night*
> *lover of right*
> *wand'ring the hills*
> *of Albion.*
> *Grail Knight.*
> *Weaver of ways*
> *starlight weft*
> *liver of myths*
> *discov'ring dim remembered*
> *truth.*
> *Grail Knight.*
> *Treasures of Earth*

> *starlight paths*
> *beaming us home*
> *across the generations.*
> *Grail Knight.*

After breakfast, Deborah, soft and smiling in her bathrobe, hands me a thermos of miso soup and kisses me farewell at the doorway. I load my essential Grail Knight equipment into her rickety green Renault (a tin box soldered to a bicycle frame, we like to joke): raincoat, galoshes, cushion, blanket, note pad, miso soup, angels. The six Blaises pile into the backseat. As I drive out of Charmouth and begin chanting to keep the Grail head happy and clear, the Blaises adjust their half-frame glasses and hold music sheets before them so they can accompany in six part *a cappella* the booming *basso profundo* in the front seat. As we drive northeast towards Avebury, the dawn breaks vaguely behind the dreary overcast and early morning drizzle.

The seventeenth century antiquarian John Aubrey, writing about the stone circle, said, "Avebury doth as much exceed Stonehenge in grandeur as a Cathedral doth an ordinary Parish Church." So convinced was Aubrey of his assessment that he proudly escorted King Charles II around the Avebury monument in 1663 and later prepared a survey of the circle under royal command. William Stukely, his successor in spirit, who visited Avebury between 1719 and 1724, commented: "Thus, this stupendous fabric, which for some thousands of years has braved the continual assaults of the weather, and by the nature of it, when left to itself, like the pyramids of Egypt, would have lasted as long as the globe, has fallen a sacrifice to the wretched ignorance and avarice of a little village, unluckily placed within it." He was referring to the destruction of many of the big stones by farmers wanting more tillable land; they dragged the stones into pits, poured boiling water over them, then pounded them with sledge hammers, until they broke into small pieces. Then in the late nineteenth century Sir John Lubbock, later called Lord Avebury, set in motion a preservation movement to secure the ravaged Avebury site against future destruction by purchasing part of the village. "The pretty little village of Avebury," Lubbock wrote, "like some beautiful

parasite, has grown up at the expense and in the midst of the ancient temple."

The ancient temple, located in Wiltshire near Marlborough, is a
stone circle occupying 28½ acres, probably the largest megalithic
site in Europe. The old village of Avebury, as Lubbock and Stukely
allude, sits rudely in the midst of the circle. But it's not just the village that intrudes itself into the once sanctified stone circle. Two
roadways divide Avebury into quarters; you can see the cross made
by their intersections in aerial photographs of the site. Not only can
you live in the Avebury monument, but you can also drive through
it. Twenty-seven sarsen stones remain from an estimated one hundred, and these stand imposingly as high as twelve feet, weigh anywhere from 40-60 tons, and have the most unusual shapes and surface textures, as if still raw, molten rock. Archeologists estimate their
age to be about 25 million years. As for the circle, experts date its
installation at approximately 2500 B.C., roughly concurrent with
Stonehenge situated thirty miles to the south. On the outside of the
stone emplacements runs a ditch with a high bank, varying in height
from 14 to 20 feet, completely encircling the site and running nearly
a mile. Within the large circle stand two smaller, incomplete stone
circles.

An old myth holds that these ancient sarsens, which seem to contain sand grains cemented with a mortar of pure silica, were artifi-
cially compounded by "wondrous stratagems" wrought by "the great
skill in Magick of Merlin." The vestiges of a ceremonial processional
called West Kennet Avenue, toothed erratically with smaller standing stones, marches across the Marlborough Downs for a little less
than two miles to Overton Hill Sanctuary, a former stone circle. In
fact, Avebury is part of an extensive megalithic temple site that occupies many acres and includes former and extant installations. The
hills around here are riddled with barrows, mounds, chambers, ancient tracks, and vestigial circles; Silbury Hill, the anomalous grass-
carpeted pyramidal cone, is just across the street and a half mile
over the fields. Beckhampton Avenue, like West Kennet Avenue,
now completely vanished, supposedly once began at Avebury Circle

and headed towards another site. The two avenues, which may have purposefully bifurcated the great wheel, helped create the impression several centuries ago that the shape of the Avebury site indicated it had once been a pagan "dragon" temple. No wonder symbol historian Harold Bayley remarked in 1913: "The English Temple of Stonehenge was a representation and a symbol of Time, but the English temple of Abury [sic] typified not only Time but also the greater Absolute, the all-embracing and more awe-full Soul of Time, the axis of Existence."

The Seraphim once told us that Avebury, like Stonehenge, Cadbury Castle, and other places, was one of the Nimitta's Wheels. And Blaise told us that somewhere on the planet there is a Master Dome that is the grid epicenter, the umbilicus for all the other domes on Earth. Gino Gennaro added another gnomic clue when he wrote of Camalate as "the royal zodiacal court of the Sun," though he didn't specify where it was located.

As he told the story, the Cosmic Chaplains, after surveying the planet, "finally landed on the spot that later became known in radical mythology as Camelot [sic]." A planetary disaster had precipitated the return of Hermes and his celestial bees to set the Earth once more in geomantic harmony with the celestial spheres, to "re-root everyone bodied or unbodied to a collective mind made of zodiacal archetypes flavored with planetary attributes." Each human would be shown the way by the "golden intellect of the Sun and the silver intuition of the Moon," and would possess a "minute personal mind, reflecting the royal court of the Sun." The human family was psychically molded in the hierarchical image of the solar system; daily celebrations and geomantic rituals were staged at Camalate by the Arch-Priest of the Pendragon Court to maintain this order, said Gennaro.

"Around the merry-go-round Arthurian table, everyone sat with equal knowledge, as children of the primal cause, who, by serving each other, honored the Creator," Gennaro wrote. In other words, the elements of the Arthurian myth formed the basis for a cycle of geomantic rituals, performed at Camalate, the site of the Master Dome and a kind of planetary umbilical point, that maintained the alignment of the Earth and its human population with the celestial spheres by virtue of the zodiacal archetypes inscribed in both humanity and planet. Thus, at Camalate, the "perpetual festivity of the cosmo-rational merry-go-round of the Arthurian round table" was upheld.

We arrive at Avebury in a morning wrapped in winter stillness. The car park is empty, the tourist shops closed, and there are almost no visitors anywhere. Unlike Stonehenge, which is fenced in, here you can touch the stones any time you wish. I stand next to a giant sarsen almost twice my height and many times my girth and press my face and palms against its pock-mocked surface. I see Elohim inside or in place of the stone. It's like glimpsing aspects of the stone's 25 million year history: white, luminous, giant human figures of light, Elohim, happy, confident, embodied, awake with God-consciousness and the knowledge of the Holy Names, invoking stones out of the ethers, setting the stones into the Earth, establishing the light circle. Stone-makers, casting *AL* into spiritual stone, turning words to stone, like Medusa, leaving their majestic traces as Avebury. Then behind them and after them, troops of humans arriving, entering life through the illuminated door of Avebury, as if born through the stones.

The stones are a dimensional doorway into an incredibly remote past, yet one that is no further away than my focussed breath at this moment. These are Elohim stones, the congealed light and intention of creator angels, words turned to stone, our prime parents setting them deep into the Earth to hold the awareness of our origins.

Avebury is girt by a massive ditch and embankment, like a record groove running the periphery of the stone circle. The ditch has a vibration that eclipses awareness of the outer environment. As I walk contemplatively through this deep channel in the Earth, it feels as if I walk under the Mother's skin, through a capillary of the Feminine somehow incarnate as earth and grass and stone and air: a *Mer*-line. I flow like a corpuscle along her veins circling the belly of light. With each step, I feel in deeper resonance with something truly beyond this Earth and yet of this Earth, indwelling, lawfully, mercifully resident. The feeling is monumentally feminine, a soft river of silent flowing light. The Mother, the great *Ave* (or Eve) whispers to her humans of the circle transiting her wheel of life. Here is the berry. She is the incalculably starry Eurynome, the great whale of space undulating through eternity with a billion billion stars scintillating in her belly. It is Ave's berry of stars the Elohim commemorated with their circle of celestial stones. You have left your mark for us in this humble ditch; in this groove, we listen to your great life. You have turned stars into stone.

The antiquarians have almost unilaterally criticized the people of Avebury village for establishing a mundane community in the midst of such obviously sacred ground and for despoiling its inherent energy configurations with roads and byways, not to mention uprooting and destroying numerous sarsens several centuries ago when the farmers wanted more tillable land. Even so, I have the growing certainty that there has always been a village within the circle, that such a village was intended as part of the original plan.

Avebury was meant to be residential, though not necessarily secular; my impression is that originally the residency was primarily sacerdotal, a community of geomancers, if you will. And I feel equally certain that the two public roads that make a cross in the center of Avebury are but latter-day versions of ancient tracks that, too, were purposely inscribed on the Earth here to mark energy lines of prime geomantic significance and to provide grounding for the geomantic temple. The roads and houses, in other words, mark the spot, and, in so doing, keep the secret public and open, should we ever discern the clues.

Standing on the slight upland of the West Kennet Avenue from where I can survey Avebury, many things come into focus. The circle is a wheel with twelve spokes like so many of the Michael and Nimitta wheels I have encountered, yet this one has a unique function. Entering the hub of the Avebury wheel of light, at the place where the two roads cross (a tiny grass-carpeted traffic island) is a dual-weaved cord of light; one strand is golden, one silver, interwoven like the DNA helix. Its origin is somewhere in the cosmos; its termination, or umbilical connection, is the traffic island specifically, and Avebury circle, generally. Where the two roads intersect, there the double helix unwraps itself; the gold line follows the track of one road, the silver line parallels the other. I contemplate this geomantic marvel for some time before its significance dawns on me. This is where the Earth plugs into the galaxy! It's Gaia's umbilicus. The central "socket" for the 1746 gold and silver dome lines around the planet, where the Buddha gathers up the gold and silver threads of the fishnet web.

I remember Blaise's image of the Earth energy matrix as a fishnet made of the gold and silver dome lines, how that flexible sack was bundled up into one slender cord. Avebury is that one slender bundled-up cord, the place of primary connection: the gold line comes from Sirius, the silver from Canopus; they enter the Earth plane as a dual-weaved heliacal cord, then at Avebury they unravel and deploy across the planet as the two primary Oroboros lines, positive (gold or "male," the Michael Oroboros Line) and negative (silver or "female"). Wait a minute. If Avebury is where the Earth grid plugs into the cosmos, which is to say, the umbilicus for the myriad of dome lines around the planet, then this must be Gennaro's Camalate and Blaise's Master Dome. Avebury, then, is the Ur-Camalate, the prime wheel among wheels.

Even the name, if a little punningly, suggests as much: assuming for the moment that AVE is a Qabalistic name, and we transpose letters for numbers, we get 161, which is the Golden Mean or phi spiral, 1.618034.... And that number, when rounded off to 162, spells AWR, which is Hebrew for light. Avebury is the AWR-Camalate. There is a further mathematical elegance at play in the number-name of Avebury. Two of gematria's prime numbers (and numbers highly relevant to matters of the grid matrix) are 666 (the prime "solar" number) and 1080 (the prime "lunar" number); their sum is 1746, which is the "mustard seed" and the number of domes on the planet. Their ratio is 1.62, the phi-cycle, or AWR—light (and AVE). And it all happens here at Avebury, the place of balanced cosmic light. The AWR-berry, the place where they buried the Ofanim's seed of light on Earth.

The entire Avebury site, I see now, is capped by a tremendous emerald-hued dome, yet there is something additional installed in the spiritual ethers above the light circle. From one perspective, it looks like a majestic Mother Ship, yet I know that's a convenient, probably distorted image; it also resembles a rosy Grail chalice filled to the brim with light, as if poised to be slowly emptied over Avebury and, through its Oroboros conduits, to irrigate the world with spiritual energy and consciousness.

Doris Lessing, in her visionary-occult novel *Shikasta*, called it The Lock: this was the connection between Earth and the cosmos (principally with the "mind" of Canopus) established in the time of the Giants on behalf of Earth evolution. "The minds of the Giants—or to put it accurately, factually, the Giant-mind—had become one with the mind of the Canopean System, at first partially and tentatively, but it was an ever-growing and sensitizing current." The Lock— "this precise and expert exchange of emanations" —facilitated a planetary energy shift capable of receiving higher and finer vibrations, said Lessing; it enabled the "strong, quiet purpose of the Necessity" to be continuously beamed from Canopus into the Earth (called Rohanda in the earliest days, says Lessing), and this was "the prime object and aim of the galaxy," to create "ever-evolving Sons and Daughters of the Purpose." Between Rohanda and Canopus "swung the silvery cord of our love," comments a galactic emissary—but that was before The Lock failed and was, in effect, turned off. Unlike Lessing's apocalyptic vision, all signs at Avebury today point to either a restoration of The Lock or the fact that it never failed or waned.

At the place where the umbilical weave of the gold and silver lines touches into Avebury, I notice a conflagration, as if a dense, compacted point of intense light has just radically expanded into effulgence. The 28 acre complex itself is like an Earth fitting for this massive crystal of light that is both set securely into the ground yet towers above everything in sight. It's hard to bring its multidimensional scale into focus. I could say this huge crystalline form occupies all of Avebury; yet I could also with equal accuracy say its epicenter is the unassuming traffic island at the intersection of the two roads and two primary Oroboros lines.

All the while I notice the Blazing Star at my belly has grown piercingly bright and much larger. As I walk down the Avenue towards the traffic island, it continues to enlarge to the size of a tennis ball and then a soccer ball. It's as if that traffic island is a kind of superpotent magnet that draws me, draws the Blazing Star, inexorably into its field. Like drawing like, Earth Star drawing Human Star. I halt in my tracks and gasp. That's Blaise's Star, the Nimitta. Avebury is where they planted the Blazing Star in the Earth, at Gaia's umbilicus. Gaia's Nimitta, her berry. The Star in the human is at the belly, so the Star for the planet is at its belly: it's an umbilical Star in either case. Ave-bury, bury the *AWR*, the light, the Nimitta: This is where they *buried the light*, which really means, where they grounded it, birthed it, incarnated, secured it, on Earth. This is where we find Ave's (Gaia's) berry of light, the planetary version of the Blazing Star at our belly. Avebury is the Nimitta for Gaia and the touchstone for our spiritual presence in Her planetary domain.

I sit down on the tiny, grassy traffic island amidst the steady flow of traffic through Avebury. The Blazing Star in my belly is growing rapidly in a slow explosion of light. Just consider: short of a journey through space, this is the closest you can get on Earth to Sirius and Canopus, to the energetic core of the galaxy and its two brightest stars. You can touch the live wires from Sirius and Canopus. Here on this diminutive traffic island is the cosmic marriage of Sirius and Canopus most intensely consummated on Earth; this rich blend is available to any who wishes to sit here. Meanwhile, the Blazing Star within me keeps enlarging until it fills me entirely, and still it keeps expanding, heading towards supernova.

I breathe as Love from Above within an inferno of white fire. As if seeing myself from across the road, I observe that my body has disappeared. In its place stands a huge cubic stone of light aflame with white fire: the Nimitta resplendent, the Philosopher's Stone ignited, Merlin's Stone completed. Here at the planetary umbilicus, the Blazing Star in me and the Blazing Star in Gaia have become one Star.

72

"We Bring Each of You into Memory Now"

couple of days later, I say goodbye to Deborah and take the train up to Cambridge to rejoin Russell and Berenice at Hilary's house before leaving for America. It feels like the end of a chapter but the beginning of a book. After a rich dinner and lively conversation, we retire to her upstairs study and prepare ourselves for Blaise's visit. Blaise comes through strong and lucid, making an angelic nimbus around us in Hilary's book-strewn room. It feels so profoundly good and right to be doing this. To be with Blaise, again. To receive the benediction, the envoi.

"We come as we are. We come as a Blazing Star. We greet you all. We ask you to feel the vibration, feel the sound. We surround you all in a wall of lilac flames. It stretches from the Earth to a pinpoint of light above. We place above each of you a single lilac flame. We surround each of you with a sphere of sapphire radiant blue. We place at each of your hearts a green emerald of six sides. Beneath which we place at the center of your physical organism behind the navel and a little way up, a brilliant pinpoint of light. It glows. We ask you to remain with this image. We will provide the flames around the brilliant blue spheres....

"Good. We come as Love from Above. We come as we are. We come as a Blazing Star. We make this our last visit in this form for some time. We will be with each of you individually from now on until we speak to you like this again. We come with a general remark.

"Each of you lacks memory. None of you puts enough emphasis on remembering. Each of you needs to remember; you are too many parts. Remember yourselves. While you consider your selves as separate parts, you will never be whole. Re-member. We bring each of you into memory now. You are not separate. You are one with us. We are the Blazing Star at the center of yourselves. We speak from that place within you. We are that point in consciousness that is a single point, a brilliant point of light beyond any division, beyond any notion of separateness, beyond all duality, that single point, the Nimitta of consciousness, the Blazing Star that we are. We are the expression in time and space of the first cause, the last effect. We are the point at the center of the wheel that is beyond time and space. We come as we are. We come as a Blazing Star.

"Now we relate to you not in terms of separation but in terms of individuated consciousnesses, with bodies and names. One name, one thought, one Blazing Star, but in an embodiment: four bodies in existence. We ask you now to remember. All things coincide; nothing is not a coincidence. Consider this. This information we present you with is startling but only to those bits of your fragmented selves that do not recognize us as Love from Above, as what you were as a Blazing Star before the Fall. We ask you to remember. 'But Blaise, how do I begin?' I is undone in this. Be as you are. Be that Blazing Star. A little light gleams in the darkness of mind. A twinkle from a Star not too far. Twinkle, twinkle, little star, how I wonder what you are, up above the sky so high, like a diamond. Re-member.

"Nothing is a coincidence. Everything coincides. It is impossible for us to be here without the necessary coincidence. Re-member. If we could return your memory that you could remember, then each of your lessons and each of your purposes would be much clearer to you. This is not a coincidence. Everything coincides. Each moment your inner and outer worlds co-incide. There is no separation. There is no difference, only that which comes after the Fall recognizes a difference and a separation. You cannot see something in another unless you have it in yourself.

"Everything *co-in-cides*. Everything is an expression of Love from

Above. If you perceive it differently, then it is because you prefer fear to love. We ask you to be as Love from Above. We are never far. We are your Blazing Star. So at this time we come as the manifestation of six angels, two more yet to be found. When will you remember them? We wonder. We look around: where are we? Oh, here we are! Not too far, your Blazing Star.

"We are most grateful to each of you, contributing equally to this coincidence, this event, this point of light within the Mind of Man, within the Mind of Mind, within the point of light in consciousness beyond Mind, within the point of light at the center beyond time and space, the single tiny point of light that is the point beyond the beyond. We will take a little break now but will return soon."

We are all silent for a few minutes, a little stunned, a little bright, as Blaise recedes from the room. Then Russell snaps his fingers in my direction. "How about some Grail Knight tea?" "Some biscuits would be lovely, too, please," Berenice says. "The Earl Grey is on the top shelf on the left," Hilary adds. We take advantage of the respite in Blaise's visit for our own debriefing. Blaise returns as we're finishing off the last of the biscuits.

"We are available now purely to answer any questions you may have for us."

"Why does the Avebury ditch feel like the Mother?" I ask.

"The earth has been taken out of a hole and removed. Look at it like a giant record. Each of these ditches are grooves. If you play the record with the needle of your spirit, then you hear some hi-fi sounds. The stones are the amplifiers. The actual original count is 94 stones inside the ditch. [If nothing else 94 means *Mazal Tov*, "good fortune, good star"—in effect, may an auspicious constellation shine over you.] When there were 94 stones, 72 of these, as you suspected, were brought into manifestation by the Elohim prior to human embodiment. [These are familiar numbers, I realize. The Avenue of Cedars, which is Morgan's sheath for the Sword of King David, had 94 trees. The Avenue of Oaks in Glastonbury had 72 trees on each side; 72, as I learned at Oath Hill, is the number of the *Shemhamforesch*, the chorus of 72 Divine Names, evidently a key design feature here at Avebury as well.] We introduced the giant crystal at the center of Avebury which, after the advent of human embodiment, made it possible to complete the pattern with the prescribed number of stones from elsewhere. The two smaller circles are much later additions and are not terribly significant. They are dealing with particular polarizations of magnetic energy made by naive architects who were not in contact with the architect of the original site. They do not, however, interfere with its purpose."

"What is Avebury's purpose, then?"

"It is for tuning human consciousness to its purpose on Earth. It will be used again. When the room in the Great Pyramid that is to be opened is used again, then Avebury will be re-energized. We have placed in the etheric over Avebury a mechanism already preprogrammed for total activation of its original purpose."

"I had the impression that the solar and lunar Oroboros lines come into Avebury from above."

"Yes, there are two major grid lines coinciding at Avebury. Each grid line, vertical and horizontal, connects with the whole pattern covering the globe. Avebury is the planetary umbilicus. Each of the two lines coming into Avebury are connected at other points with each of the other thirteen Oroboros lines."

"How long ago were the stones placed at Avebury by the Elohim?"

"There is no point in too much specificity for this period of time. We could say fifty million years ago, for example, but it wouldn't matter nor would it be accurate. The Buddha, a very wise incarnate being who took on human form, said human beings go infinitely into the past and will go on infinitely into the future. This is true."

"What does Avebury's name signify?"

"As you surmised, bury the Eve, the berry of Eve, Eve-berry, Josephs Seed."

"Blaise, we've come all this way, but I'm still not sure I know what Joseph's Seed is."

"Joseph's Seed is the seed of hope. It is the seed of the only true connection with the potential of the Dharmakaya in the physical plane available to many at this time. It is the introduction to many of what they only have in their dim recesses of their unconscious as a Christ impulse. It is a Blazing Star. It is brighter by far. It is Joseph's Seed. We say, let them pour water on it. Give their consciousness to it. It will grow into a magnificent tree in each of them as something they will get by reading this book."

"Why do people need to find Joseph's Seed?"

"Oroboros, the world dragon, has many eggs over the Earth. They hatch. The dragon sheds its skin. The Earth is about to shed its skin. Through us, you will focus some energy at nodal points to prevent too much loss of human life. You know by now we are dealing in the realm of multiple probability. We have a number of possibilities, one of which would be the shift of axis of the Earth within the next decade. There are numerous others. Gaia will cleanse herself. We will assist her in this cleansing or birthing process. So as you are aware, the Earth is in the process of detoxifying itself, or herself. We are attempting, where possible, to stabilize through the grid as many of these detoxifying impulses as is feasible to prevent much loss of life. This process is necessary for the future conscious evolution of humankind.

"Joseph's Seed prepares the people of Earth for living in a situation of chaos and turbulence during the next 10-20 years. It explains means of harmonizing personal and planetary energies. Those that are availed of the symbol through the stages in the book and who hear the message we have given will be preserved. Those that aren't ready will not hear or even see the book; they will be unprepared. We will lose them this time. They will return later."

"Is all this related to the opening of the planetary heart chakra at Glastonbury?" Berenice asks.

"It is all coincident."

"So this is a deeper explanation of why Joseph came to Glastonbury with the Christ. From your perspective, what did he come here to accomplish?" Russell asks.

"Joseph brought the Christ with him in his journeys to England. Joseph's Seed is the implantation of the Christ in His thought body in the heart chakra of the planetary consciousness. Bury the Heart in Glastonbury. Bury the Nimitta at Avebury. It is the germination of Christed thought in the heart of Gaia. It is what this book is about. It is Joseph's Seed, the germinal vessel by which the Christ and Shambhallic focus are brought together as an introduction to the Christed initiation in the Buddha Body through Joseph's Seed."

"And this initiation needs to happen in the zodiacs?"

"Correct, and before this can happen, they must be brought into activation."

"Of the landscape zodiacs on Earth today, how many are active or running?"

"Of the zodiacs, there are only a very few operative. Only three are partially operative on the planet at this time. Of these three zodiacs partially activated, they are almost at that point of being equal in their physical and etheric parts. The rest are inactive, unserviced. We are not sure what the probability of their reactivation is. Many are in the initial stages of redefinition, which is a pre-requisite for activation. The zodiac system is largely shut down. Gaia has lost much consciousness. In the future, many more may be reactivated through our guidelines. Gaia requires a minimum of seven to eight activated zodiacs for minimal consciousness. Obviously much work must be done soon."

"It seems to me our time at Wick was somehow important for the activation of the Somerset zodiac," Russell says.

"Correct. The warmth in the belly of the Dog was stimulated by the fire in the Dragon's mouth. This was the primary activation. The Dog, as you know, is the guardian. You couldn't even enter the zodiac without the blessings of the Dog. Without the warmth in the belly of the Dog, the zodiac is inaccessible."

"And I guess the gnome egg at the Fairy Dell was central to all this, too." I remark.

"It was an important place for the birthing of the first Grail Knight in this time. The interface between the Earth and the angelic kingdom is very strong at this point. We facilitated the cracking of the gnome egg. It was also warmed by the resident gnomes when you arrived. Then you meshed into the time-space sequence already programmed for you. The gnome egg thus was the egg preprogrammed for your work and also for the beginning of a new cycle."

"What was that bright blazing stone my body seemed to become at the traffic intersection at Avebury?"

"This is what you will remember in the coming years as you meet your function and your purpose. The experience will be aligned in your psyche, and its memory will become accessible.

"You came to Earth as a Blazing Star. You were close to us. You worked on the lines of light from dome to dome. You brought them into focus for the benefit of the organic film on the planet. We are aware that much has happened from that time when your original purpose on first leaving us is now coincident with your life this time. We say to you, you are very fortunate.

"We say, Grail Knight, that the time the Earth faces now is unprecedented in Earth's history. It is coincident with an event that happened on another planet many, many years ago when life was destroyed and many developing spirits who were emerging again to the universality of consciousness were deprived wrongly of their opportunity. We are redressing that balance.

"You're here—you four and many others—to help prevent the same mistake from happening again. There are many beings on this planet at this time. They are not all the same. In fact, there is a greater diversity of human souls on this planet, probably a greater variety of beings at different stages of evolution, than anywhere else in the conceptual universe. If you remembered, you would know. The ones that have already chosen themselves, the ones that begin to remember, will not be removed. They will have an opportunity this time to fulfill their destiny."

I suddenly saw what Blaise meant. I remembered my visions of Morgause and her planetary mort-house. The world as we know it is already under deconstruction; Gaia will detoxify herself, and this radical purge of our planetary body will be, no doubt, profoundly unsettling for all of us. Earthquakes, floods, fires, social upheaval, turbulent weather, stormy psyches—it's all part of the purgation. After all, all of us have helped create the toxic conditions that now must be transmuted for the planet to survive and flourish. So things will be problematic for some time, probably for most of our lives. We knew this before we came in this time, didn't we? But this is the prime reason for understanding the principles of geomancy, of what we might call the plan of the net—plan-net geomancy. Build the zodiacs, hatch the eggs, mobilize the gnomes, cooperate with the Hierarchy, acknowledge the Star, make the earth circles, love the Dog, invoke the rays, ignite new nodes, awaken Albion, heal the Fisher King. That is incumbent upon us now, pressingly so. Building—that's the key. While Gaia deconstructs the old world, we must be earnestly and prodigiously at work constructing the new—from out of ourselves. Refound Camalate, recognize the emerald, sit at the round table, behold the Grail, take the initiation, speak the words, wield Excalibur. All of this is eminently, urgently practical: it is the very stuff of myth, and that is the very stuff of redemption. Why, otherwise, have voices proclaimed over the centuries that Arthur would return if not that this return would be salutary, indispensable? We must stand up for what we know, for what we have remembered, for what we've glimpsed of a positive outcome to it all. The world as we know it may be apocalyptically deconstructed, but the planet will remain and its offer of conscious human existence in its—Her—domain. Camalate must be again, a global impulse, a spiritual insight for reformulating culture, an initiative founded on the Blazing Star at the heart of it all.

"Will we see you again, Blaise?" I ask.

"Of course. We are never too far. We say to you, Grail Knight, as you fly across the sea, remember the whales and the creatures of the sea. Send them your love. Be aware of the energy lines as you travel across the globe. We will be with you. We will roll towards you. We look forward to your progress in remembering. We leave you now with these thoughts.

"Love coincides everywhere. No act of love is not a coincidence. We say, remember. We say it often. Why not? We love to remember you all as you were before the Fall. We give you our Love from Above. We'll see you, Grail Knight, in Norway for the Christed initiation in the Buddha Body. As ever, we're not going far. We are your Blazing Star."

BIBLIOGRAPHY

Alcock, Leslie. 'By South Cadbury is that Camelot...' Excavations at Cadbury Castle 1966-70. Thames and Hudson. London, 1972.
———— Arthur's Britain. History and Archeology A.D. 367-634. Penguin Books, Hammondsworth, U.K., 1971.

Ashe, Geoffrey. King Arthur's Avalon: The Story of Glastonbury. Fontana/Collins, Glasgow, 1980.

Bailey, Alice A. A Treatise on Cosmic Fire. Lucis Publishing Company, New York, 1962.
———— The Rays and the Initiations. Vol. V, A Treatise on the Seven Rays, Lucis Publishing Company, New York, 1960.
———— Esoteric Astrology. Vol. III, A Treatise on the Seven Rays, Lucis Publishing Company, New York, 1951.

Bayley, Harold. The Lost Language of Symbolism. J. B. Lippincott Company, Philadelphia, 1913.

Beckett, Michael. The Pyramid and the Grail. Lailoken Press, Romsey, U.K., 1984.

Benham, Patrick. The Avalonians. Gothic Image Publications, Glastonbury, U.K., 1993.

Bernbaum, Edwin. The Way to Shambhala. Jeremy P. Tarcher, Los Angeles, 1989.

Blake, William. Complete Writings, with Variant Readings. Edited by Geoffrey Keynes. Oxford University Press, London, 1966.

Blavatsky, H. P. The Secret Doctrine. Theosophical University Press, Pasadena, 1977.

Blech, Benjamin. The Secrets of Hebrew Words. Jason Aronson, Inc., Northvale, N.J., 1991.
———— More Secrets of Hebrew Words. Jason Aronson, Inc., Northvale, N.J., 1993.

Blyth, R. H. Zen and Zen Classics, Vol. 4, Mumonkan, The Hokuseido Press, Tokyo, 1966.

Bond, Frederick Bligh. The Gates of Remembrance. Thorsons, Wellingborough, U.K., 1978.
———— "Memories of the Monks of Avalon," in Psychic Science, Vol. 1, No. 4, January 1923.
———— The Company of Avalon. Blackwell, Oxford, U.K., 1924.

Bromwich, Rachel, editor. Trioedd Ynys Prydein, The Welsh Triads. University of Wales Press, Cardiff, U.K., 1978.

Burl, Aubrey. Prehistoric Avebury. Yale University Press, New Haven, 1979.

Burrows, Ray. Beckery Burrows. Somerset in the Thirties. Research Publications, London, 1978.

Caine, Mary. The Kingston Zodiac. 2nd Ed. Revised, Mary Caine (self-published), Kingston, U.K., 1978.

Castaneda, Carlos. *The Fire from Within.* Century Publishing, London, 1984.
—— *The Eagle's Gift.* Simon and Schuster, New York, 1981.
—— *The Art of Dreaming.* Harper Collins, New York, 1993.
Clarke, Arthur. *Childhood's End.* Harcourt, Brace & World, New York, 1953.
Compton, Madonna. *Archetypes on the Tree of Life: The Tarot as Pathwork.* Llewellyn Publications, St, Paul, 1991.
Cooke, Grace, and Cooke, Ivan. *The Light in Britain.* White Eagle Publishing Trust, Newslands, U.K., 1971.
Coon, Robert. *Elliptical Navigations Through the Multitudinous Aethyrs of Avalon.* Excalibur Press, Street, U.K., 1984.
—— *Voyage to Avalon: An Immortalist's Introduction to the Magick of Glastonbury.* Griffin Gold Publications, Glastonbury, U.K., 1986.
Daumal, René. *Mount Analogue: A Novel of Symbolically Authentic Non-Euclidian Adventures in Mountain Climbing.* Trans. by Roger Shattuck, Penguin Books, New York, 1974.
de Troyes, Chrétien. *Arthurian Romances.* Trans. by W. W. Comfort, Everyman's Library, J. M. Dent & Sons, London, 1977.
Diodorus of Siculus. *Book II, 47.* Loeb Classical Library, No. 303, Harvard University Press, Cambridge, 1935.
Dowman, Keith. *Sky Dancer: The Secret Life and Songs of the Lady Yeshe Tsogyel.* Routledge & Kegan Paul, London, 1984.
Fitzgerald, Robert, trans. *Homer: The Odyssey.* Doubleday & Company, New York, 1961.
Fortune, Dion. *The Mystical Qabalah.* Ernest Benn Limited, London, 1935.
—— *Avalon of the Heart.* Samuel Weiser, York Beach, M.E., 1971.
Gennaro, Gino. *The Phenomena of Avalon: The Story of This Planet as Recounted by the Fairies.* Cronos Publications, London, 1979.
Geoffrey of Monmouth, *The History of the Kings of Britain,* Trans. by Lewis Thorpe, Penguin Books, New York, 1966.
—— *The Vita Merlini.* Edited by John Parry, University of Illinois Studies in Language and Literature, Vol. X, No. 3, August 1925.
Govinda, Lama Anagarika. *Foundations of Tibetan Mysticism.* Samuel Weiser, York Beach, M.E., 1969.
Halevi, Z'ev Ben Shimon. *Introduction to the Cabala: Tree of Life.* Samuel Weiser, York Beach, M.E., 1972.
Hearne, Thomas. *The History and Antiquities of Glastonbury.* Oxford, 1722.
High History of the Holy Grail. Trans. by Sebastian Evans, James Clarke & Co., Cambridge, U.K., 1969.
Hurtak, J. J. *The Book of Knowledge: The Keys of Enoch.* The Academy for Future Science, Los Gatos, C.A., 1977.
Jenkins, Stephen. *The Undiscovered Country.* Neville Spearman, Sudbury, U.K., 1977.
Jocelyn, John. *Meditations on the Signs of the Zodiac.* Steinerbooks, Blauvelt, N.Y., 1970.

Johnson, Buffie. *Lady of the Beasts: Ancient Images of the Goddess and Her Sacred Animals*. Harper & Row, New York, 1988.

Kaplan, Aryeh. *Sefer Yetzirah: The Book of Creation*. Samuel Weiser, York Beach, M.E., 1990.

———— *The Bahir*. Samuel Weiser, York Beach, M.E., 1979.

Knight, Gareth. *Experience of the Inner Worlds*. Samuel Weiser, York Beach, M.E., 1993.

———— *A Practical Guide to Qabalistic Symbolism*. 2 volumes, Helios Book Service, Cheltenham, U.K., 1965.

Lagorio, Valerie M. "The Evolving Legend of St. Joseph of Glastonbury," in *Speculum*, Vol. XLVI, No. 2, April 1971.

Lawlor, Robert. *Sacred Geometry: Philosophy and Practice*. Thames and Hudson, London, 1982.

———— *Voices of the First Day: Awakening in the Aboriginal Dreamtime*. Inner Traditions, Rochester, V.T., 1991.

Lewis, Rev. Lionel Smithett. *St. Joseph of Arimathea at Glastonbury*. James Clarke & Co., Cambridge, U.K., 1922.

Lessing, Doris. *Canopus in Argos: Archives. Re: Colonised Planet 5, Shikasta*. Vintage Books, New York, 1981.

Maharshi, Ramana. *The Spiritual Teaching of Ramana Maharshi*. Shambhala, Boston, 1972.

Malory, Sir Thomas. *Le Morte d'Arthur*. Edited by John Lawlor, Penguin Books, Hammondsworth, U.K., 1969.

Maltwood, K. E., *A Guide to Glastonbury's Temple of the Stars*. James Clarke & Co., Cambridge, 1982.

———— *The Enchantments of Britain*. James Clarke & Co., Cambridge, 1982.

Mathers, S. L. MacGregor. *The Kabbalah Unveiled*. Samuel Weiser, York Beach, M.E., 1968.

Michell, John. *The Traveler's Key to Sacred England*. Alfred A. Knopf, New York, 1988.

———— *The New View Over Atlantis*. Thames and Hudson, London, 1983.

———— *The Dimensions of Paradise: The Proportions and Symbolic Numbers of Ancient Cosmology*. Harper & Row, New York, 1988.

———— *New Light on the Ancient Mystery of Glastonbury*. Gothic Image Publications, Glastonbury (U.K.), 1990.

Nance, Robert Morton, and Pole, Wellesley Tudor. *Michael, Prince of Heaven*. J. M. Watkins, London, 1951.

Ovid. *Metamorphoses*. Trans. by A. D. Melville, Oxford University Press, New York, 1986.

Phelps, Rev. W. *The History and Antiquities of Somerset*. J. B. Nichols, London, 1836.

Pole, Wellesley Tudor, and Lehmann, Rosamond. *A Man Seen Afar*. Neville Spearman, Sudbury, U.K., 1965.

—————— *My Dear Alexias: Letters from Wellesley Tudor Pole to Rosamond Lehmann*, Edited by Elizabeth Gaythorpe, Neville Spearman, Jersey, U.K., 1979.

—————— *Writing on the Ground*, Pilgrims Book Services, Tasburgh, U.K., 1984.

Powys, John Cowper. *A Glastonbury Romance*. John Lane/The Bodley Head, London, 1933.

Rahtz, Philip, and Hirst, Susan. *Beckery Chapel, Glastonbury 1967-8*. Glastonbury Antiquarian Society, Glastonbury, U.K., 1974.

Raine, Kathleen. *Golgonooza, City of Imagination: Last Studies in William Blake*. Lindisfarne Press, Hudson, N.Y., 1991.

Regardie, Israel. *A Garden of Pomegranates*. 2nd Edition. Llewellyn Publications, St. Paul, M.N., 1987.

Rilke, Rainer Maria. *Duino Elegies*. Trans. by Stephen Mitchell, Shambhala, Boston, 1992.

Roberts, Anthony. *Sowers of Thunder: Giants in Myth and History*. Rider & Company, London, 1978.

—————— "Glastonbury—The Ancient Avalon," in *Glastonbury: Ancient Avalon, New Jerusalem*, Edited by Anthony Roberts, Rider, London, 1978.

—————— *Sacred Glastonbury: A Defence of Myth Defiled*. Zodiac House Publications, Westhay, U.K., 1984.

Roberts, Jane. "Somerset Legendary Geomancy," in *Glastonbury: Ancient Avalon, New Jerusalem*, Edited by Anthony Roberts, Rider, London, 1978.

Robinson, J. Armitage, *Two Glastonbury Legends: King Arthur and St. Joseph of Arimathea*, Cambridge at the University Press, U.K., 1926.

Roshi, Yasutani. "Makyo," in *The Middle Way*, Vol. XXXVI, No. 1, May 1961.

Schwartz, Howard. *Gabriel's Palace, Jewish Mystical Tales*. Oxford University Press, New York, 1993.

Seung Sahn. *Only Don't Know: The Teaching Letters of Zen Master Seung Sahn*. Four Seasons Foundation, San Francisco, 1982.

Schimmel, Anne Marie. *The Mystery of Numbers*. Oxford University Press, New York, 1993.

Scholem, Gershom. *Origins of the Kaballah*. Edited by R. J. Werblowsky, Princeton University Press, Princeton, N.J., 1990.

—————— *Kaballah*. New American Library, New York, 1978.

Sharp, Daryl. *Dear Gladys: The Survival Papers*, Book 2. Inner City Books, Toronto, 1989.

Shunryu Suzuki. *Zen Mind, Beginner's Mind*. John Weatherhill, New York, 1970.

Simpson, Jacqueline. "Fifty British Dragon Tales: An Analysis," in *Folklore*, Vol. 89, No. 1, 1978.

Sir Gawain and the Green Knight. Trans. by Brian Stone. Penguin Books, Hammondsworth, U.K., 1959.

Sitchin, Zecharia. *The 12th Planet*. Bear & Company, Santa Fe, 1991.

Stein, Walter Johannes. *The Death of Merlin: Arthurian Myth and Alchemy*. Floris Books, Edinburgh, 1984.

—— *The Ninth Century and the Holy Grail*. Temple Lodge Press, London, 1988.

Steiner, Rudolf. *The Mission of the Archangel Michael*. Anthroposophic Press, Spring Valley, N.Y., 1961.

Suarés, Carlo. *The Qabala Trilogy*. Shambhala, Boston, 1985.

Tain, The. Trans. by Thomas Kinsella, Oxford University Press, London, 1970.

Tennyson, Alfred Lord. *The Works of Alfred Lord Tennyson*. A. R. Mowbray & Co., Oxford, 1910.

Tolkien, J. R. R. *The Silmarillion*, Edited by Christopher Tolkien, Houghton Mifflin, Boston, 1977.

—— *The Book of Lost Tales*, Part II. Edited by Christopher Tolkien, Unwin Paperbacks, London, 1984.

Tomas, Andrew. *Shambhala: Oasis of Light*. Sphere Books, London, 1977.

Treharne, R. F., *The Glastonbury Legends*, The Cresset Press, Aberystwyth, Wales, 1967.

White, T.H. *The Once and Future King*. Flamingo/Fontana Paperbacks, London, 1984.

William of Malmesbury. *The Early History of Glastonbury*. Edited by John Scott, Boydell Press, Suffolk, U.K., 1981.

Wright, G. W. "The History of Glastonbury During the Last 40 Years," *Avalon Independent*, Glastonbury, U.K., 1890.

INDEX